Oman, UAE & Arabian Peninsula

THIS EDITION WRITTEN AND RESEARCHED BY

Jenny Walker, Anthony Ham, Andrea Schulte-Peevers

PLAN YOUR TRIP

ON THE ROAD

JUSTIN FOULKES/LONELY PLANET ©
DESERT CAMELS P413

S-F/LONELY PLANET ©
LIONFISH IN DUBAI AQUARIUM, UAE P313

JUSTIN FOULKES/LONELY PLANET ©

Contents

THE EMPTY QUARTER IN OMAN P220

Contents

ON THE ROAD

RICHARD SHARROCKS/GETTY IMAGES ©

SHEIKH ZAYED GRAND MOSQUE, ABU DHABI P351

Contents

JUSTIN FOULKES/LONELY PLANET ©
ASSORTED NUTS IN NIZWA SOUQ, OMAN P169

JUSTIN FOULKES/LONELY PLANET ©
MUGHSAIL, OMAN P203

UNDERSTAND

SURVIVAL GUIDE

SPECIAL FEATURES

Welcome to Oman, UAE & Arabian Peninsula

The spectacular emptiness of the Arabian landscape provides a blank canvas upon which is projected a riot of cultural, religious, intellectual and trading wonders.

The Desert

'No man can live this life and emerge unchanged,' wrote Wilfred Thesiger of his travels with the Bedu across the Empty Quarter in *Arabian Sands*. 'He will carry, however faint, the imprint of the desert.' The austere allure of the desert has attracted travellers to Arabia for centuries. Ibn Battuta, Marco Polo and TE Lawrence are among many famous travellers beguiled by the beauty and challenge of the barren landscapes. Thankfully, modern travellers no longer need risk life and limb to encounter the wilderness as roads and camps make encounters with the desert possible for all.

Urban Landscapes

When asked what they most like about their land of sand dunes, the Bedu near Al Hashman in Oman reply, 'Coming to town'. Town! This is the Arabia of the 21st century, built on oil and banking – sophisticated communities looking to the future and creating empires out of sand, or at least on land reclaimed from the sea. For those looking for a dynamic urban experience, the Gulf cities are the place to find it. With high incomes per capita, elegant towers, opulent hotels and eccentric malls, these cities offer the 'pleasure domes' of the modern world.

Legendary Hospitality

The essence of the Arabian Peninsula lies in its people: good-natured haggling in souqs, cursing on long journeys, sharing of sweet tea on the edge of wild places. Unifying all is Islam, a way of life, the call to prayer carried on an inland breeze, a gentle hospitality extended towards strangers. This is what many travellers most remember of their visit here – the ancient tradition of sharing 'bread and salt' and of ensuring safe passage, albeit given a modern context. Visitors can expect equally friendly exchanges in supermarkets as remote desert villages.

Cultural Riches

It's hard to think of Arabia without conjuring the Queen of Sheba and camel caravans bearing frankincense from Dhofar in Oman; dhows laden with pearls from Dilmun; the ruins of empire in Saudi Arabia's Madain Saleh. The caravans and dhows may be plying different trades these days, but the lexicon of *The Thousand and One Nights* that brought Sheherazade's exotic, vulnerable world to the West still helps define the Peninsula today. Visit a fort, barter in a souq or step into labyrinthine alleyways and you'll immediately discover the perennial magic of Arabia.

Why I Love the Arabian Peninsula

By Jenny Walker, Writer

Mention 'Arabia' and a host of familiar, media-weary images probably appear. I've spent half my life studying these images – of wilderness, wealth and war – in various academic pursuits. But there's so much more to the sophisticated culture of modern Arabia than is conjured by these stereotypes. I love the Peninsula because each day I encounter the complexity of Arabia in the dynamic, warm-hearted people who lie at the core of the region's enduring appeal. And of course the desert, with its life against the odds, has inevitably crept into my soul.

For more about our writers, see page 480.

Above: Wadi Ghul, Oman (p177)

Oman, UAE & Arabian Peninsula

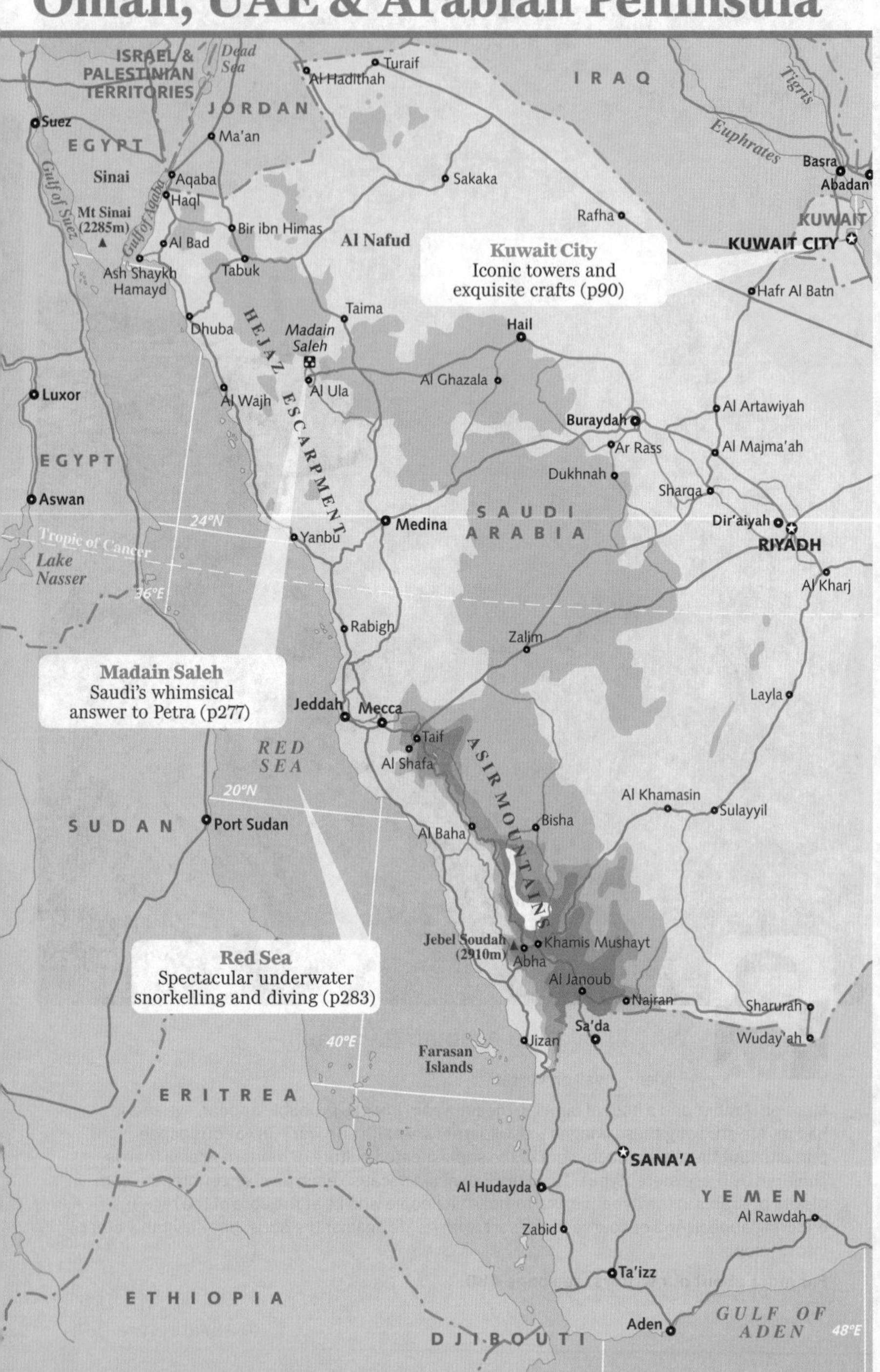

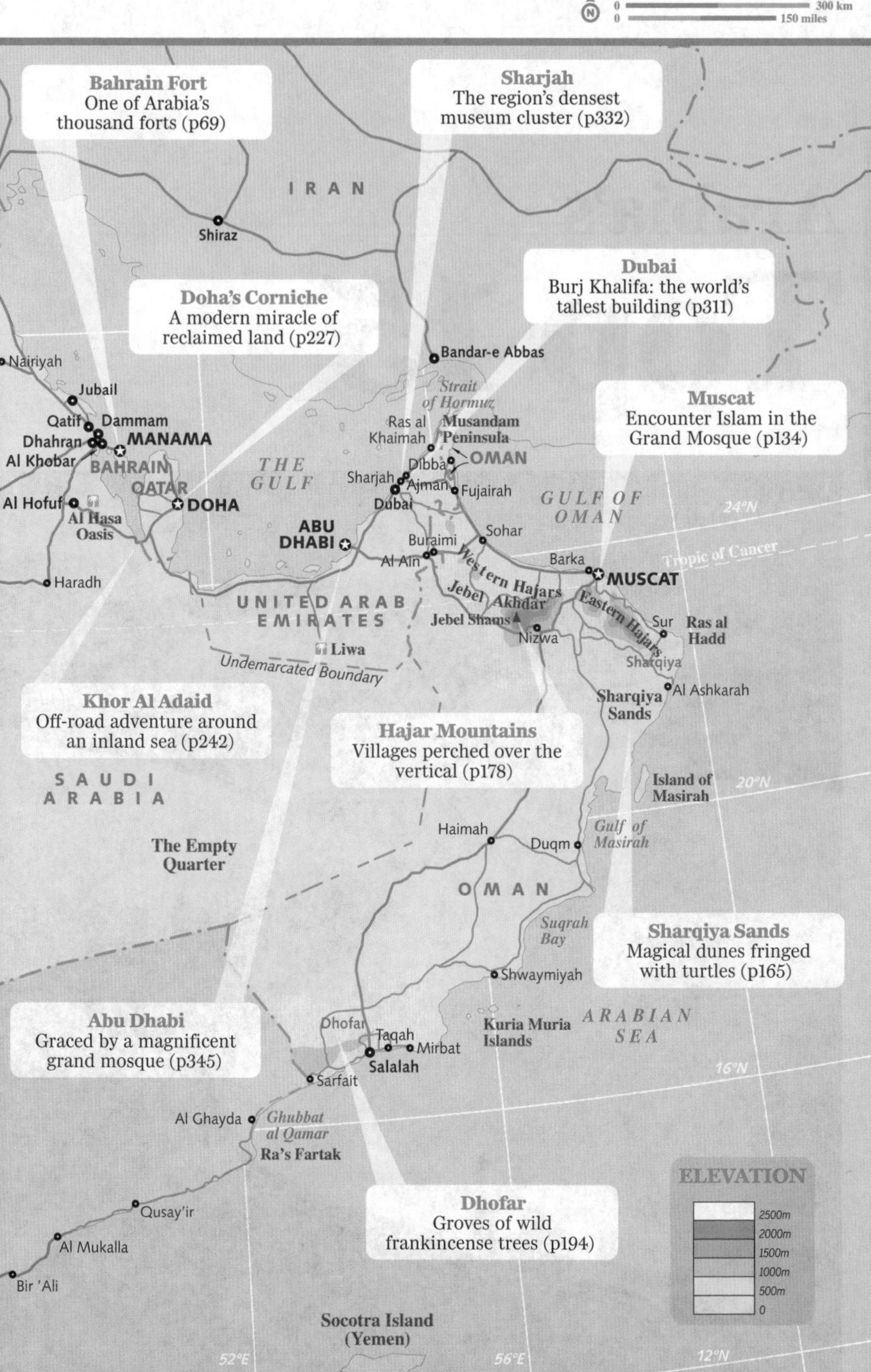
0 300 km
0 150 miles
Bahrain Fort
One of Arabia's thousand forts (p69)
Sharjah
The region's densest museum cluster (p332)
Dubai
Burj Khalifa: the world's tallest building (p311)
Doha's Corniche
A modern miracle of reclaimed land (p227)
Muscat
Encounter Islam in the Grand Mosque (p134)
Khor Al Adaid
Off-road adventure around an inland sea (p242)
Hajar Mountains
Villages perched over the vertical (p178)
Sharqiya Sands
Magical dunes fringed with turtles (p165)
Abu Dhabi
Graced by a magnificent grand mosque (p345)
Dhofar
Groves of wild frankincense trees (p194)
IRAN
Shiraz
Bandar-e Abbas
Strait of Hormuz
Nairiyah
Jubail
Qatif
Dammam
Dhahran
MANAMA
Al Khobar
BAHRAIN
QATAR
DOHA
Al Hofuf
Al Hasa Oasis
Haradh
THE GULF
Ras al Khaimah
Musandam Peninsula
OMAN
Dibba
Sharjah
Ajman
Fujairah
Dubai
GULF OF OMAN
ABU DHABI
Buraimi
Al Ain
Sohar
Barka
MUSCAT
24°N
Tropic of Cancer
Western Hajars
Jebel Akhdar
Eastern Hajars
Jebel Shams
Nizwa
Sur
Ras al Hadd
Sharqiya
UNITED ARAB EMIRATES
Liwa
Undemarcated Boundary
Al Ashkarah
Sharqiya Sands
SAUDI ARABIA
Island of Masirah
20°N
The Empty Quarter
Haimah
Duqm
Gulf of Masirah
OMAN
Suqrah Bay
Shwaymiyah
ARABIAN SEA
Kuria Muria Islands
Dhofar
Taqah
Mirbat
Salalah
16°N
Sarfait
Al Ghayda
Ghubbat al Qamar
Ra's Fartak
Qusay'ir
Al Mukalla
Bir 'Ali
Socotra Island (Yemen)
52°E
56°E
12°N
ELEVATION
2500m
2000m
1500m
1000m
500m
0

Arabia's Top 15

1

Desert Dunes

1 For centuries Westerners have been attracted to the great desert wildernesses of Arabia, drawn by its limitlessness yet repelled by the void. 'This cruel land can cast a spell which no temperate clime can hope to match,' wrote Wilfred Thesiger in *Arabian Sands* after crossing the Empty Quarter on foot with the Bedu. Feel the desert's allure in Oman's Sharqiya Sands (p165), or in the dunes of Liwa in the UAE, but beware: the summer sands don't take prisoners, and the only stranger you're likely to meet between dunes is yourself.
Rub' al-Khali desert, Saudi Arabia

Modern Architecture

2 Competitively slicing the sky, the audacious tower blocks that rise from the cities of the Gulf are a potent symbol of the region's ambitions. At 828m, Burj Khalifa (p311) in Dubai is the tallest building in the world. Dine at the top of this, or any of the region's futuristic totems of steel and glass, such as the Etihad Towers in Abu Dhabi or the Kingdom Tower in Riyadh, and you could quite literally be accused of burying your head in the clouds.
Burj Khalifa, Dubai, UAE

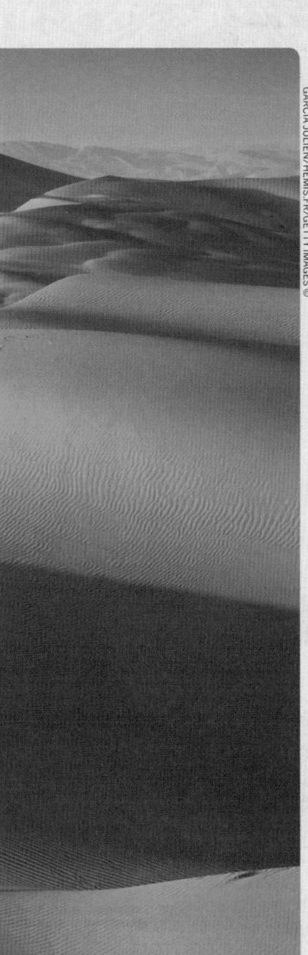

GARCIA JULIEN/HEMIS.FR/GETTY IMAGES ©

LUCIANO MORTULA/SHUTTERSTOCK ©

Encountering Islam

3 In Arabia, the birthplace of Islam, faith is a living, breathing reality inextricably entwined in the daily lives of Peninsula inhabitants and encountered in the haunting call to prayer, the warmth of welcome enshrined in the Muslim code of conduct and, for Muslim visitors, in pilgrimage to the holy cities of Saudi Arabia. Visit magnificent Sheikh Zayed Grand Mosque (p351) in Abu Dhabi or the Museum of Islamic Art in Doha, and see how faith has also been expressed in masterpieces of ceramic, carpet and furniture design. Sheikh Zayed Grand Mosque, UAE

Souqs – Arabia's Trading Places

4 They may not match the stock exchanges of New York, London or Tokyo in terms of dollars traded, but Arabia's souqs claim a far more ancient lineage. Get lost in any of the region's labyrinthine souqs, especially Doha's Souq Waqif and Muscat's Mutrah Souq (p127), and participate in the brisk trade in olives, the haggle-to-the-death of cloth merchants and a collusive wink-and-a-nod over gulled customers. Souq Waqif, Doha

3

MAREMAGNUM/GETTY IMAGES ©

ALFRED KNIPPER PHOTOGRAPHY/GETTY IMAGES ©

JOHN SEATON CALLAHAN/GETTY IMAGES ©

Jebels High, Wadis Low

5 In contrast to its vast interior desert plains, the Peninsula also boasts some of the highest mountains and deepest wadis (dry riverbeds) in the Middle East. Camp near Oman's Jebel Shams in winter for the spectacle of hail thundering into the wadis below. Watch how the precious water is channelled through ancient irrigation systems to plantations and high-altitude villages. Or for a dramatic drive, try the mountain road that takes you almost to the top of the UAE's Jebel Jais (p342), where you can expect matchless views of the surrounding cliffs and canyons. Jebel Shams, Oman

R&R on a Deserted Beach

6 Ever dreamed of staring up at a night sky so packed with stars you can read a book by their light? Opportunities for wild camping abound across the Peninsula, not least on Oman's desert island of Masirah (p159), or any of the beaches along Oman's eastern shore. Wilderness camping offers plenty of creatures (adapted to nocturnal living to escape the desert heat) but few comforts. If creature comforts are important to you, the resorts in the frontier town of Duqm (p204) offer less-rugged R&R. Masirah island, Oman

Ruins of Empire & Saudi's Petra

7 The ruins rise out of the gravel plains like lost camels, or sit crumbling to dust on mountain ridges. They speak of past greatness, prophets, kings and forgotten dynasties. Some, like the thousands of burial mounds that dot the landscape in Bahrain, have been accommodated in urban landscapes. Others, such as the superb Nabataean ruins at Madain Saleh (p277) in Saudi Arabia, stand proud on forgotten plains. Sit among these ruins of empire and it's easy to contemplate human frailty. Madain Saleh

Red Sea Diving

8 Flanking the shores of Saudi Arabia, the crystal-clear waters of the Red Sea are home to epic dramas. In some of the world's finest diving sites, clown fish play the comedians in coral gardens fit for a Zefferelli stage set, while sharks wait in the wings for heroic small fry. You don't need to dive for a balcony view: don a mask, snorkel and flippers and swim anywhere off the coast at Jeddah (p266) and you can't help but applaud the spectacle. Coral reef in the Red Sea, Jeddah, Saudi Arabia

7

8

IAIN MASTERTON/GETTY IMAGES ©

CHRISTINA-J-HAURI/GETTY IMAGES ©

LEONID ANDRONOV/GETTY IMAGES ©

Sharjah – A Cultural Cornucopia

9 It may not generate the headlines of Dubai or the sophisticated capital, Abu Dhabi, but Sharjah (p332) has quietly grown into the cultural hub of Arabia. In a celebration of local and indigenous heritage, Sharjah boasts the largest cluster of museums in the region with gems such as the Sharjah Heritage Museum among them. With the historic old quarter and chaotic alleyways undergoing major renovation in a project called 'Heart of Sharjah', the city offers a sense of Arabia in the midst of the modern. Central Souk (p336), Sharjah, UAE

A Craft Tradition

10 Arabia's riches can be counted by more than the latest car or designer handbag. Gold twine in a dress cuff, a bead of carnelian threaded for a loved one, a basket woven with camel leather, words of wisdom entwined in a silver amulet – these are the riches of the region's ancient craft heritage. Find the most precious pieces collected under one roof in the enchanting, underground Tareq Rajab Museum (p93) in Kuwait City. Brass coffee pots in Abu Dhabi, UAE

High-Rise Living

11 From the cooling wind towers of Muharraq Island in Bahrain to Saudi watchtowers and the enigmatic tombs of mountain burials in Bat in northern Oman, the architects of Arabia have for centuries favoured the vertical over the horizontal. Visit Al Hamra (p171) in Oman's Hajar Mountains, or just about any village in southern Saudi Arabia, to see where the fashion for high-rise living originated. Walk the capital corniches of the Gulf states to see how the modern Manhattans of Arabia continue the trend.
Skyscrapers in Downtown Dubai (p311), UAE

Heaven Scented Frankincense

12 Gifted by wise men to babes (according to the Bible) and queens to kings (Queen Sheba to King Solomon), and harvested from the bark of ugly trees in the mist-swirling magic of summertime in Oman, frankincense is responsible for the history of Arabian empires. Catch its tantalising aroma in the house of a newborn, buy the curdled beads of amber-coloured sap in the souq or, better still, visit the living trees in Dhofar (p194) in the middle of the region's unique and remarkable July *khareef* (rainy season).

Arabia's Formidable Forts

13 Cresting a hilltop, guarding a coastline, walling a village or securing a dried-out riverbed, there is barely a town in Arabia without some kind of crumbling battlement. Oman has some of the best preserved of the Peninsula's forts in Bahla, Nizwa, Nakhal and Rustaq, but for a whole day out, Bahrain's Fort Complex (p69) with its museum, coffeehouse and night-time illuminations, is hard to beat. Learn your forts (military only) from your castles (fortified residence) before exploring some of these mighty and magnificent buildings. Nizwa Fort (p169), Oman

12

LEAH-ANNE THOMPSON/SHUTTERSTOCK ©

13

JUSTIN FOULKES/LONELY PLANET ©

SHAHINOLAKARA/GETTY IMAGES ©

TOMAS ZRNA/GETTY IMAGES ©

Walking on Water along Doha's Corniche

14 Modernity in many Peninsula countries can be summed up in two words: reclaimed land. Take part in the promenade of nations along Doha's corniche (p227), or indeed any of the Gulf corniches, and chances are you'll be walking on water – or at least where water once was. But then again, you can climb any mountain in Arabia and claim the same: most of it was once under the sea and it would appear that modern architects are keen to reverse the tide on prehistory.

Off-Road Adventure

15 The ubiquitous 4WDs on Arabian roads are the modern 'ships of the desert' and can transport travellers into unimagined dimensions – including stuck in sand and mired in mud. However, with some careful planning, and sticking to existing tracks, an off-road trip to Qatar's Khor Al Adaid (p242) or Oman's Jebel Akhdar is unforgettable. Follow the locals over the dunes, through floodwater and up mountains to see the best of the Peninsula's varied landscape and discover the myriad plants and animals calling it home.

Need to Know

For more information, see Survival Guide (p435)

Currency

Bahraini dinar (BD); Kuwaiti dinar (KD); Omani rial (OR); Qatari riyal (QR); Saudi riyal (SR); UAE dirham (Dh)

Language

Arabic (English widely spoken)

Visas

Visas, required by all visitors, are available for many nationalities on arrival at airports and most land borders (except Saudi Arabia).

Money

ATMs widely available; credit cards accepted by most hotels and city restaurants.

Mobile Phones

Local SIM cards available for international calls, topped up with prepaid cards.

Time

Saudi Arabia, Kuwait, Bahrain and Qatar are three hours ahead of GMT/UTC. The UAE and Oman are four hours ahead of GMT/UTC.

When to Go

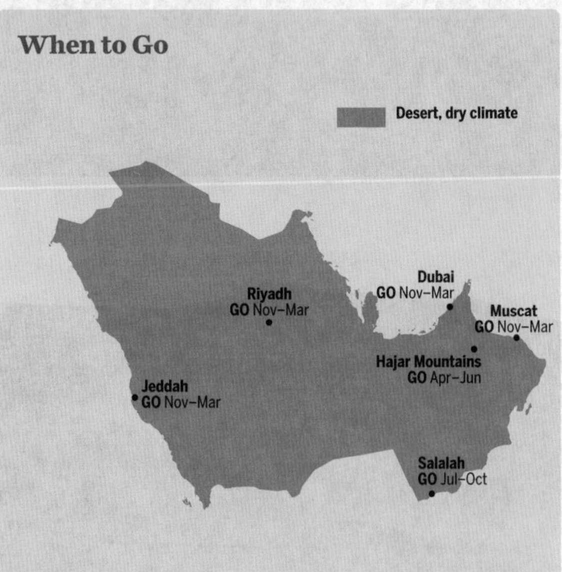

High Season (Nov–Mar)

- Perfect weather at sea level with clear, sunny days and cool evenings.
- Shopping festivals and sporting events coincide with these cooler months.
- Booking accommodation is necessary; expect highest rates in December.

Shoulder Season (Jul–Oct)

- Good time to visit southern Arabia with light rains turning the desert hills green.
- The *khareef* (rainy season) festival in southern Oman attracts many Gulf visitors, leading to higher accommodation prices.

Low Season (Apr–Jun)

- Extreme heat and high humidity make this a season to avoid in most parts of Arabia.
- Big discounts often available for accommodation.
- Best time to visit mountain areas.
- June is harvest time for fresh dates.

Useful Websites

Al Bab (www.al-bab.com) Links to dozens of news services, country profiles, travel sites and maps.

Al Jazeera (www.aljazeera.com/news/middleeast) Popular news-and-views-oriented website.

Arabnet (www.arabnet.me) Useful Saudi-run encyclopedia of the Arab world.

InterNations (www.internations.org) Information service with networking opportunities exclusively for expats.

Lonely Planet (www.lonelyplanet.com/middle-east) Destination information, hotel bookings, travel forum and photos.

Important Numbers

Precede the following country codes with ☎00.

Bahrain	☎973
Kuwait	☎965
Oman	☎968
Qatar	☎974
Saudi Arabia	☎966
UAE	☎971

Exchange Rates

	US$1	UK£1	€1
Bahrain (BD)	0.38	0.54	0.42
Kuwait (KD)	0.30	0.43	0.33
Oman (OR)	0.38	0.55	0.42
Qatar (QR)	3.64	5.19	4.01
Saudi Arabia (SR)	3.75	5.66	4.13
UAE (Dh)	3.67	5.23	4.05

For current exchange rates, see www.xe.com.

Daily Costs

Budget: Less than US$200

- Shared room in budget guesthouse: US$100
- Street fare or self-catering at local markets: US$15
- Public transport and occasional taxi: US$25
- Entry costs: US$10

Midrange: US$200–US$500

- Double room in a midrange hotel: US$200
- Local-style dining in restaurants: US$30
- Car hire: US$100
- Entry costs/unguided activities: US$50

Top End: More than US$500

- Double room in five-star hotel or resort: US$300
- International-style buffet lunch/dinner: from US$50
- 4WD vehicle hire: US$200
- Entry costs/guided activities: US$100

Opening Hours

Opening times vary widely across the region and are erratic at best, especially during Ramadan and holidays. The weekend is Friday and Saturday in all countries except Saudi Arabia. The Saudi weekend is Thursday and Friday.

Banks 8am–noon or 1pm (closed Fridays)

Restaurants noon–midnight

Cafes 9am–midnight

Shops 10am–10pm (reduced hours Fridays)

Souqs 10am–1pm & 4–9pm (closed Friday mornings)

Arriving in the Arabian Peninsula

The main international airports are listed here. Airport taxis and hotel shuttles are the main methods of transport from airport to city centre.

Bahrain Airport (p69)

Kuwait Airport (p119)

Muscat Airport (p219), Oman

Doha Airport (p240), Qatar

King Khaled Airport (p302), Riyadh, Saudi Arabia

Abu Dhabi Airport (p390), UAE

Dubai Airport (p328), UAE

Getting Around

The Arabian Peninsula is a car-centric destination and most people rely solely on their own transport to get around. As such, hiring a car is a sensible option if you're brave enough to drive alongside the often-reckless locals. Note that 4WD is necessary for exploring the interior deserts and mountains. Road infrastructure is generally excellent. If you attempt to use public transport outside capital cities, pack water – and patience!

Plane Numerous daily, good-value flights connect all the cities of the region.

Car The most convenient option but beware of long distances, high temperatures, empty roads and hairpin mountain tracks.

Bus Modern, air-conditioned, long-distance buses connect all capitals with regional cities; a few international routes (particularly between Oman and the UAE) are feasible for travellers.

For much more on **getting around**, see p451

First Time Oman, UAE & Arabian Peninsula

For more information, see Survival Guide (p435)

Checklist

- Obtain relevant visas – required in advance for Saudi Arabia
- Arrange travel insurance (p442)
- Avoid Israeli stamps in your passport
- Be aware of alcohol restrictions
- Understand the do's and don'ts of travelling in Ramadan (p446)

What to Pack

- Hat and sunglasses – the sun is ferocious year-round
- Modest clothing – essential for all
- A warm layer – locals like their malls chilly
- Sturdy, closed shoes – desert hiking is a highlight, and there are scorpions about!
- Drivers' licence – car is king across the region
- Mosquito repellent
- Patience – not much happens quickly, except in the capital cities

Top Tips for Your Trip

- Make a point of staying in the desert. Organised desert camps and opportunities for driving off-road make it easy to visit this varied landscape.
- Accept coffee and dates if invited. Whether in city shops or mountain villages, you're bound to be asked to pause for a chat – there's no better way of getting to grips with local culture.

What to Wear

Visitors to Arabia need to respect local dress codes, even in Gulf cities.

For men, it's unacceptable to be seen anywhere in public, including hotel foyers and souqs, in shorts and vests. Avoid wearing local *thobes* and *dishdashas* (floor-length shirt-dresses) – at best, Arab people think it looks ridiculous.

For women, dressing 'modestly' means covering knees, upper arms, shoulders and neckline. It also means wearing a bra and loose, climate-suitable clothing. Women are only expected to wear an *abeyya* (but not cover their hair) in Saudi Arabia.

On public beaches, women will attract less unwanted attention in shorts and a loose T-shirt rather than in swimming costumes. Bikinis (except in tourist resorts) cause a local sensation. Topless or nude sunbathing or swimming is against the law.

Sleeping

Between December and February, and during *eid* (Islamic feast) holidays, it's important to book accommodation up to a month in advance. Except in Salalah in Oman, there are usually special offers in summer (May to October).

- **Hotels** Hotels range from five-star opulence in Gulf cities to simple transit hotels along major highways. Top-end and midrange hotels offer best value.
- **Desert Camps** Organised camps offering tented or cabin accommodation, usually in stunning locations.

Safety

Many people shy away from visiting the Arabian Peninsula, afraid of the troubles afflicting parts of the Middle East. With the exception of Yemen, however, at the time of writing there is no greater likelihood of encountering terrorism on the Peninsula than anywhere else. The main threat to safety is on the road: Peninsula countries have a very high incidence of traffic accidents. Theft and assault are extremely rare.

Bargaining

Bargaining over prices (except in malls) is still very much a way of life on the Peninsula, although to a lesser extent than in some other Middle Eastern countries. Oman is perhaps the exception, where aggressive bargaining can offend.

Prices rarely come down below half the original quote; 25% to 30% discount is around the norm.

Tipping

- **Coffeehouses** Not required.
- **Hotels** Equivalent of a couple of dollars for bags; entirely discretionary for cleaning staff.
- **Restaurants** Discreet tipping for exceptional service only (a service charge is usually included).
- **Taxis** Not expected but appreciated for other than short, metered city hops.
- **Guides** Ask the tour operator before engaging a guide as rates vary in each country.

SUSANNA WYATT/GETTY IMAGES ©

A woman bargaining for scarves in Salalah, Oman

Mosque Etiquette

The impressive grand mosques that grace each Peninsula capital city are often open to non-Muslims. A mosque tour can be inspirational in terms of cultural insights. The following advice will help ensure no offence is unwittingly caused during visits.

Do...

- Dress modestly in loose clothing, covering shoulders, arms and legs (plus cleavage and hair for women); some mosques require women to wear an *abeyya* (full-length black robe).
- Remove shoes before stepping into the prayer hall.
- Sit on the carpet, enjoy the ambience and marvel at the usually exquisite interior design.
- Take photographs unless otherwise directed.

Don't...

- Enter a mosque during prayer times (non-Muslims).
- Wear frayed denim jeans or any clothing that may be deemed disrespectful.
- Enter the women's prayer hall if you're a man (women may enter the men's prayer hall in most mosques open to the public).
- Use the ablution area – it's for the preparation of worship.
- Touch the Holy Quran.
- Extend your feet out front while sitting; tuck them underneath in a slouched kneeling position.
- Speak in a loud voice, sing or whistle.
- Take inappropriate selfies or photographs of people praying.

What's New

Indigenous Fare

It used to be the case that it was almost impossible to sample indigenous cuisine unless you were the lucky invitee to somebody's home. With the new inclination of locals to travel beyond their home towns, however, demand for restaurants selling national favourites is increasing. Look out for our reviewed listings highlighting 'Emirati', 'Omani' and 'Bahraini' food – for the Arabian ambience as much as the distinctive flavours.

National Museum, Muscat, Oman

This major new contribution to the cultural archive of Oman is housed in a purpose-built marble treasure, opposite the Sultan's Palace in old Muscat. (p131)

Bahrain National Theatre, Manama

With 1001 seats, paying homage to *The Thousand and One Nights,* this theatre appears to float on water, presenting a spectacle in its own right. (p66)

Dar al Athar al Islamiyya, Kuwait City

At last the Al Sabah collection, looted in the Iraq invasion of the 1990s, finds a home in the impressive galleries of this cultural centre. (p93)

Abu Dhabi Louvre, Saadiyat Island, UAE

Due to open in 2016, and inspired by the pattern of light in a palm plantation, this remarkable building designed by Jean Nouvel will hold an international collection of fine art. (p351)

Old Castle Museum, Al Kamil, Oman

The almost-obsessive displays of household items housed here are heaven for those curious about regional social history. (p163)

Burj Khalifa At the Top Sky, Dubai, UAE

At 555m this elevation deck, the highest in the world, is as near as you can get to flying without leaving the ground. (p311)

Alila Jabal Akhdar, Oman

On an isolated plateau in the mountains, you can go wild at this remote luxury resort and spa without having to go wanting. (p177)

Road from Shwaymiya to Hasik, Dhofar, Oman

A spectacular new road across rugged Jebel Samham makes it possible now to drive along almost the entire coast of Oman. (p199)

Jebel Jais Drive, Ras al Khaimah, UAE

Corkscrewing to the top of the Emirates' highest peak, this new road ascends to almost 2000m and is dusted in snow in winter. (p342)

Hop-on, hop-off bus, Doha, Qatar

Finally earning its spurs as a city worthy of an open-top bus ride, Doha has joined other cities in the double-decker tour craze. (p231)

For more recommendations and reviews, see lonelyplanet.com/Traveller Destination

If You Like...

Shopping

Browse the old, covered alleyways known as souqs for traditional crafts. Malls (their modern, air-conditioned equivalents) are mostly found in cities and offer a day's entertainment and shelter from the heat.

Souq Waqif Doha's tasteful reinvention of its Bedouin roots includes traditional coffee-houses. (p225)

Mutrah Souq Indian Ocean trade remains unchanged in Muscat's aged souq. (p127)

Dubai Mall This Emirates pleasure dome includes a walk-under aquarium. (p327)

Yas Mall Giving access to Ferrari World, this Abu Dhabi mall delivers burgers via roller coaster. (p364)

Nizwa Souq Famed for Omani silver daggers, but also brisk trading in goats. (p169)

Jeddah Souq Saudi's gold souqs sell 22-carat jewellery by weight not craftsmanship. (p266)

Souq Al Jamal You're welcome to browse rather than buy at this ancient camel market. (p263)

Bab al Bahrain Pearls are still found in this gritty warren of shops. (p56)

Mabarakia Souq Heaped-high olives and dates, headdresses and perfumes in the heart of Kuwait City. (p92)

Sinaw Souq The Bedu travel across the neighbouring sands to buy life's essentials from the town's marketplace. (p169)

Forts & Castles

While every country on the Arabian Peninsula has its own set of crenelations, the best forts and castles are found in eastern Arabia, keeping back trouble from the sea.

Jabrin Castle Unique painted ceilings distinguish this perfectly formed Omani castle. (p179)

Qal'at al Bahrain Spectacular by night, Manama's fort looms over the sea. (p69)

Nakhal Fort Guarding what was once the regional capital, this fort appears to emerge from the rock. (p183)

Al Jahili Fort This Al Ain fort honours British desert veteran Wilfred Thesiger. (p366)

Fujairah Fort Part of a village reconstruction demonstrating that the UAE has a history and not just a future. (p374)

Al Zubara Fort Interesting mostly for its location at the end of nowhere in the middle of nothing. (p244)

Bahla Fort This Unesco World Heritage Site dominates Oman's village of magic, potters and ancient walls. (p179)

Nizwa Fort Castle buffs will spot that a round tower makes this Oman fort unique in Arabia. (p169)

Rustaq Fort Guarding the passes between desert plain and mountain interior. (p185)

Museums

Museum of Islamic Art Doha's world-class museum is housed in an iconic IM Pei building. (p225)

Tareq Rajab Museum Stunning collection of regional crafts mercifully saved from the Gulf War devastation of Kuwait's National Museum. (p93)

Bahrain National Museum This excellent ethnographic museum in Manama proves there was indeed life before oil. (p53)

National Museum, Riyadh A full-scale reconstruction of a Nabataean tomb avoids the need to journey to Madain Saleh. (p257)

Sharjah Heritage Area A living museum of restored houses, museums and souqs captures the tiny emirate's heyday. (p332)

Oil Museum, Bahrain Marks the place where black gold was first struck in Arabia. (p74)

Khasab Fort Houses one of the best little ethnographic museums in Oman. (p189)

Bayt al Zubair Housed in a Muscat residence, this eclectic collection has become Oman's contemporary art hub. (p131)

National Museum, Muscat Brand new showcase of regional artefacts opposite the Sultan's Palace. (p131)

Museum of the Frankincense Land, Salalah Explores the supposed southern Arabian haunts of the legendary Queen of Sheba. (p194)

Desert Landscapes

If you thought 'desert' meant sand, think again. The Peninsula (in particular Oman, Saudi and the UAE) is full of diverse and spectacular landscapes that redefine the term.

Sharqiya Sands, Oman A fraction of the size of the Empty Quarter dunes, but just as beautiful and much more accessible. (p165)

Khor Al Adaid, Qatar An inland sea, netted by high dunes, sparkling with shoals of silver sardines. (p242)

Wadi Dharbat, Oman Camels and cows share abundant herbage in the region's seasonal mists. (p202)

Jebel Shams, Oman Vertiginous glimpses into the Grand Canyon of Arabia from atop Oman's highest mountain. (p177)

Al Ula, Saudi Arabia Magnificent wind-blown pillars of sandstone turn copper-coloured at sunset. (p275)

Liwa Oasis, UAE Date plantations punctuate the sand dunes on the edge of the Empty Quarter. (p370)

Mughsail, Oman Blowholes fling fish, seaweed and unsuspecting crabs into the air beneath

EMAD ALJUMAH/GETTY IMAGES ©

DANITA DELIMONT/GETTY IMAGES ©

Top: Kuwait Towers (p91)

Bottom: Wadi Dharbat, Oman (p202)

Dhofar's dramatic undercliff. (p203)

Musandam, Oman Deeply incised fjords with leaping dolphins and dotted with hidden villages. (p188)

Jebel Hafeet, Al Ain, UAE Drive to the top of this rocky spine to peer across to the Empty Quarter. (p369)

Architecture

Dubai, Abu Dhabi and Doha are putting the Arabian Peninsula on the map for innovative architecture. A few ancient wonders in Saudi and Oman show it has ever been thus.

Madain Saleh, Saudi Arabia The Nabataean monuments of this 'petite Petra' lie in a wind-sculpted desert of sandstone. (p278)

Burj Khalifa and **Burj Al Arab** Both equally cutting edge, and winning the prize for height and flare respectively. (p311; p314)

Beit Sheikh Isa bin Ali Al Khalifa, Bahrain Best example of the air-conditioning wizardry of 18th- and 19th-century wind-tower architecture. (p74)

Arab Fund Building, Kuwait The interior is a demonstration of the unity of Islamic art. (p96)

Al Corniche, Qatar A monument to 21st-century postmodern architecture, setting a benchmark for daring design. (p227)

Sheikh Zayed Grand Mosque, Abu Dhabi World-class masterpiece of modern mosque design. (p351)

Kuwait Towers These iconic towers have come to symbolise more than just water in the desert. (p91)

Yas Viceroy Abu Dhabi The only hotel in the world to straddle a Formula One racetrack. (p358)

Mutrah Corniche, Muscat A picture-perfect sweep of balconied houses, mosques and forts in the heart of Oman's capital. (p126)

Abu Dhabi Louvre Famed for its beautiful domed roof filtering a 'rain of light' inspired by palm trees. (p351)

Wildlife

With the exception of Bahrain, Qatar and Kuwait, the Arabian Peninsula countries offer spectacular wildlife experiences. Go dolphin and whale watching, see turtles lay their eggs, or track oryx across the plains and you'll quickly realise that desert does not mean deserted.

Turtles Watch record numbers of turtles return to the beach of their birth at **Ras al Jinz** in Oman. (p157)

Dolphins Sail by dhow from Muscat to enjoy the company of acrobatic **dolphins**. (p138)

Whales Look out for the gentle giants of the Indian Ocean around Muscat in December.

Dugongs Go diving for pearls in Bahrain or Qatar and you may come face-to-face with a sea cow.

Oryx Get up close to the endangered 'unicorn of Arabia' at **Al Areen Wildlife Park & Reserve** in Bahrain. (p72)

Hyrax Meet the unlikely relative of the elephant when the desert turns green in summertime in southern Oman.

Gazelles Discover the indigenous fauna of Arabia in the UAE's **Sir Bani Yas Island**. (p372)

Desert adaptations Learn how animals survive the heat in **Sharjah Desert Park**. (p338)

Mangroves Kayak through the shallows off Abu Dhabi's coast to witness this rich ecosystem up close. (p356)

Adventure

Travellers have been attracted to the Peninsula for centuries in search of adventure. Follow in the footsteps of Marco Polo, Richard Burton and Wilfred Thesiger in some of the region's best outdoor pursuits.

Snorkelling and diving Swim anywhere along the Red Sea coast for one of the world's great underwater spectacles.

Wild camping Pitch a tent by the Indian Ocean and listen to ghost crabs scuttling through the high-tide line.

4WD excursions Drive at high altitude through the Hajar Mountains and discover gears you didn't know you had.

Sand driving Let down the tyres and get revving in the sand dunes of Qatar's **Khor Al Adaid**. (p242)

Wadi Walks Plunge from pool to pool in Oman's **Snake Gorge**. (p172)

Camel riding Put your riding skills to the test in Oman's **Sharqiya Sands**. (p165)

Dhow rides Hold on to your wits as your captain steers you round the bend in the *khors* (creeks) of **Musandam**. (p189)

Skating and skiing Head for the snow in Dubai's **Mall of the Emirates** or don skates in any Gulf capital. (p328)

Top: Dubai Mall (p312), UAE

Bottom: Camels crossing the Sharqiya (Wahiba) Sands desert (p165), Oman

Month by Month

TOP EVENTS

Muscat Festival, January

Dubai Shopping Festival, February

Jenadriyah National Festival, March

Salalah Tourism Festival, August

Formula One Abu Dhabi, November

January

Bitterly cold in the mountains and at night on the desert plains, but gloriously warm and sunny everywhere else, this is the peak season for visiting the Arabian Peninsula. Expect the odd rain shower though!

Muscat Festival

The Omani capital comes alive with top-class acrobatic acts, international craft shopping and Omani heritage displays in venues across the city for a month around January and February. Details at www.muscat-festival.com. (p139)

Dubai Marathon

This event (www.dubaimarathon.org) attracts thousands of runners and is the world's richest long-distance-running event.

Qatar Open

Qatar's sporting year begins with this international tennis event (www.qatartennis.org), which has included top players such as Roger Federer.

February

Still cool at night and warm in the day, but without the rush of New Year visitors, February is one of the best months to enjoy the bustle of high season in the Gulf.

Shopping Festivals

Straddling January and February, the month-long Dubai Shopping Festival and the Hala Festival in Kuwait City offer big discounts in shops and firework displays. (p319)

Desert Master Trek

During this taxing sand race (www.liwachallenge.com), international runners tackle the dunes of the Empty Quarter near Liwa over distances of 100km and 200km.

March

A flush of lime green clads the desert as spring brings an intense and brief flourish of flowers and butterflies before the onslaught of summer scares them away – along with the tourists.

Jenadriyah National Festival

Saudi Arabia's largest cultural event embraces the King's Cup camel race, falconry and traditional crafts. (p261)

Horse Racing

The Dubai World Cup is the world's richest horse race, worth US$10 million, and is a major event on the UAE's social calendar. Details at www.dubairacingclub.com. The Emir's Sword Race, held in Qatar, is one of the biggest international racing events of Arabian horses in the year. Details at www.qrec.gov.qa.

April

With the plains hotting up, this is a great month to be in the mountains of Oman or Saudi, with wild and cultivated roses in full bloom, ready to be plucked for rosewater.

Formula One Bahrain

One of the biggest events in Bahrain, this glamorous race (www.bahraingp.com) is held annually.

May

Few visitors are brave enough to experience May in Arabia – it's intensely hot and overbearingly humid. With Ramadan falling partly in May between 2017 and 2019, this is a month many people will choose to avoid.

June

With miserable heat and humidity, the only good thing to be said for June is that hotels offer discounts. Camping and 'glamping' in the mountains of Oman offer a respite from the heat.

Power Boat GP, Doha

Watch the wake being carved up by speed merchants in this championship grand prix (www.qmsf.org).

Ramadan

The holy month of Ramadan is marked by fasting between dawn and dusk and visitors must take care to avoid eating or drinking in public. Ramadan evenings, however, are marked by socialising and seasonal delicacies.

Eid al Fitr

Marking the end of the month of fasting, Eid al Fitr is generally celebrated at home with the family, with little of note for tourists.

FRANCKREPORTER/GETTY IMAGES ©

PETER J FOX/CONTRIBUTOR/GETTY IMAGES ©

Top: New Year's Eve fireworks above Dubai Marina (p315), UAE
Bottom: Abu Dhabi Grand Prix (p356), UAE

July

Excessively hot in the desert, this is the season of the *khareef* (rainy period) in southern Oman. Regional visitors pour into the area to enjoy the relative cool.

Turtle Nesting

Throughout the year, turtles return to the beaches of their birth to lay their own eggs, but July is the peak season in Oman when 100 green turtles lumber up the beach at Ras al Jinz each night. (p157)

August

High season in the misty, green, bug-laden haven of southern Arabia, while the rest of the region pants in desiccating temperatures. A challengingly hot month for hajj from 2017 onwards.

Salalah Tourism Festival

Regional visitors flock to the festival ground in Salalah to picnic in the drizzle and enjoy a program of international entertainment and Omani cultural shows. (p196)

September

The impact of millions of pilgrims heading to Mecca is felt at airports and on highways across the whole region, and Saudi is closed to non-Muslim visitors.

Eid al Adha

Families gather to eat the fatted calf and celebrate the return of pilgrims from Mecca and Medina.

Classical Music

The season opens with the Royal Opera House in Muscat staging concerts, opera, ballet and jazz from internationally renowned companies. (p133)

Dance Festival

The annual three-day Dubai International Dance Festival (www.dubaidancefestival.com) showcases renowned performing artists.

October

A slight lowering of temperatures, with a return to school and college locally, make this a tolerable low season for a visit.

November

As the summer heat subsides, occasional rains help the wadis flow. Visitors begin to return to enjoy the reawakening of the Peninsula.

Oman Desert Marathon

International runners are faced with a tough challenge in the dunes of Oman's Sharqiya Sands as they head across the wilderness to the Indian Ocean. (p165)

Formula One Abu Dhabi

Showcasing one of the most glamorous circuits in the world, the Abu Dhabi Grand Prix is a highlight of the racing year. (p356)

December

The end of the year marks the peak tourist season for good reason – the sea is still warm, the air is crisp and clear and evenings are warm enough for dining al fresco.

Dubai International Film Festival (DIFF)

Abu Dhabi and Doha host film festivals, but DIFF is the star of the show. Running since 2004, it showcases cinematic excellence and casts a spotlight on Arab film. (p319)

New Year

Although the Arab New Year falls on a different day each year, the region is never one to resist a party. Dubai offers some of the finest firework shows in the world to celebrate 31 December.

Mubadala World Tennis Championship

The most prestigious tennis tournament (www.mubadalawtc.com) in the region is hosted in Abu Dhabi and attracts the world's best players.

ISLAMIC HOLIDAYS

Ramadan, the month of fasting, and the two main Islamic holidays in the year, Eid Al Fitr and Eid al Adha (marked by feasting and festivities), are observed across the region. The dates are governed by the lunar calendar and advance by roughly 10 days each year.

Itineraries

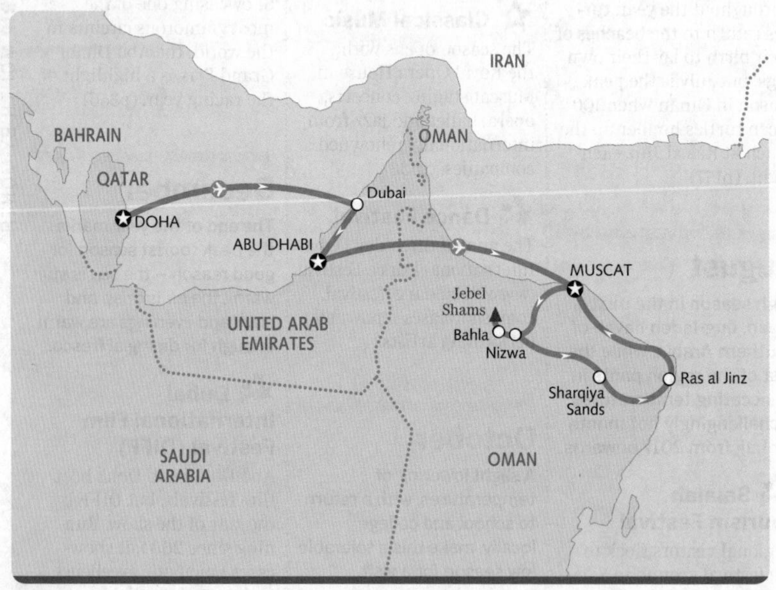

Best of the Peninsula

Weaving between the sites of modern and ancient Arabia, this itinerary highlights the best Peninsula experiences feasible in the least amount of time. If focuses on three Gulf cities and then offers a relaxing contrast to the urban pace in the wilds of Oman.

Begin with two days in **Doha**, with its skyline of modern architectural gems. Loiter with falcons in Souq Waqif and visit the Museum of Islamic Art to understand that the Gulf is built on ancient values.

Fly to **Dubai**, a city obsessed with the newest, biggest and best, for a two-day stop, including that totem of superlatives, Burj Khalifa. Spend a day in **Abu Dhabi**, the UAE's cultured capital, visiting Sheikh Zayed Grand Mosque – proof there's more to the Emirates than shopping.

For a complete contrast, fly from Abu Dhabi to **Muscat**. See how 40 years of 'renaissance' has created a modern nation underpinned by respect for heritage – evident during a four-day tour of **Nizwa** and **Bahla**. Allow three further days to forget history by hiking at **Jebel Shams**, camel riding across **Sharqiya Sands** and watching turtles return to the beach of their birth at **Ras al Jinz** before returning to Muscat.

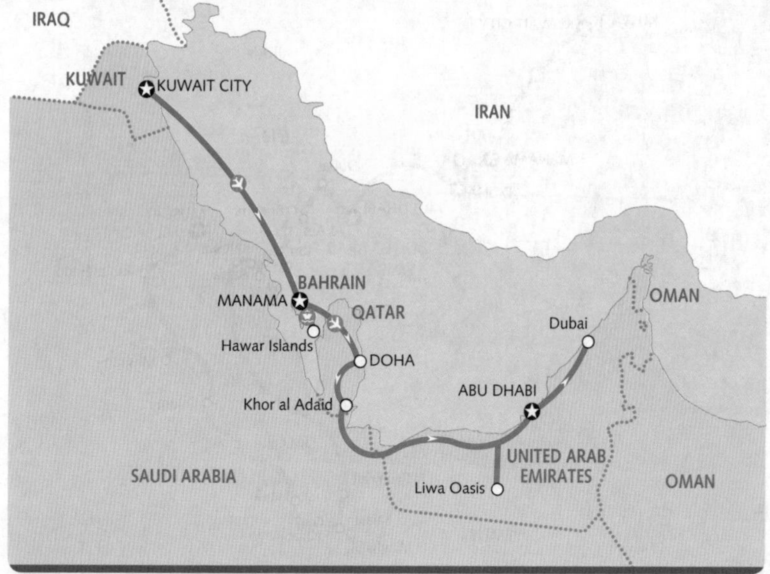

The Gulf Experience

Many people visit one of the Gulf capitals as a stopover en route to somewhere else. There are more than enough diversions and experiences on offer, however, to make it worthwhile to combine these city states as a destination in their own right.

Spend four days in each of the five main Gulf cities, flying between each. Begin in dry, traditional **Kuwait City**. Learn here the sensory vocab of Arabia – the haggling in Souq Marbarakia, the haunting call to prayer and wafts of sheesha from outdoor coffeehouses. Add to the Arabian lexicon by tracing similarities between Peninsula cultures at Tareq Rajab Museum and leave time to explore the urban landscape of high-rise towers – the quintessential icons of Gulf modernity.

Oil is responsible for Arabia's rapid propulsion into the 21st century: see how in nearby Bahrain, home to the Oil Museum. Enjoy the glamour associated with black gold at the Formula One racing circuit. Pearls gave the Gulf its former livelihood: buy a string at Gold City in **Manama** or dive for your own off the **Hawar Islands**.

Fly to neighbouring Qatar, renowned for its commitment to hosting international sports. **Doha** also boasts one of the most spectacular modern skylines in the world built on reclaimed land. Visit **Khor Al Adaid** in southern Qatar and watch the inland sea get its own back as it encroaches into the dunes.

Abu Dhabi, the cultural and political capital of United Arab Emirates, is another city reliant on reclaimed land – which becomes obvious on a walk along the beautiful Corniche. Punctuate your high-voltage city tour with an escape to **Liwa Oasis**, where life moves at the pace of a camel's stride.

If you miss the dynamism of the urban experience, then the best has been kept until last. Spend four days in and around **Dubai**, discovering what makes it the region's most internationally famous city. Cook with chefs, shop with sharks, view the city from the world's tallest tower and dine underwater in the Gulf's most can-do city.

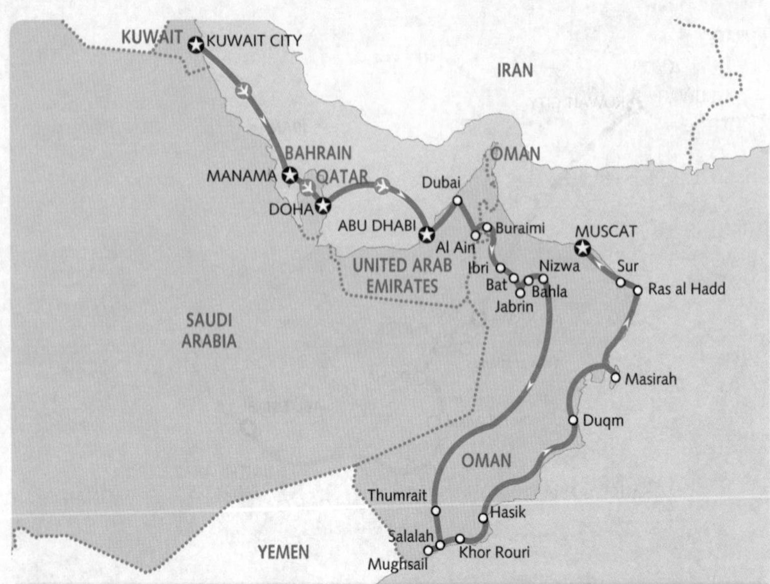

Pan-Peninsula: Five Countries in Five Weeks

They may share the same Peninsula, but arid Kuwait City in the north and subtropical Salalah in the south are so different in character they may as well belong to different continents. Explore the diversity of Arabia by spending three days in each of the five main conurbations of the **Gulf**, enjoying the modern miracle of these virtual city states.

With the city-centric part of the journey over, escape from **Dubai** at the start of week three to the starry skies and apricot-coloured dunes of **Al Ain**. Allow time to wander through souqs of grumbling camels and listen for the ghost of intrepid desert explorer Wilfred Thesiger, commemorated in the fort museum.

End week three by crossing the border via **Buraimi** to **Ibri** in Oman – the land of 1000 towers and fortifications, cresting mountain tops and looming over wadis. The building of towers in the region has been a tradition for millennia, as pre-Islamic burial towers at **Bat** testify. Continue through the castle towns of **Jabrin** and **Bahla** to **Nizwa**, where the mighty Jebel Shams looms over the heritage city.

Begin week four taking a break from the vertical in the ultimate horizontal bus ride – crossing the edge of the Empty Quarter on the flat and utterly featureless highway to **Thumrait**. The descent into **Salalah**, Oman's southern capital, after 10 hours of stony-plain monotony is sublime, especially during the rainy season when the desert turns green. End week four among frankincense trees near **Mughsail** and see where the precious resin was traded at Al Baleed and the ancient harbour of **Khor Rouri**.

With a car, begin week five skirting the Arabian Sea from Salalah to **Hasik** and the remote coast road north. Pause for a night or two of wild camping, or press on to the frontier town of **Duqm** for unexpected five-star luxury in the new resort developments in the booming port town. Complete a lap of **Masirah** to understand the true meaning of the term 'desert island' before continuing along the edge of the Sharqiya Sands to **Ras al Hadd**. Spend a day in **Sur**, where the lighthouses of Ayjah guide dhows to safe haven, before heading to journey's end in the hospitable city of **Muscat**.

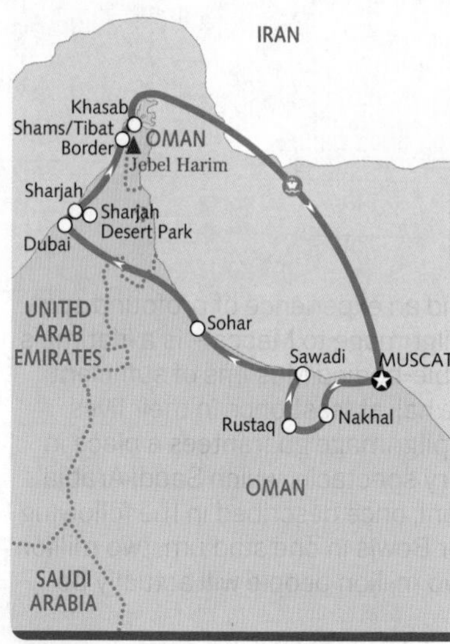

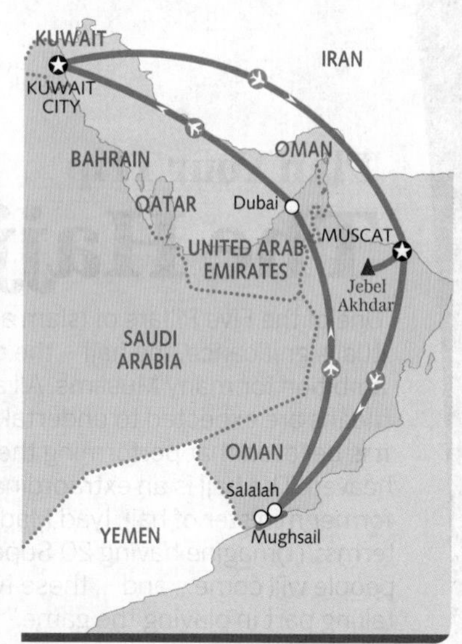

Easy Escape from Dubai

If the intensity of Dubai begins to take its toll, a trip into the neighbouring Emirates and Oman provides an enjoyable antidote. Oman's Musandam Peninsula makes a good weekend break, but with an extra day or two, a mini-tour of northern Oman is possible.

From **Dubai** head north to **Sharjah**, a hub of heritage and Islamic arts. On day two, wind through the northern Emirates to the **Shams–Tibat border** and enter Oman's fabled Musandam Peninsula. Enjoy the spectacular drive along the cliff-hugging road to **Khasab** and time your arrival for a dhow cruise in Musandam's celebrated *khors* (creeks).

Spend day three in a 4WD, exploring **Jebel Harim** and Rawdah Bowl with its 'House of Locks'. Return to Khasab and on day four take the ferry to **Muscat**: entering Mutrah harbour at night is a magical experience. Visit Mutrah Souq and Muscat's old quarter and on day five meander west via **Nakhal** and **Rustaq** with their magnificent forts and pause for a swim at **Sawadi**. Stretch to an extra day by overnighting in the growing town of **Sohar**.

Easy Escape from Kuwait

Kuwait is a fascinating country to explore, but as a conservative, flat, dry state, hemmed in by travel-restricted neighbours, it doesn't offer many opportunities to let your hair down. For the complete antithesis of life in **Kuwait City**, take the following trip to Oman and the UAE.

Fly to **Muscat** and enjoy the tolerant, cosmopolitan nature of the city. Spend a day at a beachside hotel and enjoy the novelty of a sea with waves, followed by sundowners and dancing in a nightclub. On day three be reminded of what mountains and orchards look like by hiking in clear fresh air, blissfully devoid of humidity, on **Jebel Akhdar**.

On day four, fly to **Salalah**, where the subtropical climate, summer greenery, cooler climate and casual atmosphere will remind you of Africa. On day five, visit the spectacular blowholes at **Mughsail** in a landscape untrammelled by oil pipelines and nodding donkeys. On day six, swap the rural idyll for the urban wild side by flying into **Dubai** for extreme shopping, dining and partying. On day seven, button up the collar for the journey back to **Kuwait City**.

Plan Your Trip
The Hajj

One of the Five Pillars of Islam and an experience of profound spiritual significance, the hajj – the pilgrimage to Mecca – is a lifetime's ambition for many Muslims. All able-bodied Muslims of sufficient means are expected to undertake hajj at least once in their lives: it is believed that performing the pilgrimage guarantees a place in heaven. The hajj is an extraordinary spectacle, which Saudi Arabia's former minister of hajj, Iyad Madani, once described in the following terms: '(I)magine having 20 Super Bowls in one stadium, two million people will come… and … these two million people will actually be taking part in playing the game.'

What to Bring

Label everything and attach a coloured ribbon to your belongings to help identify them.

- two to three *ihram* (white garment)
- towels
- indoor scarf (for women)
- surgical mask for crowds
- non-stitched sandals
- pyjamas (for women only)
- band-aids
- hand sanitiser
- travel belt
- pillow
- umbrella
- sunscreen
- water-bottle carrier
- toiletries (non-perfumed) and medications
- camp stool
- Quran
- shoulder bag
- pocket notebook to record thoughts

The Hajj Experience

Performed at the Great Mosque of Mecca and its immediate surrounds – Mina, Muzdalifah and Mt Arafat – hajj takes place each year on predetermined dates, and commemorates the Prophet Ibrahim's acts of surrender and devotion to God. The dates advance annually by 10 days in line with the lunar calendar on which the Islamic year is based.

Before the Pilgrimage

Most pilgrims arrive in Saudi Arabia by air, landing at the Hajj terminal of Jeddah's airport (p271). Come prepared for the fact that more than two million pilgrims flood through the terminal – waiting times for buses to Mecca can last up to 12 long, hot and humid hours. Drinking water is provided, but bring snacks. You can buy food at the airport.

Before arriving in Mecca, local pilgrims stop at *miqats* (areas designated by the Prophet) to shower and change into their *ihram* outfit, a two-piece seamless white garment. International pilgrims landing at Jeddah airport will usually have already crossed this area. Women are not permitted to wear the *niqab* or *burqa*. There is no

Top: Kaaba, Mecca , Saudi Arabia (p288)

Bottom: Koran verses on the Kaaba's door

HAJJ CALENDAR

ISLAMIC CALENDAR	ESTIMATED EQUIVALENT IN WESTERN CALENDAR
8-12 Dhul Hijja 1437H	9-12 Sep 2016
8-12 Dhul Hijja 1438H	30 Aug-2 Sep 2017
8-12 Dhul Hijja 1439H	19-22 Aug 2018
8-12 Dhul Hijja 1440H	8-11 Aug 2019

gender segregation during the rituals, as a sign that all pilgrims are equal.

An invocation in Arabic is performed – aloud, under one's breath or privately in one's head – at certain points on the way to Mecca depending on which direction pilgrims are coming from. This invocation is given as pilgrims reach the *miquat* near Mecca:

Here I am, oh God, at Your command! Here I am at Your command! You are without associate! Here I am at Your command! To You are all praise, grace and dominion! You are without associate!

The First Day

Arriving at Mecca's Grand Mosque, worshippers perform the *tawaf al qudum* (*tawaf* of arrival) by circling counter-clockwise seven times around the Kaaba. Then comes the *sa'ee*, which involves walking between the hills of Safa and Marwah (which are within the Grand Mosque grounds) seven times to simulate the desperate search for water by Hajar, the wife of Ibrahim.

The next stop is the 'tent city' of Mina, a short distance from Mecca. It's a time for rest and for reading the Quran and praying. Depending on the tour package, worshippers sleep in tents that accommodate up to 12 people each.

The Second Day

This is the most significant day of the hajj. The 'Day of Arafat' begins after sunrise, as worshippers leave Mina to travel to the Plain of Arafat. The time here is spent standing or sitting at the Mount of Mercy, asking God for forgiveness and making supplications. Some pilgrims rest in their tents. After sunset, everyone moves on to the Muzdalifah Plain to spend the whole night praying and collecting pebbles for the stoning ritual the next day.

The Third to Fifth Days

The third day begins shortly before sunrise in Mina, where worshippers once threw their pebbles at three *jamrah* (pillars) that represented the devil. In 2004, due to the many injuries caused by the fervour of the stone throwing, Saudi authorities replaced the pillars with long walls and stone basins designed to catch ricocheting rocks. The stoning can continue for three days and represents a rejection of Satan and an affirmation of Ibrahim's faith in God.

The stoning ritual is perhaps when pilgrims are most vulnerable to danger as worshippers crowd the Jamarat pedestrian bridge on their way to the pillars. Deadly stampedes have occurred here in the past, so it's important to pay close attention to instructions from guides and security personnel and to follow the multilingual signs along the route with care.

This is the first day of the three-day Eid al Adha (feast of sacrifice), and pilgrims spend the remaining days carrying out these three rites after their first round of stoning. A sheep, cow or camel is sacrificed to show God a willingness to offer up something precious, and the meat is distributed to the poor. Men shave their heads, or trim their hair evenly, and women cut off a lock of their hair to bring them out of *Ihram*. The final formal rite of hajj is the *Tawaf al Ifadah/Ziyarah*, when pilgrims return to Mecca to circle the Kaaba again, pray at the Station of Ibrahim and perform another sa'ee.

The Final Day

While the formal part of hajj is now over, many pilgrims choose to spend another day in Mina until sunset to undertake more stoning and reflection, others return to Mecca. Before leaving Mecca and starting on their journeys back home all pilgrims perform the 'farewell' *Tawaf al Wada*.

Hajj Practicalities

With so many hajj pilgrims each year – some estimates put the number at 2.5 million or more – Saudi Arabia's Ministry of Hajj has streamlined the process to obtain a visa and perform the rituals. It's still a complicated process, but remember that Muslims cannot be denied the right to perform the fifth pillar of Islam, regardless of whether they are Sunni or Shiite and regardless of their personal history.

The Hajj Ministry's website (haj.gov.sa) lists its requirements, which should be followed to the letter. The ministry requires that all pilgrims go through a licensed travel agency that operates hajj and *umrah* (a pilgrimage to Mecca outside hajj season) tours. The tour operator will do all the work after you provide it with the necessary documents.

Hajj Eligibility

The first step is to determine whether you are eligible to perform hajj. Muslims who have performed the ritual are not allowed to perform it again until five years have passed. An exception will be made for those acting as a *mahram* (guardian) to accompany a wife or family member who plans to go. All women under the age of 45 must be accompanied by a *mahram*, which must be a close male relative.

Visas & Tour Operators

Pilgrims must apply online through the Saudi Ministry of Hajj website (haj.gov.sa) and the approved tour operators listed on the website. Travel agency prices can be as low as SR6500 per person but can run as high as SR30,000 or more depending on the amenities offered. All tour companies offer meals, air-conditioned buses, transportation to Medina and side tours to significant religious sites. It is essential that you stick to the approved list of travel agencies.

These agencies handle everything, including obtaining a hajj visa (free and valid for 30 days) and permits, processing immunisation records (meningitis and hepatitis A and B are required jabs), and arranging accommodation and transportation. If the applicant is a convert to Islam, a letter from the applicant's mosque stating that he or she performed the *shahada* (statement of faith) must be produced.

Tour companies keep strict tabs on their clients once they arrive in Saudi Arabia. Worshippers give up their passport for the duration of their stay and are issued with an identity card and wristband. It is important that worshippers keep a copy of their passport, including all pages and visas, and all travel documents. Once in the Kingdom, travel for pilgrims is strictly limited to visiting Mecca and Medina and the cities and villages between the two cities.

Hajj Health & Safety

Hajj rituals can be difficult to perform for the very young and the very old. Depending on the time of year, temperatures can reach more than 40°C and crowds can be stifling.

Common sense and caution are the foundation of a safe trip. Eat and sleep when you can, drink plenty of fluids, wear a surgical mask – to protect against the small risk of MERS (coronavirus) – and never stop using hand sanitiser.

Make sure you have the requisite immunisations, although heat exhaustion is the most common enemy of the pilgrim. If you feel sweating chills, nausea or dizziness, find shade and seek medical attention from one of the hundreds of emergency-personnel stations throughout the pilgrimage route.

One of the greatest risks to pilgrims comes from the massive crowds and the danger of stampede. Always pay close attention to your surroundings and follow the instructions of officials; it's wise to keep to the outer limits of moving crowds wherever possible.

UMRAH: THE LITTLE HAJJ

Umrah (lesser pilgrimage; visitation) is a shortened version of Hajj in which rituals can be carried out within the vicinity of the Grand Mosque. *Umrah* can be performed at any time of year (except during hajj itself), and at any time of day and night. Many pilgrims say *umrah* is a quiet, peaceful and contemplative experience.

The process is similar to applying for a hajj visa. Like the hajj visa, *umrah* visas are free, but they are only valid for 15 days; overstaying the 15-day visa can have serious legal consequences. Applicants must hire a Saudi-approved tour operator and provide the required documentation as they would for hajj.

Plan Your Trip
Expats

The days of being paid well for doing little are over, while the realities of extreme temperatures and different social norms remain. So why consider an expat life? Whether motivated by the ancient culture or the thrill of rapid change, you'll find it pays to anticipate the challenges before leaving home.

Key Differences

All Countries

Extreme summer heat. Weekend is built around Friday, the region's common day of prayer.

Bahrain

Extreme humidity in summer. Tiny land mass offers limited opportunities for free-time excursions. Pockets of political unrest. Tolerant of Western customs and manners.

Kuwait

A dry state. Alcohol cannot be bought or consumed. Very little greenery. Tolerant of non-Muslim religious expression. Little to explore outside Kuwait City.

Oman

Slow pace of decision making. Tolerant of foreign customs and manners.

Qatar

Extreme humidity in summer. Quite conservative.

Saudi Arabia

A dry state. Highly conservative. Restricted movement outside city of residence. Women not permitted to drive. Non-Muslim religious expression restricted.

United Arab Emirates

Liberal exterior hides a conservative core.

Everyday Life

Not so Different from Home

For many new arrivals in the region, whether from East or West, the first few days on the Arabian Peninsula often come as a culture shock. The audible call to prayer five times a day, the extreme heat, the homogeneous clothing, the undisciplined driving and the ubiquitous aroma of *sheesha* (water pipe used to smoke tobacco) combine to create an overwhelming sense of difference. This difference is further emphasised for many by the barren desert landscape.

Give it a week, however, and the similarities start appearing and day-to-day life in Arabia appears not as 'foreign' as one had imagined. International-style clothing is worn in familiar-looking malls (albeit under an *abeyya* – a woman's full-length black robe); favourite foods from many cultures, including the likes of Marmite, soy sauce and turmeric, are widely available in corner shops; schools cater expertly for the children of different expat communities; provision is made for non-Muslim worship; drinking water is safe and health centres well-funded, and most people speak English as a common language. The drinking of alcohol is tolerated in all countries except Kuwait and Saudi Arabia, and you can even buy pork in some supermarkets.

Many expats enjoy the fact that living in any of the Peninsula countries means it is safe to leave houses and cars unlocked, for children to play in the streets and talk to strangers, and that neighbours always have time for a chat. Times are changing in the big cities, but on the whole the friendly, safe and tolerant environment of all these countries is a major contributor to the quality of life. Even in Saudi Arabia, where public life is controlled by strict codes of conduct, expats generally enjoy a safe, relaxed and crime-free experience within their own compounds.

A Multicultural Experience

Expatriate populations outnumber national populations in all Gulf States. As such, the Arabian Peninsula is one of the most multicultural places on the planet. This is both a trial and a fantastic opportunity. The trial comes in learning to cope with another layer of cultural expectation. The opportunity comes in gaining an insight into richly different ways of life, expressed most noticeably through food, festivities and workplace practices.

Perhaps the most valuable aspect of the region's multicultural experience is learning from the resident Iraqis, Afghans and Palestinians that there is another perspective on the politics of the region that is not often aired in the international media.

Gulf countries are finding their own ways of helping communities displaced as a result of war. This help has translated into cash handouts to the Syrian government, for example, but it also takes the uniquely local form of absorbing economic migration.

Regional asylum seekers are welcomed either as 'guests' or as professional or skilled employees on short-term contracts. In the absence of any formal recognition of the definition of refugee status, the emphasis is on providing temporary opportunities rather than embracing asylum seekers as fellow nationals. In other words, the expectation remains that one day these migrants will return home.

Climate

Without doubt, one of the biggest challenges of living on the Peninsula is learning to cope with the weather. If you're from a cold, wet and windy place, it is hard to imagine you would ever get bored of the endless blue skies. But in summer, the sky isn't blue; it's white with heat and the extreme temperatures from April to October (which hover, on average, around 40°C and frequently rise above 45°C) require a complete life adjustment. Learning to live in the air-conditioned indoors for those months, to live life more slowly and find ways of exercising that don't involve going outside, is as difficult as coming to terms with winter in frozen climes. The upside is six months of magnificent, benign winter warmth that bid friends and relatives to visit. Here are some key ways to beat the heat:

Embrace local timing Working hours across the region tend to favour mornings and late afternoons, either with a 7am-to-2pm regime, or a two-shift day from 7am to 7pm with a break between noon and 5pm.

Take a siesta If the job allows, follow local practice by eating your main meal at lunchtime and taking a nap in the heat of the day.

Drink plenty of water Expats often underestimate the amount of extra fluid intake they require in summer and become dehydrated and ill as a result.

Wear cotton clothing Excessive humidity in Gulf cities can make a temperature of 35°C feel more like 45°C and synthetic fibres stick to the skin, adding to the boil-in-the-bag effect. Avoid excessive use of sunscreen for the same reason.

Wear a hat and sunglasses It's no accident that local costume includes some form of head covering for all. You should also cover your neck and protect your eyes from glare (off white buildings and the sea especially). Avoid sitting in the summer sun altogether if you want to maintain supple, unwrinkled skin.

Exercise with caution Half the activity takes twice the effort in extreme heat so follow the locals by exercising just before dawn or at an air-conditioned gym. There's often a slight cooling of temperature at dusk before the night-time heat explodes.

Escape to higher ground Temperature reduces by around 5°C for every 1000m of altitude gained. A weekend break (or summer retreat to drizzling Dhofar in Oman) may just keep you sane for the rest of the week.

The Law

In most Peninsula countries the law is based on Sharia'a law, which can lead to a wide interpretation of penalties for similar illegal activities from country to country – even from judge to judge, as there is no formal penal code.

Breaking the law on the Arabian Peninsula can have severe consequences, and embassies have very little jurisdiction (or inclination) to help foreign nationals in breach of local laws.

Some things that are legal in other countries, including public displays of affection, sex out of wedlock and consumption of alcohol, are illegal in some Peninsula countries and can carry a harsh sentence. Illegal acts across the region include taking drugs, public drunkenness, driving after drinking alcohol, lewd behaviour, adultery, cohabitation and homosexuality. Depending on the country you're in, breaking the law may lead to fines (for traffic offences), jail (for causing accidental death), deportation (for cohabitation), public flogging (for adultery) or even a death sentence (for drug trafficking).

Note that penalties, and even what's considered illegal, can change frequently in some countries. As such, it is vital that you thoroughly acquaint yourself with local laws before entering the country. Consult your HR manager and the embassy of the country in which you plan to work for guidance on legal matters before you take up employment.

Links to Legal Resources

Look for *Working in the Gulf* (Explorer Group, 2011) for a list of legal services country by country.

Gulf Law (www.gulf-law.com) General introduction to Sharia'a and commercial law.

Expat Corner (www.expatcornergcc.com) Listing of Gulf Cooperation Council labour laws.

Working in the Region

Labour laws throughout the Gulf are extremely strict. It's illegal to seek work on a tourist visa and there are severe penalties for those caught working illegally. Although some travellers take the chance of applying for ad-hoc work (in Dubai, for example), to remain within the law you should secure a position before arrival. Your 'sponsor' (usually your employer) acts as a kind of guarantor of your good conduct while you reside in the country and will help you obtain a visa.

Working and living conditions are usually of a high standard. Salaries carry the enormous advantage of incurring no personal taxation. It can be tricky, however, to change jobs if you decide you're not happy with the one you have. It can also be difficult to find long-term employment; many contracts are short term, renewable annually or every two years. While it's not necessary to speak Arabic (although it's an advantage), good spoken and written communication in English, the region's second language, is a prerequisite and many jobs require qualifications that would not be expected elsewhere.

Those offering professional skills in much-needed services, such as translating, nursing, engineering and teaching (particularly English), stand the best chance of gaining employment. Many administrative positions, on the other hand, are beginning to be filled by newly trained local professionals. International recruiting agencies headhunt for positions on the Peninsula. Note that for English-language teaching you will need at least a degree and teaching experience to be eligible for most job opportunities, but you don't necessarily need to be a native speaker.

You can also enquire about job opportunities at cultural centres connected with your home country and voluntary aid organisations.

Applying the Right Attitude

The working life of an expat, which often involves confronting fundamental differences in outlook, culture and education between colleagues, can be quite a challenge. It helps, therefore, to identify these differences from the beginning and then to celebrate the 'other', rather than seek to change it. The host nations, of the Gulf in particular, do this very well, accepting the expat for who they are and rarely attempting to influence their religious or social beliefs and customs. By the same token, it is important for the expat to learn to appreciate the Arab way of doing things and not assume that your own culture is always right. The expat who *listens* to what people want, rather than *guessing* what they want, is more likely to make a genuinely valuable contribution to the emerging but complex countries of the region than those who rush in with solutions that are inappropriate to the context and then feel defeated by the lack of application or implementation.

CULTURAL DOS AND DON'TS

Do...

It is not always easy, especially in the big cities of the Gulf, to interact with the local people – and especially with the indigenous Arabs who are often outnumbered in their own countries by expat residents. Here are some simple ways to engage with the local culture.

Visit a heritage village Getting a feel for the region's Bedouin roots is a great way to understand differing concepts of time and hospitality. Visiting living heritage villages, especially during festivals and national days, provides insight into each country's rich song, dance, craft and cuisine inheritance.

Learn Arabic This is not necessary for survival, as English and other expat languages are so widely spoken, but just learning to read the street signs helps bring you closer to Arab culture.

Attend a wedding Invitations to these will surely be forthcoming and, for women especially, it's the quickest way to learn that Arab women are not the oppressed creatures portrayed in some international media.

Celebrate Eid, Diwali and Christmas Peninsula people love a party and are quick to give greetings at all religious festivals, not just those of Islam; joining them is the best way to understand the strong sense of community.

Play football Between acacia trees, on the sandy beaches or atop mountain passes, showing your interest in this regional obsession is the surest way to the Arab heart.

Don't...

Peninsula countries are, on the whole, very forgiving of the transgressions of foreigners (except in Saudi Arabia), but there is nothing to be gained by upsetting the citizens of your host country. To avoid giving offence or landing yourself in trouble with the authorities, don't do the following:

Wear revealing clothing Even in liberal Dubai nothing causes more offence than exposing shoulders or thighs in shopping centres and other public spaces, or wearing tight and provocative clothing – that goes for men as well as women.

Show affection in public Avoid holding hands, kissing or hugging with members of the opposite sex.

Indulge in excessive drinking Being drunk in public is considered thoroughly reprehensible. In many countries in the region it will get you deported or even imprisoned. In Saudi, where alcohol is strictly prohibited, the penalty is severe.

Drink and drive Even in countries tolerant of alcohol consumption, there is zero tolerance for drink driving.

Take drugs It's illegal in all countries of Arabia and can lead to severe penalties.

Eat, drink or smoke in public during daylight hours in Ramadan Some countries also enforce a ban on gum chewing, singing and loud music.

Swear or use rude hand gestures In some Arab countries this may not just be considered uncouth, it may also be illegal! It's also impolite to beckon with a finger or to use the left hand when touching, giving and eating.

Take photographs without permission This is the case when photographing people, particularly women. You should also avoid photographing anything military or 'strategic' (such as airports or bus stations).

Cohabit Despite the low risk of detection if you are discreet, it is illegal to live with a member of the opposite sex (or have a baby) unless you are married. In Saudi, men and women may not travel together (including by car) unless related.

Business Etiquette

People from the Arabian Peninsula have been eminent merchants for centuries, with global trade in copper, frankincense, pearls and, latterly, oil running through their veins. Inevitably, they have developed highly refined customs and manners when it comes to commercial interaction and they are always somewhat disdainful of their foreign counterparts whose alacrity to get straight down to business shows, in their book, a lack of finesse in the fine arts of trade.

Though urbane enough to tolerate the mores of their overseas counterparts, Arab business people are impressed with good manners. Observing the following courtesies, therefore, may just help seal the deal.

Clothing Wear a suit (with a tie for men) but avoid silk or linen, which crease badly; women should cover knees, cleavage and shoulders. Formal national dress (such as sari, salwar kameez, kaftan) are acceptable and often welcomed. Attempts at dressing local-style (in *dishdasha* or *abeyya*, for example) are deemed ridiculous.

Timing Be on time for meetings, but be tolerant of late arrivals (an accepted part of local custom). Avoid meetings or telephone calls on a Friday, which is the day of prayer and rest; during afternoon siesta (except in the UAE and capital cities, where the practice is dying out); and in the holy month of Ramadan.

Greeting Shake hands readily with men but wait for an Arab woman to proffer her hand first. Only use Arab greetings if you can master them, otherwise stick to formal English. Don't be surprised if people touch their heart after a greeting (as in Saudi), if kisses on the cheek are exchanged between men (as in the Gulf States), or noses are knocked or rubbed (as in areas of Oman) – equally, don't try to do the same.

Addressing Use Arab given names, as opposed to family names. Instead of Mr Al-Wahabbi, it's Mr Mohammed. In the same way, expect to be called Mr or Ms plus your first name or initials (Mr John, Ms Geetha or Prof KPR, for example) and don't attempt to change this polite form to your family name. The correct formal address (or equivalent of Mr) is usually *asayid* (meaning sir) or *asayida* (meaning madam).

Preliminaries Exchange pleasantries about the weather and ask after health and family for several minutes before turning to the subject in hand. It's considered rude to go straight to the point. Men, however, should never enquire after another man's wife or daughters. Exchange business cards (which are a must) with your right hand (the left hand is reserved for ablutions).

Negotiating Bargaining is an important part of discovering value to the buyer weighed against worth to the vendor. The concept of a fixed price is a largely alien one amid the highly social and personal interaction of reaching a deal in the Middle East.

PUTTING PEOPLE FIRST

Much of Arab life is underpinned by a sense of 'what will be, will be'. This fatalism stems from Islam and the belief that God determines fate and is reflected in the frequent conversational phrase, *insha'allah,* which literally means 'if Allah wills it'. A belief in God's will threads through all aspects of life: it informs the response to a car accident, a soured business deal, or the death of a loved one, and it leads to a culture where personal accountability and the culture of blame (both recognisable by those from a Western culture) have limited meaning.

For the expat who is unaware of this difference, there are many frustrations involved in social and business interactions. For example, when rushing towards a deadline (a movable concept across the region), it's not unusual to find colleagues have knocked off for a tea break. But then, from the Arab point of view, what can be more important than sharing time to discuss the day and swap family news? The deadline will be met if Allah wills it, so in the meantime take your rest and have a chat. More 'business' is conducted over a *chi libton* (cup of tea) than is ever concluded after a Powerpoint presentation because in Peninsula society, people come first. To enjoy, as well as to succeed in, living and working on the Arabian Peninsula, the expat has to learn to put people first too, and the investment in good relations invariably pays unexpected dividends, smoothing the passage of daily life and opening up social and business opportunities.

Agreement Although some of the gentility of reaching agreement has vanished during recent economic tribulations, an Arab's word is his bond and, similarly, keeping your promise is considered a matter of honour.

Problem solving Keep smiling, keep your temper and avoid raising your voice. Confrontation, criticism, blaming and swearing are highly insulting in public as they involve loss of face for those concerned. Equally, making and forcing apology is best avoided. A quiet, sympathetic word in private is much more effective.

Socialising Before any kind of transaction – at the checkout in a supermarket, if the traffic police stop you, before a meeting begins, on the telephone between strangers – people greet each other thoroughly and preferably enquire after the other person's health. They often repeat these enquiries if there is a lull in the conversation. Never refuse a cup of tea or coffee as it may offend. Take your cue from the host and avoid asking for alcohol unless it is offered.

Conversing Avoid politics, sex and religion as topics of conversation, and if you are drawn into such discussion, keep your comments general, not personal. Also, avoid any comparisons of people with animals, even in jest, especially dogs (which are considered unclean by many Muslims) and donkeys (used as a common insult).

Closing The exchange of gifts is an important aspect of conducting business in the region. Well-crafted tokens representing an aspect of your home country are the normal currency of leave-taking – poorly made or obviously cheap, mass-made items will do more damage to your agenda than good.

Women in the Workplace

In the workplace, pay and opportunities for promotion are equal for both sexes (except in Saudi Arabia, where women are only employed in certain sectors). It is the norm in most Gulf countries for men and women to work side by side in an office environment. Female professionals are respected for their qualifications and experience and although it's often harder for local women to break the glass ceiling, this is not the case for foreign female professionals, who are accorded great respect in senior roles.

General advice regarding business etiquette is the same for men and women with one exception: some devoutly religious men will not touch a woman's hand. The key is to take the cue from the other person when expecting to shake hands.

Expat Life for Children & Families

Arabs love the company of children and celebrate childhood often through large families and varying indulgences. As such, expat children are assured of a welcome and may find that they have more freedom than they do back home, as parents feel safe in the knowledge that they are not going to be preyed upon in parks or offered drugs. Here are a few key family-related considerations that expats often enquire about before signing their contracts.

Activities There is little sophisticated child-oriented entertainment outside of the big cities, but a beach is never too far away and there are often parks containing children's play areas (including swings and slides), even in small towns.

Birth and maternity leave Many expat women give birth in the region and it presents no special difficulties in the main cities. There are prenatal and postnatal groups on hand to help. Maternity leave is enshrined in law in most Arab countries.

Childcare Nannies (usually from the Indian Subcontinent or the Philippines) are one of the easily afforded perks of the region. Many mums opt for live-in home help and villas often cater for this with the provision of maid's quarters. In some cities, babysitting services are available in malls.

Coffee mornings There are many groups, such as the Women's Guild in Oman (www.womensguildoman.com), that act as a forum for non-working expat women. These groups are a lifeline for many new arrivals in the region, providing local knowledge about everything from schooling, home help and health care to voluntary work and leisure activities.

Dangers Illegal drug taking, although still a relatively minor problem, is on the increase among older teenagers. Reckless driving is prevalent in all the Peninsula countries and claims many young lives. Regional and national awareness campaigns are trying to reduce these risks.

Education The standard of international schools on the Arabian Peninsula is excellent, offering similar curricula to schools back home, enabling a smooth transition into university or college outside the region.

Healthcare The extreme heat can be debilitating for children, particularly babies. Obstetric and paediatric units in hospitals and clinics are generally of a high standard and most scourges of childhood in hot climates (such as polio, malaria and typhoid) are under control.

Hotels and restaurants In top-end and some midrange hotels, children can usually share their parents' room for no extra charge. Extra beds or cots are normally available. High chairs are often only available in top-end restaurants.

Infants Disposable nappies are not always easy to come by outside large cities. Infant formula is widely available, however, as is bottled water.

Resources Expat Woman (www.expatwoman.com) or Mums Net (www.mumsnet.com) are useful forums for sharing advice and information on expat life in the Peninsula. For further advice on the dos and don'ts of taking the kids, see Lonely Planet's *Travel with Children*.

Special needs Catering for the needs of children with disabilities is highly challenging in the region as often locals attach stigma to physical and especially mental disability. Even finding help or support with common childhood issues such as dyslexia, ADD and anorexia can be difficult.

Housing

Stories about wild parties on expat compounds where the residents never interact with people beyond the gates are largely a thing of the past. Company compounds do still exist in Saudi but many expats in the Gulf are these days given an allowance and expected to find their own accommodation. Here is some general advice regarding housing:

- Rental accommodation can be found, usually unfurnished, through embassies, cultural centres and newspapers.
- Villas with gardens, apartments with a shared swimming pool or a residency within a self-sufficient and gated compound are the preferred expat residency options. Many hotels offer long-stay arrangements.
- Check that air-con, maintenance of shared areas and mains water are included in the rent.
- Shaded, off-road parking is highly desirable.
- Unless you are a fan of early mornings, you may prefer to avoid neighbouring a mosque where a wake-up call will occur well before sunrise.
- Check your employment contract covers temporary accommodation while you house hunt.
- Relocation consultants, as well as estate agents, can be found in the telephone directories of most countries.

Health

Health care across the region is consistently of a high standard in major cities. In smaller and especially rural communities, health care may be confined to a visiting doctor at the local clinic. Health-care providers tend to be expats themselves, with many nurses from the Philippines and doctors from India.

Emergency treatment is often given free, but you shouldn't rely on this. Ambulance services are available in cities, but often a taxi is the best way to get to hospital in a hurry. Operations can be very expensive and many locals opt to have surgery in India or Thailand as they believe they will receive better care in those countries.

It's imperative to have health insurance for the whole family. Carefully check the small print of any company-issued insurance as it may well exclude dental and eye care, prenatal, delivery and maternity care, as well as exempting pre-existing conditions.

Women's personal requirements (such as tampons and sanitary pads) can be found in larger supermarkets, which tend to cater for expats. Contraception is readily available, but abortion other than on health grounds is not readily supported. The term 'abortion' is often used interchangeably with 'miscarriage' among non-native English speakers in the region.

Red Tape

The countries of the Middle East seem to have a passion for bureaucracy and have large public sectors in place to administer it. For the expat this entails various paper-

Expats enjoying a boat ride in Dubai Marina (p315), UAE

chases to ensure having the right permissions in place to work, own and drive a car, purchase alcohol and, in the case of Saudi, travel around the country. This isn't as daunting as it sounds as every company will have a fixer whose job it is to steer the employee over each bureaucratic hurdle. Note that for most countries in the region you need to test negative for AIDS and tuberculosis before you gain a residency permit. This is treated as a routine and perfunctory part of the visa-obtaining process, so don't expect any pre- or post-test counselling.

You can speed up the obtaining of various permits by having at the ready a stock of passport-size photographs, some on plain white, and some on plain blue backgrounds; multiple copies of an abbreviated CV (two pages maximum); copies of your tertiary qualifications and the original certificates attested by your embassy.

Take a number on entering queuing stations, carry a book to read, be patient and stay friendly and polite, even when at your wit's end. When at length you get your residency card, driving licence or travel permit, carry it with you at all times – this is the law in most Peninsula countries.

Many countries will permit some nationalities to drive using a licence from home. Other nationalities must pass the local driving test. Check with your embassy or HR manager.

Transport

In general, except in Dubai, the UAE and Doha, which have good public transport systems, and in Saudi, where women can't drive, it is really useful to have a car for getting to work and/or running family errands. Cities are spread out and offices, services and entertainments far flung.

The Peninsula is a good place to buy a car, but note that you can't buy one without a residency permit. Most mainstream makes and models are available, and prices are low (since there's no import duty). As when shopping for other items, bargaining is normal. A down payment of around 10% of the purchase price is usually expected if taking out a loan.

CHRISTMAS & NEW YEAR AS AN EXPAT

Christmas is celebrated with gusto on the Arabian Peninsula. In the malls and shopping centres, there are lights and carols, mangers with babies and neon cribs, cards with angels and the three wise men, and Arab Muslims queuing to take the kids to see Santa. While it's common for locals to wish you a 'Happy Christmas', the best response is 'thank you' rather than a return of the same greeting. In the UAE provision is often made for vacations to be taken at Christmas, but this is uncommon elsewhere in the region and 25 December is generally treated as a normal working day.

New Year offers several opportunities for celebration as it falls on different days among different expat communities. The Arab New Year, which moves according to the lunar calendar, is often marked by a public holiday. The night of 31 December is an excuse for parties and fireworks (most spectacularly in Dubai), but 1 January is not necessarily a holiday. Chinese New Year is becoming an important cultural event.

Because cars are cheap, they're also seen as disposable by the wealthy. There is a growing secondhand car market throughout the region. Note that change of ownership has to be completed with the local police. When buying a vehicle (or importing one), you usually have to register it with the police traffic department.

When secondhand car shopping it's essential you ensure that the vehicle you're interested in purchasing has the following:

- an up-to-date test certificate
- a registration certificate (and that the engine and chassis numbers of the car match the latter)
- a clean bill of health from a mechanic
- a clean record – fines outstanding on the car are usually transferred to the new owner.

Ramadan

The 'Holy Month of Ramadan' is a time of spiritual contemplation for Muslims. For the expat it can be a time of heightened frustration as everyone works more slowly and drives more quickly.

Muslims fast from dawn to dusk during Ramadan. Foreigners are not expected to fast, but they should not smoke, drink or eat (including gum-chewing) in public during daylight hours in Ramadan. Business premises and hotels make provision for the non-fasting by erecting screens around dining areas.

Business hours tend to become more erratic and usually shorter and many restaurants close for the whole period.

With this change of routine, and given the hardship of abstaining from water during the long, hot summer days, it's not surprising that tempers easily fray and the standard of driving deteriorates. Expats should make allowances by being extra vigilant on the roads and extra tolerant in all social interactions.

Further Reading

There are many informative books about the expat experience encompassing personal narratives and practical resources – these are readily available in capital-city bookshops and airports. In addition, there are some excellent expat websites with discussion forums dispensing advice and sharing experiences.

Internet Resources

A number of websites provide information service and networking opportunities exclusively for expats:

@llo Expat Middle East (www.middleeast.alloexpat.com)

British Expats (www.britishexpats.com)

Expat Exchange (www.expatexchange.com)

Expat Forum (www.expatforum.com)

Living Abroad (www.livingabroad.com)

Countries at a Glance

The term 'Arabian Peninsula' is such a cohesive one you could be forgiven for thinking that all the countries within it are alike. There are similarities between each – the hot, arid desert, Bedouin roots, Islamic customs and the Arabic language – but the differences are just as pronounced. Head to the United Arab Emirates (UAE) and Gulf States to experience the quintessential modern Arabian city with fine museums, marble-clad malls selling the latest international fashions, avant-garde restaurants and landscaped resorts boasting every conceivable luxury. In marked contrast, Oman and Saudi Arabia offer a glimpse of the old Arabia with characterful souqs, remote mountain villages, wild coastlines and ancient archaeological sites. At Arabia's desolate core, the Empty Quarter straddles Saudi, Oman and the UAE, giving an opportunity for desert nights in unparalleled landscapes.

Bahrain

Archaeology
Social Life
Culture

A Land of Burials

Riddling and honeycombing a surprisingly large proportion of the island, the enigmatic burial mounds at A'Ali and the tombs at Sar date back to the ancient Dilmun era and underline Bahrain's trading inheritance.

Cafe Culture

Sipping coffee shakes in Manama's fashionable Adliya district is one of the best ways to catch the social vibe of this vibrant and cosmopolitan city.

Pearling Trade

Bahrain's former wealth was built on pearls and whether you trace the new pearling path through Muharraq Island or dive with a nose peg to harvest your own, you won't escape the significance of the pearl on Bahraini culture.

p50

Kuwait

Culture
Recent History
Shopping

Museums & Monuments

From the jewels and gems of the exquisite Tareq Rajab ethnographic museum to the landmark Kuwait Towers, Kuwait's identity is defined and preserved in diverse cultural riches.

Remembering the 1990s

The Iraqi invasion and the Gulf War at the end of the last century are hidden in the psyche of modern Kuwait – and exposed in moving memorials and landmarks scattered across the city.

Souqs & Malls

From souqs where the tumbling goods and produce go unlabelled to modern malls where nothing sells without the right label, Kuwait City offers a virtual history of shopping through the ages.

p86

Oman

Landscapes
Wildlife
History

Highs & Lows

Peering from Jebel Shams (Oman's highest mountain) into Wadi Ghul, Arabia's Grand Canyon, is a vertiginous experience matched by driving through Sharqiya's almost-vertical sand dunes or diving in Musandam's cliff-hugging *khors* (creeks).

Not Deserted

Nesting turtles at Ras al Jinz, oryx and gazelles in the Huqf, leopards and wolves in Dhofar and dolphins, whales and diverse Arabian Sea shells along Oman's coast prove the desert is not deserted.

Forts & Castles

With more than 1000 forts, castles, battlements and watchtowers, it's hard to pick a favourite Omani crenellation: at a push, impressive Nakhal Fort wins it for location, location, location.

p121

Qatar

Landscapes
Architecture
Culture

Inland Sea

Beautiful Khor Al Adaid offers a dune for a pillow and stars for a blanket beside Qatar's fabled inland sea – a nostalgic landscape for camel treks, campfire barbecues and desert camps that evoke Qatar's Bedouin roots.

Urban Landscape

Competing for headroom in the clustered skies above West Bay, the creative high-rise towers of modern Doha prove that if an architect can think it, an engineer can built it.

Homes of Heritage

From Doha's superb Museum of Islamic Art to the modern revival of Souq Waqif with falcons, gold, antiques and incense on sale, Doha works hard to preserve its Arabian heritage.

p222

Saudi Arabia

History
Landscapes
Islam

Little Petra

Listen to the wind whistling around the ruins at Madain Saleh, Saudi's little Petra, and you can almost hear the ancient camel caravans grumbling across the desolate gravel plains of Arabia.

Desert & Diversity

The Rub al Khali, or Empty Quarter, has inspired travellers for centuries, while the monsoon season in Oman's Dhofar transforms the region into one of astonishingly lush green mountain scenery.

Home of the Holy Cities

You don't have to be a Muslim to appreciate the power of Mecca and Medina on the national consciousness: the holy cities' message is held in the hearts of the Saudi people and is obvious in their dress, customs and manners.

p255

United Arab Emirates

Architecture
Urban Culture
Landscapes

Urban Landscape

Dubai's Burj al Arab, with its magnificent dhow-sail design; Abu Dhabi's opulent Emirate Palace; a Formula One racing circuit straddled by a hotel; Sharjah's hub of heritage – these are a few of the UAE's many modern-day wonders.

Superlatives

The iconic Burj Khalifa, the world's tallest building, sharks swimming in the middle of a Dubai mall and free-roaming oryx on an island illustrate the UAE's can-do culture.

Back to Basics

Less known than its modern alter ego, the UAE's ancient character is defined by magnificent dunes and desert retreats in the oases of Liwa and the leafy plantations of Al Ain.

p304

On the Road

Kuwait
p86
Bahrain
p50
Oman
p121
Qatar
p222
United Arab
Emirates
p304
Saudi
Arabia
p255
Oman
p121

Bahrain 

Includes ➡

Why Go?

Like an oyster, Bahrain has a rough exterior that takes some prising open, but it's always worth the effort. Manama may lack the finesse of other Gulf capitals, but that's key to its appeal. The storied location of ancient Dilmun and the epicentre of the Gulf's pearling past – Bahrain has a history to reflect on with pride. There's even a cheeky claim that it was home to the Garden of Eden. Nowadays the country has its own Formula 1 Grand Prix, a growing art and foodie scene frequented by Manama's sizeable expat population, and all the hallmarks of wealth, modern Arabian-style. Bahrain's confidence may have been shaken by the uncertain aftermath of the Arab Spring, but its appeal endures, and the lack of visitors means you may have it all to yourself.

Best Places to Stay

➡ Fraser Suites Diplomatic Area (p58)

➡ Domain (p58)

➡ Palace Boutique Hotel (p58)

➡ Novotel Al Dana Resort (p59)

Best Places to Eat

➡ Haji Gahwa (p62)

➡ Masso (p65)

➡ Rasoi by Vineet (p65)

➡ Fish House (p63)

When to Go

Bahrain

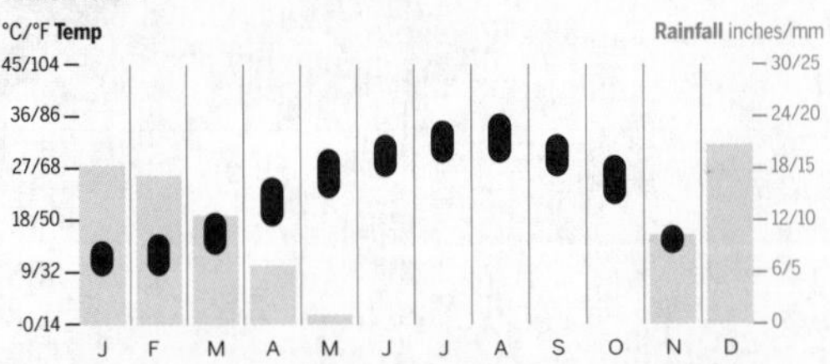

Oct–Mar Bask in the relative cool of a Gulf winter with daily blue skies.

Apr Join the fast lane during the Formula 1 Grand Prix and enjoy dancing at the Heritage Festival.

May–Sep Extreme heat; stay away if you can.

Daily Costs

Bahrain is an expensive destination, not least because budget accommodation is not recommended for Western visitors. Expect to pay at least US$100 for a comfortable room. Cheaper eating options are easier to find (starting from US$5), and with free access to many of the main sites of interest, a minimum daily cost with transport comes to around US$140. This rises to US$200 if you're staying in midrange hotels; for a top-end hotel with car hire, a starting point of US$350 is nearer the mark.

ITINERARIES

One Day

Enjoy the juxtaposition of ancient and modern at the **Bahrain National Museum** and the adjacent Bahrain National Theatre, before wandering around the real thing in the wind-tower residences of neighbouring **Muharraq**. Explore the giant **Al Fatih Mosque**, then stop for lunch at **Coco's** and a pastry at **Café Lilou** over in chic Adliya. Shop for perfumes, ice cream and gold in **Manama Souq** before having dinner at **Haji Gahwa**.

Three Days

After allowing day one for Manama, spend day two with the dead at **Bahrain Fort** and **Sar**. Admire the continuity with the ancient in the crafts of **Al Jasra**, wonder whether this is paradise at the **Tree of Life**, and complete the burial circuit at **A'Ali** for sunset. On day three, visit the **Oil Museum**, pump up the pace with a trip to the **Formula 1 Racetrack**, then slow things down at nearby **Al Areen Wildlife Park & Reserve**. If one of the days is Friday, make sure you're in Manama for a famous Bahrain brunch.

Essential Food & Drink

- **Makbous** Rice and spices with chicken, lamb or fish in a rich sauce.
- **Rangena** Coconut cake.
- **Khabees** Dates in a variety of sizes, colours and states of ripeness.
- **Tap water** Safe to drink, although most people stick to bottled water.
- **Alcohol** Widely available, with some excellent hotel cocktail bars.

AT A GLANCE

- **Currency** Bahraini dinar (BD)
- **Mobile Phones** SIM cards widely available.
- **Money** ATMs widespread; credit cards widely accepted.
- **Visas** Available on arrival for many nationalities.

Fast Facts

- **Capital** Manama
- **Country Code** 973
- **Languages** Arabic, English
- **Population** 1,346,613

Exchange Rates

For current exchange rates, see www.xe.com.

Australia	A$10	BD2.79
Euro zone	€10	BD4.14
Kuwait	KD1	BD1.25
Oman	OR1	BD0.98
Qatar	QR10	BD1.04
Saudi Arabia	SR10	BD1.01
UAE	Dh10	BD1.03
UK	UK£10	BD5.35
USA	US$10	BD3.77

Resources

- **Bahrain Tourism** (www.culture.gov.bh) Official site.
- **Clickbahrain** (www.clickbahrain.com) Privately run island guide.
- **Lonely Planet** (www.lonelyplanet.com/bahrain) Comprehensive coverage of the island.

Bahrain Highlights

1 Immersing yourself in the past at **Bahrain National Museum** (p53) then skipping forward centuries to **Bahrain National Theatre** (p55).

2 Taking a 16th-century view of the sea from the battlements of **Bahrain Fort** (p69).

3 Shopping for gold, perfumes, medicinal herbs and mango ice cream in **Manama Souq** (p66).

4 Eating to excess at Friday brunch and admiring the views from **Bahrain Bay Kitchen** (p63).

5 Sampling life in the fast lane at Bahrain's **Formula 1 Racetrack** (p71).

6 Meeting desert Bahrain's inhabitants at **Al Areen Wildlife Park & Reserve** (p72).

7 Going pearl diving like Bahrainis of old from **Dar Island** (p68).

8 Discovering what makes Bahrain what it is today at the **Oil Museum** (p74).

MANAMA المنامة

POP 330,000

Try as it might, Manama lacks the polish and in-your-face commercialism of Doha or Dubai, but therein lies its charm. Yes, you'll find here all the hallmarks of modern Gulf prosperity: vast air-conditioned shopping malls and daringly designed skyscrapers are present in abundance. But the juxtaposition of the city's pearling past and its oil-rich future is everywhere to be seen: in the National Museum set alongside the avant-garde National Theatre, and in the traditional homes of Muharraq with views across the rooftops to the skyscrapers of downtown Manama. Throw in fabulous eating options and a dynamic art scene and you'll soon discover that there's more to Manama than first meets the eye.

History

Like most Gulf cities, Manama can appear like the realisation of some wealthy developer's fantasy, and it's true that much of the city is an almost entirely modern creation built upon land reclaimed from the sea. But appearances are deceptive: Manama can trace its roots in Islamic chronicles as far back as AD 1345, and in all likelihood there were settlements on and around the best springs on the island for many centuries before that.

Invaded by the Portuguese in 1521 and then by the Persians in 1602, Manama then passed into the hands of Al Khalifa, the current ruling family, in 1783. It became a free port in 1958 and the capital of independent Bahrain in 1971.

With a third of Bahrain's population living in the city, Manama continues to grow at a steady pace. A great way to gauge that growth is to enter the National Museum and trace the myriad building projects across the satellite maps embedded into the floor. Together these projected public works, which include a soon-to-open 1000-seat National Theatre and a 'pearling pathway', make a fine foundation for the future of this easy-going city.

Sights

All of Manama's main sights are located either along Al Fatih Hwy or near (if not on) Government Ave. They are within an energetic walk of each other or a short taxi ride away. Opening hours change frequently, so call in advance to avoid disappointment.

Walking between sights, you'll notice two sets of landmark buildings: the **World Trade Centre** (Map p60; ☎17 133 666; www.bahrainwtc.com; King Faisal Hwy), with three wind turbines sandwiched between the segmented towers, and the gracefully sloping twin towers of the **Financial Harbour** (Map p60; King Faisal Corniche). Completed before the global economic downturn of 2008, they have become symbols of the city's boom years and look spectacular when lit at night.

★**Bahrain National Museum** MUSEUM
(Map p60; ☎17 298 777; Al Fatih Hwy; admission BD1; ⏲8am-8pm; P) Deservedly the country's most popular attraction, the National Museum is an outstanding introduction to Bahrain's history. The highlights of the collection, which is housed in a postmodern building with landscaping that brings the waterfront location up to the windows, are the archaeological finds from ancient Dilmun, the reproduction souq covering

IS BAHRAIN SAFE TO VISIT?

With political tensions still running high, a ban on public demonstrations, and distinguishable no-go areas around A'Ali and other towns outside the capital, there is an underlying feeling of unease in some parts of Bahrain.

At the time of our visit in November 2015, we felt no sense of danger on the streets of Manama, Muharraq or anywhere else on the island. That said, some of the more cautious Western government travel advisories warned against all-but-necessary travel to Bahrain due to concerns over political unrest and terrorism fears in the Gulf region. Travellers should take particular care in Shiite-dominated areas, such as Sitra, Sanabis and elsewhere, which have experienced continuing unrest.

Given the uncertainty, we recommend that you monitor the situation in Bahrain through your consulate and the international media before booking your stay. Once in the country, take local advice before going out and restrict your visit to the main areas of tourist interest – note that, as stated above, tourist draws A'Ali and Sitra (necessary for visiting Dar Island) were considered risky at the time of research.

You can read about the situation in more detail on p78.

Bahrain

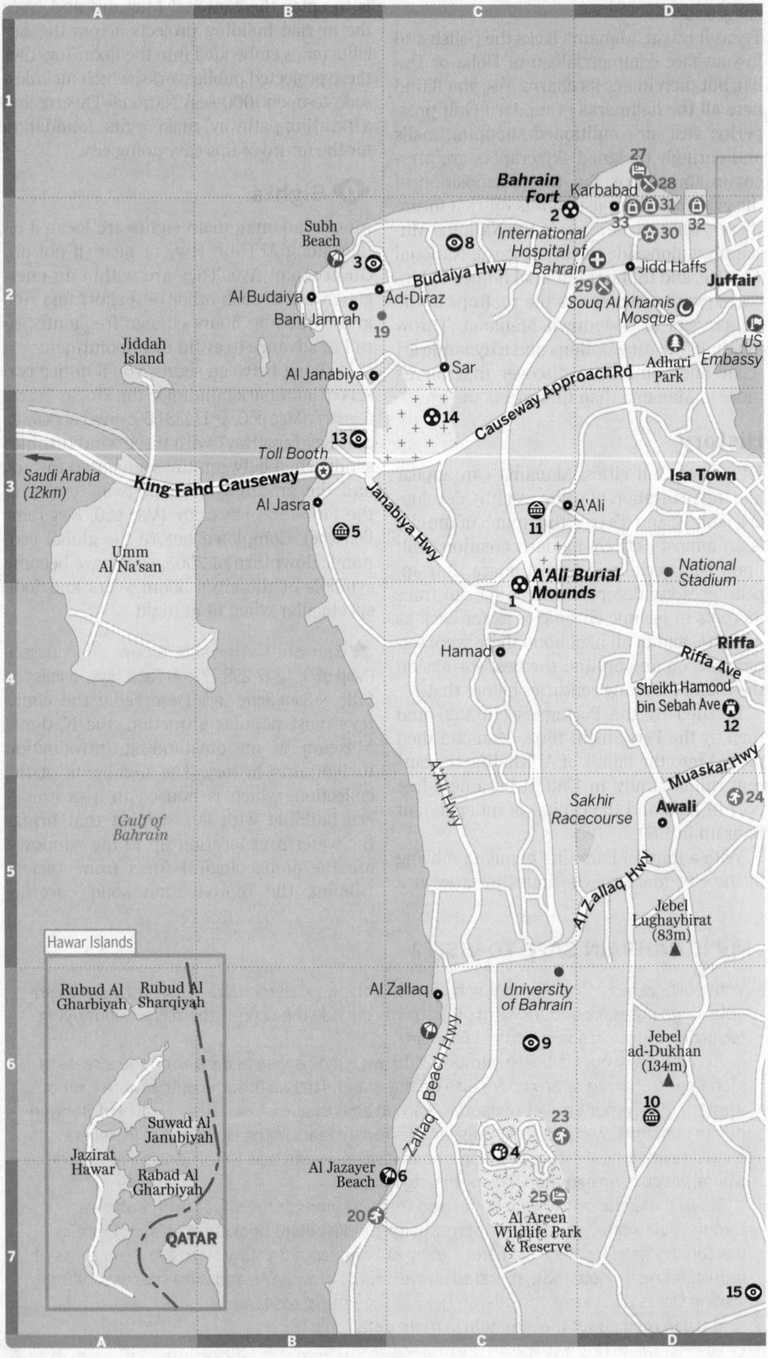

A B C D
1 2 3 4 5 6 7
27
28
Bahrain Fort
Karbabad
2
33
31
32
30
Subh Beach
8
International Hospital of Bahrain
Jidd Haffs
3
Budaiya Hwy
Juffair
Al Budaiya
Ad-Diraz
29
Souq Al Khamis Mosque
Bani Jamrah
19
US Embassy
Jiddah Island
Adhari Park
Sar
Al Janabiya
Causeway ApproachRd
14
13
Toll Booth
Saudi Arabia (12km)
King Fahd Causeway
Isa Town
Al Jasra
Janabiya Hwy
A'Ali
11
5
Umm Al Na'san
National Stadium
A'Ali Burial Mounds
1
Riffa
Hamad
Riffa Ave
Sheikh Hamood bin Sebah Ave
12
Muaskar Hwy
A'Ali Hwy
24
Sakhir Racecourse
Awali
Gulf of Bahrain
Al Zallaq Hwy
Jebel Lughaybirat (83m)
Hawar Islands
Rubud Al Gharbiyah
Rubud Al Sharqiyah
Al Zallaq
University of Bahrain
Zallaq Beach Hwy
9
Jebel ad-Dukhan (134m)
10
Suwad Al Janubiyah
23
Jazirat Hawar
Rabad Al Gharbiyah
4
Al Jazayer Beach
6
25
20
Al Areen Wildlife Park & Reserve
QATAR
15

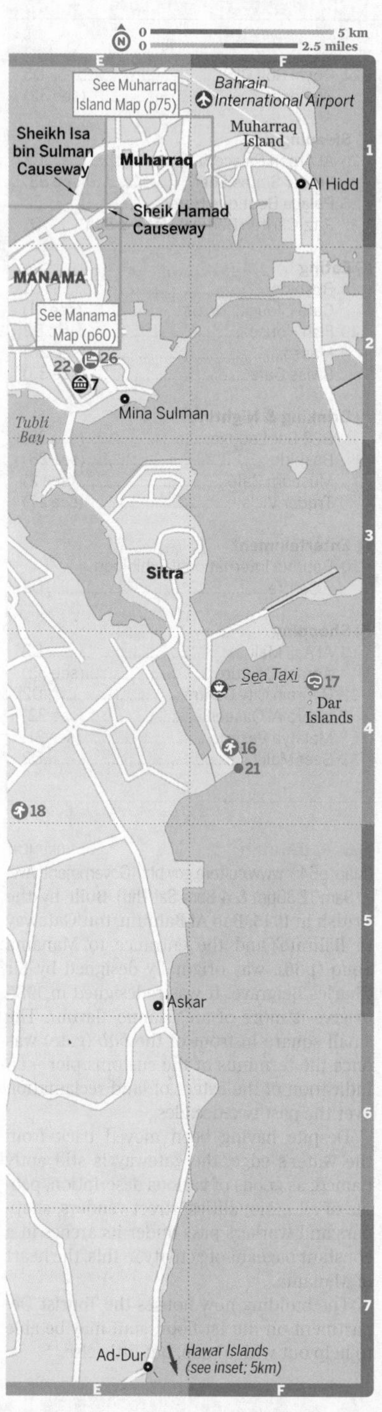

Traditional Trades and Crafts on the 1st floor (the barber could double for Sweeney Todd), and the vast satellite photo of Bahrain that takes up much of the ground floor.

Other exhibits include a Hall of Graves, Customs and Traditions, the Islamic era and Documents and Manuscripts, and we very much hope that the fine semi-permanent ground-floor exhibit on fables and storytelling continues. The museum shop is excellent, there's a chic cafe, several gallery spaces are used for contemporary exhibitions of art and sculpture, and the labelling (in English and Arabic) is first-rate throughout.

★Bahrain National Theatre ARCHITECTURE
(Bahrain National Amphitheatre; Map p60; www.culture.gov.bh; Sheikh Hamad Causeway) FREE
Adjacent to Bahrain National Museum, this stunning architectural showpiece opened in November 2012. Covering nearly 12,000 sq metres, it's the third-largest theatre in the Middle East and it's at its best up close. Appearing to float upon the water, its design owes much to local traditions – the interwoven aluminium strips that allow in air evoke the roofs of traditional local homes, while the curvaceous interior of the auditorium suggests the sea-going dhows of ancient Bahrain.

Even the number of seats in the auditorium is significant: 1001, in homage to *The Thousand and One Nights*.

Al Fatih Mosque MOSQUE
(Map p60; ☎17 727 773; www.alfateh.gov.bh; Al Fatih Hwy; ⊙non-Muslims 9am-4pm Sun-Thu; P)
Built on reclaimed land in 1984, Al Fatih Mosque is the largest mosque in the country and is capable of holding up to 7000 worshippers. The mosque was built with marble from Italy, glass from Austria and teak from India, carved by local Bahraini craftspeople, and has some fine examples of interior design. The dedicated guides lead visitors through the mosque, explaining aspects of religious etiquette while pointing out special features of mosque architecture.

Visitors begin their guided tour at the small library immediately to the right inside the main entrance, where women will be given a black cloak and headscarf to wear while visiting the prayer hall. Wearing shorts is prohibited. After the tour, visitors are offered free booklets in the Discover Islam series (published by the Muslim Educational Society of Bahrain), which help to dispel some of the commonly held misconceptions about Islam.

Bahrain

Top Sights
1 A'Ali Burial Mounds C4
2 Bahrain Fort C2

Sights
3 Ad-Diraz Temple B2
4 Al Areen Wildlife Park & Reserve C6
Al Jasra Handicraft Centre .... (see 5)
5 Al Jasra House B3
6 Al Jazayer Beach C7
7 Arabesque Art Gallery E2
Bahrain Arts Society .... (see 19)
8 Barbar Temple C2
9 Formula 1 Racetrack C6
Fort Museum .... (see 2)
10 Oil Museum D6
11 Pottery Workshop C3
12 Riffa Fort D4
13 Royal Camel Farm B3
14 Sar Burial Chambers C3
15 Tree of Life D7

Activities, Courses & Tours
16 Al Bander Hotel & Resort F4
17 Al Dar Islands F4
18 Awali Golf Club E4
19 Bahrain Arts Society B2
Bahrain Karting .... (see 9)
20 Bahrain Sailing Club B7
21 Bahrain Yacht Club F4
22 Berlitz Bahrain E2
Dragster Xperience .... (see 9)
Land Rover Experience .... (see 9)
23 Lost Paradise of Dilmun Water Park C6
24 Royal Golf Club D5
Wahooo! .... (see 32)

Sleeping
25 Al Areen Palace & Spa C7
Fraser Suites Seef .... (see 33)
26 Palace Boutique Hotel E2
27 Ritz-Carlton Bahrain Hotel & Spa D1

Eating
28 Bushido D1
Café Lilou .... (see 31)
29 Fish House D2
Masso .... (see 26)
Swiss Cafe .... (see 33)

Drinking & Nightlife
B28 Bar Lounge .... (see 33)
Bushido .... (see 28)
Museum Café .... (see 2)
Trader Vic's .... (see 27)

Entertainment
30 Bahrain International Exhibition Centre D2

Shopping
31 Al Aali Mall D2
Anmar Couture .... (see 32)
32 Bahrain City Centre D2
Kubra Al Qaseer .... (see 32)
Malatya Pazari .... (see 31)
33 Seef Mall D2

Beit Al Quran MUSEUM

(Map p60; ☎17 290 404; www.culture.gov.bh; Sheikh Hamad Causeway; ⏰9am-noon & 4-6pm Sat-Wed, 9am-noon Thu; P) FREE With its wrapping of carved Kufic script, the distinctive Beit Al Quran is a fine example of modern Bahraini architecture. It houses a large and striking collection of Qurans, manuscripts and woodcarvings and functions as a good introduction to Islam in general, and Islamic calligraphy in particular. Look out for the miniature Qurans, the smallest of which (from 18th-century Persia) measures only 4.7cm by 3.2cm. The exhibits are well labelled in English and can be superficially perused within an hour.

The main entrance and car park are at the back, on the southern side of the building; access is off Exhibition Ave. Tours are often organised – call ahead to check. Visitors should dress conservatively.

Bab Al Bahrain MONUMENT

(Map p64; www.culture.gov.bh; Government Ave; ⏰9am-12.30pm & 4-8pm Sat-Thu) Built by the British in 1945, Bab Al Bahrain, the 'Gateway to Bahrain' and the entrance to Manama Souq (p66), was originally designed by Sir Charles Belgrave. It was redesigned in 1986 to give it more of an 'Islamic' flavour. The small square in front of the *bab* (gate) was once the terminus of the customs pier – an indication of the extent of land reclamation over the past two decades.

Despite having been moved back from the water's edge, the gateway is still aptly named, as goods of various description, people of all nationalities, street vendors, shoppers and workers pass under its arches in a constant pageant of activity in this, the heart of Manama.

The building now houses the Tourist Department on the 1st floor; staff may be able to help out with a map, but little else.

Friday Mosque MOSQUE
(Map p64; Government Ave) Built in 1938, this mosque is easily identifiable by its elaborately crafted minaret, its most interesting architectural feature. The mosque is reflected in the glass windows of the neighbouring Batelco Commercial Centre, providing a suggestive reflection of old and new Manama. The mosque is not open to tourists.

Manama Central Market MARKET
(Map p60; ⏲5am-2.30pm) Malls have conquered Manama in a big way, but the antidote lies in this earthy vestige of Old Bahrain, located off Lulu Ave. Fruit and veg dominates the cavernous main space, and you'll rub shoulders with a broad cross-section of Manama society doing their shopping far from the glitz of the retail temples. Don't miss the aromatic **fish market** (Map p60; Off Lulu Ave; ⏲5am-2.30pm), in a separate building off the northwestern corner – get here before dawn to see local fishers bringing their catch to market.

Activities

Funland Bowling Centre BOWLING, SKATING
(Map p60; ☎17 292 313; www.funlandbahrain.com; Al Fatih Hwy, Marina Corniche; incl shoe hire BD2; ⏲9am-1am) Bowling is a highly popular pastime in Bahrain and Funland is a hub of activity all week. Also on site is a skating rink (BD3 including skate hire) with an ice disco – don't forget your white T-shirt for the ultraviolet lighting.

Coral Bay WATER SPORTS
(Map p60; ☎17 312 700; coral-bay.net; Marina Corniche, Al Fatih Hwy; ⏲9am-sunset Tue-Sun) Coral Bay is one of the easiest ways to engage with the sea in Manama, offering a wide range of activities including boat tours (30/60 minutes BD40/60), half- and full-day charters (BD175/325 including captain and soft drinks), jet-skiing (BD20 for 30 minutes), waterskiing and banana-boat hire. Diving is also available (BD24 for a tank dive; BD65 to BD220 for classes).

La Fontaine Spa SPA
(Map p60; ☎17 230 123; www.lafontaineartcentre.net; 92 Hoora Ave, Dhuwawdah; ⏲9am-10.30pm Tue-Sun) Not only does it nurture the soul (in the art gallery) and the stomach (in the restaurant), but La Fontaine also has one of Bahrain's best spas. There are facial and body treatments, reflexology, massages and all manner of body scrubs. Ask about its half-day packages, which combine a treatment with a meal.

Diplomat Spa SPA
(Map p60; ☎17 525 237; www.radissonblu.com/diplomathotel-bahrain/spa; cnr Sheikh Hamad Causeway & Al Fatih Hwy; ⏲9am-10pm) The Radisson Blu Diplomat Hotel's spa complex has the full range of treatments and massages with some attractive packages.

Courses

Bahrain Arts Society LANGUAGE COURSE
(Map p54; ☎17 590 551; www.bahartsociety.org.bh; Budayia Hwy) Courses in traditional Bahraini and Arabic art and music are sometimes offered for a nominal fee by the Bahrain Arts Society.

Berlitz Bahrain LANGUAGE COURSE
(Map p54; ☎17 827 847; www.berlitz-bahrain.com; Road 3605) Arabic-language courses are run by Berlitz for individual or group immersion.

Sleeping

There's a wide range of city accommodation on offer, particularly on or around Government Ave, in the heart of central Manama.

CULTURAL PASSPORT

To encourage visitors and expats to see as many of the island's attractions as possible, Bahrain's tourism authorities have initiated a scheme known as the Cultural Passport. Covering 21 sights in Manama and further afield, it involves collecting stamps at each of the sights in an impressive passport-style booklet. When it was begun in 2015, prizes (including flights) were awarded for those who visited all 21 sites and had the stamps to prove it. (We don't expect such extravagance to continue, but ask just in case.) At the time of writing, the (free) Cultural Passport was available at the **Bahrain National Museum** (p53) and the **Sheikh Ebrahim bin Mohammed Al Khalifa Centre for Culture and Research** (p75) in Muharraq.

Prizes aside, the main advantage of the scheme is the booklet itself, which is at once an attractive keepsake and a handy guide to the sights themselves, with opening hours and historical background included on a double-page spread for each entry.

BAHRAIN ACTIVITIES

As you'd expect on an island, the main activities in Bahrain focus on the sea, although very shallow coastal waters mean that swimming, snorkelling and boating are best carried out well offshore. On land, golf is popular. Expats will find that membership of a club offers big savings and a ready-made social life.

Dolphin watching Contact **Bahrain Yacht Club** (Map p54; ☎17 700 677; www.thebahrainyachtclub.com; ⏲8am-10pm) or **Coral Bay** (p57) for boat trips.

Golf Both **Awali Golf Club** (Map p54; ☎17 756 770; www.awaligolfclub.com; all-day green fees BD8.50; ⏲7am-7.30pm) and **Royal Golf Club** (Map p54; ☎17 750 777; theroyalgolfclub.com; ⏲7am-10pm) have beautiful greens – not a given in the desert!

Horse riding Dilmun Club (☎17 693 766; www.dilmun-club.com; ⏲Sat-Thu) in Sar and **Bahrain Riding School** (☎39 566 809; twinpalmsridingcentre.com; half-hour shared/private lesson per person BD12/16; ⏲7.30-11.30am & 3-7pm) offer lessons.

Pearl diving Al Dar Islands (p68) provides the nose-peg – you just bring the stamina.

Running For those who prefer to share their pain, contact the **Bahrain Hash House Harriers** (☎17 862 620; www.bahrainhash.com).

Water sports In addition to Bahrain Yacht Club and Coral Bay, check out **Al Bander Hotel & Resort** (Map p54; ☎17 701 201; www.albander.com) and **Bahrain Sailing Club.** (Map p54; ☎17 836 078)

Many of the budget and midrange hotels in this area entertain weekend visitors from Saudi Arabia – in more ways than one – so it may pay to spend a little more to enjoy one of the good-value, top-end hotels. Beautiful resort accommodation is available at the edges of the city, particularly on the causeway towards Muharraq Island and at Seef, close to Seef Mall.

All of the budget hotels reviewed have air-con, TV (many with satellite) and a bathroom with hot water, but if you can stretch your budget to midrange, it's worth it. Most of the midrange hotels listed have excellent-value rooms, but you may need to ask to see a few. Most of the top-end hotel prices listed include breakfast.

★Fraser Suites Diplomatic Area APARTMENT $$
(Map p60; ☎16 161 888; diplomaticarea-bahrain.frasershospitality.com; Road 1701, Diplomatic Area; ste from BD41) Outrageously good value, these large serviced apartments have sitting rooms, kitchens and king-size beds, a good location in Manama's Diplomatic Quarter, and contemporary decor. Many also have fine city views. Prices can go far higher, but booking ahead online should keep prices low. There's another **branch** (Map p54; ☎17 171 626; bahrain.frasershospitality.com; Road 2825, Seef) in the Seef district.

★Domain HOTEL $$
(Map p60; ☎16 000 000; www.thedomainhotels.com; Road 1705, Diplomatic Area; d/ste from BD60/70; @🛜🏊) Slick contemporary furnishings, fabulous views and exemplary service (the floors with suites have butlers) define this excellent hotel on the southern fringe of the Diplomatic Quarter. A slick spa, a fine selection of restaurants and scores of repeat guests make this an excellent choice.

Palace Boutique Hotel BOUTIQUE HOTEL $$
(Map p54; ☎17 725 000; www.thepalace.com.bh; cnr Mahooz Ave & Sheikh Isa Ave; r from BD51; P@🛜🏊) Unless you must be within walking distance of downtown, this classy, low-slung place is an excellent choice. Its four-star rooms are large, contemporary in style and supremely comfortable, and the on-site restaurant, Masso (p65), is one of Manama's best; there's also a less formal gastropub. Service is excellent, the new pool is a winner and you're close to the cool Adliya neighbourhood.

Delmon International Hotel HOTEL $$
(Map p64; ☎17 224 000; www.delmonhotel.com; Government Ave; s/d incl breakfast BD35/45; 🛜🏊) Don't be put off by the grim downtown exterior, because the well (if rather darkly) furnished rooms here come with giant mahogany beds and aren't bad value. The location's a winner for those who like to get out and walk – the Manama Souq is nearby.

Novotel Al Dana Resort RESORT $$$
(Map p75; 17 298 008; www.novotel.com; Sheikh Hamad Causeway; s/d from BD90/100;) With distinctive style and character rare in many international hotels, the Novotel is built like a *qasr* (castle or palace) around elegant central courtyards, and punctuated at the edges by whimsical Bahraini wind towers. It commands a wonderful view of the bay on Sheikh Hamad Causeway, so you can almost forget that its neighbour has built the mother-of-all-tower-blocks next door.

Ritz-Carlton Bahrain Hotel & Spa RESORT $$$
(Map p54; 17 588 000; www.ritzcarlton.com; Bldg 112, Road 40, Block 428, King Mohammed VI Ave, Seef; s/d from BD150/185;) Arguably Bahrain's most luxurious and opulent hotel, the Ritz-Carlton boasts its own private beach and secluded island, though some may find the dark, polished interior of black marble and gilt-edged furniture oppressive and pretentious. Nonetheless, service is faultless, and if yours is a Bentley, you'll be in good company.

Regency InterContinental HOTEL $$$
(Map p64; 17 227 777; www.ihg.com; King Faisal Hwy; s/d from BD100/125;) In the middle of downtown but offering uptown accommodation, this old favourite has recently enjoyed a makeover and consistently gets rave reviews. The contemporary black and grey elegance works well and the rooms make up for in pillows what they lack in window size. Bars, restaurants and impeccable service round out a superb package.

ART GALLERIES

More than any other Gulf city, Manama has a burgeoning arts scene. Its epicentre is the multicultural Adliya neighbourhood, formerly known for its nightlife. Adliya has added depth and a touch of the bohemian in recent years, with an explosion of cafes, fine restaurants and art galleries inhabiting converted Bahraini town houses.

Over in Muharraq, there are also **Bin Matar House** (p76), **Busaad Art Gallery** (p74) and **Al Oraifi Museum** (p76).

If you're here for the art, mid-October is a good time to visit, when **Art Bahrain** (www.art-bahrain.com) brings gallery owners, artists and collectors to the country for its international art fair.

La Fontaine Centre of Contemporary Art (Map p60; 17 230 123; www.lafontaineartcentre.net; 92 Hoora Ave, Dhuwawdah; 9am-10.30pm Tue-Sun) Showcasing regional and international contemporary artists, this beautiful space hosts regular exhibitions. The venue is a magnificent elaboration of a 19th-century Bahraini town house, with many features typical of Gulf Islamic architecture, including covered colonnades, archways and the signature fountain. The complex also includes an amphitheatre, a fine-dining restaurant and one of the city's best **spas** (p57).

Al Riwaq Art Space (Map p60; 17 717 441; www.alriwaqartspace.com; 3 Osama bin Zaid Ave; 9.30am-10pm) This small but dynamic space offers up some of Bahrain's best exhibitions, cultural events and film screenings and it's the heart and soul of the creative outpouring that has come to characterise the Adliya district. Great cafe, too.

Albareh Art Gallery (Map p60; 17 717 707; www.albareh.com; 7am-2pm Sun-Thu, 9am-4pm Sat) Paintings, sculptures and photography by Bahraini and other Gulf artists dominate this Adliya gallery located off Sheikh Isa Ave.

Bahrain Arts Society (Map p54; 17 590 551; www.bahartsociety.org.bh; Budaiya Hwy) One of the many centres promoting local art and artists.

Crafts Centre Gallery & Workshop (Map p60; 17 254 688; 263 Sheikh Isa Al Khebir Ave; 8am-2pm Sun-Thu) Home to a variety of studios and workshops promoting the contemporary revival of traditional crafts, such as weaving, palm-leaf papermaking, pottery and ironwork. All the work is for sale.

Arabesque Art Gallery (Map p54; 17 720 859; www.arabesque-gallery.com; Road 3703, Block 337, Umm Al Hassan; 9am-6pm Sat-Thu) Tucked away in a quiet corner southwest of Adliya, this longstanding gallery exhibits the oils and watercolours of its owner, A Weheb Al Kooheji, who specialises in painting local Gulf architecture and street scenes.

Manama

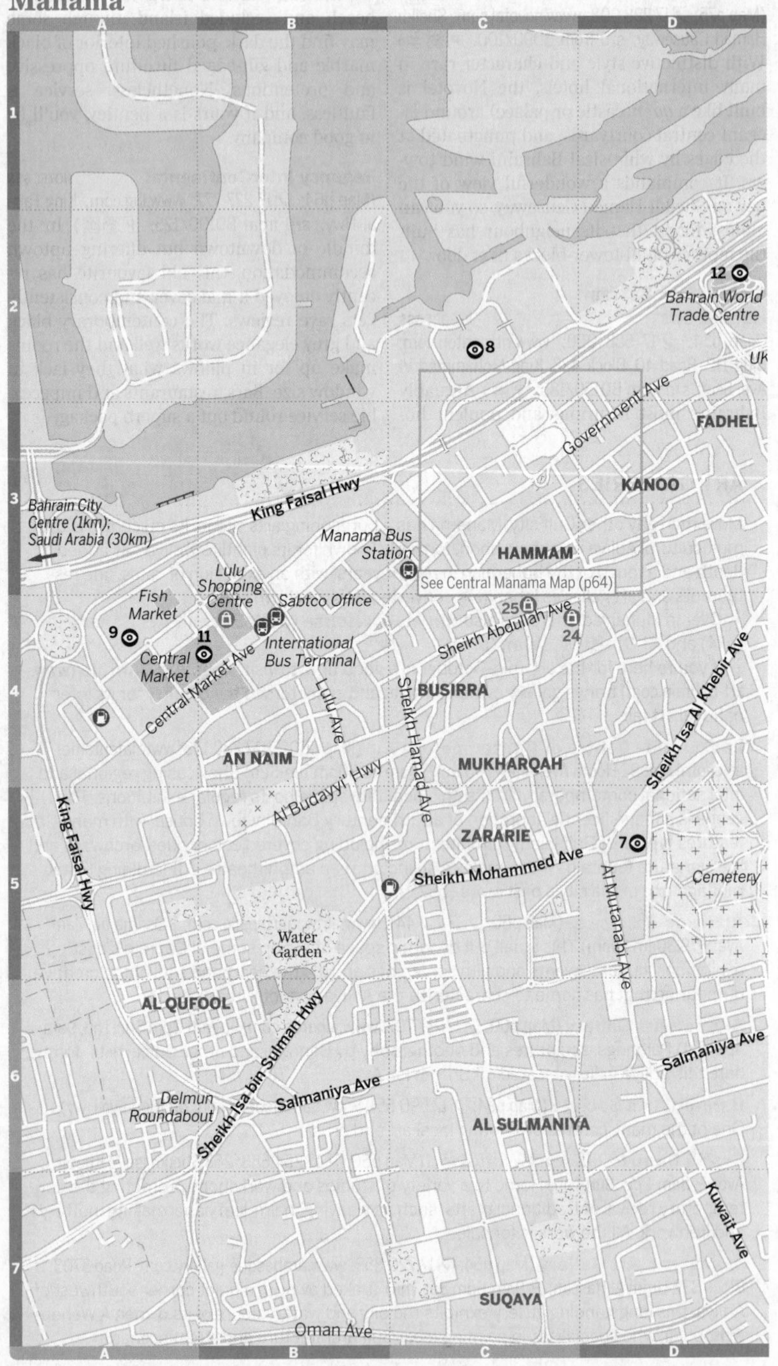

A
B
C
D
1
2
3
4
5
6
7
Bahrain City Centre (1km); Saudi Arabia (30km)
King Faisal Hwy
Government Ave
Uk
12
Bahrain World Trade Centre
8
FADHEL
KANOO
HAMMAM
Manama Bus Station
See Central Manama Map (p64)
Lulu Shopping Centre
Sabtco Office
Fish Market
9
11
Central Market
Central Market Ave
International Bus Terminal
25
24
Sheikh Abdullah Ave
Sheikh Isa Al Khebir Ave
Lulu Ave
Sheikh Hamad Ave
BUSIRRA
AN NAIM
MUKHARQAH
Al Budayyi' Hwy
King Faisal Hwy
ZARARIE
7
Sheikh Mohammed Ave
Al Mutanabi Ave
Cemetery
Water Garden
AL QUFOOL
Sheikh Isa bin Sulman Hwy
Salmaniya Ave
Salmaniya Ave
Delmun Roundabout
AL SULMANIYA
Kuwait Ave
SUQAYA
Oman Ave

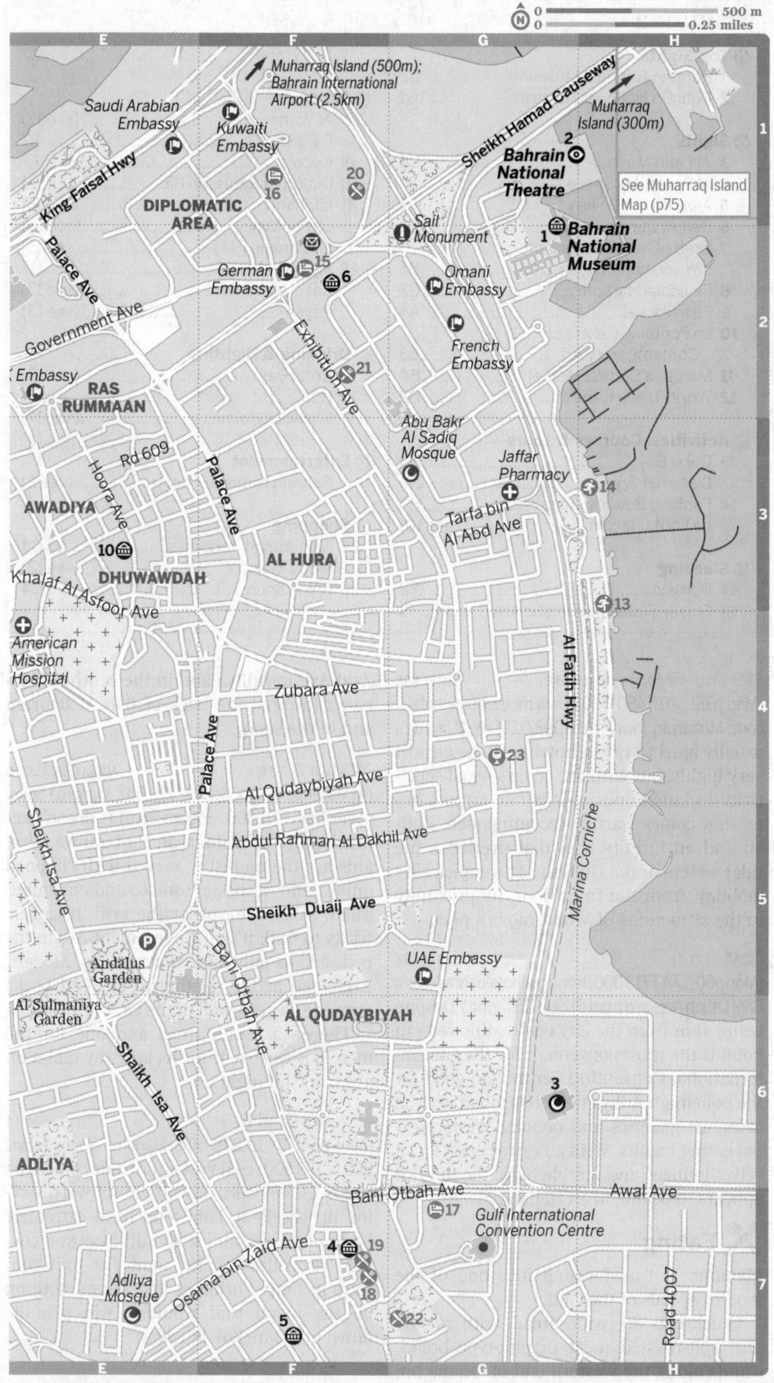

0 500 m
0 0.25 miles
Muharraq Island (500m); Bahrain International Airport (2.5km)
Saudi Arabian Embassy
Kuwaiti Embassy
Sheikh Hamad Causeway
Muharraq Island (300m)
King Faisal Hwy
Bahrain National Theatre
See Muharraq Island Map (p75)
DIPLOMATIC AREA
Sail Monument
Bahrain National Museum
Palace Ave
German Embassy
Omani Embassy
Government Ave
French Embassy
Exhibition Ave
Embassy
RAS RUMMAAN
Abu Bakr Al Sadiq Mosque
Rd 609
Hoora Ave
Jaffar Pharmacy
AWADIYA
Tarfa bin Al Abd Ave
DHUWAWDAH
AL HURA
Khalaf Al Asfoor Ave
American Mission Hospital
Al Fatih Hwy
Zubara Ave
Al Qudaybiyah Ave
Abdul Rahman Al Dakhil Ave
Sheikh Isa Ave
Marina Corniche
Sheikh Duaij Ave
Andalus Garden
Bani Otbah Ave
UAE Embassy
Al Sulmaniya Garden
AL QUDAYBIYAH
Shaikh Isa Ave
ADLIYA
Bani Otbah Ave
Awal Ave
Gulf International Convention Centre
Osama bin Zaid Ave
Adliya Mosque
Road 4007
BAHRAIN MANAMA

Manama

Top Sights
1 Bahrain National Museum ... G2
2 Bahrain National Theatre ... G1

Sights
3 Al Fatih Mosque ... G6
4 Al Riwaq Art Space ... F7
5 Albareh Art Gallery ... F7
6 Beit Al Quran ... F2
7 Crafts Centre Gallery and Workshop ... D5
8 Financial Harbour ... C2
9 Fish Market ... A4
10 La Fontaine Centre of Contemporary Art ... E3
11 Manama Central Market ... B4
12 World Trade Centre ... D2

Activities, Courses & Tours
13 Coral Bay ... H3
Diplomat Spa ... (see 20)
14 Funland Bowling Centre ... H3
La Fontaine Spa ... (see 10)

Sleeping
15 Domain ... F2
16 Fraser Suites Diplomatic Area ... F1
17 Gulf Hotel ... G7

Eating
Al Waha ... (see 17)
18 Café Lilou ... F7
19 Coco's ... F7
20 Diplomat Radisson Blu ... F1
21 Isfahani ... F2
La Fontaine ... (see 10)
Le Domain [34] ... (see 15)
22 My Cafe ... G7
Rasoi by Vineet ... (see 17)
Rayés ... (see 13)

Drinking & Nightlife
Coral Bay ... (see 13)
23 Hub ... G4
Sherlock Holmes ... (see 17)

Entertainment
Bahrain National Theatre ... (see 2)

Shopping
24 Kingdom of Perfumes ... C4
Moda Mall ... (see 12)
25 Spice Souq ... C4

Mövenpick Hotel Bahrain HOTEL **$$$**
(Map p75; 17 460 000; www.moevenpick-hotels.com; Muharraq Town; s/d BD98/120; P) It's usually hard to rate a hotel near the airport very highly, but with the chain's usual sensitivity to landscapes, this is one airport hotel that comes warmly recommended. Built around an infinity pool that overlooks the tidal waters of the Gulf, the Mövenpick says 'holiday' from the front door. Its proximity to the attractions of Muharraq is a plus.

Gulf Hotel HOTEL **$$$**
(Map p60; 17 713 000; www.gulfhotelbahrain.com; Bani Otbah Ave; s/d from BD99/115;) Despite being 4km from the city centre, this veteran hotel is the most convenient for the Gulf International Convention Centre and good for the bohemian Adliya neighbourhood with its cafes, art galleries and popular Western-expat eating haunts. With an extravagant foyer, velvet lounges and marble halls, the interior appears to belong to an Italian palazzo.

Eating

Manama is transforming into one of the foodie capitals of the Gulf.

Quick eats are widespread, with *shwarma* (spit-roasted meat in pita-type bread) stands along the western end of Osama bin Zaid Ave in Adliya and in the centre of Manama (around the back of Bab Al Bahrain and in the souq).

★**Haji Gahwa** MIDDLE EASTERN **$**
(Al Maseela; Map p64; 17 210 647; Manama Souq; mains from BD1.300; 9am-9pm) It doesn't get much more Bahraini than Haji Gahwa. Biryanis are the mainstay, served with chopped onion and a basic tomato-and-cucumber salad. After 5pm, order the grill. It can be tricky to find: it's off Government Ave in the pedestrians-only lane marked by Modern Exchange at the southern end, and backs onto the eastern wall of the Gulf Pearl Hotel.

There's a family area, and one for the men, but we love it for its laneway tables on a warm Gulf night.

Honey's Thai Restaurant THAI **$**
(Map p64; 39 238 507; Manama Souq; mains BD1.500-3.500; 11am-4am) Around since the 1980s, Honey's is a downtown stalwart, serving up excellent Thai food from extremely basic premises, and it should have you covered regardless of the hour. The tom yum soup is simply brilliant and there's nothing on the menu that wouldn't win plaudits down any Bangkok laneway.

Charcoal Grill KEBAB $

(Map p64; ☎17 223 531; Bab Al Bahrain; mains BD1.700-3.200; ⏲10.30am-12.30am) Plain, simple and clean, this no-frills grill serves meals spiced up by the panorama of life in the heart of the city. The dishes range from China to the Middle East via India; tuck into a tandoori mixed grill while watching the world pass by the city's famous gate.

Naseef ICE CREAM $

(Map p64; ☎17 208 888; Al Mutanabi Ave, Manama Souq; ice-cream cup BD1; ⏲8am-10pm) Tucked away in an air-conditioned corner of Manama Souq just south of Bab Al Bahrain, Naseef made its name with a vivid-hued mango ice cream. You *could* try other flavours, but why you'd want to is beyond us. It's Manama's most refreshing snack.

★**Café Lilou** CAFE $$

(Map p60; ☎17 714 440; Yousef Ahmed Alshawi Ave, Adliya; mains BD2.700-8.800; ⏲8am-11pm Sat-Wed, to 11.45pm Thu & Fri; ✎) This elegant balconied venue, with its velvet upholstery, wrought-iron banisters and polished-wood floors, is reminiscent of a 19th-century Parisian brasserie and is the place for a classy breakfast or lunch in particular. The handmade pastries are a standout: try the French-standard croissants or the irresistible French toast soaked in rich vanilla pastry cream with mascarpone, almonds and fresh wild berries...

The creativity is not the sole domain of the pastry chefs, with mains like grilled tamarind hammour skewers served with saffron-almond rice and rose petals in dried lime butter and chives. Service from the bow-tied waiters is attentive and discreet. There's another **branch** (Map p54; ☎17 583 939; Sheikh Khalifa bin Sulman Hwy, Al Aali Mall, Seef; mains BD2.700-8.800; ⏲10am-10pm) in Al Aali Mall.

★**Fish House** SEAFOOD $$

(Map p54; ☎17 594 040; Budaiya Hwy; mains from BD7; ⏲11.30am-11pm) Bahrain's high-end eateries have tried to wrest the mantle of the island's best seafood from this basic place out west in Budaiya, to no avail. There are no frills here, none at all, and the menu varies with the catch of the day, so it's always fresh. And *always* packed with Bahrainis and expats. It's opposite the International Hospital.

THE BAHRAIN BRUNCH

A big highlight of the Bahrain foodie's week is the institution that is Friday brunch. It usually begins around noon, runs for around three hours and involves a vast buffet with live cooking stations. The focus tends to be more on the lunch rather than the breakfast side of things, and there's often some form of live entertainment to keep things ticking over. Prices vary based on your drinks selection – soft drinks are included at the lower end, wine and beer if you pay top dinar.

➡ **Bahrain Bay Kitchen** (☎17 115 000; Four Seasons Hotel; brunch per person BD25-32; ⏲brunch 12.30-3.30pm Fri) Bahrain's most generous buffet brunch, with seemingly endless variety, great service and even a dedicated kids' area.

➡ **Bushido** (p65) A local favourite, with buffet and made-to-order dishes from the live cooking stations.

➡ **Masso** (p65) Breakfast choices share buffet space with lots of European-inspired mains, and it does it all again on Saturday.

➡ **Diplomat Radisson Blu** (Map p60; ☎17 531 666; brunch per person BD24-28; ⏲brunch noon-3.30pm) Mexican, Indian, Italian, Asian and barbecue cooking ensure ample variety here, and best of all you can break things up with a swim in the pool.

➡ **Le Domain [34]** (Map p60; ☎16 000 200; Domain Hotel, Road 1705, Diplomatic Area; brunch per person BD19-27; ⏲noon-4pm Fri) In a fabulous setting on the 34th floor of the Domain Hotel, Le Domain has fine views to go with its fabulous French and fusion cooking. It's less family friendly than many of the other places.

➡ **Al Waha** (Map p60; ☎17 713 000; Gulf Hotel, Bani Otbah Ave; brunch per person BD22-29; ⏲brunch noon-3.30pm Fri) The Gulf Hotel may have an astonishing 15 restaurants, but this one dominates proceedings on Friday, when a terrific international buffet takes over. It's family friendly and there's live music.

Central Manama

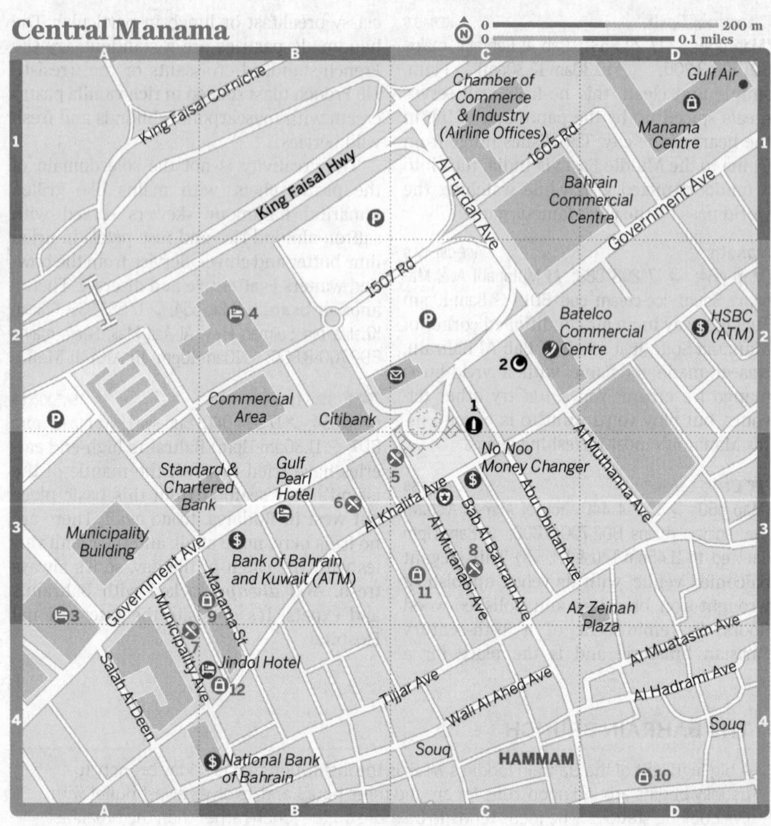

Central Manama

Sights
1 Bab Al Bahrain............C2
2 Friday Mosque............C2

Sleeping
3 Delmon International Hotel............A3
4 Regency InterContinental............B2

Eating
5 Charcoal Grill............C3
6 Haji Gahwa............B3
7 Honey's Thai Restaurant............A4
8 Naseef............C3

Shopping
9 Gold City............B3
10 Gold Souq............D4
11 Manama Souq............C3
12 World of Herbs............B4

Isfahani IRANIAN $$

(Map p60; ☎17 290 027; Exhibition Ave; mains BD2.700-4.200; ⊙noon-11pm) Excellent Iranian food at an almost-budget price is a winning combination. Take your time over the menu, but we settled on the Isfahani *juja* kebab (baby boneless chicken with Persian spices and served with rice) and were very glad we did. There are various other outposts around town, including in the **Bahrain City Centre food court** (☎17 178 382; 2nd fl, Bahrain City Centre, Sheikh Khalifa bin Sulman Hwy; mains BD2.700-4.200; ⊙10am-10pm Sat-Wed, to midnight Thu & Fri).

Rayés LEBANESE $$

(Map p60; ☎17 312 700; www.coral-bay.net; Al Fatih Hwy, Marina Corniche; mains BD2.200–16.900; ⊙noon-1am) This is one of the most attractive places to sample Lebanese food, right by the water's edge in the Coral Bay complex. The chef prides himself on the variety of salads and cold mezze, but everything's good here and there's so much choice. The bread is baked on the premises. Live Arabic music contributes to the convivial atmosphere.

My Cafe CAFE **$$**

(Map p60; ☎77 344 444; www.mycafebh.com; Block 338, Adliya; mains BD4.500-14.500; ⏰8am-midnight Sun-Wed, to 1am Thu-Sat) One of Manama's most sophisticated cafes, the elegant My Cafe, just beyond the southern end of Adliya's restaurant zone, turns out dishes like tuna carpaccio or roasted hammour, done exceptionally well. The experience is enhanced by a lovely setting, whether you choose the gorgeous salon or the garden terrace. It gets very busy at lunch or dinnertime, so book ahead.

Coco's INTERNATIONAL **$$**

(Map p60; ☎17 716 512; Yousef Ahmed Alshawi Ave, Adliya; mains BD2.700-4.900; ⏰10am-11.30pm) With indoor and outdoor seating, huge servings and an extensive menu that ranges across more than a dozen salads, pasta and other mainly Mediterranean dishes, it's hardly surprising that Coco's remains enormously popular. Too popular, perhaps, for its own good sometimes, as waiters can get a little overwhelmed when things are busy.

La Fontaine INTERNATIONAL **$$**

(Map p60; ☎17 230 123; www.lafontaineartcentre.net; 92 Hoora Ave, Dhuwawdah; mains BD6.600-11.800; ⏰noon-3pm & 6-11.30pm Tue-Sun; 🖉) This fashionable restaurant, in the outstanding La Fontaine Centre of Contemporary Art, is a magical place to enjoy lunch or dinner alongside the fountain and surrounded by one of Manama's best examples of traditional architecture. Highlights from the menu include the grilled halloumi salad and the grilled crayfish. There's also an extensive wine list with mostly European wines.

Swiss Cafe BUFFET **$$**

(Map p54; ☎66 310 041; www.swiss-belhotel.com; 10th fl, Swiss Belhotel, King Mohammed VI Ave; buffet BD7-12; ⏰12.30-3pm) One of Manama's best deals, the lunchtime buffet here offers a fine salad bar, eight main courses, barbecue area and grills, not to mention excellent views from its 10th-floor perch. The Friday version is all about seafood and worth every dinar.

★Masso INTERNATIONAL **$$$**

(Map p54; ☎17 721 061; www.massorestaurant.com; cnr Mahooz Rd & Shaikh Isa Ave; mains BD8-13, brunch per person BD26-33; ⏰noon-3pm & 7-11pm Mon-Sat, brunch noon-4pm Fri & Sat) The home kitchen of Susy Massetti wins plaudits for its cooking, born in the Mediterranean and using fresh local ingredients with class and creativity. Sample dishes include Earl Grey–marinated chicken and harissa-marinated lamb chops.

Rasoi by Vineet INDIAN **$$$**

(Map p60; ☎17 746 461; www.gulfhotelbahrain.com; Gulf Hotel, Adliya; mains BD5.500-16.500; ⏰noon-3pm & 7-11pm Sat-Thu, 1-4pm & 7-11pm Fri) Michelin-starred chef Vineet Bhatia brings Bahrain's finest Indian food to the table, showcasing what he calls 'Evolved Indian' cooking. Try the cashew-crusted asparagus, the 48-hour marinated lamb or even his clever adaptation of the Indian tiffin lunch. The hotel is off Bani Otbah Ave.

Bushido JAPANESE **$$$**

(Map p54; ☎17 583 555; www.bushido.com.bh; Ave 38, Seef; mains BD5.900-27, set menu from BD25, 3-course business lunch BD10, brunch BD22-30; ⏰noon-2am, brunch noon-3.30pm Fri) This institution is where Bahrain first fell in love with Japanese food. There are all the usual suspects, plus miso black cod, Wagyu beef cooked on a volcanic stone and 'New-Style Sashimi' such as salmon and grapefruit with yuzu black-pepper dressing or Japanese sea bream with white wine and truffle soy sauce. Its Sunday brunch is one of Bahrain's best.

There's also a teppanyaki room, a sushi bar, bento boxes for lunch, and a three-course business lunch where they promise to serve all three courses in 30 minutes. Dress conservatively; shorts are not allowed.

Drinking & Nightlife

Manama's nightlife is not what it was, although it's making something of a comeback. All top-end hotels have sophisticated bar areas, often with jazz or other live music, and usually featuring a 'happy hour' or cut-price cocktails. Serious nightclubbers should consult the English-language newspapers to track down the in-crowd.

B28 Bar Lounge COCKTAIL BAR

(Map p54; 28th fl, Swiss-Belhotel, King Mohammed VI Ave; ⏰4pm-2am Sun-Thu, 1pm-2am Fri & Sat) Plush velvet sofas, fabulous views, and brilliant bar food with Aussie steaks and lobster bisque make this intimate venue one of our favourite lounge bars in Manama.

Hub BAR

(Map p60; ☎17 296 699; Exhibition Ave; ⏰9pm-2am) In the Monroe Hotel, this place is fast becoming one of the best bars in town for live music.

Coral Bay BAR
(Map p60; Marina Corniche, Al Fatih Hwy; ⌚9am-late) By the water, with great music, next to one of Manama's best Lebanese restaurants and hosting first-rate parties – what more could you ask for in a venue?

Bushido LOUNGE
(Map p54; Ave 38, Seef; ⌚noon-3am) Is there anything they don't do well at Bushido? This fine Japanese restaurant also happens to be an uber-cool lounge bar with great views, down-tempo tunes and reassuring proximity to outstanding Japanese cooking.

Trader Vic's BAR
(Map p54; ☎17 580 000; Ritz-Carlton Bahrain Hotel & Spa, Bldg 112, Road 40, Block 428, King Mohammed VI Ave, Seef; ⌚6pm-2am) The Polynesian-themed Trader Vic's at the Ritz-Carlton has an appealing outdoor area that's perfect on a warm Bahrain night. Good bar food, too.

Sherlock Holmes BAR
(Map p60; Gulf Hotel, Bani Otbah Ave; ⌚noon-2am) The incongruously themed Sherlock Holmes in Adliya is an English pub that's still going strong well after other places have folded in Manama's fickle nightlife scene. Regular live music livens things up.

☆ Entertainment

To find out what's going on around Bahrain, see the What's On listings of the *Gulf Daily News*, *Bahrain This Month* magazine or *Time Out Bahrain*, all of which are available in bookshops.

Bahrain National Theatre CONCERT VENUE
(Map p60; www.culture.gov.bh; Sheikh Hamad Causeway; tickets BD20-70) The offerings at this stunning new venue are diverse and world-class – recent performances have included Placido Domingo, the Bolshoi Ballet and classical Arabic musicians.

Bahrain International Exhibition Centre CONCERT VENUE
(Map p54; ☎17 558 800; www.bahrainexhibitions.com; Sheikh Khalifa bin Sulman Hwy) Often has recitals of Bahraini music.

Shopping

For regional souvenirs (most of which are imported from Yemen, India, Pakistan and Iran), there are many shops selling silver jewellery, brass coffee pots, lapis lazuli and coral beads, carpets and kilims in the streets of Adliya (near the Gulf Hotel and Convention Centre), especially along Osama bin Zaid Ave.

★ **Manama Souq** MARKET
(Map p64; ⌚9am-1pm & 4-9pm Sat-Thu, 4-9pm Fri) Manama Souq, in the warren of streets behind Bab Al Bahrain, is the place to go for electronic goods, bargain T-shirts, nuts, spices, *sheesha* bottles and a plethora of other Bahraini essentials. Highlights include the Gold Souq

MANAMA FOR CHILDREN

Bahrainis welcome visiting children, and a lively expat community means that kids are never short of something to do. Look out for a handy booklet published biannually called *Fab Bahrain*, available from bookshops, schools and Seef Mall. This free directory gives a full A–Z listing of what to do and where to go in Bahrain as a family, from the story-telling activities of 'Wriggly Readers' to waterskiing and wakeboarding. It also has an excellent website (www.fabbahrain.com).

You'll also find plenty of information about what's on for children in the media; in particular, the 'Teens & Kids' section in *Bahrain this Month* magazine has heaps of information on fun activities, including lessons in hip hop and salsa.

The principal amusement area is **Funland Bowling Centre** (p57), but don't forget the **Lost Paradise of Dilmun Water Park** (p73) in Al Areen, 35km south of Manama, and the **Royal Camel Farm** (p71) near the King Fahd Causeway. Most of the malls have children's play areas of varying size and with varying facilities.

Magic Planet (☎17 173 113; Bahrain City Centre; ⌚10am-10pm Sat-Wed, to midnight Thu & Fri) This indoor play centre and amusement park on the 2nd floor of Bahrain City Centre has been recently overhauled and has rides, games and areas for all ages.

Wahooo! (Map p54; ☎17 173 000; www.theplaymania.com/wahooo; 2nd fl, Bahrain City Centre; under/over 1.2m BD12/8, under 3yr BD4; ⌚11am-8pm Sat-Tue, to 10pm Wed, to 9pm Thu & Fri) This massive indoor water park guarantees you'll get wet, with a wave pool, water slides, a slow-moving river and a number of heated swimming pools.

MANAMA MALLS

Like any Gulf city worthy of the name, Manama is a full-on subscriber to the Starbucks-and-shopping-malls approach to local culture. As elsewhere, these air-conditioned malls are as much places to eat and meet as they are purely shopping experiences.

Bahrain City Centre (Map p54; ☎17 177 771; www.citycentrebahrain.com; Sheikh Khalifa bin Sulman Hwy; ⏲10am-10pm Sat-Wed, to midnight Thu & Fri) Bahrain's true mega-mall, City Centre has something for everyone. If international brands have a presence in Bahrain, you'll most likely find them here, alongside a food court, a cinema complex, a Carrefour supermarket and even a small hub for local designers, including **Kubra Al Qaseer** (p68) and **Anmar Couture** (p68).

Seef Mall (Map p54; ☎17 582 888; www.seef.net; Sheikh Khalifa bin Sulman Hwy; ⏲10am-10pm Sat-Wed, to 11pm Thu & Fri) One of Manama's larger malls, Seef has gone for a fairly mainstream approach, with Marks & Spencer, H&M and Zara among many others, as well as the usual food court.

Moda Mall (Map p60; ☎17 535 140; www.modabwtc.com; World Trade Centre, King Faisal Hwy; ⏲10am-10pm) High-end designer retailers dominate this upmarket mall beneath the World Trade Centre. Think De Beers, Louis Vuitton and Dolce & Gabbana and you'll get an idea of what's here.

Al Aali Mall (Map p54; ☎17 581 000; www.alaalicomplex.com; Sheikh Khalifa bin Sulman Hwy, Seef; ⏲10am-10pm) This small mall next to Seef Mall has gone for quality over quantity, with a lovely reproduction of an old Gulf souq in the Souq Al Tawaweesh section, and designer brands such as Armani, Jimmy Choo and **Noof** (p68), a shopfront for local designer Noof Al Khor. Lovers of Turkish sweets will also love **Malatya Pazari** (p67).

(p67), Kingdom of Perfumes (p67), the Spice Souq (p67) and World of Herbs (p67).

★Kingdom of Perfumes — ACCESSORIES

(Map p60; ☎39 628 006; kingdom_of_perfumes@yahoo.com; Sheikh Abdullah Ave; ⏲9am-1pm & 4-9pm) You're in for a real treat at this fabulous little perfumery in the heart of Manama Souq. Try all manner of European-sourced perfumes if you must, but you're far better off sampling the locally mixed perfumes that use raw materials from India. Prices for a small bottle begin at BD1 to BD4, but even the top-of-the-range ones won't break the bank.

Gold City — JEWELLERY

(Map p64; Government Ave) Bahrain is the only country in the world to sell almost exclusively natural pearls. While the odd imported artificial pearl creeps in, shop owners are very quick to tell you which ones are and are not genuine, natural Bahraini pearls; when it comes to Bahrain's most famous heritage item, it is more than their license is worth to mislead the customer.

Gold Souq — JEWELLERY

(Map p64; Sheikh Abdullah Ave; ⏲9am-1pm & 3.30-9pm Sat-Thu, 9am-1pm Fri) Still the hub of the local gold industry, this is the place to come for both custom-made and ready-to-buy gold jewellery, with a few workshops where you can see the goldsmiths at work. Apart from anything else, come to see the locals shopping for gifts and wedding finery.

Spice Souq — FOOD

(Map p60; Road 439; ⏲9am-1pm & 4-7pm) It can be a little hard to find, but this small collection of spice sellers is a wonderfully fragrant place for a stroll as you explore one of the quieter corners of Manama Souq. Walk southeast along Municipality Ave from the Jindol Hotel and take the sixth street on the left.

Malatya Pazari — FOOD

(Map p54; ☎36 333 978; Al Aali Mall, Sheikh Khalifa bin Sulman Hwy) Lovers of Turkish sweets will love Malatya Pazari, purveyors of natural dried fruits, nuts, *halwa* (a dense Middle Eastern sweet made from flour, butter and nuts) and Turkish delight since the 19th century.

World of Herbs — BEAUTY

(Map p64; ☎17 228 218, 17 210 968; cnr Tijjar Ave & Road 470; ⏲7am-10pm) Herbal medicines are all the rage in this corner of Manama Souq; ask for the list that matches ailments to local-herb cures.

DON'T MISS

PEARLS

A highlight of shopping in Bahrain is looking for pearls. Pearls are created when grit enters the shell of, most usually, an oyster. The intrusive irritant is covered with a layer of mother-of-pearl, making it smooth and less irksome, and the longer the problem is nursed, the bigger the pearl gets. Large pearls have attracted large sums of money throughout history, but while size counts, it's not everything. Other factors taken into consideration are the depth and quality of lustre, the perfection of shape, and the colour, which ranges from peach to iron.

Commercial pearling was halted with the pioneering (in Japan) of the cultured pearl in the 1930s. Created through the artificial injection of a bead into the shell of an oyster, cultured pearls are more uniform and are created more quickly. Nonetheless, at the heart of the gem is a piece of plastic.

In Bahrain, on the other hand, natural pearls are still garnered from the island's healthy oyster beds, in a revival of this heritage industry. Occasionally, the sea bed renders up the larger, uniquely coloured pearls that once made the area so famous, but more usually Bahraini pearl jewellery features clusters of tiny, individually threaded, ivory-coloured pearls, set in 21-carat gold.

Visit the gold shops of central Manama to see how pearls continue to inspire local jewellers. A perfect pearl can fetch thousands of dollars, but a pair of cluster earrings or a ring can start at a more affordable US$100. Prices for pearl jewellery are more or less fixed, but there's no harm in asking for a discount for oyster shells (US$60 including growing pearl – or free for those willing to dive for their own).

To try your hand at pearl diving, visit **Al Dar Islands** (Map p54; ☎17 704 600; www.aldarislands.com; adult/child BD5/3; ⏰9am-5pm Tue-Sun).

Kubra Al Qaseer FASHION
(Map p54; www.kubraalqaseer.net; 2nd fl, Bahrain City Centre, Sheikh Khalifa bin Sulman Hwy; ⏰10am-10pm Sat-Wed, to midnight Thu & Fri) Arguably Bahrain's best-known designer, Kubra Al Qaseer pioneered the colourful modern interpretations of the humble *jalebiya* (long, flowing cotton garment worn by women).

Noof FASHION
(Al Aali Mall, Sheikh Khalifa bin Sulman Hwy; ⏰10am-10pm) Bahraini designer Noof Al Khor turns out modern takes on Bahraini women's fashions, with a focus on glittering sandals and *jalebiyas*.

Anmar Couture FASHION
(Map p54; ☎17 178 170; www.anmarcouture.com; 2nd fl, Bahrain City Centre, Sheikh Khalifa bin Sulman Hwy; ⏰10am-10pm Sat-Wed, to midnight Thu & Fri) All manner of colourful *jalebiyas* are the hallmark of celebrated Bahraini designer Adeeba Al Khan.

ℹ Information

EMERGENCY

Ambulance, Fire & Police (☎999)

MEDICAL SERVICES

Medical treatment is easy to obtain in Bahrain and the standard of care is high.

American Mission Hospital (Map p60; ☎17 253 447; www.amh.org.bh; Sheikh Isa Al Khebir Ave) Well-equipped Manama hospital of long standing.

International Hospital of Bahrain (Map p54; ☎17 598 222; www.ihb.net) Well-regarded hospital just off Budaiya Hwy.

Jaffar Pharmacy (Map p60; ☎17 291 039; 18 Tarfa bin Al Abd Ave; ⏰24hr) Located near McDonald's, off Exhibition Ave.

MONEY

There are several banks and moneychangers on Government Ave between Bab Al Bahrain and the Delmon International Hotel. There are ATMs at most banks including HSBC.

No Noo Money Changer (Map p64; ☎17 230 767; ⏰7am-10pm) Don't be put off by the name; this establishment behind Bab Al Bahrain Ave has grown from a hole in the wall to a fully fledged office. It still keeps late but unspecified hours.

ℹ Getting There & Away

AIR

Most airline offices are situated around Bab Al Bahrain, in the Chamber of Commerce & Industry building, or inside the Manama Centre, which is where you'll find **Gulf Air** (p84), the main national carrier.

Bahrain International Airport (Map p54; ☎flight information 17 339 339; www.bahrain airport.com; Muharraq Island) Busy Gulf airport and hub for Gulf Air.

Getting Around

TO/FROM THE AIRPORT

The airport is on Muharraq Island, approximately 6km from central Manama. A metered taxi from central Manama to the airport should cost about BD5. For trips *from* the airport there's a BD2 surcharge. Many hotels offer a shuttle-bus service.

There are ATMs for a range of bank cards, including American Express (Amex), in the transit lounge of the airport. Car-hire outlets are in the arrivals hall.

BUS

Manama Bus Station (Map p60; Government Ave) Most people get around town by car or taxi, but the expanded bus system operated by Bahrain Bus (☎66 311 111; www.bahrainbus.bh) fans out from the bus station.

TAXI

Taxis are easy to find, and there are stands outside Bab Al Bahrain and many hotels. Taxis are metered; flagfall is BD1 for the first 2km, and thereafter the meter ticks over in increments of 100 fils (or 200 fils per kilometre). You'll pay a BD1 supplement if you take a taxi at a hotel or any other taxi rank. Fares officially increase by 25% between 10pm and about 6am.

In addition to contacting the taxi companies directly you could also try www.bahtaxi.com. Uber (www.uber.com) has also recently arrived in Bahrain.

Arabian Taxi (☎17 461 746)

Bahrain Limo (☎39 666 482)

Speedy Motors (☎17 682 999; www.speedy-motors.com)

AROUND BAHRAIN ISLAND

Although it's dominated by its capital city, there's more to Bahrain Island than Manama, as those coming for the Grand Prix are sure to discover. The island is particularly rich in archaeological sites. Bahrain is small, so the main sights make easily accessible day trips from the capital by car. It's hard to get lost, because all road signs point to Saudi!

Bahrain Fort Complex قلعة البحرين

Sights

★Bahrain Fort ARCHAEOLOGICAL SITE

(Qal'at Al Bahrain; Map p54; ☎17 567 171; www.culture.gov.bh; 8am-6pm; P; 5 from Manama, then half-hour walk) FREE Overlooking the northern coast a 10-minute drive from central Manama, and standing guard on an ancient tell (mound created by centuries of urban rebuilding), Unesco World Heritage-listed Bahrain Fort was built by the Portuguese in the 16th century as part of a string of defences along the Gulf. The moated fort is particularly attractive at night, when the history of the site seems to rise out of the excavations and linger between the floodlights.

The site was occupied from about 2800 BC and seven layers of history are represented in the digs surrounding the fort, including the remnants of two earlier forts. The fort is well signposted about 5km west of Manama.

Fort Museum MUSEUM

(Map p54; Bahrain Fort; admission BD1; 8am-8pm Tue-Sun; P) This excellent museum helps

WORTH A TRIP

ARCHAEOLOGICAL SITES NEAR MANAMA

For archaeology students with a keen imagination, two temple sites near Manama are worth a visit, ideally on a guided tour – ask your hotel to make arrangements. There is no public transport, but the sites are signposted along Budaiya Hwy from Manama (but not if you're driving in the other direction) near the village of Bani Jamrah. The village is famous for textile weaving, and workshops sell hand-loomed cloth.

Barbar Temple (Map p54; suggested donation BD1; daylight hours) Barbar is a complex of three 2nd- and 3rd-millennium-BC temples, probably dedicated to Enki (the god of wisdom) and the Sweet Water from Under the Sea. The excavated complex can be seen from a series of walkways; a detailed map (such as that in *Bahrain: A Heritage Explored* by Angela Clark) or a knowledgeable tour guide are needed to make sense of the site.

Ad-Diraz Temple (Map p54; daylight hours) Ad-Diraz Temple dates from the 2nd millennium BC.

SAFETY

At the time of writing, the A'Ali area had acquired something of a reputation for unrest, and there was a heavy police presence and roadblocks restricting access. Ask locally before visiting and take the advice of your taxi driver or guide.

bring Bahrain Fort alive. How can you fail to enjoy exhibits labelled 'Looking for a Tylos Necropolis?'. Displays about snake bowl sacrifices and stamp seals from the Dilmun period help unravel some of the complexities of a site that spans nearly 5000 years.

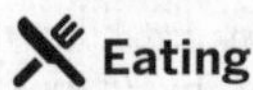

Eating

Museum Café CAFE

(Map p54; Bahrain Fort; cakes from BD1.500, light meals BD2.500-4; ⏲10.30am-7pm) With the best sea view on the island, the terrace of this cafe is a magical place to sit with a divine cake from nearby Le Chocolat Gourmet Bakery and watch the mudflats bubble with lowlife.

A'Ali عالي

A'Ali is distinguished by the extraordinary burial mounds that surround the town. It's also worth a visit for its pottery and flat bread, each produced in traditional kilns.

Sights

★A'Ali Burial Mounds ARCHAEOLOGICAL SITE

(Map p54; A'Ali; daylight hours; P) FREE To gain an idea of the significance of these burial mounds on the approach to A'Ali, visit Manama's Bahrain National Museum (p53) beforehand. The mounds, which date from the Dilmun period, encase burial chambers used for all members of society, young and old. At 15m in height and 45m in diameter, the tallest mounds are referred to as the 'Royal Tombs', and it's easy to see why: they give A'Ali, an otherwise humble town of potters and bakers, a regal presence.

From Manama, take the Sheikh Sulman Hwy south past Isa Town, then turn west along A'Ali Hwy and follow the signs to the mounds; the journey takes 20 minutes by car. Keep your eyes open either side of the highway for other burial mounds: there are more than 100,000 of them in Bahrain. An erratic bus service links Manama and A'Ali.

Pottery Workshop GALLERY

(Map p54; A'Ali; ⏲9am-1pm & 4-6pm Sat-Thu) A'Ali is the site of Bahrain's best-known pottery workshop, with traditional mudbrick kilns and a votive display of curiosities. Ceramics are on sale at several stalls nearby.

Sar سار

Sar Burial Chambers ARCHAEOLOGICAL SITE

(Map p54; Sar; ⏲daylight hours) FREE The excavations at Sar have revealed a honeycomb of burial chambers dating from the Dilmun period. They have all long since been plundered, but the systematic removal of the coping stones has at least revealed the inner sanctum of the site. There are plans to turn the site into a major tourist attraction that will include a museum, but for now there is a special privilege in being able to wander unchecked among the cradles of the dead.

Although the site is visible from the main road, there is no access from the Causeway Approach Rd. Instead, follow signs for the village of Sar, heading south from Budaiya Hwy, or from Janabiya Hwy, and then heritage signs to the site. Sar is 10km from Manama. There's no public transport.

King Fahd Causeway معبر الملك فهد

There is something immensely evocative about an international border, and there could be few more impressive heralds of one than the 26km causeway that links Saudi Arabia with Bahrain. Built in a series of humpbacked rises and long, flat stretches across the shallows of the Gulf, this remarkable piece of engineering, completed in 1986 at a cost of US$1.2 billion, is worth a visit just to marvel at its construction.

On either side of an island roughly in the middle of the causeway are two observation towers that invite visitors as close to the border as visas allow. Leave enough time to queue for the tiny lift that services the viewing platform near the top of the tower. From there it's possible to see the 26km, four-lane causeway in full, with its 12,430m of viaducts and its five separate bridges, all made from 350,000 sq metres of concrete and reinforced by 147,000 tonnes of steel.

All drivers (and passengers in taxis) must pay a toll at a booth (per vehicle BD2) along the Causeway Approach Rd, whether going to Saudi or not. The island in the middle of the causeway is 25km from Manama and it takes 30 minutes to drive there.

Sights

Royal Camel Farm FARM

(Map p54; Janabiya; 8am-4pm Sat & Sun) FREE Signposted just off King Fahd Causeway, this farm is home to hundreds of camels owned by the great and good of Bahrain. If you're lucky, one of the workers will let you ride a camel in return for a small (negotiable) fee.

King Fahd Causeway Restaurant VIEWPOINT

(17 690 674; admission 500 fils, mains from BD2; 9am-11pm) For an egg roll-up and chips while watching the sun dip behind the Saudi mainland at sunset, try the King Fahd Causeway Restaurant, halfway up the tower on the Bahraini side.

Al Jasra الجسرة

A pleasant and leafy suburb, Al Jasra is most often visited for the handicraft centre. It is worth sparing some extra time, however, to amble past villas and small, private plantations to get a sense of this typical Bahraini community.

Sights

Al Jasra House HISTORIC BUILDING

(Map p54; 17 611 454; admission 500 fils; 9am-6pm Sat-Thu, 3-6pm Fri; P) One of several historic homes around Bahrain that has been restored to its original condition, Al Jasra House was built in 1907 and is famous as the birthplace in 1933 of the former emir, Sheikh Isa bin Sulman Al Khalifa. It's constructed in the traditional way from coral stone, supported by palm-tree trunks. The gravel in the courtyard is made up of a 'hundreds-and-thousands' mixture of tiny mitre and auger shells. Opening times are erratic, so call ahead to confirm.

From the Causeway Approach Rd, look for the exit to Al Jasra (before the toll booth); the house is well signposted. The town is 15km from Manama and takes 20 minutes to travel to by bus or car.

Al Jasra Handicraft Centre ARTS CENTRE

(Map p54; 17 611 900; 10am-4pm Sat, 8am-2pm Sun-Thu; P) In the residential area of Al Jasra is the government-run Al Jasra Handicraft Centre. This collection of workshops specialises in textiles, woodwork and basket weaving. Bus 12 from Manama stops outside, but timings are unreliable.

Riffa Fort قلعة الرفاع

Riffa Fort FORT

(Sheikh Salman bin Ahmad Al Fatih Fort; Map p54; 17 322 549; admission 500 fils; 7am-2pm Sun-Wed, 9am-6pm Thu & Sat, 3-6pm Fri) Commanding the only piece of high ground overlooking the Hunanaiya Valley, this fort was originally built in the 19th century and was completely restored in 1983. The limited captions and explanations are in Arabic, and the rooms are mostly empty, but it's interesting enough and the views over a valley of a golf course, nodding donkeys and tree-lined highways are appealing.

The fort is easy to spot from several main roads near the town of Riffa and is well signposted. Access to the fort is only possible along Sheikh Hamood bin Sebah Ave, which is off Riffa Ave. Riffa is 25km from Manama and a 30-minute ride by car. Along the journey, note all the magnificent avenues of palms, orange-flowering cordias and topiaried citrus trees that line the suburban part of the highways.

Bahrain International Circuit

Bahrain's Formula 1 circuit is among the major attractions of the country and one of the main reasons for getting out of Manama to explore the island.

Sights & Activities

Formula 1 Racetrack STADIUM

(Map p54; 17 450 000; www.bahraingp.com; tours BD6; tours 10am & 2pm Sun, Tue & Thu; P) The Al Sakhir Tower of the Formula 1 Racetrack rises above the desert like a beacon. If you're visiting Bahrain out of season and want to see what a state-of-the-art track looks like, then you can join a 40-minute tour of the grounds, media centre and control room, and even take a lap around the circuit. Tours can be booked online.

Land Rover Experience DRIVING TOUR

(Map p54; 17 450 000; www.bahraingp.com; Formula 1 Racetrack, Al Sakhir; 90min passenger drive BD12, 2hr self-drive BD65) A great way to learn how to drive off-road, Land Rover Experience lets you go four-wheel driving close to the F1 Racetrack with 32 natural and artificial obstacles to negotiate.

BAHRAIN'S F1 STORY

With more than a billion people in worldwide audiences, the highlight of Bahrain's sporting calendar is undoubtedly the Grand Prix. To win the right to host the event, Bahrain fought off competition from rival bidders the UAE, Egypt and Lebanon to create the first-ever F1 grand prix to be held in the Middle East.

The first Bahrain Grand Prix was held in 2004 – Michael Schumacher, driving a Ferrari, won the first race – and it has gone ahead ever since, save for 2011. Originally part of the official 2011 program, the race was cancelled just three weeks before it was due to take place and at the height of massive street demonstrations in Manama as part of Bahrain's Arab Spring uprising – a number of drivers openly expressed concern about safety and the wisdom of holding the race at a time of such significant political uncertainty. In 2014, the race was held under floodlights, only the second track (after Singapore) to have staged a night-time grand prix. The track appears to be a particular favourite of Fernando Alonso (a three-time winner) and two-time winner Lewis Hamilton.

The magnificent Arabian-style stadium, 'tented' grandstands and allusions to the country's wind towers make a fine showcase for modern Bahrain as well as the sport.The stadium holds 70,000 spectators, and an astonishing 82,000 tyres are used to construct the barriers around the track.

There are actually six tracks as part of the complex, including a 1.2km-long drag strip and a 2km test oval. The race normally sits at second or third in the grand prix calendar, taking place in early April; the usual track is 5.412km (3.363 miles) long and is raced over 57 laps. In 2010, however, Bahrain honoured Formula 1's Diamond Jubilee and staged the opening race of the 2010 season along the full 6.299km (3.914-mile) 'Endurance Circuit'.

Out of respect for local sensibilities, winners are sprayed not with champagne but with *warrd*, made from locally grown pomegranate and rosewater, and promo models wear less revealing outfits – think Gulf Air crew uniforms rather than your usual pit-lane fare.

Bahrain Karting ADVENTURE SPORTS
(Map p54; ☎13 101 310; www.bahrain-karting.com; Formula 1 Racetrack, Al Sakhir; 15min drive BD10; ⏰3.30-10.30pm Wed, Fri & Sat) Go-karting at Bahrain's Formula 1 Racetrack is a great way to see the circuit. Several different packages are on offer.

Dragster Xperience ADVENTURE SPORTS
(Map p54; ☎17 450 000; www.bahraingp.com; Formula 1 Racetrack, Al Sakhir; per person BD40) Go from 0km/h to 100km/h in just one second – the G-force is something to behold – and reach speeds of up to 260km/h on the F1 Racetrack's drag strip. You won't be driving, of course – best leave that to the qualified driver.

Getting There & Away

From Manama, just about all roads point to the circuit. The track is 30km from Manama and it takes around 35 minutes to get there by car. There is no public transport.

Al Areen العرين

Al Areen was once little more than empty desert with a few forlorn native species roaming inside some random enclosures. Over the past few years, however, the escarpment has been transformed into a major tourist attraction with the arrival of the wildlife reserve, a resort and spa, and a water park.

Sights & Activities

Al Areen Wildlife Park & Reserve WILDLIFE RESERVE
(Map p54; ☎17 845 480; www.alareen.org; adult/child BD1/0.500; ⏰9am-4pm Sat-Thu, 2-4pm Fri; P) This 10-sq-km reserve, off Al Zallaq Hwy in the island's southwest, is a conservation area for species indigenous to the Middle East and North Africa. After a short introductory film (in Arabic only), a small bus leaves roughly every hour for a tour (with commentary in Arabic and English) past some of the park's 80 species of bird and 45 species of mammal.

There are several herds of mature oryx with fabulous horns that make it easy to appreciate, first, how this gracious animal could be mistaken for a unicorn and, secondly, what an enviable choice of national animal it makes.

Al Jazayer Beach BEACH

(Map p54) This beach has shady palm trees and reasonable swimming, though the water, like that of the entire coast of Bahrain, is very shallow.

Lost Paradise of Dilmun Water Park WATER PARK

(Map p54; ☎17 845 100; www.lpodwaterpark.com; over/under 1.2m BD15/8; ⏲10am-6pm Wed-Mon) With dozens of water-themed amenities, including slides, a rain fortress, fountains and a wave pool, Lost Paradise prompts squeals of delight you can hear for miles. There's even a sandy beach. The park is off Zallaq Hwy.

Sleeping

Al Areen Palace & Spa RESORT $$$

(Map p54; ☎17 845 000; www.alareenpalace.com; Al Areen; r from BD205; P 📶 🏊) When the sun sets in the descending pools of the resort's inner courtyards, it's obvious why the complex was built on the country's only elevated ground. The atmosphere is calm and exclusive and, apart from the soft-slippered massage therapists padding from spa to poolside, there's little to interrupt the sense of tranquility. Rooms are luxurious, with classic decor.

Getting There & Away

Al Areen's attractions are signposted off the Zallaq Hwy, 35km from Manama (40 minutes by car). There is no public transport.

Tree of Life شجرة الحياة

Tree of Life LANDMARK

(Map p54) The Tree of Life is a lone and spreading mesquite tree, famous not because it somehow survives in the barren desert (plenty of trees and thorn bushes do that) but because it has survived for so long. No one is sure what sustains this old knot of thorny branches, but it has presumably tapped into an underground spring – a miracle that has led some to suggest it is the last vestige of the Garden of Eden.

It won't be a change in the climate, however, that will signal its downfall, but the all-too-visible change in the kind of visitor it attracts, to which the daubs of spray paint all over the venerable old bark attest.

When standing under the spreading limbs of this tree that graces a patch of Bahrain's southern desert, with earth movers scraping the escarpment for cement, and oil and gas pipelines running alongside, it's hard to imagine anywhere less deserving of the name 'Garden of Eden'. And yet, modern scholars point to several ancient sources that suggest Bahrain may have been the locus of paradise. In the Babylonian creation myth, the Epic of Gilgamesh, Dilmun (Bahrain's ancient incarnation) is described as the home of Enki (the god of wisdom), the Sweet Water from Under the Sea, and Ninhursag (goddess of the Earth). Likewise, in the Old Testament, it

F1 GRAND PRIX: TICKETS & PARTIES

Tickets

The place to start when looking for tickets to or any other information about the Bahrain Grand Prix is **Bahrain International Circuit** (☎17 450 000; www.bahraingp.com). Tickets usually go on sale a few weeks before race day (join the mailing list to make sure you don't miss out), and three-day passes that include Friday practice, Saturday qualifying races and the big race itself (on Sunday) start at around BD50 for the stand at Turn 1 and go up to BD165 for a seat in the main stand. Tickets can be purchased online through the main website, although most visitors book their tickets as part of their overall travel package through their grand-prix travel agency of choice.

Parties

What the official website won't tell you is where the after-parties are to be found. Although venues change with each passing year, there are two mainstays. First, Manama's five-star hotels will be at the centre of many of the off-track celebrations, whether in their restaurants or, as the night wears on, in their bars. Secondly, it's close to guaranteed that one of the best after-parties in Bahrain – every night, but especially Sunday night after the race – will be happening at **Coral Bay** (p66). This is often where the official party's held and you can expect international live acts and DJs, and a whole lot of glamour. Door prices for Coral Bay's F1 party in 2015 were BD30 per person. **Bushido** (p66) is another reliable option.

For an updated list of party venues, check out www.timeoutbahrain.com.

is possible that Hebrew and Sumerian traditions of paradise are similarly conflated. On encountering this Tree of Life, however, you may well urge archaeologists searching for Eden to keep looking!

Follow signs to the tree along the Muaskar Hwy. It is just off the sealed road (take a right turn by Khuff Gas Well 371 and turn right again along the power lines). There's no need for a 4WD, but take care not to drive into soft sand. There is a signboard at the site telling visitors how to get there. The Tree of Life is 40km from Manama and a 45-minute drive away. Note the wind-eroded forms in the escarpment near the site.

Oil Museum

Oil Museum MUSEUM

(Map p54; ☎17 753 475; ⏲10am-5pm Fri) FREE Built in 1992 to mark the 60th anniversary of the discovery of oil, this museum is housed in a grand, white-stone building quite out of keeping with the surrounding nodding donkeys and sprawling pipelines. In the shadow of Jebel ad-Dukhan (Mountain of Smoke) – Bahrain's highest point at just 134m – the building is a befitting symbol of the country's wealth, for it marks the point at which 'black gold' was struck for the first time on the Arabic side of the Gulf.

The museum has exhibits, photographs and explanations about the oil industry in Bahrain. A few metres away, you can see the country's first oil well, which was constructed in 1932.

Ring ahead to check opening times, as the museum is seldom visited despite being clearly signposted along an unmarked road south of Awali. There is no bus service to this region. By car, it takes about 40 minutes to reach the museum, which is 35km south of Manama.

Muharraq Island

جزيرة ال محرق

POP 192,000

Just over the causeways from Bahrain Island, Muharraq Island could in many respects belong to a different country. With some beautiful old houses, a fort and a shore full of moored dhows and lobster pots, there's enough to keep visitors occupied in the atmospheric backstreets for at least half a day. The more recent addition of cultural centres, focused on preserving Bahrain's fast-disappearing heritage, may well detain you longer.

Sights

★Beit Sheikh Isa Bin Ali Al Khalifa HISTORIC BUILDING

(بيت الشيخ عيسى بن علي; Map p75; ☎17 293 820; www.culture.gov.bh; Central Muharraq; admission BD1; ⏲7am-2pm Sat-Wed, 9am-2pm Thu, 3-6pm Fri) Offering a fascinating look at pre-oil life in Bahrain, this building was constructed around 1800 and is one of the finest examples of a traditional house anywhere in the Gulf. The chief sitting room downstairs was kept cool in summer by the down draft from the wind tower (*badqeer*), the shutters on which could be closed in winter – stand beneath it to see how effective this system of natural air conditioning really is. There's some fine gypsum and woodcarving throughout.

This was the seat of Bahraini power from 1869 to 1932 and its importance is reflected in the four different sections: Sheikh, family, guests and servants. While the rooms are unfurnished, the different sections of the house are well captioned in English and a good half-hour could be spent rambling up and down the different staircases admiring the delicate arches, intricate wooden doors, courtyards and palm-trunk ceilings. Note the blackened walls and ceiling of the servants' kitchen.

From Sheikh Hamad Causeway turn right at the roundabout onto Sheikh Abdullah bin Isa Ave. Brown signs indicate the way.

Beit Seyadi HISTORIC BUILDING

(بيت سيادي; Map p75; Central Muharraq) FREE A traditional house from the pre-oil period, Beit Seyadi once belonged to a pearl merchant. The house, located off Sheikh Isa Ave and closed for restoration, boasts a fine exterior, with its peculiar rounded corners decorated with emblems of stars and crescent moons; note the filigree carved windows that allow the inhabitants to see out but no one to see in. An old mosque is attached to the house.

Busaad Art Gallery GALLERY

(Map p75; ☎17 000 020; www.busaad.com; Sheikh Isa Ave, Muharraq; ⏲9am-1pm & 4-8pm Sat-Thu) FREE In a beautifully restored Muharraq house dating to the 1930s – the elaborate wooden balconies are worth admiring from outside – this gallery is the former home of and showcases the work of Ebrahim Mohamed Busaad (b 1954). The canvases are colourful and bold, and there's a small gift shop upstairs.

Muharraq Island

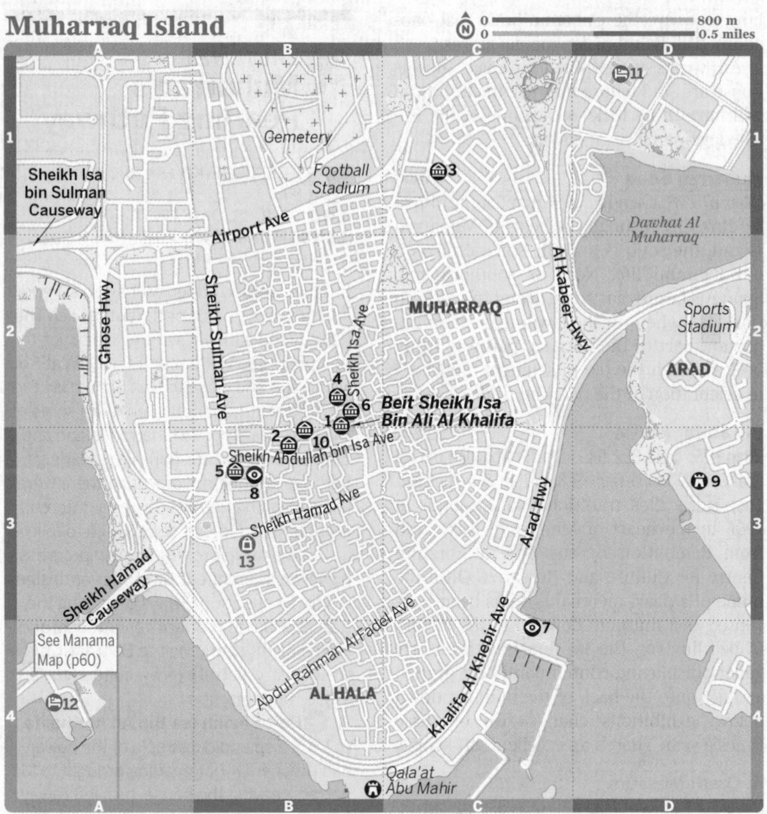

Sheikh Ebrahim bin Mohammed Al Khalifa Centre for Culture and Research HISTORIC BUILDING

(Map p75; ☎17 322 549; ⏰9am-1pm & 4-7pm Sat-Thu) FREE Inspired by the early-20th-century intellectual of the same name, this elegant centre hosts recitals, lectures and exhibitions every Monday evening. At other times it delivers a synopsis of Bahrain's history and heritage through the pages of a giant electronic book: a mere wave of the hand turns the pages on Dilmun, pearling and the Tree of Life. The building is located off Sheikh Abdullah bin Isa Ave.

Al Korar House HISTORIC BUILDING

(Map p75) FREE This house is a gathering point for Muharraq women intent on preserving the craft of *al korar* (gold-thread weaving), which three generations of a local family have saved from extinction. Once, the intricate threadwork was the occupation of all resident women; now only a handful of people know

Muharraq Island

Top Sights

1 Beit Sheikh Isa Bin Ali Al Khalifa B2

Sights

2 Al Korar House B3
3 Al Oraifi Museum C1
4 Beit Seyadi B2
5 Bin Matar House B3
6 Busaad Art Gallery B2
7 Muharraq Dhow Building Yard C4
8 Muharraq Souq B3
9 Qala'at Arad D3
10 Sheikh Ebrahim bin Mohammed Al Khalifa Centre for Culture and Research B3

Sleeping

11 Mövenpick Hotel Bahrain D1
12 Novotel Al Dana Resort A4

Shopping

13 Hussein Mohd Showaiter Sweets B3

how to weave the elaborate braid that once adorned all Bahraini ceremonial gowns.

All works the women produce in this house are sold before they are made, so you will have to be lucky to see one of the finished, gossamer-thin gowns.

Muharraq Souq MARKET

(Map p75; ⏰10am-1pm & 4-7pm Sat-Thu, 4-7pm Fri) Running through the heart of Muharraq Island, the souq is an atmospheric take on old Bahraini life. Near its southern end, Souq Al Qaisariya is still undergoing restoration that, when finished, will make it an important part of the heritage pathway being built through the old quarters of the island in celebration of the pearling trade.

Bin Matar House MUSEUM

(Map p75; ☎17 322 549; Sheikh Abdullah bin Isa Ave, Central Muharraq; ⏰8am-1pm & 4-7pm Sat-Thu) FREE This traditional house, built in 1905 in the heart of Muharraq, was saved from demolition by the Sheikh Ebrahim Centre for Culture and Research. Once the home of a pearl merchant, it has been reinvented as a museum devoted to the history of pearling (on the 1st floor), with an airy gallery displaying contemporary art grafted artfully onto the back of the building down below; exhibitions change two or three times a year. There's an excellent gift shop.

Al Oraifi Museum MUSEUM

(متحف راشد العريفي; Map p75; ☎17 535 112; admission BD1; ⏰8am-noon & 4-8pm Sat-Thu, 8am-noon Fri) Dedicated to the art and artefacts of the Dilmun era, this private collection of art and sculpture has over 100 works from the era. Inspired by these artefacts, the artist-owner paints Dilmun-related canvases that he displays in the museum's gallery. From Manama, take Sheikh Isa bin Sulman Causeway and follow the signs along Airport Ave.

Qala'at Arad FORT

(قلعة عراد; Arad Fort; Map p75; ☎17 672 278; admission BD1; ⏰9am-6pm; Ⓟ) Built in the early 15th century by the Portuguese, Qala'at Arad has been beautifully restored. There is little to see inside except the old well and the date-palm timbers used to reinforce the ceiling. Nonetheless, the location overlooking the bay makes it well worth a trip, especially at sunset, when the neighbouring park comes alive with locals. From Manama, take the Sheikh Hamad Causeway and follow the signs along Khalifa Al Khebir Ave and Arad Hwy.

City Walk Muharraq's Pearling Pathway

START BEIT SHEIKH ISA BIN ALI AL KHALIFA
END SOUQ AL QAISARIYA
LENGTH 3KM; TWO TO THREE HOURS

In 2012, Unesco added Muharraq's 'Pearling Pathway' to its World Heritage list. The 3.5km-long pathway will begin at a yet-to-be-completed visitor centre at Qala'at Abu Mahir and end close to Beit Sheikh Isa Bin Ali Al Khalifa, connecting en route some of the top sites across Muharraq Island and offering insights into Bahrain's pearling heritage. At the time of writing there were a few 'Pearling Pathway' signs scattered around the souq, but not enough to follow.

It remains an exciting work in progress, however, as architects and interior designers find inspirational ways of making the past relevant to modern generations, and is a highlight of any visit to Bahrain. Check the ministry website (www.culture.gov.bh/en) for updates.

❶ **Beit Sheikh Isa Bin Ali Al Khalifa** (p74) is a splendid example of the power and prosperity that pearling brought to Muharraq. Leaving the house, turn left (away from the mosque) and walk for around 50m, then turn right onto Road 916. Passing a school on your right, you'll soon come to the restored ❷ **Bu Khalaf Coffee Corner**, where they serve up thick Arabic coffee and dates to passing pedestrians. Take the first right after around 150m, then left after a further 50m. At this point you enter an open square – directly in front of you, behind a delightfully simple, conical minaret, is the exquisite, semi-restored facade of ❸ **Beit Seyadi** (p74). Back across the square, follow the signs east to ❹ **Busaad Art Gallery** (p74), which is on your right as you emerge onto Sheikh Isa Ave.

Retrace your steps to near to Bu Khalaf Coffee Corner, then take Lane 920 running west for 150m. Where the lane ends, turn left, then take the first right. Just 20m along on your right is the beautifully restored ❺ **Sheikh Ebrahim bin Mohammed Al Khalifa Centre for Culture and Research** (p75), its facade adorned with wooden arched windows and carved calligraphy. Di-

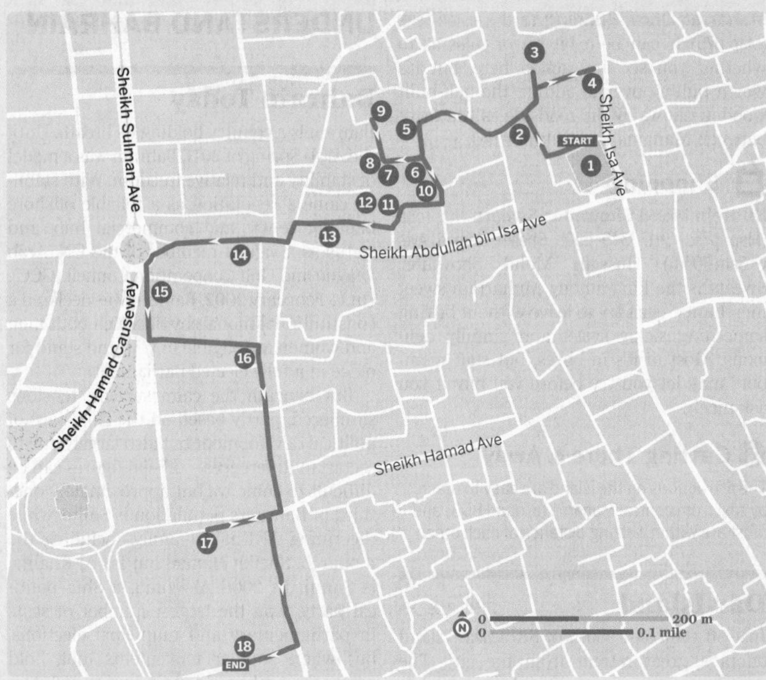

rectly across the laneway from the centre's entrance is a small **6 Children's Library**. A little further on to the west is **7 Cafe Lugmatina**, offering excellent local pastries, coffee and soft drinks in a lovely setting. Just around the corner is **8 Heraf Al Diyar**, which was closed at the time of research but may return as a handicraft centre; in the meantime, admire the restored 1st-floor wooden balconies. Just northeast of Heraf Al Diyar, **9 Beit Youssef** was undergoing substantial restoration work when we passed, while Beit Nukhida, just to the north and which once had displays on the pearling industry, was closed at the time of our visit; check to see if it has reopened.

Return to where you came from and, after passing the Sheikh Ebrahim bin Mohammed Al Khalifa Centre for Culture and Research, turn right, pass the peaceful **10 Japanese Water Garden** on your right, then follow the signs to the **11 House of Coffee**. A few doors to the west, **12 Al Korar House** (p75) keeps alive the tradition of gold-thread embroidery. A few doors west again, on the other side of the lane, **13 Abdullah Al Zayed House** is dedicated to the country's press heritage, with an old typewriter and a copy of Bahrain's first newspaper on display.

Walk down the gentle slope heading west, keeping the wavy, low wooden wall on your right, then turn left onto Road 931 where the laneway ends, then right onto busy Sheikh Abdullah bin Isa Ave. A few metres along is the **14 Vertical Garden** that acts as a landmark for entrance to the old quarter of the island. Created by European artist Patrick Blanc to evoke an oasis, and the first of its kind in the Middle East, it's home to 200 species of tropical plant from around the world in what Blanc describes as a 'living laboratory'. Continue west, then turn left at the roundabout. The sublime **15 Bin Matar House** is clearly visible on your left.

Just south of Bin Matar House, turn left along Road 1124, past the metal workshops, then turn right onto Road 1125, the starting point for Muharraq Souq. Immediately on your right is **16 Beit Bu Zaboon**, which is closed to the public but has a lovely Muharraqi facade. Continue south to Sheikh Hamad Ave, turn right and forsake all other sweet shops on your way to **17 Hussein Mohd Showaiter Sweets** (p78), the king among Muharraqi sweet merchants. Return east along Sheikh Hamad Ave and follow the signs to the under-restoration **18 Suq Al Qaisariya**.

Muharraq Dhow Building Yard HISTORIC SITE
(Map p75) It can be a bit hit or miss as to whether you see any action here, but it's worth pulling over to admire the half-built wooden dhows by the roadside as you drive between Manama and Qala'at Arad.

Shopping

Hussein Mohd Showaiter Sweets FOOD
(Map p75; 17 345 550; Sheikh Hamad Ave; 8am-10pm) Hussein Mohd Showaiter Sweets is the king among Muharraqi sweet merchants – just try to leave without buying something sickly sweet and sinfully delicious. Most of it's in boxes, but staff members may let you try before you buy if you ask nicely.

Getting There & Away

The attractions on the island are easy to reach by taxi from central Manama (around BD3) and most are within walking distance of each other.

Dar Island جزيرة الدار

Just off the coast south of Sitra, Dar Island offers a great retreat from the city. The main attraction is the sandy beach, but watersports are also available, and there is a restaurant and bar. Check out www.aldarislands.com for more information.

Possible activities include fishing, dolphin-watching and dugong-watching. One of the most popular trips is pearl collecting, which involves snorkelling to harvest oysters in shallow waters followed by a demonstration of how to find out if they are pearl-bearing.

Sea taxis to Dar Island leave daily between 9am and sunset from the scruffy harbour in Sitra, on the eastern side of Bahrain Island. The trip costs BD5 return for adults and BD3 for children. Don't forget to bring your passport as photo ID is necessary for boarding the boat.

SAFETY

The Sitra area, which you'll need to pass through en route to Dar Island, was a hot spot for unrest when we visited in November 2015. Ask locally before you go and take the advice of your taxi driver or guide.

UNDERSTAND BAHRAIN

Bahrain Today

Bahrain is a country holding its breath. Until the Arab Spring of 2011, Bahrain was a model of stability and relative freedom. With stability came a reputation as a reliable offshore banking centre and commercial hub, and status as a valued member of the UN, Arab League and Gulf Cooperation Council (GCC). On 14 February 2002, Bahrain was declared a constitutional monarchy in which both men and women are eligible to vote and stand for office in a fully elected parliament.

But beneath the calm surface, tensions simmered, partly based on the slow pace of political development but also largely due to sectarian differences – official figures can be difficult to come by, but approximately one-third of Bahrain's population is Shiite, while the ruling Al Khalifa family, including the monarch, Sheikh Hamad bin Isa Al Khalifa, is Sunni. In 2006 Al Wifaq, a Shia political party, won the largest number of seats in parliamentary and municipal elections, but when popular movements took hold across the Arab world in the spring of 2011 it became clear through the street demonstrations and major disturbances that the opposition wanted more, with many calling for nothing less than the overthrow of Bahrain's monarchy.

In scenes that echoed those of Cairo's Tahrir Sq, demonstrators occupied Pearl Roundabout in central Manama for days, effectively bringing the city to a standstill. While the opposition was predominantly Shiite, non-sectarian calls for greater democracy came from most sectors of Bahraini society. On 17 February 2011, a pre-dawn government raid on the encampment left four protesters dead and hundreds injured, while a month later, Bahrain called in troops from Saudi Arabia and the UAE to clear the protests and destroy the pearl statue that had become a symbol for the protests. Western governments and international human-rights organisations strongly criticised the use of force in dispelling protesters.

Tensions continued and, after Eid Al Adha in November 2012, the government banned public gatherings. There was a real fear that the prolonged period of civil unrest might spiral out of control. Although things have quietened down, attacks on police stations, arrests of opposition activists and government accusations of Iranian complicity in 'terrorism' on Bahraini soil ensure that the country remains tense. International tourist numbers have fallen and the Bahraini authorities remain suspicious of foreigners entering the country, in case they turn out to be journalists.

Worryingly, the ongoing uncertainty continues to threaten two of Bahrain's real success stories. The debate continues each year as to whether Bahrain's Formula 1 Grand Prix will go ahead – it was cancelled in 2011 after drivers expressed concerns about safety. Bahrain's role as an offshore banking centre and commercial hub is even more fragile, however, and some commentators suggest it won't take much to threaten international investment – greatly needed to complete the ambitious projects started in the pre-2008 building frenzy.

At the time of writing, the government held the upper hand, but the country's future stability remains far from assured.

History

Dilmun – The Ancient Garden of Eden

History in Bahrain is nowhere more intriguing than among the 85,000 burial mounds that now lump, curdle and honeycomb 5% of the island's landmass. Standing atop a burial mound at A'Ali, it's easy to imagine that the people responsible for such sophisticated care of their dead were equally sophisticated in matters of life. And, indeed, such was the case.

Archaeologists have recently confirmed Bahrain as the seat of the lost and illustrious empire of Dilmun (3200–330 BC), whose influence spread as far north as modern Kuwait and as far inland as Al Hasa Oasis in eastern Saudi Arabia. According to Sumerian, Babylonian and Assyrian inscriptions, the island's residents were not only commercially active but also attentive to matters at home. The proper burial of the sick, handicapped and young in elaborate chambers, together with their chattels of ceramics, glass and beads (carefully displayed at the Bahrain National Museum), suggest an enlightened civilisation of considerable social and economic development, assisted by the perpetual abundance of 'sweet', or potable, water on the island.

Little wonder, then, that Dilmun (which means 'noble') was often referred to as the fabled Garden of Eden and described as 'paradise' in the Epic of Gilgamesh (the world's oldest poetic saga). Dilmun's economic success was due in no small part to the trading of Omani copper, which was measured using the internationally recognised 'Dilmun Standard' (the weights can be seen in the Bahrain National Museum).

When the copper trade declined, in around 1800 BC, Dilmun's strength declined with it, leaving the island vulnerable to the predatory interests of the surrounding big powers. By 600 BC Dilmun was absorbed entirely by Babylon and was subsequently ceded to Greece. The Greeks called the island 'Tylos', a name it kept for nearly a thousand years (from 330 BC to AD 622), despite Greek rule enduring for less than 100 years. Little distinguishes the history of Bahrain from that of the rest of the Gulf thereafter until the 16th century.

Pearls & the Founding of Modern Bahrain

Take a stroll along the 'pearling path' in Muharraq and you'll quickly learn the significance of the pearl trade to Bahrain. Sweet water from springs under the sea, mingling with the brackish waters of the shallow oyster beds, contributes to the particular colour and lustre of Bahrain's pearls, and it was upon the value of these pearls that Bahrain grew into one of the most important trading posts in the region.

A 'fish eye' (the ancient name for a pearl) dating back to 2300 BC, found in the excavations at Sar, suggests that pearling was an activity dating back to the days of Dilmun – but it was an unglamorous industry. It entailed local 'divers' working with little more than a nose-peg and a knife in shark-infested waters, and being hauled up with their bounty by 'pullers' working long and sun-baked shifts from June to October. At the height of the pearling industry, some 2500 dhows were involved and loss of life was common.

Pearling was something of a mixed blessing in other ways as well, as it attracted the big naval powers of Europe, which wheeled about the island trying to establish safe passage for their interests further east. In the early 1500s the Portuguese invaded, building one of their typical sea-facing forts, Qal'at Al Bahrain, on Bahrain's northern shore. Their

BOOKS ABOUT BAHRAIN

➡ *Looking for Dilmun* by Geoffrey Bibby is a celebrated book on Bahrain in the 1950s and '60s and is arguably the best book ever written about the country.

➡ *Bahrain from the Twentieth Century to the Arab Spring* by Miriam Joyce takes a fairly dry look at Bahrain's past, but its 2012 publication date means it only touches on the 2011 demonstrations rather than their fallout.

➡ *A Winter in the Middle of Two Seas: Real Stories from Bahrain* by Ronald Kenyon is an enlightening account of the author's four months in the country.

rule was short-lived, however, and by 1602 they were ousted by the Persians.

Pearls played a hand in the country's modern incarnation, as it was this lucrative trade that first attracted the Al Khalifa, the family that now rules Bahrain, to the area from their original stronghold in Al Zubara, on the northwestern edge of the Qatar peninsula. The Al Khalifa were responsible for driving the Persians from Bahrain in about 1782. They were themselves routed by an Omani invasion, but they returned in 1820 and have not left since.

Relationship with the British

It only takes a walk through Adliya, with its emphasis on full English breakfasts and high teas, to discover that the British are part and parcel of the island's history. And it began like this...

During the 19th century, when piracy was rife in the Gulf, Bahrain gained a reputation as an entrepôt, where captured goods were traded for supplies for the next raid. The British, anxious to secure their trade routes with India, brought the island within the folds of the trucial system (the 'truce' or treaty system of protection against piracy and which included the emirates that now form the UAE). In hindsight, this could almost be dubbed 'invasion by stealth': by 1882 Bahrain could not make any international agreements or host any foreign agent without British consent. On the other hand, as a British protectorate, the autonomy of the Al Khalifa family was secure and threats from the Ottomans thwarted. To this day, a special relationship can be felt between the Bahrainis and the sizeable expatriate British community. Bahrain regained full independence in 1971.

Oil – Bahrain's Black Gold

In the middle of the desert, roughly in the middle of the island, stands a small museum sporting marble pillars and a classical architrave, wholly incongruous amid the surrounding landscape of nodding donkeys. But the museum has a right to certain pretensions of grandeur; it marks the spot where, in 1932, the Arab world struck gold – black gold, that is – and with that, the entire balance of power in the world was transformed forever.

The first well is in the museum grounds, perhaps no longer pumping oil, but with polished pipes and cocks, worthy of the momentousness of its role in modern history. The discovery of oil could not have come at a better time for Bahrain as it roughly coincided with the collapse of the world pearl market, upon which the island's economy had traditionally been based. Skyrocketing oil revenues allowed the country, under the stewardship of the Al Khalifa family, to steer a course of rapid modernisation that was a beacon for other countries in the region to follow well into the 1970s and '80s.

When the oil began to run out, the fortunes of the government started to turn, and in the last decade of the 20th century the country was shocked by sporadic waves of unrest. The troubles began in 1994 when riots erupted after the emir refused to accept a large petition calling for greater democracy, culminating in the hotel bombings of 1996 (at the Diplomat and what is now the Ritz-Carlton Bahrain). Despite many concessions, including the establishment of a constitutional monarch in 2002, the political tensions have yet to be fully resolved.

People & Society

Lifestyle

It's the prerogative of the inhabitants of busy seaports to select from the 'customs and manners' that wash up on the shore. Watching young Bahraini men on the nightclub floor in one of Manama's central hotels, for example, sporting a crisp white *thobe* (floor-length shirt-dress) or the international uniform of jeans and leather jacket, a visitor could be forgiven for thinking that the young have sold out to the West. These same young men, however, would probably have been to the barber, aged three to six years old, one auspicious Monday, Thursday or Friday in spring, and come out clutching their coins – and loins. These same young men will no doubt send their sons on similar rituals of circumcision and maturation, because beneath the urbane surface, the sweet waters of the island run deep.

As for Bahraini women, while Islam requires surrender to the will of God, it does not imply surrender to the will of man. Bahraini women play a role in many aspects of public life, and, as such, 'surrender' is the last word that comes to mind. Only an outsider considers it contradictory that women who choose to cover their hair in the presence of men should at the same time give them instructions on all matters of life, cardinal and profane.

Bahraini people have enjoyed the spoils of oil for over half a century and it's tempting to think that wealth has created a nation of idlers – you won't see many Bahrainis engaged in manual labour, for example, or waiting on tables. A modern, enterprising, wealthy nation isn't built on money alone, however, and the burgeoning financial sector is proof that the locals have chosen to invest their energies and creativity in their traditional trading strengths while importing labour for the jobs they no longer need to do themselves.

Despite the imperatives of international business, time with the family is cherished, and the sense of home is extended to the Bahraini community at large through many public-funded amenities and educational opportunities. After Ramadan, for example, Al Fatih Mosque opens its doors to free feasting for non-Muslims during Eid Al Adha: in some countries this would be interpreted as proselytising; here it is a symbol of the infectious sense of home shared with non-nationals.

Multiculturalism

Behind Bab Al Bahrain, at the heart of Manama, there is little besides shop signs in Arabic to indicate that this is indeed part of Arabia. There are Indian and Pakistani shop owners, Jewish money exchangers, Filipino hotel workers and occasional groups of US service personnel. The same could be said of Seef, where the manicured gardens and bars of the Ritz-Carlton Bahrain Hotel & Spa and the international chain stores of Seef Mall are peopled largely by Western expatriates.

In a country where an estimated 55% of residents are immigrants, it is surprising to find that a strong sense of local identity has survived the influx of migrant workers. This imbalance, however, while harmonious for the most part, has been a source of political agitation too. In 1997, for example, a series of arson attacks were carried out by unemployed local Bahrainis who were angry that jobs were being taken by workers from Asia. While the government has since actively pursued a policy favouring the indigenous workforce, tensions continue to prevail as educated Bahrainis find it difficult to compete in sectors with entrenched (and often experienced and skilled) expatriate workforces.

Arts

There's a vibrant contemporary-arts scene in Bahrain. Exhibitions of local paintings regularly take place at the Bahrain National Museum and at La Fontaine Centre of Contemporary Art. There are also a few private galleries, often showcasing the work of the owner. These include the Al Oraifi Museum on Muharraq Island.

The lanes surrounding Beit Seyadi on Muharraq Island are slowly developing into a centre for the preservation of traditional arts, crafts and social customs under the patronage of the Sheikh Ebrahim bin Mohammed Al Khalifa Centre for Culture and Research.

The best way to find out what's going on where is to consult the listings in English-language newspapers and magazines.

Environment

The Land

Most people think of Bahrain (741 sq km) as a single flat island with a couple of low escarpments in the middle of a stony desert and surrounded by a very shallow, calm sea. In fact, such is the description of Bahrain Island only, which, at 586 sq km, is the largest in an archipelago of about 33 islands, including the 16 Hawar Islands, and a few specks of sand that disappear at high tide.

LOCAL KNOWLEDGE

LOCAL CRAFTS

On the face of it, Bahrain is a modern country that looks forward more often than it looks back. This is changing, however, and Manama's recent post as Capital of Arab Culture has led to a revival of interest in Bahrain's artistic heritage. Several cultural centres, such as the Crafts Centre Gallery and Workshop in central Manama, and workshops such as Al Jasra Handicraft Centre have been set up to encourage the continuation of skills. Crafts are generally carried out in cottage industries or cooperatives, with people working from the privacy of their own inner courtyards. If you head out to the following places, especially in the company of a local guide, you may be lucky to see these crafts in progress.

Pottery and ceramics Village of A'Ali.

Traditional weaving Villages of Ad Diraz and Bani Jamrah.

Basket weaving with palm leaves Village of Karbabad.

Pearl jewellery Gold souq, Manama.

Al Kurar metal threadwork (for decorating ceremonial gowns) Al Korar House, Muharraq.

When crossing any of the causeways, including the King Fahd Causeway, which links Bahrain with the Saudi mainland, it is easy to see how the whole archipelago was once attached to the rest of the continent.

Wildlife

Bahrain's noteworthy wildlife includes the Ethiopian hedgehog, Cape hare, various geckos and the endangered Rheem gazelle, which inhabits the dry and hot central depression. The Hawar Islands, with their resident cormorant and flamingo populations, serve as a staging post for winter migrants. The Rheem gazelle, the terrapin, the sooty falcon and the seafaring dugong all appear on the endangered-species list, but some of them can be seen, along with a beautiful herd of oryx, at Al Areen Wildlife Park & Reserve.

A unique ecosystem in Bahrain is created by the seagrass *Halodule uninervis*. Important for the dugong and a large number of migrating birds, this tough plant is remarkably resilient against extreme temperatures and high salinity.

National Parks

Located in the middle of Bahrain Island, Al Areen Wildlife Park & Reserve is more a zoo than a national park and was set up to conserve natural habitats in order to support research projects in the field of wildlife protection and development. In common with most Gulf states, the 20th-century passion for hunting left the island virtually bereft of natural inheritance. At least at Al Areen visitors can see the last specimens of indigenous fauna, such as gazelles and bustards (large ground-living birds). The park also provides a free-roaming natural habitat for certain native Arabian species, including the endangered oryx.

In addition to Al Areen, there are two other protected areas in Bahrain: the mangroves at Ras Sanad (Tubli Bay) and the Hawar Islands. With a huge residential-development project under way in one and oil exploration around the other, though, it's hard to see what is meant by 'protection'.

Environmental Issues

Bahrain has made a big effort in recent years to clean up its act environmentally and beautification projects have brought a touch of greenery back to the concrete jungle, although most of the changes are cosmetic rather than meaningful – most of the damage has already been done. The main threats to the environment remain unrestrained development, perpetual land reclamation, rampant industrialisation, an inordinate number of cars (about 200 per square kilometre), and pollution of the Gulf from oil leakages and ocean acidification. In addition, little appears to have been done to curb emissions from heavy industry (such as the aluminium smelting plant) to the east of Bahrain Island.

During the stand-off between Bahrain and Qatar over ownership of the Hawar Islands, the wildlife, which includes dugongs and turtles and many species of migratory bird, was left in peace. Immediately after the territorial dispute was resolved, however, Bahrain invited international companies to drill for oil.

SURVIVAL GUIDE

 Directory A–Z

ACCOMMODATION

Bahrain's main sights are all within day-trip distance of the capital. As a result, most visitors stay in the large selection of hotels available in Manama and its suburbs.

At the budget end of things, travellers will find it difficult to find single/double rooms for less than BD15/25 per night, and many of the cheaper hotels (and some midrange hotels) double as brothels for visiting Saudi patrons. The cheaper the room, the more overt the night-time activity.

Midrange accommodation usually implies carpet, minibar, satellite TV and a view of something other than an internal stairwell.

Bahrain has some excellent top-end accommodation, including resorts. These often offer substantial discounts off the published rack rate.

CUSTOMS REGULATIONS

- Importation, purchase and consumption of alcohol is permissible.
- Non-Muslim visitors can import 1L of wine or spirits, or six cans of beer duty free.
- If you're returning to Saudi via the causeway, don't forget to empty the coolbox!

EMBASSIES & CONSULATES

The nearest embassies representing Australia, Canada and Ireland are in Riyadh, Saudi Arabia. Most of the embassies in Bahrain are in the Diplomatic Area in Manama, between King Faisal Hwy and Sheikh Hamad Causeway.

French Embassy (Map p60; ☎17 298 660; www.ambafrance.com.bh; Al Fatih Hwy; ⏲8.30am-noon Sun-Thu)

German Embassy (Map p60; ☎17 530 210; www.manama.diplo.de; Al Hassaa Bldg, Sheikh Hamad Causeway; ⏲8.30-11.30am Sun-Thu)

Kuwaiti Embassy (Map p60; ☎17 534 040; King Faisal Hwy; ⏲8.30am-noon Sun-Thu)

Omani Embassy (Map p60; ☎17 293 663; Al Fatih Hwy; ⏲8.30am-noon Sun-Thu)

Saudi Arabian Embassy (Map p60; ☎17 537 722; King Faisal Hwy; ⏲9-11am Sun-Thu)

UAE Embassy (Map p60; ☎17 748 333, 17 723 737; uaeembassybahrain@hotmail.com; Road 4007, Juffair; ⏲9am-noon Sun-Thu) Off Awal Ave.

UK Embassy (Map p60; ☎17 574 100; www.gov.uk/government/world/bahrain; 21 Government Ave; ⏲9am-noon Sun-Thu)

US Embassy (Map p54; ☎17 242 700; bahrain.usembassy.gov; Bldg 979, Road 3119, Block 331, Al Zinj; ⏲9am-noon Sun-Thu) Off Sheikh Khalifa bin Sulman Hwy.

INTERNET ACCESS

The main internet service provider is **Batelco** (Map p64; ☎17 881 111; www.batelco.com.bh; Government Ave). There are many wi-fi hot spots around town, especially in Starbucks and McDonald's and in most hotels.

LEGAL MATTERS

Breaking the law can have severe consequences. For more information, consult your embassy.

MAPS

The *Bahrain Map & Pocket Guide* (BD1), published in cooperation with Tourism Affairs, Ministry of Information, is available from the airport, Bahrain National Museum and bookshops. It has useful up-to-date information on the reverse, together with a good map of Manama.

MONEY

Bahrain's currency is the Bahraini dinar (BD). One dinar is divided into 1000 fils. There are 500-fil and one-, five-, 10- and 20-dinar notes. Coins come in denominations of five, 10, 25, 50, 100 and 500 fils. The Bahraini dinar is a convertible currency and there are no restrictions on its import or export.

ATMs & Credit Cards

Major credit cards are widely accepted throughout Bahrain. Most banks have ATMs that accept Visa, Cirrus and MasterCard cards, while the Bank of Bahrain and Kuwait (BBK) has ATMs that take Visa, MasterCard, Cirrus, Maestro and Amex cards.

Moneychangers

Money (both cash and travellers cheques) can be changed at any bank or moneychanging office. There is little to choose between banks and

SLEEPING PRICE RANGES

The following price ranges refer to a double room with bathroom and air-con in high season (November to March). Taxes are included in the price.

$ less than BD40 (US$106)

$$ BD40–BD80 (US$106–US$212)

$$$ more than BD80 (US$212)

moneychangers in terms of exchange rates and it's rare for either to charge a commission. Currencies for other Gulf states are easy to buy and sell.

Tipping

A service charge is added to most bills in restaurants and hotels in Bahrain, so tipping is at your discretion. An appropriate tip for good service would be around 10%. Airport porters expect 200 fils per bag despite their services being covered by the airport tax. Taxi drivers do not expect a tip for short journeys. For longer journeys (over 5km), 10% would be appropriate.

Bargaining

Bargaining in the souqs and in most shops, together with asking for a discount, is expected.

OPENING HOURS

The weekend in Bahrain is Friday and Saturday for most commercial and government organisations.

Banks 7.30am to 3pm Sunday to Thursday.

Government offices 7am to 2pm Sunday to Thursday.

Internet cafes 8am to 1pm and 4pm to 10pm.

Post offices 7am to 2pm (and 4pm to 6pm at alternating offices).

Restaurants 11am to 3pm and 6pm to 1am.

Shopping centres 9am to 10pm Saturday to Thursday, 10am to 10pm Friday.

Shops 8am to noon and 3.30pm to 7.30pm Saturday to Thursday.

PUBLIC HOLIDAYS

In addition to the main Islamic holidays, Bahrain celebrates a number of public holidays.

New Year's Day 1 January

Ashura The tenth day of Muharram (month in the Hejira calendar; date changeable), Ashura marks the death of Hussein, grandson of the Prophet. Processions led by men flagellating themselves take place in many of the country's predominantly Shiite areas.

National Day 16 December

TELEPHONE

Bahrain's telephone code is ☎973 and there are no area or city codes. The international access code (to call abroad from Bahrain) is ☎00.

EATING PRICE RANGES

The following price ranges refer to a standard main course. Service charges and tax are included in the price.

$ less than BD3 (US$8)

$$ BD3–BD9 (US$8–US$24)

$$$ more than BD9 (US$24)

There are several help lines, including local directory assistance (☎181) and international directory assistance (☎191).

Blue payphones take coins. Red payphones take phonecards, which are widely available from most grocery stores in denominations of BD1, BD3, BD5 and BD10.

Mobile Phones

Bahrain's mobile-phone network runs on the GSM system through Batelco and Zain. Visitors can also purchase SIM cards for BD1, BD5 and BD10 at all Batelco and Zain outlets. Recharge cards come in many denominations up to BD20.

VISAS

Visas are needed to visit Bahrain and, for people of 66 nationalities, these can be conveniently obtained on arrival at Bahrain International Airport or at the border with Saudi Arabia. A three-month, multiple-entry visa, valid for stays of two weeks to 30 days, costs BD25 and is payable in cash (either Bahraini dinars or major international currencies).

You can also apply for an e-visa online – follow the links on www.evisa.gov.bh – with the main advantage being that you'll spend less time passing through immigration on arrival.

You can check your eligibility for a visa on arrival online (www.evisa.gov.bh), as there are some restrictions currently in place (for example, for certain professions). Given the poor international press about Bahrain in recent times, and the fact that tourism outside of the Formula 1 Grand Prix has slowed to a trickle, expect to be questioned about your intentions if you're visiting as a tourist.

WOMEN TRAVELLERS

Bahrain is fairly liberal compared to some of the other Gulf countries, which can be both a blessing (less of the staring) and a nuisance (more of the hassle). Muharraq, much of the Manama Souq and Shiite-dominated areas such as Budaiya are much more traditional and female visitors should dress more conservatively in these areas as a consequence.

ℹ Getting There & Away

AIR

Bahrain International Airport (p69) is on Muharraq Island, 12km from the centre of Manama, and handles frequent services to many intercontinental destinations as well as other countries in the region.

The national carrier is **Gulf Air** (Map p64; ☎call centre 17 373 737, flight information 17 339 339, sales 17 222 820; www.gulfair.com; Manama Centre, Bldg 58, Government Rd), which flies to destinations worldwide. It has a good safety record and reliable departure times.

LAND

Border Crossings

The only 'land' border is with Saudi Arabia, across the King Fahd Causeway.

Tourists are not permitted to drive between Saudi Arabia and Bahrain in a hired car. Residents of Saudi Arabia who have their own cars may use this crossing provided they have car insurance for both countries. For those coming from Saudi Arabia this can be purchased at the border. A transit visa must be obtained from the Saudi authorities for those travelling by car between the UAE and Bahrain. This is not easy to obtain.

Bus

You must have a valid transit visa for Saudi Arabia in advance and an onward ticket and visa for your next destination beyond Saudi Arabia's borders.

Saudi Bahraini Transport Co (Sabtco; ☎17 252 959; www.sabtco.biz) The Saudi Bahraini Transport Co runs an upmarket car and bus service between Manama and Dammam in Saudi Arabia. It also acts as the agent for the Saudi bus company Saudi Arabian Public Transport Co (Saptco; ☎17 263 244; www.saptco.com.sa), with regular services to Dammam. From Dammam there are regular connections to Riyadh (Saudi Arabia) and Doha (Qatar) for those who have a Saudi transit visa.

From Manama, Saptco also has daily buses as far as Abu Dhabi, Dubai and Sharjah (UAE) and Kuwait City. All departures are from the International Bus Terminal (Map p60) in Manama.

Car & Motorcycle

All drivers (and passengers in taxis) using the causeway to Saudi Arabia must pay a toll of BD2 at the booth on the western side of the intersection between Causeway Approach Rd and Janabiya Hwy.

Anyone crossing the border from Bahrain to Saudi Arabia will be given a customs form to complete, and drivers entering Bahrain from Saudi Arabia must purchase temporary Bahraini insurance and also sign a personal guarantee.

Getting Around

BUS

Bahrain has a public bus system linking most of the major towns and residential areas, but it's designed primarily for the expatriate workforce and is of limited use to tourists. Visit **Manama bus station** (p69) for the latest information.

CAR & MOTORCYCLE

Driving around Bahrain is straightforward and roads are well signposted with regard to the main sites of tourist interest.

Speed limits, the wearing of seat belts and drink-driving laws are rigorously enforced. Speed limits are 60km/h in towns, 80km/h in the outer limits of suburbs and 100km/h on highways. Petrol stations are well signposted, especially along highways.

Hire

Car-hire companies have offices in Manama and at the airport, charging from BD20/70 per day/week for the smallest four-door sedan.

Rates exclude petrol but include unlimited mileage and insurance. To avoid the excess of BD100 to BD200 in case of an accident, it's wise to pay the extra BD2 Collision Damage Waiver (CDW) per day. Companies normally only accept drivers over 21 years old (over 25 for more expensive car models), and foreigners must (in theory at least) have an International Driving Permit, although a driving licence is often sufficient. There is nowhere to rent a motorcycle.

LOCAL TRANSPORT

Most visitors get around Bahrain by taxi, although persistence is needed to persuade drivers to use their meters. If you're visiting more than one tourist attraction outside Manama and Muharraq, it's cheaper to hire a car.

PRACTICALITIES

Magazines *Bahrain This Month* and *Time Out Bahrain* have comprehensive local listings. Both are available from Virgin Megastore and Jashanmal in Bahrain City Centre mall.

Newspapers The *Gulf Daily News* and the less-interesting *Bahrain Tribune* broadsheet are the main English-language dailies. International newspapers are available in some hotels and bookshops the day after publication.

Radio Radio Bahrain broadcasts in English 24 hours a day on 96.5FM and 101FM.

TV Bahrain TV broadcasts channel 55 in English (from late afternoon), and the BBC World Service is shown in English on channel 57. Most satellite programs, such as CNN and MTV, are available at many hotels.

Weights and measures Bahrain uses the metric system.

Kuwait الكويت

Includes ➔

Best for Culture

- Souq (p92)
- Dar Al Athar Al Islamiyya (p93)
- Tareq Rajab Museum (p93)
- Kuwait Towers (p91)
- Kuwait House of National Works: Memorial Museum (p96)

Best Places to Eat

- Burj Al Hamam (p104)
- Al Boom (p105)
- Beit Ahmed (p103)
- Le Nôtre (p104)
- Mais Alghanim (p105)

Why Go?

Kuwait, in the cradle of one of the most ancient and contested corners of the world, has a certain cachet. For a start, it may be just as oil rich as other Gulf countries, but it hasn't gone for the glitz and glamour in quite the same way – perhaps it's the years lost to the Iraqi invasion and its aftermath, or maybe it's a conscious decision not to sell its soul to the gods of commercialism. And Kuwait lies just far enough away from those self-same Gulf travel hubs to the south to mean that tourists and expats are fewer here. The result? A more authentically Arab feel to the country. At the same time, Kuwait remains an oasis in a land of desert plains, and has excellent museums, a fine souq and a corniche of combed beaches and lively restaurants. It all adds up to what could be the Gulf's most intriguing destination.

When to Go

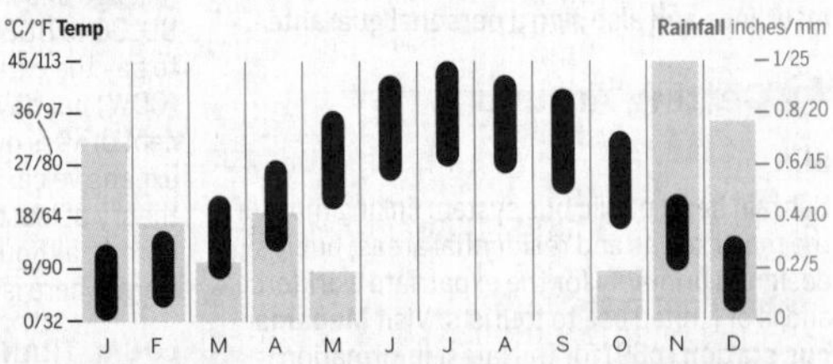

Nov–Jan Experience the relief of cool evenings after the burning heat of summer.

Feb Pick up a bargain in Kuwait's Hala shopping festival.

Mar & Apr During spring, the desert is laced in a gossamer of lime green.

Daily Costs

Kuwait is an expensive country to visit. With budget accommodation from US$100, cheap options for eating (around US$20) and museum admission charges, a minimum daily cost with transport comes in at around US$200. This rises to US$350 if you stay in midrange hotels, or US$450 for a top-end hotel with car hire.

ITINERARIES

One Day

Potter along the **corniche** (Arabian Gulf St), pausing at **Layali Al Helmeya** for a *sheesha* and **Kuwait Towers** for that quintessential Kuwait photo. Get a feel for the country's Bedouin history at **Al Sadu House**, take lunch in a heritage house at **Beit 7**, then enjoy the rich Al Sabah collection at **Dar Al Athar Al Islamiyya**. Sample local desserts in the city's most traditional souq, **Souq Marbarakia**, and return to the water (or dry dock, to be exact) for dinner on the dhow at **Al Boom**.

Two Days

After day one exploring the corniche, head inland on day two to **Tareq Rajab Museum** – a hidden gem of a collection displaying ethnographic treasures from across the Islamic world. Spend the afternoon shopping in fashionable **Salmiya** district, followed by talking to the animals at the excellent **Scientific Center**. End the day enjoying the bustle of promenading locals at nearby **Marina Crescent**, followed by dinner at **Mais Alghanim**.

Three Days

Spare a thought for the events of the past two decades by visiting the diminished **National Museum**, sense the still-smarting wounds of war in the **Kuwait House of National Works: Memorial Museum** and drive out to Al Jahra's **Mutla Ridge**. Brighten up a sobering day at the **Hilton Kuwait Resort**, on a silky stretch of coastline with sequined waters, or get away from it all on **Failaka Island**.

Essential Food & Drink

- **Baked fish** Blended with coriander, turmeric, red pepper and cardamom.
- **Hamour or pomfret** White fish stuffed with parsley, onions and dill.
- **Gulf prawns** Available late autumn and early winter.
- **Alcohol** Not available or permissible.
- **Mixed-fruit cocktails** Served in rainbow combinations.
- **Tap water** Safe to drink, although most people stick to bottled water.

AT A GLANCE

- **Currency** Kuwaiti dinar (KD).
- **Mobile phones** SIM cards widely available.
- **Money** ATMs widespread; credit cards widely accepted.
- **Visas** Available on arrival for many nationalities.

Fast Facts

- **Capital** Kuwait City
- **Country code** ☎965
- **Language** Arabic; English
- **Population** 2.79 million

Exchange Rates

Australia	A$10	KD2.19
Bahrain	BD1	KD0.81
Euro zone	€10	KD3.34
Oman	OR1	KD0.79
Qatar	QR10	KD0.83
Saudi Arabia	SR10	KD0.81
UAE	Dh1	KD0.82
UK	UK£10	KD4.64
USA	US$10	KD3.03

For current exchange rates, see www.xe.com.

Resources

- **Bazaar** (www.bazaar.town) The best of the expat and visitor resources.
- **Visit Kuwait** (www.visit-kuwait.com) Excellent site for attractions to practicalities.
- **Arab Times** (www.arabtimesonline.com) Online version of local newspaper.

Kuwait Highlights

❶ Catching a sense of Kuwait's living history at the crossroads of trade routes at **Souq Marbarakia** (p92).

❷ Marvelling at an older version of the Gulf skyscraper that trumps them all, **Kuwait Towers** (p91).

❸ Admiring ancient artefacts from the region's rich past at **Dar Al Athar Al Islamiyya** (p93).

❹ Taking a peek beneath the Gulf's waters at the **Scientific Center** (p93) in Salmiya.

❺ Exploring the fine ethnographic collection that escaped the Iraqi invasion at **Tareq Rajab Museum** (p93).

❻ Dining in a dhow at **Al Boom restaurant** (p105), in the shadow of the largest wooden boat on Earth.

❼ Revisiting the Gulf War and its heroes in the **Kuwait House of National Works: Memorial Museum** (p96).

❽ Enjoying some R&R on the beach at the **Hilton Kuwait Resort** (p103) in Mangaf.

❾ Walking amid the ruins of the ancients on the island of **Failaka** (p107).

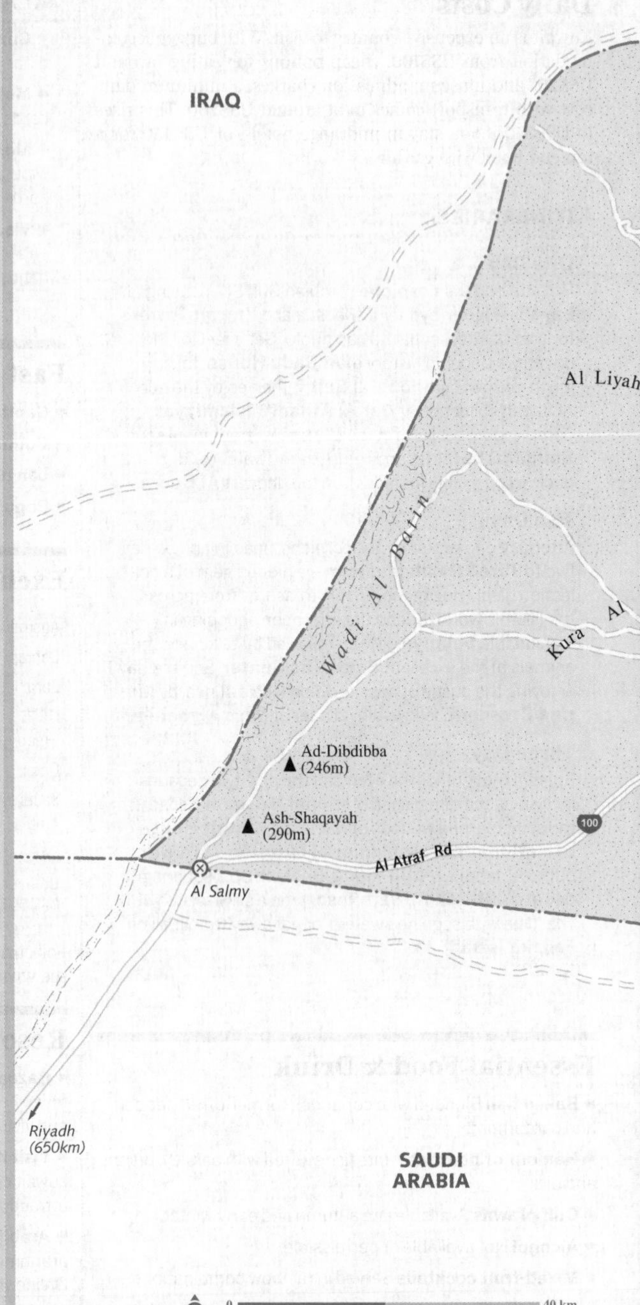

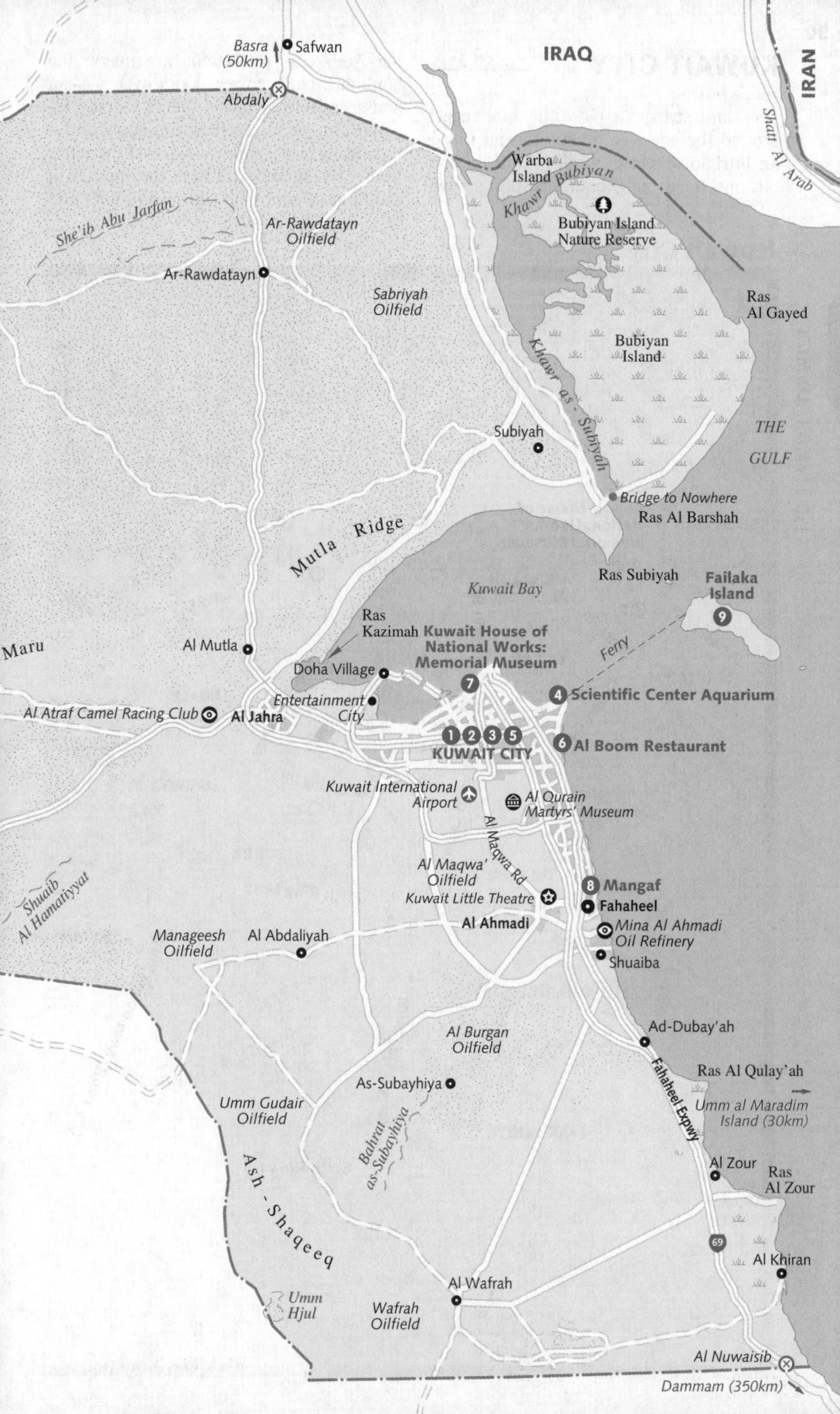

IRAQ
IRAN
Basra (50km)
Safwan
Abdaly
Shatt Al Arab
Warba Island
Khawr Bubiyan
Bubiyan Island Nature Reserve
She'ib Abu Jarfan
Ar-Rawdatayn Oilfield
Ar-Rawdatayn
Sabriyah Oilfield
Ras Al Gayed
Bubiyan Island
Khawr as-Subiyah
THE GULF
Subiyah
Bridge to Nowhere
Ras Al Barshah
Mutla Ridge
Ras Subiyah
Failaka Island
Kuwait Bay
Ras Kazimah
Kuwait House of National Works: Memorial Museum
Ferry
Maru
Al Mutla
Doha Village
Scientific Center Aquarium
Entertainment City
Al Atraf Camel Racing Club
Al Jahra
KUWAIT CITY
Al Boom Restaurant
Kuwait International Airport
Al Qurain Martyrs' Museum
Al Maqwa Rd
Al Maqwa' Oilfield
Mangaf
Kuwait Little Theatre
Fahaheel
Shuaib Al Hamatiyyat
Al Ahmadi
Mina Al Ahmadi Oil Refinery
Manageesh Oilfield
Al Abdaliyah
Shuaiba
Ad-Dubay'ah
Al Burgan Oilfield
Ras Al Qulay'ah
As-Subayhiya
Fahaheel Expwy
Umm al Maradim Island (30km)
Umm Gudair Oilfield
Bahrat as-Subayhiya
Al Zour
Ras Al Zour
Ash-Shaqeeq
69
Al Khiran
Al Wafrah
Umm Hjul
Wafrah Oilfield
Al Nuwaisib
Dammam (350km)

KUWAIT CITY مدينة الكويت

POP 1.6 MILLION

Slick and stylish in places, a little ragged around the edges in others, Kuwait City is an intriguing mix of wealthy Gulf metropolis and tough neighbourhood of a sprawling Arab city. Attractions are many: the landmark triple towers loom over a clean and accessible corniche; there's a first-class aquarium, some excellent museums and a terrifically atmospheric souq; and the selection of restaurants will whet the appetite of the fussiest gourmet. Add to its sights and

Kuwait City

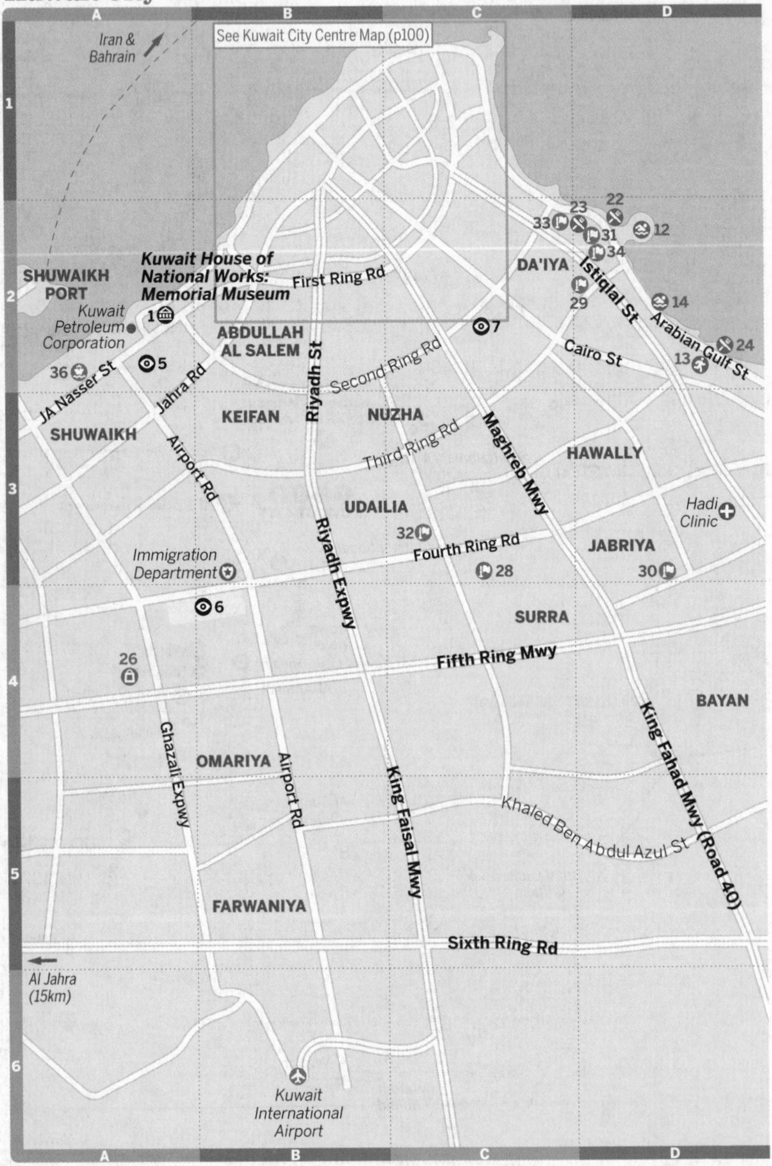

attractions a harrowing layer of modern history, the effects of which rumble invisibly below the surface, and there's enough to keep all but the dedicated nightclubber intrigued for days.

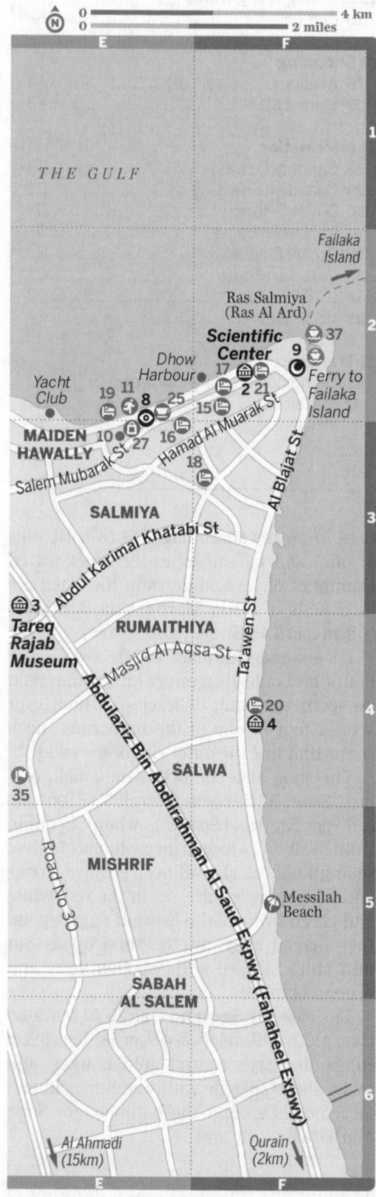

History

As improbable as it seems today, Kuwait City was until recently a nomadic port town and Salmiya consisted of a few mud huts around a tree – and that's within living memory. Suddenly, within the past two decades, a booming Middle Eastern centre has burst from its skin and the gates are all that remain of the redundant city walls. Three successive government master plans have tried to give direction to this capital growth, allowing for generous mortgages and free housing for the needy, but the growth is organic and unstoppable.

One of the few things that haven't changed is the city's name. The capital evolved from a collection of Bedouin tents around a well into a small military outpost with a *kout* (small fort adjacent to water). This *kout* was built in 1672 by the Bani Khalid tribe, who came from the Arabian interior to escape drought. The word *kout* evolved to give the city (and indeed the country) its name.

Something else that hasn't changed is the city's relationship with the sea. Its natural harbour made it an ideal location for a port. Indeed, it proved such an excellent port that it soon came to handle a lucrative trade in frankincense from Oman, pearls from Bahrain, spices from India, textiles from China and dates from just about everywhere. The port also facilitated the trans-shipment of goods across the desert to the Syrian port of Aleppo, a journey of two to three weeks. Pilgrims returned in the other direction, great caravans taking sustenance for the onward journey to Mecca. Today the port continues to play a vital role in the capital's fortunes.

The Iraqi invasion in 1990 tore a piece of the city's heart out, but remarkably most of the landmark buildings remain standing. A visitor today is unlikely to perceive just how much the city suffered.

Sights

Many of Kuwait's sights are concentrated along the corniche (Arabian Gulf St) and around the National Museum area. While some of the downtown sights are within walking distance of each other, the most convenient way of visiting outlying attractions, or of covering longer stretches of the corniche, is by taxi.

★Kuwait Towers LANDMARK
(Map p100; www.kuwaittowers.com; Arabian Gulf St, Dasman; 9am-11.30pm; P) The Kuwait

Kuwait City

Top Sights
1 Kuwait House of National Works: Memorial Museum ... A2
2 Scientific Center ... F2
3 Tareq Rajab Museum ... E3

Sights
4 Al Hashemi Marine Museum ... F4
5 Arab Fund Building ... A2
6 Friday Market ... B4
7 House of Mirrors ... C2
8 Lothan Youth Achievement Center ... E2
9 Shaikh Nasser Al Sabah Mosque ... F2

Activities, Courses & Tours
10 Beit Lothan ... E3
11 Color Me Mine ... E2
12 Green Island ... D2
13 Shaab Leisure Park ... D2
14 TEC Swimming Pool Complex ... D2

Sleeping
15 Dalal City Hotel ... F2
16 Ibis Kuwait Salmiya Hotel ... E3
17 Kuwait Palace Hotel ... F2
18 Le Royal Express Salmiya ... F3
19 Marina Hotel ... E2
20 Radisson Blu ... F4
21 Symphony Style Hotel ... F2

Eating
Al Boom ... (see 20)
22 Burj Al Hamam ... D2
23 Dukkan Burger ... D2
24 Layali Al Helmeya ... D2

Drinking & Nightlife
25 Beit Lothan ... E2

Shopping
26 Avenues ... A4
27 Marina Mall ... E3

Information
28 Bahraini Embassy ... C3
29 Canadian Embassy ... D2
30 Dutch Embassy ... D3
31 Iranian Embassy ... D2
32 Omani Embassy ... C3
33 Qatari Embassy ... C2
34 UAE Embassy ... D2
35 US Embassy ... E4

Transport
36 Combined Shipping Company ... A2
37 Kuwait Public Transport Company Ferries ... F2

Towers, with their distinctive blue-green 'sequins', are the instantly recognisable symbols of a nation. Designed by a Swedish architectural firm, they opened in 1979. The largest of the three rises to a height of 187m and houses a two-level revolving observation deck, gift shop and cafe. The towers were closed for major refurbishment at the time of research, but in any event they're much more beautiful from outside and they're visible from all along the corniche.

The lower globe on the largest tower stores around four million litres of water. The middle tower is also used for water storage, while the smallest tower is used to light up the other two.

★Souq MARKET

(Map p100; btwn Mubarak Al Kabir, Ahmad Al Jaber & Ali Al Salem Sts; ⌚9am-1pm & 4-9pm Sat-Thu, 4-9pm Fri) True to its origins, Kuwait City has retained the old souq in all of its complex, bustling and convoluted glory in the city centre. Albeit partly housed now in a series of smart, modern buildings that replicate the souqs of old with varying degrees of success, it nonetheless exudes antique practices, from the sharp haggling over ribands of offal and tails of ox to the quick-witted trading of olives and dates in the extensive food halls of **Souq Marbarakia** (Map p100; ⌚9am-1pm & 4-9pm Sat-Thu, 4-9pm Fri).

It's a wonderful place to idle away a few hours, and indeed an entire lunchtime could be spent sampling delicacies without ever setting foot in one of the numerous snack shops that line the outer rim of the souq.

The souq also comprises the small, covered **Souq Al Hareem** (Map p100; ⌚9am-1pm & 4-9pm Sat-Thu, 4-9pm Fri), where Bedouin women sit cross-legged on cushions of velvet selling kohl (black eyeliner), pumice stones and gold-spangled dresses in the red, white and green livery of the Kuwaiti flag. Beyond the covered alleyway, the souq opens out into lanes stocked with woollen vests and Korean blankets.

The close-by **Souq ad Dahab Al Markazi** (Map p100; ⌚9am-1pm & 4-9pm Sat-Thu, 4-9pm Fri) is the city's central gold market, and many shops spangle with wedding gold and local pearls around the perimeter of Souq Marbarakia.

★Tareq Rajab Museum MUSEUM

(Map p90; ☎2531 7358; www.trmkt.com; House 22, Block 12, Street 5, Jabriya; adult/child KD2/free; ⌚9am-noon & 4-7pm Sat-Thu, 9am-noon Fri) Housed in the basement of a large villa, this exquisite ethnographic museum should not be missed. There are inlaid musical instruments suspended in glass cabinets; Omani silver and Saudi gold jewellery; headdresses, from the humble prayer cap to the Mongol helmet; costumes worn by princesses and by goatherds; necklaces for living goddesses in Nepal; Jaipur enamel; and Bahraini pearls. Despite all these superbly presented pieces, it's the Arabic manuscripts in the Calligraphy Museum that give the collection its international importance.

The museum was assembled as a private collection of Islamic art by Kuwait's first minister of antiquities and his British wife. A pair of ornate doors from Cairo and Carl Haag's 19th-century painting of Lady Jane Digby el Mesreb of Palmyra, who lived in tents in the winter and a Damascus villa in the summer, mark the entrance to an Aladdin's cave of beautiful items.

The museum is in Jabriya, near the intersection of the Fifth Ring Motorway and the Abdulaziz Bin Abdilrahman Al Saud Expressway (also known as the Fahaheel Expressway). There is no sign on the building, but it is easily identified by its entrance – a carved wooden doorway flanked by two smaller doors on each side. All four of the door panels are worked in gilt metal.

Allow an hour to visit, although anyone with a passion for textiles will inevitably want to stay longer. Buses 102 and 502 stop at Hadi Clinic. Walk south along the Fahaheel Expressway for five minutes and turn right just after the Iranian School. Walk for a further 50m and the museum is on the left.

★Dar Al Athar Al Islamiyya CULTURAL CENTRE

(Amricani Cultural Centre; Map p100; ☎2240 0992; www.darmuseum.org.kw; Arabian Gulf St, Qibla; ⌚10am-7pm Mon-Thu & Sat, 2-7pm Fri) FREE This exceptional cultural centre has stunning galleries that containing some of the highlights of the world-class Al Sabah Collection, part of which was in the National Museum prior to the Iraqi invasion. With informative labels in English and Arabic, videos with experts explaining the pieces, and some exquisite sculptures and archaeological finds of great antiquity from across the region, it's everything the National Museum could be, albeit on a smaller scale. There's also an auditorium and an excellent gift shop.

★Scientific Center MUSEUM

(Map p90; ☎184 8888; www.tsck.org.kw; Arabian Gulf St, Salmiya; adult/child KD4/3; ⌚9am-9.30pm Sat-Wed, 9am-10pm Thu, 2-10pm Fri; P) Housed in a fine, sail-shaped building on the corniche, the Scientific Center boasts an aquarium that is one of the largest in the Middle East. The unique intertidal display features shoals of black-spotted sweetlips and the ingenious mudskipper. But the most spectacular part of the display (with giant spider crabs at 3.8m leg to leg, a living reef and fluorescent jellyfish coming in as a close second) are undoubtedly the floor-to-ceiling shark and ray tanks.

Ring ahead or check the website to check feeding times. There's also a section devoted to terrestrial desert animals.

The complex includes an IMAX cinema and an interactive learning centre called Discovery Place where children can make their own sand dunes or roll a piece of road. The dhow harbour is home to *Fateh Al Khair*, the last surviving dhow of the pre-oil era. Admission prices for these additional on-site attractions vary, with a variety of combination tickets available..

Salmiya bus stop, for buses 15, 17, 24, 34 and 200, is a short 10-minute (shaded) walk away.

Al Corniche CORNICHE

(Arabian Gulf St; P) Comprising over 10km of winding paths, parks and beaches on Arabian Gulf St (sometimes referred to locally as Gulf Rd), the corniche is marked at its southern end by the Scientific Center and

SAVING ANTIQUITIES

Many stories arose from the brutal Iraqi invasion and occupation of Kuwait in 1990, many of them too painful or tragic to tell. But there is one good-news story that is remarkable in its simplicity. While the National Museum was being looted by Iraqi soldiers, the custodians of the Tareq Rajab Museum bricked up the doorway at the bottom of the entry steps and littered the steps with rubbish. The Iraqis questioned why the stairs led to nowhere but mercifully didn't pursue the issue and the collection survived intact.

AL SABAH COLLECTION

Many tragic losses were brought about by Iraq's invasion of Kuwait, but the looting and partial loss of the Al Sabah Collection must rank alongside the great cultural crimes of the late 20th century.

The collection began in the mid-1970s when Sheikh Nasser Sabah Al Ahmad Al Sabah, a prominent member of Kuwait's ruling family, bought a 14th-century enamelled glass bottle from a London art gallery. What began as a hobby for the Al Sabahs became a passion for collecting and finally transformed into a world-class collection of Islamic art. By 1983, the Al Sabah Collection became the centrepiece of the **National Museum** (p95). In the space of a few short decades, the collection grew to include over 20,000 pieces, among them jewellery, textiles, calligraphy, manuscripts, miniatures, coins, ivory, carpets and wood-, metal- and stonework.

This priceless accumulation of art and archaeological treasures from across the Islamic world was famed throughout the region, and the museum was one of the first places targeted by invading Iraqi troops in 1990. The exhibition halls were systematically looted, damaged or set alight. Following intense pressure from the UN, the majority of the museum's collection was eventually returned, but many pieces had been broken in transit, poorly stored and, some suggest, deliberately spoiled. Others were lost forever.

Until a suitable home at the National Museum complex can be found for the collection, pieces from it have graced London's British Museum and the Metropolitan Museum of Art in New York. Only a fraction of the collection is back on display inside Kuwait and it will be some time before the National Museum complex is in a position to house what remains of it under one roof. In the meantime, **Dar Al Athar Al Islamiyya** (p93) showcases a wonderful, professionally displayed snapshot of the collection.

at its northernmost point by Kuwait Towers. Stop off at any of the many beaches, restaurants or coffeehouses to watch a desert sunset or, on hot summer evenings, enjoy being part of the throng of people flocking to the sea to catch the breeze.

Beit Dickson HISTORIC BUILDING

(Map p100; ☎2243 7450; Arabian Gulf St; ⏲8am-11.30am & 4.30-7.30pm Mon-Thu & Sat, 8.30-11am & 4.30-7.30pm Fri) FREE A modest white building with blue trim, Beit Dickson was the home of former British political agent Colonel Harold Dickson and his wife, Violet, whose love of and contribution to Kuwait are documented in the various archives inside the house. Highlights include a collection of photographs taken during Kuwait's British protectorate era; a replica museum of the Dicksons' living quarters; and an archive of Kuwaiti–British relations that dates from the 19th century to the 1960s, when Kuwait was granted independence.

Freya Stark spent most of March 1937 in the house and, while she adored Kuwait, she described the house as a 'big ugly box'.

Maritime Museum MUSEUM

(Map p100; Arabian Gulf St, Qibla; ⏲8.30am-12.30pm & 4.30-8.30pm Sat-Thu, 4.30-8.30pm Fri; P) FREE Giving an excellent insight into the seafaring heritage of Kuwait, the entrance of this museum is graced by three magnificent dhows. Dhows and boons like these brought water from the Shatt Al Arab waterway near Basra to the bone-dry city, making a tidy profit from thirsty inhabitants. Photographs inside the museum show the transport of water from boon to home before desalination plants brought water to the taps of all householders.

The pearling displays upstairs comprise a fascinating collection of daily-use objects, such as a heavy lead weight, a turtle-shell nose peg, leather finger ends and a wool suit to guard against jellyfish. These objects speak volumes about the deprivations of a life spent prising pearls from a reluctant seabed. The sieves of tiny mesh used to sift pearls according to size show that the effort was barely worth the dangers involved.

The museum is marooned in the middle of the *bondu* (waste ground) off Arabian Gulf St.

Modern Art Museum GALLERY

(Map p100; ☎2246 8348; www.artkuwait.org; Arabian Gulf St, Sharq; ⏲9am-1pm & 5-8pm Sun-Thu; P) This attractive, traditional-style building hosts a number of exhibitions of contemporary art throughout the year. Check the Art Kuwait website for a calendar of events.

Sief Palace PALACE

(Map p100; Arabian Gulf St) This is the official seat of the emir's court. The L-shaped Sief Palace that faces the roundabout is the original structure, dating from the early 20th century, while the new and ponderously opulent palace, complete with lake, helipad and dock for visitors' yachts, was completed around the beginning of 2000. Neither palace is open to the public. Photography is prohibited.

Grand Mosque MOSQUE

(Masjed Al Kabir; Map p100; ☎2241 8447; www.thegrandmosque.net; Mubarak Al Kabir St; ⏲24hr) The Grand Mosque was opened in 1986 and cost KD14 million to construct. The largest of the city's 800 mosques, it boasts Kuwait's highest minaret (74m) and can accommodate up to 5000 worshippers in the main hall, with room for another 7000 in the courtyard. Tours, best organised through a local tour operator, are provided by the knowledgeable mosque staff.

National Museum Complex MUSEUM

(Map p100; ☎2245 1195; kuwaitnationalmuseum.weebly.com; Arabian Gulf St, Qibla; ⏲8.30am-12.30pm & 4.30-8.30pm Mon-Thu & Sat, 4.30-8.30pm Fri; P) FREE Once the pride of Kuwait, and one of the most important collections of Islamic art in the world until the Iraqi invasion, the National Museum remains a shadow of its former self and the interminable reconstruction works were still nowhere near completion at the time of writing. Only two rooms, containing a few archaeological finds and some displays of sextants and colonial-era gramophones, were open to the public.

The museum was ransacked and largely emptied during the 1990 Iraqi invasion, and it has been under almost complete reconstruction for the past decade. Things here can only get better.

The quaint **Popular Traditional Museum** (Map p100; ☎2272 9158) – variously described as the Heritage Museum and the Culture Museum – is in Building 2, at the rear of the museum complex. It illustrates daily life in pre-oil Kuwait by means of a diorama of full-size figures going about their various business – be sure to see the bead maker and what the museum booklet describes as the 'men's over-robe tailor'.

Buses 12 and 16 (departing from the main bus station) stop a couple of blocks from the museum complex.

National Assembly Building HISTORIC BUILDING

(Map p100; Arabian Gulf St, Qibla) This interesting white building with its distinctive canopy was designed by Jørn Utzon, the Danish architect who also designed the Sydney Opera House, and was completed in 1985. The two sweeping roofs were designed to evoke Bedouin tents and the building is befitting of the first parliament of the region. The building is not open to the visiting public.

Liberation Tower TOWER

(Map p100; ☎2242 9166; Abdullah Al Salem St, Safat) Not to be confused with the distinctive Kuwait Towers, Liberation Tower in the city centre is the tallest building in the city, and at a height of 372m claims to be the fifth-tallest communications tower in the world. Started before the invasion, the tower took its new name when it was completed in 1993. Sadly,

TRACES OF OLD KUWAIT

Kuwait City's rather scruffy downtown area bears few traces of history amid the vast construction sites, but one street does carry faint echoes of the past. Al Soor St, at the southern end of the city centre, follows the line of the old city wall. Yes, this city that now sprawls seemingly forever was once restricted to the area north of the street (*soor* is the Arabic word for wall). City gates once lined up along the street (four that remain are **Al Maqsab** (Map p100), **Al Jahra** (Map p100), **Al Shamiya** (Map p100) and **Al Shaab** (Map p100) – trace a line between them on the map and you'll have a clear picture of what Old Kuwait consisted of and just how much it has grown. Despite the gates' ancient appearance, the wall and gates were only constructed around 1920. The wall was demolished in 1957.

Another interesting area lies just south of **Dar Al Athar Al Islamiyya** (p93), off Arabian Gulf St, with replica 19th-century dwellings that give a good idea of what Kuwait must have looked like prior to the discovery of oil. Their appeal has been diminished somewhat by the new motorway that runs past their front doors and separates the houses from the rest of the downtown area, although there is a pedestrian footbridge if you're coming from the city side. The restaurant **Beit 7** (p105) is part of this island of the past.

the viewing platform has not been open to the public for years, so you'll most likely have to enjoy it from ground level.

Science & Natural History Museum

MUSEUM

(Educational Science Museum; Map p100; ☎2242 1268; ksnhm.weebly.com; Abdullah Al Mubarak St, Safat; ⏰5-7.30pm Sun-Thu) FREE An eclectic range of exhibits, from electronics and space paraphernalia to fossils, stuffed animals and an 18m whale skeleton, is on display here. The museum is only open in the mornings for school visits.

Yaum Al Bahhar Village

PARK

(Map p100; Arabian Gulf St, Shuwaikh; ⏰5-11.30pm) FREE With traditional wind-tower architecture, this small area of craft workshops is part of a development along the coast that includes walking paths and fountains. The workshops are open at variable times and some of the items are for sale. Not-for-the-faint-hearted crafts include shell decorations that you wouldn't wish on your enemy. This is a good place for male visitors to enjoy mint tea in a traditional coffeehouse and listen to the clack of bone on board as locals play backgammon.

★Kuwait House of National Works: Memorial Museum

MUSEUM

(Map p90; ☎2484 5335; Block 7, 71st St, Shuwaikh; admission KD1; ⏰8.30am-1pm & 4.30-8.30pm Sun-Thu, 4.30-8.30pm Sat) This museum captures the horror of the Iraqi invasion and honours the sacrifices that Kuwaiti citizens, the Kuwaiti military and their allies made in order to repel Iraqi forces. The exhibits comprise a set of well-crafted city models that are illuminated in time with an audio recording in English. Despite the nationalist propaganda, the overall experience – walking through the darkened corridors, lit only by simulated gun blasts and mortar attacks – has a contemporary resonance that transcends the exhibit's narrow remit.

The museum is best reached by taxi and can be combined with a visit to the nearby Arab Fund Building. Alternatively, take bus 13 along Arabian Gulf St to the airport and get off at the steel and concrete headquarters of the Kuwait Petroleum Corporation (KPC). As the road bends sharply inland from here, take the first lane on the left.

Arab Fund Building

BUILDING

(Map p90; ☎2484 4500; www.arabfund.org/aohq; Airport Rd, Shuwaikh) FREE Although not strictly open to the casual caller, the impressive Arab Fund Building, with a host of exceptionally beautiful rooms, is worth the trouble of gaining access. Call first to request an appointment and explain that you wish to see the building's interior and you'll be given a guided tour by one of the employees.

The gravity of the exterior belies the light and airy interior, designed in accordance with Arabic architectural principles of integrity of space, decoration and function. The magnificent eight-storey atrium with wooden lattices, opening onto a transparent corridor or an exquisite hidden *majlis* (meeting room), is an exciting reinterpretation of a familiar theme. Traditional craftsmanship from around the Arab world is represented in lavish concoctions of ceramic, carpet and woodwork in one of the most extraordinary expressions of postmodern eclecticism in the Gulf.

Friday Market

SOUQ

(Souq Al Jum'a; Map p90; south of 4th Ring Rd & west of Airport Rd, Shuwaikh; ⏰8am-4pm Fri) This enormous semi-covered market is a shopping extravaganza – but, more importantly, it offers a look at contemporary Kuwaiti culture and cross-border relations. Five minutes shuffling between dusty textiles and sipping the coffee of a good-natured vendor delivers more in the way of insight into the complex web of Kuwaiti affairs, domestic and international, than you could absorb in a month of lectures on Arabic culture.

House of Mirrors

HOUSE

(Map p90; ☎2251 8522; House 17, Street 94, Block 9, Qadisiya) FREE For a quirky art-in-action experience, visit this small museum in the suburbs. Reputedly, 77 tonnes of mirror and 102 tonnes of white cement were used to create the mosaics that spangle the entire house. The creation of Lidia Al Qattan, the project was inspired by the decoration of an old piece of dining-room furniture and grew to incorporate epic scenes, as in the Room of the Universe (bedroom) and the Basin of the Sharks (hallway). Ring ahead to request a tour.

Al Qurain Martyrs' Museum

MUSEUM

(☎2543 0343; House 61, Street 3, Block 4, Qurain; ⏰8.30am-noon & 4.30-8.30pm Mon-Thu & Sat, 4.30-8.30pm Fri) FREE In the residential suburb of Qurain, a 20-minute taxi ride southeast of the city centre, this small museum is a memorial to a cell of young Kuwaitis who

AL QURAIN MARTYRS' MUSEUM

Early one morning during the Iraqi invasion in the early 1990s, a minibus (the one that is still parked outside) drew up outside an ordinary house in the suburbs – the house that today has been converted into Al Qurain Martyrs' Museum. When no one answered the door, Iraqi militia parked outside and began firing at the doors and windows, trying to rout a cell of the Kuwaiti resistance sheltering inside. They bombarded the house for hour upon hour with machine guns, bombs and eventually a tank, waiting for the young patriots to surrender. Eventually, they got tired of waiting. Nine of those under siege were captured and tortured to death, while four hid in a roof space.

General Schwarzkopf, who visited the house on 14 April 1994, commented that 'when I am in this house it makes me wish that we had come four days earlier, then perhaps this tragedy would not have happened'. The Iraqi occupation lasted for seven long months, during which time many similar raids on the homes of Kuwait families were made.

tried to resist arrest in February 1991. To understand what the Iraqi invasion meant to an ordinary Kuwaiti family, allow half an hour to visit this sobering museum (or what's left of it), if only to see copies of documents issuing instructions to 'burn and destroy' homes and 'fire on demonstrations'.

Bus 101 stops within a 10-minute walk of the museum, but it is difficult to find the precise location without assistance.

Al Hashemi Marine Museum MUSEUM

(Map p90; ☎2567 3000; www.al-hashemi2.com; Ta'awen St, Salwa; ⊙9am-5pm Sat-Thu, 2-5pm Fri) **FREE** This museum has an impressive collection of large, scale-model dhows. A novel shop sells 21-piece knot boards, Gipsy Moth lanterns, barometers and sextants. You can even buy your own one-armed Nelson figurine. *Al Hashemi II*, the huge and unmissable wooden dhow adjacent to the museum, is the largest wooden boat on earth, measuring a world-record-breaking 80.4m long and 18.7m wide and weighing an estimated 2500 tonnes. The museum even has a 2002 *Guinness Book of Records* certificate to prove it.

The vision of Husain Marafie, owner of the Radisson Blu hotel, *Al Hashemi II* was completed in 1998 from mahogany and ekki logs from Cameroon, planks from Ivory Coast and pine logs from Oregon. It's worth taking a five-minute walk inside the lavish, parquet-floored interior, used for conferences and banqueting.

Al Boom, a smaller dhow in the complex, is a restaurant; it's a great place for dinner. The complex is next to the Palm Gardens hotel inside the grounds of the Radisson Blu hotel.

Activities

Kuwait City's location on the seafront provides many opportunities for fun with water – in it (swimming), on it (water sports and ice skating), alongside it (jogging along the corniche) and through it (ferry rides). Contact **Touristic Enterprises Company** (TEC; ☎2562 2600; www.kuwaittourism.com) for current details of many activities in Kuwait.

Swimming

All the way along Arabian Gulf St there are splendid beaches, and there's nothing to stop a committed paddler from taking a dip at most of them, though the water tends to be on the shallow side for serious swimming and there are worries about the level of pollution in the water. One-piece swimsuits for women are encouraged.

TEC Swimming Pool Complex SWIMMING

(Map p90; ☎2562 2600; Arabian Gulf St, Dasman; admission KD2, locker 250 fils; ⊙outdoor pool 9am-2pm & 3-9pm Mon-Sat, indoor pool 9-11am, noon-2pm, 3-5pm & 6-8pm Mon-Sat) If the turquoise sea doesn't tempt, this complex has three large pools, two for men only and one for families.

Green Island SWIMMING

(Map p90; ☎2257 3542; Arabian Gulf St, Dasman; adult/child Sun-Wed KD1/500 fils, Thu-Sat KD2/1; ⊙9am-11pm) For activities ranging from strolling in the gardens, swimming in a lagoon and cycling to listening to an impromptu concert, this artificial island – joined to the mainland by a pedestrian causeway – houses a 700-seat amphitheatre and a game park for children. On Friday the increased entrance fee covers the cost of an open-air concert of Arabic music.

DON'T MISS

KUWAIT'S MODERN ARCHITECTURE

Kuwait's extraordinary modern wealth has been expressed in many pieces of architectural civic pride. If you're in town for a while, don't miss at least a drive-by of the following fine buildings.

Kuwait Towers (p91) There are few buildings in the region as iconic as these water towers. Their slender columns and plump reservoirs are symbolic of the way in which a city has blossomed from humble beginnings.

National Assembly Building (p95) Designed by Jørn Utzon of Sydney Opera House fame, this landmark building resembles a piece of unfurled silk, evoking both the canopy of a Bedouin tent and a sail-furled dhow, while expressing modernist concepts of negative space and the sculpture of light and shade.

Arab Fund Building (p96) With its expression of the integrity of space and function, light and communication, and combining modern interior design, this superb building remains true to a traditional Islamic aesthetic.

Grand Mosque (p95) Across from Sief Palace on Arabian Gulf St, Kuwait City's main mosque is graced with the tallest minaret in the country.

Fatima Mosque (Map p100; cnr Sana'a & Ibn Abbas Sts) Considerable wealth has been channelled into religious architecture, with some 60% of Kuwait's mosques financed and built by individuals, including this distinctive green-and-white domed mosque in Abdullah Al Salem.

Shaikh Nasser Al Sabah Mosque (Map p90; Arabian Gulf St, Ras Salmiya) This pyramid-shaped mosque is another example of exceptional modern mosque design.

The activities themselves are rather tame, but it's worth visiting for the chance to see Kuwaitis at leisure.

Ice Skating

Ice-Skating Rink SKATING

(Map p100; ☎2241 1151; www.kuwaittourism.com/IceSkatingRink.html; btwn Al Soor St & First Ring Rd, Shamiya; admission 500 fils, skating incl boots KD2; ⊙8.30am-10pm) One of the best in the region, this Olympic-size rink has a spectator capacity of 1600. It's home to the Kuwaiti Falcons, the country's official ice-hockey team, and the only Arab team to win membership of the International Ice Hockey Federation.

Courses

Beit Lothan CULTURAL CENTRE

(Map p90; ☎2575 5866; www.baytlothan.org; Arabian Gulf St, Salmiya; ⊙9am-1pm & 5-9pm Sun-Thu, 5-9pm Sat) This cultural centre promotes the work of Kuwaiti and Gulf artists and craftspeople through regular exhibitions in a 1930s house that was originally the home of the country's late emir, Sheikh Sabah Al Salem Al Sabah. The centre also acts as a conduit for the energies of Kuwaiti youth. It offers a range of courses, including crafts, photography, drawing and painting.

Al Sadu House COURSE

(Map p100; ☎2243 2395; www.alsadu.org.kw; Arabian Gulf St; two weekly classes over one month KD45-65; ⊙8am-1pm & 4-8pm Sat-Thu) At Al Sadu House, Bedouin craftswomen teach *sadu* (Bedouin-style) and other weaving techniques for both beginners and those with more experience. It's a terrific venue and they also run one-off family and/or children's workshops. Check with the **Kuwait Textile Arts Association** (q8textilearts.wordpress.com) for details.

Tours

Kuwait Tourism Services Company TOUR

(Map p100; ☎2245 1734; www.kts-kuwait-tourism.com; Ice-Skating Rink, btwn Al Soor St & First Ring Rd, Shamiya) Runs tours around the various city sights and out to the oilfields. Mainly caters for large tour groups but can also arrange similar tours for individuals. Excursions, which start from KD10 per person, include half- and full-day city, coastline, diving and Gulf-cruising tours.

Nuzha Tourist Enterprises TOUR

(☎2575 5825; www.facebook.com/Nuzha-Touristic-Enterprises-229701577064027/) Can organise a wide range of tours, and offers camel and horse rides, desert safaris, climbing tours and many other activities.

Festivals & Events

Hala Festival SHOPPING

(www.hala-feb.com) During the month of February, the city goes crazy with the annual shopping festival. There are lots of draws giving away valuable prizes in the shopping centres, and special promotions lure customers in. Many shops offer discounts of up to 70%. Ask your hotel reception where to go for the best bargains.

The festival coincides with National Day on 25 February and Liberation Day on 26 February. During this time, there are often firework displays and the city is draped in lights. Arts, sports, a carnival and other activities make this an exciting time to be in town. Check the festival website and 'What's On' listings in the English-language daily papers for details.

Sleeping

Most of Kuwait City's hotels have air-con, private bathrooms, satellite TVs and mini fridges, and quoted prices usually include the 15% service charge that most hotels add to their tariff. Breakfast is not generally included.

★ **Gulf Rose Hotel** HOTEL $

(Map p100; ☎2244 4800; www.gulfrosekuwait.com; Al Shuhada St; r KD29-44; @ 🛜) Fine views out over the city and the Gulf, large, well-tended rooms that would go for much more if part of a luxury chain, friendly service ... we're not quite sure why prices are so low here, but we're certainly not complaining. Breakfast is often included in quoted room prices, so we're hard pressed to find a better deal in Kuwait City.

Ibis Kuwait Salmiya Hotel BUSINESS HOTEL $

(Map p90; ☎2573 4247; www.ibishotel.com; Salem Al Mubarak St, Salmiya; r KD35-39 ; P 🛜) It's not often we recommend this international chain, but its modern rooms represent outstanding value and many on the upper floors have views out over the corniche (you can even see the Kuwait Towers in the distance). Close to the Scientific Center and Salmiya's shopping district, and just a KD2 taxi ride from the centre, the location is fine.

There's an excellent restaurant and *sheesha* cafe, too. Reception is on the 3rd floor.

KUWAIT CITY FOR CHILDREN

Kuwait is a safe, easygoing, family-oriented country, and children are welcome and catered for everywhere. Many of the city's family-entertainment activities are organised by **Touristic Enterprises Company** (p97), known as TEC. The TEC information centre can advise on facilities in town and at its resorts, and take reservations.

One standout attraction that most kids love is the **Scientific Center** (p93), with an aquarium, an IMAX cinema and Discovery Place, a zone for kids to get all creative in.

You'll find playgrounds scattered across the city, including one at the northern end of the **Sharq Marina** (Map p100; Arabian Gulf St).

Shaab Leisure Park (Map p90; ☎2561 3777; Arabian Gulf St, Salmiya; admission KD1; ⏲4pm-midnight Sun-Thu, 10am-midnight Fri & Sat) Occupying a large, open area, this leisure park offers around 70 rides, bungee jumping and pony rides. Some of the attractions are free; others cost from KD2. For a unique souvenir, try the video cinema, where visitors can make their own music video.

Aqua Park (Map p100; ☎2243 1960; Arabian Gulf St; ⏲10am-10pm) The centrally located Aqua Park, behind Kuwait Towers, is likely to come back to life once the towers reopen. Until then, call first, as it's not always open.

Color Me Mine (Map p90; ☎2224 4604; www.kuwait.colormemine.com; 1st fl, Marina Cres, Arabian Gulf Rd; ⏲10am-10pm Sat-Wed, to 11pm Thu & Fri) The motto here is 'everyone's an artist' and it's a great concept: you choose a plate, paint it in the design of your choice, they fire it so it stays and it's all yours. Kids and adults alike love this place. Prices vary depending on the paints and ceramics you choose to work with.

Music & Water Display (Map p100; ☎2242 8394; cnr Al Soor St & First Ring Rd; admission Wed-Thu KD1, Fri-Tue free; ⏲4pm-midnight Oct-Apr, 3-10.30pm May-Sep, Sun-Fri) This outdoor display is said to have the fourth-largest set of fountains in the world.

Kuwait City Centre

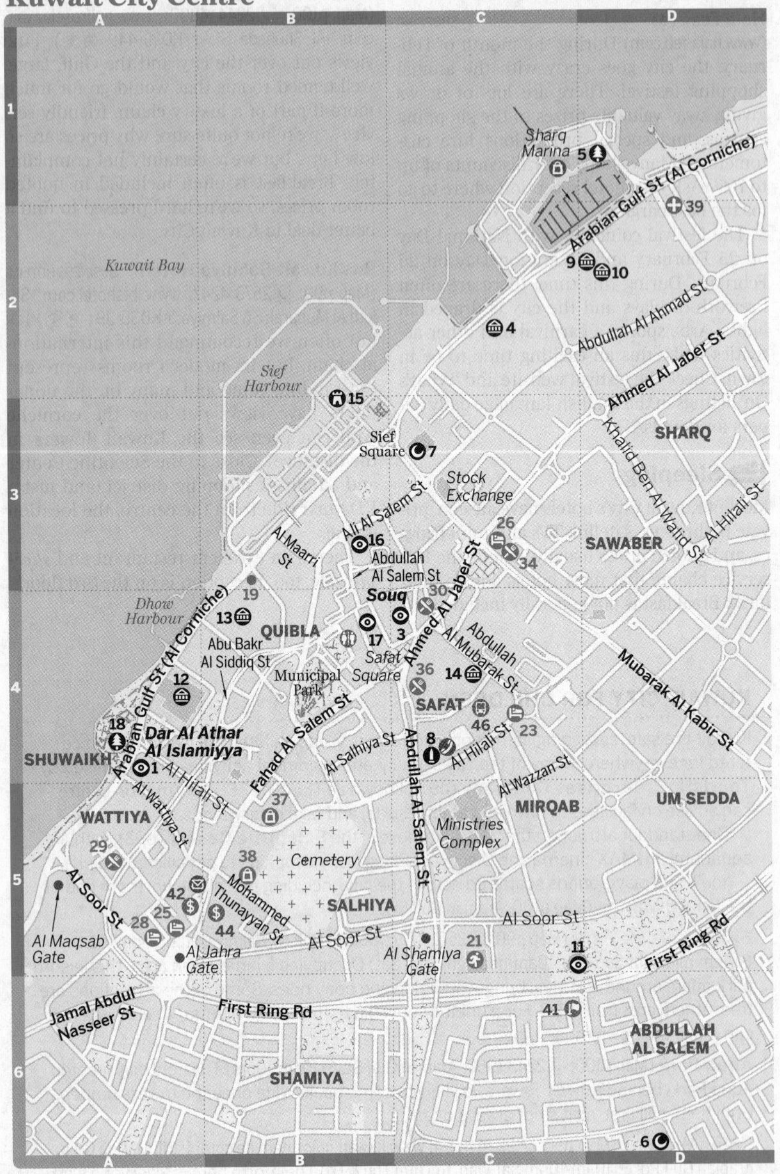

Oasis Hotel HOTEL $
(Map p100; ☎2246 5489; www.oasis.com.kw; cnr Ahmad Al Jaber & Mubarak Al Kabir Sts, Sharq; s/d KD30/36.800; 📶) This central-city hotel has simple, clean rooms with curved windowsill sofas. It's in a prime downtown location just five minutes' walk from the souq, and it's a reliable choice if the five-star hotels are beyond your reach. The upper floors have expansive views – the best are from the street-facing rooms, but they're also noisier. For a little extra you get more space and wooden floors.

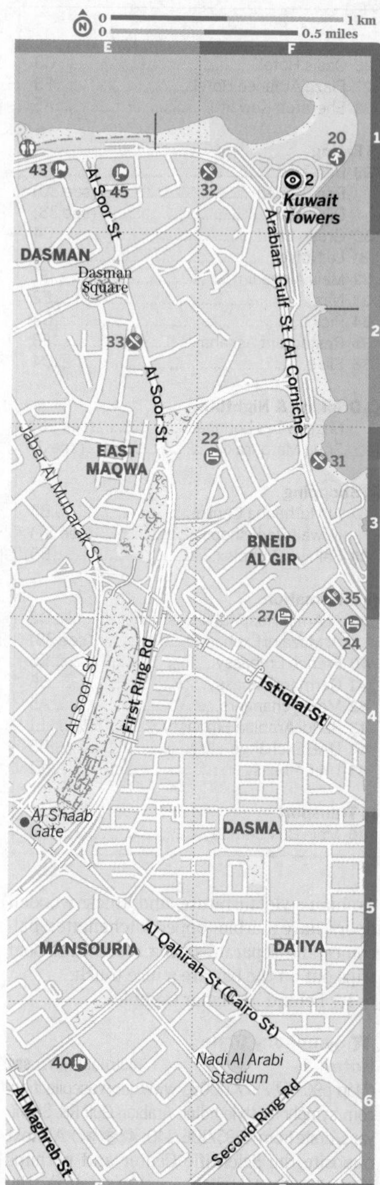

Dalal City Hotel HOTEL $$

(Map p90; www.dalalcomplex.com; Salem Al Mubarak St, Salmiya; r from KD40;) With large, attractive rooms and a location in the heart of the Salmiya shopping district – it's a short hop to Marina Mall and the corniche, and it even has its own mini mall downstairs – Dalal City Hotel is a good midrange choice. The rooftop swimming pool makes it even better.

Adams Hotel APARTMENT $$

(Map p100; 2202 0000; www.adams-hotel.com; Block 3, 64th St, Bneid Al Gir; ste from KD52;) If you're the kind of traveller who likes to rest on a sofa or cook your own meals, or even if you just value the extra space that a suite or apartment can offer, Adams Hotel is a great choice. There's an indoor pool, and some apartments have good views of the Kuwait Towers.

Not all the decor will be to everyone's taste, but with almost 75 sq metres at your disposal in even the smallest rooms, we doubt you'll mind too much.

Le Royal BOUTIQUE HOTEL $$

(Map p100; 2251 0999; www.leroyalkuwait.com; 83rd St, Bneid Al Gir; s/d from KD55/66;) This small, tasteful boutique-style hotel, on a slip road off Arabian Gulf St, offers wonderful sea views, a French-rococo foyer and a bright and intimate atmosphere. The rooms, with their CD players, polished floors, floral-design bedsteads, huge bolster pillows and enormous luxury bathrooms, are state-of-the-art. There's a cosy wicker-chair cafe in the foyer.

Le Royal Express Salmiya HOTEL $$

(Map p90; 2571 1001; Qatar St, Salmiya; s/d from KD34.500/40;) The rooms may be a little dated and nothing special, but this good-value, bright and friendly hotel, opposite the City Center shopping mall, has an appealingly busy atmosphere.

Kuwait Palace Hotel HOTEL $$

(Ghani Palace; Map p90; 2571 0301; www.kuwaitpalace.net; Salem Al Mubarak St, Salmiya; s/d KD35/45;) One of the few hotels where you don't have to check the address to remember you're in Arabia. Located in a Yemeni-style building near Central Plaza mall, the hotel sports furniture from Syria, lanterns from Morocco and local plaster work. Each wood-panelled room is split level with kitchenette and balcony and provides in character what it lacks in finish.

The sister hotel, Ghani Palace, which shares the same building, offers monthly rentals.

Le Royal Tower Kuwait HOTEL $$

(Map p100; 183 1831; www.leroyalkuwait.com/tower; Fahad Al Salem St, Wattiya; s/d from

Kuwait City Centre

Top Sights

1 Dar Al Athar Al Islamiyya A4
2 Kuwait Towers F1
3 Souq C4

Sights

4 Beit Dickson C2
5 Children's Playground D1
6 Fatima Mosque D6
7 Grand Mosque C3
8 Liberation Tower C4
9 Maritime Museum D2
10 Modern Art Museum D2
11 Music & Water Display C5
12 National Assembly Building A4
13 National Museum Complex B4
Popular Traditional Museum .... (see 13)
14 Science & Natural History Museum C4
15 Sief Palace B3
16 Souq ad Dahab Al Markazi B3
Souq Al Hareem .... (see 3)
17 Souq Marbarakia B4
18 Yaum Al Bahhar Village A4

Activities, Courses & Tours

19 Al Sadu House B3
20 Aqua Park F1
21 Ice-Skating Rink C5
Kuwait Tourism Services Company .... (see 21)

Sleeping

22 Adams Hotel F3
23 Gulf Rose Hotel C4
24 Le Royal F4
25 Le Royal Tower Kuwait A5
26 Oasis Hotel C3
27 Plaza Athenee Hotel F3
28 Sheraton Kuwait A5

Eating

29 Beit 7 .... A5
Beit Ahmed .... (see 30)
Dikakeen .... (see 38)
30 Green Land C4
31 Le Nôtre F3
32 Mais Alghanim F1
33 Naz E2
34 Pick C3
35 Restaurant Assaha F3
36 Slice C4

Drinking & Nightlife

English Tea Lounge .... (see 28)
Souq Marbarakia .... (see 3)

Shopping

37 Al Muthanna Centre B5
Kuwait Bookshops .... (see 37)
38 Salhiya Complex B5

Information

39 Al Amiri Hospital & Casualty D2
Al Muzaini Exchange .... (see 38)
40 French Embassy E6
41 German Embassy C6
42 Moneychangers A5
43 Saudi Arabian Embassy E1
44 UAE Exchange B5
45 UK Embassy E1

Transport

46 Main Bus Station C4

KD60/71; @) This stylish downtown hotel prides itself on being the first 'art and tech' hotel in the Gulf, with designer features including power showers and interactive TV. The illuminated glass panels behind the bedstead and the glass washbasin in the bathroom help complete the impression of 21st-century living.

Live cooking shows in the Cascade Restaurant (named after the water feature in the foyer) cater for individual guests.

Plaza Athenee Hotel BOUTIQUE HOTEL $$
(Map p100; 184 6666; www.plazaatheneekuwait.com; Block 18, Port Said St, Bneid Al Gir; s/d KD35/65; @) Unusually in a country more accustomed to dealing with business people than tourists, the singles here are pigeonhole size, with tiny, angular shower rooms and linoleum floors. In contrast, the doubles, with Arabian-style furniture and thick wooden doors, have marble-topped kitchenettes, balconies and separate sitting areas. Free boat trips out on the bay are a nice touch.

It's behind Al Manar Complex.

★ Symphony Style Hotel BOUTIQUE HOTEL $$$
(Map p90; 2577 0000; www.quorvuscollection.com/symphony-style-hotel; Arabian Gulf Rd, Salmiya; s/d/ste from KD95/106/140; @) Almost opposite the Scientific Center and perhaps Kuwait's most stylish accommodation, the Symphony Style Hotel boasts sea views, designer rooms with quirky, contemporary colours, a spa and fitness centre, restaurants, a children's play room and, wait for it, an iPod docking station and an espresso-coffee machine in each room. The effect is a boutique sensibility in a behemoth-size hotel.

★Marina Hotel HOTEL $$$
(Map p90; ☎2223 0030; www.marinahotel.com; Arabian Gulf St, Salmiya; s/d from KD108/124; P 📶 🏊) Situated on the edge of bustling Marina Cres and within walking distance of the shopping district of Salmiya, this low-rise hotel floats like a lily on the water's edge and offers many rooms with direct access onto the beach. Sophisticated, elegant and modern, this is one hotel that succeeds in being practical as well as aesthetically pleasing.

The hotel's Atlantis restaurant, in the shape of a ship's prow, is an excellent place to sample the catch of the day, and its Wednesday poolside barbecue (from 7pm) is excellent.

★Hilton Kuwait Resort RESORT $$$
(☎2225 6222; www.hilton.com; Coast Rd, Mangaf; from KD84; P 📶 🏊) Situated on 1.8km of white-sand beach with pristine water, this resort, 35km from the city, provides the perfect antidote to the proverbial 'hard day at the office', whether 'office' equates to a business meeting, a day of committed shopping or sightseeing, or even a day of peacekeeping over the border.

Some of the balcony rooms are a bit small, but with water views like this, you're unlikely to care.

Radisson Blu HOTEL $$$
(Map p90; ☎2567 3000; www.radissonsas.com; Ta'awen St, Rumaithiya; r from KD85; @ 🏊) It's hard to imagine that two decades ago there wasn't a window remaining in this quiet hotel. Pluses here are many: free late checkout, free airport limo service, and terrific rooms with a more contemporary look than many Radissons in the region. With excellent service and a view of palm trees and the Gulf from many rooms, it's a terrific choice.

There's also Al Hashemi Marine Museum (p97) on site and the intimate Al Boom restaurant (p105) in the back garden.

Sheraton Kuwait HOTEL $$$
(Map p100; ☎2242 2055; www.sheratonkuwait.com; Safat Tower, Fahad Al Salem St; r from KD114; P 📶 🏊) This stalwart of a central hotel has been given a recent makeover and now it glitters with dazzling chandeliers and mirror-polished treacle-coloured marble. Rooms are modern and have all the trimmings, although the look is more classic than contemporary. Afternoon tea here is a top expat experience.

Eating

Perhaps the city's best-loved activity, dining out is something of an institution here, and there are literally hundreds of restaurants to suit all wallets and palates.

A great way to get a feel for the heart of the city is to pull up a chair at one of the casual tables strewn around the western edge of Souq Marbarakia on the semi-pedestrianised Abdullah Al Salem St. If you order kebabs (around KD2), a generous helping of green leaves, pickles, hummus and Arabic bread arrives with them. Most places are open 11am till midnight.

One of the liveliest places to enjoy the night breeze over a chilled fruit juice and a choice of grilled, baked and fried fishy delights is in and around Marina Cres in Salmiya. The plaza, with its many cafes and restaurants, is linked by footbridge to Marina Mall (p106) in Salmiya and is a relaxed meeting place for Kuwaiti families throughout the weekend.

★Beit Ahmed CAFE $
(Map p100; ☎2246 7373; Souq Marbarakia; mains KD1.950-2.600; ⏰9am-1.45pm & 4-10.15pm Sat-Thu, 4-10.15pm Fri) We love this place. In a stylish homewares stall in the souq, Beit Ahmed is a small but sophisticated cafe with traditional cushions and plush sofas. It specialises in all manner of teas but serves excellent felafel, cheese platters and lamb kebabs too. You can also sit outside. Signed only in Arabic, it's just west of Green Land restaurant.

★Green Land INDIAN $
(Map p100; ☎2242 2246; Souq Marbarakia; mains KD1.700-2.500; ⏰9am-4pm & 6-11pm Mon-Sat, 9am-4pm & 6-10pm Sun; 🌿) This excellent Indian restaurant with a classy dining area is a real find. It's all vegetarian, it does a popular South Indian thali lunch or dinner for just KD1.600 and the choice of dishes seems endless. It's left off the main souq thoroughfare as you enter from Abdullah Al Mubarak St.

Layali Al Helmeya KEBAB $
(Map p90; ☎2263 8710; Arabian Gulf St, Salmiya; snacks 500 fils-KD2, mains KD1.750-3.750; ⏰8am-1am) This is a lovely place to sit and enjoy the view overlooking Kuwait Bay with a coffee and *sheesha*. A modern version of a traditional Egyptian coffeehouse, it offers kebabs and felafel sandwiches. The food's good, but it owes its popularity (it's often full) to the chance to smoke a *sheesha* (KD2) with a view.

Dukkan Burger BURGERS $

(Map p90; ☎1800 011; www.dukkan-burger.com; 83rd St, Bneid Al Gir; mains from KD2.750; ⏲8am-11pm) Very cool. Part burger joint, part modern Kuwaiti *diwaniya* (traditional gathering), Dukkan Burger effortlessly spans the two. You could order a fairly traditional if rather delicious burger, but why not go for the spiced *shwarma* burger with local aioli or a saffron pancake? Or the buttermilk fried chicken with American cheddar, cattleman's sauce, pickle, shredded iceberg, onion rings and soft roll...

Naz IRANIAN $

(Map p100; ☎2245 1892; www.naz-restaurant.com; Al Soor St; mains KD0.800-4.750; ⏲11am-midnight) The 'Persian soul food' at this casual eatery is terrific, with the full range of kebabs, salads and stews – of the latter, we especially enjoyed the *khoresht-e bademjan* (a diced-lamb stew with aubergine, onion, garlic and dried lemon).

Slice KEBAB $

(Map p100; ☎6700 9974; www.slicedoner.com; Abdullah Al Salem St; mains KD0.500-2.500) The humble doner has never looked as good as it does here. All of the essential ingredients come into play: flaky pita bread, expertly sliced chicken or beef, the full complement of lettuce, cabbage, tomato and onion. But it's the sauces that make this place stand out – choose from delicately spiced yogurt, tahini, chilli or garlic. It's just opposite the souq.

Pick FAST FOOD $

(Map p100; www.pick.com.kw; Mubarak Al Kabir St; mains KD0.950-2.800; ⏲6.30am-11pm Sat-Thu, 8am-11pm Fri) This slick little spot is best known for its frozen yogurts, smoothies and pancakes, but its concept of healthy fast food extends to ready-made sushi boxes, salads, *shwarmas* and more substantial dishes that you choose from the fridge.

★Burj Al Hamam LEBANESE $$

(Map p90; ☎2252 9095; www.burjalhamam.com.kw; Arabian Gulf St, Dasman; mains KD2.950-7.950; ⏲9am-midnight Sat-Wed, to 1am Thu & Fri; 📶) This unmissable waterfront restaurant is a terrific place to sample Middle Eastern fare. Grilled meat and seafood dominate, but how could anyone resist the hummus with lamb and pine nuts and drizzled with lamb fat? The focus is the Levant, but you'll find dishes from as far afield as Egypt and Armenia, and some real surprises (such as a raw-meat platter). There's a terrace with a 270-degree sea view.

★Le Nôtre FRENCH, MIDDLE EASTERN $$

(Map p100; ☎180 5050; www.lenotreparis-kuwait.com; Arabian Gulf St; breakfast buffet KD7, mains KD3.900-9; ⏲noon-midnight) Fantastic views of the Kuwait Towers, a discerning menu, an exclusive chocolatier, and a landmark steel-and-glass building make this one of the hippest places in town. There are so many standouts on the iPad menus, including pumpkin and quinoa soup with feta and kale, lamb and ricotta risotto, and sea bass with seaweed. Then there are the desserts...

The salted-caramel tiramisu is simply divine, but walk along the display case of sweets and you'll find it hard to resist most of them. The restaurant also serves pasta, pizza and a hugely popular breakfast buffet. Dress smartly.

KUWAIT'S WATER SHORTAGE

Kuwait has long been known for its fine natural harbour, but, like so many places in the Middle East, it is chronically short of water. Indeed, from 1907 until 1950, traders had to buy fresh water from the Shatt Al Arab waterway near Bubiyan Island, at the head of the Gulf, and ship it by dhow to Kuwait. The trade peaked in 1947, when it was estimated that 303,200L of water per day was arriving in Kuwait by boat – thankfully, the country didn't have a golf course.

Early investment of oil revenues into the search for ground water was unsuccessful, but Kuwait's first desalination plant in 1950 signalled the end of the sea trade in water. An exorbitant way to acquire fresh water, desalination nonetheless satisfies the country's huge thirst for water, which (according to some local water-resource experts) has grown to become the highest consumption of water in the world.

Natural resources are precious and, as every Bedouin knows (and any midsummer visitor can guess), in the desert, water is far more valuable than oil. In Kuwait, it's also more expensive.

★**Mais Alghanim** MIDDLE EASTERN $$
(Map p100; ☎2225 1155; www.maisalghanim.com; Arabian Gulf St, Sharq; mains KD2.650-6.950; ⊙10am-11pm) They've been serving excellent Arab cooking at this fine place for six decades and it shows in cooking that never misses a beat. The charcoal-grilled meats and seafood are the highlights, but there's so much leading up to them (salads, dips, all manner of mezze) that having enough room to fit it all in seems to be the greatest problem.

Dikakeen MIDDLE EASTERN $$
(Map p100; ☎2299 6552; www.dikakeen.net; level M2, Salhiya Complex, Mohammed Thunayyan St; mains KD5-7; ⊙8am-11pm) With a genteel air in the upmarket Salhiya mall, Dikakeen serves up classy interpretations of Arabic street food, such as *mishaltit*, an Egyptian classic of thin bread dough folded and stuffed with fillings. There are also breakfast, *shwarma* and terrific desserts to draw you here.

Restaurant Assaha LEBANESE $$
(Lebanese Traditional Village; Map p100; ☎2253 3377; www.assahavillage.com; Al Khalij Al Arabi St, Bneid Al Gir; mains KD3-7; ⊙noon-11.30pm; 📶) Built to resemble an old Kuwaiti villa, Assaha is an atmospheric place to eat. The snugs, *majlis* area, tiled floors and antiques provide an Oriental experience that's all too hard to find in the tower-block cities of the Gulf. The food's impressive too, with grilled meats and seafood, salads, and even Iraqi specialities. It's just across the corniche from the waterfront.

Beit 7 INTERNATIONAL $$
(Map p100; Behbehani Houses No 7, Usama Ben Monqiz St; mains from KD5; ⊙noon-midnight) With tables tucked around the interior courtyard of a coral-and-gypsum house dating from 1949 (and included on the government's list of heritage sites), this restaurant – with its beaded lanterns, palm fans and wicker chairs – has retained the feeling of house and home. It serves French, Italian and Middle Eastern fare and is a favourite with the expat community.

★**Al Boom** SEAFOOD $$$
(Map p90; ☎2567 3430; www.radissonblu.com/en/hotel-kuwait/restaurants; Radisson SAS Hotel, Ta'awen St, Rumaithiya; mains KD15.250-28; ⊙6-11.30pm) In the hull of a boat, this inventive restaurant takes some beating, particularly as this isn't just any old boat: this is *Mohammedi II,* built in Calicut, India, in 1979. Dishes include whole Omani lobster, Gulf shrimp skewers and grilled Kuwaiti zubeidi fish. As this is a very popular venue, it's advisable to make a reservation.

A replica of the largest dhow ever built (*Mohammedi I*, 1915), the boat took three years to construct from teak and 2.5 tonnes of copper, and was completed with 8.8 tonnes of handmade iron nails. Not that one spares much thought for the 35,000 days of labour that were invested in one of the most characterful cargo holds in the history of boat building: when you're ensconced in the curving hull, under a ship's lantern hung from the beams, your attention is much more carefully focused on the impeccable service and on the food served on a personalised brass dinner setting. It's quite an experience.

> **ALCOHOL-FREE ZONE**
>
> Kuwait is a dry state in which the consumption of alcohol is strictly forbidden. Penalties if caught in possession of alcohol or appearing under the influence of alcohol are severe. If you happen to be a hip-flask traveller, make sure you tip the contents away before you arrive at the airport.

Drinking & Nightlife

There are a number of Arabic cafes around town where mostly men go to chat over a *sheesha* and numerous small cups of sweet, black coffee. Most are the equivalent of a commercial *diwaniya* (gathering) and business preliminaries are often conducted informally on the premises. Many, such as Layali Al Helmeya (p103), blur the boundaries between restaurant and coffeehouse.

Souq Marbarakia COFFEEHOUSE
(Map p100; btwn Mubarak Al Kabir, Ahmad Al Jaber & Ali Al Salem Sts; ⊙4pm-midnight) Women may feel rather uncomfortable in the covered inner courtyard of the old souq, near the cafes on the souq's western edge, but men will love the convivial atmosphere.

Beit Lothan COFFEEHOUSE
(Map p90; ☎2575 5866; Arabian Gulf St, Salmiya; ⊙10am-10pm) Coffee, tea and a *sheesha* are available in a quiet garden adjacent to the Beit Lothan cultural centre.

English Tea Lounge LOUNGE

(Map p100; ☎2242 2055; www.sheratonkuwait.com/en/tea-lounge; Sheraton Kuwait Hotel, Fahad Al Salem St, Wattiya; high tea from KD8; ⏰10am-1pm & 4pm-midnight Sat-Thu, 4pm-midnight Fri) The Sheraton, with its multiple marble pillars, record-breaking crystal chandeliers and extravagant Persian carpets, looks like the last place to find a Welsh tea with rarebit. But if scones and cucumber sandwiches beckon, choose between a Yorkshire tea with fruit cake, and a Royal Windsor tea with smoked salmon. There's a new outpost in Avenues mall (p106).

☆ Entertainment

In the absence of bars, entertainment in the city is pretty much confined to shopping and dining, although film and theatre are popular with locals. Check Bazaar (www.bazaar-magazine.com) for what's on where.

Cinemas

Considering its size, Kuwait has an overwhelming number of cinemas, which unfortunately show the same films (usually heavily edited to exclude kissing, nudity and sex – violence, however, is left uncensored). The more popular and modern of the cinemas are in the malls. There's also an Imax cinema in the Scientific Center (p93).

Kuwait National Cinema Company CINEMA

(☎2461 0545, 24hr service 180 3456; www.kncc.com; admission KD2.500-KD5; ⏰10am-midnight Sat-Thu, 2pm-midnight Fri) Cinemas are run by the Kuwait National Cinema Company. Single men are segregated from women and families (women are not expected to go to the cinema alone). A list of banned movies appears on the website.

Theatre

Kuwait Little Theatre THEATRE

(☎2398 2680, 9937 3678; www.thekuwaitlittletheatre.com; Main St, Al Ahmadi) Arabic theatre has enjoyed a long history in Kuwait, dating back to 1922 when the first amateur plays were performed, and it's highly popular with Arab audiences. Kuwait Little Theatre has been performing comedies and dramas in its own venue in Al Ahmadi since 1948. For performance times and venues, check the website and listings in the local papers.

Shopping

Salmiya is undoubtedly *the* shopping district of Kuwait and the main street, Hamad Al Mubarak St, is lined with malls. For something more traditional, the old souq (p92) in the heart of Kuwait City is a great place to shop for anything from olives to blankets – or just to snack and watch the world go by. Alternatively, some 'old lamps for new' often turn up at the Friday Market (p96).

When it comes to museum gift shops, the two best examples are the Kuwaiti Bedouin weavings at Al Sadu House (p98) and the small but extremely tasteful selection of artistic boxes and other items at Dar Al Athar Al Islamiyya (p93).

Avenues MALL

(Map p90; ☎2259 7777; www.the-avenues.com; Fifth Ring Rd, Al Rai; ⏰10am-10pm) With its six-star hotel and valet parking, this is worth a visit just for the architecture.

Salhiya Complex MALL

(Map p100; ☎2299 6000; www.salhia-complex.com; Mohammed Thunayyan St, Salhiya; ⏰10am-10pm) The pick of the downtown shopping malls, Salhiya specialises in luxury brands.

Marina Mall MALL

(Map p90; Salem Al Mubarak St, Salmiya; ⏰10am-10pm Sat-Wed, 10am-12am Thu-Fri) One of the largest malls in Salmiya, Marina Mall is connected to the waterfront by a footbridge over Arabian Gulf St. Most of the shops are in the main mall, with numerous restaurants right by the water.

Kuwait Bookshops BOOKS

(Map p100; ☎2242 4289; kbs1935b@qualitynet.net; Al Muthanna Centre, Fahad Al Salem St, Safat; ⏰9am-1pm & 5-9pm Sat-Thu, 5-9pm Fri) With a vast collection of books (don't get too excited: their remainders policy isn't the best), Kuwait Bookshops nonetheless has a wide selection of bestsellers, books on current affairs and local-interest titles. It's in the basement of Al Muthanna Centre.

Information

EMERGENCY

Ambulance, Fire & Police (☎112)

INTERNET ACCESS

Most hotels and many cafes offer free wi-fi to guests.

MEDICAL SERVICES

Services in an emergency are provided free or at minimal charge on a walk-in basis in most city hospitals.

Al Amiri Hospital & Casualty (Map p100; ☎2245 0005; Arabian Gulf St, Dasman) The city's biggest hospital.

MONEY

Banks are evenly distributed throughout the city. Moneychangers can offer slightly better rates than banks (and usually charge lower commissions); try some of the side streets that run from Safat Sq.

Al Muzaini Exchange (Map p100; Fahad Al Salem St, Salhiya; ⊙8am-1pm & 4-7pm Sat-Thu)

UAE Exchange (Map p100; www.uaeexchangekuwait.com; Basement, Burgan Bank Bldg, Fahad Al Salem St, Salhiya; ⊙8am-1pm & 4-7pm Sat-Thu)

Getting There & Around

TO/FROM THE AIRPORT

Orange taxis charge a flat KD7 between the airport (16km south of the city) and the city centre. It's a 20- to 30-minute journey. Buses 13 and 501 run between the main bus station and the airport every half-hour from 5.30am to 9pm daily (500 fils). Car-rental agencies have booths in the arrivals hall of the airport.

BUS

Two main public bus services operate in Kuwait City: **Kuwait Public Transport Company** (KPTC; ☎2232 8501; www.kptc.com.kw) and the less reliable **City Bus** (KPTC City Bus; ☎2232 8501; www.transportkuwait.com/citybus.html). They both run air-conditioned buses with fares ranging from 250 fils to 450 fils between the hours of 5am and 10pm. The front seats of these buses are reserved for women. Route maps for both companies are available online, from the bus station and on the buses.

Bus 101 goes from the main bus station in the city centre to Al Ahmadi and Fahaheel. Bus 103 goes to Al Jahra.

Main Bus Station (Map p100) The main bus station is near the intersection of Al Hilali and Abdullah Al Mubarak Sts in the Safat district. On printed timetables the station is referred to as 'Mirqab' or 'Mirgab' bus station.

TAXI

There are several types of taxis operating in Kuwait City, including call taxis (which are 24-hour radio-controlled with the fare agreed in advance), orange cabs (which can be shared from 250 fils, plus 50 fils per kilometre, or engaged from KD1.500) and white cabs (fares negotiable, although most will use meters when asked); count on KD2 for a trip between Salmiya and the downtown area. It's easy to hail a taxi from the road or from ranks near malls and hotels.

AROUND KUWAIT

Kuwait, for all intents and purposes, is a city-state where most of the attractions and activities centre on the capital. There are few towns outside Kuwait City and even fewer in the way of physical attractions in the oil-producing interior.

Despite these drawbacks, however, Kuwait has a long, beautiful stretch of coast, and future tourist developments include a multi-billion-dollar resort and entertainment complex on Failaka Island, expected to take 10 years or so to complete.

Failaka Island جزيرة فيلكا

Failaka Island has some of the most significant archaeological sites in the Gulf. With a history dating from the Bronze Age, evidence of Dilmun and Greek settlements, a classical heritage (the Greeks called it 'Ikaros') and a strategic location at the mouth of one of the Gulf's best natural harbours, this island could and should be considered one of Kuwait's top tourist attractions.

Alas, recent history has deemed otherwise. First, Iraqi forces established a heavily fortified base on Failaka, paying scant regard to the relics over which they strewed their hardware, and then Allied personnel were billeted there, with equally pitiful regard for antiquities.

Thanks to the new resort, the island is once again open to visitors and is beginning to assume its rightful importance at last, although it will be some time before access to the archaeological sites will be possible.

Sleeping

Ikaros Hotel RESORT $$
(☎2224 4988; www.heritagevillagefailaka.com; s/d KD40/55; ❄) If you like the island enough to stay, this hotel has a range of facilities, including children's zoo, lake, horse riding, camel rides and water sports. Crafts are produced in a living heritage village and are available for sale. The hotel offers rooms in an ably refurbished police station as well as traditional houses that sleep five to 15 people.

The hotel also offers day rates of KD15 per adult and KD10 per child on Friday, Saturday and public holidays and operates a catamaran service from Marina Cres (next to Starbucks). You need to book and must arrive 45 minutes before departure.

Getting There & Away

Kuwait Public Transport Company Ferries (KPTC Ferries; Map p90; ☎2232 8814; Arabian Gulf St, Salmiya) Ferries to Failaka Island depart from Ras Salmiya (also known as Ras Al Ard). The trip takes one hour, costs KD3 and leaves daily except Saturday at 8.15am, returning at 12.30pm. If you take your own vehicle it costs KD20 (rental car KD40) return. The ferry terminal in Kuwait City can be reached via buses 15, 24 and 34.

Fahaheel الفحيحيل

POP 105,000

The traditional town of Fahaheel was, until quite recently, a separate village. It now merges into the Kuwait City suburbs but retains a distinctive atmosphere, reminiscent of its Bedouin roots. The fish souq and dhow harbour are more characterful, in many ways, than their modern counterparts in the city centre. In contrast, the oil refinery at neighbouring Mina Al Ahmadi is one of the largest in the world.

Buses 40, 101, 102 and 502 run to Fahaheel. The town, 39km from the city centre, can be reached by car on the Fahaheel Expressway.

Al Ahmadi الاحمدى

POP 750,000

Built to house the workers of Kuwait's oil industry in the 1940s and '50s, the town of Al Ahmadi, close to Fahaheel, was named after the emir of the day, Sheikh Ahmed. It remains, to some extent, the private preserve of the Kuwait Oil Company (KOC). There are some pleasant public gardens and performances in English at the Kuwait Little Theatre.

The **Oil Display Centre** (☎2386 7703; www.kockw.com; Mid 5th St; ⏲7am-3pm Sun-Thu) FREE is a well-organised introduction to KOC and the business of oil production.

Bus 602 runs from Fahaheel to Al Ahmadi (passing the Oil Display Centre as it enters town). To get here by car from Kuwait City, take the King Fahad Motorway south until Al Ahmadi exit. First follow the blue signs for North Al Ahmadi and then the smaller white signs for the display centre.

Ras Al Zour رأس الزور

Around 100km and an hour's drive south of the capital, Ras Al Zour (also spelt Ras Azzor) is one of the most pleasant beach areas in Kuwait. The Saudi Texaco compound is only open to guests of members, but the public beach alongside is clean and attractive too.

Entertainment City

Located 20km west of Kuwait City in Doha Village, **Entertainment City** (☎2487 9545, 2487 9455; admission KD3.500; ⏲3-11pm Sun-Wed, 10am-10pm Thu & Fri Oct-Apr, 5pm-1am Sun-Fri May-Sep) comprises three theme parks (Arab World, International World and Future World), a miniature golf course, a lake with landscaped parkland and railway, a small zoo and several restaurants. The entrance fee covers most of the rides, but there is an additional charge for some of the more elaborate ones.

Admission times vary slightly from season to season, so call ahead. Monday is generally reserved for women only. There is no public transport to the park, and a taxi (KD7 from the city centre) is not easy to hail for the return journey.

Al Jahra الجهراء

POP 490,000

Al Jahra, 32km west of Kuwait City, is the location of a 1920 battle against invading troops from Saudi Arabia. It was also the site of the Gulf War's infamous 'turkey shoot' – the Allied destruction of a stalled Iraqi convoy as it lumbered up Mutla Ridge in an effort to retreat from Kuwait. The highway and surrounding desert are now completely clear of evidence, picked over by scrap-metal dealers and souvenir hunters.

Sights

Red Fort FORT

(☎2477 2559; ⏲8.30am-12.30pm & 4.30-7.30pm Sun-Thu, 8.30-11am & 4.30-7.30pm Fri & Sat) FREE The town's only sight is the Red Fort, which played a key role in a 1920 battle where invading troops from Saudi Arabia were defeated (with British help). Also known as the Red Palace, this low, rectangular mud structure is near the highway: coming from Kuwait City, take the second of the three Al Jahra exits from Jahra Rd. The Red Fort is on the right, about 200m south of Jahra Rd.

✩ Entertainment

Al Atraf Camel Racing Club SPECTATOR SPORT
(☎2539 4014; Salmi Rd; ⏰7am Fri & Sat) FREE
Between November and April camel racing can be seen early in the morning on Friday and Saturday (races start around 7am or 8am). Phone ahead for details of races, or check listings in the English-language daily papers. The track is 7km west of Al Jahra.

ℹ Getting There & Away

Al Jahra can be reached conveniently by bus 103 from Kuwait City, which passes directly in front of the Red Fort. By car, take the Sixth Ring Rd west out of Kuwait City. For the racing club, take the turn-off where there is a faded sign of a camel, after skirting Al Jahra.

Mutla Ridge المطلاع

While it's not a particularly spectacular line of hills, Mutla Ridge is about as good as it gets in Kuwait – and it offers a wonderful view of the full expanse of Kuwait Bay. Although the land mines have been cleared, you should stick to the paths in case of explosive remnants.

For a taste of the desert, take the road to Bubiyan Island that runs along the south-eastern flank of the ridge. Either side of the road, large numbers of camels roam along its edge, grazing on the coarse grass that is common to the area. In spring, the slope down to the coastal marshes is pale green with new shoots and full of wild flowers. It is also a popular area for camping, both for Bedu (black tents and goats) and for city dwellers (white tents and aerials) keen to touch base for a while.

OFF THE BEATEN TRACK

BRIDGE TO NOWHERE

By following signs to Subiyah from Mutla Ridge, you'll eventually reach the Bridge to Nowhere, some 50km northeast of Al Jahra. There's a checkpoint in front of it, preventing further exploration, but the bridge spans more than just the narrow passage to Bubiyan Island; it also reinforces Kuwait's claim to the island in the face of erstwhile claims by both Iraq and Iran. So keen was Kuwait to maintain its claim to the uninhabited, flat and barren island and its neighbouring water supply that, when the Iraqis blew up the middle section of the bridge, the Kuwaitis quickly rebuilt it even though it goes to nowhere.

A brand-new, three-lane highway now goes to nowhere as well. Eventually, it will lead to the mega port planned for completion over the next decade. In the meantime, if you fancy getting off the beaten track, this is one way to do it without leaving the tarmac!

UNDERSTAND KUWAIT

Kuwait Today

If Iraq had not invaded Kuwait in 1990, Kuwait could have been the next Dubai, the next Qatar, a country made fabulously wealthy by oil and ready and able to once again take advantage of its position as a bridge between Asia and Europe. During the late 1970s Kuwait's stock exchange (the first in the Gulf) was among the top 10 in the world. And without knowing it, the country was the first to use architecture as a symbol of Gulf wealth – even after so many skyscrapers have risen along the Gulf's shores, few have come to define a country quite like the Kuwait Towers.

But Iraq most certainly did invade, and that changed everything. Iraq's brutal invasion and occupation threatened Kuwait's artistic heritage, challenged the very foundations of its wealth, and rattled its optimism in ways that still ripple through Kuwaiti society. The rebuilding of the country has been an extraordinary success, but the financial cost was similarly extraordinary, in a way that few other oil-rich corners of the region have ever had to contemplate: Kuwait is still paying back its military debts, while trying not to count the cost of rebuilding the country. The result, even more than two decades later, is a country where museums tell a story of national pain, where artistic treasures are still not on display, and where glittering skyscrapers cast long shadows over empty lots and decrepit downtown buildings.

And then there's the political uncertainty that comes from belonging to a region in the midst of great upheaval.

GROWING A SOCIAL CONSCIENCE

Mindful of the pitfalls of a modern, affluent life, several eminent Kuwaitis have introduced initiatives to help the young rediscover deeper, traditional values of self-discipline and caring for others. One such project, the **Lothan Youth Achievement Center** (Loyac; Map p90; 2572 7399; www.loyac.org; Beit Lothan), gives the privileged youth of Kuwait City the opportunity to interact with poorer communities. Organisers find this kind of community service helps young people channel their energies into positive, character-building activity. The coordinator of Loyac's International Programs told us about the scheme and the contribution it is making.

Motivation to start the project After September 11, the founder, Fare'a Al Saqqaf, recognised that one of the problems leading to extremism was the lack of alternative activities to help keep the young gainfully occupied. To address this, Loyac was designed to help secondary-school children and college students to build their personalities, raise their morale and identify goals to help them become caring individuals within society.

Kinds of activities Participants are involved in summer internships in companies, voluntary work experience, global outreach, computer and language development, summer camps, performing arts and sporting activities.

Willing participants Loyac's programs are fully booked and the message has spread to young people of all nationalities across Kuwait. It apparently comes as a shock to many youngsters in Kuwait that there are people who live quite different lives from themselves, without the benefit of wealth and modern conveniences, but they are keen to learn and to help in the community-service projects Loyac runs both nationally and abroad.

Long-term benefits The projects aim to foster the so-called '7 Habits', which include increased self-confidence, self-esteem, greater control of life, and finding a reasonable life-work balance. They also stress the need to see and experience life from other people's perspectives. By internalising these habits, youngsters develop grounded personalities and life-long values of community service and the understanding of the needs of others.

On 15 January 2006, the respected emir of Kuwait, Sheikh Jaber Al Sabah, died, leaving Crown Prince Sheikh Sa'ad Al Sabah at the helm. Poor health, however, led to Sa'ad's abdication (he died in May 2008) and the prime minister, Sheikh Sabah Al Ahmad Al Sabah, took over. While the ruling family divided the spoils among themselves, Kuwaitis were wondering when it might be their turn.

It came during the Arab Spring of 2011, when youth activists targeted the prime minister and his cabinet for removal amid allegations of corruption and the squandering of Kuwait's wealth. The prime minister was forced from office in late 2011. Opposition groups were joined in their discontent by the *bidoon*, stateless Arabs who demanded citizenship, jobs and benefits afforded to Kuwaiti nationals. A year later, electoral reform prompted even more widespread protest, and the elections of December 2012 were boycotted by Sunni Islamists, certain tribal groups and youth groups, resulting in a larger representation of Shiites in the National Assembly.

Things have settled down a little in the years since, but in 2014 a broad coalition of opposition groups that ranged from secular leftists to the local version of the Muslim Brotherhood came together to call for full parliamentary democracy. The unity of the opposition and their far-reaching demands sent a chill through other Gulf countries whose parliaments already lagged far behind Kuwait's when it came to democratic processes. For its part, the Al Sabah ruling family largely kept its own counsel, but if the reforms were successful, their grip on uncontested power would be all but over.

Behind it all lies a fear that occasional sectarian violence could become more frequent: in June 2015, a suicide bomber killed 27 worshippers and injured hundreds more at a Shiite mosque; responsibility for the attack was claimed by Islamic State.

But all is not doom and gloom. With the country home to 6% of the world's oil reserves, oil and oil-related products naturally dominate the economy and, with more than 100 years' worth of remaining oil, the need to diversify has not been as urgent as it has been in neighbouring countries. The government continues to deposit 10% of its oil revenues into a rainy-day Fund for Future Generations. The question of who will get to decide how to spend it is the issue that will determine Kuwait's future.

History

Early History

Standing at the bottom of Mutla Ridge on the road to Bubiyan Island, and staring across the springtime grasslands at the estuary waters beyond, it's easy enough to imagine why Stone Age humans chose to inhabit the area around Ras Subiyah, on the northern shores of Kuwait Bay. Here the waters are rich in silt from the mighty river systems of southern Iraq, making for abundant marine life. Evidence of the first settlement in the region dates from 4500 BC, and shards of pottery, stone walls, tools, a small drilled pearl and the remains of what is perhaps the world's earliest seafaring boat indicate links with the Ubaid people who populated ancient Mesopotamia. The people of Dilmun also saw the potential of living in the mouth of two of the world's great river systems and built a large town on Failaka Island, the remains of which form some of the best structural evidence of Bronze Age life in the world.

The Greeks on Failaka Island

A historian called Arrian, in the time of Alexander the Great, first put the region on the map by referring to an island discovered by one of Alexander's generals en route to India. Alexander himself is said to have called this, the modern-day island of Failaka, Ikaros, and it soon lived up to its Greek name as a Hellenistic settlement that thrived between the 3rd and 1st centuries BC. With temples dedicated to Artemis and Apollo, an inscribed stele with instructions to the inhabitants of this high-flying little colonial outpost, stashes of silver Greek coins, busts and decorative friezes, Ikaros became an important trading post on the route from Mesopotamia to India. While there is still a column or two standing proud among the weeds, there's little left to commemorate the vigorous Greek trade in pearls and incense. There's even less to show for the Christian community that settled among the ruins thereafter.

Growth of Kuwait City

Over time, Kuwait's main settlements shifted from island to mainland. In AD 500 the area around Ras Khazimah, near Al Jahra, was the main centre of population, and it took a further 1200 years for the centre of activity to nudge along the bay to Kuwait City. When looking at the view from the top of the Kuwait Towers, it's hard to imagine that 350 years ago this enormous city comprised nothing more illustrious than a few Bedouin tents clustered around a storehouse-fort. Its population swelled in the intense summer heat as nomadic families drifted in from the bone-dry desert and then receded as the winter months stretched good grazing across the interior.

Permanent families living around the fort became able and prosperous traders. One such family, Al Sabah, whose descendants now rule Kuwait, assumed responsibility for local law and order, and under their governance the settlement grew quickly. By 1760, when the town's first wall was built, the community had a distinctive character. It was composed of merchant traders, centred on a dhow and ocean-going boon fleet of 800 vessels, and a craft-oriented internal trade, arising from the camel caravans plying the route from Baghdad and Damascus to the interior of the Arabian Peninsula.

Relations with the British

By the early 19th century, as a thriving trading port Kuwait City was well in the making. However, trouble was always quite literally just over the horizon. There were pirates marauding the waters of the Arabian coast; Persians snatched Basra in the north; various Arab tribes from the west and south had their own designs; and then, of course, there were the ubiquitous Ottomans. Though the Kuwaitis generally got on well with the Ottomans, official Kuwaiti history is adamant that the sheikhdom always remained independent of them, and it is true that as the Turks strengthened their control of eastern Arabia (then known as Al Hasa), the Kuwaitis skilfully managed to avoid being absorbed by the empire. Nonetheless, Al Sabah emirs accepted the nominal Ottoman title of 'Provincial Governors of Al Hasa'.

Enter the British. The Kuwaitis and the British were natural allies in many regards. From the 1770s the British had been contracted to deliver mail between the Gulf

DEMOCRATIC KUWAIT?

Kuwait has an elected 50-seat National Assembly, which is sometimes described as one of the strongest in the Middle East. The powers of the emir, crown prince and cabinet are tempered by the increasingly vociferous 50-member Assembly, which must approve the national budget and can question cabinet members. That said, the emir has the power to dissolve the assembly whenever he pleases (and he has done so five times since 2006, most recently in 2013), but he is required by the constitution to hold new elections within 90 days of any such dissolution. At the time of writing, liberals (those favouring greater social and political freedoms), with 10 seats, were the largest voting bloc in the parliament.

In May 2005, after years of campaigning, women were at last enfranchised and permitted to run for parliament. In 2009 four women were elected to the National Assembly – despite the reticence of hard-line clerics and traditional tribal leaders, the move was viewed by many as a sign of a new era of transparent government.

and Aleppo in Syria. Kuwait, meanwhile, handled all the trans-shipments of textiles, rice, coffee, sugar, tobacco, spices, teak and mangrove to and from India, and played a pivotal role in the overland trade to the Mediterranean. The British helped to stop the piracy that threatened the seafaring trade, but they were not in a position to repel the Ottoman incursions – that is, until the most important figure in Kuwait's modern history stepped onto the stage. Sheikh Mubarak bin Sabah Al Sabah, commonly known as Mubarak the Great (r 1896–1915), was deeply suspicious that Constantinople planned to annex Kuwait. Concerned that the emir was sympathetic towards the Ottomans, he killed him, not minding that he was committing fratricide as well as regicide, and installed himself as ruler. Crucially, in 1899, he signed an agreement with Britain: in exchange for the British navy's protection, he promised not to give territory to, take support from or negotiate with any other foreign power without British consent. The Ottomans continued to claim sovereignty over Kuwait, but they were now in no position to enforce it. For Britain's part, Prussia, the main ally and financial backer of Turkey, was kept out of the warm waters of the Gulf and trade continued as normal.

Rags to Riches in the 20th Century

Mubarak the Great laid down the foundations of a modern state. Under his reign, government welfare programs provided for public schools and medical services. In 1912, postal and telegraphic services were established, and water-purification equipment was imported for the American Mission Hospital. According to British surveys from this era, Kuwait City numbered 35,000 people, with 3000 permanent residents, 500 shops and three schools, and nearly 700 pearling boats employing 10,000 men.

In the 1920s a new threat in the form of the terrifying *ikhwan* (brotherhood) came from the Najd, the interior of Arabia. This army of Bedouin warriors was commanded by Abdul Aziz bin Abdul Rahman Al Saud (Ibn Saud), the founder of modern Saudi Arabia. Despite having received hospitality from the Kuwaitis during his own years in the wilderness, so to speak, he made no secret of his belief that Kuwait belonged to the new kingdom of Saudi Arabia. The Red Fort at Al Jahra was the site of a famous battle in which the Kuwaitis put up a spirited defence. They also hurriedly constructed a new city wall, the gates of which can be seen today along Soor St in Kuwait City. In 1923 the fighting ended with a British-brokered treaty under which Abdul Aziz recognised Kuwait's independence, but at the price of two-thirds of the emirate's territory.

The Great Depression that sank the world into poverty coincided with the demise of Kuwait's pearling industry as the market became flooded with Japanese cultured pearls. At the point at which the future looked most dire for Kuwait, however, an oil concession was granted in 1934 to a US-British joint venture known as the Kuwait Oil Company (KOC). The first wells were sunk in 1936 and by 1938 it was obvious that Kuwait was virtually floating on oil. WWII forced KOC to suspend its operations, but when oil exports took off after the war, Kuwait's economy was launched on an unimaginable trajectory of wealth.

In 1950, Sheikh Abdullah Al Salem Al Sabah (r 1950–65) became the first 'oil sheikh'. His reign was not, however, marked by the kind of profligacy with which that term later came to be associated. As the country became wealthy, health care, education and the general standard of living improved dramatically. In 1949 Kuwait had only four doctors; by 1967 it had 400.

Independence

On 19 June 1961, Kuwait became an independent state and the obsolete agreement with Britain was dissolved by mutual consent. In an ominous move, the president of Iraq, Abdulkarim Qasim, immediately claimed Kuwait as Iraqi territory. British forces, later replaced by those of the Arab League (which Kuwait joined in 1963), faced down the challenge, but the precedent was not so easily overcome.

Elections for Kuwait's first National Assembly were held in 1962. Although representatives of the country's leading merchant families won the bulk of the seats, radicals had a toehold in the parliament from its inception. Despite the democratic nature of the constitution and the broad guarantees of freedoms and rights – including freedom of conscience, religion and press, and equality before the law – the radicals immediately began pressing for faster social change, and the country changed cabinets three times between 1963 and 1965. In August 1976 the cabinet resigned, claiming that the assembly had made day-to-day governance impossible, and the emir suspended the constitution and dissolved the assembly. It wasn't until 1981 that the next elections were held, but parliament was dissolved again in 1986. In December 1989 and January 1990 an extraordinary series of demonstrations took place calling for the restoration of the 1962 constitution and the reconvening of parliament.

The Iraqi Invasion

Despite these political and economic tensions, by early 1990 the country's economic prospects looked bright, particularly with an end to the eight-year Iran–Iraq war, during which time Kuwait had extended considerable support to Iraq. In light of this, the events that followed were all the more shocking to most people in the region. On 16 July 1990, Iraq sent a letter to the Arab League accusing Kuwait of exceeding its Organization of the Petroleum Exporting Countries (OPEC) quota and of stealing oil from the Iraqi portion of an oilfield straddling the border. The following day Iraqi president Saddam Hussein hinted at military action. The tanks came crashing over the border at 2am on 2 August and the Iraqi military was in Kuwait City before dawn. By noon it had reached the Saudi frontier. The Kuwaiti emir and his cabinet fled to Saudi Arabia.

On 8 August, Iraq annexed the emirate. Western countries, led by the USA, began to enforce a UN embargo on trade with Iraq, and in the months that followed more than half a million foreign troops amassed in Saudi Arabia. On 15 January, after a deadline given to Iraq to leave Kuwait had passed, Allied aircraft began a five-week bombing campaign nicknamed Desert Storm. The Iraqi army quickly crumbled and on 26 February 1991, Allied forces arrived in Kuwait City to be greeted by jubilant crowds – and by clouds of acrid black smoke from oil wells torched by the retreating Iraqi army. Ignoring demands to retreat unarmed and on foot, a stalled convoy of Iraqi armoured tanks, cars and trucks trying to ascend Mutla Ridge became the target of a ferocious Allied attack, nicknamed 'the turkey shoot'.

Physical signs of the Iraqi invasion are hard to find in today's Kuwait. Gleaming shopping malls, new hotels and four-lane highways are all evidence of Kuwait's efforts to put the destruction behind it. However, the emotional scars have yet to be healed, particularly as hundreds of missing prisoners of war are yet to be accounted for, despite the fall of Saddam Hussein.

Kuwait After the Demise of Saddam Hussein

The Allied invasion of Iraq in March 2003 threw Kuwait into a paralysis of fear that it heralded a return to the bad old days of 1990, and it was only with the death of Saddam Hussein (he was hanged on 30 December 2006) that Kuwaitis were finally able to rest easy. Now that it no longer has to look over its shoulder, Kuwait has lost no time in forging ahead with its ambitious plans, including its goal of attracting a greater number of regional tourists. The Hala Shopping Festival each February is proving a successful commercial venture, attracting visitors from across the region, and resorts offer R&R, mostly to the international business community. More significantly, cross-border trade with Iraq (particularly of a military kind) has helped fuel the economic boom of this decade, a boom barely affected by the global recession.

People

Lifestyle

In common with the rest of the Gulf, Kuwaiti people value privacy and family intimacy at home, and enjoy the company of guests outside. In many instances, 'outside' is the best description of traditional hospitality: while female guests are invited into the house, men are often entertained in tents at the front of the house. These are no scout-camp canvases, however, but lavish striped canopies made luxurious with cushions and carpets.

Any visitor lucky enough to partake in tea and homemade delicacies in these '*majlis* al fresco' may be inclined to think that life in Kuwait has retained all the charm and simplicity of its Bedouin roots.

Kuwaitis take a different view, however. Some blame the war for a weakening of traditional values: theft, fraudulent practice, problems with drugs, the divorce rate and the incidence of suicidal driving have all increased. Others recognise that the same symptoms are prevalent in any modern society. With a cradle-to-grave welfare system, where 94% of Kuwaiti nationals are 'employed' in government positions, and an economy that has run ahead faster than the culture can adapt, many Kuwaitis feel their society has become cosseted and indulgent, leaving the younger generation with too much time on their hands to wander off course.

Life in Kuwait has changed out of all recognition in the past decade: women work, couples hold hands in public, formerly taboo subjects find expression, and people spend money and raise debts. Indeed, the galloping pace of change is proving a divisive factor in a country of traditionally conservative people. It would be ironic if a society that survived some of the most sophisticated arsenal of the 20th century fell under the weight of its own shopping malls.

Population

Barely a third of Kuwait's population are Kuwaitis (the rest are expats) and many Kuwaitis boast Bedouin ancestry. After liberation, the government announced that it would never again allow Kuwaitis to become a minority in their own country, implying a target population of about 1.7 million. However, with an unquenchable desire for servants and drivers, and an equal antipathy for manual labour, it is unlikely the Kuwaitis will achieve this target any time soon.

There are small inland communities, but for all intents and purposes Kuwait is a coastal city-state.

Multiculturalism

The origin of the non-Kuwaiti population has changed considerably in the last two decades. Before the Iraqi invasion, 90% of the expat population was from Arab and/

DEWANIYA – KUWAITI GATHERINGS

An important part of life in Kuwait, *dewaniya* refer to gatherings of men who congregate to socialise, discuss a particular family issue or chew over current affairs. The origins of these gatherings go back centuries, but the rituals remain the same – a host entertains family, friends or business acquaintances in a room specially intended for the purpose at appointed times after sundown. Guests sit on cushions and drink copious cups of tea or coffee, smoke, snack and come and go as they please.

In the early 20th century, on the edge of Souq Mabarakia, Mubarak the Great held a famous daily *dewaniya*, walking each day from Sief Palace through the old souq to an unprepossessing building amid random coffeehouses. Here he would sit incognito, talk to the people and feel the pulse of the street. Sitting near the same place today (a renovated traditional building without signage may mark the spot), with old men nodding over their mint teas, city types trotting to work, merchants hauling their wares to the souq and groups of women strolling in the shade, it's easy to see why he chose this spot.

or Muslim countries, with large volumes of Egyptian labourers, Iranian professionals and over a million Palestinian refugees, who arrived after the creation of the state of Israel in 1948. Arab nationalities now make up less than 15% of the expat population, with large numbers of Palestinians, in particular, having been forced to return to their country of origin – a bitter phrase in the circumstances. As Yasser Arafat was widely regarded as a supporter of the invasion, all Palestinians were tarred with the same brush; some were even court-martialled on charges of collaboration.

Today Kuwait resembles other parts of the Gulf in its mix of mainly Indian and Filipino immigrants. Alas, a two-tier society appears to have developed, wherein some immigrant workers (Filipino maids, in particular) are engaged in virtual slave labour. Talk to many Pakistani or Indian traders, taxi drivers, pump attendants or restaurant workers, however, and they evince a warmth towards the country that is somewhat surprising to the Western bystander. In comparison with other countries in the region, Kuwait has a relatively small Western expat population, working almost exclusively in higher-paid professions.

Religion

Most Kuwaitis are Sunni Muslims, though there is a substantial Shiite minority. During the 1980s there was considerable tension, mostly inspired by Iran, between the two communities, a worry that has returned with sectarian violence over the border in Iraq.

Before the Iraqi invasion, Kuwait was still governed by a strict code of conduct, steered by a devout following of Islam. The invasion shook belief in all kinds of areas, including religious observance. Materialism is beginning to exert as strong an influence on the young as religion used to affect the customs and manners of their Bedouin or seafaring ancestors. Kuwaiti society certainly can't be described as permissive, but the veil in many areas of social exchange is discernibly slipping.

A tolerance towards other religions is evinced through the provision of services at Coptic, Anglican, Evangelical and Orthodox churches in Kuwait City. Kuwait is the only Gulf country to have a strong relationship with the Roman Catholic Church.

Environment

The Land

It has to be said that Kuwait is not the most well-endowed patch of earth, in terms of the sublime or the picturesque. The interior consists of a mostly flat, gravelly plain with little or no ground water. Its saving grace is the grassy fringe that greens up prettily across much of the plain late in the spring, providing rich grazing for the few remaining Bedu who keep livestock. The only other geographic feature of any note in a country that measures 185km from north to south and 208km from east to west is Mutla Ridge, just north of Kuwait City. The coast has a little more character, with dunes, marshes and salt depressions around Kuwait Bay and an oasis in Al Jahra.

Of the nine offshore islands, the largest is Bubiyan Island, while Failaka Island is the most historic: there are plans afoot to develop a container port on the former and a vast tourist complex on the latter, but at present there's nothing much to see on either island.

Wildlife

The anticlockwise flow of Gulf currents favours Kuwait's shoreline by carrying nutrients from the freshwater marshes of Shatt Al Arab and the delta of the Tigris and Euphrates in southern Iraq. The result is a rich and diverse coastline, with an abundance of marine life that even the poisoning of spilt oil has failed to destroy.

Birding highlights along the mudflats include black-winged stilts, teals, lesser crested terns, huge nesting colonies of Socotra cormorants, and flamingos. Inland, birds of prey, including the resident kestrel and the short-toed eagle, roam the escarpments.

Nocturnal desert creatures (rarely sighted) include caracals, hedgehogs, big-eared fennecs – the smallest canines in the world – and jerboas, which gain all the liquid they need from the plants and insects they eat. It is easier to spot the dhobs, a monitor lizard with a spiny tail, popular as a barbecue snack.

In terms of endangered species, given the events of the past few years, it's remarkable that a few more species have not been added to the list of desert mammals, like the oryx and the gazelle, made regionally extinct through hunting. The desert wolf has

AN ENVIRONMENTAL CATASTROPHE

On 20 January 1991, the third day of the war, Iraqi forces opened the valves at Kuwait's Mina Al Ahmadi Sea Island Terminal, intentionally releasing millions of litres of oil into the Gulf. The resulting oil slick was 64km wide and 160km long. Between six and eight million barrels of oil are thought to have been released, at least twice as much as in any previous oil spill. At least 460km of coastline, most of it in Saudi Arabia and Bahrain, was affected, with devastating consequences for the region's cormorants, migratory birds, dolphins, fish and turtles and large areas of mangroves.

The systematic torching of 699 of the emirate's oil wells contributed to the environmental disaster. By the time the war ended, nearly every well was burning. At a conservative estimate, at least two million barrels of oil per day were lost – equivalent to about 5% of the total daily world consumption. One to two million tonnes of carbon dioxide streamed into the air daily, resulting in a cloud that literally turned day into night across the country.

Like the slick, the fires devastated wildlife throughout the region, but they also had a direct impact on public health. Black, greasy rain caused by the fires was reported as far away as India, and the incidence of asthma increased in the Gulf region.

The slick was fought by experts from nine nations, and oil companies eventually managed to recover, and reuse, around a million barrels of crude oil from the slick. Initial reports that it would take five years to put all the fires out proved pessimistic. A determined international effort, combined with considerable innovation on the part of the firefighters, extinguished the fires in only eight months. The crews did the job so quickly that one well had to be reignited so that the emir of Kuwait could 'put out the final fire' for reporters in November 1991.

Cleaning up the 65 million barrels of oil, spilt in 300 oil lakes covering around 50 sq km of desert, was not so speedily effected. Through a variety of biological processes, which included composting and bioventing, more than 4000 cu metres of contaminated soil were treated, resulting in soil of such high quality that it was good enough for landscaping and could be used as topsoil.

The Japanese Garden in Al Ahmadi is a showcase for the miracle 'oil soil'. The garden's 'blooms of hope' are testament to international cooperation and the ability of humans and nature to combat the worst that disaster can throw at them. The gardens are currently undergoing rejuvenation.

apparently made something of a comeback in recent years and has been spotted near residential areas.

National Parks

Larger than the state of Bahrain, the 863-sq-km nature reserve on the northern end of Bubiyan Island is home to many species of bird and animal. Comprising marshland and creeks, it is a haven for waders. It was heavily mined during the Gulf War and the causeway destroyed. The future could be just as alarming, with a port and residential complex planned for the southern part of the island.

Environmental Issues

While Kuwait shares many of the same environmental concerns as its Gulf neighbours, it has also had to contend with the extraordinary circumstances inflicted by war. Over a decade later, the casual visitor is unlikely to detect any signs of war either in the desert or along the coast. A thorough clean-up by Pakistani and Bangladeshi troops, and subsequent diligence with regard to the removal of unexploded ordnance, means that Kuwaitis can once again enjoy the ritual camping expedition without fear of danger. Perversely, however, it is now the campers who are threatening the environment, with discarded rubbish and overuse of delicate grazing lands. In addition, relaxed standards with regard to waste and oil dumping have led to concerns about polluted seas along Kuwait's shoreline.

Every year on 24 April the country observes Regional Environment Day, with school competitions and raised public awareness regarding marine and land resources.

SURVIVAL GUIDE

Directory A–Z

ACCOMMODATION

Kuwait has a more limited hotel offering than other Gulf cities, but demand is low, so there's usually plenty of choice. At the top end, many of the international chains have hotels here, although prices are aimed at a business clientele and are usually high. It's sometimes worth asking about weekend deals, but these become less common with each passing year. There are few options for budget travellers in Kuwait but some good-value choices in the midrange category.

The northern shore of Kuwait Bay is a popular camping spot with locals: just look for the tents from October to April. Alternatively, there are some good places to camp on the coast near the Saudi Arabian border. Camping equipment is available in the many sporting-goods shops in the city malls. This isn't camping on a budget, mind: a 4WD is necessary to find a suitable spot.

CUSTOMS REGULATIONS

- No alcohol or pork-related products are permitted in the country.
- Up to 500 cigarettes and 500g of tobacco are permitted.
- Duty-free items are for sale at the duty-free shop in the arrivals and departures section of the airport.

EMBASSIES & CONSULATES

Many embassies are in the Diplomatic Area, southeast of the centre in Da'iya.

Bahraini Embassy (Map p90; 2531 8530; Villa 27, Plot 5, Surra St, Surra; 8am-noon Sun-Thu)

Canadian Embassy (Map p90; 2256 3025; www.canadainternational.gc.ca; House 24, Al Mutawakil St, Block 4, Diplomatic Area, Da'iya; 8am-1pm & 1.30-4.30pm Sun-Thu) Adjacent to the Third Ring Rd.

Dutch Embassy (Map p90; 2531 2650; kuwait.nlembassy.org; House 7, Street 11, Block 6, Jabriya; 9am-noon Sun-Thu)

French Embassy (Map p100; 2257 1061; Villa 24, Street 13, Block 1, Mansouria; 8-11am Sun-Thu)

German Embassy (Map p100; 2252 0827; www.kuwait.diplo.de; Villa 13, Street 14, Block 1, Abdullah Al Salim; 9-11am)

Iranian Embassy (Map p90; 2256 0694; Isteghlal St, Block 5, Diplomatic Area, Da'iya; 9am-noon Sun-Thu)

Omani Embassy (Map p90; 2256 1956; Villa 25, Street 3, Block 3, Udailia; 9am-noon Sun-Thu) By the Fourth Ring Rd.

Qatari Embassy (Map p90; 2251 3606; Istiqlal St, Diplomatic Area, Da'iya; 8am-noon Sun-Thu) Off Arabian Gulf St.

Saudi Arabian Embassy (Map p100; 2255 0021; embassies.mofa.gov.sa/sites/Kuwait/EN/Pages/default.aspx; Arabian Gulf St, Da'iya; 9am-3pm Sun-Thu)

UAE Embassy (Map p90; 2252 8544; Plot 70, Istiqlal St, Diplomatic Area, Da'iya; 9am-noon) Off Arabian Gulf St.

UK Embassy (Map p100; 2259 4320; www.gov.uk/government/world/kuwait; Arabian Gulf St, Dasman; 7.30am-3.30pm Sun-Wed, to 1.30pm Thu) West of Kuwait Towers.

US Embassy (Map p90; 2259 1001; kuwait.usembassy.gov; Plot 14, Al Masjid Al Aqsa St, Block 13, Bayan; 8am-4.30pm Sun-Thu) About 17km south of the city centre.

MAPS

GEO Projects publishes a good country map on the reverse of two useful maps of Kuwait City in its Arab World Map Library, available from car-rental offices, hotels and bookshops.

MONEY

The currency used in Kuwait is the Kuwaiti dinar (KD). The dinar is divided into 1000 fils. Coins are worth five, 10, 20, 50 or 100 fils. Notes come in denominations of 250 fils, 500 fils, KD1, KD5, KD10 and KD20. The Kuwaiti dinar is a hard currency and there are no restrictions on taking it into or out of the country.

ATMs & Credit Cards

Visa and Amex are widely accepted in Kuwait, and all major banks accept most credit cards and are linked to the major networks. Most banks accept Visa (Electron and Plus), MasterCard and Cirrus.

Moneychangers

Moneychangers are dotted around the city centre and main souqs, and change all major and regional currencies. Only banks and the larger money-exchange facilities will change travellers cheques, which are rapidly becoming obsolete.

The dinar is no longer pegged to the US dollar, but this has made little difference to exchange rates, which remain consistent from one moneychanger to the next.

SLEEPING PRICE RANGES

The following price ranges refer to a double room with bathroom and air-con. Taxes are included in the price. There are no particularly high or low seasons.

$ less than KD40 (US$142)

$$ KD40–KD75 (US$142–US$266)

$$$ more than KD75 (US$266)

EATING PRICE RANGES

The following price ranges refer to a standard main course. Service charge and tax are included in the price.

$ less than KD5 (US$18)

$$ KD5–KD10 (US$18–US$36)

$$$ more than KD10 (US$36)

Tipping & Bargaining

A tip is only expected in upmarket restaurants, where 10% for service is often already added to the bill. For longer journeys, 10% is a suitable tip for a taxi driver.

Bargaining is de rigueur in Kuwait's souqs but also in many Western-style shops and some hotels. It is always acceptable to ask for a discount on the original price offered, particularly as discounts have generally already been factored into the quoted price.

OPENING HOURS

These opening hours prevail throughout Kuwait.

Banks 8am to 1pm and 5pm to 7.30pm Sunday to Thursday.

Government offices 7am to 2pm (summer), 7.30am to 2.30pm (winter) Sunday to Thursday.

Internet cafes 8am to 10pm.

Post offices 8am to 1pm Sunday to Thursday.

Restaurants 11am to 3pm and 7pm to 11pm.

Shopping centres 10am to 10pm.

Shops 8.30am to 12.30pm and 4pm to 7pm or 8pm Saturday to Thursday.

PHOTOGRAPHY

- Feel free to photograph obvious 'tourist' sites, such as the Kuwait Towers or the Red Fort in Al Jahra.
- Avoid aiming a camera at military installations, embassies or palaces.
- Avoid taking pictures of people without seeking their permission first.
- Refrain from taking photographs of local women – this is considered haram (forbidden).

PUBLIC HOLIDAYS

In addition to the main Islamic holidays, Kuwait celebrates three public holidays:

New Year's Day 1 January

National Day 25 February

Liberation Day 26 February

SAFE TRAVEL

Traffic accidents The many spectacularly twisted bits of metal left by the roadside are testament to the fact that Kuwait has one of the highest road-accident rates in the world. Indeed, one third of all deaths in Kuwait are driving-related. The horrifying scenes on TV have not deterred Kuwait's drivers, despite government efforts to slow the pace down with radar surveillance – the mixture of high speed and drivers talking on their phones is an awful combination. As such, it's hard to recommend driving in Kuwait unless you're confident of holding your own in the face of sheer lunacy. A police sign at traffic lights speaks volumes: 'Crossing the red signal leads to death or prison'.

Discarded ordnance Although the country has now been cleared of mines after the Gulf War, you should still remember *not to pick up any unfamiliar object* in the desert and to stick to established tracks.

Terrorism In June 2015, a suicide bomber attacked a Shiite mosque in a suburb of Kuwait City, killing 27 people and injuring more than 220. Although such attacks are rare, it did prompt warnings from foreign governments that more attacks could take place, although the warning applied to the broader Gulf region rather than Kuwait in particular. Check government-travel-advisory websites for updates before committing to a visit.

TELEPHONE

Some useful telephone information:

- Country code: ☎965 plus local eight-digit number.
- No area codes.
- International access code (to call abroad from Kuwait): ☎00.
- Local calls are free.

Mobile Phones

Users of mobile phones can link into the GSM services of Wataniya or Zain. Prepaid SIM cards are widely available in malls and from Zain (there's a booth at the airport).

VISAS

Visas on arrival Available at Kuwait International Airport for nationals of 52 countries, including Australia, Canada, the EU, New Zealand and the USA (KD3; valid for 90 days; 30-day maximum stay). Take a number from the Fast Service Desk and buy stamps worth KD3 from the neighbouring machine (free for British, Italian, Norwegian and US passport holders). There's no need to wait again at the immigration desk downstairs, where you'll be waved through. Keep the piece of paper that you're given with the visa – you'll need to present it upon departure.

Israeli or Iraqi connections Anyone holding a passport containing an Israeli or Iraqi stamp may be refused entry to Kuwait.

Multiple-entry visas Only available for business requirements (valid for 12 months; apply in advance).

Visa Extensions

Up to two one-month visa extensions are possible, but they're a pain as you'll need to make an application to the **Immigration Department** (Map p90; 28 Street, Shuwaikh) before the existing visa expires. Alternatively, hop on a plane to Bahrain for the weekend and re-enter on a new visa. There is a hefty fine (KD10 per day) for overstaying once the visa has expired.

WOMEN TRAVELLERS

Women travellers may find the increased attention from men in Kuwait a nuisance. From being tailgated while driving to being followed around shopping centres, expat women are frequently the target of harassment. Even if you dress conservatively, and refuse to respond to approaches from and avoid eye contact with men, it's still hard to avoid attracting unwanted attention.

Generally, if the situation becomes uncomfortable, the best way to defuse it is to stop being an object and become a person: this can be accomplished by turning towards the men in question and addressing them frostily (all the better in Arabic). Ask the offending parties where they come from and to which family they belong. This is usually so unexpected and traumatising for these men that the threat disappears.

For more information for women travelling in the region, see p439.

Getting There & Away

AIR

Kuwait International Airport (Map p90; ✆flight information 161; www.dgca.gov.kw) Kuwait International Airport is long overdue for an upgrade. Visas are obtained from a counter on the upper storey of the airport (take a ticket and wait), and then you descend to passport control and baggage claim. Given the limited attractions of the airport and the heavy smoking of regional users, waiting around for a flight can seem like a long time.

Jazeera Airways (✆177; www.jazeeraairways.com; Kuwait International Airport) Kuwait has a no-frills private carrier called Jazeera Airways with flights to 30 destinations within the Middle East and the Indian subcontinent.

LAND

Border Crossings

Kuwait has borders with Iraq (currently closed to visitors) and Saudi Arabia. The crossings with Saudi Arabia are at Al Nuwaisib (for Dammam) and Al Salmy (for Riyadh). You must have a valid visa for Saudi Arabia or a transit visa, an onward ticket and a visa for your next destination beyond Saudi's borders before you can cross the border. You cannot obtain these at the border.

Bus

Kuwait Public Transport Company (KPTC; ✆2232 8501; www.kptc.com.kw) KPTC operates comfortable, modern buses to a number of destinations beyond Kuwait's borders – you'll need all the relevant visas (ie to Saudi Arabia) before buying a ticket. Agents specialising in these tickets are located in the area around the main bus station.

Saptco (www.saptco.com.sa) Modern, air-con buses, operated by Saudi bus company Saptco and handled in Kuwait by the **Kuwait & Gulf Transport Company** (✆2484

PRACTICALITIES

Magazines International glossy magazines, complete with large tracts of blackened text courtesy of the government censor, or even with pages torn out, are sometimes available from hotels, but they're not as common as elsewhere in the Gulf.

Newspapers The *Arab Times*, *Kuwait Times* and *Daily Star* are Kuwait's three English-language newspapers. They include useful 'what's on' listings. International newspapers are available (usually a day or two late) at major hotels.

Radio Radio Kuwait – also known locally as the Superstation – broadcasts on 99.7FM; it plays mostly rock and roll, with some local news and features. The US military's Armed Forces Radio & TV Service (AFRTS) can be heard on 107.9FM; it broadcasts a mixture of music, news and chat shows.

TV Kuwait TV's Channel 2 broadcasts programs in English each evening from around 2pm to midnight. Many hotels, even the smaller ones, have satellite TV.

Smoking Much more prevalent than in neighbouring Gulf countries on buses, in taxis, at the airport, and in restaurants and hotel rooms.

Weights and measures Kuwait uses the metric system.

9355), travel between Kuwait and Dammam (Saudi Arabia). The trip takes six hours and costs around KD8.

SEA

Speedboat services leave from Shuwaikh Port for the five-hour trip to Manama in Bahrain. The easiest way to book tickets for these services is through one of the city travel agents.

Combined Shipping Company (Map p90; ☎2483 0889; www.cscq8.com; 1st fl, office 119, Kuwait Port Authority Bldg, Jamal Abdul Nasser St, Shuwaikh) The Combined Shipping Company operates a return service twice a week from Kuwait's Shuwaikh Port to the Iranian port of Bushehr. Prices vary depending on the seasons. You can book online at www.irantravelingcenter.com.

Getting Around

BOAT

Kuwait Public Transport Company Ferries (p108) go to Failaka Island from Kuwait City.

Nuzha Touristic Enterprises (☎2575 5825; www.nuzhatours.com) runs half- and whole-day boat trips.

BUS

Kuwait has a cheap and extensive local bus system, but it's designed for the convenience of residents rather than tourists. The routes therefore don't often coincide with the places of tourist interest. Nonetheless, if a 10-minute walk either side of the bus stop isn't a problem, pick up a bus timetable from the main bus station in the city centre or on the bus.

Most bus routes are operated by the **Kuwait Public Transport Company** (p107), which has air-conditioned and comfortable vehicles. Intercity trips cost just a few fils per ride. The **City Bus** (p107) alternative follows KPTC routes but isn't quite as reliable. Both services are used primarily by lower-income workers travelling to their place of work.

CAR & MOTORCYCLE

If you have an International Driving Permit (IDP), or a licence and residence permit from another Gulf country, driving in Kuwait is possible, without any further paperwork, for the duration of your visa.

Hire

Car-rental costs range from KD10 (for a Toyota Corolla) to KD30 (for a Toyota Prado) per day. This rate usually includes unlimited kilometres and full insurance. Given the very high incidence of traffic accidents in Kuwait, it is worth paying the extra for fully comprehensive insurance.

Al Mulla (☎2444 8590; www.autoalmulla.com) Al Mulla is one of the better local agencies, with desks at the airport and in many of the city hotels.

LOCAL TRANSPORT

Taxi

Taxis are a useful and popular way of getting around, though they are comparatively expensive when travelling outside the city area, when costs can increase to KD10 per hour. If you want to do some exploring around Kuwait by taxi, it's better to agree on a half- or full-day rate in advance.

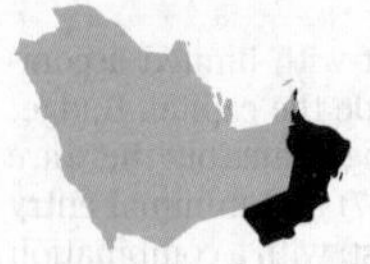

Oman عمان

Includes ➡

Why Go?

In Muscat's Grand Mosque, there is a beautiful hand-loomed carpet; it was once the world's largest rug until Abu Dhabi's Grand Mosque, in the United Arab Emirates, pinched the record. This is poignant because Oman doesn't boast many 'firsts' or 'biggests' in a region bent on grand-standing. What it does boast, with its rich heritage and embracing society, is a strong sense of identity, a pride in an ancient, frankincense-trading past and confidence in a highly educated future.

For visitors, this offers a rare chance to engage with the Arab world without the distorting lens of excessive wealth. Oman's low-rise towns retain their traditional charms and Bedouin values remain at the heart of an Omani welcome. With an abundance of natural beauty, from spectacular mountains, wind-blown deserts and a pristine coastline, Oman is the obvious choice for those seeking out the modern face of Arabia while wanting still to sense its ancient soul.

Best for Culture

- ➡ Bahla Fort (p179)
- ➡ National Museum (p131)
- ➡ Mutrah Souq (p127)
- ➡ Rustaq Fort (p185)
- ➡ Bayt al Zubair (p131)

Best for Nature

- ➡ Jebel Shams (p177)
- ➡ Sharqiya Sands (p165)
- ➡ Wadi Dharbat (p202)
- ➡ Ras al Jinz (p156)
- ➡ Wadi Shab (p154)

When to Go

Oman

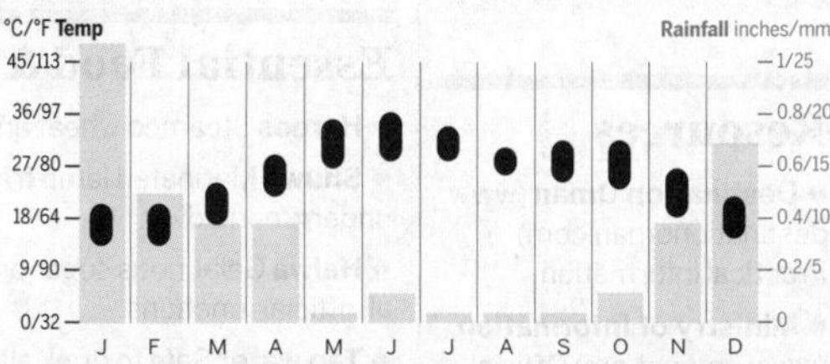

Jan–Feb Muscat Festival brings cultural shows and shopping to the capital.

Jul–Aug Salalah Tourism Festival celebrates the rainy season with entertainment and shopping.

Nov–Mar Balmy temperatures herald the high season for tourism.

AT A GLANCE

- **Currency** Omani rial (OR)
- **Mobile Phones** SIM cards widely available.
- **Money** ATMs widespread; credit cards widely accepted.
- **Visas** Available on arrival for many nationalities.

Fast Facts

- **Capital** Muscat
- **Country code** ☎968
- **Language** Arabic; English widely spoken
- **Population** 4.2 million

Exchange Rates

For current exchange rates see www.xe.com.

Australia	A$10	OR2.7
Bahrain	BD1	OR1
Euro zone	€10	OR4.2
Kuwait	KD1	OR1.3
Qatar	QR10	OR1
Saudi Arabia	SR10	OR1
UAE	Dh10	OR1
UK	UK£10	OR6
USA	US$10	OR3.8

Resources

- **Destination Oman** (www.destinationoman.com) Practical information.
- **Ministry of Information** (www.omanet.om) Official handbook of facts and figures.
- **Oman Tourism** (www.omantourism.gov.om) Official tourist website.

Daily Costs

Oman is an expensive country to visit with limited accommodation and transport options outside the capital. Budget accommodation averages US$70 for single rates but there are cheap options for eating (around US$7) and minimal entry fees to many of the main sites of interest; with a combination of public transport and taxi, a minimum daily cost comes to around US$130. This rises to US$250 staying in midrange hotels with car hire and US$500 for top-end with 4WD hire.

ITINERARIES

Muscat Stopover

Rise with the dawn to see fishermen bring in the weird and wonderful at Mutrah's **fish market**. Stroll the **corniche** and then duck into **Mutrah Souq** to lose your way among the pink, plastic and implausible. Spare an hour for the sights of **Muscat** proper, the walled heart of the capital, before a spot of respite at the **Shangri-La's Barr Al Jissah Resort & Spa**.

Two Weeks

Begin a mountain tour in the old city of **Nizwa**. Climb the beanstalk to **Jebel Akhdar**, famed for giant pomegranates and hailstones. Hike the rim of Oman's Grand Canyon for a spot of carpet-buying on **Jebel Shams**. Engage with *jinn* (genies) at the remarkable tombs and forts of **Bat**, **Bahla** and **Jabrin**. Take the long way home to Muscat via a dizzying mountain drive to **Rustaq**, and wash the dust off in the sparkling sea at **Sawadi**.

Three Weeks

Travel an adventurous route from Muscat to Oman's second city, Salalah, 1000km to the south. Follow the coast road to **Sur**, exploring the wadis (dry river beds) of **Shab** and **Tiwi**. Learn about turtles at **Ras al Jinz** before cutting inland to the **Sharqiya Sands** near Al Mintirib. Acclimatise to nights under the stars before the camping journey to Salalah via **Duqm**. Leave time to explore **Salalah** with its beautiful beaches, blowholes and frankincense.

Essential Food & Drink

- **Harees** Steamed wheat and boiled meat.
- **Shuwa** Marinated lamb traditionally cooked in an underground oven.
- **Halwa** Gelatinous sugar or date-syrup confection served at all official functions.
- **Tap water** Safe to drink although most people stick to bottled water.
- **Alcohol** Available at hotels and tourist-oriented restaurants.
- **Coffee** Laced with cardamom and served with dates, it's an essential part of Omani hospitality.

MUSCAT مسقط

☎24 / POP 1.2 MILLION

Muscat is a port the like of which cannot be found in the whole world where there is business and good things that cannot be found elsewhere.

Ahmed bin Majid al Najdi

As the great Arab navigator Ahmed bin Majid al Najdi recognised in 1490 AD, Muscat, even to this day, has a character quite different from neighbouring capitals. There are few high-rise blocks, and even the most functional building is required to reflect tradition with a dome or an arabesque window. The result of these strict building policies is an attractive, spotlessly clean and whimsically uniform city – not much different in essence from the 'very elegant town with very fine houses' that the Portuguese admiral Afonso de Albuquerque observed as he sailed towards Muscat in the 16th century.

Muscat means 'safe anchorage', and the sea continues to constitute a major part of the city: it brings people on cruise ships and goods in containers to the historic ports of Old Muscat and Mutrah. It contributes to the city's economy through the onshore refinery near Qurm, and provides a livelihood for fishermen along the beaches of Shatti al Qurm and Athaiba. More recently, it has also become a source of recreation at Bandar Jissah and Shatti al Qurm, taking advantage of the sandy beaches that stretch almost without interruption from Muscat to the border with the United Arab Emirates (UAE), over 200km to the northwest.

The opening of the Royal Opera House in 2011, with performances of acclaim from around the world, has helped place Muscat on an international stage and highlighted it as a forward-thinking, progressive city. With the imminent opening of a fine new national museum in Mutrah and the promise of new luxury hotels in the award-winning Al Mouj development near the airport, Muscat continues to be a beacon for those who live in the interior and a model of understated calm in a region of hyperbole.

History

Muscat became the capital of Oman in 1793, and the focus of the country's great seafaring empire of the 18th and 19th centuries. Having been party to the control of much of the coast of East Africa, its 20th-century descent into international oblivion, under Sultan Said bin Taimur, was all the more poignant. The tide is turning on history, however, and the capital is once more at the centre of life in Oman.

Perhaps the first documented reference to Muscat is by the 2nd-century geographer Ptolemy who mentioned a 'concealed harbour', placing the sea at the centre of Muscat's identity where it remains today. In fact, surrounded on three sides by mountains, it remained all but inaccessible from the land for centuries and the Arab tribes from Yemen who supposedly first settled the area almost certainly approached from the sea.

A small port in the 14th and 15th centuries, Muscat gained importance as a freshwater staging post, but it was eclipsed by the busier port of Sohar – something the people of Sohar's Batinah region hope may well happen again. By the beginning of the 16th century, Muscat was a trading port in its own right, used by merchant ships bound for India. Inevitably it attracted the attention of the Portuguese, who conquered the town in 1507. The city walls were constructed at this time (a refurbished set remains in the same positions), but neither they nor the two Portuguese forts of Mirani and Jalali could prevent the Omani reconquest of the town in 1650 – an event that effectively ended the Portuguese era in the Gulf.

Muscat became a backwater for much of the 20th century and the city gates remained resolutely locked and bolted against the encroachments of the outside world until 1970. Under the auspices of the current Sultan Qaboos, the city reawakened. To facilitate the growing number of cars needing access to the city, a hole was driven through the city walls. Goods and services flooded in and Muscat flooded out to occupy the surrounding coastline. Touchingly, the city gates continued to be locked at a specific time every evening, despite the adjacent hole in the wall, until the gates were replaced with an archway. In many respects, that little act of remembrance is a fitting metaphor for a city that has given access to modern conveniences while it continues to keep the integrity of its traditional character.

Sights

Wedged into a relatively narrow strip of land between the mountains and the sea, Muscat comprises a long string of suburbs spanning

Oman Highlights

1 Haggling with carpet sellers of **Jebel Shams** (p177) on a precipice above Wadi Ghul.

2 Surveying the flat panorama of the Batinah region from the battlements of **Nakhal Fort** (p184).

3 Rambling around the battlements of **Bahla Fort** (p179), a Unesco World Heritage Site.

4 Putting your driving and navigational skills to the test in the dunes of **Sharqiya Sands** (p165).

5 Attending the night-time drama of labour and delivery in **Ras al Jinz** (p157), a favourite turtle-nesting site.

6 Exploring subtropical **Salalah** (p194), a region famed for gold,

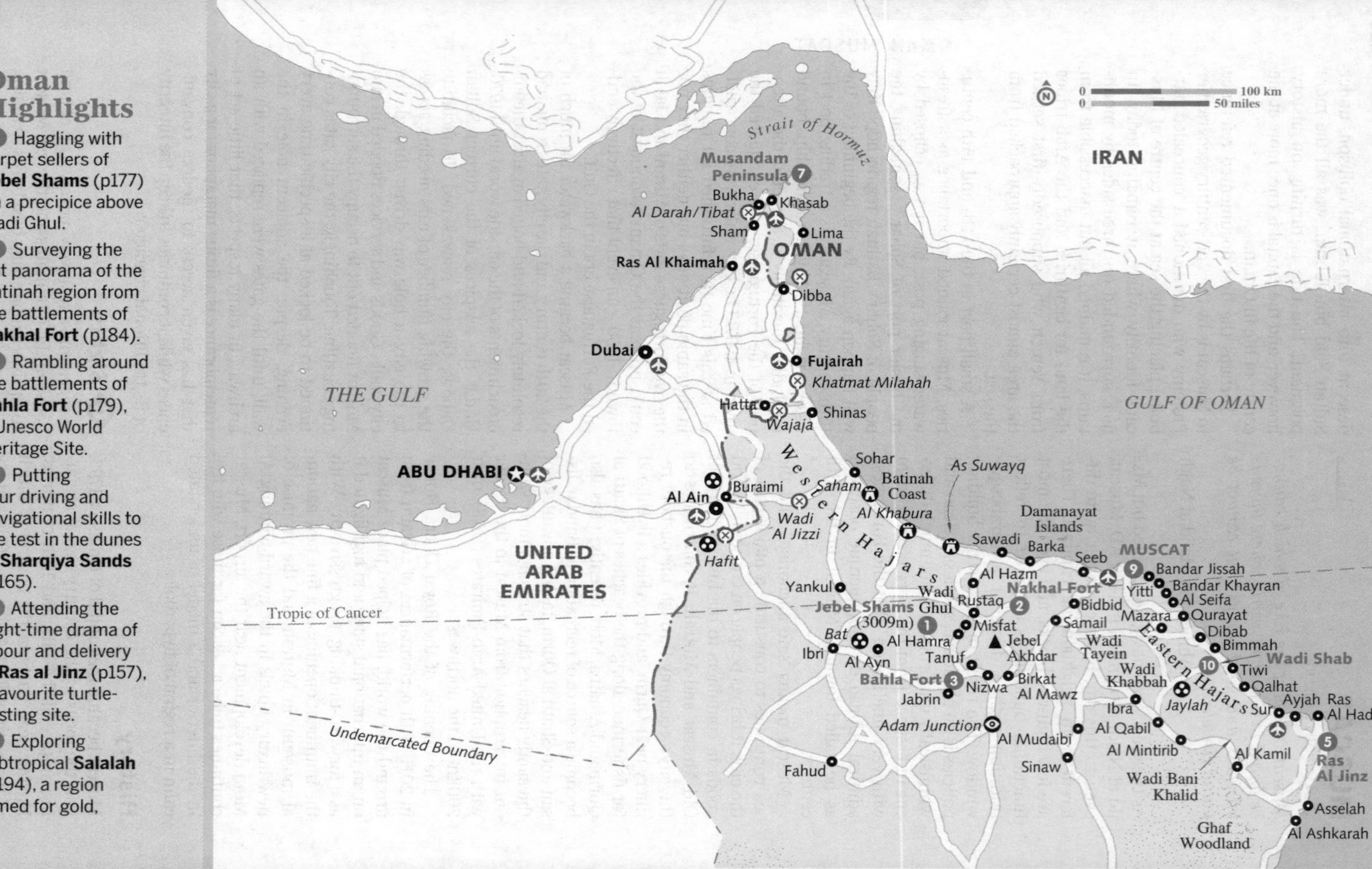

frankincense and myrrh.

7 Going round the bend on a dhow in a **Musandam** (p188) inlet.

8 Camping on a **Masirah** (p159) beach for the ultimate desert island experience.

9 Bargaining for copper pots and gold bangles in Muscat's labyrinthine **Mutrah Souq** (p127).

10 Splashing through the pools of **Wadi Shab** (p154) to the tune of croaking toads.

Greater Muscat

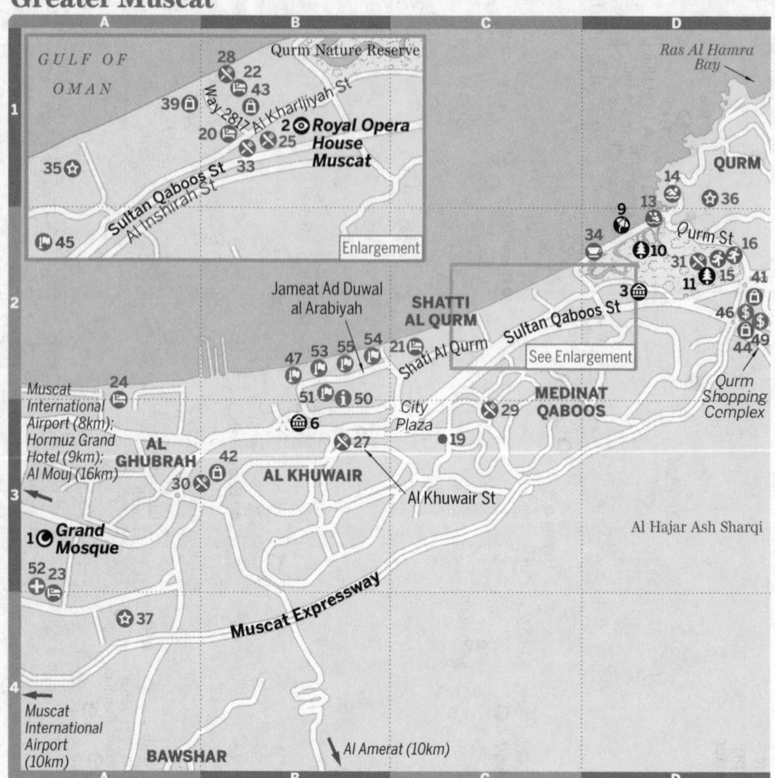

a distance of 50km or so from the airport to Al Bustan. Visiting the sights can therefore take a bit of planning, and during rush-hour periods (7am to 8.30am, 12.30pm to 3.30pm and 5.30pm to 7pm Sunday to Thursday) you may need to add an extra 45 minutes to get to your destination.

Muscat is sometimes referred to as the 'three cities': Ruwi, Mutrah and old Muscat (a small area with few shops and no hotels, comprising the diwan – palace administration – and many of the capital's sights of interest). The neighbouring port of Mutrah has the most budget accommodation, while shopping centres and transport terminals are in the commercial district of Ruwi and in the suburbs with their lovely beaches. A new development, called Al Mouj (meaning 'The Wave' in English), is fast becoming a new social hub for the city. It is a 10-minute taxi ride from the airport.

Mutrah مطرح

Mutrah's main sites are clustered along the corniche, which runs from the fish roundabout to Kalbuh Bay Park, about 4.5km east.

★ Mutrah Corniche CORNICHE

(Map p130) Mutrah stretches along an attractive corniche of latticed buildings and mosques; it looks spectacular at sunset when the light casts shadows across a serrated crescent of mountains, while pavements, lights and fountains invite an evening stroll or a bike ride (p135).

Despite being the capital's main port area, Mutrah feels like a fishing village and the daily catch continues to be delivered to the **fish market**, by the Marina Hotel, from sunrise every day. A lengthy refurbishment of the market is nearing completion as part of a larger initiative to relocate the industrial elements of the port and redevelop the dock-

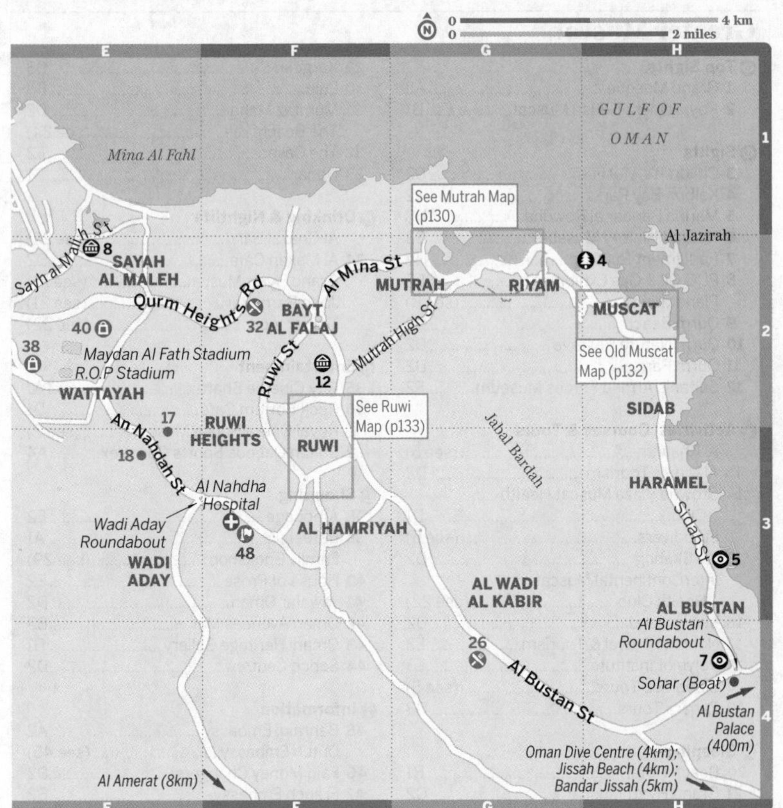

side for tourism. This will provide a permanent home for *Shabab Oman*, the country's magnificent fully rigged training ship, which is soon to be retired now that its replacement has been commissioned. In the meantime, the harbour is home to His Majesty's dhow, visiting cruise ships, the high speed ferry to Musandam and assorted naval vessels.

Bait al Baranda MUSEUM

(Map p130; ☎24 714262; http://baitalbaranda.mm.gov.om/; Al Mina St, Mutrah; adult/child OR1/500 baisa; ⏲9am-1pm & 4-6pm Sat-Thu) Housed in a renovated 1930s residence, this museum traces the history – and prehistory – of Muscat through imaginative, interactive displays and exhibits. A 'cut-and-paste' dinosaur, using bones found in Al Khoud area of Muscat and topped up with borrowed bones from international collections, is worth a look. The ethnographic displays help set not just Muscat but the whole of Oman in a regional, commercial and cultural context. The ground floor of the museum is used as an exhibition space.

★Mutrah Souq SOUQ

(Map p130; Mutrah Corniche, Mutrah; ⏲8am-1pm & 5-9pm Sat-Thu, 5-9pm Fri) Many people come to Mutrah Corniche just to visit the souq, which retains the chaotic interest of a traditional Arab market albeit housed under modern timber roofing. Shops selling Omani and Indian artefacts together with a few antiques jostle among more traditional textile, hardware and jewellery stores. Bargaining is expected although discounts tend to be small. Cards are generally accepted in most shops, but bring cash for better deals. The main entry is via the corniche, opposite the pedestrian traffic lights.

The traditional coffeehouse at the souq's entrance is a rare relic from the past and a locals-only meeting point for elderly men. Take care not to wander into the historic

Greater Muscat

Top Sights
1 Grand Mosque A3
2 Royal Opera House Muscat B1

Sights
3 Children's Museum D2
4 Kalbuh Bay Park H2
5 Marina Bandar al Rowdha H3
6 Natural History Museum B3
7 Parliament Building H4
8 PDO Oil & Gas Exhibition E2
Planetarium ..... (see 8)
9 Qurm Beach D2
10 Qurm Nature Reserve D2
11 Qurm Park D2
12 Sultan's Armed Forces Museum F2

Activities, Courses & Tours
Al Khayran ..... (see 5)
13 Al Nimer Tourism D2
14 Crowne Plaza Muscat Health Club D1
Eurodivers ..... (see 5)
15 Ice Skating D2
InterContinental Muscat Health Club ..... (see 22)
16 Marah Land D2
17 National Travel & Tourism E3
18 Polyglot Institute E3
Sidab Sea Tours ..... (see 5)
19 Zahara Tours C3

Sleeping
20 Beach Hotel B1
21 Grand Hyatt Muscat C2
22 Hotel InterContinental Muscat B1
23 Majan Continental Hotel A4
24 The Chedi A3

Eating
25 Al Angham B1
26 Al Daleh Restaurant G4
Al Fair Supermarket ..... (see 29)
27 Bin Ateeq B3
Blue Marlin Restaurant ..... (see 5)
28 D'Arcy's Kitchen B1
29 Kargeen Cafe C3
30 Lulu B3
31 Mumtaz Mahal D2
The Beach ..... (see 24)
32 The Cave F2
33 Ubhar B1

Drinking & Nightlife
Al Ghazal Bar ..... (see 22)
34 Al Makan Cafe D2
Grand Hyatt Muscat ..... (see 21)
John Barry Bar ..... (see 21)
Trader Vic's ..... (see 22)

Entertainment
35 City Cinema Shatti A1
36 Rock Bottom Café D1
Royal Opera House Muscat ..... (see 2)
37 Sultan Qaboos Sports Complex A4

Shopping
38 Amouage E2
39 Bateel A1
Family Bookshop ..... (see 29)
40 House of Prose E2
41 Jawahir Oman D2
42 Oman Avenues Mall B3
43 Omani Heritage Gallery B1
44 Sabco Centre D2

Information
45 Bahraini Embassy A2
Dutch Embassy ..... (see 45)
46 Faiq Money Changers D2
47 French Embassy B2
48 German Embassy F3
49 HSBC D2
Jordanian Embassy ..... (see 53)
Kuwaiti Embassy ..... (see 53)
50 Ministry of Tourism B2
51 Qatari Embassy B2
52 Royal Hospital A3
Saudi Arabian Embassy ..... (see 51)
53 UAE Embassy B2
54 UK Embassy B2
55 US Embassy B2

Shiite district of Al Lawataya by mistake, as the settlement is walled for a good purpose. A sign under the archway requests that visitors keep out.

Navigating the souq takes a bit of practice. You enter by going slightly uphill away from the sea. If you keep turning right at each junction, you will of course come back to the sea. If in doubt, head downhill. That said, getting lost inside the souq is part of the fun. A right fork at the first junction and a left at Muscat Pharmacy *should* lead you to an Aladdin's Cave of a bead shop and Al Ahli Coffeeshop, famed for its fresh juices, but then again...

Mutrah Gold Souq SOUQ
(Map p130; Mutrah Corniche, Mutrah; ⊙ 8am-1pm & 5-9pm Sat-Thu, 5-9pm Fri) If you're visiting Mutrah Souq (p127), don't miss a stroll through the narrow alleys that house the glittering gold shops. The bridal gold, worked into bibs, buckles and belts, may not be to everyone's taste, but the sheer accumulation of treasure in the shop windows

is exciting on the eye. To find the gold souq, enter Mutrah Souq via the main entry off Mutrah Corniche, turn right immediately through the textile shops and turn left just before re-entering the corniche.

If you feel comfortable getting lost, the alleyways behind the main gold souq are home to shops selling precious stones and silver. This is where monocled old men with beards sit in a muddle of uncut, semi-precious stones, making and mending rings and pendants in designs that are as old as the hands that craft them.

Mutrah Fort FORT

(Map p130) Built by the Portuguese in the 1580s, this fort dominates the eastern end of the harbour. Used for military purposes, it is generally closed to visitors although you can scale the flank of the fort for a good view of the ocean.

Ghalya Museum of Modern Art MUSEUM

(Map p130; ☎24 711640; www.ghalyasmuseum.com; Mutrah Corniche, Mutrah; adult/child OR1/500 baisa; ⏲9.30am-6pm Sat-Thu) This delightful little museum, which encompasses both a modern art gallery and an old furnished house, encapsulates something of the excitement of the new, tinged with the sadness of a pre-Renaissance world that has so quickly been left behind. The house unfolds like a puzzle, wrapped around a tiny central courtyard, and seems to occupy more space than logic allows.

The exhibits on display, many of which are preserved from the 1950s to mid-1970s, are centred on the private memorabilia of the family that once occupied this shore-side house. As such, the box of Kraft cheese and old biscuit tins in the former kitchen are as evocative of this bygone era as the beautifully crafted doors from East Africa that decorate the cosy interior.

Al Riyam Park PARK

(Map p130; Mutrah Corniche, Mutrah; ⏲4-11pm Sun-Thu, 9am-midnight Fri & Sat) Beyond Mutrah Fort, the corniche leads to the leafy Al Riyam Park, with fine views of the harbour from the giant, ornamental incense burner. There is a small fun fair popular with local residents at weekends. The park is on the path of a popular hike that used to link Mutrah with Muscat proper.

Watchtower TOWER

(Map p130) The restored Portuguese watchtower on a promontory out to sea, halfway along Mutrah Corniche, affords a view of the ocean and the grand sweep of Mutrah's waterfront. The area is a popular place to catch the evening breeze and is decorated with colourful fountains at night. Free bike hire is available from here in the evenings.

Kalbuh Bay Park PARK

(Map p126; Mutrah Corniche; ⏲4-11pm Sun-Thu, 9am-midnight Fri & Sat) Kalbuh Bay Park juts into a sea that's boiling with sardines. Located at the end of the corniche, it makes

MUTRAH SOUQ

Describing Mutrah's attractions, a local said 'you must visit the souq-or-market'. Thinking he said 'supermarket', it was a surprise to find a warren of alleyways with no checkouts – but there are some similarities. For a start, just when you thought you'd fathomed where to find the frankincense, you find that alleyway now stocks Thai clothing. Secondly, though you fully intended to look for a present for a favourite aunt, you came out with a toy helicopter, two melamine trays and an armful of fairy lights instead. Thirdly, even though you definitely didn't want to buy a *dishdasha* (man's shirt-dress), there was a special offer for three. And finally, although all alleyways seem to be heading for the exit, you can't actually get out.

Mind you, getting a little lost is part of the fun of the souq, as that is the most likely time you'll stumble on the 'special offers'. And Mutrah Souq has plenty of those – like the old picture frames, complete with woodworm, from the wood-crafting town of Ibra; antique *mandoos* (wedding chests) with brand-new thumbtacks brought down from the Hajar Mountains; rope-twined muskets that saw action in the Dhofar wars of the 1970s; an alleyway of sandals that complete the men's smart Omani costume; and another of aluminium serving dishes for the traditional Omani *shuwa* (marinated lamb cooked in an underground oven).

In summary, from a camel with an illuminated hump to a mosque alarm clock, Mutrah Souq sells all the things you never wanted but can afford to buy (plus a few you did and can't) and is an experience not to be missed.

Mutrah

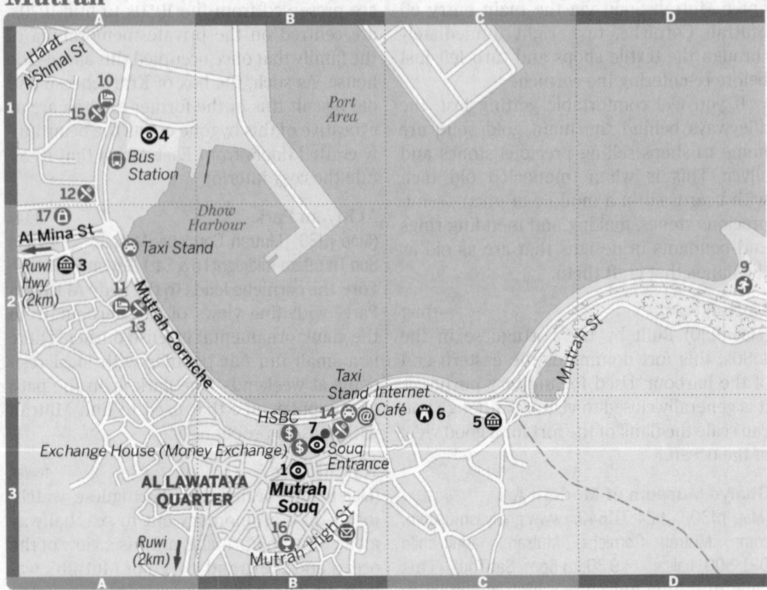

Mutrah

Top Sights
1 Mutrah Souq B3

Sights
2 Al Riyam Park F2
3 Bait al Baranda A2
4 Fish Market A1
5 Ghalya Museum of Modern Art C3
6 Mutrah Fort C3
7 Mutrah Gold Souq B3
8 Watchtower F1

Activities, Courses & Tours
9 Obike D2

Sleeping
10 Marina Hotel A1
11 Naseem Hotel A2

Eating
Al Boom & Dolphin Bar .... (see 10)
12 Bait al Luban A1
13 Cafe Chef A A2
14 Fastfood 'n' Juice Centre B3
15 La Brasserie A1

Drinking & Nightlife
16 Al Ahli Coffeeshop B3

Shopping
17 Ahmed Dawood Trading A2

a good pausing place on a hike between Mutrah and old Muscat. Swimming on the public beach is possible for those not afraid of attracting an audience.

Old Muscat

The tiny, open-gated city of Muscat, home to the Sultan's palace and the diwan (royal court), sits cradled in a natural harbour surrounded by a jagged spine of hills. Lying at the end of Mutrah Corniche, it makes a fascinating place to spend half a day with several sights of interest, including the new National Museum.

★ Sultan's Palace PALACE

(Al Alam; Map p132; off Al Saidiya St, Old Muscat) If you stand by the harbour wall on Mirani St, the building to the right with the delightful mushroom pillars in blue and gold is the Sultan's Palace. On the inland side, an avenue of palm trees leads to a roundabout surrounded by grand royal court buildings and the new national museum. Although the palace is closed to the public, you can pause in front of the gates, at the end of the colonnaded approach, for a quintessential photograph.

The palace was built over the site of the former British embassy where there used to

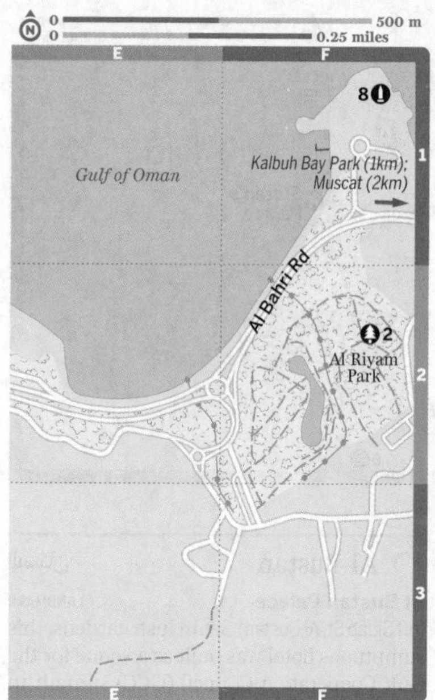

be the stump of a flagpole in the grounds: the story goes that any slave (Oman was infamous for its slave trade from East Africa) who touched the flagpole was granted freedom. The palace today is largely used for ceremonial purposes as Sultan Qaboos favours a quieter, seaside residence near Seeb.

National Museum MUSEUM

(Map p132; Al Saidiya St, Old Muscat; admission residents/tourists OR1/5) Housed in an imposing new building in the heart of Old Muscat, the National Museum makes a fitting consort for the Sultan's Palace opposite. The emphasis of this long-awaited contemporary museum is on quality rather than quantity, with space, light and height used to enhance the selective displays showcasing the heritage of Oman. Giant screens, Arabic brail and high-tech devices bring the artefacts alive. The museum was officially opened in December 2015.

Al Jalali Fort FORT

(Map p132; www.mhc.gov.om; Old Muscat; ⏲ by permit only) Guarding the entrance to the harbour to the east, Al Jalali Fort was built during the Portuguese occupation in the 1580s on Arab foundations. The fort is accessible only via a steep flight of steps. As such, it made the perfect prison for a number of years, but now it is a museum of Omani heritage. Admission is strictly by permit only – apply to the Ministry of National Heritage and Culture, through the contact page on the ministry website.

During palace military occasions, bagpipers perform from the fort battlements, and the royal dhow and yacht are sailed in full regalia into the harbour. With fireworks reflected in the water, it makes a spectacular sight.

Al Mirani Fort FORT

(Map p132; Old Muscat) Al Mirani Fort was built at the same time as nearby Al Jalali Fort. Although closed to the public, its presence looms large over the harbour and contributes to the iconic view of Muscat captured in 19th-century lithographs.

Al Mirani Fort has a special place in history as it contributed to the fall of the Portuguese. This came about through a curious affair of the heart: legend has it that the Portuguese commander fell for the daughter of a Hindu supplier, who refused the match on religious grounds. On being threatened with ruin, the supplier spent a year apparently preparing for the wedding during which time he worked an elaborate trick on the commander, convincing him that the fort's supplies needed a complete overhaul. Bit by bit he removed all the fort's gunpowder and grain and when the fort was left completely defenceless, he gave the nod to the Omani Imam, Sultan bin Saif, who succeeded in retaking the fort in 1649. The Portuguese were ousted from Muscat soon after and the wedding never took place.

★Bayt al Zubair MUSEUM, GALLERY

(Map p132; ☎24 736688; www.baitalzubairmuseum.com; Al Saidiya St, Old Muscat; adult/child OR2/1; ⏲9.30am-6pm Sat-Thu) In a beautifully restored house, this much-beloved privately owned museum exhibits Omani heritage in thematic displays of traditional handicrafts, furniture, stamps and coins. The museum has recently evolved into the cultural centre of Muscat, hosting many international exhibitions of contemporary art in **Gallery Sarah** within the museum's grounds. A modern cafe, and a shop selling quality souvenirs, usually entice visitors to stay longer than they expected.

If you're visiting the cafe, take a look at the wind tower for an idea of how old buildings in Muscat coped with the heat before the invention of modern air conditioning.

Old Muscat

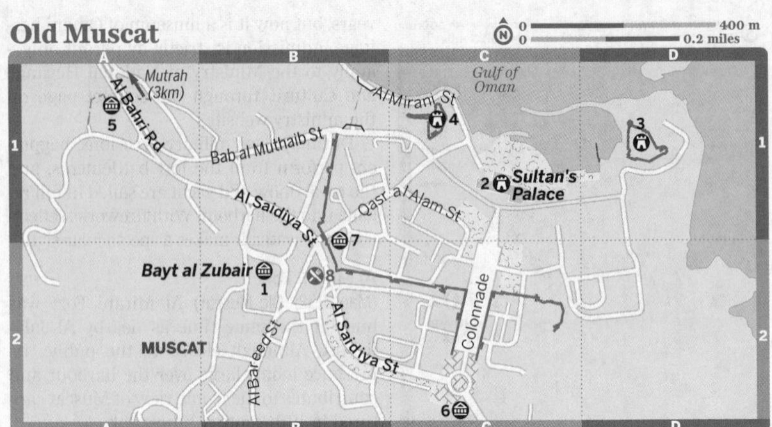

Old Muscat

Omani-French Museum MUSEUM
(Map p132; ☎24 736613; Qasr al Alam St, Old Muscat; adult/child 500/200 baisa; ⏲9am-1pm Sat-Thu) With galleries detailing relations between the two countries, this museum provides an interesting snapshot of mostly 19th-century colonial life in Muscat.

Muscat Gate Museum MUSEUM
(Map p132; ☎99 328754; Al Bahri Rd, Old Muscat; ⏲8am-2pm Sun-Thu) FREE Straddling the road between the corniche and the old walled city, this museum, with the original gates used until the 1970s to keep land-bound marauders out, marks the position of the old city wall and introduces Muscat proper. Though the museum's exhibits are of limited interest, the site provides an excellent vantage point for the corniche and the diwan.

A drive up to the aerial mast on the neighbouring hill gives an even better view of Mutrah and Muscat before dropping down to Al Riyam Park in Mutrah.

Al Bustan البستان

Al Bustan Palace LANDMARK
(off Sidab St, Al Bustan) Set in lush gardens, this sumptuous hotel was built as a venue for the Gulf Cooperation Council (GCC) summit in 1985. Remarkable for its enormous domed atrium, the hotel is worth a visit just to admire the building's interior and the location.

Parliament Building LANDMARK
(Map p126; Al Bustan Roundabout, cnr Sidab & Al Bustan Sts) This elegant building, completed in 2013, is home to the two houses of the Majlis ash Shura, Oman's parliament. It is not open to the public but it does make for a fine photo opportunity with its traditional low-rise, Omani-style, modern architecture, backed by Muscat's distinctive russet-coloured ophiolite mountains. The partially elected Majlis ash Shura assists the state in the formation of policy.

Sohar (Boat) LANDMARK
(Map p126) Just outside Al Bustan Palace Hotel, opposite the imposing parliament buildings, a small roundabout is home to the Sohar, a boat named after the hometown of the famous Omani seafarer Ahmed bin Majid. The boat is a replica of one sailed by Abdullah bin Gasm in the mid-8th century to Guangzhou in China. It was built in the dhow yards of Sur from the bark of over 75,000 palm trees and four tonnes of rope. Not a single nail was used in the construction.

Tim Severin and a crew of Omani sailors undertook a famous voyage to Guangzhou in this boat in 1980 – a journey of 6000 nautical miles that took eight months to complete.

Marina Bandar al Rowdha HARBOUR
(Map p126; ☎24 737286; www.marinaoman.net; Sidab St) Apart from offering a full range of boating amenities, Marina Bandar al Rowdha is a popular launching point for a range of watersports including fishing and diving. It's also a pleasant place to enjoy harbour activity and relax at the Blue Marlin (p141) restaurant. The marina offers free use of its pool for those dining at the restaurant, making it a potential day trip when combined with a boat trip.

The journey to the marina, along the coast road from Old Muscat to Al Bustan, offers spectacular mountain and sea views and a glimpse of local life. A **water-taxi** (☎24 749111; www.sifawyhotel.com; Marina Bandar al Rowdha; per person OR8; ⏲to Al Seifa 9am & 4pm Thu, Fri & Sat, from Al Seifa 10am, 3pm & 5pm) service connects the marina to the resort at Al Seifa (Jebel Sifah) and the marina at Al Mouj.

Ruwi روي

Oman's so-called 'Little India' is the commercial and transport hub of the capital, with plenty of budget-priced places to eat, shop (especially along Souq Ruwi St) and socialise.

Sultan's Armed Forces Museum MUSEUM
(Map p126; ☎24 312648; Al Mujamma St, Ruwi; admission adult/child 500 baisa/free; ⏲7.30am-1pm Sun-Thu & 3-6pm Sat) Despite the name, this excellent museum is far more than just a display of military hardware. The collection is housed in Bayt al Falaj, built in 1845 as a royal summer home but used mostly as the headquarters of the sultan's armed forces. The lower rooms outline Oman's history while the upper rooms explore the country's international relations and military prowess. The museum is on the itinerary of visiting dignitaries and you'll be given a mandatory military escort.

If you haven't time to visit the mountains to see Oman's ancient engineering in action, there's a working model *falaj* (irrigation channel) in the grounds outside the museum that is worth a look.

Qurm القرم

Most of this area comprises modern shopping centres and residences, but there are several places to visit and a great beach. You may like to check the Mosque Etiquette section of the First Time chapter (p21) before paying a visit to the Grand Mosque.

★**Royal Opera House Muscat** OPERA HOUSE
(Map p126; ☎24 403300; www.rohmuscat.org.om; Sultan Qaboos St, Shatti Al Qurm; Ⓟ) The arrival of the Royal Opera House Muscat in 2011 was a high point in the cultural life of Muscat. Built by the same architects as the Grand Mosque, the understated marble exterior belies the magnificent interior of inlaid wood and Arabesque designs. Even

Ruwi

Sleeping
1 Sun City Hotel B2

Information
2 Citibank B1
3 HSBC B1
4 Mustafa Jawad Exchange Company (Money Exchange) A3

Transport
5 Emirates B2
6 Europcar B2
7 Gulf Air A3
8 Intercity Microbus Station B3
9 Microbus Station (Local) A3
Mwasalat – City Bus .... (see 11)
Mwasalat – International .... (see 11)
10 Oman Air B1
11 Ruwi Bus Station B3
12 Taxi Stand B3
13 Thrifty Car Rental B2

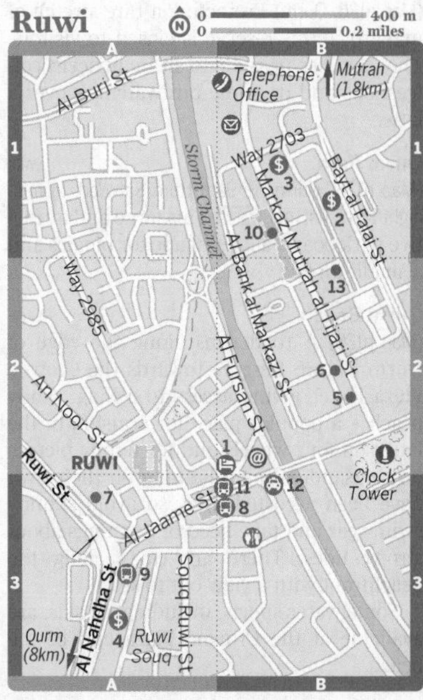

if you're not intending to catch a show, it's worth stopping by to admire the beauty of the building and enjoy window-shopping in the adjacent Opera Galleria arcade. Call the box office to check the availability of tours.

PDO Oil & Gas Exhibition MUSEUM

(Map p126; ☎24 677834; www.pdo.co.om; Sayh al Malih St, Qurm; ⊙7am-noon & 1-4pm Sat-Wed, 7am-noon Thu) FREE Petroleum Development Oman (PDO) is responsible for much of the rapid growth of infrastructure throughout the country, as outlined in the PDO Oil & Gas Exhibition. The interactive displays are of interest for anyone interested in science in general and the oil and gas industry in particular. To reach the museum from Qurm, follow the signs for the Crowne Plaza Hotel and take the first right turn along Sayh al Malih St.

Planetarium PLANETARIUM

(Map p126; ☎24 675542; www.pdo.co.om; Sayh al Malih St, Qurm; ⊙9am first Sat monthly) FREE The Planetarium offers a free show on the first Saturday of every month but book one day ahead. The website (under community) lists any additional public shows on offer. Star-gazing parties are also available. To reach the Planetarium from Qurm, follow the signs for the Crowne Plaza Hotel and take the first right turn along Sayh al Malih St.

Qurm Nature Reserve NATURE RESERVE

(Map p126; Qurm) Protecting a rare stretch of mangrove, this reserve is closed to visitors. That said, it's possible to sit in adjacent coffeeshops and do some birdwatching over a latte.

Qurm Park PARK

(Map p126; Qurm; ⊙9am-11pm Sat-Wed, to midnight Thu & Fri; P) FREE This large and attractive park boasts a lake, shade for picnics and a small fun fair.

Qurm Beach BEACH

(Map p126) A road runs along the edge of Qurm Nature Reserve towards the Crowne Plaza Hotel, giving access to a long, sandy beach – a popular place for cruising in the latest on four wheels and for family picnics on the sand. Women bathing on their own have been accosted here, so avoid skimpy swimwear and take heed of warnings about strong tides. There are cafes along the beachfront with a view out to sea.

Some water sports, including jet skis, are available at the Crowne Plaza end of the beach.

Shatti al Qurm & Al-Khuwair شاطي القرم و الخوير

Near the Hotel InterContinental Muscat, along Way 2817, there is a small shopping complex that has become the teeming heart of modern Muscat. This is where you will find young Omanis cruising the loop in their new 4WDs, families strolling along the beach amid five-a-side footballers, and expats enjoying the Western-style cafe culture and shops.

It's worth driving around the **ministry and embassy buildings** bunched in this area. Make time to stop at the beachside **Grand Hyatt Muscat** to enjoy a Yemeni prince's flight of fancy; love it or hate it, tea in the foyer is a delight.

Natural History Museum MUSEUM

(Map p126; ☎24 641374; Al Thaqafah St; adult/child 500/100 baisa; ⊙8am-1.30pm Sun-Thu, 9am-1pm Sat) The Ministry of National Heritage houses the small but quaint Natural History Museum. The museum is illuminating about the local flora and fauna, and there are some excellent displays on Oman's geography and geology, together with information about environmental protection. Entry is off Way 3413.

Al Ghubrah, Ghala & Bawshar ا وبوشر لغبرة و غلا

★Grand Mosque MOSQUE

(Map p126; Sultan Qaboos St; ⊙non-Muslims 8-11am Sat-Thu) Quietly imposing from the outside, this glorious piece of modern Islamic architecture was a gift to the nation from Sultan Qaboos to mark his 30th year of reign. The main prayer hall is breathtakingly rich. The Persian carpet alone measures 70m by 60m wide, making it the second-largest hand-loomed Iranian carpet in the world; it took 600 women four years to weave.

The mosque, which can accommodate 20,000 worshippers, including 750 women in a private *musalla* (prayer hall), is an active place of worship, particularly for Friday prayers. Visitors are required to dress modestly, covering arms and legs and avoiding tight clothing. Women and girls (aged seven and above) must cover their hair. Abeyas and scarves can be hired from the mosque cafe and giftshop for OR2.500; some form of ID is required as a deposit. Tours are available. Mwasalat buses stop outside the mosque.

Bait al Maqham HISTORIC BUILDING

(end of As Safa St, Bawshar) FREE Open on the whim of the gate-keeper, this fortified residence buried in a plantation in the suburb of Bawshar is worth a visit just for the location. Close to the city's last remaining sand dunes, Bait al Maqham is a surprise find at the crease of the Hajar mountains. New houses are slowly encroaching but for now this house presents a fascinating glimpse at Muscat's once-common plantation life. Park opposite Rashan Shopping centre to avoid getting wedged between narrow plantation walls.

Airport Area

Al Mouj AREA

(The Wave; www.almouj.com) This up-and-coming sea-board development near Muscat International Airport is fast becoming the new social hub of the capital. Planned as a mixed residential, tourism and commercial development, it remains one of only two locations where expats can purchase property. The result, a decade later, is a thriving community comprising 69 nationalities. With a marina (p136) that hosts Extreme 40 sailing, Seaoman (p138) (watersports centre), golf course designed by Greg Norman, restaurants and leafy pavement coffeeshops, this is currently Muscat's hippest meeting place.

A five-star Kempinski resort at the heart of Al Mouj complex is nearing completion and is due to open in 2016. In a sophisticated contemporary building with access to a beautiful beach, this is likely to become a Muscat favourite.

Activities

The sea and the mountains dominate Muscat, giving plenty of amenities for water-related sports and some independent hiking. Muscat Diving & Adventure Centre (p221) can help with activity-based trips in the capital area and beyond.

Beaches

Although all beaches in Oman are public, many of the big hotels have attractive beach-side facilities (pools, restaurants, gardens) open to non-guests for a fee. Women may feel more comfortable swimming in this environment than in the sea at public beaches. At present, all beaches in Muscat are 'public', so there's nothing to stop a keen walker starting at Qurm Nature Reserve and walking all the way to Seeb, a distance of some 20km or so.

Crowne Plaza Muscat Health Club SWIMMING

(Map p126; ☎24 660660; www.crowneplaza.com/Muscat; Qurm St, Qurm; adult/child OR10/6; ⏰7am-7pm) The Crowne Plaza Muscat is at the head of a beautiful, sandy bay and has access to a secluded scrap of beach. A day pass includes use of the health club sauna and steam room, tennis courts and pool. Call one day ahead to check availability.

InterContinental Muscat Health Club SWIMMING

(Map p126; ☎24 680000; www.ihg.com; Inter Coninental Muscat, Way 2817, Shatti Al Qurm; adult/child OR15/10; ⏰7am-9pm) A day pass gives access to landscaped gardens which offer a shady retreat after lengths of the training pool. Alternatively, there's more relaxed floating in the recreational pool.

Birdwatching

There are several birdwatching opportunities in Muscat and over 450 bird species to look out for in Oman. Contact the **Oman Bird Group** (www.birdsoman.com) for specialist information. A new reserve with hides is being planned at Al Ansab lagoons, part of the city's waste-water facility, but is still only at the planning stage. In the meantime, head for the Qurm Nature Reserve (p134).

Cycling

Obike BICYCLE RENTAL

(Map p130; www.obike.org; Mutrah Corniche; ⏰7-11pm) FREE A fine way to enjoy Muscat's attractive harbour, not to mention the cooler evening air, is to hire a free bike near Al Riyam Park and cycle along Mutrah Corniche. Beware the traffic – cycling is not common in the city and cars make few allowances for cyclists.

Driving

Muscat GeoSites DRIVING TOUR

(☎toll free 800 777999; www.omantourism.gov.om) FREE Oman is famous for its geological heritage and you don't have to drive miles to encounter it. Oman's official tourist website offers a smart-phone app giving GPS coordinates to some of the city's unique geological structures. Information on around 30 geological sites are offered through this excellent free download.

Hiking

There are some rewarding mountain walks in the Muscat area. Several two- to three-hour walks in and around Mutrah and Old

Muscat afford excellent views of the two port areas and take the rambler up past ruined villages. These walks are covered in Anne Dale and Jerry Hadwin's *Adventure Trekking in Oman,* with good maps, directions and safety precautions. Their Muscat–Sidab route is a one-hour walk that could be added, for those energetic walkers, onto a **walking tour** (p136) of the Mutrah–Old Muscat coastline.

The **Ministry of Tourism** (☎24 588700; www.omantourism.gov.om) has developed a set of walking tours and a booklet describing some great routes across Muscat and beyond. Brown information signs mark the trailheads of some routes. The C38 from Al Riyam Park to Mutrah (a walk of 2km taking about 1½ hours) traces the route through Muscat's distinctive ophiolite mountains on a track used by former copper miners who were active in the region 5000 years ago. Be prepared for rough conditions in remote territory on all trails: stout walking shoes, water and a hat are essential at any time of year, even on the shortest route.

Horse Riding

Qurm Equestrian School HORSE RIDING
(☎24 700844, 99 832199; www.qe.hashimani.com/; group lesson per hour adult/child OR12/10; ⏲5am-9pm) Horse-riding school with beach rides available on Thursday and Friday.

Water Sports

Water sports in Muscat include **fishing, diving** and **snorkelling**. There are also **boat trips** around scenic Bandar Khayran and the nearby rock arch. Stars of the show are the highly popular **dolphin-** and **whale-watching** trips. Kiosks along Mutrah Corniche advertise these boat rides for OR17 for a two-hour boat trip, leaving at around 8am and 10am every day from Marina Bandar al Rowdha. If you prefer less regulated activities, you can head for the beach in the village of Qantab (a left turn off the road towards Bandar Jissah), where fishermen will take visitors to see the rock arch for OR10 for an hour's boat tour.

Al Khayran BOAT TOUR
(Map p126; ☎24 737288, 97 307877; www.alkhayran.com; per trip OR25; ⏲8am, 9am, 10am & 11am May-Sep) Offering semi-submersible boat trips for a close-up of the coral gardens without getting wet.

Al Mouj Marina WATER SPORTS
(☎24 534544; www.almoujmarina.com; Al Mouj) Offering full berthing amenities and outlets

City Walk
Muscat Coastline

START FISH MARKET, MUTRAH
END AL BAHRI RD, OLD MUSCAT
LENGTH 8KM; FOUR TO FIVE HOURS

This walking tour follows the sea through the ancient ports of Mutrah and Muscat. Pack a snack and take lots of water. The walk can be segmented if time, energy or summer heat forbids the whole route.

Begin where the morning tide beaches fishermen and their catch at the ❶ **Fish Market** (p126). Stop for something fishy at nearby ❷ **La Brasserie** (p141), with delicious seafood on the menu.

Turn right at Samak roundabout, which means 'The Fish' in Arabic and is decorated appropriately with a pair of generic pisces. Call into nearby ❸ **Bait al Baranda** (p127) and learn about the history of Muscat's relationship with the sea and the origin of the city's name, meaning 'safe anchorage'. Return to the corniche and head towards the fort. Cast your eye out to sea: His Majesty's Dhow is generally harboured here, cruise ships dock by the harbour master, the ferry to Musandam sits proudly in its own berth and large cargo boats unload at the docks beyond. Inland, the merchants' houses of the Lawataya people, who built their fortunes on the seafaring trade, sport balconies that allow the inhabitants a nostalgic glance across the Arabian Ocean.

Turn into ❹ **Mutrah Souq** (p127), where items such as handmade models of silver dhows and ship chandlery are on sale; this souq grew from seaborne cargo and to this day many of the wares (Indian spices and textiles, Egyptian plastic, Iranian crafts and Chinese toys) are shipped in by sea. Ward off scurvy with a fruit juice at ❺ **Al Ahli Coffeeshop** (p142) in the heart of the souq. Return to the corniche and head east towards 16th-century ❻ **Mutrah Fort** (p129), built by the Portuguese who were unwittingly led to Muscat by the kindness of Ahmed bin Majid, a famous sailor from Sohar.

At the ❼ **goldfish monument and fountains**, a heron often snacks in view of the royal yacht and the visiting navies of other nations. Continue towards the giant incense burner; Oman's former prosperity

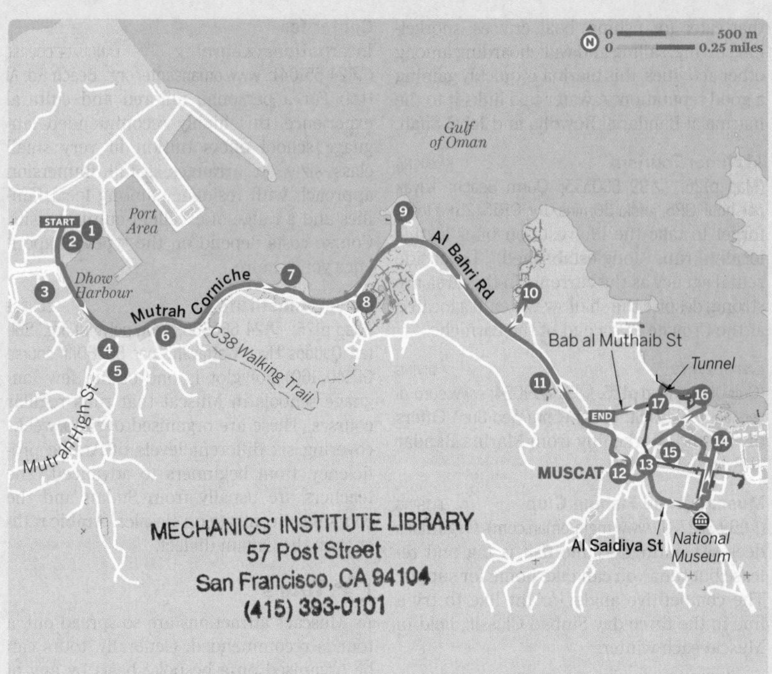

was built on Dhofar frankincense, which left the shores of Oman with other precious cargo such as Arabian horses.

On reaching **8 Al Riyam Park** (p129) you could, with stout shoes, head back to Mutrah on the Ministry of Tourism's walking route C38, past panoramic views. Alternatively, continue along the corniche to the **9 watchtower** (p129) and scan for dolphins – some real and some carved from marble.

After pausing for a rest at **10 Kalbuh Bay Park** (p129) cut inland via Al Bahri Rd and enter the 'city proper' via **11 Muscat Gate Museum** (p132). Every night until the 1970s the doors to the city were locked at this point, keeping tradition in and those from the interior out.

Turn right towards Sidab on Al Saidiya St and visit **12 Bayt al Zubair** (p131) for photographs showing the sea's influence on Muscat.

Continue along Al Saidiya St, still heading for Sidab. Pause for fried fish at **13 City Tower Grill Restaurant & Cafe** (p141) on the corner before turning right along an elegant avenue of date palms.

At the roundabout, march left through the colonnade towards the grand front entrance of the **14 Sultan's Palace** (p130). Follow the palace walls left, past beautiful gardens and mature trees (a favourite roost of myna birds) on Qasr al Alam St.

At the junction, turn left for the **15 Omani-French Museum** (p132) and a display on shipbuilding, or right for Muscat Harbour. The Portuguese built forts, such as **16 Al Mirani** (p131), towering to the left, and Al Jalali (across the bay), to protect their maritime interests. Look across the harbour for a graffiti log book etched into the promontory rocks, left by the visiting navies of Great Britain and other countries. This is a good place to admire the back garden of the palace and imagine the spectacle of the military banquets held annually here, complete with ice sculptures on the lawn, a band on each of the surrounding forts, lights from Oman's fully rigged tall ship moored in the harbour for the occasion, and fireworks mirrored in the calm waters of the bay.

Turn left at the harbour wall, and duck under the tunnel before the modern naval base. Turn right under the **17 old city gate** onto Bab al Muthaib St. This soon runs into Al Bahri Rd – and from here, it's an easy taxi ride back to Mutrah.

that cater for fishing, boat cruises, snorkelling, diving, sailing and wakeboarding among other activities, this marina is quickly gaining a good reputation. A water-taxi links it to the marina at Bandar al Rowdha and Jebel Sifah.

Al Nimer Tourism KAYAKING
(Map p126; ☎99 550535; Qurm Beach; kayak per hour OR5, jetski 30mins/1hr OR15/25) Don't forget to take the life-vests on offer at this locally run, long-established, beachside rental agency as the currents in this area are strong, despite the shallow water. It's located at the Crowne Plaza end of the corniche.

Eurodivers DIVING
(Gulf Divers; Map p126; ☎97 899094; www.euro-divers.com; Sidab St; ⊙8am-5pm Wed-Sun) Offers diving and snorkelling from Marina Bandar al Rowdha.

Muscat Game Fishing Club FISHING
(☎99 322779; www.mgfa-oman.com) Organises deep-sea outings. Game fish is tag and release but tuna you can take home for supper. The competitive angler might like to try a line in the three-day Sinbad Classic, held in Muscat each winter.

Seaoman SAILING
(Oman Sail; ☎24 181400; www.seaoman.com; Al Mouj Marina; kayak per 30min OR3; ⊙9am-5pm) Affiliated with Oman Sail with its emphasis on training and education, this watersports operator offers courses in sailing, diving, power boating, water-skiing and wakeboarding among others. It operates out of Al Mouj Marina and has outlets at the Millennium Hotel near Barka.

Sea Tours Oman BOAT TOUR
(☎99 425461; www.seatoursoman.com) Specialises in boat trips including glass-bottom boats in Muscat.

Sidab Sea Tours DOLPHIN-WATCHING
(Map p126; ☎24 736791; www.sidabseatours.com; Marina Bandar al Rowdha) Oman is a great country for naturalists, with dolphins and whales found in large numbers off the coast: early morning boat trips with a company like Sidab Sea Tours are the best way to spot them.

Courses

Muscat isn't a great place to learn Arabic, as many people speak English proficiently and relish the chance to practise. For the determined, however, there are a couple of trusted language schools in Muscat.

Center for International Learning LANGUAGE COURSE
(☎24 551041; www.omancenter.org; Beach Rd, Al Hail) For a personal, tailored and cultural experience, this highly recommended language school offers tuition in very small class sizes. It arranges a full immersion approach with residency among local families and a range of excellent cultural visits. Course costs depend on the type of experience you require.

Polyglot Institute COURSE
(Map p126; ☎24 666666; www.polyglot.org; Sultan Qaboos Hwy, Wattayah; per 50/60hr course OR140/160) Polyglot is one of the few language schools in Muscat that runs regular courses. These are organised over 10 weeks covering six different levels of Arabic proficiency, from beginners to advanced. The teachers are usually from Sudan and the courses concentrate on classical Arabic rather than the Omani dialect.

Tours

As Muscat's attractions are so spread out, a tour is recommended. Generally, tours can be organised on a bespoke basis by any of the main tour operators. An average price for a full-day city tour including lunch is OR65 per person.

Big Bus Tours CITY TOUR
(☎971 4340 7709; www.bigbustours.com; adult/child/family OR22/9/52; ⊙11am & 2pm) This popular service aboard air-conditioned, open-top double-decker buses runs through the capital on a hop-on, hop-off basis, taking in 10 of the major sites from Mutrah and old Muscat to Qurm and offering a free shuttle to the Grand Mosque. A recorded on-board commentary in six languages with free headphones is included in the price.

Buses leave from outside Mutrah Souq and the whole tour takes 1½ hours with an extra 30 minutes for a free walking tour of the palace area of old Muscat. Tickets (which are valid for 24 hours, or 48 hours for an extra fee) can be bought on the bus or from hotels. A discounted combination ticket for Muscat and Dubai or Abu Dhabi is available.

National Travel & Tourism CULTURAL TOUR
(NTT; Map p126; ☎24 660300; www.nttoman.com; Ar Rumaylah St, Wattayah; ⊙8.30am-6pm Sat-Thu) Offers an excellent, friendly and comprehensive tour service with several one-week and two-week packages on offer in addition to

popular half-day city tours of Muscat. Next to the Kia showroom in Wattayah, this is one of the best places to ask for tourist information. Staff are experienced and helpful.

Festivals & Events

Muscat Festival CULTURAL

(Jan-Feb) Lasting for a month from around the end of January, Muscat Festival is a highlight of the capital's year, featuring nightly fireworks, a 'living' replica of an Omani village with *halwa*-making and craft displays, exhibitions from regional countries and events such as laser shows and traditional dancing.

The festival is organised around several main venues – one usually in the suburbs of Al Amerat and the other in Naseem Gardens along the Muscat–Barka Hwy near Seeb. There is also a funfair, international pavilions selling crafts, bargain clothing and bedding and a range of items from cheap imports to inlaid furniture from Pakistan. International dance troupes perform on the open-air stages and fashion shows take place nightly; other acts, such as high-wire acrobatics, occupy the periphery. In addition, many shops in Muscat offer grand draws and discounts. Check the English-language newspapers and Muscat FM radio for the festival program.

National Day CULTURAL

(18 Nov) On 18 November, National Day is marked with fireworks, city buildings are draped with strings of colourful lights, and Sultan Qaboos St is spectacularly lit and adorned with flags. Petunia planting along highway verges, roundabouts and city parks is timed for maximum blooming, transforming the city into a riot of floral colour.

Sleeping

Muscat is not a cheap city to sleep in, but it does have some splendid hotels. Some are almost holidays in their own right. The hotels of Qurm, Shatti al Qurm and Al Khuwair are all on or near the same stretch of sandy beach. Alternatively, for a location within walking distance of the capital's main attractions, try the budget hotels in Mutrah.

Top-end prices quoted here are rack rates and you can almost certainly arrange a discount of some sort. Disconcertingly, rates literally change by 20% or more from one day to the next. Non-smoking rooms are available and free wi-fi is the norm. Taxes and breakfast are included in the rate unless stated otherwise.

Marina Hotel HOTEL $

(Map p130; 24 713100; www.marinahoteloman.com; Mutrah Corniche, Mutrah; s/d OR22/30;) For those wanting to discover Muscat's soul, then the Marina Hotel, overlooking the fish market and participating in the character of the corniche, offers a very good vantage point. You can feel the city's pulse over breakfast on the terrace of the popular Al Boom Restaurant. The rooms are on the cramped side but it remains a local favourite.

Naseem Hotel HOTEL $

(Map p130; 24 712418; naseemhotel@gmail.com; Mutrah Corniche, Mutrah; s/d/tr OR20/27/40, breakfast per person OR2) In need of a makeover, this tired old Mutrah favourite has large rooms, seven with grand views of the harbour. Given its prime location, plum in the middle of the city's finest row of merchant houses, it's remarkable that this hotel has survived. What it lacks in decor (and clean carpets), it makes up for in friendly, helpful service.

Sun City Hotel HOTEL $

(Map p133; 24 789801; hotel.suncity@hotmail.com; Al Jaame St, Ruwi; s/d OR20/25;) Beside Ruwi bus station, this hotel – with its bright and cheerful lobby, enormous plastic potted orange trees, and large rooms with shiny floor tiles and big windows – is recommended if you have an early bus to catch. Friendly staff can help you navigate the vagaries of the bus station.

Beach Hotel HOTEL $$

(Map p126; 24 696601; www.beachhotelmuscat.com; Way 2818, Shatti al Qurm; s/d/tr OR35/55/65;) In a pristine white building with tiled blue trim, a lobby with a dome, and big rooms with armchairs and balconies, this is a rare residential-style hotel. The breakfast menu includes *fuul medamas* (beans) and *khobz* (Arabic flat bread) and with hospitable, helpful Omani staff and an easy walk to the beach, this hotel offers a genuine Omani experience.

Majan Continental Hotel BUSINESS HOTEL $$

(Map p126; 24 592900; www.majanhotel.com; Al Ghubrah St, Al Ghubrah; s/d OR60/70;) Perched on top of a hill overlooking the pearly white suburbs of Muscat, this comfortable, Arabic-style hotel is popular with Omanis and expat business travellers. It offers a free shuttle to the airport.

★The Chedi LUXURY HOTEL $$$

(Map p126; 24 524400; www.ghmhotels.com; Way 3215, off 18th November St, Al Ghubrah North;

r from OR192; P📶❄) With a hint of the *kasbah* (desert castle) combined with Asian minimalism, the Chedi is designed to make the best of its mini sand-dune location. Don't let the occasional groan of aircraft lowering into Muscat International Airport put you off: for most of the day, the only audible sound from the poolside of Muscat's most stylish hotel is the chink of wine glasses.

The gardens, rhythmically punctuated by Zen ponds, raked pebbles and a pool virtually contiguous with the sea, are satisfying to the soul. Hanging suits and accommodating the etceteras of working life may be difficult in the minimally furnished rooms, but if all you brought is a swimsuit and a good book, then very little will intrude on your sense of getting away from it all.

Hotel InterContinental Muscat RESORT **$$$**
(Map p126; ☎24 680000; www.ihg.com; off Way 2817, Shatti al Qurm; r OR140; P📶❄) If anything is 'happening' in Muscat, chances are it is doing so at the 'InterCon' – a really excellent hotel in terms of service and amenities. While not the prettiest building, this hotel has a fine interior, quality rooms, shady gardens and beach access. Jawaharat Al Shatti Complex – a lively collection of shops, cafes and restaurants – is a stroll away.

Grand Hyatt Muscat LUXURY HOTEL **$$$**
(Map p126; ☎24 641234; www.muscat.grand.hyatt.com; Way 3033, off Al Saruj St, Shatti al Qurm; r excl breakfast from OR177; P📶❄) This hotel is pure kitsch. Allegedly designed by a Yemeni prince, the exterior owes much to Disney, while its stained-glass and marble interior is a cross between art deco and a royal Bedouin tent. With luxurious, balconied rooms, Muscat's best Italian restaurant called 'Tuscany', water sports and limitless walks along the sandy beach, this is a hotel with more than one angle.

Al Bustan Palace LUXURY HOTEL **$$$**
(Ritz-Carlton Hotel; ☎24 799666; www.ritzcarlton.com; off Sidab St, Al Bustan; r from OR160; P📶❄) In a secluded bay ringed by spectacular mountains, Al Bustan is more palace than hotel. It has an atmosphere and class of its own, partly engendered through the Arabian-style interior and top-quality restaurants. The hotel grounds are like a Garden of Eden with infinity pools and shady lawns backing onto a pristine beach. A Six Senses Spa offers luxury treatments.

Hormuz Grand Hotel HOTEL **$$$**
(☎24 350500; www.hormuzgrand.com; Bank Muscat Roundabout, Airport Heights; r from OR100; P@📶❄) If you can forgive the fact that the exterior is pink, this new, good-value hotel, close to the airport, with pleasant landscaping, and views across the mountains from large, luxurious rooms, is worth considering for those wanting easy access to routes out of Muscat. There is a very good Indian restaurant on site and a delicious daily dinner buffet (OR18.800).

Eating

There are plenty of opportunities for fine dining in Muscat, particularly at the top-end hotels. Equally, it's hard to go 10 paces without tripping over a stand selling shwarma (meat sliced off the spit and stuffed in pita-type bread with chopped tomatoes and garnish).

Dozens of what are locally termed 'coffeeshops' abound in Muscat selling a variety of largely Indian snacks, such as omelettes rolled up in Arabic bread with chilli, samosas and curried potatoes. It is more difficult to find typical Omani food, though regardless of where you end up, the best local haunts give a flavour of the region, either in menu or venue. For a comprehensive round-up of Muscat's restaurants and cafes, it's worth buying a copy of *Time Out Muscat* (OR2).

Al Daleh Restaurant INTERNATIONAL **$**
(Map p126; ☎24 813141; National Hospitality Institute, An Nuzha St, Al Wadi al Kabir; 3-course lunch OR6; ⏲1-3pm Wed & Thu; ✎) 🍃 Nervous Omani hospitality students practise their culinary and waiting skills at this exceptionally good-value restaurant. Menus comprise mostly top-notch international dishes. Encouraging these youngsters on their chosen career path is a great way to make your visit to Muscat count. Ring to book a table as it gets busy.

Cafe Chef A MIDDLE EASTERN **$**
(Map p130; ☎24 714891; Mutrah Corniche, Mutrah; mains OR3; ⏲10am-11pm Sat-Thu, noon-11pm Fri) This delightful, light-spangled addition to Mutrah's streetside restaurants offers cosy indoor dining on sedans under Turkish lanterns, or trestle tables alongside Mutrah's promenade. Try the date milkshake or opt for falafel, humus and kebabs – and try to eat them before the feral cats turn up!

Al Boom & Dolphin Bar MIDDLE EASTERN **$**
(Map p130; ☎24 713100; Marina Hotel, Mutrah Corniche, Mutrah; breakfast OR2, dishes OR5; ⏲8am-

3pm & 6pm-1am;) This intimate, licensed restaurant, with large windows and a terrace overlooking the harbour, is a good place to get a feel of Muscat's age-old relationship with the sea. A few marine favourites find their way on to the mainly Middle Eastern-style menu. The bar stays open until 3am (2am on Fridays).

Fastfood 'n' Juice Centre SHWARMA **$**
(Map p130; Mutrah Corniche, Mutrah; sandwiches 500 baisa; 9am-10pm) East of the main entrance to Mutrah Souq on Mutrah Corniche, this typical local-style restaurant with tables on the pavement is an ideal place to people-watch over a shwarma and a *chi libton* (tea-bag tea with sweet condensed milk). If the tables here are full, there are a couple of neighbouring eateries that will do just as nicely.

City Tower Grill Restaurant & Cafe CAFE **$**
(Map p132; Al Saidiya St, Old Muscat; lamb chops OR2.500, juices 800 baisa; 9am-3am) Ignore the entirely irrelevant name of this venue and have an egg roll-up in view of Fort Al Mirani in this corner street cafe, ideal as a rest stop on a walking tour of Muscat.

Bin Ateeq OMANI **$**
(Map p126; 24 478225; Al Khuwair St, Al Khuwair; meals OR5; 10.30am-midnight) Catering to homesick traders from the interior, this restaurant is one of the few to serve genuine Omani food the traditional way with seating on old carpets in private rooms with a television. Try *harees*, a glutinous Omani dish that's often mixed with chicken. Cash only.

★**Bait al Luban** OMANI **$$**
(Frankincense House; Map p130; 24 711842; www.baitalluban.com; Hai al Mina Rd, Mutrah; mains OR6, 3-course tasting menu OR10; noon-11pm;) You know you're somewhere unique when the complementary water is infused with frankincense. This delightful restaurant, housed in a renovated *khan* (guesthouse) that was built 140 years ago and which used to charge by the bed, not by the room, serves genuine Omani cuisine, homecooked by local ladies. Come just to savour the decor; it's opposite Mutrah's Fish Market.

★**Kargeen Cafe** MIDDLE EASTERN **$$**
(Map p126; 24 692269; Medinat Qaboos complex; mains from OR4; 8am-1am Sat-Thu, noon-1am Fri;) With a choice of open-air and *majlis*-style dining (on sedans in small rooms), this excellent restaurant has spilt into a courtyard of illuminated trees to create a thoroughly Arabian experience. Make sure you try Kargeen's take on the traditional Omani *shuwa* – a succulent banana-leaf-wrapped lamb dish. Also worth a try are the hibiscus drinks and avocado milkshakes.

The Cave INTERNATIONAL **$$**
(Map p126; 24 651465; www.thecave.om; Qurm Heights Rd, Darsayt; shuwa OR8; 12.30pm-1am) This Aladdin's cave-like complex of seven different restaurants includes Al Manjur, an Omani restaurant with *shuwa* (slow-cooked, marinated meat dishes) on the menu. Smart casual dress is expected here. If the slightly austere atmosphere doesn't appeal, then opt for Arab-style dining on the terrace upstairs with expansive views over the sparkling lights of Ruwi.

Ubhar OMANI **$$**
(Map p126; 24 699826; Bareeq Al Shatti Mall, Shatti Al Qurm; mains OR5; 12.30-3.30pm & 6.30-11pm) This Omani restaurant (with seating at tables rather than on the floor) offers an avante-garde menu. Camel features among other traditional meats. Leave room for dessert – the frankincense ice cream and *halwa* pastries are delicious. Within walking distance of the Royal Opera House Muscat, it's ideal for a post-show dinner.

La Brasserie FRENCH **$$**
(Map p130; Mutrah Corniche, Mutrah; mains OR7; noon-3pm & 7-11pm Mar-Nov, 7pm-1am Dec-Feb) Serving delicious French food in a small, wooden den of a restaurant opposite the fish market in Mutrah, La Brasserie is the perfect venue for coffee and a pastry on a walking tour of Muscat.

Blue Marlin Restaurant INTERNATIONAL **$$**
(Map p126; 24 740038; Marina Bandar al Rawdar; meals OR6; 8.30am-10.30pm) With cheerful cloth-covered tables under brollies alongside the harbour, the Blue Marlin offers consistentlydeliciouslightbitesatlunchtime–perfect after a boat trip from the marina. Breakfast aficionados take note: this place serves real bacon. Diners are offered free access to the marina's pool.

D'Arcy's Kitchen BREAKFAST **$$**
(Map p126; 24 600234; Way 2817, Shatti al Qurm; dishes from OR5; 9am-11pm;) Next to the Omani Heritage Gallery, this friendly, award-winning establishment serves Western favourites at reasonable prices and is open when most other cafes are taking a siesta. An English breakfast from OR5 will

set you up well for a 'constitutional' along the nearby beach.

★ **The Beach** SEAFOOD $$$
(Map p126; ☎24 524400; The Chedi, off 18th November St, Al Ghubrah North; meals from OR45; ⏲7-10.30pm Sep-May; ✎) This top-class restaurant, with a superb Arabian ambience created by fire pits and subtle lighting, serves exciting, complex fare in a luxurious beachside location. The French pastry chef at the hotel's indoor restaurant makes wicked confections, including delectable handmade chocolates. The four-course degustation menu is excellent.

Mumtaz Mahal INDIAN $$$
(Map p126; ☎24 605907; Way 2601, Qurm; mains from OR10; ⏲noon-3pm & 7pm-midnight Sat-Thu, 1-3pm & 7pm-midnight Fri; ✎) Specialising in Northern Indian Mughlai cuisine, Mumtaz Mahal is more than just the best Indian restaurant in town – it is part of the landscape of Muscat. Perched on a hill overlooking Qurm Nature Reserve, with live sitar performances, traditional seating at low tables, and lantern-light, this restaurant is a local legend.

Al Angham OMANI $$$
(Map p126; ☎22 077777; www.alanghamoman.com; Opera Galleria, Sultan Qaboos St, Shatti Al Qurm; mains OR16, set menu OR52; ⏲noon-3pm & 7-11pm) This exquisite restaurant next to the Royal Opera House offers just the kind of refined fare demanded of a special occasion, such as a night at the opera. From the silver napkin rings to the carved wooden ceiling, this stylish restaurant showcases Omani cuisine at its best.

Self-Catering

Al Fair Supermarket SUPERMARKET
(Map p126; Medinat Qaboos complex; ⏲8am-10pm) The ubiquitous Al Fair supermarket chain, found in all the main shopping areas of Muscat, is the perfect shop for picnic ingredients with an expansive fruit and vegetable counter and items to suit Western palates; the one in Medinat Qaboos makes excellent bread.

Lulu SUPERMARKET
(Map p126; Sultan Qaboos St; ⏲8am-10pm) Lulu is the region's favourite supermarket chain and its food halls include many Middle Eastern favourites such as hummus and *muttabel* (smoked aubergine dip). There is a convenient branch off Sultan Qaboos St in Al Khuwair. You can pick up a cool box and freezer packs while you're at it to keep the picnic edible in the searing summer temperatures.

Drinking & Nightlife

Arabic coffee *(qahwa)* is surprisingly hard to find in Muscat outside an Omani home, a government office or a hotel lobby. The so-called 'coffeeshops' all over town are oriented more to snacking than sipping coffee. International cafe chains have also become an addictive part of the local culture.

Each of the top hotels has an elegant cafe and a bar where alcohol is unrestricted but expensive.

★ **Trader Vic's** COCKTAIL BAR
(Map p126; ☎24 680080; Hotel InterContinental Muscat, Shatti al Qurm; ⏲6pm-2am) When it comes to cocktails (try the Samoan Fogcutter or Honi Honi), nowhere competes with this fun and lively Polynesian-style venue. Resident assistant bar manager Hubert Fernandes has been making 'em how you like 'em for a decade. With live Latin music (except Fridays) and wafts of Mongolian barbecued choice cuts, you'll probably be seduced into staying for dinner.

Al Ghazal Bar PUB
(Map p126; ☎24 680000; Hotel InterContinental Muscat, Shatti al Qurm; ⏲noon-2am Sat-Tue, to 3am Wed-Thu, 2pm-2am Fri) More of a pub than a bar, this is a popular expat meeting place, with live music, a quiz night, televised sport and excellent Western-style bar food.

Al Ahli Coffeeshop JUICE BAR
(Map p130; ☎24 713469; Mutrah Souq, Mutrah; large mixed juice 900 baisa; ⏲10am-1pm & 4-10pm Sat-Thu, 4-10pm Fri) In the middle of Mutrah Souq, this is the best place for delicious, layered fruit juices of pomegranate, custard apple and mango. There is a traditional coffeehouse, on the left, just inside the souq, where Omani elders (men) trade news.

Al Makan Cafe SHEESHA CAFE
(Map p126; ☎24 662924; Al Shatti St, Shatti al Qurm; mains OR3; ⏲noon-11pm) This popular chain of local-style coffeeshops has the advantage of a magnificent view of the sea and a small garden for *sheesha* smokers, banished from the cafe's rather cavernous interior. Drop by for mixed-juice sundowners with the locals.

Grand Hyatt Muscat HIGH TEA
(Map p126; ☎24 641234; Grand Hyatt Muscat, Way 3033, off Al Saruj St, Shatti al Qurm; afternoon tea OR9; ⏲3-8pm) If you sit sipping tea long enough in the extravagant foyer of this sumptuous hotel, chances are you'll worry

that the tea was laced: the statue of the *Arab on Horseback* that graces the central podium moves just slowly enough to make you suspect you've joined the flight of fancy that inspired the architects.

John Barry Bar LOUNGE
(Map p126; ☎24 641234; Grand Hyatt Muscat, Way 3033, off Al Saruj St, Shatti al Qurm; ⊙2pm-1am Tue & Fri, to 2am Wed & Thu) Named after the raised ship and its booty of silver treasure that made the fortunes of the Hyatt's owner, this bar is a sophisticated setting for some live piano music and a cocktail.

☆ Entertainment

Other than the Royal Opera House, Muscat is rather thin on other entertainment options, although the five-star hotels and some of the smaller ones have bars and nightclubs, usually with live acts. *Time Out Muscat* is the best source of information for current favourites.

Local 'live acts' often take the form of gyrating women (typically from India, Russia or North Africa) in skimpy outfits worn over thick leggings; the women are sometimes contained behind wire mesh in case the locals find the Arab pop irresistible and insist on dancing along. The government occasionally cracks down on such forms of entertainment but the dancing doesn't take long to return.

You can take in a football (soccer) game at **Sultan Qaboos Sports Complex** (Map p126; ☎24 592197; Al-Ghubra St, Al-Ghubra South).

★**Royal Opera House Muscat** OPERA
(Map p126; ☎24 403300; www.rohmuscat.org.om; Sultan Qaboos St, Shatti Al Qurm) Some of the most famous names in opera and ballet have performed at Royal Opera House Muscat and the quality of production has won international acclaim. There is an efficient online reservation system with collection of tickets at the door. The season extends from September to May.

Note there's a strict dress code for attending a performance: jeans and sports shoes are not permitted. Coveralls can be hired if there isn't time to get back to the hotel to change.

★**On the Rocks** LOUNGE
(☎24 346765; www.axisroyal.com; Golden Tulip Hotel Seeb Hotel, Exhibition St; ⊙6pm-3am Sat-Thu, 6pm-2am Fri) This novel lounge restaurant, with its giant psychedelic TV-screen, serves a spirited cocktail and a fine-dining menu for modest prices, but it's the music that draws the crowds. Every Tuesday is steam and beer night with dim sum and pulse and soul music; every Wednesday there is live music, and DJs pitch in from 8.30pm to 3am on other nights. Smart-casual dress is strictly enforced. It's near the airport.

MUSCAT FOR CHILDREN

Muscat is a safe and friendly city with a few attractions for children. Most malls have a themed amusement centre typically open between 10am and 10pm costing from around 350 baisa per ride or OR3 entry.

Children's Museum (Map p126; ☎24 605368; off Sultan Qaboos St, Qurm; admission 500 baisa; ⊙9am-1pm Sat-Thu) Well-signposted domed building with lots of hands-on science displays. Free for children under seven.

Ice Skating (Fun Zone; Map p126; ☎24 662928; Qurm Park, Qurm; admission incl skate hire OR4; ⊙9am-midnight Sat-Thu, 2pm-midnight Fri) A good way to beat the summer heat. Sessions last 90 minutes. Women-only sessions on Monday from 9am to 6pm. The rink is closed between 8pm and 10pm on Saturday to allow the ice hockey team to practise.

Marah Land (Map p126; ☎22 006091; www.marahland.com; Qurm Park, Qurm; admission 300 baisa plus 250-750 baisa per ride; ⊙8am-1pm & 4pm-midnight Sat-Thu, 4pm-midnight Fri) Set inside the attractively landscaped Qurm Park, this funfair with Ferris wheel is a local favourite.

Oman Avenues Mall (Map p126; ☎22 005400; www.theavenuesmall.om; Sultan Qaboos St, Al Ghubrah; ⊙10am-10pm Sun-Wed, to 11pm Thu-Sat) Muscat's newest mall comes with 150 shops, a large food court open until 1am at weekends, Funtazmo World with a rollercoaster planned for 2016 and a kids zone for the under sixes. Oman's first international gym and a cinema are also planned for late 2016.

Rock Bottom Café CLUB

(Rockies; Map p126; ☎24 651326; www.rameehotels.com; Ramee Guestline Hotel, Way 1622, Qurm; cocktails OR5; ⏰noon-3pm & 6pm-3am) For Muscat's perennial hot spot, visit Rock Bottom Café, which has live music every night with a DJ and a dance floor in case the mood takes you.

Alive Oman LIVE MUSIC

(☎97 300007; www.aliveentertainment.me/) Organises big-ticket shows in Muscat, often held on the lawns of the InterContinental Hotel or at the Shangri-La's Barr al Jissah Resort & Spa.

City Cinema Shatti CINEMA

(Map p126; ☎24 607360; http://citycinemaoman.net; Hayy As Saruj, Shatti al Qurm) One of several modern cinemas in town.

Shopping

With one of the most characterful old souqs in the region, a few classy shops such as those in **Opera Galleria** adjacent to the Royal Opera House Muscat, and some big sprawling malls (Qurm City Centre, The Avenues, Muscat City Centre near Rusayl roundabout and nearby Markaz al Bahja), there's enough to keep a dedicated shopper happy.

Souq Ruwi St is worth visiting for all manner of cheap and cheerfuls – from souvenir T-shirts to don't-ask DVDs and gold from India.

Some popular Omani-produced items include highly worked silver *khanjars* (curved daggers) that start at OR30 for a tourist replica to OR500 for an exquisite genuine item; baskets worked with pieces of camel or goat hide (from OR5); *kuma* (Omani hats), which start at OR2 for a machine-made one to OR50 for a highly crafted handmade piece; handloomed goat-hair rugs (from OR15); frankincense (from 500 baisa) and a range of local and imitation perfumes; and dates (from 600 baisa per 500g). Mutrah Souq (p127) is the obvious destination to head for, but there are a few other shops scattered around Muscat.

Omani Heritage Gallery HANDICRAFTS

(Map p126; ☎24 696974; www.omaniheritage.com; Way 2817, Jawaharat Al Shatti Complex, Shatti al Qurm; ⏰9.30am-1pm & 4-8pm Sat-Thu) For guaranteed 'Made in Oman' crafts, try the Omani Heritage Gallery, a nonprofit organisation set up to encourage cottage industries through the sale of handicrafts. Prices are high, but so is the quality.

Sabco Centre SHOPPING CENTRE

(Map p126; Qurm Shopping Complex, off Sultan Qaboos St, Qurm; ⏰10am-10pm Sat-Thu, 4.30-10pm Fri) A surprisingly comprehensive little souq located inside the Sabco Centre sells crafts (mostly from India and Iran), pashmina shawls and Omani headdresses. Bargaining is recommended, although prices are reasonable. The souq's excellent cobbler can repair any leather item. Some shops in the souq close at lunchtime.

Bateel DATES

(Map p126; ☎24 601572; www.bateel.ae; Oasis by the Sea complex, Shatti al Qurm; ⏰10am-1pm & 5-10pm Sat-Thu, 2-11pm Fri) For a regional gift with a difference, the chocolate dates from Bateel are world class.

Amouage PERFUMERY

(Map p126; Sabco Centre, Qurm Shopping Complex; ⏰9.30am-1pm & 4.30-9.30pm Sat-Thu, 4.30-10pm Fri) Amouage sells the most expensive (and exquisite) perfume in the world, produced from frankincense, musk and other exotic ingredients in premises near Rusayl. You'll find the ultimate Arabian gift here or better still, call in on the Visitors Centre & Factory on Nizwa Hwy, 3km west of the Rusayl Clock Tower, where they offer guided tours of the factory.

Jawahir Oman JEWELLERY

(Map p126; ☎24 563239; Al Wilaj St, Qurm; ⏰9am-1pm & 4.30-9pm Sat-Thu) Selling prized Omani silver, this shop's exclusive contemporary jewellery and gift items are handcrafted in a workshop in Muscat.

Family Bookshop BOOKS

(Map p126; ☎24 600084; Madinat Sultan Qaboos; ⏰10am-1pm & 4.30-8pm Sat-Thu, 4.30-8pm Fri) One of the few independent bookshops in Muscat, this Omani-run stalwart stocks a good selection of English-language titles on Oman, including Lonely Planet guidebooks, and a few bestsellers.

House of Prose BOOKS

(Map p126; ☎24 564356; Al Wadi Centre, Qurm; ⏰9am-1pm & 4-8pm Sat-Thu, 4-8pm Fri) Stocks secondhand paperbacks with a great buyback scheme.

Ahmed Dawood Trading OUTDOOR EQUIPMENT

(Map p130; ☎24 703295; Al Mina St, Mutrah) For specialised camping equipment, try Ahmed Dawood Trading.

Information

EMERGENCY

Ambulance, Fire & Police (9999) Emergency services.

Royal Oman Police (ROP; 24 569501; www.rop.gov.om) Organises emergency care at the scene of an accident.

INTERNET ACCESS

All main cafes, coffeeshops and hotel foyers offer free wi-fi. Even the new public transport service, Mwasalat, offers this service on its buses. The standard rate in the few remaining internet cafes is around OR1 per hour.

Fastline Internet (Map p133; Ruwi bus station, Al Jaame St, Ruwi; per hour 800 baisa; 10am-midnight Sat-Thu, 2pm-midnight Fri;)

Internet Café (Map p130; Mutrah Corniche, Mutrah; per hour OR1; 9.30am-1.30pm & 4pm-midnight;)

MEDICAL SERVICES

International-standard health care is available at the main city hospitals. Initial emergency treatment may be free, but all other health care is charged. English is spoken in all hospitals and clinics in Muscat.

Pharmacies rotate to provide 24-hour coverage in all regions; check the English dailies to learn which ones are on duty on a given day. Pharmacies can advise which local doctors or dentists are on duty.

Al Nahdha Hospital (Map p126; 24 837800; Al Nahdha St, Wattiyah) Emergency cases are generally brought here.

MONEY

The big banks are centred in Ruwi's central business district, although one or two bank headquarters are drifting up towards the airport into what is being dubbed as Muscat's new centre. There are numerous branches with ATM facilities throughout Muscat.

The most convenient money changers are in Qurm, along Souq Ruwi St in Ruwi, and on the Mutrah Corniche at the entrance to Mutrah Souq.

HSBC (Map p133; 80 074722; Markaz Mutrah al Tijari St, CBD Ruwi; 8am-1pm Sun-Thu) The HQ and one of many branches in Muscat.

Faiq Money Changers (Map p126; 24 565419; Qurm Shopping Complex, Qurm; 9am-8.30pm Sat-Thu) Look beyond the name – this is one of the longest-established money exchanges in town.

POST

Branch Post Office (Map p133; Markaz Mutrah al Tijari St, CBD Ruwi; 8am-1.30pm Sat-Wed, to 11am Thu)

Main Post Office (Al Matar St; 8am-1.30pm Sat-Wed, to 11am Thu) Located by the airport, but on the opposite side of the highway. There are also branches in Old Muscat and Mutrah.

TELEPHONE

Omantel and Ooredoo are the main operators. Sim cards (from OR2 with OR2 credit) are available from the arrival hall at the airport and in malls, supermarkets and corner shops.

Telephone Office (Map p133; Al Burj St, CBD Ruwi; 8am-2pm & 4-6pm) Faxes can be sent from here.

TOURIST INFORMATION

Brochures and maps are available from the tourism counter at Muscat International Airport and in the foyers of larger hotels.

Ministry of Tourism (Map p126; 22 088000, toll free 80 077799; www.omantourism.gov.om; Ministries Area, Thaqafah St, Al Khuwair; 7.30am-1.30pm Sun-Thu) Staff can answer limited telephone enquiries but this is a ministry rather than a tourist centre and staff are not prepared to receive visitors; they sometimes, however, give out brochures and their website is very informative.

Getting There & Away

AIR

Situated 37km west of Mutrah is **Muscat International Airport** (p219). At the time of writing, the only domestic flights available are with **Oman Air** (Map p133; 24 531111).

BUS

Mwasalat – National Bus (Formerly ONTC; 24 121555; http://mwasalat.om/en-us/Bus-routes; Al Jaame St, Ruwi) The national bus company provides comfortable intercity services throughout Oman. Timetables in English (with fares) are available on the website (currently under development); a summary is sometimes also printed in the *Oman Observer*. Buses to Salalah (one way/return OR7.500/14, 12 hours) currently leave at 7am and 10am, and at 7pm, but call to confirm as the whole bus company is currently being relaunched.

Ruwi Bus Station (Map p133; 24 701294, 24 708522; http://mwasalat.om/en-us/; Al Jaame St, Ruwi) The main hub of the national bus service, Mwasalat. Buses on national and international routes leave from here.

CAR

Car hire can be arranged with several agencies in Ruwi, including **Alwan Tour Rent-a-Car** (p220) and **Mark Tours** (p220), as well as at the usual desks in hotels and at the airport in Muscat and Salalah.

TAXI & MICROBUS

Taxis and microbuses leave for all destinations from Al Jaame St, opposite Ruwi bus station.

There is an additional departure point at Rusayl roundabout (also known as Burj al Sahwa – the Clock Tower), west of the airport interchange.

Keep in mind that pricing is decidedly more 'fluid' than sample taxi/microbus fares.

TO	SHARED (OR)	ENGAGED (OR)	MICRO-BUS (OR)
Barka	1	11	n/a
Buraimi	15	75	n/a
Nakhal	2	10	1.500
Nizwa	1.500	4	2
Rustaq	3	6	n/a
Samail	1	5	1.500
Sohar	3	12	2
Sur	4	12	3.500

Getting Around

TO/FROM THE AIRPORT

Blue-and-white taxis running between the airport and Qurm, Al Khuwair and Seeb cost a fixed rate of OR8; OR 10 to Ruwi; OR12 to Mutrah and Muscat; and OR15 to Barr al Jissah. They are blue-striped and have 'airport taxi' on the side. Prepay at the booth inside the arrivals hall and avoid the services of unlicensed taxi drivers who try to catch passengers from the taxi queue.

Microbuses pass the airport fairly frequently between 7am and 10pm, and cost 500 baisa to Ruwi and 800 baisa to Muscat. Buses heading in this direction leave from the other side of the footbridge over the highway outside the airport. It is a 500m walk. There is no direct bus service to/from the airport but many hotels offer complimentary shuttle services.

BUS

As part of a much-needed new strategy to curb city traffic, a new local bus service in Muscat was being introduced at the time of writing. With modern, air-conditioned buses scheduled to depart every 15 minutes along a route from Ruwi to Seeb, and with rumours of air-conditioned bus stops to match, it is hoped this initiative will greatly reduce the number of cars on the road in the capital.

Mwasalat – City Bus (Formerly ONTC; Map p133; ☎24 708522; http://mwasalat.om/en-us; Ruwi Bus Station ; ⏲6am-9.15pm, every 15 minutes) Due to offer an online booking and ticketing service. The website has a helpful destination planning feature showing the schedule, tariff and duration of journeys. Sixty stops are planned on the main route from Ruwi to Seeb with an important hub at Rusayl (Clock Tower) Roundabout, the junction for Nizwa near Muscat International Airport.

MICROBUS & TAXI

In Mutrah, local microbuses cruise the corniche and congregate around Mutrah bus station. In Ruwi they park en masse along Al Jaame St, opposite the main bus station. Trips from one suburb to the next cost 200 to 300 baisa. No microbus journey within greater Muscat should cost more than one rial.

Microbuses charge OR1.200 from Ruwi to Rusayl roundabout near the airport and shared taxis cost OR3 (OR12 engaged) for the same trip.

Muscat's non-airport taxis are orange and white and do not have meters. Even if you bargain you will inevitably pay two or three times the going rate for locals – fix the rate before you get in.

A taxi between suburbs in Muscat should cost no more than OR10 engaged or OR3 shared (getting to/from the airport excepted). Expect to be charged double the going rate to/from hotels. If you're in town for a while, collect the card of a taxi driver who proved satisfactory and call them as required.

Until the road labelling project is complete (expected 2017), landmarks (eg the HSBC in Qurm, the Clock Tower roundabout in Rusayl) are more useful for navigational purposes than street addresses when travelling by public transport or taxi.

AROUND MUSCAT

Peaceful alternatives to staying in Muscat include the traditional town of Seeb, to the west of Muscat, and the coastal resort of Bandar Jissah, to the east of Muscat.

Seeb السيب

If you are looking to experience a typical Omani town close to Muscat that barely sees a tourist, you can't do better than a trip to Seeb. A 20-minute drive northwest of the airport, this thriving coastal town has much to offer: there's a watchtower, a lively souq with a colourful textiles market, a gold souq with competitive prices, traditional Omani hat shops, *halwa* (a traditional Omani sweet) for sale, a fine corniche, a magnificent stretch of sandy beach and some of the best squid kebabs in Oman.

Sights

There are no 'tourist' sights as such but Seeb is a great place to experience everyday Omani life. It is also an excellent place to find a tailor. Bring a favourite shirt or skirt and buy some material in a Seeb textile shop. The cloth merchant will advise you which tailor to visit to make a replica in half a day for under OR20. If you've been invited to a special 'do' in Muscat and forgot to pack the dinner jacket, this is the place to get one made for a bargain OR75, including material.

Seeb Souq SOUQ
(9am-1pm & 4-9pm) One place to get a feel for local Omani culture is on the main one-way road that runs in a circle through the heart of Seeb. Alongside banks and Indian-run 'cold stores', the road is flanked by the **gold souq**, with its windows of bangles and bridal chains, and by *dishdasha* (shirt-dress) tailors, *kumar* (cap) shops and *abeyya* (full-length black robes) boutiques. A circuit only takes a few minutes by car but you could spend half a day exploring the souq on foot.

Between the main road and the sea, the **old souq** is housed in a purpose-built sandy-coloured complex of buildings near the main mosque and is a fun place to explore with camel ropes and walking sticks, piles of spices, fruits and vegetables. Thankfully the wet fish market has its own building further west along the corniche.

The road doubles back on itself just after shops selling Arabic-style sofas and sedans and Omani honey. On the return section of the loop are outlets selling Omani-style traditional ladies' clothing with colourful anklets and embroidered smocking. Interspersed with the tailors are 'wedding services' shops selling strings of lights and outrageous bridal thrones.

Towards the end of the street, and completing the loop, there are many **carpentry workshops** selling *mandoos* (bridal chests). Usually black or terracotta-red and decorated with brass tacks, these make a fun souvenir. A small box costs OR10 or a large chest OR50 with many sizes in between.

Seeb Corniche BEACH
A wonderful 8km corniche, either side of the town, has a landscaped area for walking, enjoying sea views, sniffing drying sardines and watching the fishermen mending nets while footballers compete for a pitch on the sand. Various ad hoc coffeeshops come alive in the evenings. Swimming is possible anywhere along the beach – in discreet swimwear.

For shell enthusiasts, the long flat sands at low tide make a great place to see horn, turret and auger **shells**. Al Abnah Freish Antiques & Gifts, in the town centre portion of the corniche, has a small selection of silver souvenirs and camel sticks.

Sleeping & Eating

There are a couple of pleasant places to stay in Seeb that make an alternative to the busy hotels of Muscat and you won't go hungry as there are many places to eat in town including a couple of more Western-style cafes. One of the best options is to buy squid kebabs (500 baisa per stick) from the vendors on the corniche (opposite the souq) and eat them sitting on the sea wall.

Al Bahjah Hotel HOTEL $
(24 424400; www.rameehotels.com/oman; Seeb High St; s/d OR25/28;) Right in the heart of town (turn towards the sea by Oman International Bank) and with a dhow and a giant coffee pot in the foyer, this simple hotel has basic but spotless rooms. A cosy Indian restaurant with a licence is a popular meeting place for Western expats.

Ramee Dream Resort HOTEL $
(24 453399; www.rameehotels.com; Dama St; s/d OR30/40;) To be honest, there's not much to dream about at this hotel although the sea is only a five-minute walk away and guests can watch herons parachute into the tidal pools in front of the hotel. The resort is 1km west along the corniche from Seeb fish market.

Seeb Waves Restaurant MIDDLE EASTERN $
(24 425556; Seeb Corniche; mains OR2; 9am-2am) Near the harbour in the heart of Seeb, this is a cheap and cheerful venue for roast chicken, chopped salad and hummus.

Al Hamael Trading MIDDLE EASTERN $
(Seeb Corniche; mains OR2, juices 500 baisa; 4pm-1am) This local coffeeshop prepares delicious fresh juices. You can sit at the small sea-facing terrace and watch small boats entering the new harbour, a project that has helped protect Seeb's thriving fishing industry.

Getting There & Around

Frequent minibuses connect Muscat with Seeb (OR1.200). An engaged taxi from the highway near Muscat International Airport takes 20 minutes along Sultan Qaboos Hwy (OR5).

Bandar Jissah بندر الجصة

Bandar Jissah is home to Muscat's most prestigious resort and some excellent water sports facilities. From the nearby village of Qantab, entrepreneurial fishermen will take visitors on a 30-minute/one-hour tour (OR6/OR10) to see the famous **sea arch** that is now almost incorporated into the resort.

If you have your own transport, pause at the spectacular **viewing point** (currently being redesigned) between Bandar Jissah and the long descent into Al Bustan. On the opposite side of the road, those after serious exercise can ascend to Muscat's hidden **40km cycle and walking track** that snakes above Bandar Jissah. A road cut spectacularly through the mountains links Bandar Jissah with Yitti.

Sleeping

Oman Dive Center CABIN **$$**
(Muscat Hills Dive Center; ☎24 824240; www.omandivecenter.com; Bandar Jissah; half-board in cabin s/d/tr OR62/88/114; ⏰beach bar noon-11pm, from 2pm Fri; P@≋) Offering simple *barasti* (palm-leaf) huts with attached showers on the beach, this dive centre is on a lovely sandy bay. Call by for lunch (try the camel burger) or a half-day snorkelling trip (OR20, including equipment hire; OR15 for afternoon trips). Dolphin-watching trips (OR18) offer the chance of seeing whales between December and February. There's no public transport; a taxi costs OR8 from Mutrah.

You can enjoy the peaceful, secluded beach and the club facilities for a nominal day rate of OR4 for adults and OR2 for children (OR2/1 Sunday to Thursday) and stay on for a sundowner.

Shangri-La's Barr Al Jissah Resort & Spa RESORT **$$$**
(☎24 776666; www.shangri-la.com; off Al Jissah St; Al Bandar/Al Husn/Al Waha r from OR135/181/117; P@≋) Shangri-La's Barr Al Jissah Resort & Spa comprises three kasbah-style hotels around a magnificent shared beach and landscaped garden. **Al Bandar Hotel** is the more business-oriented of the three hotels. The sophisticated six-star **Al Husn Hotel** is perched on the headland with its own private beach, and **Al Waha Hotel**, the easygoing, family accommodation, is accessed via a tunnel through the cliff.

Meandering between the hotels, a lazy river offers a fun way of getting from one watering hole to another. The richly carpeted foyers, marble corridors and designer bedrooms and bathrooms in all three hotels make choosing one over the other a matter of whim. The resort includes some of the country's top restaurants: the **Bait al Bahr** (seafood), **Samba** (international buffet) and **Shahrazad** (Moroccan).

There is a complimentary bus service from Muscat International Airport, or it is a 15-minute drive by car from Mutrah.

Yitti يتي

About 25km from Muscat, Yitti boasts a beautiful, sandy **beach** surrounded by craggy mountain scenery. The beach is at the end of a large, muddy inlet that is regularly picked over by wading waterbirds.

If the tide is low, you can wade to a sandbar and look left for a great view of Bandar Jissah's famous **sea arch**. You'll notice a clump of serrated rocks at the end of the inlet. It was believed these rocks were inhabited by *jinn* (genies) and offerings used to be left at their base. Alas, the spirits have gone somewhere more private, according to the local fishermen, due to the disfiguring earthworks on the far side of the creek. A large resort is planned for the entire bay but progress is slow due to the fall in oil prices and Yitti remains, for now at least, a peaceful backwater.

There is no public transport to Yitti, which is about a half-hour drive from Mutrah. There are three routes to Yitti from Muscat. The shortest way is to follow the signs through a deep cut in the mountains from the roundabout in Bandar Jissah. To make an enjoyable round trip, return through Wadi Mayh.

Wadi Mayh وادي مياح

For a taste of a typical Omani wadi within an afternoon's drive of Muscat, look no further than Wadi Mayh. With towering limestone cliffs, sand-coloured villages, back-garden date plantations, straying goats and feral donkeys – not to mention a compulsory watchtower or two – Wadi Mayh has it all. Look out for a pair of stout *falaj* (traditional irrigation channels) that have been shored into either side of the wadi, and carry water from one village plantation to the next.

The wadi has areas where multicoloured layers of rock have been forced into a vertical wall and there are many notable **geological forms** along the route indicated by green signs. Alternatively download the Muscat GeoSites (www.omantourism.gov.om) driving app. The steep sides of the wadi make it vulnerable to fierce flash flooding that often washes out part of the road.

The entrance to the wadi is about 24km from Wadi Aday roundabout in Muscat. To reach the wadi, follow the Qurayat road from the roundabout. After 16km, turn left at the roundabout with the gold eagle. Turn left at the sign for Yitti (at 24km) and the road eventually leads into the wadi. The wadi can be negotiated by car although the last section of road (about 10km) towards Yitti is not sealed. There is no public transport. Wadi Mayh is signposted off the Bandar Jissah–Yitti road.

Bandar Khayran بندر خيران

It's worth driving for at least 30 minutes along the Yitti to Al Seifa road to get a flavour of the inlets or *khors* that make this part of the Muscat coastline so memorable.

The first *khor* is popular with fishermen, but the second *khor* (at 4.8km) is one of those rare entities – a tidal football pitch, giving a new meaning to the term Mexican wave, perhaps, especially as the spectators of this busy pitch include crabs and mud creepers.

An Oberoi Resort is planned for the next *khor* at Shatti Masgour. Thereafter (at 6km), the road hugs the side of **Bandar Khayran**, a large, mangrove-fringed lagoon, more usually visited by boat from Muscat. It is a beautiful spectacle late in the afternoon when the sandstone, and its reflection in the water, seem to vibrate with colour.

Turn right at the mosque in the middle of Khayran village, taking care to dodge the goats and the small boys selling seashells. Turn left at the junction for Safait Al Shaikh (at 12.5km) for some excellent **snorkelling** (watch out for seahorses), or continue to Al Seifa, home to a growing resort and miles of sandy beaches.

Al Seifa السيفا

There's not much to the scenically appointed village of Al Seifa, resting in the shadow of the Hajar Mountains. Nearby beaches to the east, however, offer protected camping for those who bring equipment and provisions. The beaches are worth a closer look as they are a lapidary's dream: in between the sandy bays, pebbles of yellow ochre, burnt sienna and olive green beg to be picked up. For those interested in bugs, the giant-skipper butterfly frequents the surrounding wadis in spring. The whole bay is now the location of an ambitious but not yet wholly complete nor successful tourist development complex.

Al Seifa is clearly signposted off the Bandar Jissah–Yitti road. It is only about 25km but it takes a good 40 minutes to drive because of the winding road and some steep descents. You will need 10 minutes more and preferably a 4WD to find your own beach beyond Al Seifa along unpaved tracks. There is no public transport but a taxi to or from Mutrah costs OR15, or OR10 from Bandar Jissah. Alternatively, there is a water-taxi service to and from the hotel.

Sleeping & Eating

Sifawy Boutique Hotel BOUTIQUE HOTEL **$$**
(24 749111; www.sifawyhotel.com; Al Seifa; r from OR75, r incl half-board per person OR126;) Wrapped around a new marina with the imposing backdrop of Jebel Sifah, this boutique hotel with a range of luxurious rooms with sea views, was designed by renowned Italian architect Alfredo Freda. It will no doubt blossom once the surrounding complex is complete. For now it remains marooned in splendid isolation among a cluster of half-finished villas and unpaved roads.

The hotel's water-taxi (p133) service contributes to the sense of arriving in a remote location. The service links the hotel with Marina Bandar al Rowdha and Al Mouj Marina. Ask for the current schedule at the hotel reception.

As Sammak SEAFOOD **$$**
(24 749111; www.sifawyhotel.com; Sifawy Boutique Hotel, Al Seifa; mains OR7; noon-10pm Fri-Sat, to 6pm Sun-Thu) This atmospheric open-air restaurant on the beach, next door to the Sifawy Boutique Hotel, is a casual venue for sampling quality food. Ask for the catch of the day and the chef's choice of preparation.

Qurayat قريات

There are a number of features to enjoy in this attractive fishing village an hour's drive east of Muscat. Sights include the 19th-century **fort** and a unique triangular **watchtower** overlooking the corniche. The sandy **beach** to the east of the tower extends for many kilometres with only the occasional football team to interrupt it.

The town was once an important port, famous for exporting horses that were reared on the surrounding plains. Sacked by the Portuguese in the 16th century, the town never regained its importance, although it retains a lively fishing industry and is celebrated for its basket makers. The porous baskets are made from local mangrove, and are used for keeping bait fresh aboard the small boats that pack the harbour.

Qurayat is well signposted from the Wadi Aday roundabout in Muscat, a pretty and at times spectacular 82km drive through the Eastern Hajar foothills on a fine highway. Look out for Indian rollers (blue-winged birds) in the palm trees lining the avenue into town. Shared taxis cost OR3 and microbuses OR1.500 from the Wadi Aday roundabout. A taxi costs from OR12.

Mazara مزارع

Positioned halfway along Wadi Dayqah, protected by a fort perched on a rocky outcrop, surrounded by copper-toned mountains and half-buried in thick plantations, the picturesque village of Mazara makes for an interesting day out from Muscat. A loose assemblage of toads, kingfishers and goats congregate in the semi-permanent pools that gather in the bottom of the wadi.

Looming over the village is the enormous **Wadi Dayqah dam**, the largest in Oman. A road winds up to the reservoir, the edges of which have been pleasantly landscaped and provide opportunities for a picnic. The vista of mountains reflected in the plate-glass water is a rare sight in the desert. A seasonal coffeeshop opens up at peak times (November to January) and plans for further tourist amenities are afoot.

Brown signs indicate 'Wadi Dayqah Dam' 19km off the Muscat–Sur Hwy. To reach the crumbling fort in Mazara, follow the road through the village and across the wadi. There is no public transport.

SUR & THE EASTERN COAST

This easternmost region of the Arabian Peninsula holds some of Oman's main attractions, including beautiful beaches, spectacular wadis, turtle-nesting sites and the strawberry-blond Sharqiya sand dunes. As many of the sites of interest lie en route rather than in the towns, it's worth having your own vehicle, although tours cover the whole area.

The main artery into the region is the Qurayat–Sur coastal highway which runs along the scenic base of the Eastern Hajar Mountains. There is only one hotel between Muscat and Sur, but plenty of beaches for camping for those with equipment and supplies. The dramatic stretch of the route between Dibab and Sur is punctuated by some beautiful beaches and memorable experiences, including Oman's most accessible hike along Wadi Shab.

The route along the coast road to Sur ideally forms the first day of a two- or three-day circular tour, returning to Muscat via Sharqiya Sands and Ibra. Alternatively, it makes the first leg of an epic camping trip along the coast to Masirah or Salalah; the road cuts across the sand dunes in a remarkable feat of modern engineering.

Sur صور

With an attractive corniche, two forts, excellent beaches nearby and a long history of dhow-building, there is much to commend Sur to the visitor. In addition to its attractions, Sur is a convenient base for day trips to Wadi Tiwi and Wadi Shab and the turtle reserve at Ras al Jinz. It also makes a good halfway rest point on a round trip from Muscat via the desert camps of the Sharqiya Sands.

History

Watching the boat-builders at work in the dhow yards in Sur, hand-planing a plank of wood, it is easy to recognise a skill inherited from master craftsmen. Sur has long been famed for its boat-building industry and even in the 19th century – when the Portuguese invasion and the division of Oman into two separate sultanates had delivered a heavy blow to the port town's trading capability – Sur still boasted an ocean-going fleet of 100 or more vessels. Demand for ocean-going boats declined once the British India Steam Navigation Company became pre-eminent in the Gulf and the town's fortunes declined correspondingly. Sur is currently enjoying a resurgence, however, thanks to the ever-growing liquid gas plant and a fertiliser factory, which generate many jobs.

Sur

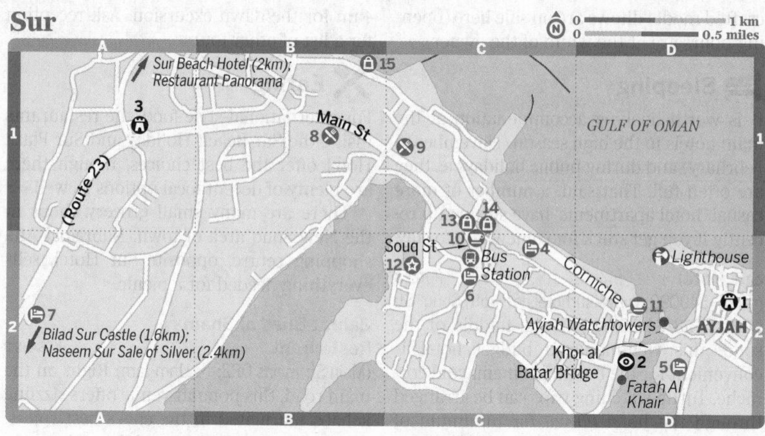

Sur

Sights
1 Al Ayjah Fort D2
2 Corniche & Dhow Yards D2
3 Sunaysilah Castle A1

Sleeping
4 Al Afiah Corniche Hotel Apartment C2
5 Al Ayjah Plaza Hotel D2
6 Sur Hotel C2
7 Sur Plaza Hotel A2

Eating
Sur Sea Restaurant .... (see 6)
8 Zahrat Bilad al Sham Restaurant B1
9 Zaki Restaurant C1

Drinking & Nightlife
Captain's Lounge .... (see 7)
10 Internet Cafe C2
11 Restaurant & Coffeeshop D2

Entertainment
12 City Cinema C2

Shopping
13 Al Haramain Perfumes C1
14 Ladies' Souq C1
15 Salef Al Khaleej B1

Sights

Bilad Sur Castle CASTLE

Built to defend the town against marauding tribes from the interior, 200-year-old Bilad Sur Castle boasts unusually shaped towers. It has been closed for an extended period for restoration, but you can wander around the outside. To reach the castle, turn left off Main St, 1.3km from the clocktower roundabout at the Muscat end of town, at an elaborately kitsch residence.

Sunaysilah Castle CASTLE

(Main St; admission 500 baisa; 7.30am-6pm Sun-Thu) Crowning a rocky eminence, this 300-year-old castle is built on a classic square plan with four round watchtowers. It was the most important part of the defensive system of Sur, a town that was greatly fortified to protect its illustrious overseas trade. A few artefacts help bring some of the rooms to life. You can't miss the castle as its presence looms over the town centre. The entrance is off Main St.

Corniche & Dhow Yards CORNICHE

The corniche affords a picturesque view across to the village of **Ayjah**. Dhows used to be led to safe haven by Ayjah's three **watchtowers**, which mark the passage into the lagoon. It is still possible to see the boats being made by hand alongside this passage. To reach the **dhow yards**, turn left at the souq end of Main St and follow the road in a crescent past the corniche to the great lagoon.

The road circles back eventually to the new souq, passing by **Fatah al Khair**, a beautifully restored dhow built in Sur 70 years ago and brought back from retirement in Yemen. A small open-air museum (open during daylight hours) in the grounds houses other traditional vessels. Look out for a small workshop opposite the dhow: Sur is famous for carpentry and some finely crafted model dhows are on sale here (opening hours are at the whim of the owner).

Sleeping

It is worth booking accommodation at the main hotels in the high season (November to February) and during public holidays as they are often full. That said, a number of more casual 'hotel apartments' have sprung up recently if you get stuck for somewhere to stay.

Sur Hotel HOTEL $

(25 540090; www.surhotel.net; off Souq St; s/d/tr OR18/24/29;) In the middle of the souq, this well-managed budget hotel is convenient for the bus stop, cinema and corniche. Turtle-watching trips can be arranged through the hotel (OR25 for minimum of two people) as well as trips to Wadi Tiwi (OR40) or Wadi Bani Khalid (price negotiable). A booking and transport service to camps in Sharqiya Sands is available.

Al Afiah Corniche Hotel Apartment HOTEL $

(25 561666; Corniche; r from OR20, excl breakfast) Don't get excited by the pink sparkling pillars holding up the porch: the glamour doesn't extend to the plain and cavernous interior. That said, if you just need a bed for the night rather than any attendant services, this hotel offers a convenient location right in the centre of the main corniche with views across to Ayjah.

★ **Sur Beach Holiday** HOTEL $$

(25 530300; http://surhotelsoman.com; Beach Rd; s/d OR45/55;) This old favourite benefits from its location on the beach and all the rooms have balconies overlooking the sea from which you can watch for phosphorescent waves at night. Reasonable Indian fare is served in the restaurant and there are two bars for a quiet drink. 'Veg' and 'non-veg' picnic boxes (OR4.500 and OR6) save the bother of self-catering.

Sur Plaza Hotel HOTEL $$

(25 543777; www.omanhotels.com; off Main St; s/d OR55/65;) This hotel, with comfortable rooms and giant oyster-shaped sinks in the bathroom, is popular with tour groups despite being inland. Oyster's Restaurant serves delicious local kingfish and Captain's Lounge acts as a local meeting place.

There is a Budget rental agency in the foyer and turtle-watching trips can be arranged (OR18 per person), departing at 7.45pm and 4am for the dawn excursion. Ask reception for a list of other tours.

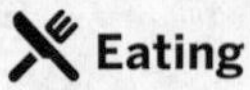

Eating

For international-style food, the restaurants inside the Sur Beach Holiday and Sur Plaza Hotel offer the best choices, though there are plenty of decent local options as well.

There are many small grocery shops in the New Souq area of town. Nabras al Afia shopping centre, opposite Sur Hotel, sells everything needed for a picnic.

Zahrat Bilad al Sham Restaurant KEBABS $

(Main St; mains OR2; 11am-1am) Right on the main road, this popular venue offers sizzling kebabs marinated in the chef's best spices, reputedly from Ottoman origin, and naughty triple-decker fruit juices. If these aren't hitting the spot, then the freshly baked baklavas right next door from the Bab al Hara sweet shop surely will.

Restaurant Panorama MIDDLE EASTERN $

(Beach Rd; snacks from OR1.500; 2pm-2am;) One of the few restaurants beside the sea, this simple eatery – with plastic chairs on a terrace and an air-conditioned interior for the hotter months – offers mezze, kebabs and friendly service at the end of the Beach Road, left of Sur Beach Holiday hotel.

Zaki Restaurant ROTISSERIE $

(off Main St; whole chicken OR2.200; noon-1am) Located next to the Oman Oil petrol station, this popular local chain serves the best rotisserie chickens in town, complete with Arabic bread, chopped salad and tasty dhal. If the roadside location doesn't appeal, then ask for a takeaway and park at one of the picnic shelters near the Sur Beach Holiday hotel, along Beach Rd.

Sur Sea Restaurant KEBABS $

(25 542516; Sur Hotel, off Souq St; mains OR2; 7am-3am) On the ground floor of the Sur Hotel (the entrance faces the other side of the block), this is a popular and lively local restaurant. It serves tasty bean dishes and biryanis for under OR2 and delicious fresh juices.

Drinking & Nightlife

Captain's Lounge BAR

(25 543777; Sur Plaza Hotel, Main St; 8pm-2am) Housed in the Sur Plaza Hotel, this bar is the best place to meet other tourists or Western expats.

Restaurant & Coffeeshop CAFE
(Corniche; ⏲10am-midnight) With old men singing sea shanties under the tree outside and dhows drifting into the lagoon, this coffeeshop is a good place to tap into the heart of traditional Sur.

Internet Cafe CAFE
(Souq St; ⏲1pm-3am) From the outdoor seating area of this place, with a cup of mint tea or a mixed fruit juice in hand, it's fun to watch the residents of Sur amble along past the brightly lit shops of the town's liveliest street.

Entertainment

City Cinema CINEMA
(☎25 540666; www.citycinemaoman.net; English film OR2.500) Screens films in English from 5.30pm daily and is a nonsmoking establishment. Opposite the Fish Market.

Shopping

Sur has grown considerably in the past few years, largely as a result of the nearby gas and fertiliser plants. The souqs of Sur reflect the town's greater prosperity and there are some interesting shops to explore.

Ladies' Souq SOUQ
(Main St; ⏲10am-noon & 5-10pm) There are many textile shops in the Ladies' Souq, some selling braided ankle parts for women's trousers.

Al Haramain Perfumes PERFUMERY
(Souq St; ⏲10am-1pm & 4.30-9pm) The elaborate bottles alone are temptation enough to enter the shop, and being daubed in exotic musk and ambergris is one of Arabia's great experiences. Adjacent to the Ladies' Souq.

Salef Al Khaleej CRAFTS
Between the Flamingo roundabout and the new harbour, this workshop sells handcrafted model wooden dhows. You'll have to take pot luck with opening hours.

Naseem Sur Sale of Silver HANDICRAFTS
(☎99 374003; Main St; ⏲8am-1pm & 4-10pm) Housed in the Global Village shopping centre near the clock tower at the entrance to Sur, this gift shop sells locally crafted items including Sur's famous miniature dhows. The large wooden dhows cost OR20; the smaller dhows are imported from India. Camel sticks make a fun souvenir ranging from OR1 for a simple cane to OR13 for a silver-tipped ceremonial version.

Information

There are several pharmacies and numerous banks, most with ATMs, along Main St and Souq St.

Getting There & Around

Public transport leaves from near the Sur Hotel off Souq St. Buses to Muscat via Ibra (OR4, 4¼ hours) depart at 6am and 2.30pm; via the coastal highway (OR3, 2½ hours) they depart at 7.30am. Shared taxis to the Rusayl roundabout in Muscat via the coastal highway cost OR4 (engaged cost OR16).

Taxis cost 200 baisa per ride anywhere in Sur.

Ayjah العيجة

Lying on the other side of the lagoon from Sur and boasting its own hotel, the pretty, whitewashed village of Ayjah is worth a visit. If you wander over to the lighthouse, there is a fine view of Sur and the dhows returning from sea.

To reach Ayjah, you can either cross Khor al Batar Bridge (Oman's first and only suspension bridge) or drive 10km around the lagoon.

Sights

Al Ayjah Fort FORT
(admission 500 baisa; ⏲8.30am-2.30pm Sun-Thu) This renovated fort which is open somewhat erratically, if at all, seems to have been built as part and parcel of the surrounding merchant houses with their elaborately carved doors and lotus-pillared porches.

Sleeping & Eating

Al Ayjah Plaza Hotel HOTEL $
(☎25 544433; www.alayjahplazahotel.com; s/d/tr OR30/40/50; P @) Ayjah boasts its own hotel. Located on the edge of the lagoon, across the water from Sur, it offers good-value modern rooms with big windows. The hotel's Turkish restaurant (open from 11am to 3pm and 6pm to 10pm) is a pleasant place to enjoy watching dhows beaching at low tide in the lagoon.

Sinkhole Park (Hawiyat Najm Park)

The blue-green, brackish water at the bottom of this peculiar 40m by 20m limestone hole invites a swim and a snorkel. The intrepid can inch round the ledges that surround the pool and dive into the deep unknown. It's known locally as Bayt al Afreet (House of the Demon); you could come face to face with more than you bargained for in the water, the depth of which is still uncertain. If the demon eludes you, look out for the equally elusive blind cavefish instead.

The sinkhole is beside the Muscat–Sur Hwy, near the village of Dibab. Follow the signposts off the highway towards a green oasis. Entry is free between 9am and 11pm and there are toilets but no changing or other facilities at this picnic spot.

From the sinkhole, you can drive along the old coast road for a closer look at the sea and rejoin the highway at the next junction in either direction.

Mountain Road to Jaylah

Along the Muscat–Sur coastal highway, you'll notice several roads zigzagging up the mountainside into the clouds that often top the Eastern Hajar range. They mostly connect with small villages, such as Umq, in the heart of the mountains from where there is no onward route except by foot.

One exception, however, is the graded track carved out of the rock face that leads to the cliff-hugging village of **Qaran**. The route is strictly 4WD and is not for the faint-hearted as the last part of the ascent is a near-vertical climb with sharp hairpin bends. The ascent offers a panoramic view of the coastal plain and an idea of the arid plateau that characterises the top of the Eastern Hajar range. If you're feeling brave, have a good sense of direction and spare petrol, you can follow the road across the plateau to the tombs at Jaylah and descend towards Ibra on the other side of the mountains.

Look out for a brown sign to 'Qaran' or 'Kbaikab Graveyard and Al Jayla Village' off the Muscat–Sur Hwy, 5km northwest of Wadi Shab. Beware, there are no facilities whatsoever on top of this desolate plateau and the nearest petrol station is in Sur (or along Hwy 23 on the Ibra side of the mountains). Watch for grazing gazelle along the route.

Tiwi طيوي

There's not much to the little fishing village of Tiwi, but being flanked by two of Oman's beauty spots, Wadi Shab and Wadi Tiwi, it has found itself very much on the tourist map. Not that it has made many concessions to tourism – there's still only one hotel and no public transport, either to Muscat or to Sur. The locals are nonetheless forbearing of the convoys of passing 4WDs and cheerful when a driver bothers to stop for a chat. If you do stop, ask about Ibn Mukarab. The story goes that this Saudi fugitive paved the steps from his house (the ruins are still visible on the hill) to his tomb in gold. As anticipated, the locals dug the steps up for the booty, making the tomb inaccessible. Ibn Mukarab has since been able to enjoy the peace in death that he couldn't find in life.

Sleeping

There is plenty of ad-hoc camping along nearby beaches. The most popular is Tiwi Beach (White Beach), a large sandy bay 9km northwest of Tiwi towards Dibab, accessed via the old coast road.

Wadi Shab Resort HOTEL $$
(☎24 757667; www.wadishabresort.com; r excl breakfast from OR60, breakfast/lunch/buffet dinner OR4/5/6; P 📶 ❄) The small but modern and stylish rooms of this low-key hotel are arranged in two tiers down the hillside with views of the sea from each verandah. A gate gives access to the beach at the bottom of the incline. Activities include fishing trips (OR45 for one hour), guided half-day hikes in Wadi Shab (OR25), snorkelling (OR2 per hour), and body surfing (OR5 per day).

Getting There & Away

Just 48km from Sur, Tiwi and the two flanking wadis make an easy day trip from Sur; the Muscat–Sur Hwy passes the very doorstep of the town. You might be able to persuade a taxi driver from Sur to take you to Tiwi (OR15) and wait for an hour or so while you explore either Wadi Shab or Wadi Tiwi. Alternatively, hotels in Sur can arrange a tour.

Wadi Shab وادي شاب

Aptly named in Arabic the 'Gorge Between Cliffs', Wadi Shab is still one of the most lovely destinations in Oman – despite the ugly Muscat–Sur Hwy slung across the entrance. The wadi rewards even the most reluctant walker with turquoise pools, waterfalls and terraced plantations; kingfishers add glorious splashes of colour and all-year-round trusses of pink oleander bloom by the water's edge. While swimming in the lower pools is forbidden (they are a source of

DON'T MISS

OMAN'S ANCIENT IRRIGATION SYSTEM

As you travel around northern Oman, be sure to look out for Oman's ancient irrigation system – an engineering highlight of such sophistication and complexity that it has earned Unesco Heritage status.

Comprised of channels, known locally as *aflaj* (plural) or *falaj* (singular), cut into mountainsides, running across miniature aqueducts and double-deckering through tunnels, this irrigation system is responsible for most of the oases in Oman. The precious water is diverted firstly into drinking wells, then into mosque washing areas and at length to the plantations, where it is siphoned proportionately among the village farms. Traditionally, a *falaj* clock, like a sun dial, was used to meter the time given to each farm; nowadays, some *aflaj* are controlled by automatic pumps.

There are more than 4000 of these channels in Oman, some of which were built more than 1500 years ago. The longest channel is said to run for 120km under Sharqiya Sands. Although they can be seen throughout the mountains, the best, most easily accessible examples are in Nizwa, Tanuf, Wadi Bani Awf, Wadi Dayqah and Wadi Shab.

drinking water), there is an opportunity for discreet swimming in the upper reaches of the wadi where you can duck into a partially submerged cave (skinny dipping is strictly taboo here).

Wadi Shab is signposted off the Muscat–Sur coastal highway. You can't miss it: the vista of mountains opening into a pea-green lake is sublime after the barren plain. Vehicles, thankfully, cannot navigate the wadi beyond a small parking area. Toilets, open from 7am to 7pm in the parking lot, are intended to dissuade visitors from urinating in the wadi. Camping and lighting a barbecue are not permitted. As with all wadis in Oman, flash flooding can make them impassable for a time. Check with recommended tour companies for up-to-date information on accessibility, especially after rains.

Activities

Wadi Shab Hike TREKKING

(return boat ride OR2; 4hr return, moderate difficulty) This hike begins with a boat ride across the deep water at the wadi's entrance, organised by enterprising locals, and continues through plantations, crisscrossing the wadi several times before reaching a small pumping-station. Be prepared to wade up to your knees in places and beware of slipping on algae-covered rocks. After heavy rains, bring a bag for your camera and dry clothes.

The path has been concreted (not very sympathetically) for part of the way and passes close to several villages that are hidden in the plantations. At times the path follows an impressive *falaj* (traditional irrigation system) complete with underground sections and laced with ferns. The wadi eventually broadens into an area of large boulders and wild fig trees with many pools of deep water. Look for a ladder descending into one of these pools as Wadi Shab bends to the left. If you duck through a short underwater channel in this pool, you will find the partially submerged cavern. Allow up to two hours of walking to reach this pool.

It's possible to walk beyond the pools to other small villages clustered along the wadi floor but the paths are not so well-trodden and they follow, sometimes steeply, goat tracks over the wadi cliffs. Walking shoes and plenty of drinking water are necessary. The wadi becomes drier the higher you climb into the mountains.

Wadi Tiwi وادي طيوي

With its string of emerald pools and thick plantations, Wadi Tiwi almost rivals Wadi Shab in beauty, especially in the spring when the allotments turn a vivid green. Known as the 'Wadi of Nine Villages', there are excellent walking opportunities through the small villages that line the road. For the more ambitious hiker, there is a strenuous but rewarding two-day hike that begins at Sooee, the last of the nine settlements. Indeed, the route over the mountain to Wadi Bani Khalid has become a popular camping excursion with walking groups.

Wadi Tiwi can be accessed by car but villagers prefer visitors to approach on foot. The road is narrow and steep in parts towards the upper reaches and it is easy to get a large vehicle stuck between the plantation walls.

LOCAL KNOWLEDGE

SPOTTING TURTLES – BEST TIME TO GO

Turtle-watching aficionados time their visit to Ras al Jinz to witness maximum traffic on the beach. This is what they recommend:

Go in July This is the peak laying season for the green turtle when more than 100 females come ashore each night.

Go between September and November Although at least one turtle arrives on the beach every night of the year, this is the best time to witness both laying and hatching at Ras al Jinz.

Go at new moon Although full-moon nights make it easier to walk and to witness the spectacle, turtles prefer dark nights so as not to attract the unwanted attentions of predators, which often dig up the eggs as soon as they are laid.

Go at dawn There is a tour at 4am perfect for seeing the last of the latecomers. At this time of day, there are fewer visitors and you can set your own limits of discretion around the few remaining laying turtles.

Go regardless If the turtles have already departed, then don't be too disappointed: at dawn the sandstone cliffs are burnished rose-red by the rising sun, and the turtle tracks of last night's heavy traffic inscribe the sand like ancient calligraphy – a rare sight that few people get to enjoy.

To reach the wadi by car, turn towards the mountains at a small junction with a signpost for Tracking Path E35 at the Sur end of Tiwi village. Donkeys and herons share the knee-deep grass at the mouth of the wadi. Unfortunately, you will also spot the giant highway pylons that stride across the once picturesque wadi entrance. The road is paved for part of the way. At the point where it meanders into the date plantations it's best to park and walk. There's no public transport but tours can be arranged from hotels in Sur.

Qalhat قلهات

The 2nd-century settlement of Qalhat is one of the most ancient sites in Oman. There's not much left to see except the ruined **Tomb of Bibi Miriam** but if you pay the site a visit, you'll be in excellent company: both Marco Polo in the 13th century and Ibn Battuta in the 14th century stopped here on their travels. You'll also have the satisfaction of knowing that your journey to Qalhat was a tad more adventurous than theirs. Marco Polo considered Qalhat a 'very good port, much frequented by merchant ships from India' and a hub for the trade in horses from the interior. Today only the tomb, water cistern and remnants of city walls are visible, and in place of barques and dhows, all that the sea brings to the shore are sharks, sardines and rays. If you camp nearby, the water is often spangled at night with green phosphorous.

The site began a major five-year redevelopment in 2014. Until the site is redeveloped for tourism, you can spot the tomb from the highway.

Ras al Jinz رأس الجنز

Ras al Jinz (Ras al Junayz), the easternmost point of the Arabian Peninsula, is an important **turtle-nesting site** for the endangered green turtle. Over 20,000 females return annually to the beach where they hatched in order to lay eggs.

Oman has an important role to play in the conservation of this endangered species and takes the responsibility seriously, with strict penalties for harming turtles or their eggs. The area is under government protection and the only way to visit the site is by joining an escorted tour.

While the tour is intended for the wellbeing of the turtle, at peak holiday times large volumes of people flock to the reserve. Thankfully groups are limited to 25 people per guide with no more than eight guides in each session. Despite the reserve's best efforts, there is something immensely intrusive about large, noisy groups gawping at such an intimate act, especially when flippers are lifted out of the way for better viewing and the frightened turtles are chased down the beach by mobile-phone wielding individuals. As such, the experience may not be to everyone's taste.

A maximum of 200 people, including those staying at the guesthouse, are given entry each evening and 100 in the morning, so booking in advance is a must.

Activities

★ Ras al Jinz Turtle Reserve ECOTOUR

(Visitors Centre; ☎96550606; www.rasaljinz-turtlereserve.com; adult/child over 5yr OR3/1, children under 5yrs free; ⏲ museum & gift shop 9am-9pm) Turtles don't approach the beach during the day, so for the best chance of seeing a turtle, join a night tour (from 9pm each evening), bookable in advance online or by phone. If you turn up without a reservation, you may miss the opportunity as maximum visitor numbers are adhered to. The beach is a 900m, 15-minute walk from the visitors centre across soft sand.

Cars are not permitted beyond the visitors centre: a shuttle bus is provided for the elderly and those with special needs. Note that photography is not permitted during the night visit.

There is an excellent museum at the visitors centre (adult/child OR1/500 baisa) with a video in English and German, a 3D cinema and an audio guide to displays and relics charting the history of local interaction with turtles since ancient times.

Between 8am and 1.30pm you can enjoy the magical bay (OR1) without an escort and it's often possible to spot turtles between the waves, waiting for nightfall before approaching the beach.

Sleeping

Desert Discovery Tours DESERT CAMP $

(☎24 493232; www.desert-discovery.com; half board per person OR25; P) Offering a number of en suite air-conditioned *barasti* huts and portacabins, Al Naseem Turtle Camp is 4km outside the turtle reserve on the approach road to Ras al Jinz – handy for a dawn visit to the beach. Children between six and 12 years of age are accommodated at half price (OR10 for children under six).

Ras al Jinz Turtle Reserve HOTEL $$

(☎96550606; www.rasaljinz-turtlereserve.com; s/d OR75/85; P @ ᯤ) Don't be put off by the ugly facade of the visitors centre at the turtle reserve: the sea-facing part is in keeping with the weather-eroded cliffs that flank the bay. The room rate includes the cost of an evening and dawn guided tour of the turtle beach at 8.30pm and 4am.

A restaurant (open noon to 10pm for non-guests) serves international-style cuisine (the buffet costs OR9.500) and there is a shop selling a range of Omani handicrafts. The reserve also offers 10 luxury two- and four-person tents in the grounds (OR120 and OR140 respectively including breakfast and free wi-fi).

TURTLE-WATCHING ETIQUETTE

Watching labour and delivery on Oman's sandy beaches can be an awe-inspiring sight. Serene and patient, the female turtles that quietly lumber up the beach are sure to win the hearts of anyone lucky enough to see the spectacle of egg-laying. Witnessing these gentle giants slip back into the darkness of the returning tide is one those unforgettable wildlife experiences – at least, that is, if the turtles are permitted to make their exit *after* rather than *before* the job is done and without the disheartening spectacle of bullish tourists trying to take a photograph at any cost.

Turtles are no land-lovers, and they are very easily dissuaded from making the journey up the beach. In fact, any disturbance during the turtle's approach to the shore will most probably result in a U-turn and it may be days before the turtle plucks up the courage to try again. Once the digging of pits is over and the laying has begun, however, the process cannot be interrupted. Nonetheless the following actions should be avoided:

- touching or approaching a moving turtle
- standing in front of a nesting turtle
- riding or sitting on a turtle (it happens)
- lighting a fire or using a torch near a turtle beach
- taking photographs with a flash or a mobile phone (cameras are not permitted on the beach at Ras al Jinz)
- leaving litter – turtles often mistake plastic bags for jellyfish, a favourite food.

Getting There & Around

Ras al Jinz can be visited as an evening or dawn trip from Sur, organised through **Sur Hotel** (p152) and **Sur Plaza Hotel** (p152). The journey time is 40 minutes each way. There is no public transport.

If you have your own vehicle, follow the signs to Ayjah and Ras al Hadd. Ras al Jinz can also be reached from Al Kamil, on Hwy 23, via Al Ashkarah (about an hour's drive south).

Ras al Hadd راس الحد

A couple of hotels, some shops and attractive lagoon scenery nearby make this fishing village a useful supply point or alternative stopover for visiting Ras al Jinz. It's not permitted to camp or picnic at night on the beaches here as they are nesting grounds for turtles.

Sights

Ras al Hadd Fort FORT
(admission 500 baisa; 7.30am-6pm Sun-Thu) Built between 1560 and 1570, this is one of many hundreds of similar picturesque forts dotted around Oman. Although empty inside, it's easy to picture the isolation of the fort's inhabitants marooned on this flat coastal plain before the small settlement grew up around it.

Sleeping

Ra's al Hadd Holiday HOTEL $
(25 569111; www.holidayhotelsoman.com; cabins OR35, r OR42; P) Offering good-value accommodation wedged between a calm lagoon full of waders and a sea bobbing with turtles queuing up to come ashore in the dark, this simple hotel is signposted from the castle in Ras al Hadd. The hotel restaurant offers a buffet of international-style dishes. Two-hour fishing boat trips are available for OR25 per boat for up to five people.

★ **Turtle Beach Resort** DESERT CAMP $
(25 543400; www.tbroman.com; half-board s/d from OR45/50, s/d without bathroom OR35/42, s/d cabin OR65/70; P) Offering accommodation in *barasti* and air-conditioned concrete huts of varying degrees of comfort, this camp is located on a glorious lagoon-side beach. The only drawback is that the huts are so close together you are at the mercy of noisy neighbours. The open-air dining area, in the shape of a wooden dhow, is a sociable spot, and there is a bar.

The camp is signposted left immediately after entering Ras al Hadd. A one-hour dolphin-watching trip in a fibreglass boat costs OR50 per boat (up to eight people); a one-hour dhow trip is OR75 per boat (up to 20 people). Other DIY water-sports facilities are available including snorkelling and kayaking (OR2 per hour).

Getting There & Around

To reach Ras al Hadd from Sur, follow the signs for Ras al Jinz but veer left after Khor Garami. It is clearly signposted. There is no public transport to this area.

Al Ashkarah الأشخرة

Wedged between two beautiful white-sand beaches, Al Ashkarah is a lively fishing village and important supply point for the Bedouin communities of the Sharqiya Sands. Umbrellas on the beaches on the southern side of town provide camping opportunities. The sea here is much rougher and more characterful than on the beaches north of town and if you choose to break your journey here, you can look forward to large waves and flocks of gulls itching to join your picnic.

Sleeping

Al Ashkarah Hotel HOTEL $
(25 566222; Main Rd, Al Ashkarah; r OR12) If you arrive too late to set up camp, Al Ashkarah Hotel with its huge whale bone in the foyer, pink doors and ill-fitting carpets, is just about clean. The Golden Beach Restaurant next door can rustle up rice and dhal or an egg roll-up for breakfast. The hotel is on the main road, on the edge of town.

★ **Arabian Sea Motel** HOTEL $$
(97794244; www.arabianseamotel.com; off Ras Al Hadd-Al Ashkarah Rd, Asselah; s/d with sea view OR30/40, per person camping incl shower & breakfast OR6; P) In a superb location at the top of the high tide, where turtles lumber up the beach at night, this low-rise hotel looks more like a government school from the distance. The rooms, however, have starched linen, huge windows, rondelles, plasterwork and equestrian paintings that give them a faded Rococo flourish. Fresh seafood is on the menu daily (from OR4.500).

A favourite with the surfing community thanks to the high waves in summer, the hotel is often full between May to October, so call ahead to check. The owner can arrange turtle-watching at Ras al Jinz for OR15 per person (minimum of two) leaving at 7.30pm for the 45-minute drive. Surfboards (OR15 per day) and stand up paddle boards (OR20 per day) are available.

Al Ashkara Beach Resort HOTEL $$
(☎94 082424; www.ashkhara.com; Al Ashkarah-Shana'a Rd; r/ste OR40/50, r with shared bathroom & fan, excl breakfast OR25) Located 13km south of Al Ashkarah, this small resort has been tastefully designed with wooden furniture and quality bathrooms. Most rooms have a jasmine-covered verandah with a view of the ocean – just as well, given it's a fair walk to the high-tide line. Boat trips (OR25 per hour), quad bikes (OR10) and horse riding (OR6) provide for the restless.

Al Ashkarah to Shana'a Road

Dubbed the 'Dunes Rd', this remarkable feat of engineering cuts a corridor through the auburn Sharqiya Sands and is almost a destination in its own right. The road links Al Ashkarah with Shana'a, the ferry terminal for Masirah. Crossing some of the most inhospitable terrain in the country, it passes small fishing villages, outcrops of aeolite (fossilised sand) blown into extraordinary formations, and the tracks of the Bedu, which ignore the road and continue across it as if it were a minor interruption to age-old caravan routes.

Fill up with petrol and supplies in Al Ashkarah as the road to Shana'a takes about two hours to drive (excluding photo stops). If you arrive too late for the ferry, you can continue on to the town of Hijj and the outpost of Mahout. The latter is at the junction with the main Sinaw–Duqm road (Hwy 32). Both towns act as staging posts for intrepid excursions into desolate **Barr al Hickman**. This shallow coastal area, centred around the recently abandoned *barasti* village of **Filim**, is a haven for birds but floods very easily and quickly often leaving the camping birdwatchers stranded. It is best to attempt a visit here with a guide or veteran of the area, or at least go in convoy with another vehicle and an off-road guidebook.

Beautiful beaches dot the coast all the way from Filim and Khaluf to Sarab, Ras Sidrah and Duqm but it is best, even in a 4WD, to drive along Hwy 32 and make sidetrips to the shore rather than risk getting stuck in soft sand and *sabkha* (thin-crusted salt pans) on the erratic coastal tracks.

Sleeping

Al Jazeera Tourist Guesthouse HOTEL $
(☎99 820882; Mahout; s/d/ste OR12/15/25; P) Given its location in the middle of almost nowhere, the well-run Al Jazeera Tourist Guesthouse in Mahout (also spelt Mahoot and Mahouth) is a surprise find with its Islamic tiles and pillars in a grand corridor punctuated with stained-glass windows. Located at the Hijj junction on the Sinaw–Duqm road, it lies 63km from the ferry.

Mahouth Guesthouse HOTEL $
(☎93 232610; Hijj; r OR15; P) If you are desperate, the Mahouth Guesthouse in Hijj, 45km from the ferry, is just about clean. There's a popular coffeeshop next door that rustles up the basics.

Masirah مصيرة

With its rocky interior of palm oases and gorgeous rim of sandy beaches, Masirah is the typical desert island. Flamingos, herons and oyster-catchers patrol the coast by day, and armies of ghost crabs march ashore at night. Home to a rare shell, the Eloise, and large turtle-nesting sites, the island is justifiably fabled as a naturalist's paradise. Expats stationed here affectionately termed Masirah 'Fantasy Island' – not because of the wildlife, but because anything they wanted during the long months of internment was the subject of fantasy only.

Little is known about the history of the island, except through hearsay. At one point it was inhabited by Bahriya tribespeople, shipwrecked from Salalah. Wiped out by an epidemic 300 years ago, their unusual tombstones can still be seen at Safa'iq. The island has been used variously as a staging post for trade in the Indian Ocean, and as home to a floating population of fishermen attracted by the rich catch of kingfish, lobster and prawn.

Masirah, 63km long, 18km wide and lying 15km from the mainland coast, is still remote, with minimal facilities. As such, it continues to offer a rare chance to see nature in the raw. A sealed road runs around the entire island but without a 4WD it is hard to get a close-up of the coast without a long walk. The northwestern tip of the island is a military zone and is off-limits.

SHIPWRECKED!

Masirah must be the only place in Oman without a fort – unless the air base counts. The local population tolerates the few remaining overseas militia with good grace, but outsiders have not always been welcome. In 1904 a British ship called the *Baron Inverdale* was wrecked off the rugged eastern coast. Her crew struggled ashore expecting Arab hospitality, but found a very different reception. A monument to their massacre in the shape of a concessionary Christian cross is all that remains of the luckless crew.

There were rumours of cannibalism and as a result the sultan decreed the destruction of all local houses – there are surprisingly few permanent settlements, even for the tiny population. A royal pardon was only granted to the islanders in 2009. You'll be glad to know that nowadays the only meat on the kebabs is likely to be camel or goat.

Hilf هيلف

The small town of Hilf, a 3km string of jetties, shops and fish factories in the northwest, is home to most of Masirah's population. Car ferries from the mainland dock at any of the three main jetties that line up along the corniche, which runs parallel with the main street in town.

There are no shops or petrol stations beyond the town, but Hilf caters for most basic needs from food stuff to simple camping and fishing gear, and the town has hotels, banks, ATMs, an internet cafe (without the coffee), post office, pharmacy and modern hospital, all within walking distance of the crossroads on the main street through town.

Limited information about the island is available from the hotels.

Beyond Hilf

You'll notice as you drive around the island that the rough Indian Ocean contrasts with the calm and shallow Masirah Channel, lending a completely different character to the island on either side. There are one or two attractions to draw the visitor away from the beach, including the **Baron Inverdale Monument**, at the far northwest of the island (currently off limits).

Masirah is internationally renowned for its turtles: four species frequent the island, including the hawksbill, olive ridley and green, but the most numerous are the loggerheads. Thirty thousand come ashore each year, making Masirah the largest **loggerhead turtle-nesting site** in the world – the favourite nesting beach is near the Masira Island Resort.

For their sheer diversity, the shells of the island are hard to beat. Spiny whelks (murex) used to be harvested here for their purple dye, and ancient shell middens near Sur Masirah indicate that clams were an important food source for early settlers. Latterly, the island has become famous for the 'Eloise', a beautiful, rare shell unique to Masirah. Needless to say, the collection of live specimens of mollusc and coral is strictly prohibited.

Nightlife on Masirah is limited to 'labour and delivery' among the turtle population – all other entertainment is left to the imagination. High tide on the southwestern shore offers idyllic swimming, but the other coast should be treated with caution due to strong currents.

Bait is available from the fish factories – during winter you can expect to catch something using the simplest hand line.

Sights & Activities

Jebel Humr MOUNTAIN

Jebel Humr (274m) is the highest point of Masirah's hilly backbone and a climb up this flat-topped mountain is recommended for the wonderful view of the island it affords, especially at sunset. The plateau is strewn with fossils. Wear good shoes as the scree can be quite dangerous towards the top. It takes about 30 minutes to hike up the left rump of the mountain and scramble over the rim.

To get there, head out of Hilf in the direction of Sur Masirah, turn left at the sign for A'Samar and scout around the wadi until the mountain comes into view.

Safa'iq Grave Site CEMETERY

They are easy to miss but the 300-year-old grave site at Safa'iq, just inland from the island road, is something of a unique sight, given the location. Look for small standing stones up the hill, 6km north of Sur Masirah. Two rocks are usually the only indication of a grave for men, three rocks for women, but some of the Safa'iq graves have surprisingly elaborate headstones.

Masirah Beach Camp KITESURFING
(☎96 323524; www.kiteboarding-oman.com; Sur Masirah) This kite-boarding camp, with its Caribbean-coloured huts, occupies a salt pan that hasn't flooded for a decade with spits of sand running far into the shallow turquoise sea. Often blowing a gale throughout the summer, it's a paradise for water sports and a sociable meeting point for the like-minded. Run by Kite Board Oman, the camp offers a peaceful retreat and various courses.

Sleeping

With a 4WD, camping in any of the deserted bays on the west coast or at the southern tip is recommended. If you choose the east coast, don't forget you cannot light fires on a turtle beach.

There are now four hotels on the island, three of which are in Hilf and within walking distance of the ferry jetties.

Danat Al Khaleej Hotel HOTEL $
(☎25 504533; www.danat-hotel.com; Main Rd, Hilf; s/d/tr OR25/30/35; P 📶) The 23 rooms of this delightful hotel, near Al Maha petrol station on the road leading southeast out of town, sport large, fancy rooms with exotic repro furniture. The custard-yellow walls and red carpet are an unusual design choice but the rooms have sea views and the management is both competent and helpful.

Masirah Hotel HOTEL $
(☎25 504401; www.almajalioman.com; Main Rd, Hilf; s/d/tr excl breakfast OR20/25/30; P 📶) With multiple beds, commodious bathrooms and a lot of Arabic chintz, you can forgive the goats sitting on the doorstep. This is the biggest and most established of Hilf's three budget hotels and it has a reasonable in-house restaurant.

Serabis Hotel HOTEL $
(☎25 504699; dira2008@omantel.net.om; Corniche, Hilf; s/d OR18/25) The gloomy lobby of this Egyptian-run hotel is a bit dispiriting, as are the basic, cavernous rooms. It is clean, however, and the location at the end of the corniche (next to Al Maha petrol station) is convenient for night-time strolls in the town.

Masira Island Resort RESORT $$
(☎25 504274; www.masiraislandresort.com; Cross-Island Rd; r OR75; 📶 🏊) This attractive, landscaped resort is a 10-minute walk across soft sand to the water's edge; turtles nest on the beach. The restaurant is the only place on Masirah for international cuisine and there's a bar. You need your own transport to reach the hotel.

Eating & Drinking

Under the guise of the ubiquitous coffeeshop, you can find Indian, Chinese and seafood, in addition to the usual Arabic fare, peppering the main street through Hilf. Ask at your hotel for current recommendations as the restaurants change as quickly as the expat staff marooned on the island.

Basic provisions can be found in the souq in Hilf. Abu Shabeeb is the most comprehensive supermarket in town but if you require any 'must-haves', bring them with you.

Turkish Restaurant TURKISH $
(Main St, Hilf; mains OR2; ⏲10am-midnight) For kebabs and whole roasted chickens, this restaurant, between the crossroads and Masirah Hotel, is an old favourite.

Getting There & Away

The ferry to Masirah leaves from Shana'a, off the Al Ashkarah–Mahout road. It is signposted in one direction only; if coming from Al Ashkarah, look for the only paved left turn leading across the salt flats. The shallow lagoons either side of the road turn a stunning red when the algae is in bloom. By car, it takes about five or six hours from Muscat to the ferry departure point, or three hours from Sur. There's no public transport but taxis often hang around the mainland jetty, charging OR40 to Muscat.

The 1½-hour ferry crossing can be characterful with impatient jostling to board the ramp, practised queue jumping, wedging of cars to within an inch of their paintwork, and then the endless wait for a last car to appear from across the desert to complete the load before sailing. At least with the new jetty, the chances of being marooned on a sandbank until high tide are more or less over.

On the old ferries, the journey costs OR10 each way per car; foot passengers travel free. The last one leaves when full at around 6pm to and from Hilf. If you don't relish the ad hoc approach, you can book a ticket on a faster, scheduled roll-on-roll-off service with National Ferries Company and travel in air-conditioned comfort.

During weekends and holidays the queue on the mainland can be very long and entail chaotic waits of up to three hours or more with no opportunity to reverse out if you change your mind about waiting.

National Ferries Company (www.nfc.om; per person OR3, saloon/4WD OR8/OR10; ⏲8am, noon, 3pm & 6pm 1hr trip to/from Hilf) Check the website for the latest sailing times as these are subject to change.

Getting Around

The only way to explore the island is by car or on foot – the taxis only service Hilf. There is no car-hire service on Masirah so the most feasible option for getting around is to bring your own vehicle. A sealed road circumnavigates the island but you'll need a 4WD to get close enough to the sea to enjoy it or to camp by it.

Jalan Bani Bu Hassan & Jalan Bani Bu Ali جعلان بني بو حسن و جعلان بني بو علي

These towns comprise a conglomeration of watchtowers, old fortified houses, forts and ancient plantation walls, all of which lie crumbling in various states of beloved dereliction. There has been little attempt to court the modern world and none at all to woo the visitor, making a visit to these sites all the more rewarding. Look out for elaborately painted metal doors and traditional carved wooden gates sported by the town's residences – both are a feature of the region.

Brown signs dot the edge of town, wistfully stating 'You are on the fringe of the sands' and warning you not to go further without 4WD. Tracks lead from either town into a uniquely wooded area of the Sharqiya Sands but should not be attempted without a guide as these routes are seldom explored by visitors and it is easy to get lost or mired in sand.

The twin towns are 17km from Al Kamil and 36km to Al Ashkarah and make a good diversion to or from Ras al Jinz. There is no reliable public transport.

Sights

Jami al Hamoda Mosque MOSQUE
(Bani Bu Ali; closed to non-Muslims) It's worth trying to stumble on this aged and revered mosque. The low-lying prayer hall is unique on account of its profusion of 52 domes. Non-Muslims are not permitted to enter but you can gain a vantage point across the mosque roof from the neighbouring buildings. A *falaj* used for ablutions runs through the courtyard and goats assemble in the shady lanes nearby. Getting to the mosque is half the fun as the road rides the fault line between settlement and sand.

Follow the signs for Jalan Bani Bu Ali at the roundabout off the Al Kamil to Al Ashkarah road, opposite the Oriental Shopping mall. Drive along the main street and head into a housing area. Turn left immediately after a dilapidated fort (obvious above the palm trees), and follow the tarmac road for half a kilometre. An alcoved water fountain, decorated with tiled butterflies, appears on the left and the mosque is around the next bend of the road.

Bani Bu Hassan Castle CASTLE
(admission 500 baisa; 7.30am-6pm Sat-Thu) This solid, squat castle in Bani Bu Hassan has been well restored and deserves a quick visit if you're passing, though you're unlikely to be passing unless you've followed the plethora of brown signs taking you into the suburban outskirts of town that have sprung up in the castle's honour. Admission is restricted to a small door within a door designed to keep marauders out.

Sleeping

Al Dabi Jalan Bani Bu Ali Tourist Motel HOTEL $
(25 553307; d/tr excl breakfast OR15/20; P) If the quiet authenticity of Bani Bu Ali or its gateway location to the sands appeals, then consider a stopover. With fancy tiling, arched corridors and carved doors, this hotel has pretensions above its ability to deliver but it does at least offer a clean bed for the night. There's a small restaurant next door for tasty biryani (OR2.500).

★ **Al Reem Desert Camp** DESERT CAMP $$
(98 089549; www.alreem-desertcamp.com; r from OR50, without bathroom OR45) This lovely little camp, remote from other camps and yet accessible by saloon car (except after rains), is on the fringe of a unique hem of desert, marked by an abundance of native *ghaf* trees. The location offers a blissfully quiet, authentic experience, in a neighbourhood frequented by the Bedouin. Book ahead to be sure of a bed and some supper (OR4).

This well-managed camp is near the town of Bani Bu Hassan and is signposted from the main road (Hwy 35). Note that for those hoping for a roll in the sands in a brutal 4WD will be disappointed as the dunes here are gently undulating and reach no great height.

Al Kamil الكامل

Despite some interesting old architecture, including a **fort** and **watchtowers**, this small town is more commonly known as an important junction with Al Ashkarah Rd and the Muscat–Sur Hwy, punctuated by local-style cafes. It is something of a rarity in Oman, however, for being one of the few towns in the country surrounded by trees. The low-lying acacia and *ghaf* **woodland** is a special feature of the area, much prized by the Bedouin who use the wood for shade, shelter (as props for their tents) and firewood. Their camels nibble the nutritious new shoots and livestock lick the moisture from the small leaves in the early morning.

Sights

★Old Castle Museum CASTLE

(☎25 557773; Al Kamil wa Al Wafi; adult/child OR2/200 baisa; ⏲9am-7pm) Home to an extraordinary museum, this private castle houses the personal collection of Sheikh Khalfan Al Hashmi. His great grandfather owned the 250 year-old castle and donated it to the government; it was restored to its former glory under the current Sultan Qaboos who gave it back to the Al Hashmi family. The current owner lives in the castle, embellishing the rooms with meticulously arranged collections of copper, ceramics, mirrors, electronics, wood and palm crafts, gleaned from homes around the country.

The museum is viewed on a guided tour and chances are, may end with coffee and dates with Sheikh Khalfan himself. If you have an interest in social history you could spend all afternoon fathoming the mechanisms of metal traps, Bakelite telephones, mincers and redundant cassette players. Alternatively, linger longest in the first room of the tour where a tray of meteorite chips jostles for pride of place among the family's inheritance of silver jewellery that somehow escaped the usual melt-down for gold. This not-to-be-missed castle is signposted from the centre of Al Kamil.

Sleeping

Oriental Nights Rest House HOTEL $

(☎99 006215; onrhoman@gmail.com; s/d from OR20/25; P 📶) Owned by the Al Hajri family, this hotel on the Muscat–Sur Hwy opposite the junction for Wadi Bani Khalid offers simple, friendly accommodation. A new block offers better grades of rooms at higher prices. A familiar choice of Indian and Arabic fare with a few international dishes is served in the hotel's restaurant. Three-hour sunset drives by 4WD (OR40) are available.

Getting There & Away

The Muscat–Sur bus passes Al Kamil twice daily (OR1, 45 minutes) and Muscat (OR3.500, 3¾ hours), but the bus doesn't always stop, especially if it's full. There is no reliable public transport from Al Kamil in any other direction.

Wadi Bani Khalid

وادي بني خالد

Justly famed for its natural beauty, this wadi just north of the town of Al Kamil makes a rewarding (and well-signposted) diversion off the Muscat–Sur Hwy or as a destination in its own right. The approach road, which climbs high into the Eastern Hajar Mountains, zigzags through some spectacularly colourful rock formations, green with copper oxide and rust-red with iron ore, and passes by an *ayn* (natural spring), which is accessed via steps by the side of the road.

Wadi Bani Khalid comprises a long series of plantations and villages that lie in or close to the wadi floor. All year round, water flows from a natural spring in the upper reaches of the wadi, supporting the abundant vegetation that makes it such a beautiful spot.

A few shops and coffeeshops in the villages near the wadi sell basic supplies. There are public toilets and a park at the base of Wadi Bani Khalid and at the picnic site at the pools.

Sights

Wadi Bani Khalid Pools SPRING

(⏲24hr) Most people visiting Wadi Bani Khalid head for the springs which collect in a series of deep pools in the narrow end of the wadi. The pools have been developed into a tourist destination with a (too) small car park, a concrete pathway and a series of picnic huts. Swimming is possible here but only if clothed in shorts and a T-shirt over the top of a swimming costume.

While the scenery is beautiful, the picnic site itself is rather unattractive, and heavily visited at weekends and during public holidays. It is possible to escape the crowds, however, by climbing above the wadi on the marked path. The path eventually leads to Tiwi by the coast. It takes three days to walk (with donkeys carrying camping equipment) and is a popular hike organised by tour agents in Muscat.

Moqal Cave CAVE

(Wadi Bani Khalid) If you want to beat the crowds at Wadi Bani Khalid, then search for

Moqal Cave in the upper reaches of the wadi. Look for a lower path above the picnic area and walk along the bottom of the wadi. You will have to scramble over and squeeze under boulders and ford the water several times. For precise directions, ask the goat herders. If they don't tell you the right place, it's because they don't like tourists penetrating deeper into the wadi. Then again, they may just be worried you'll be lured into the land of gardens and cool streams revealed to those who strike the rocks of Moqal Cave and utter the magic words 'Salim bin Saliym Salam'.

The cave, however, is more likely to reveal evidence of bats and previous visitors. The narrow entrance is finally accessed by a concrete stairway. A torch is needed to see anything, and to find the underground pools, you will need to be prepared to scramble and slither through the mud. To reach the cave, walking shoes are advisable, together with a reasonable level of fitness. If the water levels are high, the route should be avoided. It's inadvisable to enter the cave alone.

Tourist Service Centre VIEWPOINT

For a panoramic view of the wadi plantations, stop at the Tourist Service Centre on the approach road to Moqal Cave. The centre has been closed for years but it overlooks a sea of palm trees and is blissfully peaceful at sunset when most day trippers have gone home. You can bring your own picnic here and enjoy the view from the terrace of the car park.

Shopping

Oman Craftsman House CRAFTS

(hours variable Sun-Thu) This shop in Sayh al Hayl, en route to the pools in Wadi Bani Khalid, sells some handmade pots and palm-woven goods – the closest thing to a souvenir in the region.

Jaylah الجيلة

This exciting destination on top of the Eastern Hajar Mountains is worth the effort as much for the journey through crumbling cliffs and past remote mountain villages as for the reward of seeing ancient tombs on the summit.

The route, which can only be negotiated by 4WD, begins at a right turn for Souqah, just before the town of Ash Shariq (also known as Simayiah – located at the entrance of Wadi Khabbah). The start of the track moves each time it rains: look for a track across the wadi adjacent to a water station signposted for Saih Ar Rak. Make sure you have water, a map, compass and a full tank of petrol. Around 3km after you leave the sealed road, take the right fork for Jaylah (sometimes spelt Gaylah or Al Gailah). The track traces a precarious route through walls of unhinged black shale, waiting for a good storm to collapse. The last 6km of the ascent to the plateau, past shepherd enclosures, is currently poorly graded and progress is slow. At 21.4km, turn steep left by the water filling 'station' and follow the road to the top of the plateau.

Myriad car tracks thread from village to village on the top of the plateau and numerous little communities survive on very little on the more or less barren plain. Until relatively recently, the only access to many of these villages was by foot with an occasional helicopter visit bringing supplies and/or health officials.

If you are feeling adventurous, you can continue over the unmapped plateau to the village of Qaran and drop down to the Muscat–Sur coastal highway, 5km northwest of Wadi Shab. This drive is not for the faint-hearted, though, with near vertical descents and very little margin for error. If you'd rather put your faith in a local driver who knows the road, Mark Tours (p221) offer a visit to the plateau as a day trip from Muscat.

Jaylah Tombs TOMB

(24hr) The 90 or so tombs scattered across the hilltops of Jaylah date back to the Umm an Nar culture of 2000 to 2700 BC and, if you've been to Bat, you'll recognise the meticulous stone towers, carefully tracing the ridges of the high ground. Local belief has it that they were built by the spirit Kebir Keb, which is as good a way as any of describing the collective consciousness of the ancients.

Wadi Khabbah & Wadi Tayein وادي خبة ووادي الطائيين

These two wide and luscious wadis meander along the western base of the Eastern Hajar Mountains and provide a fascinating alternative route between Muscat and Sur. A 4WD is needed to navigate the off-road sections, which invariably involve fording water. The picture of rural wadi life that unfolds as you meander through the spectacular mountain scenery is a highlight. There are numerous plantations and small villages in these wadis and sensitivity is needed when driving through.

Near the point where Wadi Kabbah runs into Wadi Tayein is the village of Tool. Tool is also the gateway to Wadi Dayqah; you can park outside the village and wade across the wadi entrance. Deep pools invite a swim but don't for a minute think you're alone – the steep ravine is a favourite with silent-walking shepherds. Tool lies 10km east of the town of Mehlah, at the end of the sealed road through Wadi Tayein.

Road works were commencing in parts of these wadis at the time of writing, so check the route is easily accessible in the villages at either end of the wadis before committing to the long journey (around three hours).

Al Mintirib المنترب

This small village on the edge of the dunes is an important navigational landmark for visits to the Sharqiya Sands. Camp representatives often meet their guests here and help them navigate (by 4WD only) the route to their site – usually impossible to find independently. Al Mintirib has a picturesque **old quarter** of passing interest for those breaking the drive from Muscat, 220km to the northwest. The village is 10km southeast of Al Wasal Hotel on the Muscat–Sur Hwy.

Sights

★ Bidaya Museum MUSEUM

(admission OR1; ⏲9am-1pm) This quirky little museum on the edge of the sands preserves the history of the Hijri Tribe, written in Arabic on goat skins. A collection of old spears and swords that date back 300 years or more, together with Chinese ginger jars and dishes (an essential part of all Omani households in the last century), household implements and clothing are well displayed in a restored, cavernous old house. Located across the road from the fort in Al Mintirib, it's worth a 20-minute stop before heading into the dunes.

Al Mintirib Fort FORT

(admission 500 baisa; ⏲7.30am-2.30pm Sun-Thu) In the days before the housing of Al Mintirib encroached on its space, this solid-walled fort with its sunken door must have been an impressive sight, holding back the dunes in one direction, and repelling marauding tribes from the mountains. Timings are posted outside the fort but we have yet to find the door open.

Festivals & Events

Camel Racetrack SPECTATOR SPORT

(www.rca.gov.om) The Bedu specialise in raising camels for racing and regular camel races take place throughout the region from mid-October to mid-April. Finding information on where and when racing takes place is a challenge but asking locally is usually the most reliable source of information.

Oman Desert Marathon SPORTS

(www.marathonoman.com) In 2013, the first Oman Desert Marathon only attracted 30 runners. By 2015, 100 international participants took part in the gruelling, 165km challenge, run over six days. Runners must be self-sufficient and able to withstand the high temperatures that often prevail well into November. The marathon is hosted by the Arabian Oryx Camp near Bidayah, near to the race's starting point.

Sleeping & Eating

Al Wasal Hotel HOTEL $

(Al Wesal Hotel; formerly Al Qabil Rest House; ☎25 581243; www.alwesalhotel.com; Route 23, Al Qabil; s/d OR30/35, extra bed OR5) The new owner of this old faithful, located on the Ibra–Sur Hwy 10km northwest of Al Mintirib, has transformed this sleepy hotel into a trendy little sleep over. Simple rooms with elaborate furniture crowd the courtyard and a window in the restaurant displays the chef toiling over the tandoor. Trips into the dunes can be arranged from here.

Al Saula'ee Restaurant & Grills LEBANESE $

(☎91 163777; Route 23, Al Mintirib; lunch biryani OR2.500; ⏲6am-midnight) Sit inside the air-conditioned restaurant or do as the locals do and order a take-away, bowl up to the dunes and spread a cloth on the sand instead.

Sharqiya (Wahiba) Sands رمال الشرقية

A destination in their own right, or a diversion between Muscat and Sur, these beautiful dunes, still referred to locally as Wahiba Sands, could keep visitors occupied for days. Home to the Bedu, the sands offer visitors a glimpse of a traditional way of life that is fast disappearing as modern conveniences limit the need for a nomadic existence.

SURVEY OF THE SANDS

If you drive through the Sharqiya Sands in the spring or after rains, when a green tinge settles over the dunes, you'll notice that they are not the static and lifeless heap of gold-coloured dust that they might at first appear. Not only do they move at quite a pace (up to 10m a year) but they are also home to a surprising number of mobile inhabitants.

The Royal Geographical Society of London, in cooperation with the Omani government, conducted a survey in 1986 and concluded that among the 180 species of plants, there were 200 species of mammals, birds, reptiles and amphibians in the sands. The best way to spot these inhabitants is to look for the prints that slither, wriggle and otherwise punctuate the sand early in the evening and then lie in wait above the point where the tracks end. Sooner or later, the animal will burrow to the surface and scuttle off for twilight foraging.

While each animal has its place in the delicate ecosystem of the sands, the health of the environment as a whole is largely due to one six-legged, black-boxed insect called a dung beetle. Rolling its prize up and down the dunes, it can cover many acres of land and in so doing helps fertilise the fragile plants in its path.

The sands are a good place to interact with Omani women whose Bedouin lifestyle affords them a more visible social role. Despite their elaborate costumes with peaked masks and an *abeyya* (full-length robe) of gauze, they are accomplished drivers, often coming to the rescue of tourists stuck in the sand. They are also skilful craftspeople and sell colourful woollen key rings and camel bags at some of the camps.

It is possible to visit the sands as a day trip, but the majesty of the night sky and the pleasure of dawn in the dunes makes a stay at one of the desert camps a better bet.

Activities

Various desert experiences are available through tour companies (p221) and through the desert camps, either as day excursions or as overnight safaris. Activities include camel rides (OR10 for 30 minutes), dune-driving (from OR25 for a sunset trip with a near vertical descent), quad-biking (from OR5 for 30 minutes for 90cc vehicle), wild camping (OR40 per person), full day camel safaris (OR85), sand-boarding and trips to Bedouin settlements.

It is possible, but highly challenging, to drive right through the sands from north to south, camping under the seams of native *ghaf* trees or tucking behind a sand dune. There are, however, no provisions available, petrol stations or any other help at hand in the sands beyond the desert camps at the northern periphery and in the summer the sands rage with heat. As such, it is imperative that you go with a guide. Off-road guidebooks describe this route but all will advise you not to venture through the sands alone. Huge convoys also ply the sands with up to 100 cars ripping through the desert with little or no thought of the damage this causes to the fragile desert environment and as such cannot be recommended.

Sleeping

Accommodation in the sands takes the form of tented or *barasti* camps that offer the full desert experience. Don't confuse camping here with budget accommodation. The camps are often quite expensive for what they offer. The best-value camps are as follows and prices shown include breakfast and a barbecue dinner.

Many of the desert camps can be noisy and very busy on a Thursday or Friday evening but for the rest of the week, the silence of the sands is reclaimed. If you can't bear to be that far from normal life, there's free wi-fi at most of the camps.

Al Raha Tourism Camp DESERT CAMP $
(☎99 343851, 99 551155; www.alrahaoman.com; half board per person OR20, with air-con OR25; P) Located at the end of a long corridor of orange sand, this camp offers concrete huts decorated with *barasti* that are basic and tired. There's a play area and discounted accommodation for children (children under two years old stay for free; children between two and 12 years old pay OR10). Access is via Al Mintirib along 18km of graded track – 4WD is essential.

Al Areesh Camp DESERT CAMP $
(Desert Discovery Tours Camp; ☎24 493232, 99 450063; www.desert-discovery.com; half board per person r with/without bathroom OR25/20; P) This lovely camp lies on the edge of a silver

sand dune with local Bedouin villages nearby. Accommodation is in tents of various sizes with charpoys (lightweight bedsteads) for optional outside sleeping. A sealed road makes access easy. Call the camp for help along the last portion of track. The camp offers camel and 4WD rides with profits going to local Bedu.

★1000 Nights DESERT CAMP **$$**
(☎99 448158; www.1000nightscamp.com; half-board tent s/d OR73/62, without bathroom s/d OR27/49; P 📶 🏊) This magical camp is a haven of Bedouin-style tents, breezy Arabian-style seating areas and a swimming pool. Despite this oddity, this is one camp where you are genuinely in the heart of the dunes and the challenge of getting there, 19km over a sand ridge from Al Raha camp on the valley floor, is part of the excitement.

A retired Bedford brought the resident dhow here in three pieces; now reassembled as a bar, it makes a fun place to watch those other ships of the desert lope by. Dinner in the carpeted open-air *majlis* (seating area) is a simple buffet jollied along with the hypnotic rhythms of Bedouin drummers and dancers.

Nomadic Desert Camp DESERT CAMP **$$**
(☎99 336273; www.nomadicdesertcamp.com; half-board s/d without bathroom OR49/70; P) This intimate camp, run by a Bedouin family, offers personal service in the heart of the dunes. Accommodation is in *barasti*-style huts with shared bathrooms. Rates include guiding from Al Wasil on the Muscat–Sur Hwy in your own car (or OR10 per person return for transport) and a camel ride. There's no generator and no air-conditioning, making for a peaceful and authentic experience.

Arabian Oryx Camp DESERT CAMP **$$**
(☎94 421500; www.oryx-camp.com; half-board s/d OR45/60) This attractive camp has stolen the march on its flashy neighbour by offering a welcoming, traveller-friendly service. Providing just enough comfort to make the camp appealing to all, it lets the dunes creep in at the edges in well-thought-out excursions and facilities. Just 11km from Al Wasil, a sealed and then a graded road leads up to the camp gate.

Desert Nights Camp DESERT CAMP **$$$**
(☎92 818388; www.desertnightscamp.com; half-board s/d OR211/234; ⏲Aug-May; P @ 📶) This luxury camp offers what has been described as 'shabby sheikh' for those who want to see the sands but don't really want to engage with them. The compact, canvas-roofed cabins have boutique furnishings and the *majlis* (seating area), bar and reception area are decked with Omani antiques. A graded road leads to the camp gate from Al Wasil.

ℹ Getting There & Around

Access to the sands is by 4WD. The Muscat–Sur Hwy closely edges the sands between Bidaya and Al Kamil, giving the easiest access at Al Mintirib. Some graded tracks now penetrate the sands but they are not well maintained and the sand quickly wins back the route. If a Bedouin suggests an alternative route, expect to pay for the privilege of following in his tracks.

Desert driving brings its own set of challenges and hazards; alternatively there are plenty of tours available. Some camps will come and collect their non-driving guests from the Muscat–Sur Hwy for an extra fee (cost varies from camp to camp).

To get to the edge of the Sharqiya Sands by public transport, take a Muscat–Sur bus (from Muscat/Sur OR3/2) and ask to be dropped off at Al Wasal Hotel, located on the Ibra–Sur Hwy 10km northwest of Al Mintirib. It takes three hours from Muscat and 1½ hours from Sur but the bus doesn't stop if full.

Ibra ابراء

Ibra, the gateway to the Sharqiya Region, enjoyed great prosperity during Oman's colonial period as the aristocratic locals set sail for Zanzibar and sent money home for plantations and luxury residences, still in evidence in the old quarter of town. The tradition of farming is continued today, with rich plots producing vegetables, bananas, mangos and, of course, dates. A watchtower punctuates the top of each surrounding hill, indicating the prior importance of the town – an importance it is beginning to enjoy again with the arrival of a university and large regional hospital. Ibra makes a pleasant stop-off for those heading to Sharqiya Sands.

◉ Sights

Ibra Souq SOUQ
(⏲6am-2pm) Ibra has a lively souq that is at its most active on a Wednesday morning. Arranged around a double courtyard, the greengrocery takes pride of place in the centre, with local melons and aubergines making colourful seasonal displays. To reach the souq by car, turn right off the Muscat–Sur

Hwy at a sign for Al Safalat Ibra, just past the Sultan Qaboos Mosque, and the souq is about 500m on the right.

A working silver souq, where *khanjars* (tribal curved daggers) and veil pins are crafted, occupies several of the shops around the outer courtyard, muscling in between carpentry shops where elaborately carved doors are still made. Look out for a shop called 'Sale and Maintenance of Traditional Firearms & Rifle Making': there's always an energetic huddle of old men engaged in comparing ancient weaponry around the tables outside. You will probably also notice piles of flattened and dried fish – a local delicacy, still prized despite the modern road system that brings fresh fish to Ibra via the neighbouring wet fish market.

If trying to reach the souq by bus, say you're heading for the souq and ask to be set down near Al Yamadi turning.

Women's Souq SOUQ

(6am-1pm Wed) Once per week this souq, opposite the main souq, attracts women-only buyers and sellers from all over the region, selling a variety of handicrafts such as baskets, woven cushions and camel bags. Men are not welcome and photographs are prohibited in the only souq in the country dedicated to female shoppers.

Ibra Old Quarter RUIN

The old part of Ibra is a honeycomb of crumbling mud-built houses of two or three storeys. There's a paved walkway of several kilometres through some of the best parts of the old village, accessed by a double archway; note the well on the right of the entrance and the old **Al Qablateen Mosque** 500m along the narrow lane. Several of the houses have been restored by local residents but wander on foot as it's a struggle to get round the corners in a car.

You can reach the old quarter by walking across the wadi next to Ibra Souq and following your nose. Alternatively, follow the brown signs past the souq area and turn right for the local villages of Al Munisifeh and Al Kanatar. This route meanders round the lanes for several kilometers and ends in a parking lot. The double archway marks the village entrance.

Sleeping & Eating

There are a few accommodation options in Ibra. Eating outside these is confined to small coffeeshops. Opposite the souq is a large supermarket called Al Najah shopping centre and there are lots of small groceries, shwarma stands and rotisseries dotted along the main street.

Ibra Motel HOTEL $

(25 571666; ibramtl@omantel.net.om; Naseeb Rd; s/d OR18/20) It's cheap and central but best of all, the owner epitomises Omani hospitality. This modest hotel with a fancy foyer of outlandish plastic flowers has clean rooms and smartly tiled bathrooms. Breakfast is available (from 500 baisa) in the adjoining coffeeshop. The hotel is just off the Muscat–Sur Hwy, behind the Omanoil station.

Ibra Hotel HOTEL $

(25 571873; off Main St; s/d OR25/35;) The artist engaged to work on the exterior of this revamped hotel must have been homesick as the overflows are decorated with cashew nuts and tropical birds, while the downpipes are painted to look like palm trees. It adds heaps of character to an otherwise unexceptional hotel, located on the road connecting Ibra's main roundabout with the town's new bypass.

Al Sharqiya Sands Hotel HOTEL $

(25 587000; www.sharqiyasands.com; old Hwy 23, Ibra; s/d OR32/38;) Ignore the website blurb: on the old Ibra–Sur Hwy just south of Ibra, arranged around an unappealing pool, this once decent hotel has been thoroughly neglected. It still makes a convenient stopover, however, en route to the sands. There is a loud 'local' bar and a more family-oriented licensed restaurant with an international menu.

Rawazen Restaurant TURKISH $

(98 077980; mixed grill with appetisers OR3.300; 8am-2am;) With small cubicles, this popular restaurant on the main road in Ibra (opposite the Ibra Motel) offers cosy dining for good-value prices.

Getting There & Around

The Hwy 23 now bypasses Ibra but the Muscat to Sur bus stops in town (from Muscat OR3.700, about 2¼ hours, twice daily), usually almost alongside the Ibra Motel. A shared taxi costs OR3 to Ruwi in Muscat.

Sinaw سناو

Many people pay a visit to Sinaw just to see its rather wonderful souq, but this modest town does have one or two other, mostly overlooked attractions. If you pass the souq gate on your left and veer around to the right, a left turn after about 500m takes you up the hill towards a **cemetery**. After a couple of kilometres more, you'll come to the old town of Sinaw. Well-preserved multi-storey **mud houses** make this a fascinating place to wander around and give an idea of how this town has always been an important trading post.

Sights

Sinaw Souq SOUQ
(7-11am Thu) Like most other souqs in the country, this market place, arranged around a central courtyard, is at its most active early on a Thursday morning. What makes this particular souq such fun to visit is that it attracts large numbers of Bedouin from nearby Sharqiya Sands who throng to the town to trade livestock for modern commodities. Local ladies wearing bronze peaked masks and transparent gauzy *abeyyas* add to the spectacle.

Just before *eid* (Islamic feast), the centre of town comes to a virtual standstill as camels are loaded (with inordinate difficulty) onto pick-up trucks and goats are bartered across the street. Spirals of smoke emanating from almost every house in the vicinity over the holiday period indicate that the livestock are not traded in vain.

The souq is on the edge of the town, on the Sinaw to Hijj (also known as Hay) road. The souq gates are decorated with a green car for some reason.

Getting There & Away

Sinaw is 65km southwest of Ibra. Although you can catch a bus from Muscat (OR3, three hours), it's not very useful as it leaves late in the afternoon and there's nowhere to stay.

NIZWA & THE MOUNTAINS

This dramatic, mountainous region is one of the biggest tourist destinations in Oman, and for good reason. The area has spectacular scenery, including Jebel Shams (Oman's highest mountain), Wadi Ghul (the Grand Canyon of Arabia) and Jebel Akhdar (the fruit bowl of Oman). In addition, some of the country's best forts can be seen in Nizwa, Bahla and Jabrin.

Many of the sights between Nizwa and Jabrin can be visited on a long day trip from Muscat, and all tour companies in the capital organise such trips. The region deserves more than just a fleeting visit, however, especially if adding 4WD excursions into the mountains.

With a 4WD, an exciting three-day round trip from Muscat can be made via Nizwa, crossing over the mountains from Al Hamra and descending to Rustaq and the Batinah Plain.

Nizwa نزوى

The historic town of Nizwa, two hours from Muscat along a good highway, lies on a plain surrounded by a thick palm oasis and some of Oman's highest mountains. Marked by a grand new double-arched gateway, the town forms a natural access point for the historic sites of Bahla and Jabrin, and for excursions up the mountain roads to Jebel Akhdar and Jebel Shams.

Only half a century ago, British explorer Wilfred Thesiger was forced to steer clear of Nizwa: his Bedouin companions were convinced that he wouldn't survive the ferocious conservatism of the town and refused to let him enter. He would have been amazed to find that Nizwa is now the second-biggest tourist destination in Oman. The seat of factional imams until the 1950s, Nizwa, or the 'Pearl of Islam' as it's sometimes called, is still a conservative town, however, and appreciates a bit of decorum from its visitors. It was named the Capital of Islamic Culture in 2013 for good reason.

Sights

Nizwa Fort FORT
(admission 500 baisa; 9am-4pm Sat-Thu; P) Built over 12 years in the 17th century by Sultan bin Saif al Yaruba, the first imam of the Ya'aruba dynasty, the fort is famed for its 40m-tall round tower. It's worth climbing to the top of the tower to gauge the scale of the surrounding date plantations and to admire the view of the Hajar Mountains that dominate the town.

★**Nizwa Souq** SOUQ
(9am-1pm & 5-8pm Sat-Thu, 5-8pm Fri; P) The site of one of the oldest souqs in the country, this extensive marketplace is dedicated mostly to fruit and vegetables, meat and

fish, all of which are housed in new buildings behind the great, crenulated piece of city wall that overlooks the wadi. If you're not put off by the smell of heaving bulls and irritable goats, the **livestock souq** (in full swing between 7am and 9am on Friday) is well worth a look.

The livestock souq occupies a small plot of land beyond the main market walls, left of the entrance, and the brisk trading in goats, sheep, cattle and occasional camels is a centuries' old tradition.

Part of the souq (nearest the fort) is dedicated to handicrafts and caters specifically to the passing tourist trade. You'll have to try hard to find a bargain for antiques and silver but local craftsmanship is good. Nizwa is particularly famous for crafting silver *khanjars* (tribal curved daggers). Today Indian or Pakistani silversmiths often work under an Omani master-craftsman, especially for pieces designed for tourists, but the workmanship is often exquisite. Prices range from OR50 for a tourist piece to well over OR500 for an authentic piece.

Sleeping

All of Nizwa's hotels are located along Hwy 15 between Birkat al Mawz and Nizwa. You need to book ahead between October and April. All the listed hotels offer free wi-fi and include breakfast.

Majan Guesthouse HOTEL $
(25 431910; www.majangh.com; s/d OR28/35; P) Don't be put off by the tired astroturf at the entrance. This reliable budget hotel, with its Arab decor and carved wooden doors, offers a friendly bed for the night. Next to the Hungry Bunny fast-food outlet, the hotel is 5km east of the town centre.

The hotel is linked to Noor Majan Camp & Restaurant in nearby Manah if you fancy a night in a *barasti* hut.

★Falaj Daris Hotel HOTEL $$
(25 410500; www.falajdarishotel.com; s/d OR59/64; P @) This ever-friendly hotel, 4km east of the town centre, is wrapped around two swimming pools and a bar. With a vista of serrated mountains looming beyond, it is the most characterful hotel in Nizwa. The rooms are more pleasant in the newer block, but the older courtyard often hosts an evening buffet – a sociable, tasty affair with long tables for tour groups.

Al Diyar Hotel HOTEL $$
(25 412402; www.aldiyarhotel.com; s/d OR35/45; P) There is some charm in the gypsum and marble foyer and recent refurbishments but that charm doesn't extend to many of the plain, large, no-nonsense rooms. In a popular town with very few beds, however, this is no criticism. Ask for a room in the spanking new wing which sports modern comforts. The hotel lies 3.5km east of the town centre.

Golden Tulip Nizwa Hotel HOTEL $$
(25 431616; www.goldentulipnizwa.com; s/d OR82/94; P) This rather pretentious, marble-clad hotel has a vast foyer but somehow misses the feeling of Omani hospitality, despite previously hosting members of the royal family. Contrary to first impressions, the internal bar welcomes tourists. The hotel is some way out of town, near the Jebel Akhdar junction, 18km east of Nizwa's town centre.

Eating

★Al Mandi Al Dhahabi MIDDLE EASTERN $
(25 414121; www.mandi-dhahabi.com; opposite Nizwa Souq; mains OR2.500; 6am-midnight) A popular venue with Western expats and visitors, this friendly restaurant serves standard Middle Eastern fare despite its billing as a specialist in Omani and Zanzibari food. That said the *mandi* (rice and meat) dishes are authentic and all meals are delicious. Comfortable chairs make the best of the Nizwa Fort view and wi-fi is available.

Al Duhli Restaurant SHWARMA $
(meals OR2.500; noon-11pm) This simple venue with seating on the pavement has one of the best night-time views in Oman. Situated opposite the souq, the cafe overlooks the fort and mosque, both of which are lit up spectacularly at night. It sells shwarma and kebabs, and is always busy with locals who generally pull up in the car and toot for a takeaway.

Bin Ateeq Restaurant OMANI $
(25 410466; www.binateeqoman.com; off Main St; meals OR2.200; 11am-midngiht) Part of a small chain of Omani-style restaurants, this is one of the few places where you have the opportunity to sample genuine local dishes. It is just a pity that the restaurant hasn't risen to the challenge of increased tourists looking for an authentic experience because

the rather grubby private rooms are not the best ambience for dinner on the ground. Still, it's worth a try.

Information

Banks and ATMs are dotted along the main street that runs from the fort complex to the traffic lights at the Modern Oman Bakery. The post office is inside the souq and a small supermarket is nestled among the eateries opposite the souq. Enormous Nizwa Mall is on Hwy 15 around 10km out of town towards Birkat al Mawz.

For those with a special interest in Nizwa, a website (www.nizwa.net) offers some insider information.

Getting There & Away

Buses run from Muscat to Nizwa Souq (OR1.900, 2½ hours, 8am and 2.30pm daily). Buses for Muscat from Nizwa leave at 6am and 3.40pm.

The Muscat–Salalah bus stops in Nizwa at around 9.30am, noon and 9pm. The fare from Nizwa to Salalah is OR6, and the journey takes 10 hours. Telephone the **Ruwi bus station** (☎24 701294) in Muscat to reserve a seat and check times.

Engaged taxi/shared taxi/microbus fares from Nizwa to Rusayl roundabout in Muscat are OR20/4/2 (to Ruwi add OR1.500/1). Nizwa to Ibri costs OR20/3/2 by engaged-taxi/shared-taxi/microbus.

Coming from Muscat, the bus stop and taxi stand are in the middle of the wadi in front of the fort complex. Buses for Salalah leave from the outskirts of Nizwa, near the junction for the Muscat–Nizwa highway.

Microbuses (300 baisa) link the hotels that lie along Hwy 15, the old Muscat–Nizwa road, with the town centre.

Around Nizwa نزوى

About a 30-minute drive from Nizwa, there are a number of fine destinations that can be visited on a day trip from the town, including Tanuf, Al Hoota Cave (when it reopens), Misfat and Al Hamra. They all lie up against the sloping shoulder of the Hajar Mountain range and can be reached by turning right off the Nizwa-Bahla road, 30km from Nizwa, at the Omanoil petrol station. Brown signs lead from there to each of these destinations. There's no public transport.

There are a number of great hikes in the area, ranging from an easy 30-minute stroll through the village of Misfat to a nine-hour hike in the mountains between Jebel Shams and the Sharfat Al Alamayn viewpoint on the road to Hatt. Pick up a hiking guide from the Ministry of Tourism (p145) for details of Routes W9 and W10h.

Tanuf & Al Hoota تنوف والهوتة

Home to one of Oman's most famous mineral water plants, Tanuf is nestled at the crease between plain and mountain around 35km northwest of Nizwa. The town is sprinkled across the plain with a concentration of date palms and corn fields close to the mountains. If you're happy to follow your nose, a small rural road leads through these plantations to Al Hoota Cave, giving an interesting glimpse of plantation life.

Tanuf is worth a visit for two further reasons. The crumbling old quarter of mudbrick houses, abandoned after attack in the Jebel wars of the 1970s, makes a rich auburn foreground at sunset to the grey slab of jebel behind. If you walk behind this atmospheric collection of old houses, there's one of the best examples of an active *falaj* in the region. The water course doubles in and out of the rock high above the wadi on route to the small bottling plant nearby. For those with 4WD, the route continues on past a dam, high into the mountains beyond.

Al Hoota Cave CAVE
(كهف الهوتة; ☎24 498258; www.alhootacave.com; P) Embellished with stalactites and stalagmites, this is the only cave in Oman developed for tourism. Unfortunately it floods frequently putting it out of action for months at a time. It was closed at the time of writing. If the promise of reopening in 2016 is kept, a visit to the interactive on-site **geological museum** is worthwhile as it explores some of the features that have made Oman internationally renowned among geologists.

If the cave is closed, head for a shady natural park with flowing water on the road towards Tanuf, 2km from the cave. It makes a pleasant place for a picnic.

Al Hamra الحمراء

This venerable village at the foot of the Hajar Mountains is one of the oldest in Oman, and is interesting for its wonderfully well-preserved row of two- and three-storey **mudbrick houses** built in the Yemeni style. There are many abandoned houses in the upper parts of the village which make for an atmospheric stroll.

To reach the old part of town, follow the main road, past the turning for Misfat. The road skirts uphill above the old buildings until it reaches a tree-filled roundabout. Park near the large, square mud building and explore the town and plantation on foot.

Sights

★Bait al Sifah MUSEUM

(admission OR2; 9am-5.30pm) This quirky museum is more open-house than historical display. Three ladies accompany guests around their traditional house in the aged and crumbling village of Al Hamra. They demonstrate the culinary arts of juniper oil production, Omani bread-making and coffeebean grinding and there's an opportunity for a photoshoot in traditional regional costume. Sitting cross-legged in the *majlis* (seating area), surrounded by photos of local sheikhs, sampling coffee and dates and exchanging sign language with the ladies, is an experience not to be missed.

The museum is in the old part of Al Hamra. Park by the roundabout at the western end of town and walk along the street past the historic old Yemeni-style buildings. The ladies will spot you before you see them in the interior gloom of the downstairs entrance.

Sleeping

★The View Resort RESORT $$$

(at the lodge 97 233189, booking office 24 400873; www.theviewoman.com; half-board r with/without view OR130/110; P) This resort lives up to its name with panoramic views from Hail al Shas over Al Hamra basin, a dizzying 1400m below. Don't be put off by the portacabins, cantilevered over the drop: the spacious interiors offer an unparalleled vista from both luxury bed and bathtub. Follow the brown signs from Al Hamra; the 7.5km ascent is steep and 4WD essential.

With a temperature-controlled infinity pool that appears to hover in the sky, an upmarket restaurant with live pasta station and decked seating areas, this is a good place to relax – which is just as well as there's almost nothing else to do. A 1km walk from The View leads to some interesting villages. Alternatively bikes are for hire (OR10 per hour) or book an onward itinerary through Zahara Tours (p221) who own the resort.

Misfat مسفاه

A sealed road leads from Al Hamra up to this mountain-hugging village (sometimes spelt Misfah, and referred to in full as Misfat al Abriyyin), making it one of the few mountain villages that is easily accessible without a 4WD. The mountain flank, draped in date plantations and a terraced sequence of stone houses in the foreground, is very picturesque and often seen in promotional literature on Oman. For the best view of the entire village, turn right by the public toilets before you reach the village.

Sleeping

★Misfah Guest House GUESTHOUSE $$

(Misfah Old House; 99 338491; bandb.misfah@gmail.com; half-board d OR70, half-board s/d without bathroom OR40/55; @) This family-run enterprise is in the heart of Misfat village and a five- to 10-minute walk from the car park. It's housed in two wonderful old buildings – family heirlooms of the Al Abri family. One of the few places to sample genuine Omani home-cooked dishes, it's possible to call in just for lunch (OR25 for up to five people) if you book in advance. Reservations are essential.

Call from the car park and the guesthouse staff will meet you to ensure you find the way through a labyrinth of alleys, archways and plantations paths. If you're navigating the village on your own, look for signs for Misfah Old House. Beware though: once you have descended through the village and entered the enchanted garden of date, lemon and mango trees, you won't want to leave.

Mountain Road via Hatt & Wadi Bani Awf اهات ووادي بني عوف

This truly spectacular road over the Western Hajar Mountains affords some of the best views in Oman. It can be accomplished as a long round-trip from Muscat or as a more leisurely outing from Nizwa to Rustaq. With three sleeping options along the route, the road enables a major exploration of the mountains. Although the mountain part of the route is only 70km long, it takes at least four hours to drive and a 4WD is essential to negotiate the sustained, off-road descent into Wadi Bani Awf. This route passes through

WORTH A TRIP

MISFAT – AT THE HEART OF THE HAJAR MOUNTAINS

For a magnificent introduction to life among the date palms on the flank of Oman's highest mountain, a hike through the picture-perfect village of Misfat is highly recommended. Understandably, locals insist on visitors parking on the edge of the village and you'll see why as you begin to climb down through the narrow alleyways of the village and along the edge of the encompassed plantations. This is one of the few villages that actively welcomes tourists but in return visitors are requested to stick to the well-marked trails, respect marked no-go areas and to refrain from smoking, drinking alcohol and picking fruit – the village's main livelihood. It is also necessary to dress modestly (covering knees and shoulders).

If you're not keen on finding your own way between the flowing *aflaj* (irrigation channels) and abundant terraces of crops, the village guest house (p172) offers a three-hour guided cultural tour (OR25 for up to 10 people) with a local resident. This is quite the best way of learning about life in a traditional Omani community at the heart of the Hajar Mountains, although be sure to ask before taking photographs of local people.

It has to be said that the walking isn't easy with uneven, slippery steps leading between steeply descending plantation fields. The guesthouse offers use of its facilities (tea, coffee, dates, loos, sitting area with fan) for 500 baisa per person – a welcome pause on the long, hot pull up to the road on the return.

For a gentler experience, a 30-minute shady walk from the guesthouse to a nearby spring is one of the few almost-level routes through a mountain village. Follow the yellow, white and red markers until the main water channel and then follow the channel to the spring.

remote, rugged country and you should take the necessary precautions (spare tyre, jack, water, warm clothing, walking shoes and basic provisions). Check weather conditions before you leave and do not attempt the journey during or after rains.

Follow the signs for Al Hoota Cave from the Nizwa–Bahla road. You'll see a brown sign, just before reaching the cave, indicating Bilad Sayt (Balad Seet). The road, zig-zagging up the mountain in front of you, is sealed for the entire ascent. Look out for wild palms and clumps of aloe. Zero your odometer at the base of the road and at 23.9km you will come to the **Sharfat al Alamayn** (sometimes spelt Shorfet al Alamin) viewpoint, on the saddle of the ridge: this is the highest point in the road. It's worth spending time here (there's a small hotel on the top) to enjoy the scenery and to look for wolf traps (piles of stone with a slate trap door) before the long descent into the village of **Hatt**. This traditional mountain oasis is best explored on foot or, to avoid being intrusive, admired at a distance. It has no facilities for tourists.

After Hatt, the road continues for another 6km, skirting past **Bilad Sayt**, which is off the road to the left. The village is well worth a detour. With its picture-postcard perfection of terraced fields and sun-baked houses, it's one of the prettiest villages in the area. The villagers prefer visitors to park outside and walk in or simply view the village from a distance.

At 43.8km, the road passes the entrance to aptly named **Snake Gorge**, a popular destination for adventure hikers and climbers, and through the middle of a football pitch. From here the main track meanders around the mountain to the exit of Snake Gorge at 49.6km, signalled by a neat row of trees. If you're here in the spring, look out for a beautiful yellow-flowering tree *(Tecomella al Zamah)* that some say is indigenous to the area.

Continue along the main track into **Wadi Bani Awf**, ignoring the left fork at 57.2km that leads into Wadi Sahtan. Wadi Bani Awf runs through a magnificent canyon, with limestone cliffs towering above the wadi bottom. Plantations of dates, lemons and mangos cling to the wadi's edge providing a livelihood for small settlements that lurk in the perpetual shadow of the jebel. At 59.4km you will pass through the small wadi village of Al Teekah from where an under-construction tarmac road leads eventually to Hwy 13 at 69.7km, passing near the Tourist Village Resort Motel (p184) if you need a place to stay after the challenging journey. Turn left for Rustaq, or right for Nakhal and Muscat.

Sleeping

Al Hoota Resthouse HOTEL $

(☎92 822473; Al Hamra; s/d OR30/40, chalet OR40/50, breakfast OR2; Ⓟ) Run by the local Al Abri family, this simple guesthouse has a range of comfortable, uncomplicated rooms and chalets near Sharfat al Alamayn, the highest point on the mountain road to Hatt. A buffet dinner (OR5) can be rustled up with some notice. A 3km, four-hour trek to a local village is one of many walking options from the guesthouse.

Shorfet Al Alamin Hotel HOTEL $

(☎99 449071; www.shorfetalalaminhotel.com; Al Hamra; r OR40; 📶) Despite being perched on a ledge at the top of the mountains beside one of the most celebrated vistas in Oman, this modest, new hotel has been oddly designed to miss every hint of a view. Still, for a comfortable kip mid-excursion or a base for a hike, it serves the purpose. The restaurant can rustle up a mixed grill (OR4.500).

Birkat Al Mawz بركة الموز

The name of this village roughly translates as 'Banana Pool' – a suitable name, as a quick drive through the village plantation will reveal. Although there is a fort, **Bait al Radidah** (renovated but as yet closed to visitors) with Falaj al Hathmeen running through its ramparts, and some interesting old buildings, most people only venture into Birkat al Mawz to begin the 4WD drive (or strenuous day hike) up Wadi Muaydin to the Saiq Plateau on Jebel Akhdar.

Birkat al Mawz lies on the old Muscat–Nizwa Rd, 111km from the Rusayl roundabout in Muscat and 24km from the *khanjar* roundabout in Nizwa.

Activities

Al Kaleej Tourism ADVENTURE TOUR

(Al Mousel Rent-a-Car; ☎92 311173, 25 443767; www.gulftourism-om.com; ⏲7.30am-8pm) There are several hire car outlets in Birkat al Mawz but this family-run company has a very good reputation and the owner has extended his operation over the years into a full tour service. A 4WD (mandatory for the ascent to Jebel Akhdar) costs OR35 for 24 hours. Saloon cars are available from OR10.

Overnight half-board camping trips to Jebel Akhdar for a minimum group of four cost OR25 per person (or OR50 for one night and two full days). A guided tour through Birkat al Mawz, visiting the *falaj*, plantations and old houses is worth enquiring about.

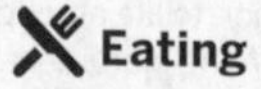

Eating

Al Mazaq al Shahi Coffeeshop MIDDLE EASTERN $

(mains OR2; ⏲8am-noon & 4-9pm Sat-Thu, 4-9pm Fri) This cheery coffeeshop at the crossroads in Birkat al Mawz makes for a friendly cuppa before the long ascent to Jebel Akhdar.

Jebel Akhdar الجبل الأخضر

Without a guide or some inside information, Jebel Akhdar (Green Mountain) may seem something of a misnomer to the first-time visitor. Firstly, Jebel Akhdar refers not to a mountain as such, but to an area that encompasses the great **Saiq Plateau**, at 2000m above sea level. Secondly, the jebel keeps its fecundity well hidden in a labyrinth of wadis and terraces where the cooler mountain air (temperatures during December to March can drop to -5°C) and greater rainfall (hailstones even) encourage prize pomegranates, apricots and other fruit. With a day or two to explore this 'top of the beanstalk', the determined visitor will soon stumble across the gardens and **orchards** that make this region so justly prized. Ask your hotel for a hand-drawn map picking out some of the highlights of the area.

Sights & Activities

It helps to think of Jebel Akhdar as two separate areas – an upper plateau, and a lower plateau on which the main town of **Saiq** is located. In a weekend, you can spend one day exploring each. On the edge of the lower plateau, in a south-facing crescent high above Wadi al Muaydin, are spectacularly arranged terraced villages, where most of the market-gardening takes place and where old men and young boys sell honey and fruit by the roadside. Head for **Diana's Viewpoint** – named after the late Diana, Princess of Wales, who visited this vertiginous vista – with its natural pavement of fossils and dizzying view of the terraces below. The viewpoint is en route to the dangling village of **Al Aqor**. **Wadi Bani Habib**, with its old ruined village and abundant walnut trees, is also located on the lower plateau and is a popular and picturesque place for a walk. For a longer hike, after allowing time to

Jebel Akhdar

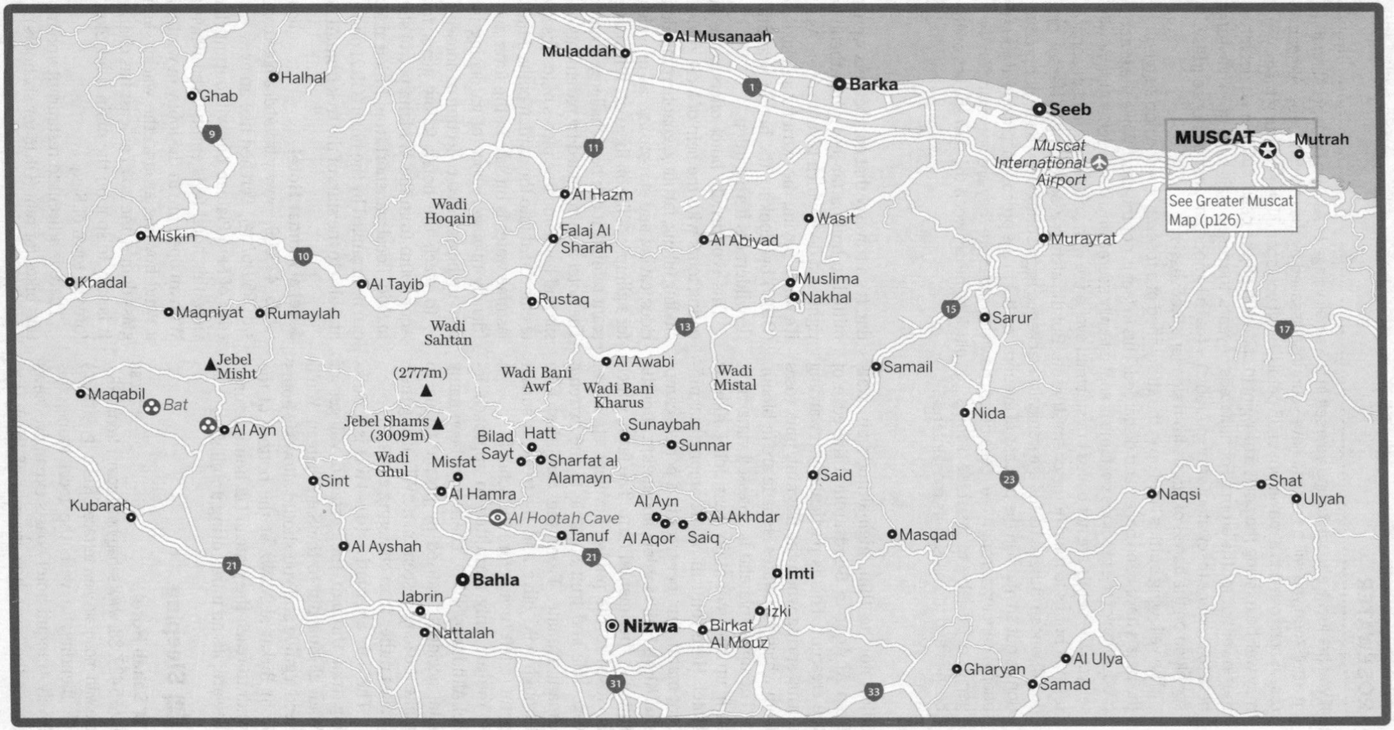
0 20 km
0 10 miles
MUSCAT
Mutrah
See Greater Muscat Map (p126)
Muscat International Airport
Seeb
Barka
Al Musanaah
Muladdah
Halhal
Ghab
Al Hazm
Wadi Hoqain
Falaj Al Sharah
Al Abiyad
Wasit
Murayrat
Miskin
Khadal
Al Tayib
Rustaq
Muslima
Nakhal
Maqniyat
Rumaylah
Sarur
Wadi Sahtan
Jebel Misht
(2777m)
Al Awabi
Wadi Bani Awf
Wadi Bani Kharus
Wadi Mistal
Samail
Maqabil
Bat
Al Ayn
Jebel Shams (3009m)
Bilad Sayt
Hatt
Sunaybah
Sunnar
Nida
Wadi Ghul
Misfat
Sharfat al Alamayn
Sint
Said
Al Hamra
Al Ayn
Al Akhdar
Al Aqor
Saiq
Naqsi
Shat
Ulyah
Kubarah
Al Hootah Cave
Tanuf
Masqad
Al Ayshah
Imti
Bahla
Jabrin
Izki
Nizwa
Birkat Al Mouz
Nattalah
Al Ulya
Gharyan
Samad
1
9
10
11
13
15
17
21
23
31
33

ROSEWATER

If you are lucky enough to find yourself in the small village of **Al Ayn** on Jebel Akhdar in April, then you will be sure to have your nose assailed by the redolent Jebel Akhdar rose. Each rose has a maximum of 35 petals, but if you spend time counting them, you may well be missing the point. The point in cultivating these beautiful briars is not for the flower but for the aroma. For hundreds of years, the rose petals have been harvested here to produce rosewater (*attar* in Arabic) – that all-important post-dinner courtesy, sprinkled on the hands of guests from slender, silver vessels.

The yellowing bottles lined up in the sticky shed of a rosewater workshop suggest the petals have been boiled and discarded. This in fact is not the case. While the exact production of the precious perfume is kept a family secret, anyone on Jebel Akhdar will tell you the petals are not boiled but steamed over a fire with an arrangement of apparatus that brings to mind home chemistry sets. But the alchemy, according to Nasser 'bin Jebel', whose father's hands are ironically blackened each spring with rosewater production, is not so much in the process of evaporation but in the process of picking. If you see people dancing through the roses before dawn, chances are they are not calling on the genies of the jebel to assist the blooms, but plucking petals when the dew still lies on the bushes and the oil is at its most intense.

adjust to the thin, high-altitude air, walk from Al Aqor to **Seeq** around the edge of the crescent. This is particularly rewarding during spring when the fragrant, pink roses from which rosewater is made are in bloom.

The upper plateau is accessed via a right turn up the mountain near Jebel Akhdar Hotel. Here you can picnic among magnificent mature juniper trees in a perfect campsite, **Khab Hail Mahlab**, about 2km after the sultan's experimental farm. The farm, which is closed to the public, develops strains of vegetable and fruit suitable to the extreme Omani climate. From the campsite, hike through wild olive and fig trees to sunset point (a left turn before the school).

You are only permitted to approach Jebel Akhdar by 4WD. There have been many fatal accidents caused by people trying to make the long descent in a 2WD, using their brakes rather than changing gears.

The only alternative to a 4WD is a walking trail through the terraced villages of Wadi al Muaydin to the Saiq Plateau. You'll need a guide and you should allow six hours from Birkat al Mawz at the bottom of the wadi to reach the plateau (12 hours return). Beware: it's an unrelenting uphill slog.

Sleeping

★Sahab Hotel HOTEL $$
(☎25 429288; www.sahab-hotel.com; r from OR83, ste with mountain view terrace OR132; P @ ☎ ≋) Blending in with the local stone, this lovely, tranquil hotel boasts expansive views across the horseshoe crescent of Jebel Akhdar. It's a travesty that competitors were permitted to build a far-less sympathetic hotel right next door which is yet to open. As such, it's worth paying the extra for a deluxe room (OR97) overlooking the hotel's beautiful little wilderness herb garden.

This eco-friendly hotel offers some fascinating tours with the help of local guides, including hiking, farming, goat-herding, donkey rides, caving and star-gazing, all of which offer a glimpse of life on the edge. When there is scant rainfall, it can be a challenge to survive. The hotel is surrounded by pavements of fossils and has some fine pieces of fossilised coral embedded into the garden paths. Mint and jasmine water is on sale in the foyer and the friendly manager's love of gardening is evident in the assorted collection of houseplants.

To reach the hotel, follow signs for Al Aqor 500m from the Al Maha petrol station in Saiq. Local transport from Birkat al Mawz can be arranged by the hotel (OR21 one-way) and also to the start of the trek from Al Aqor.

Jebel al Akhdar Hotel HOTEL $$
(☎25 429009; www.jabalakhdharhotel.com.om; s/d OR50/67; P) Perched like an eyrie on the edge of Saiq Plateau but without much of a view, this hotel feels empty even when full. With an open fire in the lobby in winter and a wind howling around the wacky stained-glass domes, the hotel at least has character. It is easy to spot on the main road, 2km before the town of Saiq.

There is a licensed restaurant and mountain bikes for rent (OR15 for six hours).

Alila Jabal Akhdar Oman BOUTIQUE HOTEL **$$$**
(☎25 344200; www.alilahotels.com; half-board package for 2 people from OR263; P@🛜❄) This is one gorgeous hotel. Overlooking a dramatic rift in the mountain floor, the 86 luxury rooms of this refined hotel command views of the 2000m desert canyon below. Built of locally hewn basalt, with hints of the juniper wood for which the upper plateau of Jebel Akhdar is renowned, the resort lives up to its Sanskrit name, 'Surprise'.

A *falaj* runs past the licensed Juniper Restaurant, which offers buffet and barbecue dining (OR15) from noon to 3pm (4pm on Fridays) and a fine dining à la carte menu (dishes around OR10) at other times. An open fire roaring in the lobby takes the nip out of the high-altitude air and a spa (OR46 for a one-hour therapeutic Balinese massage) helps ease the aches from wilderness hiking with local guides. A range of three-hour hikes can be organised through the Leisure Concierge from OR15 per person to the abandoned village of Sarab and beyond. There is a library sporting large slabs of polished fossilised coral from the jebel and a shop selling a few tasteful Omani crafts.

Getting There & Around

Access to Jebel Akhdar is via the town of Birkat al Mawz. Follow the brown signs for Wadi al Muaydin, off Rte 15, and head for the fort. After 6km you will reach a checkpoint where you will have to satisfy the police that your car has 4WD. Saiq is about 30km beyond the checkpoint and the main road, after a series of steep switchbacks up the mountainside, leads straight there.

As yet there is no public transport to the area, but several tour companies, including **National Travel & Tourism** (p138), offer day trips from OR140 per person. It is cheaper and more rewarding to hire a 4WD in Birkat al Mawz and stay at one of the three hotels.

Jebel Shams جبل شمس

Oman's highest mountain, Jebel Shams (Mountain of the Sun; 3009m), is best known not for its peak but for the view into the spectacularly deep **Wadi Ghul** lying alongside it. The straight-sided Wadi Ghul is known locally as the Grand Canyon of Arabia as it fissures abruptly between the flat canyon rims, exposing vertical cliffs of 1000m and more. Until recently, there was nothing between the nervous driver and a plunge into the abyss but now an iron railing at least indicates the most precipitous points along the track and a couple of rough car parks along the rim pick out some of the best viewpoints into the canyon.

While there is nothing 'to do' exactly at the top, the area makes a wonderful place to take photographs, hike the balcony trail, have a picnic (there are no shops or facilities so bring your own) or buy a carpet.

You need only step from your vehicle and you'll find **carpet sellers** appear from nowhere across the barren landscape clutching piles of striped red-and-black goat-hair rugs. Weaving is a profitable local industry, but don't expect a bargain. A large rug can cost anything from OR30 to OR80, depending on the colours used and the complexity of the pattern. Weaving is men's work on Jebel Shams: spinning the wool is women's work. If you can't find room for a carpet, a spindle made from juniper wood makes a more portable souvenir. Failing that, buy a woollen key fob (OR1) from the army of children who come with colourful fistfuls of them wherever you find to camp.

Jebel Shams is a feasible day trip from Nizwa (or a long day trip from Muscat), but to savour its rugged beauty, consider staying overnight on the plateau near the canyon rim at one of the low-key accommodations.

Sleeping

Jebel Shams Resort MOUNTAIN CAMP **$$**
(☎99 382639; www.jebelshamsresort.com; half-board tent s/d OR35/50, cabin s/d OR55/70; P🛜❄) Offering cosy stone cabins with bathroom, verandah and heater and some Arabic tents popular with Omanis at weekends, this camp is so close to the canyon rim, you'll have to be strapped down if you're a sleepwalker. Mountain-bike hire (OR5 per hour), pitch and putt and air-rifle practice (OR1 for 10 shots) are available. Pitch your own tent for OR6 (OR16 with food).

The camp is signposted from the Shell petrol station in Al Hamra, 39km (40 minutes' drive) up the flank of Jebel Shams. Local guides are available from OR35 to OR70 depending on which hike you choose.

Jabal Shems Heights Resort MOUNTAIN CAMP **$$**
(☎92 721999; www.jabalshems.com; half-board in tented cabin/bungalow/stone chalet with view OR55/60/75; P❄) Even with recent renovations, it's stretching the imagination to call this a 'resort'. Situated at the start of the walking route to the summit of Jebel Shams (route W4, seven to 12 hours), this simple camp

OFF THE BEATEN TRACK

ADVENTURE IN THE HAJAR MOUNTAINS

Most people would be content with peering gingerly over the rim of Wadi Ghul (Oman's Grand Canyon) but there are those for whom this isn't close enough. If you are the kind who likes to edge to the ledge, then try some of the following adventure activities in the Hajar Mountains.

Hike the Balcony Walk The return hike along route W6 from the rim village of Al Khateem (3km beyond Jebel Shams Resort) to the well-named hanging village of Sap Bani Khamis is a favourite with thrill-seekers. Abandoned more than 30 years ago, it is reached along the popular but vertiginous balcony walk: one false step in this five-hour 'moderate hike' will send you sailing (without the 'ab') 500m into the void.

Cycle at High Altitude For those with lungs built to withstand punishing altitude, try the high-altitude tour that pedals between 1600m to 2300m with two canyons thrown in.

Climb in Snake Gorge If you're comfortable with an extreme angle of dangle, then you might like the climbing opportunities in the upper reaches of this narrow gorge. Enthusiasts have thrown up 'via ferrata' lines allowing those with a head for heights to pirouette on a tightrope 60m above certain death.

Rappel into Majlis al Jinn The 158m drop into this cavern is like a descent into Hades. Fabled as the second-largest cavern in the world – bigger than St Peter's Basilica in Rome, bigger than Cheops' pyramid in Giza – this is one mighty hole. Don't count on *jinn* for company; the only spirit you're likely to feel is your own, petering out with the rope as you reach for rock bottom. Named after the first person to descend into the shaft of sunlight at the bottom of the cavern, Cheryl's Drop is the deepest free-fall rappel in Oman.

Drive the Mountain Road to Hatt You don't need to see the mangled heaps of metal at the bottom of the vertical cliffs to realise that this is one off-road route that needs extreme concentration. If impossible inclines, narrow gaps and heart-stopping drop-offs appeal, this five-hour route is for you.

With dozens of challenging hikes, 200 bolted climbing routes, and an almost uncharted cave system, Oman is one adrenalin rush still pretty much waiting to happen. If you want to be in with the pioneers, contact the mountain camps on Jebel Shams (guided hikes cost from around OR50 from the camps for a maximum of four people). Alternatively, contact **Muscat Diving & Adventure Centre** (p221) which tailor-makes trips for the extremely edgy or **Bike & Hike Oman** (p221) which offers exciting pedal-power tours.

offers a range of accommodation. There's hot water, a small restaurant on site and the chance of a barbecue in the camp cave.

If hiking up from 3000m to the summit of Jebel Shams seems too much of an effort, the kids can settle for swimming, football, volleyball, cycling (OR4 per hour) or quad biking (OR15 per hour). Transport from Al Hamra costs OR45 for a return trip while hire of a sunshade (OR40) helps make a day of it.

Sunrise Camp MOUNTAIN CAMP **$$**
(☎97 100900; www.sunriseresort-om.com; half-board s or d in Arabic tent OR50, chalet OR60; P) In a tranquil location near a dramatic mountain precipice, 50-minutes' drive from Al Hamra, this remote camp makes for a peaceful retreat. Beds are offered in Arabic-style tents or concrete chalets (all with private bathrooms). Guests huddle inside the dining room during bitter winter nights or round their own camp fires. Pitch your own tent for OR5 (OR15 including supper and breakfast).

A three-hour marked trail offers fine views of Rustaq, thousands of kilometres below. A local guide for route W6 costs OR45 and transfers from Al Hamra cost around OR55. To reach the camp, follow the directions to Jebel Shams but turn left at the camp's signboard a few kilometres after the end of the sealed road, before you reach the Jebel Shams plateau. The graded road (4WD essential) zigzags up a neighbouring flank of the mountain.

Getting There & Away

The junction for Jebel Shams is clearly signposted off the Nizwa–Bahla road, 30km or so from Nizwa. Turn right at the Omanoil petrol station then left after 12km at a Shell petrol station and follow the sealed road along the bottom of the wadi. Around 9km after the Shell petrol station, the road passes the vacant village of Ghul at the entrance of the Wadi Ghul canyon (you can access the canyon for a short distance only), providing a good photo opportunity.

The road climbs through a series of sharp hairpin bends to the top of Jebel Shams. The road then gives way to a well-graded track that climbs eventually to the military radar site on the summit (closed to visitors). There's a right turn just before the summit that leads, after 10 minutes' drive or so, to the canyon rim, 28km from the Shell station.

For a rewarding drive with spectacular views, you can continue up the graded track towards the summit of Jebel Shams (the very top is a restricted area, closed to the public) and follow the signs for Krub and Al Marrat. Continue around the loop via the Sunrise Resort, passing the ruins of ancient burial sites.

It is sometimes possible but foolhardy to attempt Jebel Shams without a 4WD, and car-hire agencies won't thank you for the uninsurable abuse of their car. Big holes in the road open up after rains. There is no public transport.

Bahla & Jabrin بهلاء وجبرين

Ask anyone in Oman what Bahla means to them and historians will single it out for its fort, expats for its potteries; but any Omani not resident in the town will be sure to respond with '*jinn*'. These devilishly difficult spirits are blamed for all manner of evil-eye activities, but you're unlikely to encounter them unless you understand Arabic, as they are considered a living legend in the folklore of the country. Nearby Jabrin, accessible via the brand new, triumphal 'Gateway to Bahla' (an enormous double-arched construction over the road with grand views of Bahla) boasts its own impressive fort.

Sights

★Bahla Fort FORT

(www.virtualbahla.com; admission 500 baisa; 8.30am-4pm Sat-Thu, 8-11am Fri) A remarkable set of battlements is noticeable at every turn in the road, running impressively along the wadi and making Bahla one of the most comprehensive walled cities in the world. These walls extend for several kilometres and are said to have been designed 600 years ago by a woman. Part and parcel of the battlements is the impressive fort, built by the Bani Nebhan tribe who were dominant in the area from the 12th to the 15th centuries.

After many years of restoration, Bahla Fort, which is one of the most comprehensive in Oman, is now open to the public and easily proves why it was granted Unesco World Heritage Site status in 1987. There are a few interpretative panels and some tourist information and you can gain a further idea of the purpose of each room by referring to the website.

The surrounding mud-brick settlement is a fine example of a Medieval Islamic community organised around the *falaj*. It is better to explore the twisting lanes on foot.

Bahla Potteries WORKSHOPS

(8am-1pm & 4.30-6pm Sat-Thu) All over Oman you'll spot terracotta pots with simple ribbed decorations at the entrances to smart villas and hotels. The famous potteries where these beloved vessels are made are humble in comparison, buried in Bahla's backstreets. To reach them, follow the main road through the town centre towards the plantations. After 500m you'll come to a number of potteries. Beware, the streets are very narrow and it's easy to get a 4WD stuck. Better to walk if you're not planning a big purchase.

The traditional unglazed water pots cost a couple of rials; a large 'Ali Baba' pot fetches around OR40.

Bahla Old Souq SOUQ

(6-10am) Bahla has a traditional souq with homemade ropes and *fadl* (large metal platters used for feeding the whole family) for sale, and a beautiful tree shading the tiny, central courtyard. To find the souq, turn off Hwy 21, the main Nizwa–Ibri road, opposite the fort; the souq entrance is 100m on the right. It was under reconstruction at the time of writing but possible to wander through regardless.

★Jabrin Castle CASTLE

(admission 500 baisa; 9am-4pm Sat-Thu, 8-11am Fri) Rising without competition from the surrounding plain, Jabrin Castle is an impressive sight. Even if you have had a surfeit of fortifications, make the effort to clamber over one more set of battlements as Jabrin is one of the best preserved and whimsical castles of them all. Head for the **flagpole** for a bird's-eye view of the latticed-window courtyard at the heart of the keep.

Built in 1675 by Imam Bil-arab bin Sultan, it was an important centre of learning for astrology, medicine and Islamic law. Look out for the **date store**, to the right of the main entrance on the left-hand side. The juice of the fruit would have run along the channels into storage vats, ready for cooking or to assist women in labour. Note the elaborately **painted ceilings** with original floral motifs in many of the rooms which seem to spring illogically from different courtyards. Finding these hidden rooms is part of the fun and the defensive mechanism of Jabrin. Try to locate the **burial chambers**, remarkable for their carved vaults. There is even a room earmarked for the sultan's favourite horse. The *falaj* was not used for water but as an early air-con system.

Sleeping

Jibreen Hotel HOTEL $

(☎25 363340; www.jibrenhotel.com; s/d/tr OR28/38/45; P 📶) Conveniently situated on the main Bahla–Ibri road by the Jabrin junction. With sky-blue rondelles in the ceiling, rag-rolled walls, Egyptian gilt-edged furniture and luxurious drapes in the wi-fi equipped bedrooms, this hotel is often full. With no other accommodation nearby, it's worth calling ahead. The attached River Nile restaurant is perhaps the best place for supper outside Nizwa.

Information

There is a branch of the Nizwa-based City Travels opposite the bus stop on the corner of the road that leads to the souq. It acts as an ad-hoc information centre. There is a branch of HSBC with an ATM nearby.

Getting There & Away

Microbuses to/from Nizwa cost OR1 and shared taxis cost OR2 (OR10 engaged). The trip takes about 45 minutes. An engaged taxi to Muscat is OR30. The bus stop outside Bahla fort advertises services at 10.55am and 5.25pm to Ibri and 8.05am and 5.12pm to Ruwi in Muscat. Probably of less interest are the services to Dubai at 2.10am and Salalah at 8.10pm.

Jabrin is clearly signposted 7km off the Bahla–Ibri road. Beware of hitching from the junction, as it is an exposed 4km walk if you're out of luck. It may be better to engage a return taxi (OR6) from Bahla.

Bat & Al Ayn بات و العين

Unlike the discreet modern cemeteries of Oman, where a simple, unmarked stone indicates the head and feet of the buried corpse, the ancient tombs of Bat and Al Ayn rise defiantly from the tops of the surrounding hills, as in a bid for immortality. The whole area feels highly charged, especially at sunset when the distinctive, triangular, tooth-edged **Jebel Misht** apears to catch alight. The mountain is one of Oman's so-called 'Exotics' – a limestone mass that is out of sequence with the surrounding geology.

Just past the sealed road to Al Ayn, a sign leads up a winding paved road to the beautiful **mountain village** of **Sint** (Sant on some maps). With a 4WD and an off-road guide, there are some exciting mountain drives in this area. There is no public transport.

Bat & Al Ayn Tombs TOMB

(⏲daylight hours) FREE Known as 'beehive tombs' (on account of their shape) these free-standing structures of piled stones were designed to protect the remains of up to 200 people. There is barely a hilltop without one, and because of the extent of the site, which lies on an ancient caravan route, the whole area has Unesco World Heritage status. Little is known about the tombs except that they were constructed between 2000 and 3000 BC, during the Hafit and Umm an Nar cultures.

While Bat has the largest concentration, the best-preserved tombs are near Al Ayn. If you time your visit for an hour or so before sunset, Jebel Misht (Comb Mountain) makes the most stunning backdrop for the highly atmospheric site.

The junction for Al Ayn is around 50km from Ibri. The tombs are arranged in a line along a low ridge on the flank of Jebel Misht. A two-bay parking slot opposite a mosque helps focus your eye in the right place; from here you can walk through the foreground plantation and up the hillside into the unfenced site. You need a 4WD and an off-road guidebook to explore the tombs at Bat.

Ibri عبري

Ibri is the capital of the northern Al Dhahirah region. A modern town with a major highway, Hwy 21, linking it to the border town of Buraimi in the north, it has a few sights to keep a visitor busy including a newly renovated fort. The town also makes a friendly stopover en route from the UAE to Nizwa and a base for visiting the Unesco-protected tombs at Al Ayn and Bat. If you have plenty of time to explore Oman, a loop can be made from Muscat via Nizwa, Bat and Ibri, through the mountains along Hwy 8 to Sohar and back along the coast to Muscat – a trip of at least three days.

In Ibri there are literally dozens of shwarma and rotisserie-chicken restaurants along Hwy 21 if you want to get a feel for local life. Banks and supermarkets are clustered around the central roundabout at the turning for Ibri Castle.

Sights

Ibri Castle CASTLE

(admission 500 baisa; 9am-4pm Sat-Thu, 8-11am Fri) Currently the more interesting and complete of the town's two forts, this imposing building has been restored and has brought the old quarter of Ibri to life. There is not too much to see inside but the views from the battlements are grand and the neighbouring gold souq and livestock markets are fun for wandering around. Follow the brown signs from the main road.

Sleeping

Ibri Oasis Hotel HOTEL $

(25 696172; iohotel@omantel.net.om; Hwy 21; s/d OR28.300/38.900; P) The Ibri Oasis Hotel is on the Buraimi side of town. With a polished marble staircase and stained-glass windows, the hotel is mainly used by local dignitaries. An English breakfast is OR3.700 and the dinner menu tends towards Indian cuisine. This is just about the only hotel in Oman to charge for wi-fi (OR1 for 24 hours – one device only.).

Getting There & Away

To reach Ibri by public transport, two daily buses leave Muscat at 6am for Ibri (OR3.700, 4½ hours), passing through Nizwa at 8am (OR1.500, 2½ hours). Buses leave for Muscat at 3.40pm. Microbuses cost OR2 from Nizwa and take two hours.

Buraimi البريمي

For many years the inseparable twin of Al Ain, in the UAE, Buraimi is now divided from its alter-ego by a large barbed-wire fence. This shouldn't be interpreted as a cooling of relations between Oman and its neighbour, just an attempt to sort out a border that leaked in both directions. It's fair to say that there's not much reason to make a special visit other than if you're using the UAE border for Al Ain and Abu Dhabi. If you do visit, take your passport: you cannot pass through the border post (which is in Wadi al Jizzi – 50km *before* the UAE border) without it.

Sights

Buraimi Fort FORT

(admission 500 baisa; 9am-4pm Sat-Thu) Buraimi has a large and interesting fort with decorations that give it a Saharan flourish in comparison with the austere exteriors of most of Oman's interior forts. The market opposite sells *barasti* – plaited palm fronds traditionally used for roofing and fencing – while just along the road, a lively souq trades in locally grown fruit and veg from neighbouring plantations, dates and honey from the mountains, and a handful of crafts (including camel sticks and Bahla pottery) from around Oman.

Sleeping

Al Buraimi Hotel HOTEL

(25 642010; www.alburaimihotel.com; Sohar-Al Ain Rd; r OR47; P @) One of several simple places to stay in town, Al Buraimi Hotel is located along the road to Sohar on the edge of town. It's dated, with a mini fort as a lobby and cavernous corridors, but it is also clean and friendly. There are lots of local eateries nearby and the rooms have been recently refurbished.

Getting There & Away

Three daily buses leave Muscat at 6.30am and 1pm for Buraimi (OR4.200, 4½ hours).

SOHAR & THE BATINAH PLAIN

This flat and fertile strip of land between the Hajar Mountains and the Gulf of Oman is the country's breadbasket and most populous area. Interesting sites include the old castle towns of Nakhal and Rustaq, exhilarating off-road destinations such as Wadi Sahtan and Wadi Hoqain, the fishing towns of Barka and Sohar, and the pristine Damanayat Islands, an hour out to sea.

Many of the sights can be managed on day trips from Muscat, with a tour company or even by public transport. A more enjoyable way of visiting, however, is to hire a car and visit Nakhal and Rustaq en route to Sohar, returning via Sawadi and Barka on a two- or three-day trip. This is difficult to accomplish if relying only on public transport, particularly as there is limited accommodation. With a 4WD (even better with camping equipment), side trips into Wadi Bani Awf or Wadi Hoqain open the door to some of the most dramatic landscapes in the country.

It's also possible to combine the above route with a visit to (or preferably *from*) the Western Hajar Mountain region by using the 4WD mountain road via Hatt and Wadi Bani Awf. In addition, there are many other spectacular wadis with remote villages and superb desert mountain scenery, accessible to those with a 4WD, an off-road guide and a sense of adventure.

On the Muscat–Sohar Hwy, elaborately decorated mosques reflect the Persian influence of the Farsi people who have settled in the region. Also look out for forts guarding the coastal strip at **As Suwayq**, **Al Khabura** and **Saham**. None particularly warrant getting off a bus for, but they may be worth a leg stretch from your own vehicle.

Sohar صحار

The rumoured home of two famous sailors, the historical Ahmed bin Majid and the semifictional Sinbad, Sohar is one of those places where history casts a shadow over modern reality. A thousand years ago it was the largest town in the country: it was even referred to as Omana, though its ancient name was Majan (seafaring). As early as the 3rd century BC, the town's prosperity was built on copper that was mined locally and then shipped to Mesopotamia and Dilmun (modern-day Bahrain).

The town boasts one of the prettiest and best-kept seafronts in the country, but little more than legend (and a triumphal arch over the Muscat–Sohar Hwy) marked its place in history until a decade ago when a vast port-side industrial area transformed the town into a city. The port has brought jobs, an influx of expatriates, new residential areas, giant malls, a five-star hotel, a regional hospital complex and a new university illustrative of Sohar's new wealth. In fact, rumour on the street is that Sohar has pretensions of grandeur that more than match its copper-mining heyday. Watch out Muscat!

Associated in 2011 with unrest during the so-called Arab Spring, the town has sought to slough off its reputation as trouble-maker and offers a relaxed destination on a tour of northern Oman, or a stop-over on the long drive from the UAE to Muscat.

Most of Sohar's sites of interest lie along or near the corniche, 3km from the Muscat–Sohar Hwy.

Sights

Sohar's Municipal Park PARK
(sunrise-sunset) FREE Sohar's glorious beach, with glossy-smooth strands of sand, runs without interruption into the distance. Access to the beach is easiest from a car park next to Sohar's municipal park. Look under the hedges for the mighty minotaur, the largest beetle in Arabia. This nicely maintained park is next to Sohar Beach Hotel, north along the sea front.

Traditional Handicraft Souq SOUQ
(8am-noon Sat-Thu) Only half the workshops in this modern arcade are open but there's a few mat-weaving establishments and an apothecary, where you can pick up some *bukhorr hassad*, a mixture of natural ingredients to ward off the evil eye. Try sage for sore throats, frankincense for constipation and myrrh for joint pains. The opening to the souq is at a bend in Sohar Rd by Al Jadeeda Stores.

Sohar Fort FORT
Built in the 13th century, Sohar's distinctive fort allegedly boasts a 10km tunnel intended as an escape route during a siege. Easier to find is the small museum in the fort's tower, which outlines local history, and the tomb of one of Oman's 19th-century rulers, Sayyid Thuwaini bin Sultan al Busaid, the ruler of Oman from 1856 to 1866. The fort has been closed for several years for restoration but work seems nearing completion.

Neighbouring the fort is Sohar's newly revamped **heritage souq**: the addition of a covered walkway, arcade and wooden doors for the shops has made it a more interesting and attractive place for a wander.

Fish Market MARKET
(7am-noon) The fish market, built in the shape of a dhow, punctuates the northern end of the corniche and is fun to visit early in the morning.

Sleeping & Eating

A Radisson Blu is due to open on the coast near Sohar Beach Hotel and there are several hotel apartments around town for longer stays. A string of unexceptional local restaurants are clustered along the highway. **Lulu Hypermarket**, selling everything you might need for tomorrow's journey, is near the main junction from the highway to the town centre.

★Sohar Beach Hotel HOTEL **$$**
(☎26 841111; www.soharbeach.com; Sultan Qaboos St; r from OR75;) Situated northwest of the corniche on a long sandy beach, the Sohar Beach Hotel has made the most of its traditional-style building to bring a bit of local character to Sohar accommodation. With a good restaurant, coffeehouse, pretty gardens and a pool, it makes a peaceful retreat while being just a few minutes' drive from the town's attractions.

Crowne Plaza Sohar HOTEL **$$**
(☎26 850901; www.ichotelsgroup.com; Sohar-Buraimi Hwy; r from OR80; @) Tiers of bougainvillea lead to the domed porch and grand foyer of this glossy hotel, on the new highway to Buraimi about 15km from the centre of town. It overlooks desolate gravel plains but work will soon begin on Sohar airport in the vacant land opposite. A jazz festival hosted by the hotel in November is tipped to become an annual event.

Al Wadi Hotel HOTEL **$$**
(☎26 840058; www.omanhotels.com; Al Barakah St; s/d OR41/53;) With a lively atmosphere (due partly to the popular 'taxi bar' – frequented exclusively by male taxi drivers), Al Wadi has nicely refurbished poolside rooms and a welcoming foyer with *majlis*-style seating. A buffet (OR8) is offered when occupancy is high. The hotel is on a service road off Sallan Roundabout on the main Muscat–Sohar Hwy, 10km from the town centre.

Dhow Marine Restaurant SEAFOOD **$**
(☎22 024077; mains OR3.500, 300gm of kingfish OR4.300 ; ⏲11.30am-4pm & 6-11pm Sat-Thu, 1-4pm & 6-11.30pm Fri;) In the heart of the busy fish market, this attractive, bright-windowed restaurant serves up the best of the catch fresh from the incoming fishing boats. Preparations range from Indian and Chinese to fish and chips with plenty of non-fish and vegetarian options.

Wardat al Fatah Trading TURKISH **$**
(Sultan Qaboos St; mains OR2.500) For a partial sea view and newly caught hamour from the fish market opposite, this simple eatery on Sultan Qaboos St serves delicious Turkish food at outdoor plastic tables. Next door, the Turkish Food Restaurant & Coffeeshop offers a 24hr service if this cafe is closed.

Getting There & Away

Buses from Muscat (OR2.600, three hours, depart 6am, 6.30am, 1pm and 3pm) drop passengers off at the small hospital near the centre of town and then continue to Buraimi or Dubai.

Microbuses and taxis assemble across the street from the hospital. Microbuses charge OR3.500 to Rusayl roundabout in Muscat and OR4.500 to Ruwi. Shared taxis charge OR10 to Rusayl roundabout and OR12 to Ruwi (OR60 engaged).

Nakhal نخل

Nakhal is a traditional town dominated by the Hajar Mountains and one of Oman's most dramatic forts. The fort was well-placed to protect the large date plantations here that flourish thanks to the presence of abundant spring water. There are a few sights of interest scattered through the plantations spread across the surrounding plain including two old mud-built houses, **Harrat Asfalah** and **Bait al Ghasham**, both of which are indicated with brown signs.

There's no accommodation in Nakhal itself but a couple of attractive resorts lie a short drive away and there are a couple of coffeeshops in town for masala tea and a sandwich.

Sights

★Nakhal Fort FORT
(admission 500 baisa; ⏲9am-4pm Sat-Thu) Built on the foundations of a pre-Islamic structure, the towers and entranceway of this fort were constructed during the reign of Imam Said bin Sultan in 1834. There are excellent views of the Batinah plain from the ramparts, and the *majlis* (seating area) on the top 'storey' of the fort makes a cool place to enjoy the tranquillity. The windows are perfectly aligned to catch the breeze, even in summer.

There are many features to look for: gaps where boiling cauldrons of honey would have been hinged over doorways; spiked doors to repel battering; round towers to deflect cannonballs; *falaj* in case of a siege. The entire structure is built around a rock – a common feature of Omani forts, which saves the problem of having to construct sound foundations. There are public toilets here.

Ain Al Thwarah SPRING

(Ath Thowra Hot Spring; 24hr) FREE Beyond the date plantations that surround Nakhal Fort, this hot spring emerges from the wadi walls and is channelled into a *falaj* for the irrigation of the surrounding plantations. There are usually children and goats splashing in the overspill. Look out for the flash of turquoise-winged Indian rollers, among other birds, attracted to the oasis. Picnic tables with shelters, a store and toilets make it popular at weekends.

Take the short cut back to the main road for a fine view of the plantations.

Eating

Abray Nakhal Coffeeshop COFFEESHOP $

(sandwich OR1; 8am-11pm) This unassuming coffeeshop offers 'Tasty Tea' in a perfect location opposite Nakhal fort.

Getting There & Away

Microbuses and taxis leave from the junction with the main road and in the area below the fort. Microbuses charge OR1 for the one-hour trip to Rusayl roundabout and 500 baisa to/from Barka (30 minutes). A taxi costs about OR7 for the same trip if you can find one that doesn't only travel locally.

Wadi Bani Kharus وادي بني خروص

Famed for its geological interest, this dramatic wadi has only recently become readily accessible to visitors with the construction of a paved road along the wadi bottom. The entrance of the wadi is marked by a small, restored fort, **Al Awabi Castle**, from where the road leads towards the village of Al Aliya, 24km into the heart of the mountains.

If you park at the first bend in the road, you'll notice a great slab of smooth pale grey rock on the other side of the wadi. On close inspection of the overhang, you'll see some of the **ancient petroglyphs** for which the wadi is noted. The rock art features figures, men on horseback and camels but some have sadly been defaced by vandals.

The whole road makes for a fascinating drive, past the terraced fields of Stal village, market gardens anchored to the rock by retaining walls in Sana village, an aqueduct in the village of Ain Karfas. It's worth parking the car and walking into the wadi at **Al Markh** to photograph a pair of venerable old houses that have towered over the plantations here for centuries.

There's a simple coffeeshop in Al Alia but no public transport.

Wadi Bani Awf وادي بني عوف

This spectacular wadi often flows year-round and looks particularly gorgeous when mountain rain causes the *falaj* to cascade over its walls. That said, the trip (currently 4WD only) should be avoided if there is any hint of stormy weather. It is possible to reach the **rock arch** (a fissure in the cliff, about 17km into the wadi) as a day trip from Muscat or Sawadi. If you follow the graded road through the rock arch into neighbouring Wadi Sahtan, you will eventually emerge in Rustaq but beware, this is a long journey.

Wadi Bani Awf can be reached via the mountain pass from Al Hamra on the other side of the Western Hajar Mountains or from the Nakhal–Rustaq road. There's no public transport.

Sleeping

Tourist Village Resort Motel HOTEL $

(99 214873; r OR25; P) This no-frills guesthouse at the opening of Wadi Bani Awf has 11 simple rooms set in a semi-wilderness of flowering trees and shrubs. Dinner is a 'bring your own' affair or you can order in advance. Bit lonesome if you're travelling alone.

Rustaq الرستاق

Some 175km southwest of Muscat, Rustaq enjoyed a spell as Oman's capital in the 17th century and it remains an important regional centre. An imposing fort dominates this friendly town and some famous **hot springs** (Ain al Kasfah) feed into neighbouring public baths (open until 9pm). Turn right at the traffic lights on the way into town and you will find them beside the mosque at the end of the road. Call into the **old souq** opposite the fort; it is used for livestock but some silver items are for sale here too.

Rustaq is an important access point to the mighty **Wadi Sahtan** which threads along the base of the Hajar Mountains behind the town and eventually connects with Wadi Bani Awf via an impressive rock arch. With Jebel Shams towering above the wadi, and impossibly lofty villages perched on

OMAN'S GEOLOGICAL HERITAGE

If geology seems like a frankly 'anorak' pursuit, then a trip through the wadis of the Western Hajar Mountains might change your mind. Seams of iridescent copper minerals; perfect quartz crystals glinting in the sun; stone pencils and writing slates loose in the tumbling cliff; walls of fetid limestone that smell outrageously flatulent when struck; pavements of marine fossils, beautiful for their abstract design and the pattern of history they reveal – these are just a few of the many stone treasures of Batinah's wild wadis.

Although many of these features can be spotted in Wadi Bani Awf, it is neighbouring Wadi Bani Kharus that excites geologists. They go in search of the classic unconformity that is revealed halfway up the canyon walls a few kilometres into the wadi. At this point, the upper half of the cliff is a mere 250 million years old while the lower half is over 600 million years old. What created this hiatus, and what it reveals about tectonic forces, is the subject of speculation in numerous international papers. For the layperson, what makes Wadi Bani Kharus remarkable is that it appears to have been opened up as if for scientific study: the opening of the wadi comprises the youngest rocks, but as you progress deeper into the 'dissection', some of the oldest rocks in Oman are revealed, naked and without the obscuring pelt of topsoil and shrubs. While you're inspecting the rocks, look out for petroglyphs – the ancient images of men on horseback are a common feature of all the local wadis.

All the main wadis in the area – Wadi Mistal, Wadi Bani Kharus, Wadi Bani Awf and Wadi Sahtan – have their share of geological masterpieces and can be easily accessed with a 4WD, a map and an off-road guidebook. Take along Samir Hanna's *Field Guide to the Geology of Oman* too, to help identify some key features. Note that there are currently major roadworks in each of the wadis – the good news is that this means they will soon by accessible without 4WD.

high-altitude ledges, a drive through this region is an off-road highlight that remains strictly 4WD-only at present.

Sights

★Rustaq Fort FORT

(admission 500 baisa; 9am-4pm Sat-Thu, 8-11am Fri) Two cannons mark the interior courtyard of this remarkable fort whose entrance alone signals its size and former importance. Recently reopened to visitors after extensive restoration work, it is a fort-lovers dream, with hidden passages, vertical stairways and massive ramparts.

Sleeping

Shimook Guesthouse HOTEL $$

(26 877071; www.alshomokh.org; r OR50) The only place to stay in Rustaq is Shimook Guesthouse, at the start of the road from Rustaq to Ibri, opposite Hoor Al Ain Hypermarket. A new hotel, it is often fully booked with expat teachers, so it's worth ringing ahead. For dinner, head for one of the small restaurants on the corner (a two-minute walk towards the great Sultan Qaboos Mosque).

Getting There & Away

Microbuses can be found a few hundred metres from the fort on the main road to Nakhal (OR1) or the Barka roundabout (OR2). For Muscat, you must change taxis in Barka.

Wadi Hoqain وادي الحوقين

This fertile wadi, accessible only by 4WD, offers one of the easiest off-road experiences of the region and an intimate view of life under the date palms. A reasonable graded road meanders through wadi-side **plantations** and **villages**, bustling with activity in the late afternoon. Add copper-coloured cliffs and a stunning **castle** to the rural mix, and it's a wonder that this wadi has remained a secret for so long.

To reach the wadi, take the Rustaq–Ibri road. Zero your odometer at the great mosque roundabout in Rustaq at the start of the road and after 15km look for a bridge over a wadi. Turn right here for Neyobet Wadi bani Henai and follow the track into the wadi bottom. At 17km, you will reach the fortified 'castle' in the middle of the wadi. On closer inspection, you'll find the castle is better described as a walled settlement. The best view of the fortification is the approach, with watchtowers and date plantations in the foreground and the wadi escarpment behind.

The track climbs out of the wadi and leads past an abandoned settlement in As Salam. It crosses the wadi once or twice more, and follows a *falaj* channel for part of the way. Eventually the track emerges in a plantation and block-making village at 35km. The local industry of concrete block-making for construction is a feature of many small towns in Oman. If you get lost in the village, locals will steer you to the other side of town, which eventually meets up with a sealed road at about 60km. Turn right for **Al Hazm** (where there is yet another magnificent fort – currently closed for repair) 20km from Rustaq, or left to reach the Muscat–Sohar Hwy. The whole route from Rustaq to Al Hazm takes about three hours.

Barka بركاء

Barka, 80km west of Muscat, is a thriving coastal town that has become something of a crossroads between the regional centes of Sohar and Rustaq and Muscat. It has to be said that the old part of town, near the sea, is looking a bit sad as the old quarters are being torn down to make way for a new coast road. In compensation, New Bahla has sprung up along the Muscat–Sohar Hwy with big shops and new restaurants transforming life in this once sleepy town.

Barka is famous for its *halwa,* a unique, laboriously made Omani confection. A pot from dedicated *halwa* shops in town costs from OR8.

There's nowhere to stay in Barka itself, but two luxury resorts run by Al Nahda are nearby. If visiting just for the day, then nearby **Naseem Gardens**, off the main Muscat–Sohar Hwy, makes a pleasant place for a picnic. It hosts part of the annual Muscat Festival with shopping stands, fun fairs and live entertainment.

Sights & Activities

Barka Fort FORT

(500 baisa; 8am-1pm Sat-Thu) With its unusual octagonal tower and location fending off incursions from the sea, Barka Fort cuts a dash along Barka's busy coastline, flanked by several adjacent watchtowers. It has been closed for restoration for some time but is still impressive from the outside. To reach the fort from the town centre (4.5km from the Muscat–Sohar Hwy), turn right at the T-intersection; it's 300m on the left.

Bayt Nua'man HISTORIC BUILDING

(admission 500 baisa; 8am-3pm Sun-Thu; P) Barka is home to the 18th-century Bayt Nua'man, a fine merchant house that has been restored and now doubles as a local museum, with a small collection of typical household items. The turn-off for the house is signposted off the Muscat–Sohar Hwy, 7km west of the main Barka junction. There's no public transport to the house.

Sleeping

Al Nahda Resort & Spa RESORT $$

(26 883710; www.alnahdaresort.com; r from OR75; P@) A night spent in a luxurious low-rise chalet, amid the 30 acres of verdant gardens at this well-established resort may trick you into forgetting the surrounding desert plain. Seeing an ostrich head appear over the wall of the neighbouring farm, then, comes as quite a shock. Located near Barka, on the road towards Nakhal. A taxi from Muscat International Airport costs OR15 (one-way).

Millennium Resort Mussanah RESORT $$

(26 871555; www.millenniumhotels.com; r from OR70, r with seaview OR80; P@) Built to accommodate athletes during regional games, this great, concrete block stuck on the seashore has something of a Soviet feel about its construction but thankfully the uninterrupted sandy beach, good facilities, lovely staff and excellent food compensate. Located near Mussanah, west of Barka, it's an hour's drive from the capital offering a weekend getaway from Muscat.

Dunes by Al Nahda LUXURY DESERT CAMP $$$

(97 235700; http://dunesbyalnahda.com; Wadi Al Abiyad; cabin OR117, breakfast buffet OR15; P) Many residents of Muscat are unaware that there are sand dunes just 45 minutes west of the capital. Access to this luxury camp involves 5km of gravel track best attempted with a 4WD. With an open-sided reception and restaurant overlooking the dunes, a sand therapy unit and attractive rooms designed to resemble tents, this camp makes for a peaceful retreat.

Transfers from Muscat International Airport cost OR45. Quad bikes cost from OR15 per hour and there are opportunities to explore the nearby wadi, famous for its pools of opaque white water.

☆ Entertainment

Bull Butting SPECTATOR SPORT

One reason for visiting Barka is to see the traditional spectator sport of bull-butting. This is where great Brahmin bulls, specially raised by local farmers, are set nose-to-nose in a push-and-shove that supposedly hurts neither party. One of the highlights can be witnessing the excitement of the locals who seem mindless of the dust bath kicked up around them.

To get to the bullring by car take the turning for Barka off the Muscat–Sohar Hwy and turn left at the T-intersection in the centre of town. After 3.4km you will see the concrete enclosure on your right.

Bull-butting rotates from village to village along the Batinah coast on selected weekends. Ask locally to find out when and where, or chance your luck at the bullring on a Friday between November and March from 4pm to 6pm.

Getting There & Away

Buses run between Barka and Muscat's Ruwi bus station (OR1, three times daily). Taxis and microbuses can be found around the T-intersection in town and at the Barka roundabout on the highway. A shared taxi from Rusayl roundabout to Barka costs OR3 per person and around OR15 engaged. Microbuses charge OR1.500.

Sawadi السوادي

A sandy spit of land and some **islands** scattered off the shore make Sawadi a popular day trip, an hour or so drive west of Muscat. At low tide, you can walk to a **watchtower** on one of the islands, but beware: the tide returns very quickly. There's good snorkelling off the islands and local fishermen will take you around for OR5.

There is an abundance of shells at Sawadi. Pick up a shell guide by the late Donald Bosch if you want help identifying the treasures on the beach.

Activities

Available to nonguests, the Al Sawadi Beach Resort has a few **bikes** (OR6 per hour for an adult, OR3 for a child), which are a good way to explore the flat headland. Children may enjoy the inflatable slides at **Aqua Fun Oman**, in the resort's grounds near the beach.

Global Scuba DIVING

(☎98 061532, 26 795545; www.global-scuba.com; Al Sawadi Beach Resort; 2 dives incl equipment OR48) A variety of water sports, snorkelling (OR23) and diving is on offer, including boat trips to the nearby Damanayat Islands that leaves at 8.30am. The dive centre operates from the beach of Al Sawadi resort. Jet skiing (OR25 per hour) and kayaking (OR12 per hour) are also available.

BORDER CROSSING: WAJAJA & KHATMAT MILAHAH الوجاجة و خطمة الملاحة

These two **border crossings** (open 24 hours) are the most common entry and exit points for the UAE. Wajaja is the post that buses use (it takes about an hour for a full bus to clear through immigration) while Khatmat Milahah is more useful for those with their own transport wanting to explore the eastern coast of the UAE. A good tip when using either border is to bring a photocopy of your passport and a pen – you may find that this helps speed up the process, which can be lengthy at weekends and on public holidays. You have to park before the border post and enter the arrivals hall to complete the formalities. The route to Dubai from Wajaja takes you in and out of Omani territory (the border is not a straight line) with checkpoints at each crossing but this usually involves a quick wave of your passport.

You can take a hire car across the border if you have insurance (available from booths at both crossings) but it is much quicker to clear immigration if you have arranged insurance in advance. Don't try to take beer in your coolbox in either direction. There's no exit tax for Oman; exit tax from UAE costs Dh36, payable only by credit card.

The rules regarding entry and exit formalities change frequently so check with the Royal Oman Police (p145) before travelling.

Horse-Riding HORSE RIDING
(☎26 795545; Al Sawadi Beach Resort; 30min/1hr OR10/15; ⏲8am-5pm) A local enterprise manages a small stable of horses (and an occasional camel) from the Al Sawadi Beach Resort. Galloping along the beach at sunset is possible for experienced riders. Short trips on a horse are available for children (OR5 for 15 minutes) and the hotel's mini zoo offers the chance to pose with a camel.

Oman World Tourism KITESURFING
(☎99 431333; www.kiteboarding-oman.com; 7hr beginner package per person in group of 2-3 persons OR160; ⏲8.30am-5.30pm) This internationally accredited kite-surfing school has two outlets – at Sawadi and on the island of Masirah. The German company also organises a number of tours and has an office in Qurm in Muscat.

Sleeping

★Al Sawadi Beach Resort RESORT $$
(☎26 795545; www.alsawadibeach.om; half-board r with garden/sea view OR100/110; P@🛜🏊) Forty minutes west of Muscat International Airport, this low-key retreat makes a peaceful alternative to city accommodation. With a limitless beach peppered with pink top-shells, bungalow-style rooms set in landscaped gardens of cacti and aloe, and lots of user-friendly services and amenities including a spa (a one-hour massage costs OR28), gym and tennis courts, this old favourite offers good value for money.

Getting There & Away

From the turn-off to Sawadi off the Sohar–Muscat Hwy, it's a further 12km to the coast. The resort is 1km before the end of the headland. There is no public transport to Sawadi. An engaged taxi from Muscat is OR20 per person from Muscat International Airport.

Damanayat Islands جزر الديمانيات

These government-protected rocky islands about an hour's boat ride off the coast of Sawadi are rich in marine life and make an exciting destination for snorkelling and diving. Turtles feed off the coral gardens here and at certain times of the year can be found congregating in large numbers. Angel and parrot fish are commonly seen and colourful sea snakes are another feature of the area – though be warned, the latter are highly dangerous if disturbed.

Day trips can either be arranged through Al Sawadi Beach Resort (p188), through Al Mouj Marina (p136) or one of the dive centres in Muscat; this includes the permit. Ad hoc camping is permissible with a 'voucher to visit' (OR1 per person payable only by credit card) from the Ministry of Environment. These vouchers are available from Al Mouj Marina or your dive centre and the instructions for use are given on the voucher. Formalities must be completed by SMS the day before use.

THE MUSANDAM PENINSULA

Separated from the rest of Oman by the east coast of the UAE, and guarding the southern side of the strategically important Strait of Hormuz, the Musandam Peninsula is dubbed the 'Norway of Arabia' for its beautiful *khors* (rocky inlets), small villages and dramatic, mountain-hugging roads. Accessible but still isolated in character, this beautiful peninsula with its cultural eccentricities is well worth a visit if you're on an extended tour of Oman, or if you're after a taste of wilderness from Dubai.

Khasab خصب

The capital of the province is small but far from sleepy. Its souq resounds to a babble of different languages, including Kumzari (a compound language of Arabic, Farsi, English, Hindi and Portuguese), and its harbour bursts with activity, much of it involving semi-illicit trade with Iran. The smugglers are distinguished by their souped-up fibreglass boats with outboard motors that line up along the creeks waiting for dusk to make the mad dash 55km across the strait to Iran. They bring money and character into town, so no one seems in a hurry to get rid of them; besides, piracy has been a tradition in these parts for well over 200 years and locals respect a good piece of tradition.

The new souq area, in the centre of town, north of the airport and south of the port, is home to banks (with ATM), the post office, pharmacies and random shops and coffeeshops.

Sights

Forget what you read about 'city tours' (typically OR10 for a three-hour tour of the fort and nearby petroglyphs), Khasab is still just a town where the biggest event of the past few years has been the building of a Lulu supermarket. That said, it makes a pleasant place to wander around and it boasts an excellent museum and a lively shopping area. If you drive past Lulu on the left and take the first right towards Khmazera Castle, you'll circuit some grand modern villas with nautical themes: one house has a scale model of a dhow over the entrance while another sports fine Iranian tiles with a seafaring theme. The town's villas, which are partially buried in date plantations, are noteworthy for their sparkling pillars, doorsteps and domes: a job lot of reflective tiles from Pakistan has recently brought glitter to the once-sober town.

★Khasab Fort FORT, MUSEUM

(admission 500 baisa; 9am-4pm Sat-Thu, 8-11am Fri) With its command of the bay sadly diminished since Lulu supermarket was built on reclaimed land opposite, Khasab Fort nonetheless cuts quite a dash with its four stone turrets and fine crenelations. Built by the Portuguese in the 17th century around a much older circular tower, this well-preserved fort now houses one of the best little ethnographic museums in Oman. The central tower displays the peninsula's flora and fauna and a video highlighting the famous sea chants of local fishermen.

Allow an hour to do a visit justice and to explore the *bait al qufl*, literally the 'house of locks', built by a master craftsman in the courtyard. Typical of the region, these houses were built with a floor well below ground level – one of several features keeping the house safe during the empty summer months when the occupants moved to the shore to fish and harvest dates. You can see remnants of these houses in Rawdah Bowl, a two-hour off-road drive through the mountains. Also on display is *'arish*, a summer house built on stilts to allow for ventilation in the sweltering summer months.

Khmazera Castle CASTLE

(8am-2pm Sat-Wed) FREE Buried in the heart of town (brown signs show the way), this small fortified house sports two cannons at the doorway, a renovated well in the courtyard and giant oyster shells in one of the rooms. It's underwhelming after Khasab Fort but worth a pause during a walk or drive around town.

Musandam Peninsula

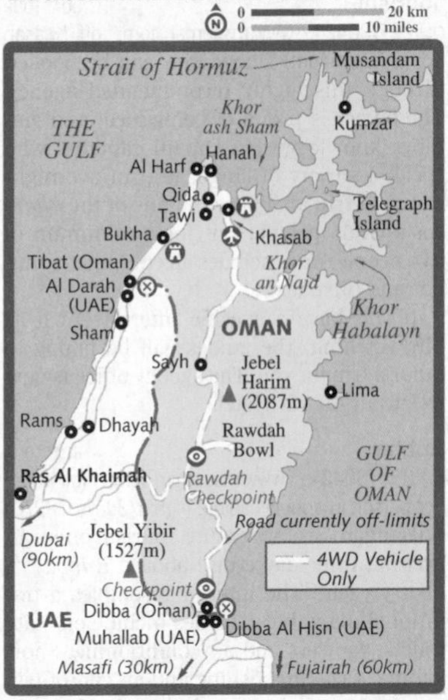

0 20 km
0 10 miles

Strait of Hormuz
Musandam Island
Kumzar
Khor ash Sham
THE GULF
Hanah
Al Harf
Qida
Tawi
Telegraph Island
Bukha
Khasab
Tibat (Oman)
Khor an Najd
Al Darah (UAE)
Khor Habalayn
Sham
OMAN
Sayh
Jebel Harim (2087m)
Lima
Rams
Dhayah
Rawdah Bowl
GULF OF OMAN
Ras Al Khaimah
Rawdah Checkpoint
Road currently off-limits
Dubai (90km)
Jebel Yibir (1527m)
4WD Vehicle Only
Checkpoint
UAE
Dibba (Oman)
Dibba Al Hisn (UAE)
Muhallab (UAE)
Masafi (30km)
Fujairah (60km)

Activities

There are two main activities accessible from Khasab: dhow cruising around the *khors* and 4WD mountain safaris to the top of Jebel Samhan. All the tour companies in Khasab offer both if you're looking for a 'one-stop' service. Book online, through your hotel or at the agencies in Khasab.

Dhow Trips

A key activity from Khasab is to explore the coastline with its rugged inlets on board a traditional wooden fishing vessel known locally as a 'dhow'. A boat ride is easy to arrange either through your hotel or through one of the many agencies in town. The trips are a great way not just to enjoy the spectacular fjord-like scenery, but also to watch the great flocks of Socotra cormorants and bridled terns that inhabit the *khors'* vertical cliffs. Equally rewarding are the antics of humpback dolphins that invariably accompany boats around the neck of each inlet. Deep-sea fishing is popular off the most northern tip of the peninsula, especially around Musandam Island.

Musandam Sea Adventure Tourism BOAT TOUR
(☎26 730424; www.msaoman.com; off Khasab Rd; ⏲10am-4pm) Dhow trips can be booked through this highly recommended agency. The owner is proud of being local and employs knowledgeable Omani captains who speak a variety of languages. An overnight camping trip on a beach in one of the *khors* costs OR55 per person (for a minimum of two people) and includes all equipment, dinner and breakfast.

If you have a specific interest (such as birdwatching) the guides will be happy to tailor a trip for you. The agency office is next to Diwan Alamir Hotel.

Rubba BOAT TOUR
(☎26 730424; www.msaoman.com; full-board per person in double cabin 2 nights/3days OR270) Musandam Sea Adventure Tourism offers an exciting three-day cruise aboard *Rubba*, its luxury yacht. The interior resembles a traditional dhow but facilities include en suite toilets, showers and air-conditioning. Snorkelling, kayaking, fishing and an end-of-trip mountain safari are included. *Rubba* sails with a minimum of four people or as scheduled on the first Sunday of every month between October and April.

Khasab Sea Tours BOAT TOUR
(☎26 731123; www.kstoman.com; Khasab Rd; ⏲8am-8pm) This agency, almost opposite Al Maha petrol station near the port, offers half-day dhow rides from 9.30am to 1.30pm to Telegraph Island for OR15 per person. Whole-day trips (9am to 5pm) press on to Seebi Island and cost OR20 and include lunch. Snorkelling equipment is provided on board.

Half/full-board beach camping (OR40/50 per person) with all equipment provided is a popular way of engaging with the wilderness.

Diving & Snorkelling

Extra Divers – Khasab DIVING
(☎99 877957; www.musandam-diving.com; incl equipment 2 dives OR53, snorkelling OR21; ⏲8am-6pm) Musandam has a reputation as an exciting destination for diving but conditions are suitable mainly for experienced divers. Extra Divers, at the Atana Khasab Hotel, organises full-day dive trips (8.30am to 3pm) for a range of capabilities.

Mountain Safaris

The most cost-effective and easiest way to explore the peninsula is to take a tour on what is locally called a 'mountain safari'. About 10 different operators offer similar trips that include a half-day 4WD to Khor an Najd and Jebel Harim (around OR25 per person or OR80 for a minimum of three people) and a full-day drive to Rawdah Bowl (OR150).

Khasab Travel & Tours TOUR
(☎26 730464; www.khasabtours.com; ⏲8am-1pm & 4-7pm) Situated at the Atana Khasab Hotel, this agency is at least efficient if rather brusque with customers. It offers dhow tours and mountain safaris and can organise transfers to the UAE border.

Swimming

Bassa Beach SWIMMING
Khasab is a good place for a swim. Bassa Beach is a walk away from the ferry terminal but has a lovely sandy beach with palm umbrellas (and toilets). Wild camping is permissible here and beautiful shells often wash up at the tent flaps when the weather is rough. Follow the road from the port towards Bukha for 2km or so.

Don't be alarmed by the 1.8m sharks that often circle in the shallow bays near Khasab – apparently they're not interested in human flesh.

Sleeping & Eating

In peak season, October to April, you need to book accommodation as Khasab is a popular weekend trip for UAE visitors. All the hotels offer a pick-up service from the airport. There are a number of restaurants around the souqs selling similar fare of roast chicken, kebabs and fresh juices from around OR1.500. Expect to keep company with a smuggler or two.

Lulu Hypermarket (⏲9am-11.45pm) sells fresh biryani, tandoori chicken, salads and pastries – all the ingredients needed for a picnic.

Khasab Hotel HOTEL $
(☎26 730267; www.khasabhotel.net; s/d Sat-Wed OR28/38, Thu & Fri OR38/47; P@🛜🏊) A kilometre inland, near the airport, this traveller-friendly hotel with its whacky mini-fort entrance offers bright rooms with views of the mountains. There's a cosy restaurant on site. Payment is preferred in

cash. There's a free shuttle to and from the ferry or airport and cheap tours are on offer.

★Atana Khasab Hotel HOTEL $$
(☎26 730777; www.atanahotels.com; d with mountain/sea view Sat-Wed OR70/80, Thu & Fri OR80/90;) Perched on a headland just outside Khasab, on the Khasab–Tibat road, this old favourite is surrounded on three sides by water and makes the most of the crystal-clear water and mountain scenery. At sunset the cliffs on the opposite side of the bay dissolve like liquid gold. Some rooms have split levels, windows for walls and balconies aligned to the sunset.

Ignore the astro-turf: take your buffet (weekday/weekend OR13/14) onto the terrace and listen to the sea lapping the rocks below for Khasab's best night out. This is the only venue in town with a bar (6pm to 1am).

Atana Musandam Resort HOTEL $$
(☎26 730888; www.atanahotels.com; Khasab-Tibat Rd; r from OR90) Using local materials, this appealingly rustic hotel attempts to blend into the environment with its sandstone-clad rooms, wooden beams and *barasti* ceilings. Arranged along the edge of two creeks that slice through the reclaimed land upon which this resort sits, together with neighbouring Lulu Hypermarket, it explodes into life twice a day when powerboats set out or return from fishing.

Diwan Alamir Hotel HOTEL $$
(☎26 833991; www.diwanelamir.com; Khasab Rd; standard/suite OR60/75) There are good views from the small rooms but what really distinguishes this new hotel is the chocolate-caramel swirls of the marble basins. An average restaurant serves average international fare. The hotel is close to the fort and walking distance from the ferry.

Shopping

Walking sticks make an unusual souvenir of the region. With their axe-tops, used traditionally for cutting wood, killing snakes and keeping children in order (at least according to one local), these sticks are the emblem of the Shihuh tribespeople – the main ethnic group in the Musandam Peninsula. They carry them in place of the camel stick on formal occasions. Ones with silver decoration cost OR55-plus and the easiest place to find one is at the gift shop in Khasab Hotel (ask at reception for it to be opened).

Getting There & Away

The Musandam Peninsula can be visited as a long weekend trip from either Muscat or Dubai (two hours by road – up to four hours depending on Dubai traffic). From Muscat, a great way to visit is to fly to Khasab for an eagle-eyed view of the mountains and take the memorable high-speed ferry around the *khors* on the way back. Another option offered by **Oman Air Holidays** (☎24 531000; www.omanair.com) is to fly both ways for OR139 per person including two nights at the Antana Musandam Resort in Khasab.

AIR

Oman Air (☎in Khasab 26 731592, in Muscat 24 531111; www.omanair.com) Flights between Khasab and Muscat cost OR24 each way (1¼ hours) and currently leave Muscat at 7.25am and 10.55am, and Khasab at 9.10am and 12.40pm daily. The office in Khasab is on the main roundabout opposite the grand mosque, and flights depart and arrive from the military air base.

BOAT

National Ferries Company (☎in Khasab 26 731802, in Muscat 24 715252, toll free 80 072000; www.nfc.om; one-way/return OR23/44) Operates a service every Thursday from Muscat at noon, arriving in Khasab at 4.30pm, returning on Saturday at 11.30am. Report two hours before sailing time. To enjoy the journey in style, consider paying the extra for business class (one-way/return OR45/85). VIP class is OR60 one-way. You can take a car (including car rental) on the ferry for an extra OR50 return.

The trip is punctuated with lunch, a film channel and attendant dolphins that can't quite keep up with the fastest catamaran in the world. The journey through one of the busiest shipping lanes in the region is worth taking for the spectacular cruise into the harbour at either end.

CAR

Driving to and from Muscat to Tibat (530km, eight hours) involves insurance for two countries, and passing through checkpoints no fewer than eight times. On an Omani visit visa, this is not the best use of time.

It is a feasible drive, however, from Dubai. The only border post allowing access to the Musandam Peninsula is at Al Darah/Tibat, on the western coast of the UAE. Expat residents in Oman and the UAE cannot currently drive through Wadi Bih. You can drive from Dibba if you have a letter of invitation from the resort at Six Senses Zighy Bay. There is a Dh36 road tax to leave the UAE. Visas on arrival are available in either direction.

A 4WD is necessary to explore the mountains. You can bring a car (including a rented car) from Muscat on the ferry.

LONG-DISTANCE TAXI

There is no public transport operating in Musandam. You can book a taxi, though, through your hotel to Bukha (OR25) or Tibat and Khor an Najd (OR25) or Jebel Harim (OR60). A taxi to Dubai costs OR30 to the border with an Omani driver and then a metered taxi to Dubai.

Getting Around

TO/FROM THE AIRPORT

It's best to arrange transfers with your hotel in advance as there are no taxis near the airport. The airport is 2km from the souq and 6km from the harbour.

CAR

Khasab Rent-a-Car (☎99 726565, 99 447400; Khasab Rd; ⏰8am-1pm & 5-10pm) Car hire (2WD/4WD OR13/40) is available from the ever-obliging Omani owner of Khasab Rent-a-Car. A 4WD with a driver costs OR60 per day. Cars can be delivered to your hotel and dropped off at the ferry terminal.

Rahaal Khasab (☎91 323440, 99 441700; hayatix5@gmail.com; Khasab Rd; ⏰8am-1pm & 5-10pm) Cheap 4WD deals from OR25 per day.

TAXI

The orange-and-white taxis in town are owned by locals running errands and are not useful as public transport. If you want to go into town, or beyond, ask the hotel or an agency to arrange transport for you. The going rate for any trip in town is OR3 per person.

Khasab–Tibat Road

طريق خصب - تيبات

The cliff-hugging 42km, 90-minute drive from Khasab to Tibat is a highlight of a trip to Musandam. The sealed road is a feat of engineering and affords spectacular views across the Strait of Hormuz. There are a few sites of interest along the way and you could spend a day pottering along the road, enjoying a swim at one of the many glorious sandy beaches – and watching very large sharks basking in the shallows.

About 8km from Khasab harbour lies the village of Tawi, site of a few **prehistoric rock carvings** of boats, houses and warriors on horseback. To reach these petroglyphs, follow a track up Wadi Qida, just before Qida village, for 2.3km. The petroglyphs are etched into two rocks on the left, just before a large white house with outdoor ovens.

Scenically positioned **Bukha Fort** commands a good view of the bay halfway along the Khasab–Tibat road. Prisoners used to be pegged to the lower courtyard and drowned by the incoming tide. The view from the fort (closed to visitors) above town shows the classic Musandam landscape of steep-sided cliffs sheltering 'bowls' (cul-de-sac plains) of flat-topped acacia trees. Often the beachside settlements are inundated by the listing flanks of sand dunes blown back from the shore. A new mosque (still under construction) sits alongside a very old **Grand Mosque** that has been newly renovated near the fort.

The road ends in Tibat at Al Darah border with the UAE; the post is open 24 hours and passing through customs on either side is quick and efficient.

The Musandam Khors

اخوار مسندم

A dhow trip around the *khors* (inlets) of Musandam, flanked by dolphins, is a must and well worth the expense. Trail a fishing line from the back of the boat, and your skipper will cook your catch for lunch. So remote are some of these *khors* that people still have their water delivered by boat and speak a dialect almost unrecognisable to Arabic speakers from Muscat. Note that you'll need a permit (which can be arranged by pre-booking with a tour company) to enter any village in the Musandam *khors*.

Khor ash Sham خور شم

This beautiful inlet is interesting for its stone **fishing villages**, accessible only by boat, and for **Telegraph Island**, which you can land on at high tide. Snorkelling and swimming in the pristine surrounding waters is a highlight, as are the dolphins which swim alongside the boat. It is the most popular dhow tour from Khasab.

Khor an Najd خور نجد

At 24.5km southeast of Khasab, this is the only *khor* accessible by vehicle (preferably 4WD). You can camp on the rim of this wild bay although it's often too shallow and muddy for a good swim. The **viewpoint** at the top of the graded road, however, is stunning and worth the visit for its own sake. This is the view that is most often chosen in tourist literature to promote Musandam.

GOING ROUND THE BEND

Ever wondered about the term 'going round the bend'? If you take a trip to Khor ash Sham, you'll learn first-hand what the saying means. In the middle of the *khor* (inlet), a tiny island, not much bigger than a postcard and considerably less attractive, was home to a British telegraphic relay station in the 19th century. The utter isolation of the island, tucked around the bend of this remote inlet, with no diversions other than sleeping and swimming, drove many of the workers stationed there to madness. The saying 'going round the bend' persists to this day...and so perhaps does the associated implication of being 'driven round the bend'. From time to time, the military set up camp on the rocks and see how long it takes to run out of things to do. Personnel stationed there run straw polls estimating the number of days endurable at a stretch. One volunteered the improvement of their fishing skills, and Captain Ahmed Saif said, 'We get very good at counting cormorants.'

To reach the khor from Khasab, head inland past the airport for 15km and follow the sign for 'Khor an Najd 6km'. Turn left and head for the obvious graded road that winds up the mountain. After a couple of kilometers you come to the pass, from where a steep 3km descent brings you to the water's edge.

From the base of the track, a road leads to Sal Ala'a and **Al Khaldiyah**, an inland bowl full of mature trees that makes for a pleasant and rare shaded picnic spot.

Kumzar كمزار

Set on an isolated *khor* at the northern edge of the peninsula, the surprisingly modern town of Kumzar is accessible only by boat. The villagers speak their own language, known as Kumzari – a combination of Farsi, Hindi, English, Portuguese and Arabic. There is nowhere to stay in Kumzar, and there are no sights of special interest in the town. It is nonetheless fascinating to wander around the **old stone houses** and the **souq** area to see how this outpost has developed its own unique character. Note that officially you are required to have a permit (arranged by pre-booking with a tour company) to enter this or indeed any village in the Musandam khors.

Water taxis travel between Khasab and Kumzar, charging an outrageous OR120 (and in excess of OR200 at weekends) for the harrowing trip in a speedboat with no seats and a maximum clearance between deck and gunwale of 15cm. It's better to organise a day-trip through a tour company.

Jebel Harim جبل حارم

If you have a 4WD, the mountain scenery around **Jebel Harim** (Mountain of Women) makes a rewarding day trip, especially in spring when the mountains are full of delicate blooms such as wild geraniums and miniature iris.

The graded road switchbacks through limestone formations until it reaches the **Sayh plateau**, a startling patchwork of fields and grazing donkeys surrounded by stone settlements. The road climbs a further 8km to a pass below the telecommunications tower (off limits to the public) that marks the top of the mountain. Even if you don't intend to make the descent to Rawdah Bowl, it's well worth unravelling the helter-skelter of road for a few kilometres beyond the pass: the views of improbable homesteads, clinging to the crescent-shaped canyons, with terraces in various states of livid green or grey abandonment, are spectacular.

Rawdah Bowl مدرج الروضة

From Jebel Harim, the descent towards Dibba is via a narrow ridge with remarkable views of striated sedimentary rock.

At the bottom of the descent, a right turn leads towards Dibba via the Omani checkpoint (no access for non-Omanis) while a left turn crosses the wadi bottom and meanders into the Rawdah Bowl – a beautiful depression of mature acacia and *ghaf* trees. The bowl has several interesting features including the local stone-built houses known as *bayt al qifl*, or the '**house of locks**'. So called on account of the elaborate locking mechanism, the homes (which were traditionally left empty during the summer months) are built low to the ground and the floor is excavated to about 1m below the door with beds and an eating area raised on platforms. The furniture and vital earthenware water jars are often placed inside before the house is roofed, ensuring that no one makes off with the contents during summer migration. Some of the rocks used in these buildings are 1m thick and take six to eight men to lift. One good example still exists in the middle of the bowl, near the road and a grave site. Note the roof made of tree trunks and insulated against the heat and cold by mud.

The area has a long history of settlement, as can be seen from the **pre-Islamic tombstones** (lying close to the road) made either from luminous yellow sandstone or grey limestone and etched with script or pictographs. The entire area, with its diagonal slants of sandstone, takes on a surreal quality at sunset.

SALALAH, DHOFAR & SOUTHERN OMAN

The southernmost province of Oman is a world away from the industrious north and is separated geographically by an interminable gravel desert. With its historic frankincense trade, great beaches, a laid-back atmosphere and an interesting ethnic mix, it's a fascinating place to visit, particularly during or just after the *khareef* (mid-June to late August season of mists and light rains).

There are many possible day trips from Salalah, including Job's Tomb, the heroic town of Mirbat with its beautiful beaches, and Mughsail, famed for some violent blowholes in the undercliff and for nearby groves of wild frankincense.

If you are travelling during the *khareef* and can put up with the unremittingly tedious journey from Muscat or Nizwa, it is worth going overland to Salalah across the largely featureless Al Wusta Region and returning by plane. This is the best way to sense the full spectacle of the *khareef* across the top of the jebel; after eight hours of gravel plains, Dhofar seems like a little miracle.

Salalah صلالة

Salalah, the capital of the Dhofar region, is a colourful, subtropical city that owes much of its character to Oman's former territories in East Africa. Flying into Salalah from Muscat, especially during the *khareef*, it is hard to imagine that Oman's first and second cities share the same continent. From mid-June to mid-August, monsoon clouds from India bring a constant drizzle to the area and, as a result, the stubble of Salalah's surrounding jebel is transformed into an oasis of misty pastures. Year-round, Salalah's coconut-fringed beaches and plantations of bananas and papayas offer a flavour of Zanzibar in the heart of the Arabian desert.

Sights

★Museum of the Frankincense Land ARCHAEOLOGICAL SITE
(Al Baleed; www.omantourism.gov.om; admission OR2; 9am-9pm Sun-Thu, 3-9pm Fri & Sat) Well-labelled and atmospherically lit at night, the ancient ruins of Al Baleed belong to the 12th-century trading port of Zafar. Frankincense was shipped across the sea to India from here in exchange for spices. Little is known about the port's demise but the excellent on-site **museum** charts the area's settlement since 2000 BC and illustrates the maritime strength of the nation including its recent renaissance. The site includes several kilometres of landscaped paths and the adjoining reed beds are good for birdwatching.

Plantations GARDENS
Salalah is famous for its plantations of coconuts, papayas and bittersweet, small bananas. Stroll through the plantation roads near the corniche (2km from the town centre) and it's hard to remember Salalah is Oman's second city. For refreshment, stop off at the many colourful fruit stands that stay open until late in the evening.

Al Husn Souq SOUQ
(Sultan Qaboos St; 10am-1pm & 4.30-9.30pm) Head for this souq to rub shoulders with the jovial Dhofari people who have been assembling in this spot, albeit under different awnings, for centuries. The souq, spread over a number of alleyways next to the sultan's palace, flap with colourful cotton headdresses, smoke with aromatic frankincense and sparkle with imitation jewellery. This is a good place to see how the Omani hats are made.

Salalah

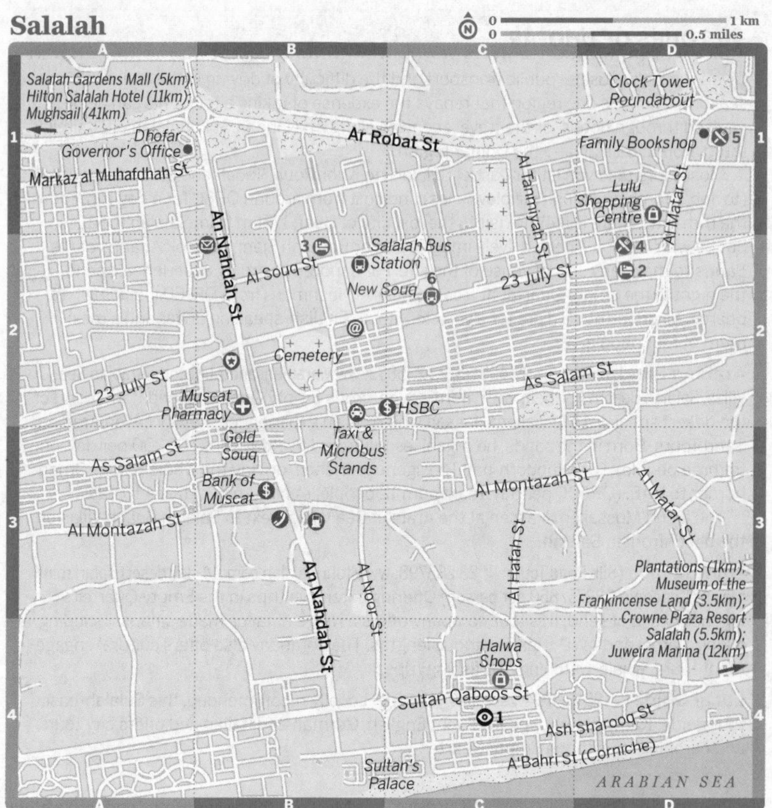

Salalah

Sights
1 Al Husn Souq....C4

Sleeping
2 Al Hanaa Hotel....D2
3 Salalah Hotel....B2

Eating
4 Al Jood Restaurant....D2
5 Marrosh Restaurant....D1

Transport
6 Gulf Transport Company....C2

Activities

Extra Divers – Salalah DIVING

(☎91 780935; www.extradivers.org; Juweira Marina, Salalah Beach; ⏲3.30-7pm Oct-May) For diving and snorkelling opportunities in the region, contact the highly competent Extra Divers. A day trip (two dives) including transport, equipment and permit costs OR40. Note that it is not possible to dive or snorkel in the summer months (June to September) due to dangerous currents. Payment can only be made in cash.

Free transport is offered from Juweira Marina to Mirbat.

Around the Ocean DHOW CRUISE

(☎98 111123; aroundtheocean@yahoo/com; Juweira Marina, Salalah Beach; 1hr dhow cruise adult/child OR10/3) Offering the only dhow cruises currently operating in Salalah. In addition to its one-hour sunset cruise, a 10-hour snorkelling trip to Mirbat from 8am to 6pm is available for OR40 (half price for children) for a minimum of two and maximum of eight people. Two-hour dolphin-watching trips (OR20) leave at 8am and 10am. Fishing trips and donuts are also available.

TOURS OF DHOFAR

Given the lack of useful public transport and the difficulty of driving in the *khareef* (rainy season), Dhofar is one region that repays the expense of taking a tour. This can be organised through hotels, or the travel agencies along An Nahdah St in Salalah offer similar tours around Salalah and the Dhofar region.

Most tours take you either east of Salalah (to Khor Rouri, Taqah and Mirbat) or west (to Job's Tomb and Mughsail blowholes) and cost from around OR80 for a day trip. For the romantic, there is a 4WD visit to the lost city of Ubar, 175km from Salalah (OR120), but be warned, you'll need a lively imagination or Ranulph Fiennes' book *Atlantis of the Sands* to make any sort of sense of the site. For a more-rewarding experience, spend the night in the Empty Quarter at a camp near Al Hashman (from OR160 including half board). All prices quoted are for a vehicle with an English-speaking driver and a maximum of four people.

Arabian Sand Tours (☎99 495175, 23 235833; www.arabiansandtours.com; Arabian Sea Villas, Salalah Beach) For help with more-adventurous Empty Quarter expeditions, contact the desert specialist Mussallem Hassan who runs an experienced agency called Arabian Sand Tours. Born in the sands, he organises full-board five-day trips (OR200 per day, one to three people). For a modern-day Thesiger experience, driving the whole Saudi–Oman border to UAE, (OR600 per day, maximum 12 people, minimum two) takes 10 days.

You'll find Mussallem Hassan at the Arabian Sea Villas, next to Salalah Beach Villas on the beachfront in Salalah.

Tour Salalah (Silk Road Tours; ☎23 288798; www.tour-salalah.com; 14-day desert safari min/max 6/12 people OR975/850 per person) Offering extensive trips in the Empty Quarter's legendary sea of sand, this tour company offers a range of tailor-made safaris, including hiking, camel and 4WD trips of various lengths. The company also offers cultural engagement tours, whale-watching and fishing trips.

Local Guide (☎95 253794; zebralfa@yahoo.de) Locally recommended, this Salalah-based tour guide, Kathy Zanchi, speaks fluent English, German and Italian and offers city tours and camping trips to the Empty Quarter.

No Boundaries Oman FISHING
(☎in UAE +971 5088 49070; www.noboundaries oman.com) This respected tour company specialises in game fishing (including world class GT or Giant Trevally) with conservation in mind. Run by an expat couple, Ed and Angela Nicholas, the company operates from Ash Shuwaymiah, a beautiful bay three hours' drive from Salalah. Accommodation is in simple lodges and trips to the nearby Hallaniyat archipelago, 50km off shore, are routine.

Festivals & Events

Salalah Tourism Festival CULTURAL
(Khareef Festival; ☎23 383333; www.traveller oasis.om; Ittin Rd; ⌚21 Jun-21 Sep) During the *khareef*, Ittin Rd is the main location of the Salalah Tourism Festival. Arab families from across the region come to picnic in paradise. Their favourite haunt is under the street lights of Ittin Rd where a large festival complex includes fun-fairs, clothes stalls, cultural villages, a theatre, restaurants and lots of small stands selling kebabs and shwarma.

Most of the restaurants and attractions are strictly seasonal, opening only between mid-June to mid-September. Check *Oman Today* for a program of nightly concerts and cultural activities.

Sleeping

During the *khareef*, all accommodation in Salalah is heavily booked and prices are often double the standard rates given here. Reservations are essential. Camping is possible around Mirbat, but you'll need to bring your own equipment. Alternatively, you can buy supplies in any of the major shopping centres in Salalah.

★ **Salalah Beach Villas** HOTEL $
(☎23 235999; www.beach-villas-salalah.com; Beach Rd; s/d sea view with balcony OR30/38; P 📶 ❄) This welcoming family-style hotel has lovely views: the sea is so close you can taste it through the window. Walk off breakfast along the magnificent white sand and splash in the surf on calmer days. Don't leave without trying the house specialty: Mr

and Mrs Kumar's fish curry (OR6) is legendary. It's one block east of the Crowne Plaza.

Tours and car hire (2WD/4WD from OR14/37, including 200km free mileage) are available. This guesthouse also runs the 65-room **Beach Resort** next door (singles/doubles OR35/50 for sea view with balcony), which has the benefit of an all-day restaurant.

Al Hanaa Hotel HOTEL $

(☎23 290274; msarawas@omantel.net.om; 23 July St; s/d/tr OR13/17/20; P 📶) This well-maintained Arabic-style hotel with a tiled foyer is recommended for its bright, clean rooms. It is situated in the middle of town, within walking distance of the bus station and the main shopping areas.

Salalah Hotel BUSINESS HOTEL $

(☎23 295332; fax 23 292145; Al Souq St; r OR15; P @) This hotel is looking a bit tired but it has large, comfortable rooms and friendly staff. Close to the new souq area and almost opposite the bus station, it is a good choice for the early morning bus back to Muscat.

Salalah Gardens Residences HOTEL $$

(☎23 381000; www.safirhotels.com; Salalah Gardens Mall, Ar Robat St; r/ste with kitchenette OR59/71 ; P 📶 🏊) At the heart of the city's busiest shopping enterprise, this hotel offers easy access to all the amenities of Salalah Gardens Mall. It is also a short distance from Ittin Rd, home of the annual Salalah Tourism Festival. With longer-stay options available, it represents good value for money out of season.

Juweira Boutique Hotel BOUTIQUE HOTEL $$

(☎23 239600; www.juweirahotel.com; Taqah Rd; r from OR70; P 📶 🏊) This hotel, marooned in the middle of lonesome Salalah Beach, some 13km from town, has at last been joined by some neighbours, including a few shops clustered around Juweira Marina. That said, it's taking time for other parts of the surrounding tourism and residential complex to take shape. In the meantime, the hotel and its quality amenities offer a peaceful retreat.

The Salalah Rotana Resort next door offers added dining options.

Hilton Salalah Hotel RESORT $$

(☎23 211234; www.hilton.com; Sultan Qaboos St; r from OR73; P 📶 🏊) It was a surprise when the Hilton chose Salalah instead of Muscat. It was an even greater surprise when the hotel was built 12km along the highway to Mughsail, within view of the enormous Raysut Port. Despite the cargo boats queuing up on the horizon, and camels charging by the rather cramped grounds, the hotel is a hit with Nordic holidaymakers.

Crowne Plaza Resort Salalah RESORT $$$

(☎23 238000; www.cpsalalah.com; Al Khandaq St; r mountain/sea view from OR100/110; P 📶 🏊) The main rendezvous for Western expats, this sociable and highly competent hotel, with rondelles of local scenes and coloured glass, is the most characterful of the large hotels in and around Salalah. It has a small golf course, beach and terraced restaurants overlooking a magnificent sandy beach, with waves illuminated each evening beneath the palms.

Eating

There are plenty of small Indian restaurants along As Salam St and Sultan Qaboos

THE KHAREEF – REGULAR RAIN IN THE DESERT

It may seem odd that while the rest of Oman suffers the summer slump in visitors, the result of insanely high temperatures, one small corner of the country enjoys an isolated high season. Dhofar, in the far south of the country catches the edge of an annual monsoon carried on winds from India. There is not much volume to the clouds as they reach the shore of Oman, but enough to disperse as a light rain or drizzle that generally persists for 60 days or so over the months of July and August.

The rain brings mists and cooler temperatures which between them transform the generally hard-baked landscape into a green oasis of flowering shrubs and grasses. This annual phenomenon is known locally as the *khareef* and is celebrated in Salalah, the capital of the Dhofar region, with a shopping and entertainment festival that attracts visitors from across the region.

It's hard for many from wet climes to understand the attraction of a picnic in the rain, with its attendant mud and swarms of flies, but to those who are enduring the hellfire heat of the rest of the Peninsula, the *khareef* offers a little slice of heaven.

St near the Crowne Plaza Resort. All the top-end hotels have good restaurants and cafes, with international menus and prices to match. There are numerous cold stores, supermarkets and hypermarkets, including Lulu, for picnic items.

Makdas Restaurant FAST FOOD $
(☎23 236234; Sultan Qaboos St; mains 300 baisa; ⏰4pm-1am) This no-frills restaurant, one in a string of cheap and cheerful eateries 1km east of the Crown Plaza Resort, serves juices, grilled chicken, burgers and pizzas. Stroll along the same road for dessert from the fruit stands.

Marrosh Restaurant SHWARMA $
(☎23 292456; Ar Robat St; shwarma with hummus OR3; ⏰9am-1am) This simple restaurant serves tasty food in a modern space, just to the southeast of the Clock Tower Roundabout at junction of Ar Robat and Al Matar Sts.

Al Jood Restaurant LEBANESE $$
(☎23 295656; 23 July St; mixed mezze per person for 2/4 people OR12/9; ⏰10am-2am) With dishes of fresh *kunifer* (an addictive syrup and cheese dessert) on display and fresh bread flipped from the ovens onto the plate, this new restaurant is worth tearing yourself away from the beach for. There's a fresh fish counter and seating for families in the basement.

Annabi Shisha Lounge MIDDLE EASTERN $$
(☎23 381000; www.safirhotels.com; Salalah Gardens Mall, Ar Robat St; executive lunch buffet OR7; ⏰12.30-4pm & 7-11pm) Tuck behind an Arabesque screen for private dining or sit outside in the landscaped terrace and watch the shoppers go by at this attractive restaurant. You don't have to be a smoker to enjoy a whiff of peach sheesha from neighbouring tables as you tuck into hot mezze and mocktails.

★Dolphin Beach Restaurant INTERNATIONAL $$$
(☎23 238000; Crowne Plaza Resort Salalah; buffet OR14; ⏰noon-3pm & 6pm-midnight) One of the few places in Salalah to offer dining with a sea view, this open-air restaurant under the coconut palms offers a different themed buffet each night. Call ahead to reserve a beachside table if you want to watch the wading birds dash in and out of the flood-lit waves, finding their supper as you eat yours.

☆ Entertainment

Both the Crowne Plaza Resort Salalah and the Hilton Salalah Hotel offer live music.

Palmyra 7D Simu(lator) CINEMA
(Salalah Gardens Mall; 5-12min film OR1.500; ⏰10am-11pm, shows every 30 minutes) Offering terrifying thrills such as cold water showers, shaking seats and snow, this simulator offers a horror-movie experience that affects all the senses. Safety belts are mandatory.

Fun Station FUN FAIR
(Salalah Gardens Mall; admission OR2, plus extra per ride; ⏰10am-10pm Sun-Wed, to midnight Thu & Sat, 2pm-midnight Fri) This small indoor fun fair is designed to keep kids and young teens entertained.

Shopping

Don't visit Dhofar without treading in the paths of ancient traders. A small bag of locally harvested frankincense costs from 500 baisa, and a decorative locally made pottery incense burner costs OR3.500 to OR10. There are different grades of incense: Somali frankincense is cheaper but not so aromatic while the milky, greenish resin from Dhofar is highly prized. A whole kit with burner and charcoal costs OR1 or buy a local perfume made from frankincense (OR5 to OR50 per bottle).

Baskets made of rush and camel's leather, from the fishing village of Shwaymiyah, make another good souvenir (OR8 to OR30), together with colourful woven rice mats. Among Dhofar's most distinctive souvenirs are small, bead-covered *kohl* (black eyeliner) bottles (OR4 to OR10).

Visit the **gold souq** on An Nahdah St for Salalah's distinctive silver necklaces and bracelets, which cost around OR25 (depending on weight).

Halwa shops selling Oman's traditional confection monopolise the corner of Al Hafah and Sultan Qaboos Sts.

For camping equipment and supplies, visit Lulu Hypermarket or Salalah Gardens Mall.

Oman House Handicrafts HANDICRAFTS
(☎98 218700; dhofarfrankincense1@gmail.com; Aswaq, Salalah Gardens Mall; incense burner from OR3.5; ⏰10am-10pm) Hidden in the traditional souq ('Aswaq') in the middle of Salalah Gardens Mall, this craft shop is owned by an expert in the properties and production

MUSCAT TO SALALAH OVERLAND

Inland Route

It comes as some surprise to see a sign off the Rusayl roundabout in Muscat that says 'Salalah 998km'. Salalah may be Oman's second city, but there are few destinations that are sign-posted from such a distance. The signs imply that there is precious little in between – that once on the lonely Hwy 31 from Nizwa, there is nothing between you and Salalah.

And that's pretty much the case. The eight-hour journey between Nizwa and Thumrait across Al Wusta Region is punctuated by one lone limestone hump near Adam, the excitement of a scruffy little town at Hayma and very little else. One Thorn Tree correspondent called it 'the least memorable journey in the world' and, as you gaze across the big sky, midpoint along Hwy 31, without a rock, a bush, or any kind of interruption of the level plain, it's hard not to agree.

With your own 4WD, however, there are a few points of interest en route. If the prospect of exploring this 'Road Across Nowhere' appeals, you can make the interminable drive more bearable by stopping off at the basic but friendly hotels in Hayma. There's no need to book ahead.

➡ **Oasis of Muqshin** Relatively easy access to the magnificent ghaf woodlands and seams of Sodom's apple that decorate the edge of the Empty Quarter.

➡ **Oases of Muntasar** (near Qitbit) Famous for the daily fly-by of thousands of sand grouse.

➡ **Shisr** Chance to exercise the imagination at the supposed site of the fabled gold-pillared city of Ubar, a shortish detour along Hwy 43.

Top Tip If you drive this route between July and mid-September there is a point along Hwy 31, just after Thumrait, where you will notice something quite remarkable: the jebel, suddenly, unexpectedly and with rulerlike precision, turns green. After hours of hard desert driving, it is an unforgettable, almost Zen-like experience.

Coastal Route

There is an altogether more scenic way of getting to Dhofar along the shores of the beautiful Arabian Sea but it is not for those in a hurry. The coastal trip from Muscat to Salalah takes at least three days and the beauty of the coast will make you wish you'd allowed more time. There are hotels at Al Ashkarah, Mahout and Duqm but you'll need camping equipment for the last leg. The route includes the new, spectacular, coast-hugging road from Shwaymiyah to Hasik, wrapped around brooding Jebel Samhan. If you want to explore the best of the coastal route, you'll need a 4WD to reach the shore or explore the wadis. For full descriptions of how to make the best of this area, refer to an off-road guide. Some of the highlights include:

Filim to Khaluf A few examples of traditional barasti fishing houses survive in this area of salt lagoons and unnerving off-road races against the tide.

Wadi Shuhram Ancient rock formations such as blue-green algae (the earth's original animate form) can be seen in the laminations of Wadi Shuhram (near Shital).

Duqm Wind-eroded sandstone make the rock garden at Duqm a national treasure.

Ras Madrakah Superb shells and cosy camping abound in the coves of this candy-striped headland.

Al Kahil Pink, algae-blown lagoons make seasonal homes here for flamingoes.

Shwaymiyah Famous for basket-weaving and its long bay, this village cowers under the looming presence of Jebel Samhan, lair of the leopard.

Hasik Curtains of dripping limestone, more usually seen in a cave, bedeck the roadside.

of frankincense, Dr Mohammed Al Mashani. He has researched the subject in depth and will show you some highly prized green frankincense, the colour of jade.

Information

There is no information centre as such, but the travel agencies on An Nahdah St are helpful and some of them can arrange local tours. Banks with ATMs, including HSBC, and a few exchange houses can be found around the intersection of An Nahdah and As Salam Streets. **Muscat Pharmacy** is on An Nahdah St just near the Gold Souq and Salalah has good, modern medical facilities at **Sultan Qaboos Hospital**.

Family Bookshop (23 290027; Ar Robat St; 9am-1pm & 4-8pm Sat-Wed, 4-8pm Fri) One of the very few bookshops selling English-language publications and maps. Located near the Clock Tower Roundabout at junction of Ar Robat and Al Matar Sts.

Internet Café & Computer Services (23 July St; per hour OR1; 9am-2am) Opposite the bus station, this is one of several internet cafes dotted around 23 July St.

Main Post Office (An Nahdah St; 8am-2pm Sat-Wed, 9-11am Thu) Entrance is at the rear of the building.

Telephone Office (cnr An Nahdah & Al Montazah Sts; 8am-2.30pm & 4-10pm) Offers fax facilities.

Getting There & Away

AIR

Salalah Airport (24 518072; www.omanairports.co.om) This beautiful new airport puts other airports in Oman to shame. Car hire companies are well represented beyond the arrivals hall.

Oman Air (Muscat 24 531111, Salalah Airport Office 23 368201, Salalah City Office 23 295747) The national carrier flies to Muscat (one-way/return from OR32/64, 1½ hours) around six times daily at variable times.

BUS

Mwasalat (23 292773; http://mwasalat.om/en-us/;) Mwasalat (formerly ONTC) buses to Muscat (one-way/return OR7.500/12, 12 hours) travel via Nizwa (OR6) and leave from the bus station in the new souq at 7am, 10am and 6pm. You can store luggage in the adjoining ticket office free of charge. There is also a service to Dubai (one-way/return OR11/18) at 3pm. Mwasalat runs air-conditioned, non-smoking buses with toilet and TV on all services.

Gulf Transport Company (Muscat Office 24 790823, Salalah Office 23 293303; Jnct 8, 23 July St; 5am-11pm) Services on modern buses to Muscat currently leave Salalah for Muscat at 7am and 10am, at 1.30pm and on the hour between 5pm and 9pm (one-way/return OR7/13, 12 hours). A service to Dubai leaves at 3pm (one-way/return OR10/18) and takes 16 hours. Tickets should be bought in cash a day in advance of travel.

Getting Around

TO/FROM AIRPORT

The new airport terminal is still very new and as yet there are no public bus services to the town centre. The 20-minute journey by taxi costs around OR10.

CAR

Hiring a car in Salalah is recommended for exploring, especially during the *khareef*. You don't strictly need a 4WD unless you want to enjoy some of the country's best camping, or explore the more rugged roads, but beware of the soft sand on the beaches.

The main car-hire companies can be found on arrival at the airport and Budget is represented at the Crowne Plaza Resort. Many local companies offer cars for hire, especially along 23 July St. For competitive rates and help with where to explore, **Salalah Beach Villas** (23 235999) hires 2WD/4WD from around OR14/37, with 200km free and reductions for week-long rental.

During the *khareef* the roads into the jebel are notoriously dangerous. They are slippery and local drivers fail to make allowances for the fog. Camels often cause accidents by wandering onto the road – if you hit one, you can be sure it will be an extremely expensive female, prize-winning, racing camel.

TAXI & MICROBUS

Salalah's taxis and microbuses loiter behind HSBC on As Salam St.

Microbus fares from Salalah include Mirbat (OR2) but there's a long walk from the drop-off point into town. A microbus ride within the city costs around 500 baisa.

Some sample fares on engaged taxis from the city centre include Crowne Plaza (OR5), Hilton (OR6), Juweira Marina (OR7), Taqah (OR15), Mirbat (OR25) and Salalah Marriott Resort (OR30).

Around Salalah

Salalah is sandwiched in the middle of a plain between the mountains and the Indian Ocean. This plain, with its horseshoe crescent of hills, extends east towards Jebel Samhan, and west towards the Yemeni border. For a day trip, it's feasible to go east or west, but not to tackle both.

The hillsides at any time of year are a fascinating product of human interaction with centuries of livestock grazing (mostly camels, cows and goats) helping to shape the contours, while nature takes care of the rest. Ancient trees and striking limestone formations are just some of the unique natural wonders of the region.

Many facilities at Dhofar's sights, such as restaurants and teashops, are only open in the *khareef*.

Sights & Activities

Job's Tomb HISTORIC BUILDING
(قبر النبي أيوب; daylight) FREE In religious terms, this tomb is probably the most important site in Dhofar. Regardless of your religious convictions, the tomb, situated on an isolated hilltop overlooking Salalah, is a must-see for the beautiful drive, especially during the *khareef*, and for the view over the Salalah plain on a clear day. The tomb is around 30km northwest of Salalah. Follow the signs along Ittin Rd and turn left at the signpost for An Nabi Ayyub after 22km.

A small restaurant below the tomb has wonderful views – and good egg roll-ups. There is no public transport.

If you are visiting Job's Tomb during the *khareef*, return to the main road and turn right to **Ayoon**. If you continue along here for another 22km, past dotted frankincense trees, you'll reach the end of the monsoon catchment. The contrast between the green slopes and the desert floor beyond is remarkable. Below the village of Ayoon, there are some natural pools, via a 3km off-road drive, which make for a pleasant picnic spot.

You can continue along the main road for another 22km until you meet the Thumrait road where a right turn brings you back to Salalah.

Beaches & Springs

There are glorious white-sand beaches along the entire coastal plain of Salalah, extending from the corniche in the heart of the city. Beware of strong currents anywhere along the coast during the *khareef*: swimming is prohibited at this time and challenging for weak swimmers at any time of year.

The whole area surrounding Salalah is dotted with *ayns* (freshwater springs) and any of these make a good half-day trip from the city. They are all signposted off the Salalah–Mirbat road. Some of the most picturesque springs include **Ayn Razat**, set in gardens; **Ayn Tabraq** and **Ayn Athum**, in the heart of a subtropical thicket; and **Ayn Garziz**, which can be visited off the Ittin Rd on the way to Job's Tomb. With eccentric limestone cliffs, gnarled with wild fig-tree roots and hanging with maidenhair ferns, this is a good spot to appreciate the transformation brought about by a drop of water.

East of Salalah

Taqah طاقة

This pretty fishing village, at the end of the magnificent white-sand beach that extends from Salalah, has several attractions, including a landscaped *khor*, a fine corniche, a fort on the hill (closed to visitors) and, for some inexplicable reason, a multi-storey branch of Bank Dhofar.

★Taqah Castle CASTLE
(adult/child OR500/200; 9am-4pm Sat-Thu, 8-11am Fri) This small but well-preserved castle was built in the 19th-century. With a furnished interior, video display, excellent signage, craft shop and an accompanying booklet explaining the history of this sardine-producing town, this is one of the best fort museums in Oman.

Khor Rouri خور روري

Looking across one of Dhofar's prettiest bays at peacefully grazing camels and flocks of flamingos, it's hard to imagine that 2000 years ago Khor Rouri was the trading post of the frankincense route and one of the most important ports on earth. Today little remains of the city except the painstakingly excavated ruins of Sumhuram Archaeological Park.

Sumhuram Archaeological Park ARCHAEOLOGICAL SITE
(admission per car OR2; 8am-9pm) This fascinating park is part museum and part archaeological site and you can wander around the ruins and watch the archaeologists at work. Visit the gallery within the site to see some of the 1st century BC to 3rd century AD finds from the site including some evocative Kursi inscriptions. There are toilets but no other facilities here.

Khor Rouri is about 35km east of Salalah. Take the Mirbat road and follow the brown signs. A microbus to the junction on the highway is 500 baisa. A new amphitheatre may soon offer a sound-and light-experience.

Wadi Dharbat وادي دربات

A popular picnic site during the *khareef* and a great place to enjoy the jebel in any season, Wadi Dharbat is the source of the estuary that flows into Khor Rouri. During a good *khareef,* an impressive waterfall spills over the cliff face, 300m to the plain below. Above the falls, water collects in luminous limestone pools. In the dry months, October to May, the Jebbali tribespeople set up their camps in this area.

The surrounding caves were used by the sultan's forces, together with the British SAS, to infiltrate areas of communist insurgency in the mid-1970s. Now the most surreptitious activity you are likely to see is the scuttling away of a small, fur-clad rock hyrax (an unlikely relative of the elephant) that lives among the rocks. Chameleons share the same territory and are equally clandestine, changing colour when abashed.

To get to Wadi Dharbat, follow the signs off the Mirbat road and climb 3km to the Wadi Dharbat junction (a small coffeeshop with toilets marks the entrance). A sealed road leads to the top of the waterfall and eventually to an unlikely lake (which shrinks to a pond after a poor rainy season) with a tea shop open in the *khareef.* Don't be tempted to swim as bilharzia is present here. A sealed road at the bottom of the cliff leads to the seasonal pool at the base of the waterfall, a haven for butterflies.

Mirbat مرباط

The town of Mirbat, just over 70km east of Salalah, has seen better days, but it has considerable historical significance. The town's main **fort** is now derelict despite being the site of the well-documented Battle of Mirbat in which nine soldiers kept 300 insurgents from taking Mirbat in July 1972 during the Dhofari insurrection. Two British Victoria Crosses were earned by the SAS but not awarded, to help keep the war out of the public eye. A much older fort, by the shore, has recently been restored but remains closed.

Notice the old **merchant houses** with their wooden, latticed windows. The onion-domed **Bin Ali Tomb**, 1km off the main road, marks the entrance to the town.

Sights & Activities

Glorious **beaches** stretch east and west of Mirbat, though a 4WD is necessary if you want to get close enough to the sea for wild camping (there are no facilities).

Salalah Marriott Resort (p202) has a dive centre that offers comprehensive underwater experiences.

Sleeping

Salalah Marriott Resort RESORT $$$

(☎23 275500; www.marriottsalalahresort.com; half-board r from OR110; @⊠) Bringing luxury and comfort to the coastal experience for those who'd rather not camp, this resort is a 10-minute drive east of the town of Mirbat. Transport is free from the airport and there's a complimentary shuttle to Salalah at 4.30pm, returning at 8.45pm on Mondays and Thursdays. There's also an on-site dive centre.

Getting There & Away

Microbuses to Mirbat from Salalah cost OR2; taxis cost OR30.

Jebel Samhan جبل سمحان

Although you need a permit and a good reason to visit the leopard sanctuary at Jebel Samhan, the sealed road up to the reserve entrance makes a rewarding day trip from Salalah. The road passes the entrance to Tawi Attair, a deep sinkhole known as the 'Well of Birds' which has a viewing platform but is really only accessible with a guide. Further up the Jebel Samhan road, signs lead to Taiq Cave, a vast limestone complex deep in the hills. En route to the cave, you'll pass lots of low-lying roundhouses belonging to the Jebbali (the indigenous residents of Dhofar's mountains), traditionally constructed with sticks and more recently covered with tarpaulins and tyres.

Continuing towards Jebel Samhan, the road climbs up through a variety of different flora, including rocky fields of leafless desert roses. Sometimes known as elephant plants, they have huge bulbous trunks and beautiful pink flowers in spring. As you near the summit (around 1300m) drive towards the cliff edge for a panoramic view of the coast. There are many exceptional vistas in Oman and this is one of them. If you're wondering about the odd spiky tree on the plateau, it's called a dragon tree and is confined to high, semi-arid elevations. The road ends at a couple of ad hoc teashops.

To reach any of these sights, take the Tawi Attair road after the fishing town of Taqah, and follow the brown signs. If you return to the coast from Tawi Attair following the signs to Mirbat, you'll pass (on the right of the descent) a wadi of tall, bulbous **baobab trees** – the only such trees in Arabia.

Hasik حاسك

Positioned at the most eastern end of the Dhofar coast before the cliffs of Jebel Samhan interrupt, Hasik is worth the two-hour drive from Salalah for the journey more than the destination. The road is sealed and not particularly exceptional in winter, but in summer luminous clouds billow down from the jebel and high winds whip across the water, sending the surf backwards as the waves roll inexorably forwards. Glossy cormorants cluster like oil slicks in the coves and waders shelter from the seasonal fury amid the drifts of pink top shells.

There is not much to see in Hasik itself, but if you continue along the road towards Hadraban, look out for an interesting limestone formation overhanging the sandstone cliffs. A small car park and toilet block marks the spot. The spectacular road across Jebel Samhan, linking Hasik to Shwaymiyah, is a tourist attraction in its own right.

West of Salalah

Mughsail مغسيل

Mughsail is 48km west of Salalah on Oman's most spectacular bay, ending in a set of sheer cliffs that reaches towards the Yemeni border. Immediately below the start of the cliffs (turn left opposite Al Maha petrol station) the rock pavement is potholed with **blowholes** that are active year-round, but particularly volatile during the high seas of the *khareef*. Toilets are available on the beach nearby and the enterprising **Restaurant for Local Food** offers roasted camel for OR3 per kilo.

Sarfait Road طريق صرفيت

If you have your own transport, continue from Mughsail towards the Yemeni border. The road is an impressive feat of engineering, zigzagging 1000m to the top of the cliff. Look out for a wadi full of **frankincense trees** 8km from Mughsail. Three or four kilometres after the top of the road, there are stunning views back towards Mughsail and inland across some of the wildest wadis in Arabia. The vegetation in this area is entirely different from that on the Salalah plain, with yuccas and succulents clinging to the limestone ledges.

At 13.5km from Al Maha petrol station in Mughsail, there is a small sign for **Fizayah**, 6km down the cliff face from the Sarfait road. It's just about possible in a 2WD in the dry season. The effort will be rewarded by one of the most dramatic spectacles in Dhofar: lunging cliffs and limestone pinnacles, decorated at the base with perfect sandy coves and grazing lands for the numerous camels owned by Jebbali (the indigenous residents of Dhofar's mountains).

The Sarfait road continues to the Yemeni border, a two-hour drive from Salalah along a sealed road, passing the endearingly dubbed **Sea Overlooking Site**, 31km from Al Maha petrol station. There is no accommodation in this area.

Shisr (Ubar) اوبار

Shisr has little of note except that it is possibly built on the ancient site of an old caravan post that some have identified as legendary Ubar. The equally legendary Empty Quarter beckons beyond. Ask tour companies in Salalah about overnight camping trips to the edge of these famous sands from the settlement of **Al Hashman**, an hour's rough ride from Shisr along a badly weathered unsealed track. The attempts at farming in the area quickly peter out beyond Shisr.

Ubar ARCHAEOLOGICAL SITE
(Wubar; 24hr) FREE Ubar, in the village of Shisr, is an archaeological site of potentially great importance. Lost to history for over a thousand years, the rediscovery of the remains of this once important trading post on the frankincense route caused great archaeological excitement in the 1990s. It may be hard for the ordinary mortal to appreciate what all the fuss is about as there is little to see.

A small, dusty museum (currently being rehoused in a much more recent fort tower) will eventually show the limited finds from the digs but you can wander around the unearthed settlement walls and get a feeling for

WORTH A TRIP

LOST CITY OF UBAR

In early 1992 the British explorer Ranulph Fiennes, together with a group of US researchers led by Nicholas Clapp, announced that they had found, with the use of satellite imagery, the remains of Ubar, one of the great lost cities of Arabia. According to legend, Ubar, otherwise known as the Atlantis of the Sands, was the crossroads of the ancient frankincense trail. Scholars are fairly certain that the place existed, that it controlled the frankincense trade and was highly prosperous as a result, but therein lies the end of the certainties.

The Quran states that God destroyed Ubar because the people of Ad were decadent and had turned away from religion, but archaeologists are more inclined to believe that it fell into a collapsed limestone cavern or sink hole. The site of this calamity is easy to see today, the remains shored up rather unsympathetically in concrete.

Predictably, there are many who dispute the rediscovery of Ubar. Excavations at the site have shown nothing of sufficient age to verify the claims and some chess pieces suggest a much later inhabitation. So is it worth the effort of bouncing along a graded track into the middle of nowhere to see not very much? For the historian, the romantic, or the plain curious, the site, in the middle of a great stony plain, offers the chance to peer through a hole in the desert at a legend laid bare.

the old walled community. The fabled golden pillars of antiquity, however, are probably just that: a fable elaborated from Bedouin tales. The route from Thumrait is now paved and signposted from the main road.

Hayma هيما

Hayma is the chief town of the region and an important transit point between the interior and the coast. Although there is little to commend the town itself, it does have basic accommodation and makes a good base for visiting the (relatively) nearby wildlife reserve, once famous for its oryx.

Sights

Al Wusta Wildlife Reserve NATURE RESERVE
(Formerly Arabian Oryx Reserve; ☎99 356002; half-/full-day guided tour in own vehicle OR25/40; ⏰7am-noon & 3-5pm) FREE A guided tour, usually by a member of the Harsusi tribe, is the only worthwhile way to visit the reserve although you can visit the porta-cabin information centre and captive oryx herd for free. The guides don't speak English and act as navigators only. The reserve, access to which is by 4WD only, is 50km off the Hayma–Duqm road (Hwy 37) on a poorly graded track marked 'Habab', 110km from Hayma. After 23km along the track, veer right.

A full-day's tour includes the remarkable windblown formations of the Huqf Escarpment, deep in the reserve but it has to be said that even here there is only a slim chance of spotting gazelles, hares or ibex let alone wild oryx.

Since its fall from grace (p205), wild camping with your own equipment outside the reserve is the only accommodation at present and you need to bring all your own supplies of food and water. Keep clothes under canvas as there is always a heavy dew by the morning – this is how the animals survive in the absence of surface water.

Sleeping

Don't expect more than a pitstop from accommodation in Hayma which caters mostly for truck-weary drivers. Equally, there are a number of unremarkable chicken-and-rice restaurants dotted around the petrol station opposite the motel.

Hayma Motel HOTEL $
(Himah Motel; fax 23 436061; Hwy 31; s/d OR15/20; P) On the highway opposite the main road turning into town, this motel primarily caters for Asian businesspeople. It is partially redeemed by the friendly staff.

Arabian Oryx Hotel HOTEL $
(☎23 436379; arabianoryxhotel@gmail.com; Hwy 31; s/d excl breakfast OR20/30; P 📶) This very basic hotel offers a clean bed for the night and basic Indian cuisine next door.

Duqm الدقم

Duqm's port may not yet have reached anything like its hyped potential but it has transformed the once tiny fishing community into a sprawling, busy town. Set to become a city of 40,000 people, construction is taking place across the barren shores of this wild coastline with two hotels and sets of improbable luxury housing cropping up in various scattered developments.

Thankfully, construction teams are being mindful to preserve the Duqm's main attraction, the beautiful natural **rock garden** of wind-eroded forms. Chosen as the location for a cultural centre there is as yet a fence around the site, but no gate. In case you're wondering, the stone plug out to sea is called **Nafun Island**.

Sleeping

★Crowne Plaza Duqm HOTEL $$

(☎25 214444; www.ihg.com/crowneplaza; r from OR60; P@☎≋) Whether you welcome the prospect of resorts mushrooming along this once remote beach or not, the Crowne Plaza has to be congratulated at least for building a beautifully landscaped hotel with first-class amenities. The deck to the pecten-strewn high-tide line invites a late-afternoon swim if nature wins out over the infinity pool.

There's a decent, well-priced buffet buffet and a bar with live entertainment, making this hotel altogether an extremely good-value experience.

Park Inn & Residence HOTEL $$

(☎24 507777; www.parkinn.com; r from OR59; P@☎≋) The second of several planned hotels and resorts along the beach south of the port complex, the individual chalet-style rooms here lend themselves to longer-term stay. Set back from the shore, however, there is no ready access to the sea.

City Hotel Duqm BUSINESS HOTEL $$

(☎25 214900; www.cityhotelduqm.com; s/d OR50/60) This modern, low-key business hotel is signposted off the highway with friendly, helpful management.

Getting There & Away

Duqm Jaaluni Airport (www.omanair.com) Oman Air flies into this desert airport (no amenities) four times a week (Muscat–Duqm one-way/return OR35/64; 1¼ hours). Check the website for the latest schedule.

Happy Line Oman (☎24 798470; www.happylineoman.com) Modern, air-conditioned buses make this epic journey from Muscat daily (one-way OR10, 8¼ hours), departing at 7am and arriving at 3.15pm. The return service leaves at 6am, reaching Muscat at 1.15pm.

DWINDLING ORYX HERDS

Until recently, watching the magnificent oryx paw the dust in the summer heat, or slip gracefully through the dawn mists in winter, made the long journey to the desolate Jiddat al Harasis plain worthwhile. Watching the mature bull, with rapier-like antlers and white, summer coat, level up to a rival in profile, you could be forgiven for thinking you'd seen a unicorn. In fact some trace the unicorn myth to the ancient Egyptian practice of binding the antlers of young oryx so they fuse into one. Fact or fiction, there's no doubting this magnficent animal caught the public imagination and great efforts were made to protect the species.

In 1962 the Fauna Preservation Society captured the last remaining oryx in Oman close to the border with Yemen and sent them to a zoo in the USA. By 1982, protected by new laws banning the hunting of wild animals, a herd of 40 Arabian oryx was returned to Jiddat al Harasis. Despite intermittent bouts of poaching the program met with initial success, in part due to the commitment of the Harasis tribe designated to look after them, and earnt the reserve Unesco World Heritage status.

But sadly much of these efforts have been in vain. Poaching has been harder to control than anticipated and the discovery of oil in the reserve resulted in a drastic 90% reduction in the animal's protected habitat. As a result, and to the country's embarrassment, the oryx reserve became in 2007 the first Unesco site ever to be delisted. This is bad news not only for the oryx which has shrunk from a herd of 450 in 1996 to only around 60 (with only four mating pairs) two decades later, but also for the endangered houbara bustard, honey badger and caracal who also call the diminished Huqf wilderness their home.

UNDERSTAND OMAN

Oman Today

The Rebirth of Oman

'Renaissance' is a term any visitor to Oman will hear, as it refers to the current period under Sultan Qaboos, a leader held responsible by most of the population for easing the country into modernity. Before he came to the throne in a bloodless coup in 1970, Oman had no secondary and only two primary schools, two hospitals run by the American mission and a meagre 10km of sealed roads. In addition, the country was in a state of civil war.

The country has since caught up with its more affluent neighbours. It now boasts efficient, locally run hospitals, respected colleges and universities, electricity to remote villages and an ever-improving infrastructure of roads. In January 1992 an elected Majlis al Shura (Consultative Council) was convened as a first step towards broader participation in government. Female representation on the council is growing (Omani women were the first in the Arab Gulf states to participate in this way) and women continue to hold high office in government, including at ministerial level (the ministers of education and higher education are both women). The country enjoys an enviably low crime rate and a well-trained and highly educated workforce.

It is perhaps this latter point that led to the Arab Spring of 2011 in Oman which took its toll on the country's stability. Oman fell 20 points on the Global Peace Index 2012, published by the US Institute for Economics and Peace, although it still ranks among the most peaceful countries in the Arab world. Local protests, particularly in the northern town of Sohar, focused less on calls for greater democracy (the sultan is the ultimate authority, with jurisdiction over even minor policy decisions) than on the lack of opportunities for job seekers and the slow progress of Omanisation – the process of replacing expatriates with Omani nationals. The government response was to offer a generous scholarship system for Omani citizens to study at tertiary level free of charge with the result that a large proportion of the population now studies at under- and postgraduate level, although there is some speculation that this may not be sustainable if the low price of oil continues.

Throughout the political and economic challenges of the past five years, Sultan Qaboos remains a popular leader whose reign is celebrated with due pomp and ceremony each year. Aging and failing in health, his return to Oman in 2015 after a prolonged health-related absence was the occasion of genuine relief and excitement in the country. Until his illness, the Sultan's 'meet the people' tour, where he and his ministers used to camp each year in different regions of the country to listen to local requests, was a good metaphor for his success. These tours, during which any visiting dignitaries were obliged to go camping too, were often marked by pennant-carrying camel riders bringing their petitions across the desert with gifts of goats for His Majesty. Requesting lighting in their village on day two of the sultan's visit, petitioners were often gratified to see the pylons delivered by day four of the same trip. It was this accessibility on the part of the sultan, together with his reputation for delivering promises, and for promoting tolerance and dialogue in a region not wholly typified by either quality, that has made him a national treasure.

Sultan Qaboos is not married and has no children. As he celebrates 45 years of a benign and enlightened reign, thoughts inevitably are turning to what the country will do without him. Whereas five years ago this was a source of anxiety, his prolonged absence in 2015 has suggested that the legacy of sound governance that he has put in place will endure.

Education & Diversification

In building a modern state, Sultan Qaboos' chief strategy has been to create a highly trained local workforce through intensive investment in education. Schooling is free, even partially at tertiary level, and provision is made for children of even the remotest villages. There has been no distinction in this approach between the genders. Indeed, girls account for almost half of the students in public and private schools while around half of the students at Sultan Qaboos University, the country's leading educational establishment, are women. Women are outperforming male students in engineering and medicine, traditionally male disciplines: the first female flight engineer in the region is from Oman and women are peforming to a high level in the military.

With limited oil revenues, Oman cannot sustain costly expatriate labour, so a policy of 'Omanisation' in every aspect of the workforce is rigorously pursued. In contrast to the rest of the region, it is refreshing to find locals – often of both sexes – working in all sections of society, from petrol-pump attendants to senior consultants.

Two central planks of the economy are self-sufficiency in food production, realised through intensive agriculture along the Batinah coast, and diversification of the economy. These schemes include the export of natural gas from a successful plant near Sur; giant ports in Salalah and Duqm; and methanol and aluminium plants in Sohar. The decision to disperse new economic initiatives across the regions has helped keep local communities buoyant and helped slow the exodus of villagers migrating to the capital. Tourism is the one major plank of the economy that enjoys a mixed fortune, vulnerable as it is to the negative effect on tourism confidence of Middle Eastern security concerns.

Much investment continues to be made in Oman's infrastructure – no mean feat given the challenges presented by the country's size, remoteness and terrain. It is now possible to drive on sealed roads to most towns and villages across the country. A similar surge in IT infrastructure is ensuring that Oman is connected effectively to the world's information highways, with e-government and telecom developments revolutionising the way business is conducted at home and abroad.

It is probably fair to say that Oman's approach to investment in new projects is cautious and this has slowed the recent pace of development to the frustration of many who see the country's potential. That said, a new government-led emphasis on entrepreneurialism is helping to create a sector of small- and medium-sized enterprises, run by Omanis for Omanis, which will inevitably lead the way to a more sustainable, homegrown future.

History

Gold, Frankincense and...Copper

The term 'renaissance' applied to Sultan Qaboos' reign is an appropriate one, as it suggests equally rich periods through Oman's long history.

As far back as 5000 BC, southern Oman (now called Dhofar) was the centre of the lucrative frankincense trade. This highly prized commodity, produced from the aromatic sap of the frankincense tree, was traded for spices with India and carried by caravans across all of Arabia. While the trees grew in Yemen and one or two other locations, they grew best in the monsoon-swept hills of Dhofar, where they continue to be harvested to this day. So precious was the sap of these trees that even the Queen of Sheba hand-delivered Dhofari frankincense to King Solomon. Equally legendary, of course, are the gifts borne by the three wise men of biblical report.

The Bible also mentions the golden-pillared city of Ubar, built by the people of Ad. This fabled city, which has excited the curiosity of explorers for hundreds of years, grew out of the frankincense trade to become one of the most powerful cities in the region. The remains of the city were reputedly rediscovered in the 1990s by English explorer Ranulph Fiennes. Nonetheless, it is hard to believe this claim, looking at the virtually barren plot near Thumrait. Much more persuasive is the fact that the presumed descendents of the remarkable civilisation of Ad still occupy the surrounding desert, speaking the distinct and ancient language of Jebbali, whimsically known as the 'language of the birds'.

Oman, or 'Majan' as it was then called, enjoyed further prosperity in pre-Islamic times through the trading of copper. Indeed, Oman is referred to in some sources as 'the Mountain of Copper', and the Bahrain National Museum provides evidence of vigorous trading in copper between Oman and its Gulf neighbours. The country then slipped into a long period of isolation that prevailed until the 7th century AD when Islam was introduced by Amr ibn al As, a disciple of the Prophet Mohammed. Oman was quick to embrace the new faith – it even gained a reputation for its proselytising zeal.

For about the next 500 years Oman came under the leadership of the Bani Nabhan dynasty (1154–1624).

Hostilities: the Portuguese

Frequent civil wars during the Bani Nabhan dynasty, between the sultan's forces and tribal factions, left the country vulnerable to outside hostilities that eventually came in the form of the Portuguese.

Alarmed by Oman's naval strength and anxious to secure Indian Ocean trade routes, the Portuguese launched a succession of attacks against Omani ports; by 1507 they managed to occupy the major coastal cities of Qalhat (near Sur, and mentioned in the journals of Ibn Battuta and Marco Polo), Muscat and Sohar. Ironically, it was a talented sailor from Sohar, Ahmed bin Majid, who unwittingly helped Vasco da Gama navigate the Cape of Good Hope in 1498, leading to the Portuguese invasion a few years later.

Over the next 150 years Oman struggled to oust the occupying forces. Eventually, under the guidance of the enlightened Ya'aruba dynasty (1624–1743), Oman was able to build up a big enough fleet to succeed. The Portuguese were interested in Oman only as a sentry post for their maritime adventures and had barely ventured into the country's interior. They were therefore easy to rout, given Oman's newly established naval might. Other than Al Jalali Fort, Al Mirani Fort and Mutrah Fort, all of which dominate the centre of Muscat, the Portuguese left little behind, although their legacy of military architecture continued to shape fort construction in Oman for centuries.

Unified & Wealthy

By 1650 Oman became a settled, unified state of considerable wealth and cultural accomplishment, with influence extending as far as Asia and Africa. Many of Oman's other great forts were built during this period, including the impressive, round-towered Nizwa Fort.

By the 19th century, under Sultan Said bin Sultan (r 1804–56), Oman had built up a sizeable empire controlling strategic parts of the African coast, including Mombasa and Zanzibar, and parts of what are now India and Pakistan. Today it is easy to see the influence that Oman had on the coastal areas of those countries, and even more tangibly the extent to which its own culture and population was enriched by the contact. The Batinah coast, for example, is home to the Baluchi people originally from Pakistan; as a result, mosque design along the highway between Barka and Sohar bears more resemblance to the florid architecture across the neck of the Gulf than it does to the more austere Ibadi tradition of Oman's interior.

When Sultan Said died, the empire was divided between two of his sons. One became the Sultan of Zanzibar and ruled the African colonies, while the other became the Sultan of Muscat and ruled Oman. The division of the empire cut Muscat off from its most lucrative domains, and by the end of the century, the country had stagnated economically, not helped by British pressure to end its slave and arms trading.

Coast Versus Interior: Isolation

The new century was marked by a rift between the coastal areas, ruled by the sultan, and the interior, which came to be controlled by a separate line of *imams* (religious teachers). In 1938 a new sultan, Said bin Taimur, tried to regain control of the interior, sparking off the Jebel Wars of the 1950s. Backed by the British, who had their own agenda, Said successfully reunited the country by 1959.

In all other respects, however, Said reversed Oman's fortunes with policies that opposed change and isolated Oman from the modern world. Under his rule, a country that a century earlier had rivalled the empire builders of Europe became a political and economic backwater. While neighbours such as Bahrain, Qatar and Kuwait were establishing enviable welfare states and sophisticated modern patterns of international trade, Oman slumped into poverty, with high rates of infant mortality and illiteracy. Even the communist insurgency in Dhofar during the 1960s failed to rouse Said from his reclusive palace existence in Salalah, and by the end of the decade his subjects, the most powerful of which had been either imprisoned or exiled, lost patience and rebellion broke out across the country.

The unrest led to a palace coup in July 1970 when Said's only son, Qaboos, covertly assisted by the British, seized the throne. With a face-saving shot in the foot, Said was spirited off to the Grosvenor Hotel in London, where he spent the remainder of his days. Some suggest that Said was not a greedy or malicious leader, just fiercely protective of his country's conservative traditions, which he feared would be eroded by the rapid modernisation experienced in neighbouring countries. Perhaps the country's contemporary balance between old and new, so skilfully maintained by his son, owes something to Said's cautious approach to Western influence.

People & Society

The National Psyche

Since the sultan came to power in 1970, Oman has trodden a careful path, limiting outside influence while enjoying some of the benefits that it brings. The result has been a successful adoption of the best parts of the Gulf philosophy, marked by a tolerance of outside 'customs and manners'. This has been achieved, thanks to the slower pace of change, without the sacrifice of national identity that often characterises rapid modernisation.

Oman takes pride in its long history, consciously maintaining customs, dress, architecture and rules of hospitality, as well as meticulously restoring historical monuments. With relatively modest oil revenues, Omani people have had to work hard to make their country what it is today, and perhaps that is why the arrogance that may be seen in neighbouring countries is conspicuously absent here. It is refreshing to find Omani nationals in all walks of life, from taxi drviers to university professors.

Lifestyle

It would be hard to imagine any country that has changed so dramatically in such a short space of time. Within the living memory of most middle-aged people outside Muscat, travelling to the next village meant hopping on a donkey or bicycle, education meant reciting the Quran under a tree, and medication comprised of a few herbs (very effective ones) from the mountainsides. Modern farmers contemplate GMC crop rotations, yet also look at the cloudless sky and realise that their grandmothers and children haven't been praying loudly enough. Modern medics administer the latest drugs while nipping back to grandmother for a herbal remedy for their own headaches. Little wonder that some families have buckled under the pressure of such an extraordinary pace of change; alcoholism, divorce, drug abuse and manic driving are all social ills that have increased proportionately.

On the whole, however, Oman is a success story; it has embraced the new world with just enough scepticism to allow people to return to their villages on the weekend, park their Toyotas at the end of the tarmac and walk the rest of the way to see grandfather.

Multiculturalism

Oman's population is predominantly Arab, although the country's imperial history has resulted in intermarriage with other groups, particularly from East Africa. As such, some Omanis speak Swahili better than Arabic. An Indian merchant community has existed in Muscat for at least 200 years, and people of Persian or Baluchi ancestry dominate the Batinah coast, with many still speaking Farsi or the Baluchi language.

OMANI DRESS

While many modernising countries have rushed headlong into international-style clothing, marked by business suits or jeans and a t-shirt, the people of Oman have made a conscious effort to maintain their sartorial heritage. While this is beginning to change in certain circumstances (in Muscat women often wear trousers under abeyyas, for example), on the whole visitors to the country can't fail to note the uniformity – not to mention the elegance – of the costume worn by young and old alike.

Traditional Omani dress is revealing of ethnic and regional origins. Heads, arms and legs are always covered, but costumes for women range from a long velvet train traditional to Dhofar, to a transparent *abeyya* (woman's full-length black robe), worn over colourful tunics with a peaked face worn by the Bedouin. During festivals, sisters and even friends often wear clothes cut from the same fabric. Elaborate trouser cuffs with silver embellishment, embroidered tunic yolks and long veils bedecked with gold jewellery form dazzling ensembles on special occasions.

Men wear a *dishdasha* (shirt-dress, usually white) and a white *kumar* (cotton, brimless hat), traditionally embroidered by a loved one. At work, men sport pastel-coloured turbans made of pashmina imported from Kashmir, tied according to the traditions of their home region. During ceremonies, a silver *khanjar* (dagger) is tucked into the belt and on an especially formal occasion, a *bisht* (transparent silk outer garment with gold trim) is worn while carrying a short, simple camel stick.

The Jebbali people form a separate group in Dhofar. Many Jebbali live a mostly nomadic life with their own distinct customs and language. Another unique language, Kumzari (a mixture of Portuguese, Arabic and Farsi), is spoken at the opposite end of the country in parts of the Musandam Peninsula.

Omani people have a strong sense of tribe and their tribal names (for example, Al Nabhani, Al Wahaybi, Al Balushi) indicate very clearly to which area they belong. Some families, such as Al Abris from Wadi Sahtan, can be pinpointed to specific wadis in the Hajar Mountains.

Attracted by work and modern amenities, many people are moving to the capital, Muscat, which is spreading along the coast towards Seeb. In an effort to stem this flow, graded roads, electricity and water have been supplied to even the smallest *willayat* (village). It is not unusual in even these far-flung outposts of the country to see expatriates, mostly from India, working in shops, schools and clinics.

Religion

About 75% of Omanis follow the Ibadi sect of Islam, an austere form of Islam that eschews decadence of any kind, even in mosque architecture. That said, modern Omanis tend to be pragmatic in their interpretation of religion, are tolerant of other forms of Islamic worship and allow expats to express their own religions in and around Muscat.

Magic plays a tangible role in the spiritual life of many Omanis. The 'evil eye' is not mere superstition; it is regarded as a hazard of everyday life. Amulets containing verses from the Quran, or hung around the necks of infants, are considered an effective way of warding off such adversities.

Arts

In a village between Dibab and Tiwi on the old Qurayat–Sur coast road, the porches of several houses sport splendid pink or lime-green bathroom tiles, complete with fern motifs. Next door to one of these houses, the remains of an intricately hand-carved door lay disintegrating for years until weather, or an entrepreneur from Muscat, or both, put paid to it.

It's not a case of out with the old and in with the new, but a demonstration of Oman's commercial relationship with art: a job lot of Indian tiles for a camel-bag of incense (or the modern-day equivalent) is the kind of international exchange that has characterised the pragmatic nature of Omani arts and crafts for centuries. It's not unusual, for example, to find the family silver (particularly grandmother's jewellery) making the journey to Muscat because wife number two prefers gold. Before they became items of tourist value, exquisite pieces of silver were readily melted down and returned in kind from the gold souq. In fact, for centuries most silver jewellery was fashioned from Oman's old currency (smelted Maria Theresa dollars, or *thalla*), prized for its 80%-plus silver content.

In other words, Oman's arts and crafts are all about the living rather than the dead, the practical rather than the purely decorative. Whether this heritage can withstand rapid modernisation is another matter.

Traditional Crafts

There are many crafts in Oman, all of which have been meticulously documented through the Omani Craft Heritage Documentation Project, under the auspices of His Highness Sayyid Shibah bin Tariq al Said and endorsed by Unesco.

Each region of Oman is associated with a different craft – Bahla is famous for pottery, Nizwa for silver jewellery, Jebel Shams for rug-weaving, Sur for boat-building, Shwaymiyah for basket-making. For a definitive survey of Omani crafts, the twin-volume *The Craft Heritage of Oman*, by Neil Richardson and Marcia Dorr, makes a weighty souvenir. Avelyn Forster's book *Disappearing Treasures of Oman* focuses on the silver Bedouin jewellery of Oman.

For more information on Oman's rich craft industry, see the website of the Public Authority for Craft Industries (www.paci.gov.om).

Music & Dance

There are dozens of traditional song and dance forms in Oman, over 130 of which have been documented by the Oman Centre for Traditional Music (www.octm-folk.gov.om), which was established in 1984 to preserve the country's musical heritage. Oman was the first Arab country to become part of the International Council for Traditional Music, under Unesco.

Oman's music is diverse, due to the country's seafaring and imperial heritage. The *naham* is a particularly famous call to crew members to pull together during a long sea voyage.

Sultan Qaboos is a Western classical-music lover. The Royal Oman Symphony Orchestra set up in his honour has been a surprising success, given the difficulties involved in learning a completely different musical idiom. The opening of the magnificent Royal Opera House Muscat in 2011, to mark the occasion of the 40th anniversary of the sultan's reign, has enabled the hosting of world-class opera, ballet and classical-music orchestras from around the world.

Each branch of the armed forces has a band of international calibre, including the highly popular bagpipe contingent – no official ceremony in Oman would be the same without the pipes and drums. The massed bands perform annual tattoos, giving lavish horse- and camel-back displays. Some of the military bands have regularly participated in the Edinburgh Tattoo to much acclaim.

Architecture

Oman may no longer boast pillars of gold like the fabled city of Ubar, but it does have another architectural trump card: its forts. There is barely a village without one and crenellations turn up as a motif in many public buildings, from bus stops and telephone kiosks, to ministries and courts of law.

The country has mercifully largely escaped the skyscraping obsession of its neighbours, settling for more restrained public buildings in keeping with a more modest budget. However, what the buildings lack in multiple floors, they make up for in imaginative design. Muscat, in particular, abounds with serene and elegant examples, such as the ministry buildings and embassy buildings in Al Khuwair. The Grand Mosque in Al Ghubrah, completed in 2001, is the ultimate expression of restraint, with the simplicity of its exterior masking an exuberantly rich interior.

Barasti (palm-leaf) and other palm-constructed housing is no longer common but a few examples can still be seen along the coast from Duqm to Shwaymiyah. In the Sharqiya Sands, Bedu use goat-hair tents, and a few people in the mountains live in caves with an improvised front door.

Finding a balance between old and new is a challenge. Young Omani engineers are disappointed in the low rise constructions of their capital and yet at the same time, it has been difficult convincing some communities to move the goats out of the municipal housing built for their benefit. For the time-being, at least, architectural ambition is held in check by the falling price of oil and visitors will appreciate the resulting and unique homogeneity of the built environment.

Environment

Oman is blessed with a remarkable environment of spectacular desert landscapes and a wealth of flora and fauna. However, it doesn't render up its treasures easily and a 4WD is required to visit many of the places of natural beauty and interest. Accommodation near these places is often restricted to ad-hoc camping, but many regard this as a joy in its own right. Indeed, waking up to the sound of a turtle retreating down the beach, or falling asleep to the croak of toads, is an unforgettable experience.

The Land

Geographically, Oman is large and diverse, with a coastline over 2000km in length, rugged mountains, a share of the Empty Quarter and a unique monsoon catchment. It extends from the fjords of the Musandam Peninsula to the seasonally green Dhofar region.

Most of the country's population is concentrated on the Batinah coast, a semi-fertile plain that runs from the border with the United Arab Emirates (UAE) to Muscat, and is separated from the rest of Arabia by the Hajar Mountains. These mountains are internationally famed for their geological heritage and even the layperson will enjoy the candy-striped rocks. The highest peak is Jebel Shams (Mountain of the Sun) at 3009m, alongside which runs Wadi Ghul, dubbed the Grand Canyon of Arabia. On the slopes of nearby Jebel Akhdar (Green Mountain), temperate fruits are grown.

Much of the country between the Hajar Mountains and Dhofar is flat and rocky desert, but there are also areas of sand dunes. Most notable are the Sharqiya Sands, informally known as Wahiba Sands, and the less-accessible sands of the Rub al Khali (Empty Quarter). Oman is not as rich in oil as its neighbours, but it does have some extensive fields in the gravel plains around Marmul in Al Wusta region and Fahood in Al Dakhiliyah region.

Thriving and diverse marine life exists off Oman's long coastline and there are many islands, the chief of which is the desert island of Masirah.

Wildlife

ANIMALS

Oman's isolated mountains and wadis are a haven for a variety of animals. These include over 50 types of mammals, such as wolves, foxes, hedgehogs, jerboas and hares. The largest land mammal that a visitor is likely to see is the gazelle which occupy the Huqf in Al Wusta region.

There are 13 different species of whale and dolphin in Omani waters, including the world's biggest living creature, the blue whale – a skeleton of which can be seen in Muscat's Natural History Museum. Oman also has an important biodiversity of molluscs: it's quite possible to identify over 30 different species along a 1km stretch of beach, even in the capital.

The *Oman Bird List* is updated regularly and published by the Oman Bird Records Committee (available in Muscat bookshops); there are nearly 500 recorded species. Spoonbills and flamingos frequent salt lagoons, even in Muscat, but the country is internationally renowned for its migrating raptors. For more information, *Birdlife in Oman*, by Hanne and Jens Eriksen is an excellent resource produced by two expats renowned for their superb bird photography. Keen ornithologists should contact the Oman Bird Group (p135).

There is a wide diversity of insects in Oman – from the mighty minotaur beetle to the fig tree blue, orange pansy and other butterflies – attracted to Oman's fertile wadis or desert acacias. Dhofar, with its unique microclimate, is particularly rich in entomological interest.

ENDANGERED SPECIES

Oman is of global importance to the survival of the endangered green turtle and has one of the largest nesting sites in the world at Ras al Jinz. There are five endangered species of turtle supported by the coasts of Oman, all protected by royal decree.

Oman's varied terrain is home to a large number of endangered species, including houbara bustard, ibex, *tahr* (an Omani species of a goatlike animal) and Arabian leopard which is native to Dhofar. There are also declining numbers of sand cat, caracal, honey badger and mongoose.

Al Wusta Wildlife Reserve (p204) in Jiddat al Harasis protects a herd of dwindling wild oryx, reintroduced in the 1980s. The future of this magnificent antelope, however, is looking bleak.

PLANTS

Oman built an empire on the frankincense trees that grow in Dhofar. The trees are still bled for the aromatic sap, but dates, covering 49% of cultivated land, have overtaken them in economic importance. Oman has a very rich plant life thanks to its fertile wadis, many irrigated year-round by spring water. It is common to see tall stands of pink oleander flowering in the wadis throughout the year.

A government-sponsored herbal clinic in Muscat uses many locally occurring plants and shrubs to treat a wide range of illnesses, most commonly diabetes and hypertension.

A national collection of plants is being assembled as part of the world-class Oman Botanic Garden (www.bgci.org), the first of its kind in Arabia. When complete (in 2017), every habitat in Oman will be represented in two giant biomes.

National Parks

While there are several reserves, such as the Qurm Nature Reserve in Muscat set up to protect the endangered mangrove, there are no formal national parks. The Damanayat Islands are designated as a national nature reserve and access to this marine environment is controlled.

Environmental Issues

Oman used to enjoy an enviable record with regard to its protection of the environment – a subject in which the sultan has a passionate interest. His efforts were even acknowledged by the International Union for the Conservation of Nature (IUCN), which awarded him the John C Phillips Prize in 1996, and cited Oman as a country with one of the best records in environmental conservation and pollution control. The sultanate's first environmental legislation was enacted in 1974, and in 1984 Oman was the first Arab country to set up a ministry exclusively concerned with the environment. The prestigious Sultan Qaboos International Prize for Environmental Preservation, first awarded in 1991, has been given every two years to a conservation body or individual chosen by Unesco for environmental performance. On 8 January each year the sultanate celebrates Environment Day, when children learn about habitat erosion, rubbish dumping and depletion of freshwater reserves.

Despite this exemplary record, increased tourism has led to a recent increase in littering, especially of plastic, and oil waste is being washed up on Oman's hitherto pristine beaches, dumped illegally from container ships. Despite heavy penalties if caught, offenders often get away with it, as it's almost impossible for Oman's military services to police such a long and exposed coastline.

Landfill and waste management issues are being tackled through various research initiatives, together with schemes to make solar energy more reliable in a dust-blown climate and water conservation more sustainable. A circular economy of recycling and energy generation through waste, however, is still a long way off.

To find out more about the steps Oman is taking to preserve the environment and the unique flora and fauna within it, contact the Environmental Society of Oman (www.eso.org.om). There is also a highly successful Outward Bound initiative, endorsed by the government, bringing environmental awareness to the nation's youth.

Food & Drink

Omani cooking is nutritious and varied with a heavy emphasis on cardamom, saffron and turmeric, reflecting the country's ethnic diversity. Until recently it was difficult to sample much Omani cuisine as there were few restaurants offering the genuine article. That is beginning to change, at least in the capital, as the habit for eating out, combined with more women seeking careers, has led to an increased demand for Omani traditional dishes outside the home.

With access to a long coastline, Omanis are particularly fond of fish – sardines can be seen drying in noisome piles from Sohar to Salalah. Until recently, shellfish, including

OMAN'S FAVOURITE SWEETS

Omanis have a decidedly sweet tooth, which they indulge during every important social occasion – a factor that has contributed over the past few decades to a high incidence of diabetes. It's polite to participate in the communal eating of sweetmeats – using the right hand only, of course.

Halwa At official ceremonies, such as event openings and National Day celebrations, *halwa* is offered to guests. Lumps of the sticky, glutinous confection are pinched out of a communal dish between the right finger and thumb, much to the chagrin of those who forgot to bring a hanky. Made of sugar or dates, saffron, cardamom, almonds, nutmeg and rosewater, *halwa* is prepared in huge copper vats heated over the fire and stirred for many hours by men wielding long, wooden pestles; it's hard and hot work and its production is displayed as an entertainment during *eids* (Islamic feasts) and festivals. Every region thinks it produces the best *halwa* but Barka is generally understood to have the edge and many outlets around the town sell it piled up in colourful plastic bowls or glazed ceramic dishes.

Dates If no one quite got round to buying the *halwa* for a party, then dates will suffice. Dates are not only an indispensable part of a meal, but also of Omani hospitality. Dates are always served with one or two cups of strong *qahwa* (Arabic coffee laced with cardamom) and it is impolite to refuse to share at least one date with at least two cups with a host (but not too many more).

Honey Dubbed by some as the 'liquid gold' of the region, honey costs OR10 to OR70 a kilo. As such, it's easy to see why apiculture is on the increase. It's not a new trend, however: boiling honey was used in Oman as a weapon against enemies – just look for the holes above fort doors. The most expensive honey is still collected in the traditional way from wild beehives in the upper reaches of the Hajar Mountains. Pale, golden honey indicates the bees were raised on date-palm pollen; deep amber suggests sumar-tree blossom; while *sidr*, a mountain shrub, produces a molasses-coloured honey.

the local lobster (actually a large, clawless crayfish), were not considered fit for eating. Tastes have now changed and lobster is a popular dish even in small regional restaurants. One delicacy worth sampling from southern Oman is *rabees*. Made from boiled baby shark, stripped and washed of the gritty skin, and then fried with the liver, it is a nutritious dish from a sea where sharks are plentiful.

Perhaps the most typical Omani dish is *harees,* made of steamed wheat and boiled meat to form a glutinous concoction. It is often garnished *ma owaal* (with dried shark) and laced with lime, chilli and onions, and is a popular dish used to break the fast during Ramadan. Few Omani dishes are especially spicy although some form of chilli paste usually crops up as a garnish.

The dish of parties and festivals is *shuwa*; goat, mutton, calf or camel meat is marinated with date juice and spices, wrapped in banana leaves and buried in an earthen or underground oven. The result, at least 12 hours later, is a mouth-wateringly tenderised piece of meat, aromatically flavoured with wood smoke and spices. It is served with *rukhal* (wafer-thin Omani bread) and rice on a *fadhl* (giant, communal eating tray), and eaten, of course, with the right hand only. Guests traditionally eat first, followed by men, who are expected to reserve the best pieces for women, who eat with the rest of the family after the guests are gone. This does not represent as long a wait as it might seem as traditionally guests 'eat and go', having dispensed with all the news before the meal commences. Many modern families these days eat together.

As Oman grows its own prize pomegranates, bananas, apricots and citrus fruit, mainly on the terraced gardens of Jebel Akhdar, fruit is not surprisingly an important part of an Omani meal. What is surprising to many visitors, however, is that it is traditionally served before the meat course.

Camel milk is available fresh and warm from the udder in Bedouin encampments. Like mare's milk, it's an experience many prefer to miss! Alcohol cannot be purchased 'over the counter' in Oman without a resident permit. It is available, however, in most of the more expensive hotels and restaurants where it must be consumed on the premises.

SURVIVAL GUIDE

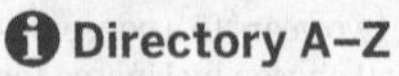

Directory A–Z

ACCOMMODATION

In general, accommodation in Oman is limited and expensive. The following notes may be helpful when booking accommodation:

- Discounts can often be negotiated in the low season (May to September, except in Salalah where peak season is June to August).
- In many places, there's no alternative to the single midrange to top-end hotel, and smaller towns often have no hotels at all.
- Almost all hotels, including the most basic and some desert camps, offer free wi-fi, at least in the lobby area.
- There are no campsites in Oman as such, only the desert camps of Jebel Shams, Ras al Hadd and Sharqiya Sands. These vary in price and amenities but most offer the chance of erecting a tent on the premises and using the camp facilities for a fee.
- Wild camping is one of the highlights of Oman, providing you are discreet, outside urban areas and don't require creature comforts. Finding somewhere suitable to camp can be difficult without a 4WD vehicle.

ACTIVITIES

Oman is a large country with a sparse population. There are still vast tracts of land without a road that are virtually unmapped. This is excellent news for anyone interested in the outdoors, as you have the chance of coming across an uncharted wadi or hidden cave system, finding a bed of undisturbed fossils, or discovering a species unnamed by science – the possibilities are endless. However, there is a responsibility, firstly, to avoid getting into a dangerous situation (rescue services are either not available or stretched to the maximum in taking care of road traffic accidents) and, secondly, to limit the negative impact of each activity on the environment.

Off-Road Exploration

One of the highlights of visiting Oman is off-road exploration of its mountains, wadis, sand dunes and coastline, particularly in a 4WD with some camping equipment. A detailed off-road guide for this activity is essential. Hiring a 4WD can be expensive, but tour companies offer all the main off-road destinations as day trips or on overnight tours.

Companies that aggressively promote 'wadi bashing' should be viewed with caution: driving irresponsibly across virgin desert terrain, ripping up the sides of pristine dunes and pounding at speed along delicate wadi floors causes great damage to the environment and destroys the local flora and fauna. One shower of rain and the desert comes alive, showing just how problematic it is to treat the land as a waste-ground for car chases. Stick to prior tracks and confine extreme driving to designated areas.

Hiking, Rock Climbing & Caving

With a pair of stout boots, a map, water and *Adventure Trekking in Oman*, by Anne Dale and Jerry Hadwin, you can access superb walking territory all over the country. Unless you are an accustomed outbacker, however, it is advisable to take a tour that can help tailor a trip to suit your interests.

Rock climbing and caving are increasingly popular activities in Oman, but they tend to be conducted on a 'go-it-alone' basis. *Rock Climbing in Oman*, by RA McDonald, lists some exciting routes, but you need a climbing partner and equipment.

Oman has some rich cave systems, of which many have never been explored. *Caves of Oman*, by Samir Hanna and Mohamed al Belushi, gives a good account of speleology in Oman and points out some local safety advice.

Although these activity guidebooks are now out of print, they are readily available second-hand in Muscat bookshops.

Watersports

Alongside turtle-watching at Ras al Jinz and dolphin-watching from Muscat and Khasab, fishing and watersports are offered in various locations around the country. Kitesurfing is gaining in popularity near Ashkara and on the island of Masirah. Diving and snorkelling are other popular activities. What the Indian Ocean lacks in clarity off the shores of Oman, it makes up for in the pristine nature of the relatively unexplored dive sites.

CHILDREN

Oman is a friendly and welcoming place for children. For younger children, beachcombing, sandcastle building and paddling make Oman a dream destination. That said, there are few specifically designed amenities for children, except for a park with swings in most town centres.

CUSTOMS REGULATIONS

- Non-Muslims travelling by air can bring in two bottles of wine or spirits.
- It is illegal to cross by land from Oman into the UAE and vice versa carrying alcohol.
- A 'reasonable quantity' of cigars, cigarettes and tobacco can be imported.
- It is illegal to bring in banned substances of any kind and penalties for possession are severe.

ELECTRICITY

The mains electricity in Oman is 220V to 240V. Adaptors are widely available at hotel shops and from supermarkets such as Al Fair.

EMBASSIES & CONSULATES

Unless indicated otherwise, all the embassies listed are on Jameat ad Duwal al Arabiyah St in the district of Shatti al Qurm, Muscat. The British embassy looks after Irish nationals, processes visas and handles emergencies for Canadian citizens. Australians should contact the Australian embassy in Riyadh, Saudi Arabia.

Consular sections of the embassy often close an hour or two earlier than the rest of the embassy, so try to go as early in the day as possible or ring first to check.

Bahraini Embassy (Map p126; ☎24 605133; muscat.mission@mofa.gov.bh; Way 3017, Shatti al Qurm; ⏲8am-2.30pm Sun-Thu)

Dutch Embassy (Map p126; ☎24 603706; www.mfa.nl/mus; Villa 1366, Way 3017, Shatti al Qurm; ⏲9am-noon Sun-Thu)

French Embassy (Map p126; ☎24 681800; www.ambafrance-om.org; ⏲9am-2.30pm Sun-Thu)

German Embassy (Map p126; ☎24 832482; www.maskat.diplo.de; Al Nahdha St, Ruwi; ⏲9am-noon Sun-Thu)

Jordanian Embassy (Map p126; embhkjom@omantel.net.om; ⏲8am-noon Sun-Thu)

Kuwaiti Embassy (Map p126; ☎24 699626; fax 24 604732; ⏲8am-12.30pm Sun-Thu)

Qatari Embassy (Map p126; ☎24 701802; muscat@mofa.gov.qa; ⏲8am-2.30pm Sun-Thu)

Saudi Arabian Embassy (Map p126; ☎24 698780; omemb@mofa.gov.sa; ⏲8.30am-2pm Sun-Thu)

UAE Embassy (Map p126; ☎24 602531; uaeoman@omantel.net.om; ⏲8am-1.30pm Sun-Thu)

UK Embassy (Map p126; ☎24 609000; www.britishembassy.gov.uk; ⏲7.30am-2.30pm Sun-Thu)

US Embassy (Map p126; ☎24 643400; www.oman.usembassy.gov; ⏲8am-12.30pm Sun-Thu)

SLEEPING PRICE RANGES

The following price ranges refer to a double room with bathroom and air-con in high season (November to March). Taxes, breakfast and wi-fi are included in the price, unless otherwise stated. Listings are arranged by price and then by author preference within a price category.

$ less than OR45 (US$120)

$$ OR45–OR100 (US$120–US$265)

$$$ more than OR100 (US$265)

EATING PRICE RANGES

The following price ranges refer to a standard meal. Service charge and tax is included in the price.

$ less than OR5 (US$14)

$$ OR5–OR10 (US$14–US$28)

$$$ more than OR10 (US$28)

FOOD

Local restaurants selling genuine Omani food (p213), with its emphasis on fish and dates, represent a new trend in the cities. Although alcohol is served in many city restaurants and regional hotels and resorts, note that it can't be bought or consumed outside licensed premises. Provision is made for eating during Ramadan for those who are not fasting, but discretion is key to avoid causing offence – or indeed, breaking the law.

INTERNET ACCESS

Internet access is available throughout Oman and free wi-fi is available in most hotels and leading cafes. Internet cafes are becoming less common.

LEGAL MATTERS

Breaking the law can have severe consequences (p38). For more information, consult your embassy.

MAPS

Up-to-date maps are hard come by in Oman. The Ministry of Tourism desk at the airport offers a reasonably accurate, free road map of Oman, which is also available from many hotels.

MONEY

The official currency is the Omani rial (OR but widely spelt RO). One rial is divided into 1000 baisa (also spelt baiza and shortened to bz). There are coins of 5, 10, 25 and 50 baisa, and notes of 100 and 200 baisa. There are notes of a half, one, five (which looks unfortunately similar to a one rial note), 10, 20 and 50 rials.

ATMs & Credit Cards

ATMs are widespread in Oman and many of them, particularly those belonging to HSBC, are tied into international systems. The most popular credit card in Oman is Visa, but MasterCard is also widely accepted. Amex is not accepted in many shops, and you may incur a fee of 5% for using it in some restaurants and hotels.

Moneychangers

Most banks will change US-dollar travellers cheques for a commission. Money changers keep similar hours to banks, but are often open from around 4pm to 7pm as well. They usually offer a slightly more competitive rate than the banks, and most charge only a nominal commission of 500 baisa per cash transaction.

Tipping & Bargaining

A tip of 10% is customary only in large hotels and restaurants if a service fee hasn't been included in the bill. It is not the custom to tip taxi drivers or smaller establishments.

Discounts are available for most items in all shops other than supermarkets and Western-style chain stores. Haggle for taxi fares and souvenirs but don't expect too much of a bargain.

OPENING HOURS

Oman's weekend is on Friday and Saturday.

Banks 8am to noon Sunday to Thursday; some reopen between 5pm to 8pm.

Government Departments & Ministries 7.30am to 2.30pm Sunday to Thursday; closing 1.30pm during Ramadan.

Post Offices 8am to 1.30pm Sunday to Thursday; 8am to 11am Saturday.

Restaurants 11.30am to 2pm and 5pm to midnight Saturday to Thursday; 5pm to midnight Friday.

Shops 8am to 1pm and 4pm to 7pm Saturday to Thursday; 5pm to 7pm Friday; Mutrah Souq and upmarket Muscat shopping centres open to 9pm or 9.30pm.

Sights 9am to 4pm Saturday to Thursday; closed or reduced hours on Friday; many sights open on an ad hoc basis and timings change frequently.

PHOTOGRAPHY

- Memory cards and batteries are widely available in Muscat. Most studios can print digital photos from a memory card and transfer photos to a CD.
- It is important to be discreet photographing people, especially women, as it can cause great offence, especially in rural and remote areas.

POST

Sending a postcard to any destination outside the Gulf Cooperation Council costs 150 baisa. Postage for letters is 250 baisa for the first 10g and 400 baisa for 11g to 20g. For parcels of up to 1kg it is around OR5.

PUBLIC HOLIDAYS

In addition to the main Islamic holidays (p446), Oman observes these public holidays:

Lailat al Mi'raj (Ascension of the Prophet) The exact date is dependent on the sighting of the moon – the date is never given until the last minute.

Renaissance Day (23 July) A day's holiday is given to mark the beginning of the reign of Sultan Qaboos, generally credited for the modern rebirth of the country.

National Day (18 November) Marked by at least two days of holiday, camel-racing, military parades and flags decorating the highway.

RESPONSIBLE TRAVEL

Westerners are often seen wandering around supermarkets or hotel foyers in shorts, dressed in bikinis on public beaches and skinny-dipping in wadis. These practices are highly resented, though Omanis are too polite to say as much. In order to respect local customs, knees and shoulders should be covered in public and both men and women should observe this. Women should cover their cleavage but do not need to wear *abeyya* or head scarf.

It's tempting when exploring off-road destinations to drive straight through the middle of villages. This is about as sensitive as taking a lorry through a neighbour's garden back home. If you want to see the village, it's better to park outside and walk in, preferably with permission from a village elder.

In addition, Oman's wild environment requires special consideration. Tyre tracks leave marks on the desert floor, often forever. Litter has become a major problem as even a banana skin does not biodegrade in the hot, dry climate. Please don't add to this sadly ever-growing problem.

SAFE TRAVEL

Oman is a very safe country. Three dangers that may escape the attention of visitors, however, are high volumes of traffic accidents due to tailgating and speed, flash floods and the isolation of many off-road destinations.

SHOPPING

Oman is a great centre for handicrafts, with expertise in silversmithing. Exquisitely crafted *khanjars* (traditional curved daggers) can cost up to OR500 but tourist versions are available from OR30. Genuine Bedouin silver is becoming scarce due to the tradition of melting it down rather than handing it on to the next generation. Besides, most modern Omani women prefer gold. Silver Maria Theresa dollars, used as Oman's unit of currency for many years, make a good buy from OR3. Wooden *mandoos* (chests) studded with brass tacks cost from OR10 for a new one and start at OR100 for an antique.

Other items commonly for sale include coffee-pots (not always made in Oman), baskets woven with leather, camel bags, rice mats and cushion covers. Many items are imported, as per centuries of tradition, from India and Iran.

Frankincense is a 'must buy' from Salalah, together with a pottery incense burner (both available in Muscat). Amouage (from OR50), currently the most valuable perfume in the world, is made in Muscat and comes in different fragrances and preparations, some of which is derived from frankincense. A visit to one of the outlets (at city centre, Qurm or the airport) is a treat in itself. Omani dates make another excellent gift.

SOLO TRAVELLERS

Travelling beyond Muscat and the main towns of Nizwa, Sohar, Sur and Salalah can be a lonely experience. The interior is sparsely populated and, with no established circuit of travellers' meeting places, bumping into other foreigners is rare outside the holiday period. While Omani people are very friendly and hospitable, they are also private and you are unlikely to be invited to stay for longer than the customary bread and salt. If you hitchhike to somewhere remote, you may have a very long wait before you find a ride out again. On the whole, as with any country with large expanses of remote territory, it's better to have backup in the form of a vehicle, a companion, or at least water, a map and a compass.

BEST BOOKS

➡ *The Doctor and the Teacher: Oman 1955–1970*, by Donald Bosch – includes an interesting account of life before the 'renaissance'.

➡ *On the Track of the Early Explorers*, by Philip Ward – combines modern travel narrative with the accounts of earlier travellers.

➡ *Arabian Sands*, by Wilfred Thesiger – the final part of Thesiger's 1959 classic describes Oman's interior.

➡ *Atlantis of the Sands*, by Ranulph Fiennes – an account of the Dhofar insurgency in the 1960s, and also describes the search for the lost city of Ubar. On the same subject, *The Road to Ubar*, by Nicholas Clapp, is worth a read.

➡ *Adventure Trekking in Oman*, by Anne Dale and Jerry Hadwin – lists some great hikes.

➡ *Oman – a Comprehensive Guide*, published under the auspices of the Directorate General of Tourism. It includes interesting anecdotal information.

PRACTICALITIES

Magazines *What's On in Muscat* gives a useful listing of events.

Newspapers *The Times of Oman* and *Oman Daily Observer* are local English-language newspapers. Foreign newspapers are available (three days old) from hotels and major supermarkets.

Radio The BBC World Service is available on 103.2FM. The local English-language radio station broadcasts on 90.4FM (94.3FM from Salalah) from 6.30am to midnight daily. High FM (95.9FM) is Oman's most popular English-language commercial radio station, playing contemporary music and promoting local events. There is a home-grown classical music station (97FM) reflecting the Sultan's passion for orchestral music.

TV Oman TV broadcasts the news in English nightly at 8pm and shows English-language films two or three nights a week (usually around 11pm). Satellite TV is also widely available.

Smoking A no-smoking policy is enforced in interior public places. This includes inside restaurants and on public transport.

Weights & Measures Oman uses the metric system.

TELEPHONE

Each area of Oman has its own code (for example, ☎24 is the prefix for Muscat). Note that you need to use this code even if calling from within the same area.

Phonecards are available from grocery stores and petrol stations. International phone calls can be made with a phonecard by dialling direct from most public phone booths throughout Oman. The cost of a two-minute call to Europe and the US is approximately 200 baisas.

Mobile Phones

Temporary local GSM connections can be made through the purchase of an Omanmobile Hayyak SIM card (www.omanmobile.om; starter pack OR2), which includes OR1 worth of call time. Alternatively, Ooredoo (www.ooredoo.om) and Friendi Mobile (www.friendimobile.om) offer a similar service. These cards can be purchased on arrival at the airport and from shopping centres in Muscat.

TRAVELLERS WITH DISABILITIES

Oman does not cater particularly well for the needs of disabled travellers with ramps and disabled parking being the exception rather than the rule except in Muscat. The **Oman Association for the Disabled** (☎99 329030) primarily assists nationals but they may be able to help if you call with enquiries.

VISAS

A visit visa, required by all nationalities except for citizens of Gulf countries, can be obtained by many foreign nationals (including those from the EU, the Americas, Australia and New Zealand) online through the Royal Oman Police (ROP) or on arrival at Muscat International Airport.

It is also possible to obtain a visa at border crossings. Currently those with a Qatar or UAE tourist visa may visit Oman without paying for an Omani visa if travelling on direct flights or overland.

Royal Oman Police (ROP; www.rop.gov.om; Muscat International Airport; visits of 10 days OR5, 10-30 days OR20; ⏲7.30am-1pm Sun-Thu) Visas can be obtained in advance using the ROP's E-visa application service. Admission may be refused if you have an Israeli stamp in your passport. Visa regulations change frequently, so check the website for updates. Multiple-entry visas cost OR50 (valid for one year) and are good for three-week visits for bona fide business travellers.

Visa Extensions

A 10-day extension (OR5) on a 10-day visa and a one-month extension (OR20) on a one-month visit visa are available from the ROP Visa Information counter at Muscat International Airport. No extensions on multiple-entry visas are available. Overstaying a visa will incur charges on departure (OR10 per day).

WOMEN TRAVELLERS

Women travelling alone may feel uncomfortable, particularly on public transport, eating in restaurants and when visiting public beaches. Omani men mostly ignore women out of respect and it's hard to meet Omani women. Many of the country's attractions lie off-road where travelling solo (for either sex) is inadvisable unless you are highly resourceful and, if driving, strong enough to change a tyre.

Harassment is not a big problem. It helps, in addition to being culturally sensitive, to be discreetly dressed in loose-fitting clothing, and to wear shorts and a T-shirt for swimming.

WORK

To work in Oman you have to be sponsored by an Omani company before entering the country (ie you have to have a job). Although it is illegal to work on a tourist visa, some expats take a short-term contract and hope their employer will arrange a labour card for them. The reality is a fretful experience best avoided.

Getting There & Away

ENTERING OMAN

Visas (required for most nationalities) are available on arrival. Fill in a form in the immigration hall and take it to the visa-collection counter before queuing up to have your passport stamped. E-visas are available through the Royal Oman Police website (www.rop.gov.om).

AIR

Airports

There is only one truly international airport in Oman, and that is Muscat International Airport in Muscat. That said, Qatar Airways offers direct flights between Doha and Salalah and Fly Dubai offers direct flights between Dubai and Salalah.

Muscat International Airport (☎24 519223; www.omanairports.com) This small airport is surprisingly efficient, queues are kept to a minimum (outside holiday periods), the sense of hospitality begins at the immigration counter and your luggage is often waiting on the carousel before the formalities are complete. A new airport should be open by 2017.

Regional Flights

There are direct flights to each of the destinations below daily. Frequent single-stop flights connect all these destinations.

FLIGHT DESTINATION	PRICE
Abu Dhabi (UAE)	OR67
Doha (Qatar)	OR120
Dubai (UAE)	OR27
Kuwait City (Kuwait)	OR45
Manama (Bahrain)	OR33
Riyadh (Saudi Arabia)	OR158

Airlines Flying to/from Oman

British Airways (☎80 077694; www.ba.com) Hub: Heathrow, London

Emirates (Map p133; ☎24 404444; www.emirates.com) Hub: Dubai. Has an office in Ruwi.

Fly Dubai (☎24 765091; www.flydubai.com) Hub: Dubai

Gulf Air (Map p133; ☎24 703222; www.gulfair.com) Hub: Bahrain. Office in Ruwi.

Oman Air (☎24 531111; www.omanair.com) Hub: Muscat. Office in Ruwi.

Qatar Airways (☎24 162700; www.qatarairways.com) Hub: Doha, Qatar.

Saudi Arabian Airlines (☎24 789486; www.saudiairlines.com) Hub: Jeddah, Saudi Arabia.

LAND

Oman borders the UAE, Saudi Arabia and Yemen. Current practicalities mean, however, that you can only enter UAE. The situation changes frequently and it's worth checking with the **Royal Oman Police** (p218) before planning your trip to see which crossings are open to non-GCC (Gulf Cooperation Council) visitors. Visas are obtainable at all Oman border posts.

Border Crossings

There were six Oman–UAE border posts open to foreigners at the time of research: these are at Buraimi, Hafit, Khatmat Milahah, Tibat and Wajaja. All are open 24 hours. There are sometimes long delays at the Buraimi and Wajaja borders, especially during regional public holidays.

Bus

Mwasalat – International (Formerly ONTC; Map p133; ☎24 708522; http://mwasalat.om/en-us; Al Jaame St, Ruwi) Has buses on the Oman–Dubai express service at 6am, 3pm and 11pm (OR5.500, 5½ hours) departing from Ruwi Bus Station.

Car

It's possible to drive through any of the open borders in your own vehicle if you obtain insurance to cover both countries.

You need extra insurance if you wish to take a hired car over the border to/from UAE and you must return the car to the country in which you hired it (unless you're willing to pay a huge premium).

SEA

There are no passenger services to/from Oman, although Muscat is a port of call for cruise liners.

Getting Around

AIR

Besides Muscat International Airport in Muscat, there are domestic airports in Salalah, Duqm, Sohar and Khasab.

The national carrier is Oman Air (p219). It services the domestic airports, as well as a selection of Middle East and subcontinental destinations. Tickets can be booked through any travel agent or online.

A new Oman-based low-cost airline is planned for 2016. The only domestic flights currently available in the country at the time of writing are on Oman Air.

MUSCAT TO/FROM	ONE-WAY/ RETURN	DURA-TION	FREQUENCY
Duqm	OR35/64	1hr 20mins	4 times weekly
Khasab	OR24/48	1hr	twice daily
Salalah	OR35/64	1hr 20 mins	4 times daily
Sohar	OR18/26	50 mins	twice weekly

BUS

The intercity buses are operated by **Mwasalat** (p145), which has daily services to/from the main provincial cities for less than OR10. Buses are usually on time, comfortable and safe. It is worth making reservations for longer journeys. Tickets can be bought with cash from the bus driver.

CAR

- Road signs are written in English (with inconsistent spelling) and Arabic throughout Oman.
- Brown tourist signs signpost most sites of interest.
- Petrol, all of which is unleaded, is widely available and cheap.
- Al Maha petrol stations usually have modern, well-stocked shops and clean(ish) toilets.

Driving Licence

Most foreign driving licences are accepted in Oman but an International Driving Permit is preferable.

Hire

International car-hire chains in Oman include Avis, Budget, Europcar and Thrifty, but dozens of local agencies offer a slightly reduced rate.

- Rates for 2WD cars start at about OR15 and 4WD vehicles at OR40.
- Carrying water is essential (a box of a dozen 1.5L bottles costs OR1.700 from petrol stations)
- Tow-ropes (OR5) are available from any large supermarket.
- 'Freezer packs' (around 600 baisa each) will keep cool boxes cold for a day, even in summer, and hotels will refreeze the packs at night.

Alwan Tour Rent-a-Car (☎99 833325; www.alwantour.com) Large selection of saloon and 4WDs.

Mark Tours (☎24 782727; www.marktours oman.com/rentacar) A reliable local rental agency.

Insurance

Check the small print on all car-hire documents to see if you are covered for taking the vehicle off-road.

Road Conditions

Travellers comment that some roads indicated in this book as '4WD only' are passable in a 2WD. Often they are right, until something goes wrong – 2WDs are not built to withstand potholes, washboard surfaces and steep, loose-gravel inclines, let alone long distances to the next petrol station.

If travellers' letters are anything to go by, who knows over what terrain the previous driver dragged your hire car! Bear in mind, you'll get no sympathy from hire companies if your 2WD breaks down off-road (and don't forget you're not insured to be off-road in a 2WD). With virtually zero traffic on some routes you are very vulnerable, especially in extreme summer temperatures.

In short, saving on the expense of a 4WD might cost more than you bargained for. Investing in an off-road guide is also essential as the available maps for Oman are often inaccurate.

A JOURNEY ACROSS THE EMPTY QUARTER

On 10 December 2015, one English and three Omani explorers set out from Salalah in Oman to re-create the first documented crossing of the Empty Quarter. Walking in the footsteps of Bertram Thomas's epic journey of 1930–31, and accompanied for part of the journey by the great-great-grandson of Thomas' Bedouin guide, the team's mission was to raise awareness of the Outward Bound movement, with its emphasis on youth, the environment and leadership.

Their greatest challenge in crossing the largest sea of sand in the world proved to be the fitness of their camels. Unused to the rigours of long desert journeys, today's modern ships of the desert have grown soft on milk and honey.

Unlike the former journey, undertaken in the days before satellite communications, the modern team was being followed on social media around the globe. This did not make the 50-day, 1300km journey across the heart of the Arabian Peninsula any less arduous and a very weary team reached Doha in February 2016, full of admiration for the bravery and endurance of their predecessors.

When travelling offroad, be sure to stick to prior tracks to avoid harming the fragile desert environment.

Road Hazards

Watch out for the following potential problems on the road:

- Aggressive tailgating and fast, aggressive driving.
- Camels and goats wandering onto the road.
- Exceptionally slippery conditions after rain.
- Failing brakes on mountain roads (low gear is a must).
- Soft sand and a salty crust called *sabkha* that looks and feels hard until you drive on it.
- Flash-flooding occurs frequently in wadis.

Road Rules

The following traffic laws are strictly enforced, especially in Muscat:

- Seatbelt use is mandatory.
- Hand-held mobile phone use is forbidden.
- The drink-driving limit is zero.
- The maximum speed limit is 120km per hour.
- Speeding and parking fines must be paid by credit card before exiting Muscat International Airport.
- There's an OR5 fine for a dirty car.

HITCHING

Hitching is possible but inadvisable as most roads outside the capital area have low volumes of traffic. Plan the return journey to avoid getting stranded. Always carry water and avoiding hitching off-road. It is the custom to offer the driver some remuneration. If you're driving, you will often be asked to give a ride to locals but do this only with caution.

LOCAL TRANSPORT

At the time of writing a new bus system was being introduced in Muscat and between cities – a welcome move in a country that has very little reliable public transport.

Long-distance shared taxis, painted orange and white, and microbuses (hard to use without some rudimentary Arabic) travel between most major towns. They do not wait until full to leave – drivers pick up and drop off passengers along the way.

For most places of interest, it's only possible to take an 'engaged' taxi (ie private, not shared) – four times the price of a shared taxi to cover the cost of the empty seats. Settle the price before you get in and expect costs to vary.

Beware that public transport isn't networked yet – a bus or taxi may go from A to B and B to C but not from C to A. This means it's easy to get stranded in a town with no onward connections.

TOURS

Tours in Oman are generally tailor-made for the customer in private vehicles (often 4WD) with an English-speaking driver-guide. This is great for your itinerary, but painful on the pocket unless you can muster a group of three or four.

The following are average prices per vehicle for a full-day tour from Muscat. Picnic lunch costs an extra OR5.

TOUR	COST
Nizwa, Bahla & Jabrin	OR100
Nakhal & Rustaq	OR90
Jebel Shams	OR130
Wadi Shab & Wadi Tiwi	OR110
Sharqiya Sands	OR130
Dolphin-watching	OR20 (per person); dhow cruise OR25 (per person)

Tour companies abound in Muscat, Salalah and Khasab; they offer city tours, camel safaris, 4WD touring, camping, caving, rock climbing, dhow rides, dolphin watching, boating, diving and snorkelling, and combinations thereof. Some recommended agencies, in addition to **National Travel & Tourism** (p138) are as follows.

Bike & Hike Oman (☎24 400873; www.bikeandhikeoman.com) Offers a number of spectacular cycling and hiking tours in the Hajar Mountains.

Explore Oman (☎in UK (0044) 1252 884 738; www.explore.co.uk/destinations/middle-east/oman) A UK-based company with many years of experience in Oman.

Mark Tours (☎24 782727; www.marktoursoman.com) One of the most experienced and enduring tour companies in Oman. Can make tailor-made study tours and adventure trips.

Muscat Diving & Adventure Centre (☎24 543002; www.holiday-in-oman.com) One of the best companies through which to organise caving, hiking and other outward-bound activities. They cater for individuals as well as small groups.

Zahara Tours (Map p126; ☎24 400844; www.zaharatours.com) This comprehensive and well-respected tour company has been in business since the 1970s and has won several awards for excellence. Specialising in small group cultural and adventure tours, it runs a modern fleet of 4WD vehicles and the iconic hotel, The View, in the Hajar Mountains.

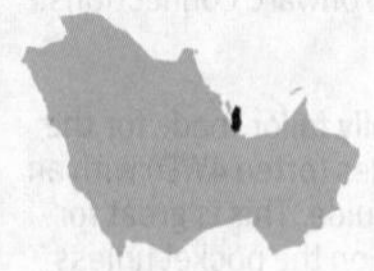

Qatar

Includes ➡

Best for Culture

- ➡ Museum of Islamic Art (p225)
- ➡ Souq Waqif (p225)
- ➡ Falcon Souq (p226)
- ➡ Qatar National Museum (p229)

Best Places to Stay

- ➡ Arumaila Boutique Hotel (p232)
- ➡ W Hotel Doha (p234)
- ➡ Banana Island Resort (p234)
- ➡ Al Najada Boutique Hotel (p233)

Why Go?

Just over a decade ago, we labelled Qatar one of the most boring places on Earth. Now it's fast becoming one of the most exciting. Doha is a world-class city in the making, with the peerless Museum of Islamic Art, perhaps the finest traditional souq in the Gulf region, and burgeoning arts and culinary scenes. Qatar is the kind of place where you can learn about the ancient pursuit of falconry or watch camels ridden by remote-controlled robot jockeys race across the desert, admire traditional dhows bobbing on the water alongside one of the world's most spectacular modern skylines, or sample Doha's portfolio of sophisticated restaurants and then watch the sun set over sand dunes that seem to spring from an Arabian fairy tale. Put simply, Qatar is racing headlong into the future without losing sight of its past – and it's one pretty exciting ride.

When to Go

Qatar

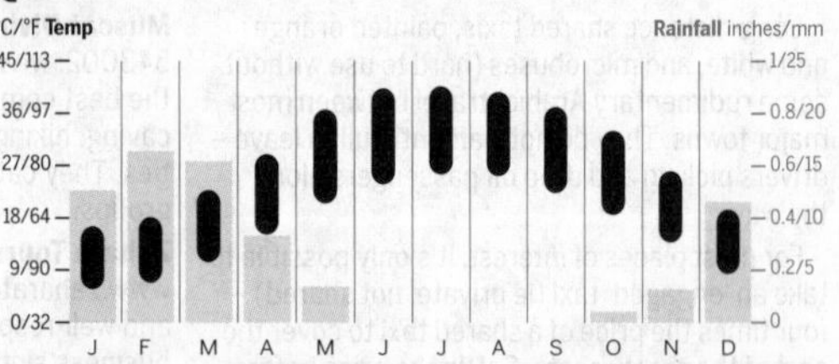

Oct–Mar Enjoy a break from the intense heat and humidity of summer.

Mar & Apr Cheer on the favourite at the Emir's GCC Camel Race – camel racing at its best.

May–Sep Extreme daytime temperatures – avoid this time if you can.

Daily Costs

Qatar is a relatively expensive destination. With the few budget hotels being swept away in the name of development, accommodation costing less than US$100 per night is hard to find. Factoring in cheap options (around US$10) for eating and the cost of a sight or an activity, a minimum daily cost with transport comes to around US$150. This rises to US$250 if you're staying in midrange hotels; for a top-end hotel with car hire, US$400 is nearer the mark.

ITINERARIES

Qatar Stopover

Spend a morning absorbing the best of Doha in a promenade along the **corniche**, watching the city's stellar skyline dance in the heat. Use the afternoon in cooler contemplation at the **Museum of Islamic Art**, Doha's priceless treasure house. Seek out gems of a different kind among the silks and spices for sale in **Souq Waqif**, and admire the feathered plumage on display in the neighbouring **Falcon Souq**. Complete the evening in the company of Qataris at one of the souq's teeming restaurants.

Three Days

Recharge on day two by the beach at **Katara**, where there are also fine restaurants and art galleries to fill your day, before a sunset **dhow trip**. On day three hire a car and tour the peninsula, stopping off at **Al Khor** for lunch at Al Sultan Beach Resort. Head north to explore the ancient **rock carvings** at Jebel Jassassiyeh and end the day at far-flung **Al Zubara**, visiting its fort.

For Expats

Camp out under the escarpment at **Bir Zekreet** and search for a pearl on a shore full of washed-up oysters. Cast an eye over the historic interior at **Umm Salal Mohammed** and neighbouring Umm Salal Ali, or enjoy some R&R and water sports at **Sealine Beach Resort**. For something more adventurous, stay overnight at the enchanting inland sea of **Khor Al Adaid**, picnic in the dunes and sleep on a magic carpet of sand.

Essential Food & Drink

- **Makbous** Rice and spices with chicken, lamb or fish in a rich sauce.
- **Grilled lobster** Local crayfish are a popular choice.
- **Khabees** Dates in a variety of sizes, colours and stages of ripeness.
- **Tap water** Safe to drink, although most people stick to bottled water.
- **Alcohol** Available only in top-end hotel restaurants and bars.
- **Coffee** Traditionally served pale and spiked with cardamom or dark, strong and with plenty of sugar.

AT A GLANCE

- **Currency** Qatari riyal (QR)
- **Mobile phones** SIM cards widely available
- **Money** ATMs widespread; credit cards widely accepted
- **Visas** Available on arrival for many nationalities

Fast Facts

- **Capital** Doha
- **Country code** ☎ 974
- **Language** Arabic (English widely spoken)
- **Population** 2.195 million

Exchange Rates

For current exchange rates see www.xe.com.

Australia	A$1	QR2.65
Bahrain	BD1	QR9.72
Euro zone	€1	QR4.13
Japan	¥100	QR3.05
Kuwait	KD1	QR12.09
Saudi Arabia	SR1	QR0.97
UAE	Dh1	QR0.99
UK	£1	QR5.64
USA	US$1	QR3.64

Resources

- **Lonely Planet** (www.lonelyplanet.com/qatar) In-depth coverage of Qatar and the Thorn Tree forum.
- **Al Jazeera** (www.aljazeera.com) Arab-world, Qatar-based equivalent of the BBC.
- **Qatar Tourism Authority** (www.qatartourism.gov.qa) Official tourism website.

Qatar Highlights

1. Stepping into the past in the cardamom-scented alleyways of **Souq Waqif** (p225).
2. Ruffling feathers at the **Falcon Souq** (p226) by bidding for a peregrine.
3. Joining the locals in a game of aldama (similar to backgammon) while smoking a *sheesha* at **Majlis Al Dama** (p238).
4. Ordering a serve of *kunafa* (syrupy pastry) and other local sweets in the souq at **Al Aker** (p238).
5. Gazing at a skyline in the making by walking along **Al Corniche** (p227).
6. Taking a dune for a pillow and the stars for a blanket at beautiful **Khor Al Adaid** (p242).
7. Finding fish inland at the rock carvings of **Jebel Jassassiyeh** (p241).
8. Visiting an exhibition, enjoying opera, swimming at the beach and dining at **Katara** (p227).
9. Setting up camp under a desert limestone mushroom at **Bir Zekreet** (p244).

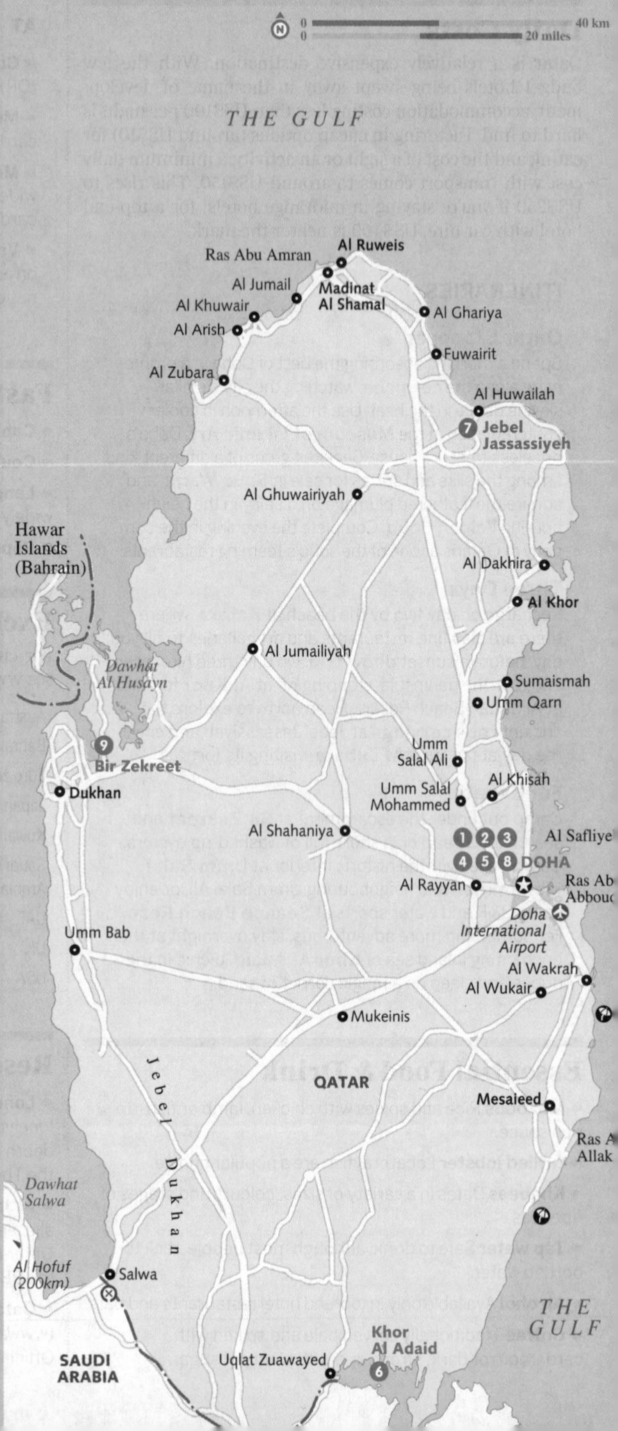

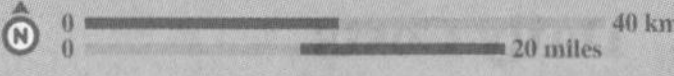

DOHA الدوحه

POP 956,460

It's rare to see a great city in the making these days, but here's your chance. Whether it's the stunning and constantly changing skyline or the massive investment the Qatari authorities are making in landmark cultural icons, this is a city oozing confidence and style, as at ease in its modern shopping malls as in its traditional souqs. Wander the reinvented and fabulously atmospheric Souq Waqif, wonder at the sheer beauty of the world-class Museum of Islamic Art and its exhibits or head out to Katara to explore – wherever you look, Doha is threatening to eclipse Dubai as the Gulf's most dynamic city. Throw in a new Metro system in the making and the 2022 FIFA World Cup on the horizon, and the chances are that things are only going to get better.

History

Doha was a small, inconsequential fishing and pearling village up until the mid-19th century, when the first Al Thani emir, Sheikh Mohammed bin Thani, established his capital at Al Bida, now the port area of town. Once a notorious safe haven for Gulf pirates, it became the British administrative centre in 1916 and the capital of the independent state of Qatar in 1971.

The University of Qatar (1973) and Qatar National Museum (1975) brought education and culture to the city, and slowly the shape of Doha changed, one ring road at a time, from an ugly concrete rash to the elegant city of today. The master stroke was the early construction of Doha Bay, carved out of reclaimed land, and giving harbour to Doha's shrimp industry, leisure for inhabitants and a vantage point that architects have exploited to the full in West Bay.

Sights

Doha's main sights are along and just off the corniche. Note that some attractions can only be visited by appointment; this is most easily arranged through a tour company.

★Museum of Islamic Art MUSEUM

(Map p232; ☎44 224 444; www.mia.org.qa; ⏰10.30am-5.30pm Sun, Mon & Wed, noon-8pm Thu & Sat, 2-8pm Fri; P) FREE Rising from its own purpose-built island, and set in an extensive landscape of lawns and ornamental trees off the corniche, this is a fabulous museum. It's shaped like a postmodern fortress with minimal windows (to reduce energy use) and a 'virtual' moat, and the views across the water are splendid. With the largest collection of Islamic art in the world, collected from three continents, the museum is so rich in treasure that it rewards short, intense visits.

The museum was designed by IM Pei (architect of the Louvre pyramid), and you know that something special awaits from the minute you lay eyes on the grand palm-lined entrance. Inside, the building is a masterpiece of light and space, drawing your eyes up to the dome, a clever modern take on the dome so prevalent in Islamic architecture.

The collection is spread over three floors. The 1st and 2nd floors house the permanent collection, which ranges across exquisite textiles, ceramics, enamel work and glass, all showcased conceptually: a single motif, for example, is illustrated in neighbouring display cases in the weave of a carpet or a ceramic floor tile, or adapted in a piece of gold jewellery, allowing visitors to gain a sense of the homogeneity of Islamic art.

Pace yourself by visiting the cafe downstairs or punctuate your visit with a browse in the extensive museum shop (also on the ground floor) to avoid sensory overload. A good option can be the free 40-minute guided tours (in English and Arabic) of the permanent collection on Thursday at 2pm and Saturday at 4pm, and of the temporary or special exhibitions on Wednesday at 2pm. Avoid strappy tops and shorts or you may be refused admission.

★Souq Waqif MARKET

(Map p232; btwn Al Souq & Grand Hamad Sts; ⏰9am-1pm & 4-9pm Sat-Thu, 4-9pm Fri; P) Reincarnated in the last decade as the social heart of Doha, Souq Waqif is a wonderful place to explore and an undoubted highlight of the city. There has been a souq on this site for

SOUQ WAQIF

Until land was reclaimed along Doha's waterfront in the 1970s, Souq Waqif was a waterfront market, one where traders were just as likely to arrive by boat as by camel. The first semi-permanent stalls or shops here were first built around 250 years ago. Prior to that, vendors stood and sold their wares from makeshift stalls, so often did the market flood, and it is from this tradition that the souq's name derives: *waqif* means 'standing' in Arabic.

DON'T MISS

FALCONRY

Falconry is an ancient art that dates at least from the 7th century BC. The first falconer, according to Arabic tradition, was a violent king of Persia who was so entranced by the grace and beauty of a falcon taking a bird on the wing that he had it captured so he could learn from it. What he learned, according to legend, changed him into a calm and wise ruler.

It is no easy task to train birds of prey. Bedu, falconers par excellence, traditionally net their falcons (usually saker or peregrine) during their migration, using pigeons as bait. They train the birds through complex schedules of sleep deprivation and sparse feeding, retain them for as long as it takes to harvest fresh meat, and then set them free again at the onset of summer. Despite the rigorous training regimen, animal-welfare groups tend to focus on the falcons' prey (namely the rights and wrongs of hunting animals using falcons) rather than the welfare of the falcons themselves.

It is estimated that 2000 falcons are still employed on the Arabian Peninsula each year. Today, birds are more usually bred and 'imprinted' from hatchlings to create a bond that lasts a lifetime. Sporting achievement is measured not by the number of quarry caught but by the skill of the catch – and by the wisdom of leaving enough prey for tomorrow.

centuries; the Bedu would bring their sheep, goats and wool here to trade for essentials, and the entire market area has been cleverly redeveloped to look like a 19th-century souq, with mud-rendered shops, exposed timber beams and some beautifully restored original Qatari buildings.

With booming prosperity, the advent of vast, air-conditioned shopping malls and Qatar's rush to embrace the new, Souq Waqif fell into serious decline by the 1990s and much of the souq was destroyed in a fire in 2003. The outcry from Qataris prompted the authorities to undertake a massive rehabilitation program, one that continues to this day. Such has been the success of this venture that the souq keeps growing to accommodate new 'old alleyways'.

Despite the ongoing gentrification of the area, the chief business of the souq continues unabated and it remains one of the most traditional marketplaces in the region. This is the place to look for the national Qatari dress, including the beautifully embroidered *bukhnoq* (girl's head covering), spices, perfumes and *oud* (an exotic incense made from agarwood). Watch for the *alhmalah* (porters in numbered maroon waistcoats who transport shoppers' purchases in wheelbarrows) – they're an essential element in the souq's story. Even the souq's functioning **Heritage Police Station** (Map p232; ☎44 441 303; Souq Waqif Rd, Souq Waqif; ⊙8am-noon & 3-7pm Sun-Thu) gets in on the act: its officers dress in uniforms from the 1940s while they keep an eye out for trouble.

Falconry is not the only traditional Qatari leisure pursuit you can see around the souq. Not far from the Falcon Souq, **stables** (Map p232) house Arabian horses, and no-one seems to mind if you wander in and have a look. And just off the corniche end of Al Jasra St, a **pen** (Map p232) is filled with feeding camels most of the day.

Most of the shops in the souq close around 1pm and reopen at 4pm, but the many cafes and restaurants remain open all day.

The excellent little **Souq Waqif Information & Tourism Center** (Map p232; Souq Watif Rd, Souq Watif; ⊙8am-1pm & 3-10pm Sat-Thu, 3-11pm Fri) has maps and printed information on the souq and friendly staff who are eager to help.

★**Falcon Souq** MARKET
(Map p232; ⊙9am-1pm & 4-8pm Sat-Thu, 4-8pm Fri; Ⓟ) If you want a glimpse of heritage, don't miss the Falcon Souq. You only have to see the scale of the souq, afforded its own traditional arcaded building off Souq Waqif, to understand the place of falconry in Qatari society. It can be quite unnerving entering a falcon shop: birds, most of them hooded in black leather, perch on an open railing a handspan away, waiting to be taken home, fed less than a square meal and put straight to work.

The best time to come (although it can be a little hit or miss) is in the evenings, especially Thursday, when you can watch customers examining the birds and discussing the finer points of falconry with the shopkeepers. Next door to the Falcon Souq is the Souq Waqif Falcon Hospital – if you stop by when things are quiet and ask nicely, the staff *might* be willing to show you around.

Gold Souq MARKET

(Map p232; 9am-1pm & 4-7pm Sat-Thu, 4-10pm Fri; P) This pageant of glorious design and spectacular craftsmanship is fun to see even if you've no intention to buy. The souq comes alive later in the evening, especially before a holiday, when men traditionally express the value of their relationships by buying 22-carat gold bangles, or a 'set' comprising earrings, necklace and bracelet, for the women in their family. Qatari bridal jewellery can cost thousands, but sometimes pieces can be traded back after the wedding for something more readily usable.

Bird Souq MARKET

(Map p232; Salwa Rd; 9am-1pm & 4-7pm Sat-Thu, 4-7pm Fri) Located behind the colourful spice section of Souq Waqif, this collection of caged birds (as well as occasional cats, rabbits and dogs) has pigeons, parrots, cockatiels and budgerigars. It comes alive with local Qatari families just before the *eid* holidays; even when it's not busy, the birds make up for the lack of customers.

Doha Fort FORT

(Al Koot Fort; Map p232; Jasim bin Mohammed St; P) Built during the 19th-century Turkish occupation, this fort has been used as a prison and as an ethnographic museum. During restoration in the late 1970s, however, many of the structure's original features were lost. It's increasingly overshadowed by the redevelopment of the surrounding Souq Waqif and is still in need of a modern mission in life; it was fenced off when we visited as part of work on the souq, so we hope that it will soon receive a makeover. Camels are grazed outside during *eid*.

Al Corniche WATERFRONT

(Map p232) More than most other Gulf cities, Doha makes full use of its attractive waterfront promenade, helped by the fact that Doha Bay was carefully constructed with landfill to make an attractive crescent. The best views are from the water's edge close to the Museum of Islamic Art, with dhows in the foreground and the skyscrapers of West Bay across the water. And the best time to come is late afternoon on Friday, when families of all nationalities throng here.

KATARA & THE ARTS

There's something stirring north of downtown Doha and it promises to be big. Katara, a custom-built cultural village on West Bay, with some stunning replica architecture on show from across the Islamic world, is fast becoming one of the most important creative hubs of the Gulf region, with a buzzing gallery scene, dozens of restaurants, and even a striking open-air amphitheatre facing the sea and providing a fantastic venue for opera, concerts and other live entertainment. For more details, stop by the **Katara Information Center** (Map p228; 182; www.katara.net; 9am-9pm Sat-Thu, 1-9pm Fri). The website also has helpful event listings and booking options.

Katara is particularly well served when it comes to art galleries, but when you've had your fill of art and history, the village also has Doha's best **beach** (p231), and two excellent restaurants, **Khan Farouk Tarab Cafe** (p236) and **L'Wzaar** (p237).

Katara Art Center (Map p228; 44 080 244; www.kataraartcenter.com; Bldg 5; 10am-9pm Sun-Thu, 2-9pm Fri & Sat) Local contemporary art and design are the focus of this expansive beachfront complex.

Qatar Fine Arts Association (Map p228; 44 081 469; Bldg 13; 10am-10pm Sat-Thu, 2-10pm Fri) This gallery draws some of the better-known artists from across the region.

Qatar Museums Authority (Map p228; www.qm.org.qa; Bldg 10; 10am-10pm Sat-Thu, 2-10pm Fri) Stages interesting art exhibitions, usually with a strong historical focus.

Qatar Photographic Society (Map p228; 44 081 812; Bldg 18; 8am-10pm Sat-Thu, 2-10pm Fri) The society stages some excellent exhibitions by photographers from across the Arab World.

Arab Postal Stamps Museum (Map p228; 44 091 077; Bldg 22; 9am-9pm Sun-Thu, 9am-noon & 5-8pm Sat) Philatelists will love this journey through the world of postage stamps from the 22 countries of the Arab world.

Greater Doha

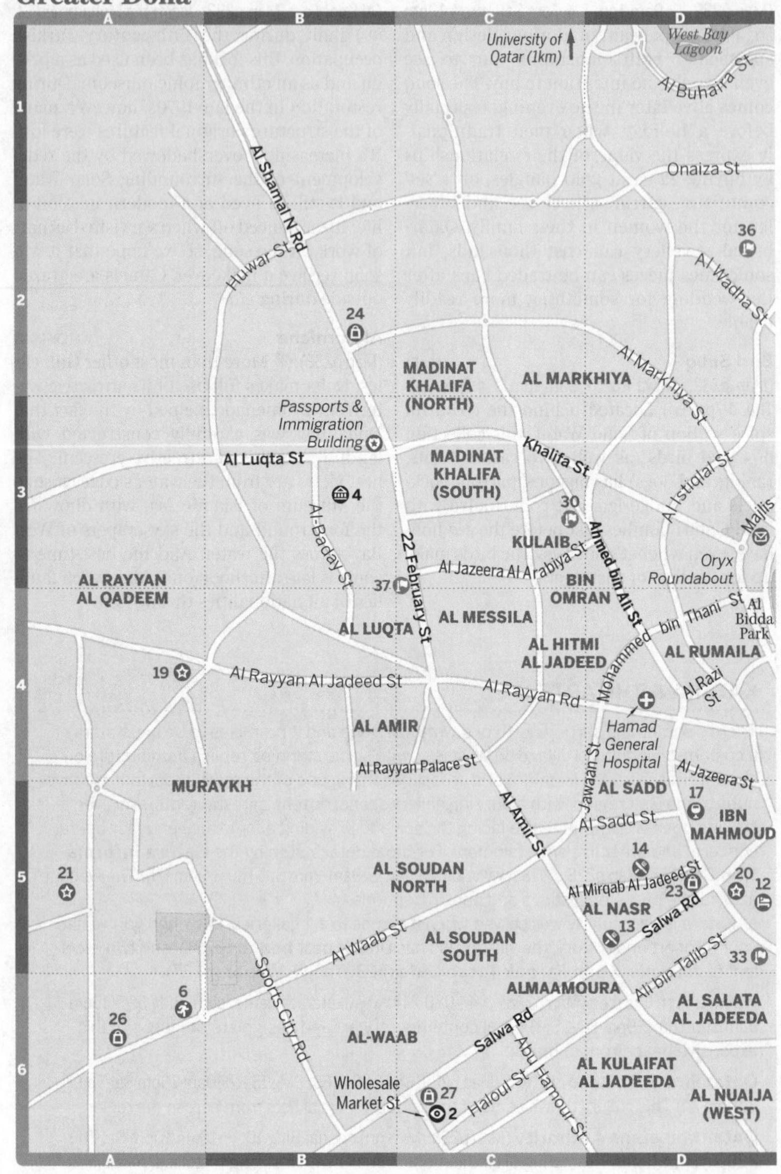

It could take an hour and a half, but the 5km walk from the Museum of Islamic Art to the Sheraton around on West Bay is a wonderful late-afternoon stroll in a city not known for its pedestrian-friendly streets.

At the southern end of the corniche, at the Ras Abu Abboud St Flyover, a small park with ornamental wind towers introduces the 'heritage' zone of the corniche. The collection of whitewashed traditional-style buildings on the far right belongs to the

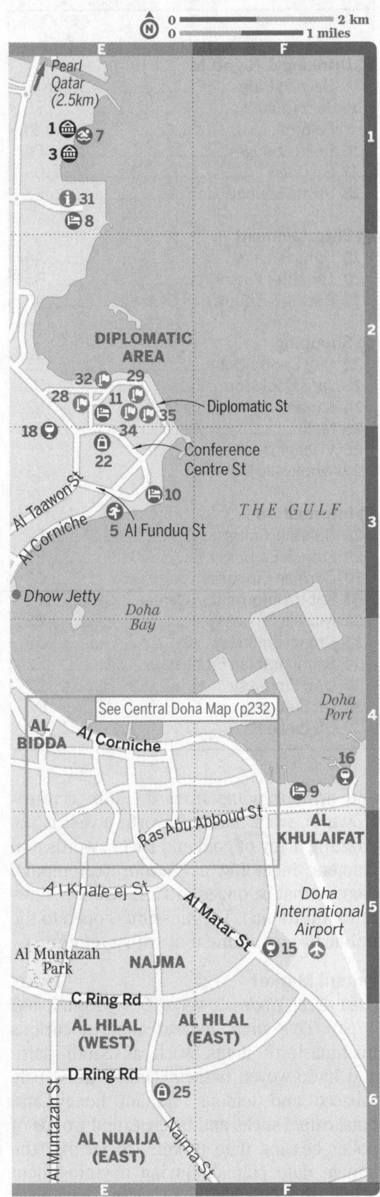

exquisite five-star Al Sharq Village Resort & Spa. A must-stop down this end is the traditional Halul Coffeehouse (p238), a local-style coffeehouse that has somehow escaped the modernisation of the area.

Further north is the 'sea' zone of the corniche, with Doha's busy port marked by the monumental anchors on the shore and the cream-coloured flour mills at the end of the jetty. Along the corniche north of the Museum of Islamic Art, the entrance to the dhow harbour is marked by the famous **pearl monument** (Map p232), a popular spot for photos. Enjoy the spectacular view of West Bay from the end of a jetty full of lobster pots and lazy dhows, moored between night-time fishing trips. It's hard to believe that this remarkable skyline of futuristic towers was built entirely on land reclaimed from the sea.

MIA Park PARK

(Map p232; 10am-midnight Wed-Mon Oct-May, 6pm-midnight Wed-Mon Jun-Sep; P) One of many beautiful green spaces along or just back from the Doha waterfront, MIA Park is home to Richard Serra's vertical steel sculpture, known as '7' – the first public piece of art by this celebrated artist in the Middle East. On the first Saturday of every month from October to March, stalls sell arts and crafts, clothing and souvenirs from the Park Bazaar (noon to 7pm).

Gallery Al Riwaq GALLERY

(Map p232; 44 525 555; www.qm.org.qa/en/project/qm-gallery-al-riwaq; Al Corniche; 10.30am-5.30pm Sun, Mon & Wed, noon-8pm Thu & Sat, 2-8pm Fri) At the edge of MIA Park, this modern gallery space hosts some terrific temporary exhibitions – check the website to see what's on. Recent artists to exhibit here include Damien Hirst and Takashi Murakami.

Qatar National Museum MUSEUM

(Map p232; www.qm.org.qa/en/project/national-museum-qatar) When it reopens after a massive renovation, the Qatar National Museum, just off Al Corniche, will be one of Doha's standout attractions. No-one seems to know the reopening date, but everyone agrees that architect Jean Nouvel's desert rose–inspired structures, which will form the museum's centrepiece, will be worth waiting for. Remarkably, the new edifice will be superimposed upon the Fariq Al Salata Palace, built in 1901 and used by Sheikh Abdullah bin Mohammed, Qatar's ruler from 1913 to 1949.

Mathaf GALLERY

(Arab Museum of Modern Art; 44 028 855; www.mathaf.org.q; Education City; admission to exhibitions QR25; 11am-6pm Sat, Sun & Tue-Thu, 3-8pm Fri; P) This exceptional new exhibition space was

Greater Doha

Sights

- Arab Postal Stamps Museum .... (see 3)
- 1 Katara Art Center E1
- 2 Omani Market C6
- 3 Qatar Fine Arts Association E1
- Qatar Museums Authority .... (see 3)
- Qatar Photographic Society .... (see 3)
- 4 Weaponry Museum B3

Activities, Courses & Tours

- Arabian Adventures .... (see 10)
- 5 Children's Playground E3
- 6 Jungle Zone A6
- 7 Katara Beach E1
- Regatta Sailing Academy .... (see 8)
- Winter Wonderland .... (see 22)

Sleeping

- 8 InterContinental Doha E1
- 9 Sharq Village & Spa F4
- 10 Sheraton Doha Hotel & Resort E3
- 11 W Hotel Doha E2
- 12 Zubarah Hotel D5

Eating

- 13 Batteel Café D5
- Gordon Ramsay Doha .... (see 8)
- Khan Farouk Tarab Cafe .... (see 3)
- L'Wzaar .... (see 3)
- Opal by Gordon Ramsay .... (see 8)
- 14 Turkey Central D5

Drinking & Nightlife

- Belgian Cafe .... (see 8)
- 15 Jazz Club F5
- Paloma .... (see 8)
- 16 Pearl Lounge F4
- 17 Sky View D5
- 18 Strata Lounge E3

Entertainment

- 19 Doha Players A4
- 20 Laughter Factory D5
- 21 Racing & Equestrian Club A5

Shopping

- 22 City Centre Doha E3
- 23 Jarir Bookstore D5
- 24 Landmark Shopping Mall B2
- 25 Mall E6
- 26 Villaggio Mall A6
- 27 Wholesale Market C6

Information

- 28 Bahraini Embassy E2
- 29 French Embassy E2
- 30 German Embassy C3
- 31 Katara Information Center E1
- 32 Kuwaiti Embassy E2
- 33 Omani Embassy D5
- 34 Saudi Arabian Embassy E2
- 35 UAE Embassy E2
- 36 UK Embassy D2
- 37 US Embassy C3

opened in 2010 to provide a home for international art with an Arab connection. Housed in an old school off Al Luqta St near Education City, the building was redesigned by French architect Jean-François Bodin. The venue hosts a variety of exhibitions, workshops and lectures through the winter months.

Heritage House HISTORIC BUILDING

(Map p232) Formerly an ethnographic museum, this restored traditional house (built 1935) offers one of the best opportunities in Doha to see a *badghir* (wind tower). The square wind tower was commonly used as a form of pre-electric air-conditioning throughout the Gulf, sucking fresh air into the house and channelling it into the ground-floor rooms. The house is closed to visitors but is worth a look from the outside. It's in the Al Najada Shopping Centre courtyard, just off Grand Hamad St.

Weapony Museum MUSEUM

(Map p228; 44 867 473; btwn Al Luqta & Makkah Sts; by appointment) FREE This small museum has an impressive collection of arms and armour, some from the 16th century. However, what makes it worth a visit is the dazzling array of gold and silver swords and daggers, including a *khanjar* (ceremonial dagger) that belonged to TE Lawrence ('Lawrence of Arabia'). The museum is open to the public by appointment or with a tour guide.

Omani Market MARKET

(Map p228; Wholesale Market St; 10am-1pm & 4-7pm) This small market offers a curious mishmash of items, such as Saudi dates and hand-woven baskets, Omani dried fish, tobacco and lemons, Iranian honey and pots, camel sticks and incense, and fronds of pollen-bearing date flowers (to fertilise the female date palms). Buying anything here brings the satisfaction of taking part in a trade that has existed between Oman and the Gulf for centuries.

Activities

To see the corniche from the sea, consider taking a dhow ride around Doha Bay. Local fishing boats leave from various points along the corniche (QR20/10 adult/child), and all the tour companies offer three- to four-hour evening dhow cruises with dinner, traditional music and entertainment for around QR200 per person.

Doha Golf Club GOLF
(☎44 960 777; www.dohagolfclub.com; West Bay Lagoon; visitor green fees per 9/18 holes from QR420/650; ⏲6.30am-11pm) A sight to behold amid the surrounding barren desert, the green Doha Golf Club has an internationally recognised 18-hole course, which hosts the annual Qatar Masters in March. Open to nonmembers, it also has a floodlit, nine-hole academy course for those in a hurry.

Katara Beach SWIMMING
(Map p228; ☎44 081 017; www.katar.net; Katara; adult/child QR100/25; ⏲9.30am-sunset) If you fancy a swim, the 1.5km beach at Katara Cultural Village also offers the chance of dinner and a show at the adjoining arts centre when the sun goes down. Children under six gain free admission to the beach and there's a ladies-only section. One-piece costumes are advised.

Courses

Thanks to the vibrant expatriate community in Doha, there are many courses available, from line dancing to karate, ice skating and scuba diving. Anyone in town for a while and interested in any of these activities is advised to pick up a copy of *Marhaba, Qatar's Premier Information Guide*, available from some hotels, supermarkets and bookshops, and consult its 'Leisure Activities' section.

FANAR Qatar Islamic Cultural Center LANGUAGE COURSE
(Map p232; ☎44 250 173, 44 250 175; www.fanar.gov.qa/TrainingCenter.aspx; Medinat Khalifa South; 2-month course QR300; ⏲7.30am-1.30pm & 5-8pm Sun-Thu) Near the Doha English Speaking School, FANAR offers courses in Arabic language and culture.

University of Qatar LANGUAGE COURSE
(☎44 034 584; www.qu.edu.qa; Jelaiah St, Tarfa) Runs a year-long course in Arabic.

Regatta Sailing Academy SAILING
(Map p228; ☎44 424 577; www.regattasailingacademy.com; InterContinental Doha, Al Isteqlal Rd, West Bay; ⏲7am-9pm) Offers a variety of casual and certified sailing courses from beginner to advanced levels for all ages.

Tours

Doha Bus BUS TOUR
(☎44 422 444; www.dohabus.com; adult 24/48hr QR180/225, child QR90/110, family QR455/681; ⏲9am-9pm) You know a city has made it as a tourist destination when it gets its own hop-on, hop-off open-top sightseeing bus. The Doha version ranges from the Marriott Hotel south of the city centre and goes all the way to the new Pearl development in the north. The journey takes 2½ hours. Tickets cost 10% less if you book online.

Major stops include the Museum of Islamic Art, Souq Waqif, City Centre mall, Katara and the Pearl. Buses pass every 45 minutes, and if you've bought your ticket online and can't print it, there are kiosks at Souq Watif and City Centre mall where you can pick up your ticket.

Arabian Adventures CULTURAL TOUR
(Map p228; ☎44 361 461; www.arabianadventureqatar.net) Recommended operator with a range of tours, including dhow cruises, a Doha city tour (per person QR250) and half-/full-day desert safaris (QR300/450).

Gulf Adventures TOUR
(Map p232; ☎44 221 888; www.gulf-adventures.com; Aspire Zone St) Offers friendly and knowledgeable advice. Located off the B Ring Rd.

Qatar International Tours TOUR
(☎44 551 141; www.qittour.com; tours per person from QR175) Desert safaris with overnight camping offered. Historical heritage tours a strong point.

Festivals & Events

Doha hosts a huge variety of events and entertainment, with sports high on the agenda. With each new event comes a flurry of construction activity. And of course there's the 2022 FIFA World Cup to look forward to.

Check listings in the newspapers, and consult *Marhaba, Qatar's Premier Information Guide* (published quarterly) for a month-by-month guide to Doha's busy calendar.

Emir's GCC Camel Race SPORTS
(☎44 872 028; ⏲Mar or Apr) Riders compete for the prestigious 'Golden Sword' in Qatar's most important camel race at Al Shahaniya, 60km west of Doha along the Dukhan Rd.

Sleeping

Doha's accommodation offering is arguably the best in the Gulf, from stunningly

Central Doha

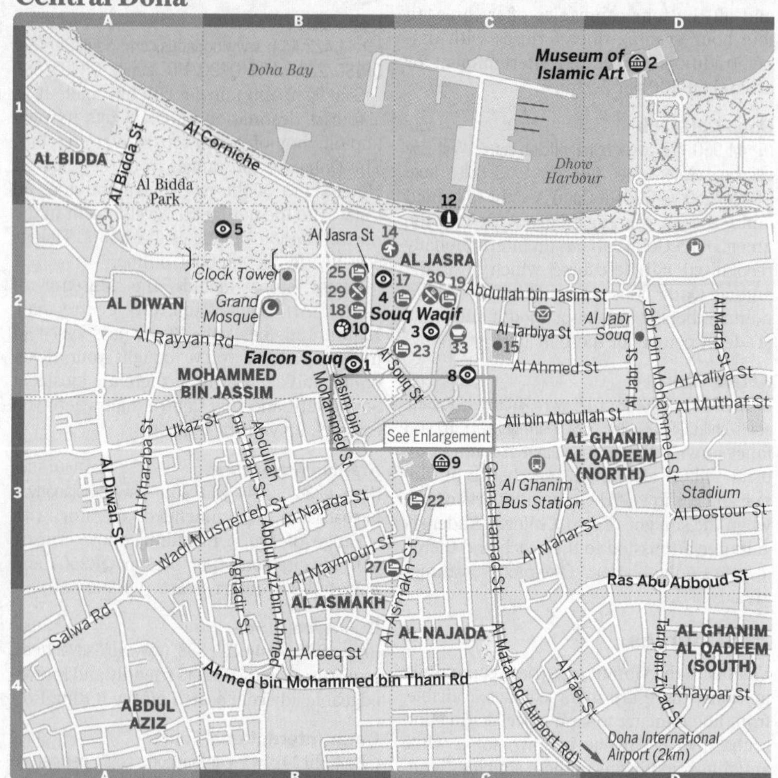

converted boutique hotels in the souq to five-star palaces in the skyscrapers; Doha even has its own island resort. Cheaper accommodation is conveniently located near Souq Waqif, although none of the options could be termed genuinely 'budget'. The basic, men-only budget hotels are intended largely for Asian expats and are not reviewed by Lonely Planet.

All rooms at the hotels reviewed have air-conditioning, TV (normally satellite), fridge and bathroom but do not usually include breakfast.

Qatar Palace Hotel HOTEL $
(Map p232; ☎44 421 515; www.qatarpal.com.qa; 44 Al Asmakh St; s/d QR275/400; wi-fi) The rooms – decorated in pastel shades and with large sofas – are homely and comfortable, but beware: some are virtually windowless. The furnishings will be a little over the top for some tastes, but staff members are friendly. The Maharajah Restaurant, with a chef from Mumbai, is a local favourite.

Al Nakheel Hotel HOTEL $
(Map p232; ☎44 283 221; www.alnakheel-hotel.com; 101 Al Asmakh St; s/d QR250/350) With an excellent location close to Souq Waqif, this basic hotel with mirrored ceilings in the corridors has large rooms with somewhat heavy and dark furnishings. Ask to see your room first to avoid a view onto a brick wall.

★Arumaila Boutique Hotel BOUTIQUE HOTEL $$
(Map p232; ☎44 336 666; www.swbh.com/arumaila boutique; Souq Waqif; s/d from QR750/800; @ wi-fi) Truly one of the loveliest hotels in Doha, the Arumalia inhabits a gorgeous old souq building with stunning rooms with wooden floors, soothing grey walls and beautiful lamps and partitioning with elaborate filigree design. The view from the roof terrace

is rather special, there's a mini gym and you have access to spa facilities nearby.

★Al Najada Boutique Hotel BOUTIQUE HOTEL **$$**
(Map p232; ☎44 336 444; www.swbh.com/alnajadaboutique; Souq Waqif St, Souq Waqif; s/d from QR650/750; 📶) This superb hotel at the southern end of Souq Waqif was among the first of the souq's boutique hotels and remains one of the best. With its courtyard design, wattle-and-daub rooms and wooden-beamed ceilings, it's also the most traditional. The architect has recreated a rambling Qatari-style building but added stylish modern features such as granite flooring and walls of water.

With a spa and an inspiring rooftop view, it offers a haven of quiet in the heart of the bustling souq. Dozens of restaurants are a few steps away.

★InterContinental Doha RESORT **$$**
(Map p228; ☎44 844 444; www.ihg.com; Al Isteqlal Rd, West Bay; r from QR780; P📶🏊) This genteel luxury hotel has been dwarfed by lofty neighbours in recent years, but continues to thrive regardless. InterCon hotels have an excellent reputation in the Gulf for the 'common touch': providing high-quality facilities without being snooty. This attractive resort, with its appealing beach area, matches the chain's reputation, and is fantastic value to boot.

Zubarah Hotel HOTEL **$$**
(Map p228; ☎44 470 000; www.zubarahhotels.com; Al Rawabi St; d/ste from QR550/700) The Zubarah is proof that excellent value still exists in Doha, despite the profusion of five-star hotels across the city. Rooms here are excellent, with some showing contemporary designer touches, while service is also good. There's a 1st-floor spa, a gym, good restaurants and plenty of repeat visitors.

Al Bidda Boutique Hotel BOUTIQUE HOTEL **$$**
(Map p232; ☎44 336 666; www.swbh.com/albiddaboutique; Souq Waqif; s/d from QR650/750; @📶) We like the blend here of contemporary and traditional, which leans a little more towards the former than most others in the souq. The main patio evokes an old Arab courtyard, with abundant marble, water and geometric designs, while the rooms have warm and welcoming colour schemes, pleasing arches, fluffy cushions and even hanging basket chairs in some alcoves. It's also on one of the quieter souq thoroughfares.

Al Mirqab Boutique Hotel BOUTIQUE HOTEL **$$**
(Map p232; ☎44 336 666; www.swbh.com/almirqabboutique; Souq Waqif; s/d from QR650/750; @📶🏊) Elegant, spacious rooms with marble floors and minimalist decor offset occasional flourishes such as filigree stonework at this fine place. There are no views here, but there is a sense of refinement and privacy, in keeping with the large Doha houses of old. There's an on-site spa and the souq location is ideal.

Musheireb Boutique Hotel BOUTIQUE HOTEL **$$**
(Map p232; ☎44 336 666; www.swbh.com/musheirebboutique; Al Jasra St, Souq Waqif; s/d from QR750/800; @📶🏊) Studded velvet sofas, plush carpets, gilded mirrors – Musheireb has gone for the extravagance of traditional Arab design, but the lush purples and sky blues ensure that it's neither dark nor overwhelmingly heavy. The hotel is nicely removed from the souq hubbub and some

Central Doha

Top Sights
- 1 Falcon Souq ... B2
- 2 Museum of Islamic Art ... D1
- 3 Souq Waqif ... C2

Sights
- Bird Souq ... (see 3)
- 4 Camel Pen ... B2
- 5 Diwan (Parliament) Building ... B2
- 6 Doha Fort ... E1
- 7 Gallery Al Riwaq ... E1
- 8 Gold Souq ... C2
- 9 Heritage House ... C3
- 10 Horse Stables ... B2
- 11 MIA Park ... E1
- 12 Pearl Monument ... C2
- 13 Qatar National Museum ... E2

Activities, Courses & Tours
- 14 Children's Playground ... B2
- 15 FANAR Qatar Islamic Cultural Center ... C2
- 16 Gulf Adventures ... E4

Sleeping
- 17 Al Bidda Boutique Hotel ... C2
- 18 Al Jasra Boutique Hotel ... B2
- 19 Al Jomrok Boutique Hotel ... C2
- 20 Al Mirqab Boutique Hotel ... F1
- 21 Al Najada Boutique Hotel ... E1
- 22 Al Nakheel Hotel ... C3
- 23 Arumaila Boutique Hotel ... C2
- 24 Bismillah Boutique Hotel ... F1
- 25 Musheireb Boutique Hotel ... B2
- 26 Najd Boutique Hotel ... F1
- 27 Qatar Palace Hotel ... C3

Eating
- 28 Al Bandar ... E1
- Al Matbakh ... (see 23)
- 29 Argan ... B2
- 30 Bandar Aden ... C2
- 31 Café-Tasse ... E1
- Damasca One ... (see 24)
- IDAM ... (see 2)
- MIA Cafe ... (see 2)
- 32 Zaatar W Zeit ... F1

Drinking & Nightlife
- Al Aker ... (see 37)
- Al Mandarine ... (see 31)
- Cafe Brouq ... (see 20)
- 33 Coffee Asherg ... C2
- 34 Halul Coffeehouse ... E1
- Majlis Al Dama ... (see 3)

Shopping
- 35 Handicrafts Souq ... F1
- 36 Souq Waqif Art Center ... E1
- Spices & Sweets Souq ... (see 3)
- Zubeir ... (see 24)

Information
- 37 Heritage Police Station ... F1
- 38 Souq Waqif Information & Tourism Center ... F1

rooms have views towards the corniche and beyond to West Bay. There's also an on-site spa and gym.

★W Hotel Doha HOTEL **$$$**

(Map p228; ☎44 535 000; www.whoteldoha.com; Street 831, West Bay; r from QR999; @ 📶 🏊) With stunning designer rooms, many shaped like a pearl, W Hotel Doha is taking on the five-star chains of longer standing and winning. Everything about this place, from the outrageously attractive rooms and top-class restaurants to the excellent service and tech-savvy rooms, screams cool and contemporary.

★Sharq Village & Spa RESORT **$$$**

(Map p228; ☎44 256 666; www.ritzcarlton.com/sharqvillage; Ras Abu Abboud St; r from QR1245; P 📶 🏊) With its Arabian-heritage architecture, its exquisite desert landscaping and its beach location, this is one superb hotel. The intimate, super-luxurious rooms with four-poster beds and diaphanous silken drapes are arranged around sand-coloured courtyards and cactus gardens. Lanterns, shadows dancing across the marble and Ali Baba pots bubbling with water all play their part in creating an *Arabian Nights* experience.

★Banana Island Resort RESORT **$$$**

(☎40 405 050; www.doha.anantara.com; Banana Island; r/ste/villas QR1190/1828/4208; @ 📶 🏊) Inhabiting its own island out in the Gulf and reached via a luxury yacht transfer service, Banana Island Resort is exclusive and beautiful in all the right places. Discretion and calm are recurring themes and the luxurious rooms and sense of closeness to the sea make this a unique Gulf experience.

Sheraton Doha Hotel & Resort HOTEL **$$$**

(Map p228; ☎44 854 444; www.sheraton.com/doha; Al Funduq St, Al Corniche; r from QR1050; @ 📶 🏊) The Sheraton Doha is more than a place to stay; it's an institution. It's the oldest of Doha's five-star hotels, and still boasts one of the best locations, with wonderful views from light-filled, split-level, recently

BOUTIQUE HOTELS IN THE SOUQ

As Souq Waqif expands further with each passing year, one of the more welcome developments has been the conversion of old or remodelled souq buildings into boutique hotels that combine intimacy, luxury and traditional Qatari decor. Run by the same owners, there are nine in all, and they share a website (www.swbh.com) and have a single reservation desk located at the Al Jomrok Boutique Hotel. The conversions of such places into hotels have added considerable depth to Doha's accommodation scene, making it one of the more impressive anywhere in the Gulf region.

In addition to those covered in this guide, there's also:

Al Jasra Boutique Hotel (Map p232; ☎44 336 666; www.swbh.com/aljasraboutique; Al Jasra St, Souq Watif; s/d from QR750/800; @📶)

Al Jomrok Boutique Hotel (Map p232; ☎44 336 666; www.swbh.com/aljomrokboutique; Souq Watif; s/d from QR650/750; @📶)

Bismillah Boutique Hotel (Map p232; ☎44 336 666; www.swbh.com/bismillahboutique; Souq Watif Rd, Souq Watif)

Najd Boutique Hotel (Map p232; ☎44 336 666; www.swbh.com/najdboutique; Souq Watif; s/d from 750/800; @📶)

renovated rooms with balconies, and a private beach. Rates include breakfast delivered to the room on silver salvers.

Eating

Many of Doha's more celebrated restaurants inhabit the city's five-star hotels and there's an ongoing battle as each tries to outdo the others. Famous international chefs are increasingly turning up here.

Unless you've a particular restaurant in mind, there are two excellent areas to wander in search of a meal: the main thoroughfare through Souq Waqif and the Katara cultural precinct north of the city. Pick up a copy of the monthly *Time Out Doha* for the latest restaurant listings.

★Bandar Aden MIDDLE EASTERN $
(Map p232; ☎44 375 503; www.bandaraden.com; Souq Waqif; mains QR10-50; ⏰8am-11pm Sat-Thu, 12.30-11pm Fri) This market institution is a fabulous place to eat. Its traditional Yemeni cooking draws a predominantly local crowd, who just love to sit on the carpeted floor (shoes off, please) and share a great mound of rice and all manner of meats. The stews, too, are exceptionally good. Don't worry: there are also tables for less flexible diners.

MIA Cafe CAFE $
(Map p232; www.mia.org.qa/en/visiting/cafe; ground fl, Museum of Islamic Art; sandwiches from QR40, mains QR36-55; ⏰10.30am-5.30pm Sun, Mon & Wed, noon-8pm Thu & Sat, 2-8pm Fri) Cafeteria-style salads and snacks nicely complement the light Arabic and French mains that fill the short, carefully selected menu at the Museum of Islamic Art's cafe. But more than the food it's the chance to sit in the light-filled atrium and gaze out across the water that you'll enjoy.

Turkey Central TURKISH $
(Map p228; ☎44 432 92744 432 927; Al Mirqab Al Jadeed St; mains QR10-50) No frills but utterly delicious Turkish food is worth the trek out here, west of the downtown area. Fantastic breads (cooked on site) and mezze in truly epic portions may leave little room for the kebabs, which would be a terrible shame.

Zaatar W Zeit MIDDLE EASTERN $
(Map p232; ☎44 315 224; Souq Waqif St, Souq Waqif; mains QR8-29; ⏰8am-midnight) Lebanese fast food has proved a big hit here in the heart of the souq. The menu is built around *manakeesh* (a cross between pizza and Arabic flat bread, sprinkled with *zaatar* (thyme) and served in numerous varieties). It also does tasty wraps.

Café-Tasse ITALIAN $
(Map p232; ☎44 447 017; Souq Waqif; mains QR40; ⏰8am-2am; 📝) If you've reached the limit of your fascination for Middle Eastern food, one venue worth singling out is this Italian-style place, offering all-day dining of pasta, salads and snacks. A quick bite generally turns into something longer as diners enjoy the Souq Waqif pageant flowing past the cafe doors. It's almost always full, even when the surrounding eateries are empty.

DOHA FOR CHILDREN

Qatar is a safe, easy-going, family-oriented country, and children are welcome and catered for everywhere. Even the Gulf, with its gently sloping shores and flat, waveless seas, lends itself better to paddling about and building sandcastles than to extreme sports. The large resorts all have plenty of activities for young children and Doha has a heap of attractions to keep even the most overactive kids amused.

There are playgrounds at the **Sheraton end of Al Corniche** (Map p228) and between the entrance to **Souq Waqif and Al Corniche** (Map p232).

Winter Wonderland (Map p228; ☎44 839 163; www.citycenterdoha.com; Conference Centre St, City Centre Doha, West Bay; per person from QR30; ⏲10am-9pm Sat-Wed, 10am-11pm Thu, 1-10pm Fri) Snow in Arabia? Inside the City Center Doha mall, Winter Wonderland features an ice-skating rink, a 10-pin bowling alley and a water park.

Jungle Zone (Map p228; ☎44 694 848; www.hyattplaza.com; Hyatt Plaza, Al Waab St; admission Thu-Sat QR55, Sun-Wed QR40; ⏲noon-10pm Sun-Wed, noon-11pm Thu, 1-11pm Fri, 10am-10pm Sat) Jungle Zone offers 3500 sq metres of animal-themed children's attractions.

Batteel Café CAFE **$**
(Map p228; ☎44 441 414; www.batteel.com; Salwa Rd; snacks QR50; ⏲8am-midnight) With a range of delicious freshly baked pastries, homemade ice creams and sorbets, and some innovative sandwiches, this cafe, set in a traditional Qatari house with Arabic cushions and *barasti* (palm-leaf) ceilings, is a firm favourite with residents. It also serves some of Doha's more reasonably priced seafood.

★Argan MOROCCAN **$$**
(Map p232; ☎44 336 686; www.swbh.com; Al Jasra St, Souq Waqif; mains QR59-75; ⏲noon-4pm & 6pm-midnight Sun-Wed, noon-midnight Thu-Sat) One of the premier dining experiences in the souq and removed from the main restaurant strip, Argan serves excellent Moroccan cooking in a classy setting. The seafood tajine is spectacular and the couscous outstanding, and there are many other options (soups, salads, mezze) from North Africa. There's a formal section, but we recommend the more convivial *majlis* area in the centre.

Khan Farouk Tarab Cafe EGYPTIAN **$$**
(Map p228; ☎44 080 845; www.khanfarouktarabcafe.com; Bldg 7, Katara; mains QR42-98; ⏲noon-midnight) So powerful is the sense of Old Cairo here that you half expect to find Naguib Mahfouz writing his novel at a corner table. Instead, there's live traditional Egyptian tarab music in the evenings and a menu brimming with *kushari* (noodles, rice, black lentils, fried onions and tomato sauce), felafel (deep-fried chickpea balls) and signature Egyptian dishes like grilled pigeon.

Damasca One SYRIAN **$$**
(Map p232; ☎44 759 088; www.damascarestaurant.com; Souq Waqif; mains QR86-137; ⏲noon-11pm Sat-Thu, 1-11pm Fri) Stepping across the threshold of this expansive place is like entering the lost culinary world of Damascus. *Sheeshas* outside, and within everything from Arabic breakfasts to the subtle flavours of paprika-inflected hummus and other dips, salads such as *fattoush* (bread salad) and perfectly grilled meats make this one of our favourite, most atmospheric places to eat in the souq.

Al Bandar SEAFOOD **$$**
(Map p232; ☎44 311 313; Souq Waqif Rd, Souq Waqif; mains QR35-110, set menus QR85-104; ⏲12.30-11.30pm) With perhaps the best seafood in the souq – or anywhere in downtown Doha for that matter – Al Bandar is a wonderful choice. Its seafood casserole is tasty and packed with seafood, but we like it fresh, grilled and unadorned: the mixed seafood for QR75 could just be Doha's best-value feast.

Al Matbakh MIDDLE EASTERN **$$**
(Map p232; ☎44 336 666; www.swbh.com; Arumaila Boutique Hotel, Souq Waqif; mains QR85-270; ⏲6pm-midnight) Rock lobster, Australian steaks and slow-cooked camel may be reason enough to come to this dinner-only restaurant, but it's the rooftop perch with fine views over the souq and city skyline that may live just as long in the memory.

★IDAM FRENCH **$$$**
(Map p232; ☎44 224 488; www.mia.org.qa/en/visiting/idam; 5th fl, Museum of Islamic Art; lunch menu per person QR200, mains QR170-400, 3/5 mezze QR300/450; ⏲noon-2pm & 7-10pm Wed, Thu, Sat &

Sun, 7-10pm Fri) From the Alain Ducasse stable, the restaurant that crowns the Museum of Islamic Art is one of Doha's best. Try the whole blue lobster, or the tender camel with duck foie gras, black truffle and souflééd potatoes. Alternatively, you could just surrender and let the chef make all the decisions for you as part of the 'Experience menu' (QR810). The mezze are also incredible.

Gordon Ramsay Doha MEDITERRANEAN **$$$**
(Map p228; ☎44 460 105; www.gordonramsaydoha.com; St Regis Doha, West Bay; mains from QR150; ⏲6-11pm Mon-Sat) Gordon Ramsay brings his star appeal to Doha's St Regis Hotel, north of the city centre. The main restaurant concentrates on the best in Sardinian, Spanish and southern French cooking and takes it in unexpected directions, for example in the risotto served with wild mushrooms, pecorino Romano and Italian black truffle.

For something less formal, though with similar prices, try **Opal by Gordon Ramsay** (Map p228; ☎44 460 116; www.opalbygordonramsaydoha.com; St Regis Doha, West Bay; mains QR130-275; ⏲noon-4pm & 6-11pm) in the same complex.

L'Wzaar SEAFOOD **$$$**
(Seafood Market; Map p228; ☎44 080 710; www.lwzaar.com; Bldg 27, Katara; mains QR150; ⏲noon-4pm & 7-11.30pm Sat-Thu, 1-4pm & 7-11.30pm Fri) There's a separate fish-and-chip shop in this glamorous, choose-your-own-fish restaurant. Just back from the beach in the cultural village of Katara, it gives a rare opportunity to mingle with Qatari families and sample what claims to be Doha's best, freshest seafood. The traditional fish soup followed by grilled mixed seafood would be our choice, but it also does excellent sushi.

Drinking & Nightlife

In the absence of nightclubs or pubs, hotel bars usually double as nightlife in Doha, and while there's not a whole lot happening, there's enough to make a night of it. Old-style coffeehouses, particularly around the souq, are perfect daytime haunts.

Bars

★Belgian Cafe BAR
(Map p228; ☎44 844 444; InterContinental Doha, Al Isteqlal Rd, West Bay; ⏲noon-2am) One of the most enduringly popular pubs in Doha, Belgian Cafe gets packed to the rafters on weekends (ie Thursday and Friday nights) and they're here for the imported Belgian and other European beers, great bar food (mussels or waffles, what else?) and laid-back atmosphere (the dress code is one of Doha's more relaxed).

If you're unsure where to start, ask the knowledgeable bar staff for guidance – if you can get a word in edgeways.

★Sky View BAR
(Map p228; ☎44 288 888; La Cigale Hotel, 60 Suhaim Bin Hamad St, Bin Mahmoud; ⏲7pm-2am) Travel a few blocks west of the centre for an incredible perspective on the city's skyline from the rooftop bar of La Cigale. The well-to-do but young and professional crowd doesn't flinch at the tab for what are some of Doha's pricier drinks. Great sushi-bar food and a strict door policy have made this one of *the* places to be seen.

Strata Lounge COCKTAIL BAR
(Map p228; ☎44 158 888; InterContinental Doha – The City, West Bay; ⏲6pm-2am) On the 56th floor of the InterContinental's city branch, off Al Wahda Rd, this is a head-spinning venue, a state of affairs that has as much to do with the mixologist's concoctions as the vertiginous views. The only challenge is working out which 'vertical bus' delivers you to the top floor. Happy hour runs from 6pm to 8pm.

Paloma BAR
(Map p228; ☎44 944 919; InterContinental Doha, West Bay; ⏲6pm-2am) One of the most lively bars in town, the Paloma also happens to be the best place for live music. If the band's not to your taste, glide over to the much cooler, more sedate Lava Lounge.

Jazz Club COCKTAIL BAR
(Map p228; ☎44 023 333; Oryx Rotana, Al Nahda School St) Decent jazz (some of it live) provides something a little different at this bar in the Oryx Rotana Hotel southeast of the city centre, but it's the cocktails that are the real stars of the show. Happy hour is a generous 5pm to 8pm; you'll need to dress nice, but there's no need to go over the top.

The hotel is off Old Airport Rd.

Pearl Lounge COCKTAIL BAR
(Map p228; ☎44 298 888; Doha Marriott Hotel, Ras Abu Abboud St; ⏲9pm-3am Mon-Sat, 5-8pm Sun) Draped across two floors of an opulent central hotel; has a large menu of tasty temptations to accompany the bangs, sours and fizzes.

Cafes & Coffeehouses

The *majlis* (meeting room) is a Qatari institution, where men congregate over tea or coffee for a chat, to share news or to watch TV together.

★ Majlis Al Dama COFFEEHOUSE
(Map p232; Spice Souq, Souq Waqif; ⏲7am-1pm & 4-11pm Sat-Thu, 4-11pm Fri) They don't get many tourists in here, but that's the point. Majlis Al Dana is old school, the sort of place where old timers pop in for thick Arabic coffee and a game of aldama (similar to backgammon). It's a place to be a fly on the wall, but it's really only worth it when there are people at the boards.

★ Al Aker CAFE
(Map p232; Souq Waqif Rd, Souq Waqif; ⏲9am-midnight Sat-Thu, noon-midnight Fri) Now here's something special. The main events here are simply splendid Arabic and Turkish sweets to go with your coffee. On no account miss an order of *kunafa* (a soft or crispy pastry filled with white cheese and soaked in syrup). A couple of large pieces should set you back around QR15. More importantly, your life will never be the same again.

Staff can also box up a selection of sweets for you to take away and enjoy.

Cafe Brouq CAFE
(Map p232; ☎44 336 648; Al Mirqab Boutique Hotel, Souq Waqif; ⏲8am-10.30pm) In the new Doha, not all coffeehouses are about cushions on the floor and men playing board games. Cafe Brouq is the height of sophistication, with classy decor and service to match the menu of teas, coffees and divine desserts; there are more substantial meals (salads, sandwiches and paninis) and breakfast if you're really hungry.

Halul Coffeehouse COFFEEHOUSE
(Map p232; Al Corniche; ⏲9am-1pm & 4-10pm Sat-Thu, 4-11pm Fri) This local-style coffeehouse has somehow escaped the modernisation of the area and makes a suitable place to pause for a *shay* (tea) on a hike round the corniche or en route to or from the new National Museum.

Coffee Asherg COFFEEHOUSE
(Map p232; ☎44 367 776; Souq Waqif; ⏲8am-11pm) On the eastern (sea-facing) edge of the souq, this traditional rooftop coffeehouse is welcoming of all comers, if a little touristy. Then again, lying stretched on a divan under the stars, sipping mint tea and listening to the muezzin call prayers at dusk while the city lights sparkle into life is the quintessential Arabian experience.

Al Mandarine CAFE
(Map p232; Souq Waqif Rd, Souq Waqif; ⏲8am-1.30am Sat-Thu, 8-11am & 1pm-1.30am Fri) This place serves some of the best juices in the souq, with a range of cocktails on its rather long (and rather small-print…) menu.

☆ Entertainment

With the mushrooming number of luxury hotels in Qatar, there's plenty of entertainment on offer. Jazz evenings, live entertainment and international food promotions are held frequently. Check listings in *Time Out Doha* and *Marhaba, Qatar's Premier Information Guide,* as well as in English-language newspapers, for anything from line dancing at the rugby club to cookery classes at the Ritz-Carlton.

The best cinemas are in the City Centre Doha (p240), **Mall** (Map p228; D Ring Rd) and Landmark Shopping Mall (p240) shopping complexes. They show the latest Hollywood blockbusters and the occasional film from Iran or Europe. Tickets cost about QR30. For upcoming shows at these and other cinemas, visit www.cinemaqatar.com.

Horses are in the hearts of most Qataris, so for a chance to meet the locals, consider attending one of the weekly horse races that occur throughout the season (October to May).

Doha Players THEATRE
(Map p228; ☎44 474 911; www.thedohaplayers.com; Al Gharrafa St) In existence for 50 years, the Doha Players stages amateur productions, with an emphasis on Shakespeare.

Laughter Factory COMEDY
(Map p228; ☎44 281 673; www.thelaughterfactory.com; Radisson Blu Hotel, Salwa Rd) The Laughter Factory organises monthly tours of professional comedians from the international circuit around the Gulf. Tickets sell like hot cakes.

Racing & Equestrian Club HORSE RACING
(Map p228; ☎44 803 01644 803 016; www.qrec.gov.qa; Al Furousiya St) FREE Every Thursday at 4pm races of pure-bred Arabian horses take place here.

Shopping

Doha is full of wonderful shopping opportunities: options range from a camel to a racing car, an Armani suit to a sequinned *abeyya* (woman's full-length black robe) and a fishing rod to a peregrine falcon. While

WORTH A TRIP

WHOLESALE MARKET

If you have an hour to spare, head to Doha's **Wholesale Market** (Map p228; Salwa Rd) for sales of produce, fish and meat. It's worth visiting just for the sideshows: cockerels unbagged in a flourish, children tugging at rabbit ears, hooded peregrines balancing on a white-robed arm and women in black picking their way through the mayhem of one of the great bazaars of modern times.

There's also a livestock market, which may be of interest to anyone who hasn't seen pink, yellow and lime-green chicks before. Why the birds are dyed is a mystery of the region. Fortunately, they leave the spotted guinea fowl, ring-necked parakeets, African greys and cut-throat zebra finches untinged – possibly because the plumage of these domestic birds is outrageous enough already.

The day before an *eid* (Islamic feast), the market heaves with goat buyers, camel traders and sheep shoppers, all looking for a suitable *eid* supper, but the animals are well shaded and watered, and respect for the livestock is shown by much inspection of teeth and smoothing of coats.

It's all a world away from the sanitised experience of a Western supermarket meat counter, but it is very much part of the Middle East, repeated in similar scenes from Yemen to Kuwait.

there aren't many locally produced crafts, half the fun of shopping here is ambling through the souqs or brand-new shopping malls, stumbling over things you couldn't imagine people would want to buy and then buying them anyway, like a house (complete with letter box) for the garden birds or a dyed-pink hair extension made of ostrich feathers – the possibilities are endless.

Jarir Bookstore BOOKS
(Map p228; ☎44 440 212; Salwa Rd; ⏰9am-10pm Sat-Thu, 4-10pm Fri) Doha's best bookshop, Jarir has books, magazines, newspapers, stationery and electronics.

Souqs

One of the joys of shopping in Doha's traditional souqs is that the shopkeepers take the time to chat with customers, whether buying or not, making shopping one of the best ways to engage with the locals. Despite a bit of push and shove when it's crowded, all the souqs are safe places to visit and bargaining is expected. Souq Waqif (p225) is the overarching name for a host of subsidiary souqs that fall within its boundaries. Particular highlights include the Falcon Souq (p226), the Gold Souq (p227) and the Bird Souq (p227).

Aside from these easily discernible sections of the souq, there are other areas where traders of the same genre cluster together, although you'll find that the boundaries are often blurred. Next to the Gold Souq, the **Handicrafts Souq** (Map p232; Souq Watif; ⏰9am-1pm & 4-9pm Sat-Thu, 4-9pm Fri) is a short but densely packed thoroughfare filled with souvenir shops of varying quality, from musical instruments or baskets to Gulf evening wear and hand-sewn shoes.

A particularly fragrant corner of Souq Waqif is the **Spices & Sweets Souq** (Map p232; Souq Watif; ⏰9am-1pm & 4-7pm Sat-Thu, 4-9pm Fri). It's just south of the Bird Souq.

Zubeir MUSIC
(Map p232; Handicrafts Souq, Souq Waqif; ⏰9am-noon & 4.30-9pm Sat-Thu) Signed only in Arabic, this musical-instrument shop sells drums and authentic ouds, the stringed lute of Arabian lore, as well as a few CDs of oud music. It's the second shop on your left as you enter the Handicrafts Souq from next to Al Mirqab Boutique Hotel.

Souq Waqif Art Center ARTS
(Map p232; ☎44 176 204; Souq Waqif Rd, Souq Waqif; ⏰8am-2pm & 4-10pm Sat-Thu, 4-10pm Fri) Housed in an attractive building that fronts onto the main souq, this centre for the arts has a number of showrooms for paintings, sculpture and other artistic pursuits. If you're lucky there might be an artist in residence.

Malls

There is a kind of subversion of expectation inside the great shopping malls of the Gulf. They appear to be even more opulent versions of American malls, complete with themed entertainment and Starbucks, but then you'll find an *abeyya* shop selling women's cloaks or a prayer-bead counter next to a waffle stand that confirms that you are, indeed, shopping in the Middle East.

In the heat of summer, they become much more than a place to shop, as people congregate in them to escape the ravages of the sun and to be entertained by the prospect of other worlds. Each of the malls has some form of entertainment for the family, from skating rinks to cinemas, and as such they make for a popular day's outing. Numerous new malls were under construction when we visited, so expect the offerings to get bigger and better with each passing year.

City Centre Doha MALL
(Map p228; ☎44 839 990; www.citycenterdoha.com; ⌚10am-10pm Sun-Wed, 10am-midnight Thu & Sat, 3pm-midnight Fri) With its 350 shops, tented architecture, marble flooring and glass-fronted lifts, its ice-skating rink, bowling alleys and climbing walls, its congregations of juice-sipping Qataris and huddles of homesick expatriates, and its trolleys laden with eggs, packets of *khobz* (Arabian flat bread) and Egyptian olives, City Centre Doha is more an event than an errand.

Villaggio Mall MALL
(Map p228; ☎44 135 222; www.villaggioqatar.com; Al Waab St; ⌚10am-11pm Sat-Thu, 1-11pm Fri) In this Venetian-themed mall, you can shop under a diorama of fluffy white clouds, eat pizza at Paul's and take a ride on a gondola along the grand canal. It includes lots of entertainment opportunities, including a cinema.

Landmark Shopping Mall MALL
(Map p228; ☎44 875 222; www.landmarkdoha.com; cnr Al Shamal N Rd & Al Markhiya St; ⌚9am-10pm Sat-Wed, to 11pm Thu & Fri) This enormous shopping centre, with a multiplex cinema, a Marks & Spencer department store and a Virgin Megastore, is home to dozens of other international chain stores.

Lagoona Mall MALL
(☎44 335 555; www.lagoonamall.com; Zone 66, West Bay; ⌚10am-10pm Sat-Wed, 10am-midnight Thu, 2am-midnight Fri) Facing across the eternal construction sites towards the Pearl precinct, Lagoona Mall has the usual range of international designers as well as the FNAC department store, with music, books and electronics.

Information

DANGERS & ANNOYANCES

Doha is one of the safest cities in the Middle East. Even women travelling on their own late in the evening are unlikely to feel threatened, provided they are dressed appropriately. The only danger worth commenting on is the volume of traffic, and the speed, as drivers don't always obey the rules.

EMERGENCY

Fire, Police & Ambulance (☎999)

MEDICAL SERVICES

Hamad General Hospital (Map p228; ☎44 395 777; www.hmc.org.qa; Al Rayyan Rd) Subsidised medical and dental treatment is available for tourists on a walk-in basis.

MONEY

There are plenty of moneychangers just south of Doha Fort. ATMs that take Visa, MasterCard, Cirrus, Maestro and Amex cards are available throughout Doha.

TOURIST INFORMATION

Qatar Tourism Authority (www.qatartourism.gov.qa) There are no tourist-information centres as such, but the Qatar Tourism Authority provides good general information on its website.

Getting There & Away

Hamad International Airport (dohahamadairport.com) Doha's swish international airport opened for business in April 2014 and has grown into one of the region's busiest airports.

Getting Around

There are ambitious plans for an extensive underground Metro system that will connect all points of Doha, from the airport to the Pearl, and will revolutionise travel within the city. Although construction was well under way when we visited, it seems unlikely that works will meet the original 2016 completion deadline.

TO/FROM THE AIRPORT

Hamad International Airport is 13km southeast of the city centre and many top-end hotels and resorts provide free transport to/from the airport.

Taxis (turquoise in colour) are clean, safe and metered, and the journey between the airport and central Doha starts at QR25. Avoid taking unofficial taxi rides from the touts at the airport who illegally claim business for their private car.

Karwa buses between the airport and the Al Ghanim bus station leave every hour between 5.50am and 11.50pm from Saturday to Thursday. The service starts an hour later on Friday. A 24-hour Karwa Smartcard, valid for two trips within Greater Doha within a 24-hour period, costs QR10. Alternatively, you can buy a one-way ticket for QR5.

BUS

The government-run national bus company provides comfortable city services around Doha in environmentally friendly, battery-powered and LPG-fuelled vehicles. Timetables are displayed at each of the sheltered bus stops.

Karwa Public Bus (☎44 588 588; www.mowasalat.com; ⏲4.30am-10.30pm) Operates buses every 15 to 30 minutes along many city routes; most start from Al Ghanim bus station and have stops every 750m. To travel by bus, you must purchase a Karwa Smartcard. Without a card, there's a QR10 fee for a single journey. Cards are available at the bus station and at some supermarkets. Check online for details (www.karwasmartcard.com).

The free West Bay Shuttle loops through the West Bay area and can be handy for getting from one end of West Bay to the other. Route maps are posted at bus stops and are available on www.mowasalat.com.

Al Ghanim Bus Station (Map p232; ☎44 588 888; www.mowasalat.com) Most public buses begin their route at this station.

CAR

There are a string of car-rental companies in the arrivals area of the airport.

Driving in Doha is easy enough if you watch out for impatient drivers overtaking on both the left and right, honking the horn at roundabouts and at free-roaming pedestrians. Parking, except in the souq areas, is not too much of a problem: most hotels and malls have car parks or parking services. A lack of street signs can make navigation difficult and most people navigate by landmark not by road sign.

TAXI

Despite the efficient bus system, most people get around Doha by taxi. The best taxi service is run by **Mowasalat Karwa** (☎458 8888). Although very few taxis use their meters these days, in theory journeys cost QR4 plus QR1.200/1.800 per kilometre during daylight/night-time hours; waiting time costs QR8 for each 15 minutes. In practice, agree a price before getting in. The minimum fare is QR10.

The bright-turquoise cars can be hailed by the side of the road or found at the airport and outside malls and hotels.

AROUND DOHA

While Qatar isn't exactly blessed with sights and activities outside the capital, it does have several attractions that justify the cost of hiring a vehicle for a day or two, including a few coastal villages where life still revolves around fishing and the local mosque.

The land is arid in the extreme, but that's not to say it's featureless: there are some beautiful beaches, interesting wind-eroded escarpments and large areas of sand dunes. The country's biggest natural attraction is undoubtedly Khor Al Adaid, a salt-water inlet in the south surrounded by a magical landscape of sand and salt. Camping at Khor Al Adaid or at Bir Zekreet is a reminder of the achievement of the Qataris (which they have in common with their Gulf neighbours) in fashioning a complex modern state from a virtually barren plot of land.

OFF THE BEATEN TRACK

THE PETROGLYPHS OF JEBEL JASSASSIYEH جبل الجساسية

The petroglyphs of northern Qatar have been seen by very few visitors. This is largely because until very recently their whereabouts was all but a secret and only those in the know with a 4WD could find them.

A low-lying rocky outcrop about 60km north of Doha, the apparently unprepossessing Jebel Jassassiyeh is home to a remarkable 900 rock carvings, strewn across 580 sites. Some of these ancient incisions are said to depict aerial views of boats, which is interesting given that, in an utterly flat country, bounded by a (usually) utterly flat sea, there would have been no opportunity for people to have an aerial view of anything. While some archaeologists have suggested the carvings could date back to the 3rd century BC, most experts agree that they were created between the 10th and 18th centuries AD.

To reach the main concentration of petroglyphs, take the road to Jassassiyeh off Hwy 1 and then the first (unmarked) road on the left. After 8km you will come to some fenced-off areas with warnings not to trespass. The gates are left open, however, and you are free to wander around providing you are sensitive to the antiquity and importance of the sites. There are no signs, so look for uniform grooves and incisions on top of flat rocks: once you've spotted one, you'll find you are surrounded by many similar carvings.

WORTH A TRIP

CAMELS AT AL SHAHANIYA الشحانية

If you've come to the Middle East hoping to see camels, then there's one place you're guaranteed to find them. At Al Shahaniya, 60km west of Doha along the Dukhan Rd, camels roam freely around the desert, or you can see them being exercised before the famous local camel races.

Camel races (known as the 'sport of sheikhs') can be seen from a purpose-built stadium, and they involve remote-controlled robot jockeys(!) that weigh 25kg. If you have a car – a 4WD is not necessary – it's fun to drive along the 8km racetrack during the race. It can be quite an event, as female camels can maintain a speed of 40km/h for an entire hour and are often better at keeping in their lane than motorists. Check the English-language daily newspapers for race times or contact a tour company, most of which organise trips to the races during the season (November to April). Most races take place on Friday, but call ☎44 872 028 to confirm.

It's easy to spot the stadium, as long before it comes into view the approach is marked by 5km of stables, exercise areas, lodgings for the trainers and breeders, and all the other facilities required of a multimillion-dollar sport, not to mention a national passion befitting Qatar's Bedouin origins. The season culminates in the prestigious Emir's GCC Camel Race (p231).

Al Wakrah & Al Wukair الوكرة و الوكير

The old pearling villages of Al Wakrah and Al Wukair are rapidly stringing out to meet the Doha suburbs. They make a pleasant afternoon outing from the capital, however, and there are several interesting old mosques and traditional houses in and around the gracious modern villas. The old souq along the shoreline is being given a makeover following the success of Souq Waqif (p225) in Doha.

The beaches south of Al Wakrah offer glorious stretches of sand, interspersed with the odd *khor* (creek). The shallow water makes paddling a better option than swimming. At least the determined wader is in good company: small flocks of flamingos roost along the coast between Al Wakrah and Mesaieed during winter. Fishing is a popular pastime in the area, as the limestone shallows act as fish traps when the tide goes out.

Both Al Wakrah and Al Wukair are an easy 15-minute drive from Doha, following Al Matar St past the airport and heading south. The bus from Doha leaves every 20 minutes and costs QR5.

Mesaieed مسيعيد

Mesaieed is an industrialised town about 45km south of Doha, and although it's not particularly attractive in itself, the nearby beaches with deep water make for some of the best swimming in Qatar.

Sleeping

Sealine Beach Resort RESORT $$
(☎44 765 299; www.sealinebeachqatar.com; r from QR850; P @ 🛜 🏊) This lovely low-rise, beach-side resort is just south of Mesaieed; it's far enough away to be unaffected by Mesaieed's heavy industry, and the ring of glorious amber sand dunes doubles the entertainment opportunities. The beach shelves quite steeply, allowing for good swimming, and the resort hires out desert quad bikes for exploring the local dunes, known as the 'singing sands'.

Day visitors are welcome to use the hotel facilities, including pools and the beach; camel and horse rides are available; and there's a clown to entertain the children, as well as activities like face painting. Day admission costs QR25 for children and QR50 for adults from Sunday to Wednesday and QR75 and QR125 respectively from Thursday to Saturday.

Getting There & Away

To reach Mesaieed from Doha, follow the road past the airport and through Al Wakrah. A taxi to the resort from Doha costs around QR200.

Khor Al Adaid خور العديد

Without a doubt, the major natural attraction in Qatar is the beautiful 'inland sea' of

Khor Al Adaid, near the border with Saudi Arabia. Often described as a sea or a lake, the *khor* is in fact neither: rather it is a creek surrounded by silvery crescents of sand (known as *barchan*). All sand dunes look wonderful in the late-afternoon sun, but those of Khor Al Adaid take on an almost mystical quality under a full moon, when the *sabkha* (salt flats) sparkle in the gaps between the sand.

While a night under the stars on a camping expedition is a special experience in the right company, not everyone goes to the area to enjoy the tranquillity. Sand skiing, quad-biking and 4WD racing compete with the time-honoured picnic and a song, much to the consternation of some and the pleasure of others. The area is big enough, thankfully, to satisfy both, although environmental concerns are being expressed as more and more travel agencies make the area the central attraction of their tours.

This region is *only* accessible by 4WD, and independent travellers should accompany someone who knows the area and really can drive a 4WD. Being stuck in the sand is no fun after the first hour and in summer it is very dangerous. If you're determined to do it yourself, make sure you have at least a box of water bottles on board for each passenger, a map and compass, very clear directions of the best route currently navigable, a tow rope and a shovel. If you get stuck, don't dig: let out the air in the tyres and return to the nearest petrol station immediately to reinflate.

Going on an organised tour is probably the safest way to see Khor Al Adaid; overnight tours often include folkloric entertainment and a barbecue, as well as camping equipment. Rates vary, but a six- to seven-hour day excursion usually costs around QR750 per person for two people; add another QR100 per person for an overnight trip.

Umm Salal Mohammed ام صلال محمد

There are several old buildings dating from the 19th and early 20th century dotted around this small, modern residential district 22km north of Doha.

Sights

Umm Salal Mohammed Fort FORT

(8am-1pm & 4-7pm) FREE The ruined Umm Salal Mohammed Fort was built for military and civil use.

Barzan Tower TOWER

The triple-decker, T-shaped Barzan Tower is unique in the Gulf; however, this white-washed building was closed to the public at the time of research and is unlikely to reopen any time soon.

Getting There & Away

Umm Salal Mohammed is just west of the main highway to Al Ruweis.

Umm Salal Ali ام صلال علي

A small field of six Iron Age grave mounds, dating from the 2nd millennium BC, makes it worth a visit to Umm Salal Ali if you're coming to nearby Umm Salal Mohammed, especially if you have a guide. If not, look for rounded bumps in otherwise flat land just north of the town; more mounds are scattered among the buildings in the town centre. Umm Salal Ali is clearly signposted off the main highway north to Al Ruweis, about 27km from Doha.

Al Khor الخور

Al Khor, once famous as a centre for the pearling industry, is a pleasant town with an attractive corniche, a small dhow yard and a lively fish market. The small museum (if it ever reopens) displays archaeological and cultural artefacts from the region including traditional clothing. Several old watchtowers are scattered around town; many have been restored to their original form.

The nearby mangroves are a good place for birdwatching.

Sleeping

Al Sultan Beach Resort RESORT $$$

(44 722 666; www.alsultanbeachresort.com; r incl breakfast from QR1100; @) Situated just off the corniche, Al Sultan is a quirky place with cast-iron horses in the drive, tigers in the foyer and paintings of camels decorating the rooms. With comfortable accommodation (albeit with slightly dated decor), an infinity pool and sea views, it's a fine getaway.

Getting There & Away

Al Khor is a drive of around 45 minutes, or 40km, from Doha.

Al Ghariya الغارية

All round Al Ghariya there are excellent birdwatching possibilities (4WD or a strong pair of boots permitting).

Sleeping

Al Ghariya Resort RESORT $$$
(☎44 728 000; www.algharivaresorts.com; villas from QR2000;) Given Qatar's picturesque coastline, it's surprising there aren't more resorts like this. With apartment-style accommodation and a kitchen area for self-catering, it's popular with Doha families – be warned, the noise of children on sand buggies can be deafening! There's an indoor pool for ladies and an outdoor pool for men; sea swimming is only possible at the neighbouring beach.

Getting There & Away

Al Ghariya is signposted off the northern highway from Doha, some 85km from the capital.

Al Ruweis & Around الرويس

Situated at the northern tip of the peninsula (at the end of the northern highway about 90km from Doha) lies Al Ruweis, a typical fishing village where the age-old industries of net mending and fish-pot cleaning take place on board the stranded dhows while their crews wait for the tide to return.

Several abandoned villages, like Al Khuwair and Al Arish, mark the road between Al Ruweis and Al Zubara. They were vacated in the 1970s as the inhabitants were drawn to new areas of industry.

The lovely, unspoilt beaches around the northern coast are a joy, but access is only possible in a 4WD; extreme care should be taken to follow previous tracks, both for environmental and for safety reasons.

Al Zubara الزبارة

Qatar's only Unesco World Heritage–listed site, Al Zubara occupies an important place in Qatari history, as it was a large commercial and pearling port in the 18th and 19th centuries when the area was under the governance of Al Khalifa (now the ruling family in Bahrain).

Nearby, work is under way to open up the ongoing excavations of an old pearling village to visitors. There's not too much to see, but the enthusiasm of the archaeologists is infectious.

Sights

Al Zubara Fort FORT
(⏲5.30am-5.30pm) Al Zubara Fort was built in 1938 and used by the military until the 1980s. The archaeology and pottery exhibits have sadly been neglected, but the fort is still worth visiting for the bleak views from its battlements. The fort is at the intersection of the road from Doha and the road from Al Ruweis, 2km from Al Zubara.

Getting There & Away

Al Zubara is 105km northwest of Doha along Hwy 1.

Bir Zekreet بئر زكريت

There is not much in the way of altitude in Qatar, which only serves to exaggerate the little escarpment on the northwestern coast of the peninsula, near Dukhan. The limestone escarpment of Bir Zekreet is like a geography lesson in desert formations, as the wind has whittled away softer sedimentary rock, exposing pillars and a large mushroom of limestone. The surrounding beaches are full of empty oyster shells, with rich mother-of-pearl interiors, and other assorted bivalves. The shallow waters are quiet and peaceful and see relatively few visitors, making the area a pleasant destination for a day trip. Camping is possible either along the beach or less conspicuously under the stand of acacia trees near the escarpment. There are no facilities or shops nearby, so campers should come prepared, bringing plenty of water especially in the summer months.

To reach Bir Zekreet from Doha, head west past Al Shahaniya and take the signposted turn-off on the right about 10km before Dukhan. A new road is under construction, which will make reaching the area easier, but a 4WD is advisable for exploring the escarpment. To reach the desert mushroom, turn right 1.5km past the school at a gap in the gas pipes and bear left before the trees.

The remains of the 9th-century Murwab Fort, about 15km further up the northwestern coast from Dukhan, may be worth a visit with a guide. Five groups of buildings, including two mosques and an earlier fort, have been partially excavated, but a lack of information makes the site of limited interest.

UNDERSTAND QATAR

Qatar Today

Since June 1995, when Sheikh Khalifa bin Hamad Al Thani was replaced as emir by his son Hamad Khalifa Al Thani in a bloodless coup, Qatar has been transformed.

On one level, it has tried to court friendships with odd bedfellows – allowing American troops to launch operations in Iraq and Afghanistan from Qatar, for example, while courting the Taliban, Iran, Hamas and militant Islamist rebels fighting in Libya and Syria. This dichotomous approach may have caused consternation in Arab and Western capitals, but when a country has the world's largest gas fields and is consistently among the world's three richest countries in per-capita terms, there's little appetite for rocking the boat.

Besides, the lack of democracy in Qatar has not proved too much of an issue among the native population. In 2011, Qatar was notable among its regional neighbours for the lack of Arab Spring protests, despite having no elected representatives in government and despite key government posts being occupied by members of the emir's family. The most likely explanation for Qatar's lack of protests is the ruling family's generosity in spreading the country's wealth and allowing a degree of (albeit limited) free speech.

Instead of democracy, the ruling family has accelerated the modernisation of the country through encouraging education and training (in which women make up the majority of university students), investing in independent media, and opening the country to tourism – the stunning rise of Qatar Airways and the country's dazzling new international airport are the most obvious signs of this latter ambition.

In 2013, in a peaceful transition rare in this part of the world, Hamad abdicated as emir and elevated his 33-year-old son Tamim bin Hamad Al Thani to the throne. The early signs are that Al Thani the Younger has little intention of altering the course set by his father. Cleverly, his early years as ruler have seen him make a priority of boosting the private wealth of ordinary Qataris, as well as investing heavily in the country's health and education systems. And all the while, the massive investment in infrastructure continues as Qatar seeks to boost its profile by hosting some of the world's most prestigious sporting events.

It hasn't all been smooth sailing. Qatar's successful bid for the 2022 FIFA World Cup was marred by controversy: in the fallout from the troubles at FIFA, football's world governing body, from 2015, claims were widely aired in the international media that bribery and corruption had played a role in Qatar's winning bid. In late 2014, the UK's *Guardian* newspaper also reported that more than 1200 Nepalese workers alone had died on construction sites at the World Cup stadiums; these latter accusations have shed uncomfortable light on Qatar's broader treatment of migrant workers. And Qatar's bids for the 2016 and 2020 Olympics were both unsuccessful – Doha's searing summer temperatures were widely viewed as the main reason the country never made it past the first round of voting.

Proof that money can't buy everything or a mere blip in Qatar's seemingly inexorable rise? Perhaps the truth lies somewhere in between. But with Qatar's phenomenal wealth seemingly assured for generations to come, it's difficult to find too many Qataris who spend much time worrying about the setbacks.

History

Early Inhabitants

The written history of Qatar begins in grand fashion with a mention by the 5th-century Greek historian Herodotus, who identifies the seafaring Canaanites as the original inhabitants of Qatar. Thereafter, however, Qatar appears to be the subject more of conjecture than of history. Although there is evidence – in the form of flint spearheads, pottery shards (in the National Museum), burial mounds near Umm Salal Mohammed and the rock carvings of Jebel Jassassiyeh – of the early inhabitation of Qatar (from 4000 BC), the peninsula has surprisingly little to show for its ancient lineage.

Take Al Zubara, for example: the famous ancient Greek geographer Ptolemy tantalisingly includes 'Katara' in his map of the Arab world. This is thought to be a reference to Al Zubara, Qatar's main trading port right up until the 19th century. A visitor to the small modern town, however, would have difficulty imagining a dhow dodging the sandbanks at low tide, let alone a fleet of cargo ships moored in the harbour and, bar a few minor archaeological remains, the surrounding desert is marked by absence rather than historical presence.

The Rise of Islam

The history of Qatar, in many respects, is the history of the Bedouin, who traverse the land 'taking only memories, and leaving only footprints'. As such, history in Qatar is easier to spot in the living rather than the dead, for example, by the racing of camels at Al Shahaniya, the trading of falcons in Doha's souqs, the hospitality towards guests in the coffeehouses of the city, and the building of camps (albeit with TV aerials and 4WDs) in the sand dunes of Khor Al Adaid.

Documents indicate that Qatar played an important role in the early spread of Islam through the assembling of a naval fleet used to transport the warriors of the Holy Jihad. Again, however, Islam is carried rather more stoutly in the conservatism of the modern people than in any monuments to that era.

Even the Portuguese, who left forts in every country in the Gulf like modern businessmen leave calling cards, bequeathed only hearsay to Qatar's coastline. The Turks helped drive out the Portuguese in the 16th century and Qatar remained under the nominal rule of the Ottoman Empire (and the practical governance of local sheikhs) for more than four centuries. Yet the comings

AL JAZEERA TV

A Unique Forum

Al Jazeera has transformed the press in the Arab world. Established as Al Jazeera Independent Satellite TV Channel in November 1996, it differed from all that went before it because it was free from censorship or government control, it offered regional audiences a rare opportunity for debate and independent opinion, and it opened up an alternative perspective on regional issues for the world at large. Its call-in shows were particularly revolutionary, airing controversies not usually open for discussion in the autocratic Gulf countries.

Origins

Al Jazeera, which means 'The Island' in English, was originally launched as an Arabic news and current-affairs satellite-TV channel, funded with a generous grant from the emir of Qatar. It has been subsidised by the emir on a year-by-year basis since, despite the airing of criticism of his own government. The station was originally staffed by many former members of the BBC World Service, whose Saudi-based Arabic-language TV station collapsed under Saudi censorship; a close relationship with the BBC continues to this day.

The station has always been viewed with suspicion by ruling parties across the Arab world: on one occasion in the early days (on 27 January 1999), the Algerian government reportedly pulled the plug on the capital's electricity supply to prevent the population from hearing a live debate that alleged Algerian military collusion in a series of massacres.

International Significance

Al Jazeera only became internationally significant after the September 11 attacks on New York in 2001. The station broadcast video statements by Osama bin Laden (incidentally earning the station $20,000 per minute in resale fees) and other Al Qaeda leaders who defended the attacks. The US government accused the station of a propaganda campaign on behalf of the terrorists; however, the footage was broadcast by the station without comment. Al Jazeera continued to air challenging debate during the Afghanistan conflict, bringing into sharp focus the devastating impact of war on the lives of ordinary people. In 2003 it hired its first English-language journalist, Afshin Rattansi, from the BBC's *Today Programme*.

Al Jazeera has earned its spurs on the frontline of journalism and is today the most widely watched news channel in the Middle East. In November 2006 a 24-hour, seven-day-a-week news channel called Al Jazeera English was launched and it currently broadcasts to more than 260 million households in more than 130 countries. It has won many international awards for risk-taking journalism both on TV and through its website (www.aljazeera.net, in Arabic, and aljazeera.com – with more than 20 million visits every month), which was launched in January 2001. In 2012 Al Jazeera won the prestigious Royal Television Society Award for news channel of the year.

and goings of even that great empire made little impression on Qatar's sands of time, metaphorically or physically. Indeed, what is remarkable about the history of Qatar is not what has been left behind but the almost magical erasure of any visible sign of the 6000 years of its human evolution.

Al Thani Family Dynasty and the British

The transience of historical record changes in the mid-18th century with the arrival of the ruling Al Thani family. Al Khalifa (the current ruling family of Bahrain) controlled much of the peninsula until the arrival, in the mid-18th century, of the charismatic Al Thani family, which remains in power to this day.

Al Thani is a branch of the ancient Tamim tribe of central Arabia. Originally they were nomadic Bedu, but the region's sparse vegetation led them to settle in the peninsula's coastal areas around Zubara, where they fished and dived for pearls. The first Al Thani emir, Sheikh Mohammed bin Thani, established his capital at Al Bida in the mid-19th century, thereby laying the foundations of modern Doha.

Sheikh Mohammed strengthened his position against other local tribes by signing a treaty with the British in 1867. In 1872 the second Al Thani emir, Jasim, signed a treaty with the Turks allowing them to build a garrison in Doha (Doha Fort). The Turks were expelled under the third Al Thani emir, Sheikh Abdullah (the emir who lived in the palace that now houses the National Museum), after Turkey entered WWI on the opposite side to Britain. Thereafter, the British guaranteed Qatar's protection in exchange for a promise that the ruler would not deal with other foreign powers without British permission – an agreement that endured until independence was proclaimed on 1 September 1971.

Rags to Oil Riches

Qatar's history from WWI to the end of the 20th century reads rather like a fairy tale. Life in Qatar, even before the collapse of the pearl market in the 1930s, was marked by widespread poverty, malnutrition and disease. The arrival of oil prospectors and the establishment in 1935 of Petroleum Development Qatar, a forerunner to today's state-run Qatar General Petroleum Corporation (QGPC), signalled the beginning of a brave new world, even though WWII delayed production of oil for another 10 years.

Although not huge in comparative terms, the oil revenue instantly turned the tiny, impoverished population into citizens of one of the richest per-capita countries in the world. Qatar's first school opened in 1952 and a full-scale hospital followed in 1959, marking the beginning of long-term investment in the country's modernisation. Most of these improvements occurred under the leadership not of Sheikh Abdullah's son Ali or his grandson Ahmed but of his nephew Khalifa bin Hamad Al Thani, who, over a period of 15 years, ran many of the country's ministries, including foreign affairs, oil and the police.

On 22 February 1972 Khalifa ousted his politically apathetic kinsmen in a palace coup. Astutely, one of his first gestures was to crack down on the extravagance of the royal household. Celebrating the stability that his reign and increasing oil prices brought to Qatar, Sheikh Khalifa invested in Qatar, particularly in terms of developing an all-encompassing welfare state that provides free education and health care, job opportunities in the public sector and generous pensions for Qatari nationals.

BOOKS ABOUT QATAR

➡ *Qatar and the Arab Spring*, by Kristian Coates Ulrichsen, looks at how Qatar weathered the Arab Spring and emerged stronger than ever.

➡ *Qatar: A Modern History*, by Allen James Fromherz, is a 2012 study of Qatar's past and its modern place in the world.

➡ *Qatar: Small State, Big Politics*, by Mehran Kamrava, was published in 2015 and is the most recent book to examine Qatar's emergence as a regional power.

People

Qatar's population may seem in balance: just 25% of the population is under 25 (a far lesser proportion than other countries in the region). But that's where any sense of equilibrium ends. More than 99% of the population lives in urban areas, there are three

FRIENDSHIP CAUSEWAY

Relations between Qatar and its neighbour, Bahrain, have not always been the best. Shared royal family has been a bone of contention for one thing, and it was only relatively recently that the two countries stopped haggling over ownership of the Hawar Islands. Driven by a growing sense of community within the Gulf region, however, and with a shared mission to attract higher volumes of tourists, the two countries have at last put their differences aside. As if consolidating the friendlier relations, work is scheduled to begin on a 40km road link between Qatar and Bahrain. The scheduled (if somewhat optimistic) completion date is 2022, in time for the FIFA World Cup in Qatar, and will involve multiple bridges supported on reclaimed land – similar to King Fahd Causeway, which links Bahrain to Saudi Arabia. When complete, it will form the longest fixed link across water in the world.

Qatari males for every female and Qatari nationals make up just 40% of the population; there are almost as many immigrant workers from the Indian subcontinent in Qatar as there are locals.

Lifestyle

Despite its significant neighbour, Saudi Arabia, with which it shares a religion (the Wahhabi sect of Islam) as well as a border, Qatar has managed to steer a remarkably independent course.

While observant of a conservative form of Islam, Qataris are not afraid of extending hospitality to those of a different mind; while it is still unusual to see Qataris drinking alcohol, there is a tolerance of visitors who do, and while men and women are discreetly dressed, there's no harassment of the disrespectful tourist. Wahhabism does not preclude women from working outside the home or driving, but it does forbid any activity that may incite illicit relationships between men and women. In Qatar, unlike in Saudi Arabia, driving and working are not considered areas of likely temptation. Most significant is Qatar's press, which has enjoyed complete freedom of expression since 1995, resulting in one of the most exceptional media phenomena of modern times: the Al Jazeera independent satellite-TV channel.

In public, the country reflects the espousal of Western materialism while paradoxically retaining something of the Bedouin simplicity of life: the day can stop for tea with a stranger; the emergency exit on a plane is spread with prayer carpet; and a business dinner may be rejected in favour of kebabs with friends because in the private sphere family life lies at the heart of Qatari society.

Multiculturalism

An arriving visitor will be stamped into the country by a Qatari, but thereafter they could be forgiven for thinking they had stepped into another country – or at least pockets of many. There are car-hire attendants from Pakistan, shopkeepers from India, nightclub entertainers from the Philippines, and Brits turning pink in the afternoon sun during a day off from the oil and gas industries. Qatari men are recognisable in the multiethnic crowd by their impeccable white *thobe* (floor-length shirt-dress), *gutra* (white headdress) and long, black-tasselled *agal* (head rope), and women by their narrow-eyed *yashmak* (veil).

The broadmindedness of an otherwise conservative nation stems not only from interaction with the thousands of immigrant workers who have helped build the country but also from the fact that so many Qataris have travelled or studied abroad. Alas, that broadmindedness doesn't always translate into fair treatment of the immigrant population, many of whom continue to be treated as second-class citizens. This issue came to the fore in 2013 when the International Trades Union Confederation published a report claiming that 1200 workers from India and Nepal alone had died while working on construction projects associated with the 2022 FIFA World Cup. Qatar denied the accusations, but the fact remains that migrant workers very often live and work in appalling conditions that have everything and nothing to do with the glossy facade that Qatar likes to present to the world.

Arts

Although the rapid modernisation of Qatar has encouraged a certain Westernisation of culture, some distinctive elements of traditional cultural expression remain, particularly in terms of music and dance, as evident during Eid al Adha and Eid al Fitr or on social occasions such as weddings. Only a specialist is likely to pick up the nuances that distinguish Qatar's music or dance from that of other Gulf states, given their shared Bedouin inheritance, but numerous events throughout the country make Qatar one of the easier places to encounter these art forms. Check listings in the *Gulf Times*, the *Peninsula* or the *Qatar Tribune* to see what's happening where.

Interest in orchestral music is enjoying a revival with the Qatar Philharmonic Orchestra (qatarphilharmonicorchestra.org), sponsored by the charitable Qatar Foundation and playing at venues around town.

For contemporary arts and crafts, spare an hour to browse around the new galleries in Souq Waqif.

Poetry & Dance

On National Day (3 September), you may be lucky to see a troupe of male dancers performing Al Ardha in a display of patriotic affection. It's hard to know whether to call the performance a dance with words or a poem in motion, as during Al Ardha, a poet chants celebrations of horsemanship and valour while threading a path between two opposing lines of dancers, each of whom echoes a verse of the poem while fluttering his sword in the air.

Another fascinating spectacle sometimes seen on National Day is Al Qulta. Witnessing this kind of spontaneous poetry-making is remarkable for those who understand Arabic, as two facing poets improvise with great skill on a given topic. Even without knowing what is being said, the occasion is exciting, as the poets are accompanied not by instruments but by syncopated *tasfiq* (the slapping of palm to palm), while the audience gets carried away with the rhythm of the poetry.

There is a long association between the Gulf countries and those of the east coast of Africa, and an interchange of culture is an inevitable bonus of trade. One dance that reflects East Africa's more relaxed integration of the sexes is Al Lewa, performed by a mixture of men and women for pleasure.

At weddings it is a traditional mark of respect for young women, who are often daringly dressed in the absence of men in low-fronted, backless ball gowns, to dance for the bride. Today, the music is often imported from Egypt and is a sort of pan-Arabic pop, performed by men hidden

BONDING BEADS

Sit in a coffeehouse in Qatar, be present at a business meeting or watch a party of *sheesha* smokers and you will notice that they are bonded by a common activity: they are twirling a set of beads between thumb and forefinger, or flicking the entire set of 33, 66 or 99 beads around the wrist. At a party or wedding, they may even be whirling them overhead like a rattle.

These are not any old beads: they could be pearl or jade; bought in the local souq, or collected bead by bead and at great cost from around the world. Qataris favour amber beads, however, and a trip to a specialist *misbah* (prayer bead) shop in Souq Waqif will gladden the eye with strands of yellow, gold and treacle-coloured amber.

Men have carried *misbah*, traditionally threaded by women, since the early days of Islam to help in the contemplation of God. A user usually rolls each bead while reciting the names or attributes of Allah.

While many continue to use the beads for religious purposes, prayer beads in Qatar have become a social item, and if you really want to be in with the in-crowd then you'll acquire this necessary accessory. Let them sit in your pocket ready to be whipped out when the haggling gets tough or, like the 'How are you?' that can be repeated 10 times or more in the course of an evening's engagement, bring them out when a pause threatens conversation. If you let them function like a piece of intuited discourse, as well as talisman and storyteller, comforter and companion, you'll find you are holding the ultimate symbol of Qatari male bonding.

behind a screen. If lucky enough to be invited to a wedding, the visitor (strictly women only) may be treated to Al Khammary, performed by a group of masked women, or to Al Sameri, a thrilling spectacle in which the dancers gyrate their loosened hair in time with the accelerating beat.

Crafts

The traditional Bedouin skill of weaving carpets, tents, rugs and curtains was practised by modern Qataris until only about two decades ago, when machinery and cheap imports shut down the industry. Carpet wool, however, is still often prepared in the traditional way. The wool is washed and soaked in lemon juice and a crystalline mixture to remove impurities and oil, boiled for about 10 hours, dried in the sun and then dyed (often with imported dyes from India and other Gulf states). Goat hair is still used to make tents (particularly the black tents with white stripes that are now seen more readily in the garden of a wealthy villa than in the interior). Camel hair, plaited using two hands, one foot and a strangely shaped piece of wood, is used for ropes and bags. A form of basket weaving called *al-safaf* (using palm leaves and cane) is still practised in the villages.

Jewellery making is a craft that continues to thrive: while the traditional Bedouin pieces of silver and stone are now difficult to find, expert local goldsmiths and jewellers engage in centuries-old practices of sword decoration and bridal ornamentation. The *burda* (traditional Qatari cloak) is still worn in Qatar and the cuffs and sleeves are decorated by hand, using thin gold and silver threads.

GYPSUM

Look up at the door lintels or window frames of any old house or mosque in Qatar and chances are it will be decorated with a filigree of white plaster – only it isn't plaster, it's gypsum, otherwise known as calcium sulphate. Found in abundance locally, and sometimes combined with chippings of driftwood washed up on the beach, it was used to clad the exterior of houses, forts, mosques and wind towers, as an improvement on mud. Able to withstand extreme changes in temperature and humidity, this durable material lent itself to moulding and carving. Some of the abstract plant designs and geometric patterns that can be seen on important buildings across the Gulf illustrate how working with gypsum has evolved into a complex craft.

Environment

The Land

One would expect the area of a country to be finite. Not so in Qatar, where extensive reclamation programs keep adding a square kilometre or two to the total with each passing year. The area of the Qatar peninsula is generally given as 11,586 sq km – about 160km long and 55km to 80km wide – with 700km of shallow coastline. It includes one or two islands, but not the neighbouring Hawar Islands, which were a bone of contention until the International Court of Justice awarded the oil-rich islands to Bahrain in 2001. While Qatar is mostly flat, the oil-drilling area of Jebel Dukhan reaches a height of 75m.

The sand dunes to the south of the country, especially around the inland sea at Khor Al Adaid, are particularly appealing. Much of the interior, however, is marked by gravel-covered plains. This kind of desert may look completely featureless, but it's worth a closer look: rain water collects in *duhlans* (crevices), giving rise intermittently to exquisite little flowering plants. Roses even bloom in the desert, though not of the floral kind: below the *sabkha* (salt flats that lie below sea level), gypsum forms into rosettes, some measuring 20cm to 25cm across.

Wildlife

A passion for hunting, traditionally with falcons or salukis (Bedouin hunting dogs), has marked Qatar's relationship with birds (particularly the tasty bustard) and mammals, with the unsurprising consequence that there is little wildlife left.

The gazelle, oryx (Qatar's national animal) and Arabian ibex are all locally extinct, but ambitious breeding programs aim to reintroduce the animals into the wild. A herd of oryx can be seen, by permit only or while on a tour, at a private reserve near Al Shahaniya. There are also protected areas north of Al Khor for the endangered green turtle, which nests on the shore.

Altogether easier to spot, a rich and diverse number of birds (waders, ospreys, cormorants, curlews, flamingos, larks and hawks) frequent the coastal marshes and the offshore islands. A golf course may seem an unlikely birding venue, but the lush oasis of Doha Golf Club occasionally attracts the glorious golden oriole and crested crane. The mangrove plantations north of Al Khor are another good place to get the binoculars out.

Qatar's Natural History Group (www.qnhg.org) has some information on local wildlife and runs occasional excursions.

Environmental Issues

Qatar has virtually no naturally occurring fresh water and it relies increasingly upon hugely expensive desalination plants for its burgeoning water needs. And what little water there is may be getting harder to find. Qatar is now 2m higher than it was 400 years ago thanks to 'geological uplift', a phenomenon by which movements in the Earth's crust push the bedrock up. As a result, the underground water table sinks, or at least becomes more difficult to access. In Qatar, uplift has resulted in increasing aridity and sparseness of vegetation. This, combined with encroaching areas of sand and *sabkha*, has given environmentalists much to be concerned about.

Qatar's mangrove wetlands, which provide a breeding ground for waders and crustaceans such as shrimps, are threatened by the multiple hazards of grazing camels, oil seepage and land reclamation. Various projects are afoot to protect this important coastal habitat, including the replanting of mangroves north of Al Khor, but there are no official nature reserves as yet.

SURVIVAL GUIDE

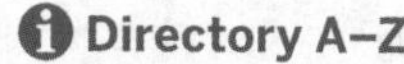

Directory A–Z

ACCOMMODATION

Qatar's main sights are all within day-trip distance of the capital. Unless you plan on camping out overnight in the desert (something you'll need to arrange through a travel agency), your best bet is to stay in Doha or neighbouring West Bay and West Bay Lagoon, where the choice of accommodation is exceptional, with boutique hotels carved from traditional buildings in the souq and five-star temples to luxury in the city's skyscrapers. There's even an offshore resort...

> **SLEEPING PRICE RANGES**
>
> The following price ranges refer to a double room with bathroom and air-con in high season (November to March). Taxes are included in the price.
>
> **$** less than QR500 (US$140)
>
> **$$** QR500–QR1000 (US$140–US$280)
>
> **$$$** more than QR1000 (US$280)

A few things to consider:

- As a general rule, Doha's budget accommodation is rarely suitable for Western travellers and never so for women. As a bare minimum, count on paying QR350/450 per night for a single/double room.
- At the lower end of the midrange category, expect carpet, minibar, satellite TV and a view of something other than an internal stairwell. Some of the upper-midrange places are world class.
- Qatar has some of the world's best top-end accommodation. Most offer weekend (Friday and Saturday) specials and other deals in association with selected airlines.
- 'Wild camping' is possible in some parts of the country, but you will need to be self-sufficient and preferably have a 4WD to gain access to beaches or sand dunes. Basic camping equipment is available from Carrefour in the City Centre Doha mall.

ACTIVITIES

Beaches

The coast of Qatar is almost a continuous line of sandy beaches with pockets of limestone pavement. As pretty as it looks, the sea is very shallow, making it almost impossible to swim. There are some good beaches, however, at the top resorts in Doha, at **Sealine Beach Resort** (p242) near Mesaieed and at **Al Ghariya Resort** (p244). The nearest public-access beach close to Doha is at **Katara** (p231). None of the wild beaches have facilities, and lack of shade is a problem in summer.

> **EATING PRICE RANGES**
>
> The following price ranges refer to a standard main course. Service charge and tax are included in the price.
>
> **$** less than QR50 (US$14)
>
> **$$** QR50–QR150 (US$14–US$40)
>
> **$$$** more than QR150 (US$40)

SAFETY

Many Western visitors have been deterred from coming to the Gulf on account of the hostilities in the Middle East and unrest in neighbouring Bahrain. Qatar, however, is one of the safest and most politically stable countries to visit and it experiences minimal crime.

The poor quality of driving is the only danger worth pointing out, especially as intolerant local drivers are not very cautious about pedestrians.

For those hiring a 4WD, beware the pockets of soft sand and *sabkha* (salt flats) around the coast and in the interior that are not always apparent until it's too late. Drivers should always stick to tracks when going off-road and make sure they have all the necessary equipment (water, tow rope, jack, spare tyre etc) for an emergency, as passing cars are sometimes few and far between, especially in the interior.

Sand Sports

The sand is beginning to attract people to Qatar in the same way that the snow draws the crowds elsewhere, with sand skiing, quad-bike racing and sand-dune driving all becoming popular sports, though largely for those with their own equipment. The **Sealine Beach Resort** (p242), south of Mesaieed, is the best place for these activities, offering quad bikes and helpful assistance if you get stuck. For 4WD trips into the dunes, contact any tour agency or pitch up at Sealine.

CUSTOMS REGULATIONS

No alcohol, narcotics or pork-related products may be brought in through customs – and no pornography from back home. Goods originating from Israel may also pose problems if you're stopped by customs.

EMBASSIES & CONSULATES

Most embassies are in the 'Diplomatic Area', north of the Sheraton Doha Hotel & Resort.

Bahraini Embassy (Map p228; ☎44 839 360; www.mofa.gov.bh/doha/Home.aspx; ⏲8-11am Sun-Thu)

French Embassy (Map p228; ☎44 021 777; www.ambafrance-qa.org; Al Corniche, West Bay Diplomatic Area; ⏲8am-noon Sun-Thu)

German Embassy (Map p228; ☎44 082 300; www.doha.diplo.de; Al Jezira Al Arabiyya St; ⏲8am-noon Sun-Thu)

Kuwaiti Embassy (Map p228; ☎44 832 111; kweqatar@kuwaitembassy.com.qa; Diplomatic St, West Bay Diplomatic Area; ⏲8-11am Sun-Thu)

Omani Embassy (Map p228; ☎44 931 910; doha@mofa.gov.om; C Ring Rd; ⏲8-11am Sun-Thu)

Saudi Arabian Embassy (Map p228; ☎44 832 030; Diplomatic St, West Bay Diplomatic Area; ⏲8-11am Sun-Thu)

UAE Embassy (Map p228; ☎44 838 880; www.uae-embassy.ae/embassies/qa; ⏲8am-noon Sun-Thu) Off Al Khor St.

UK Embassy (Map p228; ☎44 962 000; www.gov.uk/government/world/organisations/british-embassy-doha; Onaiza, Dafna Area; ⏲11am-2pm Sun & 8-10am Mon-Thu)

US Embassy (Map p228; ☎44 966 000; www.qatar.usembassy.gov; 22 February St; ⏲7-10am Sun-Thu)

INTERNET ACCESS

There's (usually free) wi-fi at most hotels, some restaurants, and the Museum of Islamic Art.

MONEY

The currency of Qatar is the Qatari riyal (QR). One riyal is divided into 100 dirhams. Coins are worth 25 or 50 dirhams, and notes come in one-, five-, 10-, 50-, 100- and 500-riyal denominations. The Qatari riyal is fully convertible.

ATMs & Credit Cards

All major credit and debit cards are accepted in large shops. Visa (Plus and Electron), MasterCard and Cirrus are accepted at ATMs at HSBC, the Qatar National Bank and the Commercial Bank of Qatar, which also accepts American Express (Amex) and Diners Club cards.

Moneychangers

Currencies from Bahrain, Saudi Arabia and the UAE are easy to buy and sell at banks and moneychangers. Travellers cheques can be changed at all major banks and the larger moneychangers. Moneychangers can be found around the Gold Souq area of central Doha. There is little difference in exchange rates between banks and moneychangers.

Tipping & Bargaining

A service charge is usually added to restaurant (and top-end hotel) bills. Local custom does not require that you leave a tip and, although it is certainly appreciated, there is a danger of escalating the habit to the detriment of the workers involved (some establishments reduce wages in anticipation of tips that may or may not be forthcoming). It is therefore recommended that local custom is followed, unless exceptional service or assistance warrants an exceptional gesture.

Bargaining is expected in the souqs and, although Western-style shopping centres have fixed prices, it's still worth asking for a discount in boutiques and smaller shops.

OPENING HOURS

Qataris love their 'siesta', and Doha resembles a ghost town in the early afternoon. These opening hours prevail throughout Qatar.

Banks 7.30am to 1pm Sunday to Thursday.

Government offices 7am to 2pm Sunday to Thursday.

Internet cafes 7am to midnight.

Post offices 7am to 8pm Sunday to Thursday, 8am to 11am and 5pm to 8pm Saturday.

Restaurants 11.30am to 1.30pm and 5.30pm to midnight Saturday to Thursday, 5pm to midnight Friday.

Shopping centres 10am to 10pm Saturday to Thursday, 4pm to midnight Friday.

Shops 8.30am to 12.30pm and 4pm to 9pm Saturday to Thursday, 4.30pm to 9pm Friday.

PUBLIC HOLIDAYS

In addition to the main Islamic holidays, Qatar observes the following public holidays:

Accession Day 27 June

National Day 3 September

TELEPHONE

All communications services are provided by **Ooredoo** (www.ooredoo.qa). Local calls are free, except from the blue-and-white phone booths, which charge a nominal fee. Phonecards (which come in denominations of QR10, QR30 and QR50) are available in bookshops and supermarkets around Doha and can be used for direct international dialling.

The cost of an International Direct Dial call is cheaper between 7pm and 7am, all day Friday and on holidays. At peak times international calls cost around QR2 per minute.

Mobile Phones

Qtel operates a prepaid GSM mobile phone service called Hala Plus. Cards in a variety of denominations are widely available in shops.

IMPORTANT PHONE NUMBERS

There are no area or city codes.

- Country code: ☎974
- International access code (to call abroad from Qatar): ☎0
- Local directory enquiries: ☎180
- International directory enquiries: ☎150

TRAVELLERS WITH DISABILITIES

Little provision has been made in Qatar for travellers with disabilities, although the new resorts have tried to make accommodation wheelchair accessible. The corniche area of Doha and the new malls are easily accessed, but many of the other sights and souqs are not. No provision is made for the visually or hearing impaired.

VISAS

- All nationalities need a visa to enter Qatar.
- Around 33 nationalities can obtain a one-month, single-entry visa on arrival.
- Click on the links on the **Hamad International Airport** (p240) website for the latest visa requirements.
- To avoid being turned back after reaching the head of a lengthy queue, fill out the application card (in piles on top of the visa counter) before you reach the visa counter.
- Payment is by credit card only.
- Multi-entry tourist and business visas are applied for through a Qatari embassy or consulate. Three passport-size photos, an application form filled out in triplicate and a letter from the hosting company is required. These visas are issued within 24 hours.
- Visa extensions valid for two weeks can be obtained through your hotel or a travel agent.
- Charges for overstaying are high.

Getting There & Away

AIR

Hamad International Airport (www.dohahamadairport.com) World-class airport and Doha's international gateway.

Qatar Airways (☎44 496 666; www.qatarairways.com; Al Matar St) National carrier Qatar Airways has transformed itself into one of the world's best airlines.

LAND

Border Crossings

Residents of Qatar, Saudi Arabia and the UAE can drive across the Qatar–Saudi Arabia border, providing they have insurance for both countries. Bear in mind that if you want to travel *from* Qatar, you must have a Saudi visa in advance.

Bus

Saudi Arabian Public Transport Co (Saptco; www.saptco.com.sa) From Doha, Saptco has daily buses (from QR50 to QR150 depending on destination) to Dammam (Saudi Arabia) with onward connections to Riyadh (Saudi Arabia), Manama (Bahrain), Abu Dhabi and Dubai (UAE), and Kuwait City (Kuwait).

PRACTICALITIES

Magazines *Marhaba, Qatar's Premier Information Guide*, published quarterly, is an excellent source of information regarding events in Qatar, and includes some interesting feature articles on Qatari life and culture. It costs QR20. *Time Out Doha* gives the most comprehensive listings for dining and entertainment.

Newspapers Qatar's English-language newspapers, the *Gulf Times* and the *Peninsula*, are published daily, except Friday. International newspapers and magazines are available one or two days after publication at major bookshops in Doha.

Radio Programs in English are broadcast on 97.5FM and 102.6FM each afternoon from 1.15pm until 4pm. The BBC is available on 107.4FM.

TV Channel 2 on Qatar TV (QTV) broadcasts programs in English, and international satellite channels are available at the majority of hotels. The renowned Al Jazeera Satellite Channel is broadcast in English and Arabic from Doha: it has become one of the most watched and most respected news channels in the Arab world.

Weights & Measures Qatar uses the metric system.

Getting Around

The Qataris have big plans for transport around the island. Once Doha's urban Metro system is complete, there are plans for a rail system that connects most of Qatar's population centres.

BUS

The public bus system operates from the central **Al Ghanim Bus Station** (p241), with air-conditioned services to Al Khor, Al Wakara and Masaieed among other destinations. Prices range from QR3 to QR10.

CAR & MOTORCYCLE

If you're driving around Doha, you'll discover that roundabouts are very common, treated like camel-race tracks and often redundant in practice. Finding the right way out of Doha can also be difficult: if you're heading south towards Al Wakrah or Mesaieed, take the airport road (Al Matar St); the main road to all points north is 22 February St (north from Al Rayyan Rd); if you're heading west, continue along Al Rayyan Rd.

- Driving in Qatar is on the right-hand side.
- Numerous petrol stations are located around Doha, but there are few along the highways.
- Authorities are strict with anyone caught speeding, not wearing a seat belt or not carrying a driving licence: heavy on-the-spot fines are handed out freely.
- Don't even think about drink driving. The maximum legal blood alcohol concentration if you're behind the wheel is zero.

Hire

- A visitor can rent a car if they have a driving licence from home – but only within seven days of arriving in Qatar (although expats resident in other Gulf Cooperation Council (GCC) countries can drive for up to three months).
- After seven days, a temporary driving licence – issued by the Traffic Licence Office – must be obtained. It lasts for the duration of your visa and rental agencies can arrange this for you.
- The minimum rental period for all car-hire agencies is 24 hours and drivers must be at least 21 years old.
- Major agencies charge about QR150/750 per day/week for the smallest car.
- The cost of a 4WD can be very high (around QR500/3000 per day/week); an ordinary car is perfectly suitable for reaching most of Qatar's attractions, with the exception of Khor Al Adaid and some of the sand-dune seas.
- A 4WD is essential, however, for those wanting to explore the interior in greater depth or wishing to camp on a remote beach.
- All of the international car-rental companies have local offices in Qatar.

Al-Muftah Rent-A-Car (☎70 634 433, 44 634 433; www.rentacardoha.com; Doha International Airport; ⊙24hr) With over 40 years of experience in Doha, this is a reliable option and a cheaper local alternative to the major car-hire companies.

LOCAL TRANSPORT

Taxi

The turquoise taxis belonging to Mowasalat-Karwa offer a good service, charging QR4 plus QR1.800 for each subsequent kilometre.

The easiest way to catch a taxi is to ask your hotel to arrange one, although technically you can wave one down from the side of the road. To visit most sights outside Doha, it's better to hire a car or arrange transport with a tour company as it usually works out considerably cheaper and it saves long waits for return transport.

Saudi Arabia
المملكة العربية السعودية

Includes ➡

Best Places for Culture

- ➡ Madain Saleh (p277)
- ➡ National Museum (p257)
- ➡ Old Dir'aiyah (p264)
- ➡ Old Jeddah (p268)
- ➡ Camel market & races (p263)

Best Places for Nature

- ➡ Red Sea Diving, Yanbu (p273)
- ➡ Al Wajh (p283)
- ➡ Al Nu'man Island (p283)
- ➡ Jebel Al Lawz (p284)
- ➡ Red Sands (p266)

Why Go?

The birthplace and spiritual home of Islam, Saudi Arabia is as rich in attractions as it is in stirring symbolism. It is also one of the most difficult places on Earth to visit.

For those who do get in, rock-hewn Madain Saleh is Arabia's greatest treasure. Other wonders abound, from the echoes of TE Lawrence along the Hejaz Railway to the mud-brick ruins of Dir'aiyah. Fascinating Riyadh is a showpiece for modern Saudi Arabia, Jeddah blends ancient and modern and has an enchanting old city made of coral, while the Red Sea coast has world-class diving. And for Muslim travellers, Mecca and Medina represent the most sacred destination you can imagine.

There are few places left that can be said to represent the last frontier of tourism. Whether you're an expat or a pilgrim, Saudi Arabia is one of them.

When to Go

Saudi Arabia

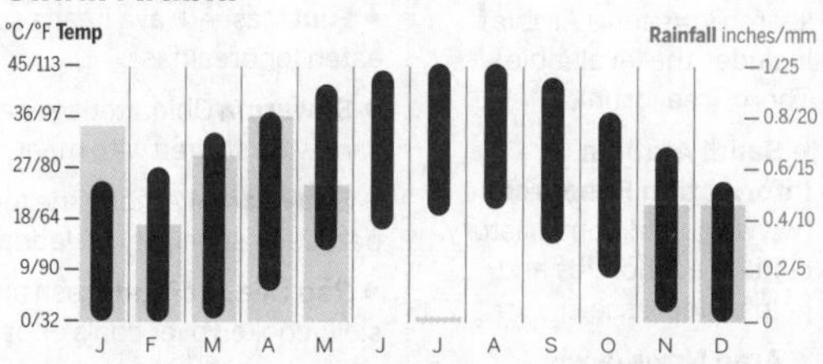

Nov–Mar Cooler temperatures make daytime weather bearable and nights surprisingly chilly.

Apr–Oct Daily temperatures above 40°C, high humidity along the coast; Ramadan; April sandstorms.

Year round Red Sea diving has excellent visibility all year, but in summer morning dives are best.

FAST FACTS

- **Capital** Riyadh
- **Area** 2,149,690 sq km
- **Population** 27.8 million
- **Country code** ☎966

At a Glance

- **Currency**: Saudi riyal (SR)
- **Money**: ATMs widespread, credit cards widely accepted
- **Visas**: Only business visas possible (no tourist visas)
- **Mobile phones**: GSM phone network widespread

Exchange Rates

Australia	A$1	SR2.73
Canada	C$1	SR2.91
Euro zone	€1	SR4.26
Japan	¥100	SR3.14
New Zealand	NZ$1	SR2.56
UK	£1	SR5.80
USA	US$1	SR3.75

Resources

- **Lonely Planet** (www.lonelyplanet.com/search?q=saudi+Arabia) Includes the invaluable Thorn Tree forum.
- **Saudi Arabian Information Resources** (www.saudinf.com) History, culture, economics and helpful addresses.
- **Arab News** (www.arabnews.com) Up-to-the-minute news from a Saudi perspective.

Daily Costs

Saudi Arabia isn't a budget destination. Eating well for SR50 to SR75 per day is rarely a problem, but few budget hotels accept Westerners – expect to pay at least SR500 for a double in a decent midrange hotel. It is, of course, easy to pay much more than this for both food and accommodation; a more realistic midrange budget, once you factor in transport, is around SR1000 per day.

ITINERARIES

One Week

Begin in Riyadh, with a couple of days exploring the modern architecture, Masmak Fortress, the National Museum and the nearby camel races. On the third day, factor in an afternoon at Dir'aiyah and camp in the Red Sands. Fly to Medina and drive, with one or two stops along the Hejaz Railway en route, to Al Ula; spend a day amid the wonderful Nabataean ruins of Madain Saleh. Fly down to Jeddah, Saudi Arabia's most beguiling city, and lose yourself in the souqs and coral houses of Old Jeddah and a stroll along the corniche.

Two Weeks

With an extra week, head for the hills (especially in summer) of pretty Taif; make it a weekend if you want to catch the camel races. Then allow for a couple of days' diving around Yanbu before continuing your way north along the Red Sea coast, with numerous fine beaches to pause in along the way. Then cut inland to Tabuk in the Kingdom's far north, one of Saudi Arabia's most intriguing cities.

Essential Food & Drink

- **Mezze** Truly one of the joys of Arab cooking and similar in conception to Spanish tapas, with infinite possibilities.
- **Fuul** Mashed fava beans served with olive oil and often eaten for breakfast.
- **Shwarma** Ubiquitous kebab- or souvlaki-style pita sandwich stuffed with meat.
- **Baby camel** Among the tenderest of Saudi meats, it's a particular speciality of Jeddah and the Hejaz.
- **Red Sea seafood** Fresh and varied and at its best when slow-cooked over coals or baked in the oven; try *samak mashwi* (fish basted in a date puree and barbecued over hot coals).
- **Khouzi** A Bedouin dish of lamb stuffed with rice, nuts, onions, sultanas, spices, eggs and a whole chicken.

RIYADH الرياض

POP 5.3 MILLION

Once a walled, mud-brick way station along desert trading routes, Riyadh ('The Garden') is the Kingdom's political, financial and administrative capital and one of the wealthiest cities in the world. It also has a very Saudi subtext: nowhere are the contradictions of modern Saudi Arabia more evident than in Riyadh. Seen from afar, soaring, sparkling, stunning modern towers rise above the desert and shiny 4WDs throng modern highways. Up close, Riyadh is cautious and sober (certainly compared to Jeddah), not to mention conservative and deeply rooted in Saudi traditions. Throw in fine hotels and restaurants and some excellent sights, and it's a fascinating place to spend a few days.

> **WARNING**
>
> At the time of research and writing most of Saudi Arabia's Eastern Province and the Kingdom's southwest (including Abha and Najran) were considered off-limits to travellers. For this reason, we have not updated our coverage of these places.

Sights

Riyadh's architecture is mostly modern, including contemporary high-rise towers, but Al Diriyah district, the nucleus of the city, has been rebuilt in a style meant to evoke the old mud-brick buildings of the pre-20th century.

National Museum MUSEUM

(King Abdul Aziz Museum; Map p260; ☎01-402 9500 ext 2030; www.nationalmuseum.org.sa; King Saud Rd; adult/child SR10/free; ⏰men 8am-noon Sun, Tue & Thu, women & families 8am-noon Mon & Wed, open to all noon-2pm Sun, noon-2pm & 4-8pm Mon-Thu, 4-8pm Fri, 9am-1pm & 4-8pm Sat) This state-of-the-art museum is one of the finest in the Middle East. Encased within modernist architecture, it*s two floors contain eight well-designed and informative galleries covering Arabian history, culture and art. The galleries beautifully display evocative rock carvings, engaging models and a full-scale reconstruction of a Nabataean tomb from Madain Saleh. Films (in English via headphones) shown on 180-degree screens complement the exhibits, as do virtual visits to sites and other excellent interactive displays.

Masmak Fortress HISTORIC SITE

(Qasr Al Masmak; Map p262; ☎01-411 0091; Al Imam Turki Ibn Abdullah Ibn Muhammad St, Al Diriyah; ⏰men 8am-2.30pm & 4-9pm Sun, Tue & Thu, 9am-noon Sat, women & families 8am-2.30pm & 4-9pm Mon & Wed, 4-7.30pm Fri & Sat) FREE It's a scene out of the movies: a big fortress representing an empire. Surrounded by sand, this squat fortification was built around 1865 and was the site of Ibn Saud's daring 1902 raid, during which a spear was hurled at the main entrance door with such force that the head still lodges in the doorway. Highlights among the exhibits include maps and a fascinating range of photographs of Saudi dating from 1912 to 1937 in galleries converted from *diwans* (living rooms).

The roofs are covered with painted palm-tree, taramic and ethel wood and exude an old-world charm that evokes an Arabian painting. Inside, the information panels and short, chest-thumping films on the storming of the fortress and the 'reunification' of Saudi Arabia are reverential towards the Al Sauds but worth watching nonetheless.

Al Faisaliah Tower BUILDING

(Map p260; ☎01-273 3000; www.rosewoodhotels.com; King Fahd Rd; viewing platform adult/child SR60/free; ⏰11am-11pm) Designed by British architect Norman Foster and built in 2000 by the Bin Laden construction company, Al Faisaliah Tower was the first of the startling new structures to rise above Riyadh's skyline. It's most famous for its enormous glass globe (24m in diameter and made of 655 glass panels) near the summit. Its 44 floors contain a five-star deluxe hotel and four exclusive restaurants, offices, apartments, the Sky shopping mall (p263) and a fabulous viewing platform (Globe Experience).

The needlepoint pinnacle (with a crescent on the tip) sits 267m above the ground. The tower is off Olaya St.

Kingdom Center BUILDING

(Map p260; ☎01-211 2222; kingdomcentre.com.sa; Olaya St) Riyadh's landmark tower is a stunning piece of modern architecture – it's particularly conspicuous at night, when the upper sweep is lit with constantly changing coloured lights. Rising 302m high, its most distinctive feature is the steel-and-glass 300-ton bridge connecting the two towers. High-speed elevators fly you (at 180km/h) to the 99th-floor **Sky Bridge** (Map p260; ☎01-201

Saudi Arabia Highlights

1. Marvelling at **Madain Saleh** (p278), the 'other Petra', with its evocative tombs in a sublime desert setting.
2. Diving the dazzling depths of Saudi's Red Sea and spotting sharks, sea turtles and stunning coral reefs at **Yanbu** (p273).
3. Meandering among the old merchants' houses, ancient markets and myriad museums of Jeddah's **old city** (p268) and enjoying delicious coffee and conversation along the **corniche** (p266).
4. Wandering the mud-brick ruins of **Dir'aiyah** (p264), a Unesco site and birthplace of modern Saudi Arabia.
5. Listening for the ghost of TE Lawrence along the **Hejaz Railway** (p279).
6. Escaping the summer heat like a Gulf Arab and heading for the hills of **Taif** (p271).
7. Finding the perfect Red Sea beach and having it all to yourself at **Al Wajh** (p283).
8. Taking in one of Arabia's best-kept secrets by visiting **Tabuk** (p279).

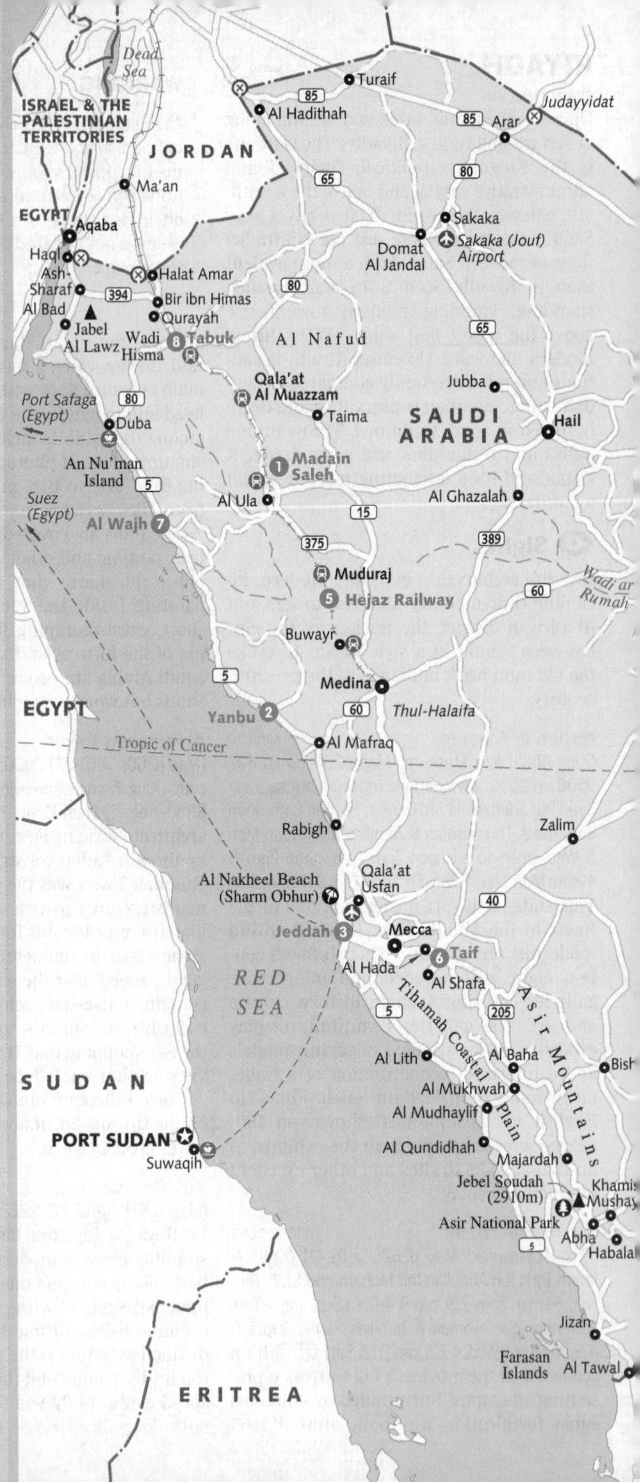

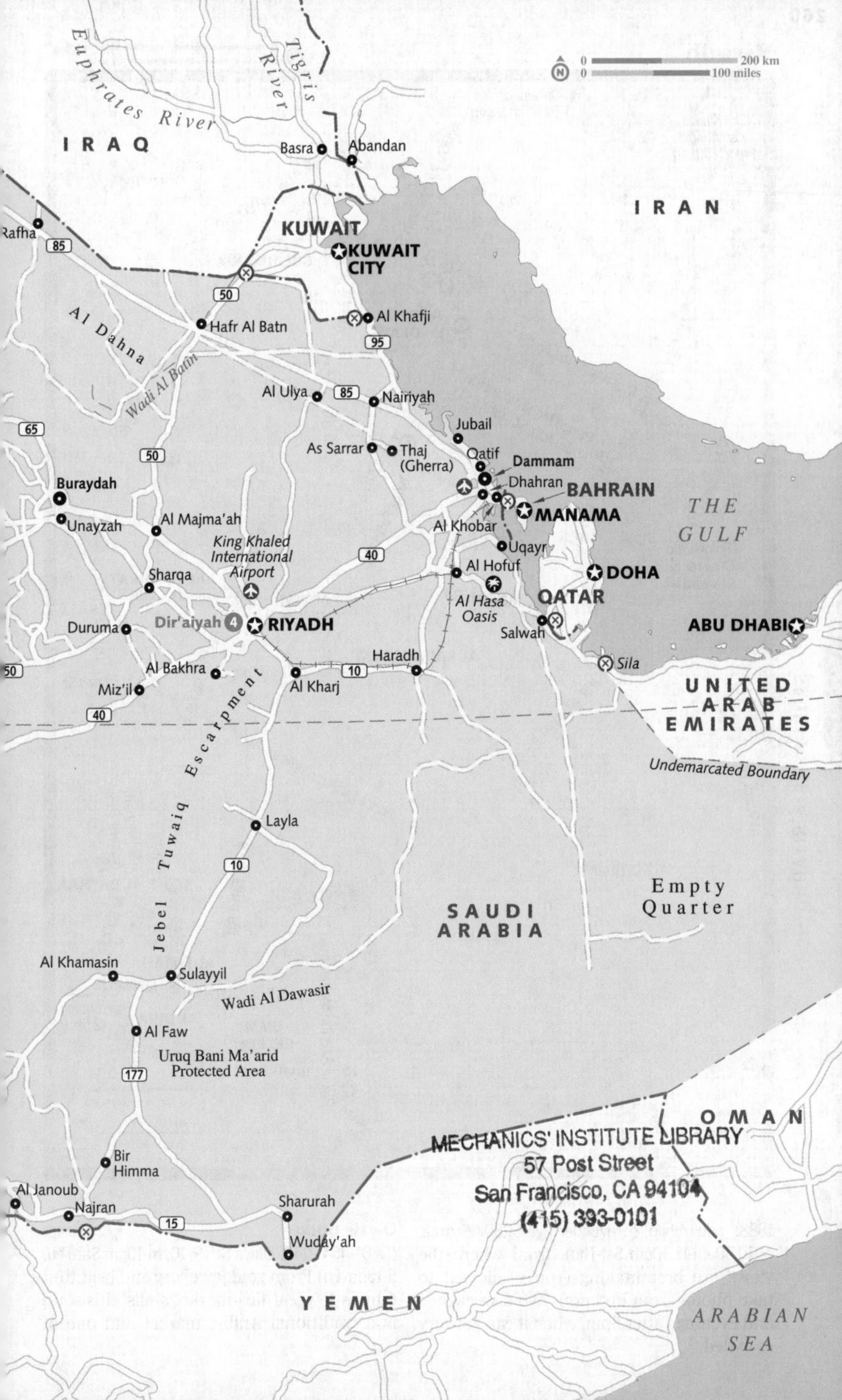

0 200 km
0 100 miles
Euphrates River
Tigris River
IRAQ
Basra
Abandan
IRAN
Rafha
85
KUWAIT
KUWAIT CITY
50
Al Khafji
Hafr Al Batn
95
Al Dahna
Wadi Al Batin
Al Ulya
85
Nairiyah
Jubail
65
50
As Sarrar
Thaj (Gherra)
Qatif
Dammam
Dhahran
BAHRAIN
MANAMA
THE GULF
Buraydah
Unayzah
Al Majma'ah
Al Khobar
King Khaled International Airport
Uqayr
40
Al Hofuf
DOHA
Sharqa
Al Hasa Oasis
QATAR
Dir'aiyah
4
RIYADH
Salwah
ABU DHABI
Duruma
50
Al Bakhra
Haradh
10
Sila
Miz'il
Al Kharj
UNITED ARAB EMIRATES
40
Tuwaiq Escarpment
Undemarcated Boundary
Layla
10
Jebel
Empty Quarter
SAUDI ARABIA
Al Khamasin
Sulayyil
Wadi Al Dawasir
Al Faw
Uruq Bani Ma'arid Protected Area
177
OMAN
Bir Himma
Al Janoub
Najran
Sharurah
15
Wuday'ah
YEMEN
ARABIAN SEA

Riyadh

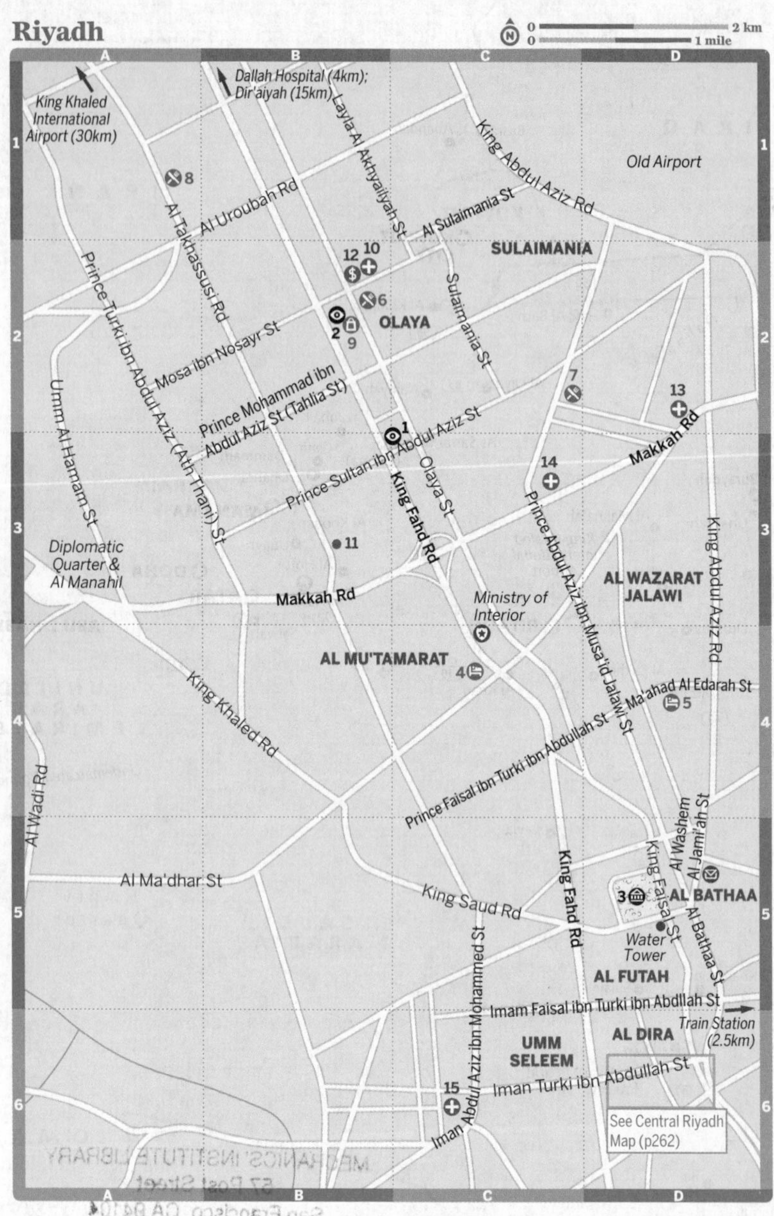

1888; adult/child 2-9yr/under 2yr SR60/20/free; ⏲10.30am-11.30pm Sat-Thu), from where the views are breathtaking (you're allowed to take photos from up here). Avoid weekends and evenings after 6pm, when it can get very crowded.

Owais Souq MARKET

(✆01-454 2146; Olaya St; ⏲10am-10pm Sat-Thu, 5-10pm Fri) From gold jewellery and beautiful fabrics to great flea-market stalls, this souq is a traditional Arabic market and one of

Riyadh

Sights

1	Al Faisaliah Tower	C3
2	Kingdom Center	B2
3	National Museum	D5
	Sky Bridge	(see 2)

Sleeping

	Al Faisaliah Hotel	(see 1)
	Al Khozama Hotel	(see 1)
4	Riyadh Intercontinental Hotel	C4
5	Riyadh Palace Hotel	D4

Eating

6	Ata bin Ali Restaurant	B2
	Globe	(see 1)
7	Mama Noura	C2
8	Najd Village	A1
	Spazio 77	(see 2)

Shopping

9	Jarir Bookstore	B2
	Sky Shopping Mall	(see 1)

Information

10	24-Hour Pharmacy	B2
11	Al Tayyar	B3
12	Arab National Bank	B2
13	Armed Forces Hospital	D2
14	King Fahd Medical City	C3
15	Riyadh Central Hospital	C6
	Saudi American Bank	(see 2)

the most popular among locals. Bargaining is a must.

Riyadh Zoo ZOO
(☎01-477 9523; Mosab bin Umair, Al Malaz; adult/child SR10/5; ⏲variable) The largest zoo in Saudi Arabia began in 1957 as a small-scale zoo that housed animals gifted to members of the Al Saud ruling clan. Refurbished and opened to the public in 1987, its highlights include the houbara bustard, which is almost extinct in the wild in Saudi Arabia. Opening hours are complicated and vary with prayer times – ring ahead for details.

Late afternoon is the best time to visit, when the weather is cooler. Kids can sit in the mini train rides designed for entertainment.

Antiquities Museum MUSEUM
(☎01-467 5063; King Saud University, Prince Abdullah St; ⏲8am-2pm Sat-Thu) This museum belongs to the College of Tourism and Antiquities at King Saud University and is home to objects discovered during the Faw and Rabdha excavations (archaeological sites in southern and northern Saudi Arabia respectively) that were carried out by the university. The collection also includes inscriptions, writings, porcelain, pottery, jewellery, coins, statues, frescos and more.

Festivals & Events

Jenadriyah National Festival CULTURAL
(janadria.org.sa; ⏲late Feb or early Mar) Saudi Arabia's largest cultural festival runs over two weeks at Al Janadriyah heritage village, 42km northeast of Riyadh. Commencing with the King's Cup (an epic camel race with up to 2000 participants racing across a 19km track), the program includes traditional songs, dances and poetry competitions, as well as demonstrations of falconry and exhibitions of traditional crafts from around the Kingdom.

Sleeping

Riyadh's hotels fill up during the week with business travellers. Things are quieter at weekends. Most budget hotels won't accept bookings from non-Arabs.

Al Khozama Hotel HOTEL **$$**
(Map p260; ☎01-465 4650; www.alkhozamahotels.com; Al Faisaliah Tower, Olaya St; r from SR750; @ ≋) Though the rooms here aren't large, they are comfortable, well furnished and squarely aimed at the modern business traveller. With a lively lobby, a good patisserie and two reputable restaurants, it's a popular choice.

Riyadh Palace Hotel HOTEL **$$**
(Map p260; ☎01-405 4444; www.riyadhpalacehotel.com; Al Amir Abdul Bahman Ibn Abdul St, Ministries Area; r from SR750; P @ ≋) The decor here is a little tired, but it's actually not a bad place to stay. The rooms are good sized, the staff is very friendly and there is no restriction on foreign women dining in the main restaurant. Al Amir Abdul Bahman Ibn Abdul St is off Al Bathaa St.

★**Ritz-Carlton Riyadh** HOTEL **$$$**
(☎01-802 8020; www.ritzcarlton.com; Mecca Rd, Al Hada; r from SR1500; P @ ≋ ≋) With 210,000 sq m of lavishly landscaped gardens, a panoramic view and a Hollywood-like driveway, not to mention the gold and mahogany interiors and lavish dining halls, the Ritz-Carlton is a reminder of the time when guests of the royal family spent their days here. There's also a bowling alley, five restaurants and an exclusive spa for men.

Central Riyadh

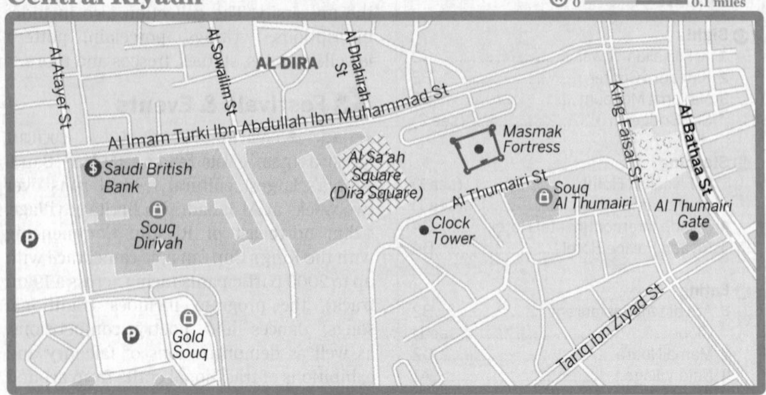

Riyadh Intercontinental Hotel HOTEL $$$
(Map p260; ☎01-465 5000; www.intercontinental.com; Al Ma'dhar St; r from SR1400; P@☜≋) Many rooms at the luxurious InterContinental feature fine city or golf-course views. There's a nine-hole course on site, a 12-lane bowling alley, a gym, a sauna, tennis and racquetball courts, and indoor and outdoor pools. The hotel's two restaurants are popular dining venues, or visit the Addiwan Tea Lounge for a snack, coffee or afternoon tea.

Al Faisaliah Hotel HOTEL $$$
(Map p260; ☎01-273 2000; www.rosewoodhotels.com; Al Faisaliah Tower, Olaya St; r from SR1500; P@☜≋) All the details of a fabulous modern hotel are present at Al Faisaliah, including fresh orchids and chocolates delivered daily to your room and your own butler 24 hours a day. Il Terrazzo restaurant enjoys a fine reputation and the hotel is hugely popular with Riyadh's upper crust for celebrating weddings and birthdays.

Eating

Riyadh is full of eating choices, from *shwarma* (spit-roasted meat in a pocket of pita-type bread) stands along Prince Mohammad ibn Abdul Aziz St (Tahlia St) to fine-dining choices at five-star hotels around town.

Mama Noura MIDDLE EASTERN $
(Map p260; ☎01-470 8881; King Abdullah Branch Rd, Ar Rahmaniyah; mains SR13-30; ⏲6am-3.30am) Large, bright and clean, this Turkish place remains perennially popular among Riyadhis, who come for the succulent *shwarma* (sandwich/plate SR4/12) or famous felafel (SR4 to SR15). There's no family section, but takeaway is possible.

★Najd Village MIDDLE EASTERN $$
(Map p260; ☎01-464 6530; Al Takhassusi Rd; mains SR15-30; ⏲noon-midnight) Serving Saudi food in a Saudi setting (designed like a central-region village), this place is almost unique in the Kingdom. It's the perfect place to sample *kasba* (meat with rice) or the Najd-region speciality, *hashi* (baby camel). The set menu (SR100; minimum five people) includes 14 mains, coffee, dates and *bachoor* (incense). Friday is the only day when families are welcome. Prices are reasonable and it's much loved by locals.

★Ata bin Ali Restaurant MIDDLE EASTERN $$
(Map p260; ☎01-219 7676; Prince Sultan bin Abdul Aziz St, Al Olaya; mains SR30-50; ⏲1pm-12.30am Sun-Thu, from 1.30pm Fri & Sat) Ata bin Ali comes from the heart of Jordan, bringing to Riyadh all the delicious traditional food of the region as cooked at home. Not surprisingly, it's extremely popular with locals and deservedly so.

★Globe INTERNATIONAL $$$
(Map p260; ☎01-273 2222; www.rosewoodhotels.com; Al Faisaliah Tower; mains from SR100; ⏲noon-2.30pm & 8pm-12.30am) One of five restaurants in Al Faisaliah Tower, Globe is one of the most romantic spots in town. Cosy, dimly lit and with spectacular views, this is one of the best restaurants in Riyadh.

Spazio 77 INTERNATIONAL $$$
(Map p260; ☎01-211 1888; www.spazio77.com; Kingdom Tower; mains from SR100; ⏲10am-1am Sat-Thu, 1pm-1am Fri) Located in the nook of

the 'necklace' of the Kingdom Tower, Spazio 77 is a brasserie, coffeehouse, sushi bar, cigar bar and oxygen bar. Michelin-starred French chef Alain Solivérès oversees the kitchen, but there's a family-friendly Friday buffet. It's where the great and good (presidents and the like) come when in town.

Shopping

In a country where public diversions are few, shopping has become a national sport.

With more designer outlets than you can shake a Gold Amex card at, **Kingdom Tower** (☎01-211 2222; Al Mamlaka Mall; ⏲9am-noon & 4-11pm Sat-Thu, 4-11pm Fri) even has a floor for women only (Ladies' Kingdom), and the **Sky Shopping Mall** (Map p260; ☎01-273 0000; ⏲10am-11.30pm Sat-Thu, noon-11.30pm Fri) in Al Faisaliah Tower is also popular.

Souq Al Thumairi HANDICRAFTS
(Map p262; Al Thumairi St; ⏲9am-noon & 4-9pm Sat-Thu, 4-9pm Fri) For authentic handicrafts, head to Souq Al Thumairi, immediately south of Masmak Fortress in the Al Diriyah area. The shops in the small lanes offer everything from carpets to coffee pots, silver daggers to silver jewellery.

Jarir Bookstore BOOKS
(Map p260; ☎01-462 6000; www.jarir.com; Olaya St; ⏲9am-2pm & 4-11pm Sat-Thu, 4-11pm Fri) The excellent Jarir Bookstore has extensive selections in Arabic and English. This branch is the most accessible.

Information

EMERGENCY

Emergency (☎112)
Ambulance (☎997)
Fire (☎998)
Police (☎999)
Traffic Accidents (☎993)

INTERNET ACCESS

There are loads of internet cafes across Riyadh and the restrictions on foreign women using them seem to have relaxed. Most hotels and chain coffee shops offer free wi-fi.

MEDICAL SERVICES

24-Hour Pharmacy (Map p260; Mosa ibn Nosayr St; ⏲24hr) In Al Akariya Centre.

Dallah Hospital (☎9200 12222, 01-454 5277; cnr King Fahd & Al Imam Saud ibn Abdul Aziz ibn Mohammad Rds) This hospital northeast of Riyadh accepts emergency cases on a walk-in basis.

TO/FROM RIYADH

DESTINATION	AIR	BUS
Jeddah	17 daily flights from SR280	12 daily, SR150
Al Ula	Mon & Sat, from SR280	2 daily, SR190
Taif	3 daily flights, SR250	over 10 daily, SR125

TRAVEL AGENCIES

Al Tayyar (Map p260; ☎9200 12333; www.altayyargroup.com; Al Takhassusi Rd; ⏲9am-1.30pm & 4.30-8pm Sat-Thu) The largest travel company in the Kingdom and one of the most reputable, Al Tayyar can organise car hire, air tickets, accommodation and tours.

Getting There & Away

The **airport** (p302) is 25km north of the city centre.

Al Aziziyah Bus Station (Saptco Bus Station; ☎01-288 4400) Located 17km south of the city centre.

Getting Around

TO/FROM THE AIRPORT

Buses (SR15, every two hours) run from 8am to 10pm daily between Al Aziziyah Bus Station and the airport, via the main bus stop in Al Bathaa.

A taxi from the airport to the city centre costs around SR80 to SR100 depending on the traffic. Make sure the driver turns on the meter.

TAXI

Riyadh's white taxis charge SR10 for a journey of 1km to 2km, but always negotiate the price first.

You can also download Uber, Easy Taxi or Careem to book private taxis.

AROUND RIYADH

Camel Market & Around

Sand dunes, motorbikes and tents in the desert. Riyadh's camel market is full of Saudi men and young boys who travel to Riyadh for a traditional Hejazi experience.

Sights

Souq Al Jamal MARKET
(⏲sunrise-sunset) FREE One of the largest in the Arabian Peninsula, Riyadh's camel market is a fascinating place to wander. Late

WORTH A TRIP

JUBBA

Northwest of Riyadh, the Najd plateau is hemmed in by the Hejaz Mountains to the west, with sand deserts surrounding the other three sides. Crossing the plateau, the drive between Riyadh and Madain Saleh is mostly a long, lonely stretch of road. Fortunately, close to the midpoint is one of Saudi Arabia's more intriguing sites: Jubba.

These days Jubba is a sleepy frontier town 100km northwest of Hail, but it's rightly famous for its impressive petroglyphs (rock carvings) of prehistoric animals and is arguably the premier pre-Islamic site in the country. In 1879 intrepid British explorer Lady Anne Blunt described Jubba as 'one of the most curious places in the world, and to my mind, one of the most beautiful'.

Between 9000 and 6000 years ago this desert landscape was lush savannah grassland that supported cattle. Archaeologists have found evidence of four major periods of settlement at Jubba stretching back through the Middle Paleolithic period, 80,000 to 25,000 years ago. The finest carvings date from around 5500 BC, when much of this area was an inland lake and inhabitants carved game animals that came to the waters. Elegant rock-cut ibex and oryx abound, and there are also significant inscriptions in Thamudic (a pre-Arabic alphabet) dating to 1000 BC. Among the enigmatic stone circles are crude carvings of camels and other domesticated animals dating from AD 300.

The huge site covers 39 sq km. The closest carvings to Jubba are 3km away.

A permit from the **Director General of the Department of Antiquities** (fax 01-411 2054) at the National Museum in Riyadh is necessary to visit the site. Contact local guide and site warden **Atiq Al Shamali** (☎057 494 877): note that he speaks Arabic only, so email Hadi Abdullah (hadi1500@yahoo.com), the local English teacher, if you have any queries in advance.

The town of Hail has the nearest habitable accommodation, with the simple but adequate **Al Jabalain Hotel** (☎06-532 0402; King Abdul Aziz Rd; s/d SR250/300) and **Hotel Sahari Hail** (☎06-532 6441; King Khaled St; r SR110). Also in Hail, the **Lebanese House Restaurant** (☎06-532 6736; King Khaled St; mezze SR5, mains SR5-20; ⏲1pm-1am) is good for a meal.

Saptco (☎531 0101) has buses to Hail from Riyadh, Al Ula, Jubba and Jeddah. Schedules and fares are constantly changing, so confirm details in advance.

afternoon is when the traders really find their voices. If you want to put in a bid, you'll need a good SR5000 to SR10,000. The market is north of the Dammam road 30km from the city centre (take the Thumamah exit).

☆ Entertainment

Camel Races SPECTATOR SPORT

At 4pm on some Thursdays, camel races take place at the track along the extension of Al Uroubah St in the Thumamah district, 10.5km from Riyadh.

Dir'aiyah

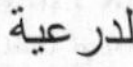

The ancestral home of the Al Saud family in Wadi Hanifa and the birthplace of the Saudi-Wahhabi union, the Turaif district in Dir'aiyah was declared a Unesco World Heritage Site in 2010 and is one of the most evocative places in the Kingdom. Since receiving Unesco recognition, the site has been closed to the public for restoration works, although special permission allows you to enter with a private guide (arranged through any travel agency) and explore the site.

The Turaif quarter, on the site's southwest, is the heart of the historic centre, while the Ghusaiba quarter was the first Saudi capital up to 1683. On the eastern bank of Wadi Hanifa a visitor centre, cultural centre and museum were also under construction at the time of research.

ℹ Getting There & Away

There's no public transport to Dir'aiyah, which is 25km northwest of Al Bathaa. A one-way taxi costs SR50, or expect to pay at least SR150 for a return taxi, including waiting time.

If driving, take King Fahd Rd north and follow the signs off to the west after passing Dallah Hospital. The road then turns north again – follow the brown signs marked 'Old Dir'aiyah'.

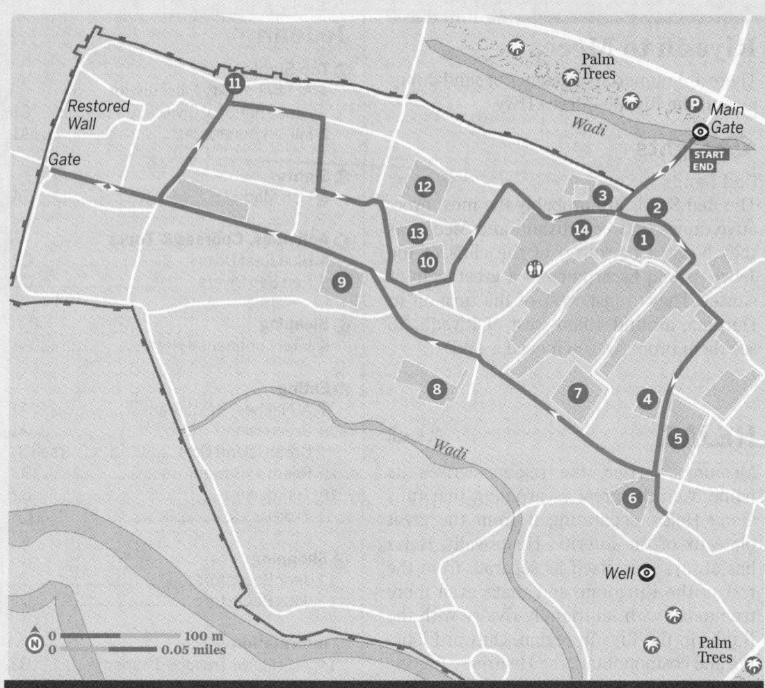

Walking Tour
Dir'aiyah

START MAIN-GATE CAR PARK
END VISITOR CENTRE
LENGTH 2KM, ONE TO TWO HOURS

As you climb up from the car park, the 1 **Palace of Salwa** – once a four-storey complex of palaces and residential and administrative buildings, and the home of Mohammed ibn Abd Al Wahhab – towers above the 2 **visitor centre** on your left. Directly opposite, the 3 **Al Saud Mosque** was once connected to the palace by a bridge.

The main path continues south, then east, then south again to the 4 **Palace of Fahd** and the 5 **Palace of Abdullah bin Saud**. Further south are the somewhat nondescript ruins of the 6 **Palace of Thunayyan bin Saud**, behind which are good views out over the palm groves.

Returning to the main path, walk west for around 250m, passing the ruined 7 **Palace of Mishaari** on the right and the newly restored 8 **Al Turaif Bath**, with its decoratively painted doors. After a further 100m to the west and northwest, respectively, you'll find the restored 9 **Palace of Nasser** and the 10 **Palace of Saad bin Saud**, which has turrets and wall and door decorations. This is how much of Dir'aiyah must once have looked.

The main lane continues west before entering an open area where few houses remain. You can continue on to the restored sections of the wall (which once ran for 15km around the perimeter of Dir'aiyah) or branch off to the north to the 11 **Tower of Faisal**. A different path twists back to the Palace of Saad bin Saud, passing en route the ruined 12 **Palace of Fahran bin Saud** and the 13 **Saad bin Saud Mosque**.

Circle the Palace of Saad bin Saud, from where a path heads north and then east back to the entry gate, passing some of the best-preserved 14 **houses** along the way.

Riyadh to Mecca

There are numerous stretches of sand dunes just off the Riyadh–Mecca Hwy.

Sights

Red Sands SAND DUNE

The Red Sands are probably the most evocative dunes between Riyadh and Mecca, as they boast a backdrop of the cliffs of the Jebel Tuwaiq Escarpment – a great sight at sunset. They're just west of the turn-off to Duruma, around 40km west of Riyadh. To see them properly, you'll need a 4WD.

HEJAZ الحجاز

Meaning 'barrier', the region derives its name from the great escarpment that runs along Hejaz, separating it from the great plateaux of the interior. Historically, Hejaz has always seen itself as separate from the rest of the Kingdom, and that's even more true today with its friendly rivalry with the Najdis in the Riyadh region. Outward looking and cosmopolitan, the Hejazi are fiercely proud of their heritage. Explore the Red Sea coastline and make time for languid Jeddah, rarely visited Yanbu and bustling, family-oriented Taif.

Jeddah جدة

POP 3.5 MILLION

The country's commercial capital, and a point of convergence for pilgrims and traders for centuries, Jeddah is the most easygoing city in the Kingdom – not to mention its most beguiling. The Al Balad district, the heart of Old Jeddah, is a nostalgic testament to the city's bygone days, with the beautiful coral architecture of historic buildings casting some welcome shade over the bustling souqs where shopkeepers hawk their goods.

Jeddah has done much to improve its image over the years. North Jeddah in particular has undergone massive redevelopment to make the Corniche more attractive to visitors, while upscale department stores and malls have expanded shoppers' choices. The city is also famed for its international cuisine and seafood, and it remains a sweet spot for seasoned and novice scuba divers.

Jeddah

Top Sights

1 Al Tayibat City Museum for International Civilisation C1
2 Fakieh Aquarium A1

Sights

3 Fish Market C4

Activities, Courses & Tours

4 Blue Reef Divers C2
5 Red Sea Divers C2

Sleeping

6 InterContinental Hotel B3

Eating

7 Al Nakheel Restaurant A1
8 Green Island A1
Green Island Café ..... (see 8)
9 Reem Al Bawadi B2
10 Turkouise B2
11 Yildizlar C3

Shopping

12 Jarir Bookstore B1
13 Jarir Bookstore D3

Information

14 Al Shitaiwi Travel & Tourism B3

Sights

North Jeddah & the Corniche

Take a walk along the 35km-long Corniche alongside Saudis and expats to enjoy the warm breeze off the water. This is the place to get a real sense of Jeddah, especially in the evenings – students sit stooped over books, families share picnics, and men gather to gossip and cut commercial deals. Kiosks offer chair and bicycle rentals and sell candy, coffee and ice cream.

Look out for the famous sculptures that line the wide pedestrian areas for 30km north from the port. Among the highlights are four bronzes by British artist Henry Moore, as well as work by Spaniard Joan Miró, Finnish artist Eila Hiltunen and Frenchman César Baldaccini. It can get crowded after sunset prayers, so try to arrive early to grab a spot. Bring a blanket, a thermos of Arabic coffee and a box of dates and experience a warm Arabian night as the King Fahd Fountain shoots water nearly 300m into the sky.

Jeddah

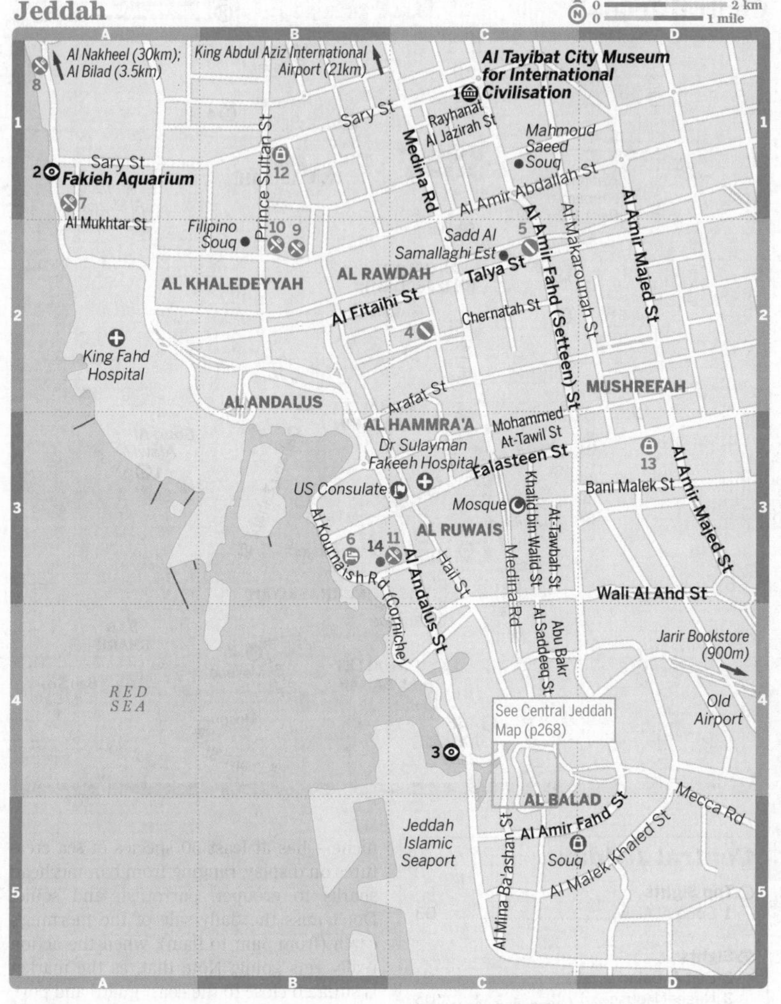

★Al Tayibat City Museum for International Civilisation MUSEUM

(Map p267; ☎02-693 0049; Rayhanat Al Jazirah St; admission SR50; ⏰8am-noon & 5-9pm Sat-Thu) This privately owned four-floor collection ranges from pre-Islamic artefacts, exquisite Islamic manuscripts, old coins and weaponry to stunning furniture, pottery and traditional Saudi dress. Replicas of home interiors from each region are also featured. Exhibits are accompanied by excellent information panels, as well as some dioramas of the Kingdom's provinces. If you get here early enough, you may get lucky and receive a private tour.

★Fakieh Aquarium AQUARIUM

(Map p267; ☎02-880 2081; www.fakiehaquarium.com; N Corniche; admission SR50; ⏰10am-10pm daily) This aquarium offers a wide range of fish species, including sharks, as well as turtles and other marine life. Ladies-only night is Wednesday. The complex also features an ice-skating rink and an arcade for the children. An on-site buffet-style restaurant overlooks the Red Sea and is family friendly, although no strollers are permitted in the aquarium. Traffic is heavy and parking virtually non-existent in the evenings: arrive early. The aquarium is next to Al Nawras.

Central Jeddah

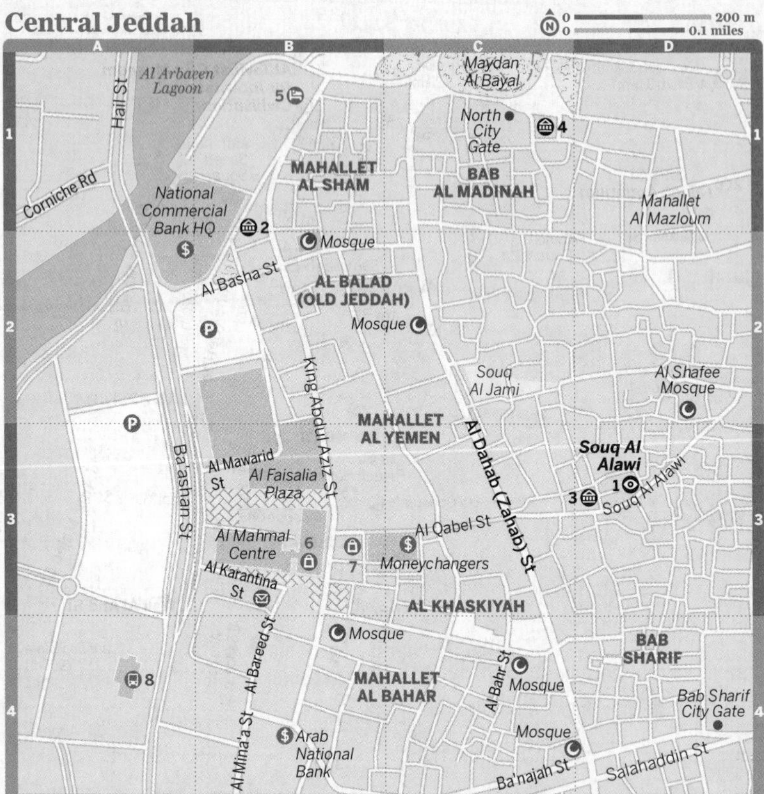

Central Jeddah

Fish Market MARKET
(Map p267; 5am-9pm) **FREE** The colourful and frenetic fish market – west of the Corniche – has at least 50 species of sea creatures on display, ranging from hammerhead sharks to grouper, parrotfish and squid. Don't miss the daily sale of the morning's catch (from 5am to 9am), when the action really gets going. Note that, as the market is situated close to the coast guard and port, photos are not permitted.

Old Jeddah (Al Balad)

★**Souq Al Alawi** SOUQ
(Map p268; 8am-1pm & 5-9pm Sat-Wed) This souq runs off Al Dahab St and is the most extensive in the Kingdom. The market stalls cut into the heart of the old city and buzz with the activity of traders and pilgrims. Search long enough and you will find genuine Arabian jewelry, Islamic art and traditional dress. Be here at sunset when the call to prayer fills the lanes – this is Arabia at its best.

The atmosphere is especially cosmopolitan during the hajj season, and the municipality has made efforts to keep the souq clean and pedestrian-friendly. Bargaining with merchants is encouraged, so never settle for the price listed on the tag.

Naseef House HISTORIC BUILDING
(Map p268; ☎02-647 2280; Souq Al Alawi; admission SR25; ⏲5-9pm) Jeddah's old coral houses are in a sorry state. Unique among the sea of dilapidation is the restored Naseef House, which belonged to one of Jeddah's most powerful trading families. It's set back from Souq Al Alawi – look out for the wide ramps installed by King Abdul Aziz in place of staircases so that camel-mounted messengers could ride all the way to the upper terrace in order to deliver messages.

Sharbatly House HISTORIC BUILDING
(Map p268; Maydan Al Bayal) Built in 1930, this historic structure also boasts some lovely *mashrabiyya* (balconies with perforated screens to allow the air to circulate and inhabitants to look out without being seen). Though restored during the 1980s, it has since been allowed to deteriorate. It is officially closed to visitors, but the staff at Naseef House may be able to arrange access. Discussions have continued over the years about refurbishing Sharbatly House as a museum.

Beit Al Balad MUSEUM
(Map p268; ☎020-880 8855; King Abdul Aziz St, Al Balad; ⏲10am-1pm & 5-11pm Sat-Thu) FREE Built in the early 20th century to be the British legation's headquarters in Jeddah, and serving in that role from about 1915 to the mid-1930s, Beit Al Balad is now a museum housing artefacts, photographs and ephemera documenting Jeddah's history. The structure is a typical cream-coloured example of Hejazi architecture.

Activities

Scattered around the city are dive shops that specialise in finding remote spots in the blue waters of the Red Sea. Pay extra for an instructor willing to give one-on-one lessons.

Red Sea Divers DIVING
(Map p267; ☎02-660 6368; redseadivers@arabnet.com.sa; Tahlia St; per person per day SR350; ⏲9am-11pm) One of the oldest dive shops in the city, Red Sea Divers uses Sheraton and Al Nakheel beaches, the most common areas for diving. Rental of buoyancy control device, regulators, weights and one tank starts at SR70. It's opposite Danube Hypermarket.

Blue Reef Divers DIVING
(Map p267; ☎02-618 1777; info@bluereefdivers.com; Tahlia St; per person per day SR250; ⏲9am-11pm Sat-Thu, 7am-11pm Fri & Sat) Blue Reef Divers starts its trips from Durrat Al Arus, 45km north of Jeddah. Rental of buoyancy control device, regulators, weights and one tank costs SR70. It's behind Danube Hypermarket.

Sleeping

Most of Jeddah's budget and midrange hotels are in Al Balad. On the edge of Al Balad are more up-to-date midrange hotels that cost a bit extra but are within easy walking distance (in the evening) of Old Jeddah. More upscale lodgings are found along the Corniche – perfect for families – while business travellers may prefer a more central location like Madinah Rd or Palestine St.

Al Bilad Hotel HOTEL $$
(☎02-694 4777; www.albiladhotel.net; N Corniche; s/d SR520/650, bungalows SR950; @ 🏊) Situated halfway between the airport and downtown, the Bilad is much loved for its 'escape the crowds' feel and cosy atmosphere. Facilities include a bakery, a lovely covered verandah (with aircon) and landscaped gardens with sea glimpses and birdsong. Some rooms have been recently renovated.

Bhadur Resort RESORT $$
(☎02-234 4400; N Obhur Rd; s SR600, villas SR2500; @ 🏊) Overlooking the Red Sea in North Jeddah, the Bhadur is a kid-friendly resort with floating water park and swimming pool. Each room features a kitchenette. Management can arrange fishing, cycling and snorkelling trips, and the resort also provides dive services (a 45-minute dive in 12m of water costs about SR375). There's a cafe for light snacks and a buffet-style restaurant.

The resort is affordable for families on a budget. Expect to share space with a *lot* of children.

Red Sea Palace Hotel HOTEL $$
(Map p268; ☎02-642 8555; www.redseapalace.com; King Abdul Aziz St; d/ste SR475/950; 🏊) Large, comfortable rooms, albeit with slightly tired decor, and reasonable prices make this a viable alternative to the luxurious options elsewhere in town. The hotel has two restaurants.

InterContinental Hotel HOTEL $$$
(Map p267; ☎02-661 1800; www.intercontinental.com; Corniche; r/ste SR1225/1676; @ 📶 🏊) The chic InterContinental boasts three main

PRAYER TIMES

Saudi Arabia is the only Muslim country that requires all businesses to close during prayer five times each day: morning (*fajr* prayer), late morning (*dhuhr*), afternoon (*asr*), dusk (*mahgreb*) and evening (*isha*).

Saudis' and expats' daily routines revolve around these prayer times, as all shops and government offices, except emergency services and hospitals, close for prayer – arrive at the wrong time and you'll be forced to wait outdoors in the heat for a shop or museum to open its doors. Strictly enforced, the closure can last for up to 30 minutes. If you're already inside a restaurant and eating, you'll usually be allowed to finish your meal (with the curtains drawn and door locked), but note that most places won't let you in unless they think you can finish in time. In shops, banks and other places, you will usually be asked to leave to avoid problems with the *mutawwa* (religious police).

Prayers are set according to the lunar calendar, so they can vary by a minute or two from day to day. The first is performed just before sunrise then (usually, depending on the time of the year) between noon and 1pm for the noon prayer, between 3.30pm and 4.30pm for the afternoon, 6pm and 7pm for early evening and between 8pm and 9pm for the last prayer of the day. Note that the last two prayers – *maghreb* and *isha* – occur close together, which requires close attention when scheduling outings in the evenings. Consult local daily newspapers (eg page two or three of the *Arab News*) for exact timings.

drawcards: a waterside location with a private beach, good facilities (including decent restaurants) and attention to detail – right down to complimentary underwater cameras and playing cards for the kids.

Waldorf Astoria Qasr Al Sharq HOTEL **$$$**
(☎02-659 9999; www.waldorfastoria3.hilton.com; N Corniche; s/ste SR2764/4864; P@☎≋) Decorated by the same designer who worked on Dubai's famous Burj Al Arab, the self-described seven-star Al Sharq prides itself on luxury. The dazzling decor includes no less than 60kg of gold leaf, silk curtains and a 12m chandelier; rooms all come with 42-inch plasma TV (with obligatory gold panelling) and 24-hour butler service.

Eating

To catch the buzz surrounding Jeddah's burgeoning food scene, head to Al Rawdah S in North Jeddah – it's virtually become restaurant row. Consult www.jeddahfood.com for up-to-date reviews of Jeddah's eateries.

For a table with a view, the 7th floor of the **Al Mahmal Centre** (Map p268; King Abdul Aziz St; ⏲8am-11.30pm Sat-Thu, 1-11.30pm Fri) has several small restaurants serving Turkish, Lebanese and Filipino fast food (mains SR7 to SR22).

★**Yildizlar** TURKISH, LEBANESE **$$**
(Map p267; ☎02-653 1150; Al Andalus St; mains SR29-98; ⏲1pm-1am) With appealing decor and a comfortable atmosphere, Yildizar is a local institution serving a splendid mix of Turkish and Lebanese food. Dishes range from grilled quail and boneless pigeon to caviar, fabulous fish dishes and appetising grills. It can get busy and more than a bit noisy. It's behind Ruby Tuesday.

Al Nakheel Restaurant MIDDLE EASTERN **$$**
(Map p267; ☎02-606 6644; Al Mukhtar St; mains SR30-50; ⏲9am-3am) Styled like a traditional tent (with open sides to let in the sea breezes), this is the place to come for a taste of Jeddah. It's wildly popular and the food is good, with seafood a speciality.

Green Island SEAFOOD **$$**
(Map p267; ☎02-694 1234; N Corniche; mains SR45-110; ⏲5pm-1.30am) Spread across the water in the form of little chalets on stilts – complete with glass floor panels that reveal the fish below – Green Island is a little worn around the edges but remains the place to come if you're after a final splurge or a romantic revival. The menu spans Lebanese, Indian and continental cuisines, with seafood dominating most dishes.

The **cafe** (Map p267; ☎02-694 0999; N Corniche; mains SR20-40; ⏲8am-2am Sat-Thu, 1pm-2am Fri) is also excellent.

Reem Al Bawadi MIDDLE EASTERN **$$**
(Map p267; ☎02-661 7059; Al Rawdah St; mains SR50-150; ⏲1pm-11pm) In the heart of North Jeddah, opposite King Faisal Hospital, this two-level Lebanese eatery with outdoor dining offers a sweets counter on the ground

floor and family dining upstairs. Appetisers start at about SR15, and the excellent mains range from tender mixed grill to fresh seafood. The Middle Eastern decor is fresh, the seating comfortable and the service top notch.

Turkouise TURKISH $$
(Map p267; ☎02-683 2128; Al Rawdah St; mains SR50-150; ⊙noon-midnight) The decor is contemporary, if a bit cold, but the food provides a taste of authentic Turkey – it's no wonder that the restaurant draws many Turkish expats. The Tarsus kebab is a local favourite, while the lamb shish and kofta kebab also top the list of best dishes. Bread is served with every meal.

Shopping

Jarir Bookstore BOOKS
(Map p267; ☎02-673 2727; www.jarir.com; Falasteen St; ⊙9am-2pm & 4.30-11pm Sat-Thu, 4.30-11pm Fri) Jeddah's best bookstore also has branches on **Sary St** (Map p267; ☎02-682 7666; Sary St) and **Jamea Plaza** (☎02-687 2743; Jamea Plaza).

Khayyam Al Rabie Est FOOD
(Map p268; ☎02-647 6596; ⊙9am-2pm & 4.30-11pm Sat-Thu, 4.30-11pm Fri) For dates, nuts and nibbles at discount prices, head straight for the famous Khayyam Al Rabie Est, off Al Qabel St. With its fairy lights and floor-to-ceiling rows of goodies (including more than 50 varieties of date in all shapes, shades, colours and textures), it's like an Aladdin's cave for the sweet-toothed.

Information

EMERGENCY
Ambulance (☎997)
Fire (☎998)
Police (☎999)
Traffic Accidents (☎993)

MEDICAL SERVICES
Dr Sulayman Fakeeh Hospital (Map p267; ☎02-665 5000, 02-660 3000; Falasteen St) Has a good emergency department.

MONEY
A central row of **moneychangers** (Map p268; Al Qabel St, Al Balad; ⊙9am-1.30pm & 4.30-10pm) offers good rates with no commission.

TRAVEL AGENCIES
Sadd Al Samallaghi Est (Map p267; ☎02-668 5054; www.samallaghi.com; Talya St) This one-stop shop arranges flights around the peninsula, day trips around Jeddah, longer excursions to Madain Saleh, car rental, diving, desert safaris and boat trips. It's one of Saudi Arabia's best operators.

Al Shitaiwi Travel & Tourism (Map p267; ☎02-271 1770; www.alshitaiwitours.com; Salman bin Abdul Aziz St) Runs tours and can arrange flights and car rental.

Getting There & Away

AIR
King Abdul Aziz International Airport (☎02-688 5526, 02-684 1707; Medina Rd) Jeddah's King Abdul Aziz International Airport is 17km north of the city centre. **Saudi Arabian Airlines** (Saudia; ☎02-632 3333; King Abdul Aziz St) and **Nas Airlines** (☎02-650 3419; www.flynas.com; Medina Rd) depart from the south terminal. Foreign airlines use the north terminal.

Daily domestic departures include Medina (SR139), Riyadh (SR259), Taif (SR488) and Yanbu (SR848). For Al Ula you'll need to fly via Riyadh or drive from Medina.

BUS
Buses for the following destinations depart daily from the **Saptco Bus Station** (Map p268).

For Al Ula (SR125) some services travel via Medina. If you're a non-Muslim, inform the ticket vendor when you buy your ticket. The driver of your bus should drop you outside the haram boundaries and another bus should come and pick you up from there.

DESTINATION	DURATION (HR)	FREQUENCY	COST (SR)
Abha	9	every 2hr	125
Dammam	14-15	3 daily	210
Jizan	9	every 2hr	120
Riyadh	12	every 2hr	160
Taif	3	hourly	45
Yanbu	5	every 2hr to 3hr	65

Getting Around

A taxi from the town centre to the south/north airport terminal costs SR75/100 (add SR15 to SR25 in high season). A short hop in town costs around SR20.

Taif الطائف

POP 987,900

Situated 1700m above sea level, Taif can seem like a breath of fresh air in summer, and compared to humid Jeddah it truly is. Its gentle, temperate climate is its biggest attraction. Watch for wild baboons along the mountain roadside on the way into the city from Jeddah.

Taif is family friendly, with over 3000 garden parks scattered throughout the city and outlying areas; in the evening the parks are packed with families spreading out a full supper on blankets. Some bring *sheesha*, filling the night air with a sweet, smoky aroma. Taif is not known for its restaurants, so buying everything you need at a market and settling down for a picnic is a wonderful alternative. The city is popular among visitors for its roses and fruit – particularly honey-sweet figs, grapes, prickly pears and pomegranates.

In summer Taif becomes the Kingdom's unofficial capital when the king relocates here.

Sights

Taif has wide, tree-lined streets and plenty of traditional Hejazi-Ottoman-Roman architecture, including perhaps the best 19th- and early-20th-century architectural examples in the Kingdom. It also features a lively souq, amusement parks and beautiful surrounding scenery.

Shubra Palace MUSEUM, PALACE
(02-732 1033; Shubra St; 8am-2pm Sat-Wed Sep-May, 8am-noon & 5-7pm Sat-Wed Jun-Aug) FREE The city's museum occupies a beautiful house built in 1905 on the orders of Sharif Ali Pasha. The palace is the most stunning vestige of old Taif, with latticework windows and balconies and interior marble from Carrara. King Abdul Aziz used to stay here and the palace was later the residence of King Faisal.

Al Gadhi Rose Factory BUILDING
(02-733 4133; 9.30am-2.30pm Sat-Thu) FREE The largest rose factory in Taif, the 120-year-old Al Gadhi Rose Factory is well worth a visit, particularly at harvest time (May to July), when it's open 24 hours. Rosewater (SR12 per bottle), used in Arabia to scent clothes, baths, cooking and drinks, is sold here. The factory is off As Salamah St.

Souq Gazzaz SOUQ
(9am-2pm & 4.30-11pm Sat-Thu) Taif's souq is one of the largest in the Kingdom and is worth a wander, particularly on a summer evening, when the people of Taif take to its streets. The souq is southeast of the Great Mosque.

Beit Kaki HISTORIC BUILDING
(As Salamah St; 8am-2pm Sat-Wed Sep-May, 8am-noon & 5-7pm Jun-Aug) FREE Built in 1943 as a summer residence for one of Mecca's most important merchant families, Beit Kaki is among Taif's finest buildings. The intricately carved balconies and window and door frames have all been sympathetically restored and the building is now a small museum.

Al Kateb House HISTORIC BUILDING
(As Salamah St; 8am-2pm Sat-Wed Sep-May, 8am-noon & 5-7pm Jun-Aug) FREE Built by Mohammed bin Abdul Wahed in 1897, this historic building features a mix of Hejazi and Roman architecture with Islamic flourishes. Last occupied as a residence in 1968, it has been home to Taif's top officials.

Sleeping

Taif is a popular summer retreat (May to September) and advance reservations are advised.

Safari Hotel HOTEL $
(02-734 6660; Mussel St; s low/high season SR150/200, d SR175/220) The best budget choice, with pleasantly furnished rooms, all with balconies. Ask for a 'mosque-side' view, although be prepared for an early wake-up call if you do. It's near Shubra St.

FESTIVALS & SIGHTS AROUND TAIF

Souq Okaz Festival (9am-2pm & 4.30-11pm Sat-Thu late Aug) About 40km northeast of the city, Souq Okaz stands on the same site as its ancient predecessor and features the annual Souq Okaz Festival. The location was once the cultural and economic center of the Kingdom. The festival runs for eight days each year and features cultural seminars, lectures, poetry readings, traditional dancing, Arab products and Bedouin handicrafts.

Al Shafa Al Shafa, 25km southwest of Taif, is the highest mountain in the Taif region and accessible via modern, paved roads. The 10,000-sq-m Daka Mountain Park is perched on the peak and offers terraces for barbecues and picnics. Mountaineering is a favourite sport among tourists, but there are no organised tours.

Shubra Palace Hotel HOTEL $
(☎02-737 4747; fax 02-736 2822; Shubra St; r from SR250) The no-frills Shubra Palace Hotel offers clean, spacious rooms and a nice-size lobby. Shubra Historic Palace is a half-block away and it's a three-minute walk to the city centre.

Al Barraq Hotel HOTEL $$
(☎02-650 3366; fax 02-651 1322; Shehar St; s low/high season SR251/300, d SR450/500) Al Barraq is popular among the diplomatic expat community and it's easy to see why: rooms are spacious and comfy, and the luxurious lobby, laden with marble and chandeliers, offers old-world glamour. There are also two restaurants, health club and hot tub.

InterContinental Hotel HOTEL $$
(☎02-750 5050; www.intercontinental.com; Airport Rd; r/ste from SR564/1080; @≋) Around 10km from Taif's airport, the refurbished InterContinental offers great facilities and services.

Eating

As Shafa MIDDLE EASTERN $
(☎02-733 0332; mains from SR1.50; ⊙noon-1am) Off Shubra St, behind the Saudia office, As Shafa serves delicious Saudi/Turkmenistan dishes, including *manti* (like ravioli; two pieces SR2) at unbeatable prices. It's much admired locally, but there's no family seating.

Ahlan Wa Sahlan TURKISH $
(☎02-732 7324; Shubra St; sandwiches from SR7, mains SR20-26; ⊙7am-noon & 1pm-1am) Light, bright and clean, the Ahlan has a great pick-and-point counter containing fresh Turkish dishes that change daily and include veggie and seafood options.

Mirage Indian Restaurant INDIAN $$
(☎02-370 0563, 02-748 4444; As Saddad Rd; mains SR25-75; ⊙5pm-1am) Although light on atmosphere, with small touches of Indian decor, the Mirage offers an excellent biryani rice dish cooked with saffron and accompanied by marinated chicken or lamb. A traditional treat for the timid diner might be the tandoori chicken cooked in yogurt and spices.

Getting There & Away

There are bus services to Riyadh (SR135, nine hours, 10 daily), Jeddah (SR45, three hours, 20 daily) and Abha (SR125, eight hours, three daily).

CAMEL CHAOS

Every other weekend (Thursday and Friday) during July and August, the town of Taif departs for the races. Open to all, the spectacular events feature camels from far and wide, including other peninsula countries. Held 10km outside Taif, the four races are run from 3pm to 5.30pm, and each attracts between 25 and 100 participants. It's no wonder: first prize is SR150,000 in cash, 10 cars and 100 bags of wheat!

Taif Airport (☎02-685 5527) Taif airport is 25km north of the town; both **Nas Airlines** (☎02-731 1435; www.flynas.com; Bab Al-Rei/Al-Amana St) and **Saudia** (☎02-732 2251; www.saudiairlines.com; Shubra St) operate from here. There are flights to/from Riyadh (SR229) and Dammam (SR478).

Getting Around

Taxis charge SR20 for short journeys around town (including to/from the bus station) and SR45 to the airport. From the airport, they charge SR75. Limousine service (in a four-door sedan) is offered to tour the city and surrounding areas by some of the more upscale hotels. The cost is about SR100 per hour.

Yanbu ينبع

POP 299,000

At first glance, with its port, refineries and petrochemical plants, Yanbu is hardly the Kingdom's most attractive spot. But it's fast becoming the top tourist destination in the country, with its premier scuba-diving locations and pristine white sandy shores, many with resorts and private beaches geared towards families. The industrial section of Yanbu is a good 10km to 15km south of the city centre and has little impact upon the region's gorgeous beaches to the north. The downtown area is small but quaint, with an unhurried atmosphere not found in the larger cities.

Just outside town is vast, open desert that gives way to the water, and it's here that most visitors spend their time: imagine sitting on the beach with few, if any, people on either side of you. Hajj season, which draws big crowds, is the exception.

Sights

Historic Quarter HISTORIC SITE

Northwest of the city centre, at the edge of the commercial zone and 1km from the beach, is the city's historic area. The recently restored residence of TE Lawrence, who helped the Arabs defend Yanbu against the Turks in 1916, is the shining centrepiece of this small district. (Neighbouring structures, dating to the 19th century, are in extreme disrepair but are targeted for refurbishment.) A historic wall built in 1885 is also part of the neighbourhood's appeal.

Yanbu Lakes PARK

(Almenaa St) It's not really a lake but, as one of the greenest spots in the area, it's beautifully landscaped and maintained, making it suitable for family picnics. There's space for jogging and a play area for children. It's a perfect spot for lounging around on the weekend and watching the sun set.

Activities

Dream Divers DIVING

(☎04-322 0660; www.dreamdiver.net; Ibis Hotel, King Abdul Aziz St; per person per day for 2 dives incl tanks, weight belt & lunch box SR350; ⏰9am-noon & 2-10pm) Dream Divers has the best reputation of the various dive centres in Yanbu. If you're without equipment, buoyancy control devices and regulators can be hired for SR150 each, a mask and snorkel for SR95. PADI scuba-diving courses are also offered, including a seven-day open-water course (SR1850 per person all inclusive). Bring your own boots, fins and wetsuit.

Sleeping

Danat Apartment Hotel HOTEL $

(☎04-391 2222; danat_hotel@yahoo.com; King Abdul Aziz St; s/d SR180/215) Decorated in browns and creams like a giant crème caramel, the rooms are nevertheless comfortable and clean. The hotel is conveniently situated two doors down from Dream Divers.

Radhwa Holiday Inn HOTEL $$

(☎04-322 3767; www.holiday-inn.com/yanbu; King Abdul Aziz St; s/d SR765/850; 📶🏊) A five-minute drive from the city centre, this hotel caters to business travellers, but the large pool makes it attractive to families too. Rooms may be a bit cramped, but the decor is modern, the facilities clean and well maintained, and the staff helpful. The restaurant serves an excellent breakfast buffet with a chef on duty for special orders.

Arac Yanbu Resort RESORT $$$

(☎04-328 0888; www.arac.com.sa; cnr Prince Abdul Majeed & King Salman Rds; villas with general beach access for 1/2/3 people SR1890/2590/3200, chalets with private beach access for 1/2/3 people SR2200/3200/3900, r SR990; 📶🏊) A families-only resort 17km from town and 10km from the airport, Arac boasts a good location and great facilities. These include a private beach where women can swim in modest attire, a host of water sports, a cafe and a restaurant. The comfortable two-storey chalets are built on the waterfront. All prices include service charge.

Dolphin Resort RESORT $$$

(☎04-357 0444; Omar bin Khatteb St, Al Sharm; s/d SR900/1500; @🏊) A family resort, Dolphin has a playground, a fitness centre, family and games rooms and a sauna. The beach is private and management offers services for water sports, fishing and diving. The resort is located off Hwy 5.

Eating

Iskenderun Restaurant TURKISH $

(☎04-322 8465; King Abdul Aziz St; mains from SR13-25; ⏰1pm-2am) Canary coloured, cheap and cheerful, this is Yanbu's favourite eating establishment. Try the speciality: *shwarma skandar*, served with a secret sauce (SR20). Mixed grills, Turkish pizza, barbecued hamoor fish and fresh fruit juices are also served.

Seafood Time SEAFOOD $$

(☎04-393 3300; Omar bin Abdulaziz Rd; mains from SR30-60; ⏰1-11.30pm) This out-of-the-way establishment is Yanbu's best-kept secret. Family dining is on the 2nd floor. The decor is simple, but the dishes are some of the best in town. Try a half-kilo of barbecued shrimp, fresh chicken, fish or shrimp baked in a clay pot, or the tasty *kufta* (a ground-beef dish).

Getting There & Away

The airport is 10km northeast of the town centre. **Saudia** (☎04-322 6666; King Abdul Aziz St) has twice-daily flights to Jeddah (SR978) and Riyadh (from SR618). Nas Airlines has no Yanbu office, but flights can be booked through its call center: ☎920 00 1234.

Yanbu is 230km (around 2½ hours by car) from Jeddah.

MADAIN SALEH & THE NORTH مدائن صالح و الشمال

Madain Saleh is without doubt the most impressive site in Saudi Arabia and should be on every visitor's must-see list.

Al Ula العلا

Al Ula – gateway to Madain Saleh – is a small town about 400km north of Medina. Once an oasis with fertile soil and abundant water, it was founded in the 6th century BC and originally inhabited by the Lihyanites. The town was formerly a strategic trade route for spices and incense from the Levant, Egypt and North Africa.

Situated in a valley, Al Ula has an exceptional view of snowcapped mountains in winter, palm groves running down the centre of the wadi (river bed) and forbidding red-sandstone cliffs rising up on two sides.

As well as extraordinary Nabataean tombs in the vicinity, the town has the delightful ruins of Old Al Ula – one of the best examples of traditional Arab architecture. With a little imagination, its winding narrow alleys and high watchtowers can bring back the sights and sounds of Al Ula's origins.

Sights

★Old Al Ula HISTORIC SITE

Old Al Ula is one of the most picturesque old towns on the Arabian Peninsula. The mud-brick town of about 800 structures stands on the reputed site of the biblical city of Dedan, mentioned in Isaiah (21:13) as home base of Arab caravans, and in Ezekiel (27:20-21) as trading partner of the Phoenician city of Tyre. The buildings you'll see have repeatedly been rebuilt over the centuries, although the foundations are believed to date to the 13th century.

Some foundation stones still bear Lihyanite inscriptions. The village was walled, with two gates protecting about 800 families, and was occupied until the late 1970s. Throughout the atmospheric ruins there are superb house doors made from tamarisk. Rising up from the centre of the old town are the remnants of the fortress Umm Nasir. The palm trees and maze of low mud-brick walls, directly across the road from the old town, were once farms whose owners lived in the town. Look out for Dedan pottery, hastily produced for everyday purposes in the 2nd century BC.

★Jebel Khuraibah MOUNTAIN, RUINS

The fortress and three peaks of Jebel Khuraibah once formed part of the capital of the ancient Kingdom of Lihyan. Rock-cut tombs squat at the foot of the peaks, the most impressive being the 'Lion Tomb' – named for the two lions carved on either side of the entrance. At Khuraibah is a huge, headless sandstone figure, while climbing to the top of the central peak reveals stone stairs and walls linking all three crags together into a ruined fortress city.

THE NABATAEANS

There are many theories about where the Nabataeans came from, although most scholars agree that they were early Bedouins who lived a nomadic life before settling as farmers in the area in the 6th century BC. They developed a specialised knowledge of desert water resources (using water channels known as *qanats*) as well as the intricacies of the lucrative trade caravan routes.

Nabataean merchant families grew incredibly wealthy from 200 BC, organising caravans of frankincense and feeding the insatiable markets of the ancient world. Nabataean wealth, which had derived initially from plundering trade caravans, shifted to exacting tolls (up to 25% of the commodities' value) upon these same caravans as a means of securing Nabataean protection and guiding the caravans to water. The Nabataean capital was at Petra (Jordan) and Madain Saleh was their second city.

Through a mixture of shrewd diplomacy and military force, the Nabataeans kept at bay the Seleucids, the Egyptians, the Persians and later, for a time, the Romans. The Nabataeans never really possessed an 'empire' in the common military and administrative sense of the word. Instead, from about 200 BC they had established a 'zone of influence' that stretched to Syria and Rome and south into the Hadramaut (modern Yemen). But it was all undone when the Romans cleverly cut out the middlemen by building fleets on the Red Sea and importing frankincense directly. An impoverished Nabataean kingdom staggered on for a few years but was formally absorbed as a province of the Roman Empire in AD 106.

Al Ula Museum of Archaeology & Ethnography MUSEUM
(☎04-884 1536; Main St; ⏰8am-2.30pm Sun-Thu) FREE This small museum is attractively designed with some intriguing and informative displays on the history, culture, flora and fauna of the area, as well as on Madain Saleh and Nabataean culture.

Umm Al Daraj HISTORIC SITE
A few kilometres north of Old Al Ula, Umm Al Daraj (Mother of Steps) is worth a detour. Climbing the hill reveals three red-sandstone religious structures, a former Lihyanite sacrificial altar and some beautiful Lihyanite inscriptions; ancient petroglyphs – depicting people and camels – graffiti the site. From the top of the steps there are stunning views over the wadi. You'll need a guide to find Umm Al Daraj, but try to get there for sunset – it's well worth the climb.

Castle Al Ula CASTLE
To protect the ancient village, inhabitants in the 6th century used red-sandstone blocks to build a castle on a promontory, giving a 360-degree view of the surrounding valley. The 45m climb to the castle is of moderate difficulty but worth the effort once you see the red-tinged cliffs of the sweeping valley below.

Mount Almejder MOUNTAIN, RUINS
This 300m-high mountain east of Al Ula features stone settlements and caves with pre-Islamic inscriptions and drawings.

Tours

Arac Hotel Al Ula TOUR
(☎04-884 4444; www.arac.com.sa) The Arac Hotel Al Ula can organise group day tours to Madain Saleh using local guides. If you're travelling on your own, a guide may take you, but you would need to pay the entire group rate (around SR800 including vehicle). Other options include guided 4WD excursions into the desert. Lunch boxes can be prepared on request.

Hamid M Al Sulaiman TOUR
(☎055-435 3684) Local tour guide Hamid is also the author of a splendid coffee-table book on Madain Saleh. With intimate knowledge of the area, he offers 4WD tours of all local sites and the Hejaz Railway, camel excursions, and a few trips not offered by the hotels. Though his English is limited, he is reliable, keen to please and good company.

Haya Tours TOUR
(☎011-450 7167; www.hayatour.com) This Riyadh-based company offers two-day trips to Al Ula and Madain Saleh with meals and accommodation included. Prices start at SR2500 per person.

Sleeping & Eating

★ **Arac Hotel Al Ula** HOTEL $$
(☎04-884 4444; www.arac.com.sa; Madain Saleh Rd; s/d/ste from SR360/440/1600; P 📶 🏊) The only hotel close to Madain Saleh, the three-star Arac offers attractive, well-sized rooms 7km from Al Ula on the main road to Madain Saleh. The restaurant serves up good buffets during high season as well as a la carte offerings at other times, while the large, inviting swimming pool is open to both men and women at different times.

The staff are especially friendly, the gardens make a nice contrast to the arid surrounds and the hotel can arrange a site permit for Madain Saleh.

Al Ula Matam Buchary MIDDLE EASTERN $
(☎04-884 1124; Khaled bin Walid St; mains SR5-13; ⏰1pm-1.30am Sat-Thu) Of Al Ula's small selection of restaurants, Al Ula Matam Buchary, which lies 100m south of Saptco, has the best reputation. It's signposted in Arabic only and there's no family section, but it does do takeaway. Try the flavoursome barbecue half-chicken (SR10).

Getting There & Around

There are direct Saudi Arabia Airlines flights to Al Ula from Riyadh (SR430) on Thursday and Saturday. From elsewhere in the Kingdom you'll need to fly via Riyadh. Otherwise, Medina's Prince Mohammad bin Abdulaziz International Airport is accessible to non-Muslims. At the airport, a car can be rented for the three-hour drive to Al Ula.

Saptco (☎04-884 1344) runs buses to Al Ula from Jeddah (SR145) and Riyadh (SR200).

Around Al Ula

Sights

Ekma LANDMARK
Around 3km northwest of Al Ula off Rte 375 lies Ekma, a huge stone believed by some to be where the Prophet Saleh delivered a camel – a gift from God to the Thamud peo-

ple, who had challenged Saleh to perform a miracle. Archaeologists consider Ekma, also spelled Ikma, a vital window into Madain Saleh's past.

Elephant Rock LANDMARK

(Sakharat Al Fil, Mammoth Rock) A wonderful natural rock formation, Elephant Rock towers above the sands in a landscape of red rocky monoliths. It lies 11km northeast of Al Ula, just off the road to Hail, some 7km from the Arac Hotel Al Ula.

Madain Saleh مدائن صالح

If you can only visit one place in Saudi Arabia, make it Unesco World Heritage–listed Madain Saleh. This crossroads of ancient civilisations, pilgrims, explorers, trade caravans and armies finds its most remarkable expression in the elaborate stone-carved tombs of the Nabataeans. Although the tombs are less spectacular than the Treasury at better-known Petra in Jordan, the setting of sweeping sand and remarkable rock formations is unique and unsurpassed.

Madain Saleh

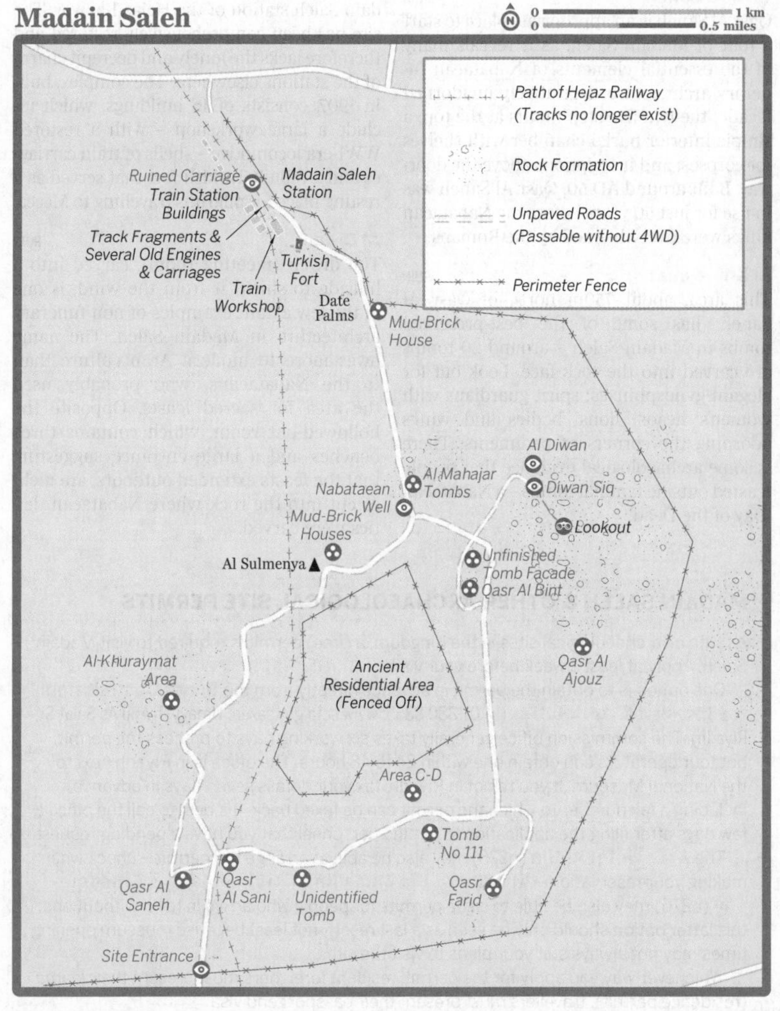

Sights

The extraordinary **Madain Saleh** (9am-6pm Sat-Thu, 2-6pm Fri) FREE is home to 131 tombs, 45 of which carry inscriptions in late-Aramaic script above the entrance. These inscriptions detail the tomb's builders; many were constructed by wealthy women. The enigmatic tombs combine elements of Greco-Roman architecture with Nabataean and Babylonian imagery. The park is well signposted, but as you drive deeper in it's highly recommended that you use a 4WD vehicle.

Qasr Al Saneh RUIN

Qasr Al Saneh is an appropriate place to start a tour of Madain Saleh, as it reveals many of the essential elements of Nabataean funerary architecture: a relatively unadorned facade; the two five-step motifs at the top; a simple interior burial chamber with shelves for corpses; and inscriptions above the doorway. Built around AD 50, Qasr Al Saneh was in use for just 50 years before the Nabataean kings were overwhelmed by the Romans.

Al Khuraymat RUIN

This area, about 750m north of Qasr Al Saneh, has some of the best-preserved tombs in Madain Saleh – around 20 tombs are carved into the rock face. Look out for elegant gynosphinxes: spirit guardians with women's heads, lions' bodies and wings adorning the corners of pediments. There is some archaeological evidence that people feasted outside familial tombs – a Nabataean 'Day of the Dead'.

Nabataean Well & Al Mahajar Tombs RUIN

The Nabataeans were masters of hydrology and manipulated rain run-off and underground aquifers to thrive in this desert landscape. This great well was one of over 60 wells currently known in the city. The wall supports – added in the 20th century – were built from railway sleepers pilfered from the Hejaz Railway. The Al Mahajar tombs are especially photogenic and some of the oldest at Madain Saleh.

Hejaz Railway Station HISTORIC BUILDING

At the northern edge of the site is the Madain Saleh station of the Hejaz Railway. The site has been comprehensively restored and therefore lacks the lonely and decrepit charm of the stations elsewhere. The complex, built in 1907, consists of 16 buildings, which include a large workshop – with a restored WWI-era locomotive – shells of train carriages and a rebuilt Turkish fort that served as a resting place for pilgrims travelling to Mecca.

Al Diwan RUIN

The diwan (meeting room), carved into a hillside to shield it from the wind, is one of the few extant examples of non-funerary architecture in Madain Saleh. The name owes more to modern Arab culture than to the Nabataeans, who probably used the area for sacred feasts. Opposite the hollowed-out room, which contains three benches and a large entrance suggesting that the feasts extended outdoors, are niches cut into the rock where Nabataean deities were carved.

MADAIN SALEH & OTHER ARCHAEOLOGICAL SITE PERMITS

As with all archaeological sites in the Kingdom, a (free) permit is required to visit Madain Saleh. Apply at least a week before your visit.

One option is to obtain the permit in advance directly from the **Saudi Commission for Tourism & Antiquities** (01-880 8855; www.scta.gov.sa/en; Umayyah Abu As Salat St, Riyadh). The commission office generally takes six working days to process the permit, but tour operators can obtain one within 24 to 48 hours. The office is in Riyadh next to the National Museum. If you're not in Riyadh, fax your details seven days in advance, including a fax number to which the permit can be faxed back. It's best to call the office a few days after filing the application to remind personnel that you have a pending request.

The **Arac Hotel Al Ula** (p276) may also be able to arrange the permit – check when making your reservation – while the **Al Ula Museum of Archaeology & Ethnography** (p276) may also be able to issue permits for people who arrive in town without one; this latter option should only be seen as a last resort, not least because museum opening times may not always suit your plans to visit the site.

Whichever way you apply for the permit, resident foreigners must present their *iqama* (residence permit); travellers must present their passport and visa.

WORTH A TRIP

THE HEJAZ RAILWAY

The Hejaz Railway, with its echoes of TE Lawrence and the Arab Revolt, cuts across northwestern Arabia in the form of abandoned and evocative stations, substations and garrison forts.

The official idea of the railway was to make it easier for pilgrims to reach Medina and Mecca, cutting the journey time from Damascus from six weeks to just four days. In addition to the tracks and station buildings, forts were also built every 25km for garrisons of Turkish soldiers, whose role was to protect the railway from bandits. The line opened in 1908, stretching over 1600km through largely desert terrain; the planned extension to Mecca was never built.

During WWI, the Ottomans sided with Germany (who had helped build the railway). Sherif Hussein, the Hashemite ruler of the Hejaz, made an alliance with the British to drive out the Turks. Harnessing the hostility of some local Bedouin, TE Lawrence helped to orchestrate the Arab Revolt, attacking trains and sabotaging the tracks. Most tribes, however, supported the railway because of its potential economic advantages. The Turkish garrison in Medina was soon cut off from the remainder of the Ottoman forces, whose empire was crumbling. The railway became unviable and ceased to run after 1918.

Many of the stations and substations remain, with at least 19 substations between Medina and Madain Saleh, including many alongside the Medina–Al Ula road. North of Madain Saleh there are a further 13 substations.

Running south from the diwan is the Siq, a narrow passageway measuring about 40m wide between two rock faces lined with more small altars. At the far end is a striking natural amphitheatre. Climb along the southeastern slope up to a number of altars. From here, look west for breathtaking views.

Qasr Al Bint RUIN

(Palace of the Daughter) Qasr Al Bint consists of a wonderful row of facades that make for dramatic viewing from across Madain Saleh. The east face has two particularly well-preserved tombs, the largest 16m tall. If you look up near the northern end of the west face, you'll distinguish a tomb that was abandoned in the early stages of construction and would, if completed, have been the largest in Madain Saleh – only the step facade was cut. These tombs date to about AD 31.

Qasr Farid RUIN

Qasr Farid in the south is the largest tomb of Madain Saleh and perhaps the most stunning, if not the most iconic in the region. Carved starting from the top – but never completed – from a free-standing rock monolith, its location gives it a rare beauty. Try to arrive as late in your visit (and as close to sunset) as you can, as the enigmatic tomb passes through shades of pink and gold until darkness falls: breathtaking.

ℹ Information

Video cameras are not allowed inside the site; be aware that surveillance is carried out. Bring your passport and visa – you will need to present them at the gate along with the permit. You must leave the site before sunset.

ℹ Getting There & Away

Madain Saleh is 23km from Al Ula. The site entrance is marked off the road with a blue 'Antiquities' sign.

Tabuk

POP 668,000

Tabuk, now a bustling tourist destination, was a strategic stopping place for pre-20th-century hajj pilgrims trekking on foot from Damascus (Syria) to Medina and onward to Mecca. The city's culture was deeply influenced by Egyptian travellers (one of the largest groups of land-travelling pilgrims) from the west and the Ottomans (who controlled pilgrimage routes for centuries) from the north.

Defying the perception that Saudi Arabia is all desert sand and sun, Tabuk also serves as a gateway to a pristine region of white beaches, virtually untouched islands and coral reefs, and snowy mountains in winter. An archaeologist's paradise, Tabuk was once home to the Nabateans, who populated the region

Tabuk

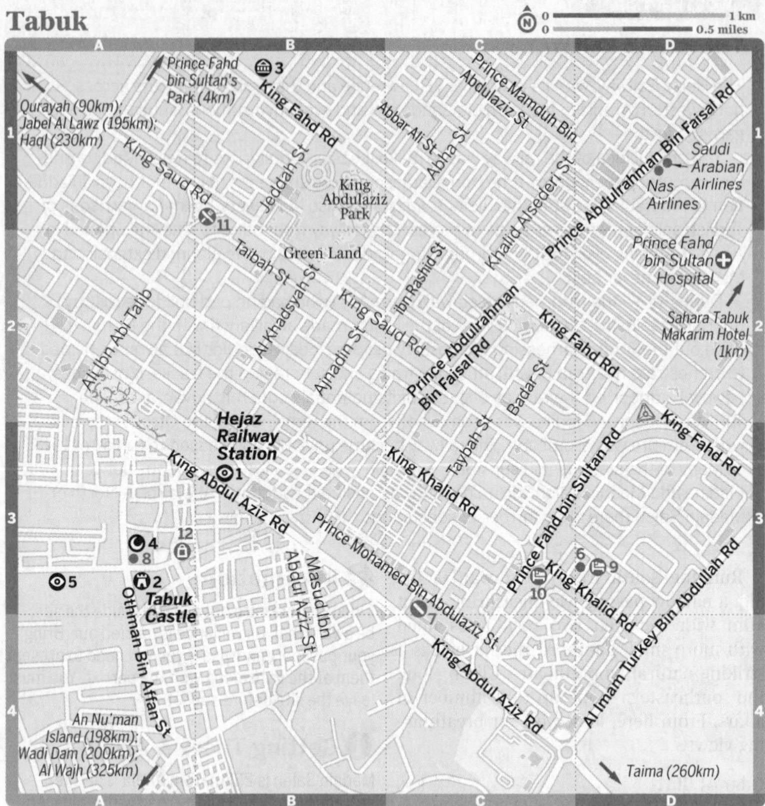

700 years before the birth of the Prophet Mohammed. The region's rock formations reveal thousands of examples of pre-Islamic art.

History

Tabuk's historical identity is dominated by the Prophet Mohammed's visit to the area and the Battle of Tabuk, though the battle never came to pass. In AD 630 the Prophet organised an army of 30,000, then the most powerful force on the Arabian Peninsula. His men travelled to Tabuk to engage the Byzantines, who had planned an invasion to stamp out the growing influence of Islam. When the Prophet's army arrived, the Byzantines were nowhere to be found.

Muslims worldwide journey to Tabuk because the Prophet visited Tabuk Castle and the Prophet's Mosque to pray before the battle. A Hadith (a collection of the Prophet's sayings) mentions Tabuk, giving the city special meaning for Muslims. According to the Hadith, Mohammed said, 'If you live long enough…you will see this place (Tabuk) filled with gardens'.

Sights

★Tabuk Castle CASTLE
(☎04-421 6198; Prince Fahd bin Sultan Rd; ⏲9am-5pm Sat-Thu, 3-5pm Fri) FREE Dating to 1559, Tabuk Castle was refurbished in 1950 and underwent full restoration in 1992. It's now a museum, with thorough signage and a room reserved for video presentations. The castle features a ground-floor mosque, an open courtyard and a stairway that ascends to the castle's second mosque and watchtowers. Outside are cisterns (c AD 650) that captured spring water. The museum has a large collection of antiques and documents dating to the time of the Prophet.

Tabuk

Top Sights

1 Hejaz Railway Station....B3
2 Tabuk Castle....A3

Sights

3 Museum of Antiquities and Traditional Heritage....B1
4 Prophet's Mosque....A3
5 Souq Twaheen....A3

Activities, Courses & Tours

6 Al Tayar Travel & Tourism Agency....D3
7 Tabuk Divers....C3
8 Tabuk Tourist Sights....A3

Sleeping

9 Tabuk Plaza Apartments....D3
10 Tulip Inn....C3

Eating

11 Bella Serra....B1
Tabuk Zaman Restaurant & Coffee Shop....(see 8)

Shopping

12 Jada Mall....A3

There is even a VIP room for international guests, who are served Arabic coffee and dates (museum personnel often coordinate with the restaurant across the street to treat visitors to Saudi hospitality).

★Hejaz Railway Station HISTORIC SITE
(☎04-421 6198; King Abdul Aziz Rd; ⌚9am-5pm Sat-Thu, 3-5pm Fri) This outpost of the early-20th-century Hejaz Railway is in the heart of the city, with 13 recently refurbished Hejazi-inspired buildings stretching over 80,000 sq metres. The station includes a workshop, a handicrafts centre and a building housing a locomotive and freight car. Adjacent is a state-of-the-art modern museum, scheduled to open in late 2016, dedicated to the railway's history and Tabuk's cultural history. Two other stations lie in Tabuk's hinterland.

Museum of Antiquities and Traditional Heritage MUSEUM
(☎04-422 1290 ext 287; khrisin@scth.gov.sa; Prince Sultan Cultural Centre; ⌚8am-2.30pm & 4-9pm Sat-Thu) The museum focuses on archaeological research and includes a restoration lab and lecture hall. A special treat is the exhibit on the pre-Islamic era. It's located off King Abdullah bin Abdulaziz Rd.

Prophet's Mosque MOSQUE
(Prince Fahd bin Sultan Rd; ⌚24hr) FREE The Prophet Mohammed offered prayers at the mosque after arriving with an army of 30,000 men for the Battle of Tabuk against the Byzantines. Originally constructed of bricks, mud and palm-tree trunks, the mosque was restored in 1652 and again in the early 20th century.

Souq Twaheen MARKET
(Windmill Souq; Othman bin Affan St) In the old quarter of Tabuk, the souq is dominated by grain and vegetable wholesale sellers bargaining with shopkeepers and restaurant owners. It's a good place for travellers to pick up items on the cheap for those out-of-the-way picnics. It's not much to look at, but the souq is a genuine Saudi marketplace where they bake the best bread in the region.

Prince Fahd bin Sultan's Park PARK
(Al Khawarazmi St) Although a bit sparse in amenities, Prince Fahd bin Sultan Park is a perfect spot for families to relax in the late afternoon and early evening. Even in summer the temperatures are relatively mild. A carpet of lush grass stretches along Rte 15, giving visitors an opportunity to take long walks or jog along the cement pathway that runs the length of the park.

Activities

Tabuk Divers DIVING
(☎04-450 0365; tabukdivers@hotmail.com; Al Jada St) A popular dive shop, Tabuk offers PADI-certified lessons and dive excursions. From the Jordan border along the entire length of the coastline of Tabuk Province there are around two dozen dive and swimming sites.

Tours

Tabuk Tourist Sights BUS TOUR
(☎055 537 0555; Prince Fahd bin Sultan Rd) Offers all-day bus tours with light breakfast and lunch buffet at SR250 per person. Tours include historic sites, museums and horse and camel rides. The owner, Hatim Al Jalawi, takes special pride in providing VIP treatment to Westerners as a way of introducing guests to Saudi culture and history. The office is opposite Tabuk Castle.

Al Tayar Travel & Tourism Agency TOUR
(☎04-428 1219) Operates tours and arranges flights and car rental. The office is near the corner of King Khalid and Prince Sultan Rds.

Sleeping

Tabuk Plaza Apartments APARTMENT $
(☎04-476 9511; Al Khamsin St, Al Solaimaniah District; s SR185, 1-/2-bedroom apt SR285/385; P 📶) Somewhat utilitarian apartments that provide more privacy than a hotel. This budget accommodation choice is located off King Khalid Rd.

Tulip Inn HOTEL $$
(☎04-423 0721; Al Olaya St; s/d/apt SR400/450/500; P 📶 🏊) The recently renovated Tulip Inn caters to families and is a favourite among airline crews and vacationers. The hotel's restaurant is open all day and a small cafe offers snacks and coffee. The rooms are priced reasonably, so go for the self-catering apartment for extra privacy and modest luxury appointments.

Sahara Tabuk Makarim Hotel HOTEL $$
(☎04-422 1212; Prince Fahd bin Sultan Rd; s/d/ste from SR 653/700/800; P 📶 🏊) Attractive to business travellers and only 3km from Tabuk regional airport, the rooms here are no-frills but comfortable. There's a fitness centre and an outdoor pool for evening swims. The hotel's Al Walima restaurant serves a middling buffet breakfast. Note that smoking is permitted just about everywhere in the hotel and no-smoking signs in a few spots are routinely ignored.

Eating

Bella Serra CAFE $
(☎04-443 4225; admin@bellaseracafe.com; Centria Centre, cnr Ali ibn Abi Talib & King Saud Rds; mains from SR18; ⏲4pm-midnight) Another operation with all female staff, this coffee shop specialises in Saudi sweets, cakes and fresh juices. The cafe opens into a lobby from the street and features large partitioned rooms for patrons' privacy. It also provides free transport to female patrons.

Tabuk Zaman Restaurant & Coffee Shop MIDDLE EASTERN $$
(☎04-421 5888, 055 113 4544; Prince Fahd bin Sultan Rd; mains SR40-150; ⏲mornings & evenings, hours vary) In a city not known for its restaurant diversity, Tabuk Zaman provides the biggest bang for your buck with a decent selection of Saudi dishes. Try the *mensaf* (lamb or chicken on a bed of rice; SR60 for chicken, SR70 for lamb). Only women – including the chefs, who specialise in home-cooked Saudi dishes – operate the restaurant and coffee shop.

The decor features genuine Saudi handicrafts and art, and customers can sit Saudi-style on the floor or at a table. Traditional Saudi clothing is also sold here.

Shopping

Jada Mall MALL
(Avenue Mall; cnr Othman bin Affan St & Prince Fahd bin Sultan Rd, Old Quarter; ⏲9am-noon & 4-11pm Sat-Thu, 5-11pm Fri) Jada Mall is a cluster of hundreds of shops on what can be loosely described as a pedestrian mall over several blocks. Closed to traffic, the mall teems with buyers on warm weekend (Thursday and Friday) nights. It offers virtually every product imaginable, from children's clothes at discount prices to high-end gold jewellery from the Gold Market section. Part of the fun is bargaining with gold sellers for 18-carat and 21-carat-gold bracelets and anklets.

Information

Bureau of Exchange (☎04-422 1501; Tabuk Airport Rd; ⏲9am-midnight) The best place to

TABUK: A PLACE APART

The Tabuk region is unlike any other in Saudi Arabia and often seems like a separate country. While Taif and Jeddah are family friendly with myriad amusement parks and public gardens for evening picnics, the residents of Tabuk lead starkly different and in some ways more traditional lives.

Although customs are slowly changing, families rarely venture out in public together and more often stay at home for entertainment. In public there is, for the most part, strict social segregation. Yet the contradictions are inescapable. Female-owned and operated businesses flourish in the region and women occupy very public jobs as, for instance, hotel and restaurant hosts and sales clerks. As a general rule, the people of Tabuk are open, friendly and generous with strangers, have a great affection for babies (don't be surprised if a woman reaches to hold an infant without asking permission first), and are immensely proud of their heritage.

WORTH A TRIP

THE NORTHERN RED SEA COAST

Saudi Arabia's northern Red Sea coast has some of the least visited beaches and stretches of coastline in the country, with some good diving spots if you're carrying your own equipment.

Al Wajh

Al Wajh (population 27,000) is unknown to many visitors – unspoilt beaches stretch for 100km on either side of the city. Scuba divers will find exceptionally clear water teeming with marine life. Al Wajh is 240km west of Al Ula or 325km southwest of Tabuk via Rte 80, then Rte 5. There are also Saudi Arabian Airlines flights to Al Wajh Airport from Tabuk.

Hawaz Beach

Around 60km north of Al Wajh is 6km-long Hawaz Beach. Shelters and barbecue pits dot the coastline here and are just off the highway.

An Nu'man Island

An Nu'man Island is a mountain slope rising from the sea. What could be better than hiking a mountainous island surrounded by crystal blue-green water? Think Tom Hanks in *Cast Away* but a bit closer to the mainland. The island is 198km southwest of Tabuk via Rte 80 on Rte 5.

Haql

In the country's extreme northwest, Haql is the only coastal village in Saudi Arabia from which the coastlines of Jordan, Israel and Egypt can be seen. Offshore from the crescent-shaped Bi'r Al Mazhi Beach is a ship sunk in 1975 that attracts adventurous divers. Nearby is Al Sultaniyyah Beach on the Aqaba Gulf, directly opposite Egypt and perfect for swimmers. Haql is also home to the more popular Al Wasl Island, which is accessible by boat or a short swim.

Al Sharim Beach

About 30km south of Haql, Al Sharim Beach also sits on a gulf. Rich in coral reefs and natural beauty, this portion of the coast has yet to be explored in depth by tourists.

change money is at Tabuk's Prince Sultan bin Abdul Aziz Airport.

Prince Fahd bin Sultan Hospital (☎ 04-428 2987; cnr Prince Sultan & Al Khalell bin Ahmad Rds) This medical facility has a good accident and emergency department.

ℹ Getting There & Around

Saudi Arabia's two domestic airlines use Prince Sultan bin Abdul Aziz International Airport. Airfares from Jeddah cost from SR252 with **Saudi Arabian Airlines** (☎ 04-422 1763; www.saudiairlines.com; Prince Abdulrahman Bin Faisal Rd; ⏰ 8am-4pm Sun-Thu) and SR209 on budget carrier **Nas Airlines** (☎ 04-421 5609; www.flynas.com; Prince Abdulrahman Bin Faisal Rd; ⏰ 10am-6pm Sun-Thu).

There are no taxis in Tabuk. Car rentals from the airport start at SR100 per day, plus SR15 daily for insurance, for a compact car.

Saptco (☎ 04-422 5357, 02-884 1344) The fare from Jeddah to Tabuk is SR160.

Around Tabuk

In Tabuk's hinterland you could scuba dive and play on the beaches of the Red Sea in the morning, then spend the afternoon hiking around the rocky hills and discovering what ancient civilisations brought to northwestern Saudi Arabia.

Qurayah

POP 27,000

Qurayah has seen considerable growth over the last decade. Its agricultural development and irrigation system date back 3000 years and the area has ancient pottery kilns, with pottery shards commonly found. Resist the temptation to take them home, though, as they're an important part of the region's heritage. The town is 90km northwest of Tabuk, off Rte 15.

WORTH A TRIP

TAIMA

Taima, 260km southeast of Tabuk via Rte 15, is rich in archaeological discoveries reaching as far back as the Bronze Age. In 2010, the Saudi Commission for Tourism & Antiquities announced that an inscription of the Egyptian pharaoh Ramesses III had been discovered on a rock near the city: the inscription dates to between 1185 and 1153 BC and is the first royal Egyptian artefact discovered in Saudi Arabia. Archaeologists believe the discovery lends credence to the theory that Taima and Tabuk were important destinations along a land route between the Arabian Peninsula's Red Sea coast and the Nile Valley.

In 2012, the Saudi government gave German archaeologists permission to continue excavation of the area until 2017. Among Taima's important discoveries accessible to visitors are a collection of brick tombs from 600 BC and the Hadaj Well from 500 BC. The well is 13m deep and has been restored. Nearby is the Rumman Palace, a castle constructed of clay and bricks. About 50km from Taima is the Qarat Al Hairan, featuring Thamud inscriptions. Permits to visit the site must be obtained through the Saudi Commission for Tourism & Antiquities (p278) in Riyadh.

Wadi Dam

At Wadi Dam, 200km southwest of Tabuk via Rte 80, the Paleolithic to Islamic eras are represented in hundreds of pieces of rock art. Images by the Nabatean, Greek and Thamudic peoples depict animal and human figures.

Hejaz Railway

In addition to Tabuk's downtown station, two remnants of the Hejaz Railway lie not far beyond the city limits.

Just 36km south of the city is Al Muazzam Station No. 27, a six-room structure with three arched openings and a water tower. Nearly in ruins, Al Akhdhar Station No. 30 is only for hardcore railway enthusiasts. It's 68km south of Tabuk.

Jebel Al Lawz

Jebel Al Lawz, rising 2785m above sea level, provides an unexpected treat in a land of blinding sun and barren landscapes. The slopes are blanketed with snow in winter.

Camping amid wild almond-tree groves on the eastern slopes in spring and summer is the main attraction for visitors, while hiking can be moderate to difficult through valleys rich in flora and fauna. Look out for rock formations with pre-Islamic petroglyphs and inscriptions.

There are no formal tours or guides for hiking, but local villagers – who welcome visitors warmly – are often willing to bargain for services.

MECCA

POP 1.3 MILLION

Muslims often describe the moment they step inside Mecca's Grand Mosque as an overwhelmingly emotional experience. For those living outside Saudi Arabia, a visit to Mecca – generally spelt 'Makkah' by Muslims and in Saudi Arabia – is a lifelong dream as they prepare for the hajj pilgrimage, an obligation that all Muslims must perform if they are financially and physical able to do so.

But Mecca, the birthplace of the Prophet Mohammed, is not limited to satisfying the spiritual thirst of visitors. Born of the desert, this is a city with the heart of a village, conjuring images of historic Arabia. Sun-bleached homes nestle in rocky hillsides and visitors bargain with shopkeepers with the largest mosque in the world rising above them. It's here that modernity, thanks to extensive building improvements, mixes with the Arabia of the past.

History

Mecca's recorded origins are vague, but evidence suggests it existed as early as 30 BC, when Greek historian Diodorus Siculus wrote of Bakkah and a holy shrine revered by inhabitants in a narrow valley on the Arabian Peninsula.

Islamic tradition holds that Mecca dates back even further, to 2000 BC, when Ibrahim (Abraham) rebuilt the Kaaba (House of God), the holy shrine that all Muslims face when performing prayers five times a day. By the 5th century AD the Quraysh tribe ruled Mecca and the city became known for its savvy spice merchants, who developed overland trade routes to avoid pirates at sea. The birth of Mohammed in AD 570 forever transformed Mecca from a trading post to the birthplace of Islam. By 610, Mecca's inhabitants were known for their pagan worship. Islamic scholars agree that Mohammed attempted to introduce monotheism but endured 13 years of persecution by the Quraysh and ultimately departed Mecca for Medina.

In AD 630, Mohammed's 10,000-man army marched in, destroyed the pagan idols and declared Mecca an Islamic city. The aim was to take the city as peacefully as possible, and it's believed to have happened with minimal bloodshed. Today, Mecca's population swells to nearly 4.5 million during each hajj pilgrimage.

Sights

Grand Mosque MOSQUE

(Al Masjid Al Haram; Great Mosque; 24hr) The focal point for every Muslim performing hajj, the Grand Mosque encompasses 356,800 sq metres. It can accommodate as many as 820,000 worshippers within its confines and more than one million outside the perimeter, where worshippers can pray. The Kaaba is in the central courtyard. The mosque dates to the 7th century under the leadership of Caliph Omar bin Al Khattab, who expanded the structure to accommodate the growing number of pilgrims each year.

Birthplace of Mohammed LIBRARY

(She'eb Banu, Hashim District; 10am-1pm & 5-9pm) FREE The birthplace of the Prophet still survives, although it faces threats of demolition to make way for the expansion of the Grand Mosque. Adjacent to the mosque across an expansive courtyard, the two-story structure is now a library. At this site it's believed that Aminah gave birth to the Prophet around six months after the death of the Prophet's father, who had been on a trading journey and had stopped in Medina. It's west of King Fahd Rd and the Second Ring Rd.

Makkah Museum MUSEUM

(012-547 1044; Medina Rd, Al Zahir District; 8am-12.30pm & 4-9pm Sat-Thu, 5-8.30pm Fri) FREE Once the Al Zahir Palace, the 3435-sq-metre Makkah Museum has a collection ranging from images of Saudi Arabia's important archaeological discoveries to exhibits on pre-Islamic history. An interesting presentation traces the origins of Islamic calligraphy by reference to Arabic fonts and samples of inscriptions discovered in archaeological digs. A hall on Islamic art complements the calligraphy displays.

Museum of the Prophet MUSEUM

(055-285 0031; 7th fl, World Trade Tower, Al Aziziyah St; 10am-noon & 5-9pm Sat-Thu, 5-9pm Fri) FREE Hajj and *umrah* pilgrims flock to this privately owned museum dedicated to study of the Quran, the Prophet's life and his Hadiths (traditions). The museum features a scientific examination of Mohammed's life, and there are also displays of utensils, furniture and weaponry used by the Prophet. Be sure to allow plenty of time to take in the collection, particularly the several versions of the Quran.

Al Haramain Museum MUSEUM

(025-549 0942; General Presidency for Haramain Bldg; by appointment) FREE Be persistent

Mecca

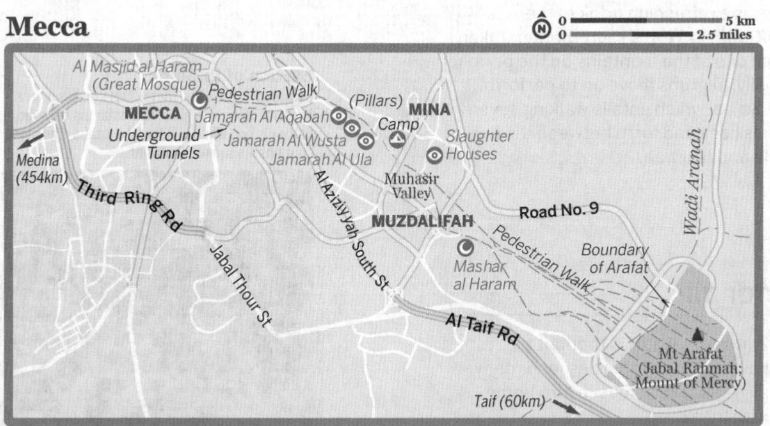

Grand Mosque (Al Masjid Al Haram)

Welcome to the world's largest mosque. The Grand Mosque (Al Masjid Al Haram) complex is the beating heart of Mecca, and home to the ❶ **Kaaba**, Islam's holiest site.

The mosque can hold almost a million worshippers at once, and plans for colossal expansion are underway to accommodate the huge numbers of pilgrims who visit the site each year.

During these pilgrimages, the flow of humanity never stops as worshippers try to get close enough to the Kaaba to touch or kiss it. If crowds – or sometimes security – prevent them from touching the black, veiled cube, they point at it instead.

This is part of the ritual of ❷ **tawaf**, one of the most significant parts of hajj and umrah. To perform the ritual, worshippers circle the Kaaba seven times counterclockwise, keeping it on their left.

Once they have completed the seventh round, they offer a prayer of two units, called rak'ahs, at the ❸ **Station of Ibrahim**, a small structure sitting about 1.5m from the door of the Kaaba.

Next is a refreshing drink of the ❹ **Zamzam Well's** sacred water, taken from one of the fountains on the periphery. Finally, pilgrims move on to perform ❺ **Sa'ee**, which entails walking seven times back and forth between the hills of Safa and Marwah.

TOP TIP

Zamzam's water is thought to have healing properties, and many pilgrims take at least a litre home with them.

AZAHAR PHOTOGRAPHY/GETTY IMAGES ©

Kaaba
The Kaaba was not always an Islamic place of worship but stood in the pre-Islamic era as a pagan shrine. Some scholars also claim that the Kaaba was once dedicated to the Nabataean deity Hubal.

Station of Ibrahim
Enclosed in glass and metal, this stone is where Ibrahim, often with his son, Ishmael, is believed to have stood while building the Kaaba. The stone contains his sunken footprint.

REZA/CONTRIBUTOR/GETTY IMAGES ©

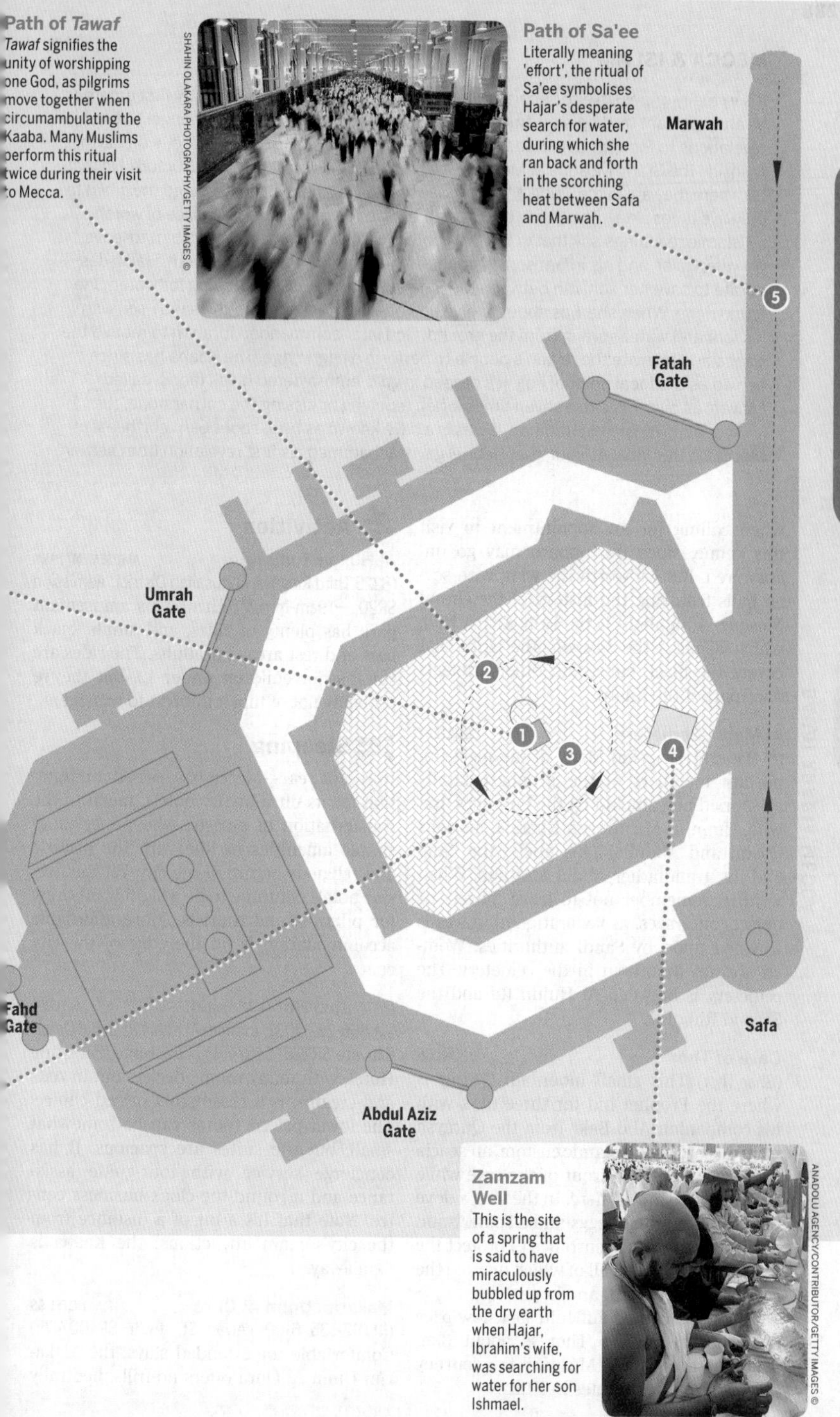
Path of *Tawaf*
Tawaf signifies the unity of worshipping one God, as pilgrims move together when circumambulating the Kaaba. Many Muslims perform this ritual twice during their visit to Mecca.
SHAHIN OLAKARA PHOTOGRAPHY/GETTY IMAGES ©
Path of Sa'ee
Literally meaning 'effort', the ritual of Sa'ee symbolises Hajar's desperate search for water, during which she ran back and forth in the scorching heat between Safa and Marwah.
Marwah
5
Fatah Gate
Umrah Gate
2
1
3
4
Fahd Gate
Safa
Abdul Aziz Gate
Zamzam Well
This is the site of a spring that is said to have miraculously bubbled up from the dry earth when Hajar, Ibrahim's wife, was searching for water for her son Ishmael.
ANADOLU AGENCY/CONTRIBUTOR/GETTY IMAGES ©

MECCA & ISLAM

It's virtually impossible to separate Mecca from its religious roots. The city first emerged as an important trading stop, but according to Islamic tradition, the archangel Gabriel's revelations to Mohammed made it the birthplace of Islam and the holiest city on Earth.

Inside the Grand Mosque at Mecca is the Kaaba, Islam's most revered structure. No matter where they are in the world, Muslims face the Kaaba (the direction is called the *qibla*) to pray five times a day. The Quran describes the Kaaba as the world's first place of worship.

Islamic teachings say that in the 3rd century BC God commanded Ibrahim to leave his wife, Hajar, and his infant son, Ishmael, in the desert as a test of his faith. Hajar, desperate to save her son, ran between the Safa and Marwah hills searching for water. She found none. When she was about to give up hope, Ishmael dug into the sandy soil with his foot and water sprang from the ground. God later commanded Ibrahim to rebuild the Kaaba and to invite the region's people to perform a pilgrimage. The Kaaba has since served as the focal point of hajj. It's draped in gold-embroidered black fabric, called *kiswah*, as pilgrims circle seven times, often touching or kissing the cornerstone.

According to Islamic tradition, it was in a cave known as Hira, about 6km northeast of Mecca on the Jabal Al Nour, that Gabriel gave Mohammed his first revelation from heaven.

when calling for an appointment to visit this venue, since the phones may go unanswered. But it's worth the wait, with seven halls featuring the history of the Grand Mosque. A highlight is the Holy Kaaba Hall, which displays the *kiswah*, the cloth that covers the black cube, and other artefacts once part of the Kaaba.

Al Malaa Cemetery CEMETERY

(Al Masjid Al Haram Rd) Many of the most important members of the Prophet's family are buried here, including the Prophet's first wife, Umm ul Mu'mineen Khadija, his sons Qasim and Abdullah, his uncle Abu Talib and his grandfather Abdul Muttalib. When visiting, remember not to leave flowers or objects on graves, as veneration of graves is frowned upon by Saudi authorities. Women are not permitted in the cemetery. The cemetery is between Al Hujun Rd and the Second Ring Rd.

Cave of Thor MOUNTAIN

(Ghar Thor) This small mountain (761m) is where the Prophet hid for three days with his companion Abu Bakr from the Quraysh tribe. According to Islamic custom, an acacia tree grew rapidly in front of the cave while the men were hiding here. In the tree, a dove built a nest and laid eggs and a spider spun a web over the cave's entrance to protect the men from detection, all of which marked the cave as a sign of faith and hope.

The climb can be difficult, so a slow pace is encouraged. Ghar Thor is about 3km south of the Grand Mosque; the journey takes around 30 minutes in a taxi.

Activities

Al Hukair Funland AMUSEMENT PARK

(8225 Third Ring Rd, Al Rusaifah District; admission SR20; 9am-1pm & 5-11pm) This amusement park has plenty of rides, and ample snack bars and rest areas for adults. The rides are suitable for children under 12, but they're probably not of much interest to teenagers.

Sleeping

In recent years, Mecca has earned a reputation for its ultra-luxury hotels, much to the consternation of purists, who prefer more simple amenities in line with the historic and religious nature of the city. Yet the five-star hotels continue to be a significant draw for pilgrims and tourists. More affordable accommodation is on the edge of the city centre.

Palestine Hotel Makkah HOTEL $

(866-232 5031; Ibrahim Al Khalil St, Jabal Omar; d/tr/ste SR228/348/461) The huge Palestine Hotel, with many rooms decked out in reds and creams, is a reasonably priced choice. The lower-priced rooms can be somewhat small, but the suites are spacious. It has concierge service with tour-guide assistance and a round-the-clock business centre. Note that it's a bit of a distance from the city's main attractions: the Kaaba is 5km away.

Makarim Umm Al Qura HOTEL $$

(012-535 6100; Aiyad St; tw/tr SR400/475) Comfortable for extended stays, the Makarim Umm Al Qura offers no-frills, neutrally decorated rooms; the spacious triples are worth the extra SR75. The hotel's Al Taai restaurant serves an excellent breakfast and lunch. The Grand Mosque is 2km away, but don't let that fool you: the heat means it's not within easy walking distance; take a taxi.

Other perks include concierge service, a 24-hour business centre, and friendly front-desk staff.

Hyatt Regency Makkah HOTEL **$$**
(☎012-577 1234; makkah.regency.hyatt.com/en/hotel/home; Ibrahim Al Khalil St, Jabal Omar; r SR533-703;) This high-end hotel offers large rooms with partial views of the Grand Mosque from floor-to-ceiling windows. The bathrooms are the height of luxury, with walk-in marble rain showers.

Fairmont Makkah Clock Royal Tower HOTEL **$$$**
(☎012-571 7777; fairmont.com/makkah; Abraj Al Beit, Uum Al Qura St; r SR1061-5266) The Fairmont may have an air of controversy around it for its association with the complex's clock tower (p290), but there is no question that it is every bit the five-star hotel it claims to be. Rooms offer panoramic views of Mecca and the Kaaba in the Great Mosque.

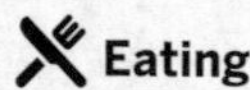

Eating

Unless visitors choose to eat at one of the many five-star hotels surrounding the Grand Mosque, there are few high-end restaurants in town. Not particularly known for its cuisine, Mecca offers mostly Arab-style, Pakistani and Indonesian fare, reflecting local and tourist tastes, at modest prices. Many midrange and fast-food eateries do not offer family seating.

Al Tazaj FAST FOOD **$**
(☎012-557 2003; Haram Commercial Centre, Al Azizia St; mains SR10-45; ⏲1pm-2am) This little fast-food restaurant has great barbecue chicken and hamburgers. Try the tikka rolls (SR10). Customer queues are often long, and they're out the door at peak dining hours.

Kholood Restaurant & Café MIDDLE EASTERN **$**
(☎012-545 4704; Abdullah Oraif St, Rte 40; mains SR10-45; ⏲noon-11pm) This inexpensive but quality cafe specialises in kebabs garnished with vegetables and olives. The atmosphere is generic, but you come for the good food and cheap prices. Try to go between *asr* (afternoon) and *mahgreb* (dusk) prayers because it's crowded after *mahgreb*.

SACRED SITES

In a city rich with religious sites it can be difficult for the first-time visitor to absorb the significance of each place. Complement your visit to the Grand Mosque with trips to key mosques and mountains just outside Mecca to more fully appreciate the city's cultural and religious importance.

Masjid Al Bi'ah Found off Al Haramain Rd near Mina, Masjid Al Bi'ah marks the spot where tribal leaders pledged their allegiance to Mohammed in AD 621. Simple in design, but carrying Hejazi architectural touches, it features arched entryways opening to a large courtyard. It's easily accessible from the street and can accommodate visitors with disabilities.

Masjid Al Khayf According to a Hadith of Bin Abbas – a cousin of the Prophet and an early Islamic scholar – numerous prophets prayed here. It's south of Mina.

Jabal Al Nour (Mountain of Light) The 640m-tall Jabal Al Nour is the location of the tiny Hira cave and one of the most important pilgrimage sites. According to Islamic tradition, it was here that the archangel Gabriel gave the Prophet his first revelation. Although the mountain is actually a hill, reaching the cave entails a difficult hike that takes even the fittest hiker as much as two hours. Temperatures can reach 45°C and extreme caution should be exercised before making the climb.

You'll find Jabal Al Nour east of Al Hajj Rd and north of King Faisal Rd.

Jabal Rahmah (Mt Arafat) Known as the Mountain of Mercy, this granite hill is an important part of performing hajj as pilgrims leave Mina for Arafat on the ninth day to recite the Quran and pray. The Prophet gave his last sermon at the site shortly before his death. Stairs leading to the hill's peak provide relatively easy access. Vendors may be selling markers here, but be aware that writing names on the hillside is illegal.

WORTH A TRIP

MEDINA

Whenever Medinans return home after a long absence they relish the peaceful atmosphere of their city. Nestled against the Uhud Mountain range that rises to 1077m, the city twists around rocky hills, some of which feature flowing human-made streams tumbling down the granite. In the evening the hills near the city centre are illuminated, giving Medina a magical vibe. The air is breathtakingly clean, even in summer, when temperatures can reach 42°C, and especially in winter, when temperatures can drop to 10°C during the day.

Hajj pilgrims usually visit the city as part of their itinerary, since Medina is Saudi Arabia's second holy city, where Mohammed made his home following his exile from Mecca. The sprawling Prophet's Mosque (Al Masjid An Nabawī) – on the site of the Prophet's home – and the Quba Mosque, believed to be the oldest mosque in the world, are must-sees for pilgrims.

The Prophet's Mosque, which never closes, becomes the centre of bustling crowds during hajj. Four- and five-star hotels line the perimeter of the grounds to accommodate the hundreds of thousands of visitors, and during hajj season the hotels' ground-floor malls and shops are thronged. The Prophet's Mosque is especially crowded during Eid Al Fitr, following Ramadan. During Eid, tens of thousands of worshippers stream through the small confines of one portion of the mosque in a single day. They offer supplications and prayers in an area called Al Rawdah between the Prophet's tomb and the site of his house.

If visitors are lucky enough to have family or friends living in Medina during Eid, their hosts will drive to the edge of the western portion of the city to purchase a lamb, have it slaughtered according to Islamic tradition and serve it barbecued on a single bed of rice on a huge platter. Supper is eaten Arabian style on the floor late in the evening.

Tayyibah Restaurant MIDDLE EASTERN $
(☎055-625 7134; Ajyad St; mains SR20-50; ⊙noon-11pm) At this ragged little restaurant the waiters are a little slow in cleaning dirty tables, but the food, particularly the lamb biryani, is very good at modest prices. It's no-fuss Middle Eastern– and Pakistani-style fast food, and ideal if you're in a hurry.

Al Deyafa FAST FOOD $$
(☎012-571 4444; Al Marwa Rayhaan, Abraj Al Beit, Uum Al Qura St; mains SR100-150; ⊙6-10.30am, 1-3.30pm & 7-11pm) On the 12th floor of the Al Marwa Rayhaan hotel, with a spectacular view of the Grand Mosque, Al Deyafa offers European cuisine along with a selection of Arab and Mediterranean offerings.

Shopping

Makkah Mall MALL
(☎012-528 2211; www.makkahmall.com; King Abullah bin Abdulaziz Rd; ⊙10am-11pm Sat-Thu, 5-11pm Fri) This shopping centre has an extensive range of retail outlets, including designer and luxury brands. On Friday most shops don't open until after *asr* (afternoon) prayers, which is about 5pm.

Abraj Al Beit Towers MALL
(Fairmont Makkah Clock Royal Tower; Uum Al Qura St; ⊙10am-noon & 5-11pm) They've been criticised for their modern architectural design overlooking the historic and holy Grand Mosque, but these 601m-tall, postmodern towers are perhaps Mecca's most visited non-religious landmark. They feature a prayer hall that can accommodate up to 10,000 people and – perhaps incongruously – a five-storey mega shopping mall.

Information

EMERGENCY

Ambulance (☎997)
Fire (☎998)
Police (☎999)
Traffic Accidents (☎993)

MEDICAL SERVICES

King Abdulaziz Hospital (☎012-544 2400; Qasr Al Dhiyaafah St, Al Zahir) Good emergency department.

MONEY

Said MA Al Amoudi & Partners Co (☎012-647 4515; Umm Al Qura Rd, Jabal Omar; ⊙9am-1.30pm & 4.30-10pm)

TRAVEL AGENCIES

Abdel Al Lehaibi Travel Office (☎012-548 7314; Biban Dist)

Getting There & Away

Al Shitaiwi Travel & Tourism (p271) in Jeddah runs tours and can arrange flights and car rental for trips to Mecca.

AIR

Mecca has no major airport, so you must fly to Jeddah and then take a taxi to Mecca. Arriving at Jeddah airport, avoid the illegal cab drivers and head for the taxi queue. Fares from the airport to Mecca start at SR100 to SR150. The highway between Jeddah and Mecca can be dangerous. Although it's a relatively straight shot between the two cities, motorists speed and illegally use the left and right shoulders to pass. Urge your driver to be cautious and tip him well if he follows your instructions.

Saudi Arabian Airlines (9200 22222; www.saudiairlines.com; Al Shohada Rd, Mecca-Medina Expressway; 8am-10pm Sat-Thu, 3-10pm Fri) Flies daily between Riyadh and Jeddah (SR460 return).

Flynas (012-567 0000; www.flynas.com; Al Rusaifa District Branch, Al Nakheel Centre; 9am-6pm) Flies between Riyadh and Jeddah (from SR650 return).

BUS

Saptco fares from Jeddah to Mecca are about SR40 for the one-hour trip. The Saptco Al Haram bus station in Mecca is on Jabal Al Kaabah Rd at Omar bin Abdulaziz Rd.

Getting Around

Taxis in Mecca start at about SR20 to get just about anywhere in the city.

UNDERSTAND SAUDI ARABIA

Saudi Arabia Today

On the face of it, the Arab Spring had little impact in Saudi Arabia, although pockets of unrest did occur in mainly Shiite areas of the Eastern Province. But it has been terrorism that has dominated so many headlines in recent years. Mass arrests and trials of suspected Islamist militants have become all too common, while a suicide attack on a Shiite mosque in the east of the Kingdom in 2015 suggested that things may get worse before they get better.

The country's internal war against extremism has been mirrored by Saudi Arabia's participation in wars across the region: Saudi Arabia has been heavily involved in the conflict in neighbouring Yemen, while the Saudi air force has joined the international coalition of Western forces carrying out air strikes on Islamic State positions in Syria and Iraq.

Similarly complicated has been the path of reform. King Abdullah appointed 30 women to the previously all-male Shura Consultative Council (the first time Saudi women have held any positions of political power), but any signs of dissent still provide a trigger for repressive government crackdowns. The death of King Abdullah in January 2015 and his replacement by the conservative King Salman suggest that the reform agenda could slow, and King Salman's appointment of his nephew, Mohammed bin Nayef, as his crown prince and successor was widely seen as the first sign of generational change in the Kingdom's political power balance – the new crown prince is the first of his generation to be in line for the throne.

History

Ancient Arabia

The myriad kingdoms and empires that grew from the desert sands of Arabia prior to the Prophet Mohammed all had one commonality: frankincense. Ancient gods were placated with holy smoke and the peoples of Arabia got very rich providing frankincense to eager worshippers in ancient Egypt, Persia and Rome. One of the most intriguing groups of these trading states were the Nabataens: Bedouin clans who gathered at the extraordinary rock-hewn twin cities of Madain Saleh (Saudi Arabia) and Petra (Jordan).

The phenomenal explosion of Islamic-inspired armies out of Arabia shattered the weary Byzantine and Sassanid Empires, but following the Prophet Mohammed's death in 632, Arabia slumped into torpor again and was economically insignificant to the sophisticated Umayyad and Abbasid caliphates. Arabia was only saved from irrelevance by the utmost spiritual significance of the holy cities of Mecca and Medina.

Trade caravans still crossed the desert, linking the cities and small towns of the Hejaz and the interior with the great cities of the wider Islamic world, but in 1517 the powerful Turkish Ottomans, under Salim I, invaded Arabia and took control of the two holy cities, a most unwelcome development in the peninsula.

BOOKS ABOUT SAUDI ARABIA

Some of the following titles are available from any branch of the Jarir Bookstore. Those that aren't are probably banned inside the Kingdom, for obvious reasons.

Arabian Sands (by Wilfred Thesiger) If you only read one book about the early explorers, make it this one.

Travels in Arabia Deserta (by Charles M Doughty) A rival to Thesiger's meditations on the Bedu and their desert home.

Arabia of the Bedouins (by Marcel Kurpershoek) A nuanced account of a Dutch diplomat's search for the magic of poetry among Bedouin nomads.

Desert Treks from Riyadh (by Ionis Thompson) Excellent for excursions around the capital.

The Saudis: Inside the Desert Kingdom (by Sandra Mackey) A searing expat account from the early 1980s.

Inside the Kingdom (by Robert Lacey) Gripping and succinct analysis and probably the best (and most frightening) overview available of the Kingdom today.

Cities of Salt Chronicles (by Abdelrahman Munif) The impact of oil money and modernisation on a deeply traditional society; banned in the Kingdom.

Women and Words in Saudi Arabia (by Saddeka Arebi) A fascinating insight into the world of Saudi women.

Girls of Riyadh (by Rajaa Alsanea) A sensational first novel that lifts the lid on the lives of young Saudi women.

Wahhabi Islam & the Al Sauds

In 1703 a seemingly insignificant man was born in the then-insignificant oasis village of Al Uyaynah in the Wadi Hanifa of central Arabia. Yet this man – Mohammed ibn Abd Al Wahhab – would ultimately transform the lives of all inhabitants of the Arabian Peninsula. After a period of itinerant religious scholarship, Al Wahhab returned to Al Uyaynah and preached his message calling for the purification of Islam and a return to the original values proclaimed by the Prophet Mohammed.

Al Wahhab's reform agenda was initially successful and he converted the local sheikh to his message. But the severe punishments Al Wahhab meted out to those he accused of sorcery, adultery and other crimes unnerved the local authorities and he was exiled. Al Wahhab sought refuge in Dir'aiyah, 65km from Al Uyaynah, where he was granted protection by Mohammed ibn Al Saud, the local emir. Al Wahhab provided religious legitimacy to the Al Sauds, who in turn provided political protection for Al Wahhab. Together they built a power base that relied on the formidable combination of politics and religion.

With growing anger throughout Arabia that the holy cities of Mecca and Medina were under Ottoman control, the Saudi-Wahhabi emirate expanded rapidly. Upon his death, Al Saud was succeeded by his son Abdul Aziz, who captured Dir'aiyah's rival city in central Arabia – Riyadh – in 1765. In 1792 Al Wahhab died, but the inexorable expansion of the Saudi-Wahhabi emirate continued.

In 1803 the Saudi-Wahhabi army finally marched on the holy cities of the Hejaz and defeated Sherif Hussain of Mecca. The Saudi-Wahhabi emirate was recognised by the Mecca authorities, whereupon this first Saudi empire stretched from Al Hasa in the east to Hejaz in the west and Najran in the south.

The Birth of Saudi Arabia

It didn't last long. Ottoman sultan Mahmoud II ordered his over-powerful viceroy of Egypt, Mohammed Ali, to retake Hejaz in the sultan's name. Supported by many Arabian tribes who resented domination by the Saudi-Wahhabis, Mohammed Ali's armies successfully captured Mecca and Medina in 1814 and conquered the Saudi-Wahhabi stronghold of Dir'aiyah on 11 September 1818. Mohammed Ali topped off his triumph by executing Abdullah ibn Al Saud (Abdul Aziz's successor).

The Al Sauds spent the rest of the 19th century fighting the Ottomans, rival tribes and themselves to no apparent gain. The decisive battle for the future of modern Arabia came in 1902, when a 21-year-old Abdul Aziz ibn Abdul Rahman ibn Al Saud (Ibn Saud) and his small band of followers successfully stormed Riyadh under cover of night and daringly captured the fortress.

With deft diplomacy and the momentum of a successful military campaign, Ibn Saud orchestrated a conference at which Arabia's Islamic clergy condemned Sherif Hussain (ruler of Mecca) as a mere puppet of 'The Turk'. Sherif Hussain promptly responded by proclaiming himself king of the Arabs. In 1925 the Saudi-Wahhabis took Mecca and Medina; the following year Ibn Saud proclaimed himself king of the Hejaz and sultan of Najd, and on 22 September 1932, Ibn Saud announced the formation of the Kingdom of Saudi Arabia.

The Power of Oil

In 1933 Saudi Arabia signed its first oil concession. Four years later, the Arabian American Oil Company (Aramco) discovered commercial quantities of oil near Riyadh and around Dammam in the east. In 1943 President Roosevelt established the Kingdom's political importance by grandly stating that the Kingdom was 'vital for the defence of the USA'.

In 1964, King Faisal began to provide his subjects with a stake in the economic benefits of oil. He introduced a free health service for all Saudi citizens and began a building boom that has transformed Saudi Arabia from an impoverished desert kingdom into a nation of modern infrastructure.

In response to the USA's unconditional support for Israel, Saudi Arabia imposed an oil embargo in 1974, a move that quadrupled oil prices globally and reminded the world of the country's importance in an economy dependent upon oil.

A Kingdom of Contradictions

On 25 March 1975 King Faisal was assassinated by a nephew and the throne formally passed to Faisal's brother Khaled. Real power, however, lay with another of Faisal's brothers, Fahd.

In November 1979 the Great Mosque of Mecca was overrun by 250 fanatical followers of Juhaiman ibn Saif Al Otai, a militant Wahhabi leader, who claimed that the Mahdi (Islamic Messiah) would appear in the mosque that very day. During two bloody weeks of fighting, 129 people were killed. In 1980, riots broke out in the towns of the Qatif Oasis (the heartland of the Kingdom's 300,000 Shiites). The riots were brutally repressed.

On 14 June 1982 the figurehead King Khaled died aged 69. Fahd became king and set about reinforcing the twin pillars of modern Al Saud rule. He made a priority of proving himself a moderate and reliable friend of the West, but in 1986 he proclaimed himself the 'Custodian of the Two Holy Mosques', the coveted title that confirms Saudi sovereignty over the holy cities of Mecca and Medina and seeks to bestow legitimacy upon the Saudi royal family in the wider Islamic world.

When Iraq invaded Kuwait in August 1990, Saudi Arabia made the hugely controversial decision to allow foreign military forces to operate from Saudi soil. In 1991 a petition calling for reforms and greater openness was sent to King Fahd by liberal intellectuals. It was quickly followed by a contrary petition by conservative Islamic scholars – a struggle within Saudi politics that continues to this day.

After a great deal of fanfare, the feeble Consultative Council (Majlis ash-Shoura) was opened on 20 August 1993. When Fahd died in August 2005, his half-brother

THE BEDU

The Bedu (Bedouin) represent 15% of the Saudi population and, although they're looked down upon by many city-dwelling Saudis, the Bedu remain the bedrock of Saudi society. The traits historically associated with the Bedu are legendary and include a refusal to surrender to outside authority; a fierce loyalty to one's family and tribe; the primacy of courage and honour; the purity of language and dialect as preserved in poetry and desert legends; a belief in the desert codes of hospitality, blood feuds and mutual obligations; and the tradition of *razzia* (raiding travellers or members of other tribes).

Some 1.8 million Bedu still claim to lead a semi-nomadic lifestyle in Saudi Arabia, living for at least part of the year in movable encampments of black goat-hair tents and following grazing fields for their livestock and sources of water.

CREATIVE CRUISING

If you think it might be difficult to survive in cities with the most restricted entertainment scenes in the world, spare a thought for young Saudis. In a country where cinema is banned, singles are kept strictly separated from the opposite sex and nightclubs are nonexistent, young Saudis have resorted to novel means of making contact.

The least subtle of these are the *shebab* (teenage boys) with little else to do but 'impress' other drivers with their speed. Cars cruise up and down outside girls' schools and the *shebab* sometimes throw their phone numbers from the window in the hope of receiving a call on their mobile.

The *shebab* try a similar gambit while cruising on foot in the shopping malls in Riyadh (particularly Al Faisaliah and Kingdom Towers). Called 'numbering', it's the Saudi version of a casual encounter. Bluetooth technology has facilitated things still further by allowing total strangers to text each other without even knowing each other's numbers.

Abdullah ascended the throne and Prince Sultan bin Abdulaziz Al Saud became crown prince.

People

Saudi society is still strictly segregated between the public (male) and private (female) domain. Family and Islam form the twin pillars of Saudi society.

Population

Around 80% of Saudi Arabia's population is concentrated in urban areas, with more than one-third of the population in the megacities sprawling around Riyadh, Jeddah and Mecca.

Saudi's population is very young (almost 47% of the population is under 25 years old), with an annual population growth rate of 1.5% – meaning the population doubles around every 30 years. Saudi authorities are confronted with the dilemma of providing for a disaffected, young, Islamicised population with not enough jobs to go around.

The Lives of Women

Despite the opening of the country's first co-educational university in 2009, education remains strictly segregated. The education system is strongly criticised by educated Saudis for its reliance on rote learning and heavy emphasis on Wahhabi Islam to the exclusion of much else. Official school curricula are under review, but change happens at a glacial pace, with reformers ever wary of a conservative backlash.

A woman's life in Saudi Arabia is more controlled than it is anywhere else in the industrialised world, particularly with regard to freedom of movement. Women are officially forbidden to drive within the country's cities – although this only became a formal law in 1990, following protests by 47 women deploring restrictions to their day-to-day lives. Yet Saudi and foreign women drive freely within the oil-company compounds of Aramco and have done so for years.

Saudi Arabia has signed the UN Convention on the Elimination of All Forms of Discrimination Against Women, and girls officially enjoy the same right to attend a segregated school and university as boys and later to work as teachers, doctors, nurses, social workers, business managers and journalists. Visible Saudi and Arab female journalists on the satellite news channels beamed daily from the Gulf into Saudi homes are altering both private and public perceptions of a woman's role. Many Saudis (including women) also say that women in Saudi Arabia live free from the fear of public harassment and sexual assault.

Multiculturalism

Modern Saudi Arabia is a paradox; it's one of the most insular societies on Earth, yet a large proportion of the population are foreigners. Around one-third of all Saudi Arabia's inhabitants are expats, although this is widely believed to be a gross understatement, and the large cities can feel distinctly Asian rather than Arab.

Westerners often work in high-skilled and technical jobs for which Saudis do not yet have qualifications or experience – something King Abdullah's educational reforms aimed to address. Non-Western expats (primarily Pakistanis, Bangladeshis, Indians and Filipinos) perform mostly unskilled labour such as taxi driving, construction work and domestic help. However, a substantial and growing cadre of medical professionals and information-technology specialists from the Indian subcontinent has altered Saudi perceptions. Many of the unskilled labourers in particular complain of ill treatment, exploitation and abuse, although Saudi law in theory protects its legal immigrants.

As the location of Islam's holiest sites, Saudi Arabia receives millions of hajj and *umrah* (a pilgrimage to Mecca that's not hajj) pilgrims from poor Islamic countries, and many of these stay on in the Kingdom to work illegally. The local media often attribute crime to illegal immigrants, stoking traditional prejudices.

Religion

Islam is not just the religion of Saudi citizens; it's the religion of Saudi society and the Saudi state, and it's all-encompassing.

Officially, all Saudi citizens are Muslim; 15% are Shiites who live particularly in the Eastern Province. The practice of other religions is strictly forbidden in Saudi Arabia. Non-Muslims cannot even be buried within the borders of the Kingdom.

Wahhabi Islam

Islamic orthodoxy in Saudi Arabia is Wahhabi Islam (an offshoot of Hanbali or the 'literalist' school of Islamic interpretation). Named after the 18th-century cleric Mohammed ibn Abd Al Wahhab, Wahhabi doctrine calls for a return to the Arab purity of Islam and rejection of Sufism and Turkish and especially Persian influences on Islamic thought and practice.

At the heart of Wahhabi Islam is a denunciation of all forms of mediation between Allah and believers, and a puritanical reassertion of *tawhid* (the oneness of God). Under the Wahhabis, only the Quran, the Sunnah (the words and deeds of Mohammed) and the Hadith (Mohammed's sayings) are acceptable sources of Islamic knowledge. Under Wahhabi doctrine, communal prayers are a religious duty and rulings on personal matters are interpreted according to Sharia'a.

Environment

The Land

Saudi Arabia takes up 80% of the Arabian Peninsula. Over 95% of Saudi Arabia is desert or semi-desert, and the country is home to some of the largest desert areas in the world, including Al Nafud (Nafud Desert) in the north and the Empty Quarter in the south.

Just 1.5% of Saudi territory is considered to be suitable for agriculture and just 0.5% of the land is covered by forest.

THE RETURN OF THE ARABIAN ORYX

Just 200 years ago, the Arabian oryx (*Oryx leucoryx*), with its distinctive white coat and curved horns, roamed across much of the Arabian Peninsula, especially in the Nafud Desert in northern Arabia and the Rub' Al Khali (Empty Quarter) in the south. Hunting devastated the population, which retreated deeper into the desert, pursued by automatic weapons and motorised vehicles. The species was wiped out in the northern Nafud in the 1950s, and the last wild oryx was killed in the Dhofar foothills of Oman in 1972.

But all was not lost, and it wasn't long before an ambitious program of reintroducing the Arabian oryx to its former territories was launched. A captive breeding program had begun in the early 1960s when four wild oryx (three males and a female) were caught in southeastern Saudi Arabia. In 1964, nine Arabian oryx (gifts from Gulf sheikhs) were taken to Phoenix Zoo in the US. By 1977, the 'World Oryx Herd' in America had grown to almost 100. Between 1978 and 1992, members of the herd were transported back to the Middle East, including 55 oryx to Saudi Arabia and smaller populations to Jordan, Israel, the UAE and Oman.

In Saudi Arabia, Arabian oryx from the breeding program of the National Wildlife Research Center (NWRC; www.nwrc.gov.sa) in Taif were released into the fenced, 2244-sq-km Mahazat as-Sayd protected area. Since 1995, 149 oryx have been released into the 'Uruq Bani Ma'arid protected area in the northwestern part of the Rub' Al Khali near Sulayyil. Oryx territory now measures 12,000 sq km and, despite the challenges of poaching and drought, the remaining herd (estimated to number over 500 animals) is the only viable population of Arabian oryx in the wild.

Wildlife

Illegal hunting is still a major problem in Saudi Arabia and according to the International Union for the Conservation of Nature (IUCN), the list of endangered mammals in Saudi Arabia includes the dugong, Arabian oryx, Arabian leopard and Nubian ibex. Successful captive breeding and reintroduction programs for species such as the Arabian oryx, Arabian leopard and houbara bustard are at the forefront of the government's work to arrest the slide.

The waters of Saudi's Red Sea are teeming with wildlife, and include five species of marine turtle. Whales and dolphins are also present in the Red Sea and the Gulf.

Environmental Issues

Saudi Arabia's environmental problems are legion and include desertification, pollution, deforestation, lack of local education and awareness, and critical depletion of underground water. Illegal hunting – even of endangered species – is a particular problem. Once a Bedouin survival strategy, hunting is now an enjoyable sport for many Saudis and the Kingdom is still a popular hunting destination for wealthy Gulf Arabs.

The Kingdom's water shortages are especially worrying for the ruling family. Expensive seawater-desalination plants are all over the country, but the depletion of underground aquifers continues at an alarming rate.

SURVIVAL GUIDE

Directory A–Z

ACCOMMODATION

The quality of accommodation varies widely throughout the Kingdom. Budget accommodation is rarely an option for Western travellers (and never so for women travellers) for reasons of both security and cleanliness. Midrange hotels range from places of dubious repute to some outstanding places; most have private bathrooms.

Saudi Arabia has a generous selection of top-range, international-standard hotels and the government is keen to get Westerners on business trips to stay in them. Most offer the usual five-star facilities, including business centres, internet access, swimming pools and fitness centres. If you're travelling for business ask your company to fax the hotel with your dates to ensure a discount.

> **SLEEPING PRICE RANGES**
>
> The following price ranges refer to a double room with private bathroom; unless otherwise stated, prices do not include taxes or breakfast.
>
> **$** less than SR400 (US$106)
>
> **$$** SR400–1000 (US$106–266)
>
> **$$$** more than SR1000 (US$266)

Check when making a reservation whether quoted room rates include the 15% service charge that is added to your bill by all five- and some four-star hotels and restaurants.

In the high season – during hajj (particularly in Jeddah), at the end of Ramadan, during school holidays and in summer (June to August) – prices in Taif and other mountain regions can increase anywhere between 50% and 150%. At these times, advance reservations are strongly recommended.

ACTIVITIES

4WD Excursions

There are ample opportunities to leave tarmac roads behind and explore Arabia's desert interior. Among the most rewarding are the sand seas of the Empty Quarter, following the Hejaz Railway, and excursions into the Al Nafud desert.

Locally produced guides to off-road excursions within the Kingdom can be found in any branch of the Jarir Bookstore, while most of the country's travel agencies can arrange guided expeditions.

Beaches

Saudi's beaches fall into two categories: some of those on the Red Sea coast are long, empty and utterly splendid. Many others, particularly those close to towns, are built on, strewn with litter and very crowded at weekends. They're almost all men-only. The best bet is to head for the five-star coastal hotels, which often have their own private beach where women can also swim (usually covered up by a T-shirt and trousers).

Diving

Those who know Saudi Arabia rank it among the best diving countries in the world. Its relative obscurity is its greatest advantage and its reefs remain nearly empty of divers and boats.

Note that women (local and foreign) are permitted to dive, although conservative behaviour is still sometimes expected, such as wearing loose clothing over your wetsuit until just before you get into the water.

Even in winter, the water temperatures rarely drop too low (at the southern sites from 24°C to 26°C), though wetsuits of between 5mm and 6mm are advised in winter, 3mm to 4mm in summer. Visibility ranges from good to astonishing (up to 35m to 40m is not uncommon). In general, there are few currents to contend with.

Where to Dive

The safest and most accessible dive sites are those at Jeddah and Yanbu, with reputable operators in both places.

Jeddah has more than 50 dive sites, and a number of wrecks (accessible even to inexperienced divers) can be reached by day boats operated by local dive clubs. Expect a colourful selection of hard and soft corals, and a good variety of smaller reef fish, including anthias, sergeant majors, large-sized trevally jacks, kingfish and Spanish mackerels, as well as rays, moray eels and turtles.

Yanbu, 230km north of Jeddah, is well known for outstanding visibility (34m to 40m on average). You'll find hammerheads here at deeper depths (from around 40m), while other highlights include Napoleon wrasse, blue-spotted rays, moray eels and turtles.

CHILDREN

Saudi Arabia has numerous amusement parks for children – just about every medium-size town has one. They're usually family-only affairs and cost around SR15/8 per adult/child.

CUSTOMS REGULATIONS

Despite all warnings, some travellers continue to try to enter Saudi with alcohol. If you are caught with any amount, you will be returned home on the next flight. If you're deemed to be in possession of a quantity that exceeds 'personal consumption', punishments are severe (they include flogging and even the death penalty if you're convicted of smuggling).

DVDs, videos or suspect-looking books are passed to Ministry of Information officials for inspection. Unfamiliar or suspect-looking items may be confiscated for further inspection for up to 48 hours. Receipts are issued for later collection once items have been inspected and passed. Laptops and computer media are not checked unless officials are suspicious.

EMBASSIES & CONSULATES

Australian Embassy (☎01-250 0900; www.saudiarabia.embassy.gov.au; Abdullah bin Hozafa Al Sahmi Ave, Diplomatic Quarter; 🕒9am-4pm Sun-Thu)

Bahraini Embassy (☎01-488 0044; www.mofa.gov.bh; Diplomatic Quarter; 🕒8am-2pm Sat-Wed)

Canadian Embassy (☎01-488 2288; www.canadainternational.gc.ca; Diplomatic Quarter; 🕒8am-4pm Sun-Thu)

French Embassy (☎01-434 4100; www.ambafrance-sa.org; Diplomatic Quarter; 🕒7.45am-3.30pm Sun-Thu)

German Embassy (☎01-277 6900; www.riad.diplo.de; Diplomatic Quarter; 🕒8.30-11.30am Sun, Mon, Wed & Thu)

Irish Embassy (☎01-488 2300; www.embassyofireland.org.sa; Diplomatic Quarter; 🕒9-11am Sun-Thu)

Kuwaiti Embassy (☎01-488 3500; www.mofa.gov.kw; Abdullah bin Hozafa Al Sahmi Ave, Diplomatic Quarter; 🕒9-11am Sun-Thu)

New Zealand Embassy (☎01-488 7988; www.nzembassy.com/saudi-arabia; Diplomatic Quarter; 🕒9am-noon & 12.30-3pm Sun-Thu)

Qatari Embassy (☎01-482 5544; https://qatar.visahq.com/embassy/saudi-arabia/; Abdullah bin Hozafa Al Sahmi Ave, Diplomatic Quarter)

UAE Embassy (☎01-488 1227; www.uae-embassy.ae/Embassies/sa; 🕒9am-noon Sun-Thu)

UK Embassy (☎01-481 9100; ukinsaudiarabia.fco.gov.uk; Diplomatic Quarter; 🕒8am-3pm Sun-Thu)

PRACTICALITIES

Discount cards Although there is no official discounting policy for holders of student cards, some places will offer discounts if you ask for them and upon presentation of official student accreditation (international or local).

DVDs Like much of Europe and the Middle East, Saudi Arabia belongs to DVD region 2.

Electricity Both 110VAC and 220VAC; European two-pin plugs are the norm, but three-pronged British plugs are also present, so bring both just in case.

Smoking Banned in most public spaces, including restaurants, coffee shops and shopping malls.

Weights and measures Saudi Arabia uses the metric system.

EATING PRICE RANGES

The following price ranges refer to a standard main course. Unless otherwise stated, service charges and taxes are included in the price.

$ less than SR30 (US$8)

$$ SR30–120 (US$8–32)

$$$ more than SR120 (US$32)

BANNED ARTICLES

The following items are banned in Saudi Arabia. If you try to bring any of them into the country, penalties range from confiscation for minor offences to imprisonment or deportation for more serious offences.

- Alcohol
- Artwork considered un-Islamic or items bearing non-Islamic religious symbols
- Many books, DVDs and videos
- Firearms and explosives
- Illegal drugs, or medication without a doctor's prescription
- Politically sensitive material and material overly critical of the government or royal family; this may include seemingly innocent newspaper articles
- Pork products
- Pornography or any publications containing pictorial representations of people (particularly women) in a less than conservative state of dress
- Symbols or books of other religions (including the Bible)

US Embassy (☎01-488 3800; riyadh.usembassy.gov; Diplomatic Quarter; ⏰8am-5pm Sun-Thu)

INTERNET ACCESS

Internet cafes are present in larger Saudi towns and they're men-only domains outside of Jeddah and Riyadh. Connections are generally adequate and cost SR3 to SR10 per hour.

Most four-star and all five-star hotels and many coffeehouses now offer free wi-fi.

The internet is strictly policed, with over 6000 sites currently blocked. Most are pornographic, but they also include sites discussing politics, health, women's rights and education.

LEGAL MATTERS

Saudi Arabia imposes strict Sharia'a (Islamic law), under which extremely harsh punishments are imposed. For more information, see p38 and consult your embassy.

If you're involved in a traffic accident, call ☎993 or 999 (it doesn't have to be an emergency), don't move your car (even by 1m) and don't leave the scene until the police arrive. Try to get the name of the other driver and the registration and insurance numbers of the vehicle. To claim insurance a police report is obligatory. Sometimes Saudis in a hurry offer to pay for minor damage on the spot, but you should insist on a police report as garages are not allowed to carry out repairs without one.

MAPS

The best maps of Saudi Arabia are produced by Farsi Maps. Costing SR25 each, they're available at branches of the Jarir Bookstore throughout the Kingdom. The series includes many general maps of most regions and excellent city maps for Riyadh, Jeddah, Yanbu, Taif, Mecca and Medina, among other locations.

MEDIA

The English-language dailies *Arab News* (www.arabnews.com) and *Saudi Gazette* (www.saudigazette.com.sa) are surprisingly frank, although they steer clear of any criticism of the royal family or Islam.

International newspapers (the *Guardian*, the *Times*, the *International Herald Tribune* and *Le Monde*) and magazines (*Time* and *Newsweek*) are available from any branch of the Jarir Bookstore, usually within three days of publication. Don't expect your foreign newspaper to include all of its pages – censors routinely extract articles about Saudi Arabia and any photographs considered vaguely risqué or controversial.

Jeddah Radio (96.2FM) broadcasts in English and French, while the **BBC World Service** (www.bbc.co.uk/worldserviceradio) is available online and on short-wave frequency (11.760kHz or 15.575kHz).

MONEY

Credit Cards

Many establishments accept credit cards, including most medium to large hotels, restaurants, airline offices and shops. Surprisingly, some tour operators don't – check first.

Currency

The unit of currency is the Saudi riyal (SR). One riyal (SR1) is divided into 100 halalas. Coins come in 25- and 50-halala denominations. Notes come in SR1, SR5, SR10, SR20, SR50, SR100, SR200 and SR500 denominations. The Saudi riyal is a hard currency and there are no restrictions on its import or export.

Exchanging Money

Banks and ATMs that accept international cards are ubiquitous throughout Saudi. For exchanging cash, you'll get a much better rate at a money-exchange bureau. All major hard currencies are exchanged and commission is not usually charged, but check this first. Exchange desks at hotels offer poor rates.

OPENING HOURS

In Saudi, the weekend is Thursday and Friday. Note that during prayer times – five times a day – everything shuts. In general, hours are as follows.

Banks 8.30am to noon and 4.30pm to 8pm Saturday to Wednesday. At airports, banks are open 24 hours.

Offices 7.30am to 2.30pm or 3.30pm Saturday to Wednesday.

Post offices 7.30am to 10pm Saturday to Wednesday, 4.30pm to 10pm Friday.

Restaurants 7am to 10.30am, noon to 3pm and 6pm or 7pm to midnight (to 1am or 2am at weekends).

Shopping centres 9am or 10am to midnight Saturday to Thursday.

Shops and souqs 8am or 9am to 1pm or 2pm and 4.30pm or 5pm to 9pm Saturday to Wednesday.

PHOTOGRAPHY

Photography in certain areas is still off-limits due to security concerns – government buildings, embassies, airports, sea ports, desalination or electricity plants, oil rigs, royal palaces and police stations or anything vaguely connected with the military or security services. Don't photograph people without their permission, and never photograph women (even in a general street scene).

Filming is still prohibited at some archaeological sites; if you get caught, your video camera may be confiscated. If you're coming to Saudi with a tour operator, it can organise a video permit for you, as well as a letter to customs (stating that you'll arrive with a camera).

PUBLIC HOLIDAYS

No holidays other than Eid Al Fitr (dates vary), Eid Al Adha (dates vary) and National Day (23 September) are observed in the Kingdom.

SAFE TRAVEL

Dos & Don'ts

- Conservative dress is the rule of thumb in Saudi Arabia. Shorts in public are a big no-no (except at the private beaches operated by some top-end hotels and expat compounds); if males wear shorts, they must reach over their knees, while women must cover themselves with the traditional *abeyya*.
- Unmarried couples shouldn't travel together and if they do they may be stopped and investigated.
- Alcohol is strictly illegal in Saudi Arabia.
- You should carry your passport with you at all times. While travelling on business carry a letter of introduction (and many copies) from your company.
- Greetings are considered to be extremely important. The most common greeting is *salaam alaykum* (may peace be upon you), to which the reply is *wa alaykum as salaam* (and peace upon you too).
- Shaking hands (between men) is an important gesture of mutual respect.

Mutawwa

Formally known as the Committee for the Propagation of Virtue and the Prevention of Vice, the *mutawwa* (religious police) have an infamous reputation as moral vigilantes out to enforce strict Islamic orthodoxy. Operating independently of other branches of the security services, the *mutawwa* are at their most authoritative (and hence not to be argued with) when accompanied by uniformed police.

They became less visible (and less welcome) in cities like Jeddah following a horrific fire at a Mecca girls school in 2002. The *mutawwa* pushed schoolgirls back into the burning building because they weren't dressed 'correctly'. Fifteen girls died.

Ramadan

For Muslims, public observance of the fast is mandatory. For non-Muslims, smoking, eating or drinking in public could result in arrest.

Road Safety

Saudi Arabia has one of the highest incidents of road fatalities in the world. Some of the worst hazards:

> **MINDING THE MUTAWWA**
>
> The *mutawwa* (religious police) are a source of both fear and fascination for many travellers, but if you dress and behave appropriately, you have little to fear. Indeed, some *mutawwa* are known to give *hawajas* (Westerners) a wide berth.
>
> The *mutawwa* are conspicuous for their *thobes* (men's shirt-dress), which are worn above their ankles, and for wearing *gutras* (white head cloths) without *agals* (head ropes), since God alone is entitled to wear 'crowns'.
>
> The places you're most likely to encounter *mutawwa* are, in descending order: Al Ula, Jizan, Abha, Hail, Al Hofuf, Riyadh, Taif and Najran.

- The coastal road that links Jeddah to Jizan (Road No 55), which has the highest fatality rate in the Kingdom.
- Camels wandering onto unfenced roads, particularly at night.
- Buses and taxis suddenly veering across the road to pick up or drop off passengers.
- Pick-up trucks suddenly pulling out at junctions or after petrol stations.
- Vehicles driving outside towns at night with one light or no lights on.
- Vehicles trying to overtake on corners. Saudi drivers expect you (and sometimes oncoming traffic too) to pull over so that they can pass.

Sexual Harassment

Stares, leers and obscene comments are sometimes reported by Western women travellers.

It's rarely more than this, however, and the social disgrace that comes from having touched a woman in public is one of your most effective weapons. If your harasser persists, report him to the police or security men that can be found on most streets and in most malls in the Kingdom.

The more conservatively you dress, the more conservatively you will be treated, particularly with regard to wearing a headscarf.

Terrorism

Security has been tight around residential compounds and embassies for more than a decade and shows no signs of relaxing. Nevertheless, security incidents still occur in the Kingdom and isolated attacks on foreigners have taken place in both the country's east and in Riyadh.

Simmering unrest in eastern Saudi Arabia and the ongoing war with Yemen mean that both the east and southwest of the country are best avoided for the foreseeable future. The biggest current security concern remains Islamist acts of terror against government installations and public gatherings. It pays to remain vigilant at all times. While in Saudi Arabia, you should register with your embassy and keep a close eye on warnings issued by it in the form of emails or text messages.

TELEPHONE

The mobile-phone network run by STC operates on the GSM system.

At the time of writing, mobile networks were offering myriad rapidly changing deals, usually to attract migrant workers wanting to call home. The major networks:

- STC (www.stc.com.sa)
- Zain (www.zain.com)
- Mobily (www.mobily.com.sa)

For directory assistance, call ☎905 (domestic) or ☎900 (international).

VISAS

Saudi bureaucracy is at its most opaque when you're applying for a visa, but one thing is clear: independent leisure travel to Saudi Arabia does not currently exist.

Top of the restricted list of travellers into Saudi Arabia remain citizens of Israel but people of Jewish faith from other countries are also restricted. All visitors to Saudi must declare their religion – those declaring 'Jewish' or 'none' will usually be refused a visa.

Any evidence of travel to and from Israel will result in refusal of entry into Saudi. If you have *any* evidence of travel to Israel in your passport and intend to travel to Saudi Arabia in the future use a brand-new passport for your Saudi visa application.

For a full list of possible visa types, see www.saudiembassy.net/services.

VISA RULES

When planning your Saudi visa, keep the following in mind:

- A Saudi sponsor is necessary for any visit to the Kingdom, and they are legally responsible for the conduct and behaviour of visitors whilst in the Kingdom.
- Passports must be valid for a minimum of six months.
- When applying for a visa, women under 30 years old must be accompanied by either their brother or their husband, who must also arrive in and leave Saudi at the same time.
- Men and women are only allowed to travel together and are granted a visa to do so if they (a) are married (with an official marriage licence) or (b) form part of a group.
- It's not permitted for an unmarried couple to travel alone together in Saudi Arabia and doing so runs the risk of arrest.

Hajj & Umrah Visas

For hajj visas there's a quota system of one visa for every 1000 Muslims in a country's population. For more on hajj and *Umrah* visas, see p37. The system of administration varies from country to country but typically involves an application processed by a Saudi-authorised hajj and *umrah* travel agency. Every Saudi embassy has a list of authorised hajj and *umrah* travel agencies for that particular country.

Umrah (any pilgrimage to Mecca that is not hajj) visas are granted to any Muslim requesting one (in theory), although if you are not from a Muslim-majority country or don't have an obviously Muslim name, you'll be asked to provide an official document that lists Islam as your religion. Converts to Islam must provide a certificate from the mosque where they underwent their conversion ceremony.

Umrah and hajj visas are free but are valid only for travel to Jeddah, Mecca, Medina and the connecting roads.

There has been a recent crackdown on hajj and *umrah* visa holders illegally staying on to work in the Kingdom, and security roadblocks for checking visa permits are common throughout the Hejaz region.

Residence (Work) Visas

Residence (work) visas are arranged via a Saudi employer who is also an individual's visa sponsor. There are annual job-category quotas in place for residence (work) visas and individuals are regularly assigned a different visa category from the job actually being performed. For example, a nurse may receive an engineer's visa, or vice versa, as the various annual job quotas are filled.

Visa categories can and do provide a major source of headaches for expat workers to Saudi Arabia, especially in relation to the nature of the stay offered to accompanying family members. The visa restrictions and length of stay in Saudi Arabia granted to each family member will often differ depending on gender and age. These details should not be assumed to be the same for younger children, teenagers or spouses and should be carefully checked before arrival in the Kingdom.

Tourist Visas

At the time of writing no tourist visas were being issued. A brief period in which tourist visas were issued by authorised Saudi travel agents to groups of at least four individuals ended in 2010.

Business Visas

Business visas are arranged via an employer and a sponsoring Saudi partner for a specific business purpose. Depending on the Saudi embassy where you are applying for a visa (always phone ahead to double-check requirements), typically you will require a letter from your employer or company outlining the nature of your business in Saudi Arabia and a letter of support from your local chamber of commerce.

The Saudi sponsor (either an individual or a company) then applies to the Saudi Chamber of Commerce and Industry for approval. If approval is granted, an invitation letter will be sent to you, or directly to the Saudi embassy in your home country. Note that you must make your visa application in your country of nationality or permanent residency.

Note that in theory a single businesswoman is not allowed to check into a hotel without the presence of her Saudi sponsor or a male representative of her Saudi sponsor. In the larger cities such as Riyadh and Jeddah this rule is not usually applied, but in smaller towns and more conservative regions of the Kingdom this rule may be upheld by hotel check-in staff. Be prepared.

WOMEN TRAVELLERS

Saudi Arabia is rightly considered one of the most difficult countries in which to travel if you're a Western woman. The strict segregation of the sexes and the prohibition on female drivers leads to obvious limitations on freedom of movement; even in elevators, women should not be accompanied by anyone other than their families. However, women are also accorded (officially) great respect and are typically urged to the front of queues and served first at banks, check-in desks and ticket offices.

Saudi men's attitudes towards women do vary from the big cities to the smaller rural towns, and many urban, educated Saudi men will make a point of shaking hands with Western women, especially in social or business settings. Take your cue from those around you and remember that in traditional Saudi eyes it never hurts (them at least) for you to be too covered up.

Restrictions

Access to some internet cafes, and most mid- and budget-range hotels is impossible, as is access to many restaurants. Most towns and villages have at least one restaurant with a 'family section' where women, whether accompanied or not, must sit – those that do not have such a section provide takeaways. Museums and some sights have special family-only hours, and banks have 'Ladies' branches'.

What to Wear

Women must by law wear an *abeyya* (full-length black robe). Though a headscarf is not compulsory, you should always have one at hand as the *mutawwa* may insist that you wear it.

ℹ Getting There & Away

ENTERING SAUDI ARABIA

Immigration is much quicker than it used to be (except during hajj and Ramadan, when you can expect long queues). All bags including hand luggage are x-rayed but are usually only opened when further investigation is warranted.

Note that departure security is vigorous and time consuming. You're advised to arrive early – three hours before international flights.

If you're arriving by land, procedures are similar, although expect long delays if you're bringing your own car into the Kingdom.

AIR

The national carrier is **Saudi Arabian Airlines** (Saudia; ☎01-488 4444; www.saudiairlines.com), which flies to dozens of destinations across the Middle East, Europe, Asia and the USA. It has a respectable safety record and is usually on time and comfortable. Saudia usually offers a free domestic flight with an international ticket.

International Airports

King Abdul Aziz International Airport (☎02-684 2227; www.jed-airport.com) Jeddah's international airport.

King Khaled International Airport (☎01-221 1000; www.riyadh-airport.com) Lies 25km north of the city centre. Look out for the royal terminal, which is for the exclusive use of the Saudi royal family and their guests.

Prince Mohammad bin Abdulaziz International Airport (☎04-842 0000) Medina's international airport.

LAND

Border Crossings

At the time of research there were problems with a number of Saudi border crossings – the land borders with Iraq, Jordan and Yemen were closed to non-Arab travellers. Check with your embassy for the latest information.

Bus

Saptco (☎800 124 9999; www.saptco.com.sa) Saptco offers the best international bus services; other companies from surrounding countries also cover the same routes for similar prices. Saptco prices are kept low by the government. Departures are primarily from Riyadh, Jeddah and Dammam.

ℹ Getting Around

AIR

Checking in 1½ hours prior to departure is advised for domestic flights. Note that Medina airport lies outside the haram (forbidden) area, so it can be used by non-Muslim tourists; it can be a useful gateway for Al Ula in particular.

Saudi Arabian Airlines (www.saudiairlines.com) Excellent state-run airline with the largest domestic network.

Nas (www.flynas.com) A low-cost domestic rival to Saudi Arabian Airlines.

BUS

Unaccompanied foreign women can travel on domestic buses with their *iqama* (residence permit) if they're an expat, or with a passport and visa if a visitor. The front seats are generally unofficially reserved for 'families' (which includes solo women), and the back half for men.

Check in half an hour before domestic departures, one hour before international departures (although passengers with only hand luggage can arrive 10 minutes before).

Note that during hajj, services are reduced across the country as buses are seconded for the pilgrims.

Saudi Arabian Public Transport Company (Saptco; ☎800-124 9999; www.saptco.com.sa) All domestic bus services are operated by Saptco, which is professionally run and has a good safety record. The well-maintained buses are comfortable, air-conditioned and clean. All buses have on-board toilets, and make rest stops every few hours.

Costs

Bus fares are approximately half of the equivalent airfare. Return tickets are 25% cheaper than two one-way fares. Online booking is now available.

Reservations

When purchasing your ticket, you'll need to show your passport (visitors) or *iqama* (expats). During hajj season, Ramadan or in summer, booking at least a week in advance is advisable.

Tickets can be bought up to three months in advance for domestic journeys, six months for international. If tickets are cancelled or unused, you can get a refund: less 10% for a one-way ticket (or unused return), and less 30% for a return ticket if it hasn't expired (within three/six months for domestic/international destinations).

Tickets are best bought from Saptco itself.

CAR & MOTORCYCLE

Despite its impressive public-transport system, Saudi Arabia remains a country that glorifies the private car (the shiny 4WD is king). Roads are generally sealed and well maintained.

Motorcycles are rare and generally considered a vehicle of the rural poor.

Driving Licence

If you'll only be in the country for less than three months and want to rent a car, you should always have your International Driving Permit (IDP) available to show.

If you're going to be in the Kingdom for more than three months, you'll need to get a local driving licence, which is arranged by your employer. You'll also have to do a driving test and purchase insurance.

Fuel

It seems miraculous to a Westerner, but it's still only around 60 halalas per litre for unleaded petrol. All petrol stations charge the same (by law). Petrol stations are ubiquitous throughout the country.

Hire

International and local car-hire agencies can be found in the larger towns in the Kingdom, as well as at international airports. Local companies tend to be significantly cheaper, but always check that *full* insurance is included. Prices usually stay the same throughout the year.

Rates at international agencies generally start at SR120 per day (including full insurance) for the smallest cars, and SR600 for 4WDs. For rental of a month or more, prices drop significantly. Be sure to negotiate.

There's usually an additional charge of around SR0.75 to SR2 per kilometre, although most agencies offer the first 150km free. Women travellers (who are not permitted by law to drive) will need a driver, which will cost around SR125 per eight-hour day, plus SR30 per extra hour.

Insurance

If you are travelling with a car from another Gulf Cooperation Council (GCC) country, insurance and the Collision-Damage Waiver (CDW) are mandatory. With car hire it's usually included in the price, but it pays to check very carefully.

Road Rules

The main rules:

- Drive on the right-hand side of the road.
- Leaving the scene of an accident is a serious offence and can result in fines of over SR1000, imprisonment and deportation.
- Not carrying a valid driving licence can result in a night in jail and a hefty fine.
- Right turns are allowed at red lights unless specifically forbidden.
- The speed limit in towns is 60km/h, 70km/h or 80km/h.
- The speed limit on open highways is 120km/h (but can drop to 90km/h or 100km/h).

TAXI

Taxis are found in most of the larger towns and are known as 'limousines'; they can be hailed anywhere. Note that it's much cheaper to negotiate the fare first (as locals do) rather than use the meter.

TRAIN

Saudi Arabia currently has only one stretch of train track in the entire country, between Riyadh and Dammam via Al Hofuf. Visit www.saudirailways.org for details.

Classes

There are three classes: 2nd, 1st and VIP class. The main difference between them is legroom (plus TV and a meal in the splendidly named 'Rehab' VIP class). All classes have access to the train restaurant.

Women can travel unaccompanied (with ID) and sit in any class. In 2nd there's a separate women's carriage and in VIP and 1st there are special designated areas.

Reservations

Reservations (☎92 000 8886) can be made a minimum of 24 hours before departure and a maximum of 90 days in advance, by phone, online or at any station.

During school holidays, Ramadan and hajj, book well in advance. At weekends (Thursday and Friday), book three to four days in advance.

United Arab Emirates

الإمارات العربية المتحدة

Includes ➡

Best Places for Culture

- ➡ Sheikh Zayed Grand Mosque (p351)
- ➡ Sharjah Heritage Museum (p332)
- ➡ Sheikh Mohammed Centre for Cultural Understanding (p313)
- ➡ Deira Souqs (p311)
- ➡ Sharjah Museum of Islamic Civilisation (p333)

Best Places for Nature

- ➡ Liwa Oasis (p370)
- ➡ Sir Bani Yas Island (p372)
- ➡ Al Ain Zoo (p366)
- ➡ East Coast (p375)
- ➡ Jebel Jais Mountain Road (p342)

Why Go?

For most people, the United Arab Emirates means just one place: Dubai, the sci-fi-esque city of iconic skyscrapers, palm-shaped islands, city-sized malls, indoor ski slopes and palatial beach resorts. But beyond the glitter awaits a diverse mosaic of six more emirates, each with its own character and allure.

An hour's drive south, oil-rich Abu Dhabi, the UAE capital, is positioning itself as a hub of culture, sport and leisure. Beyond looms the vast Al Gharbia region, which is dominated by the northern reaches of the Rub' Al Khali desert. Its magical silence is interrupted only by the whisper of shifting dunes rolling towards Saudi Arabia.

North of Dubai, Sharjah does art and heritage best, while tiny Ajman and Umm Al Quwain provide glimpses of life in the pre-oil days, and Ras Al Khaimah snuggles against the mighty Hajar Mountains. For the best swimming and diving, though, head across the range to Fujairah to frolic in the clear waters of the Gulf of Oman.

When to Go

UAE

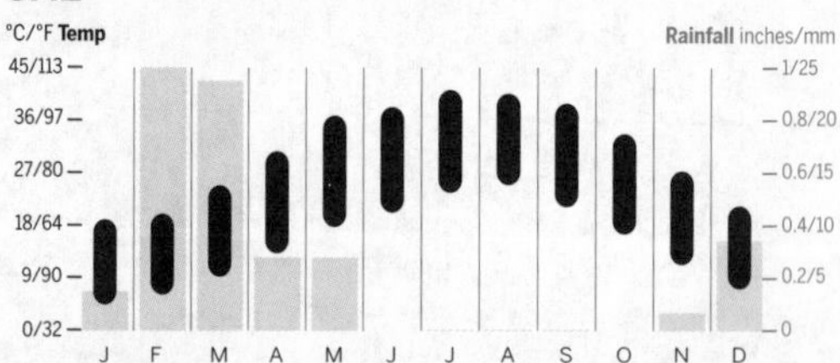

Nov–Mar Moderate temps, higher room rates, major festivals and events; good for outdoor activities.

Mar–May & Oct Hot days, balmy nights, good for beach vacations; desert camping still OK.

Jun–Sep Hot and humid, steep hotel discounts; life moves indoors; summer sales; good for diving.

Daily Costs

The sky's the limit when it comes to spending money in the UAE, but it's possible to keep expenses down, for example by forgoing the glitzy five-stars for a midrange hotel, where standard doubles can be had for Dh400 to Dh600. A glass of beer or wine will cost around Dh30 or Dh50, respectively, but if you stick to water, you can get a nice two-course meal for around Dh70, and a shwarma to go costs just Dh4. Museums are free or cheap, but expect to pay Dh200 and up for guided tours and admission to water parks and other big attractions.

ITINERARIES

Two Days

If you're in the UAE just on a short layover, base yourself in the Downtown Dubai area. Spend day one checking off the iconic sights on a **Big Bus tour**, then head up to the **Burj Khalifa** at sunset (book ahead), take a spin around **Dubai Mall** and have dinner in **Souk Al Bahar**, with a view of the **Dubai Fountain**. The next day, take a cab to Sharjah for a glimpse into the past in the **Heritage Area**, stocking up on souvenirs at the **Central Souq** and enjoying dinner in bubbly **Al Qasba**.

One Week

Spend two days in futuristic Dubai and one in retro Sharjah before heading south to Abu Dhabi to marvel at the **Sheikh Zayed Grand Mosque**, zoom around **Ferrari World** and learn about the new Cultural District on **Saadiyat Island**. For total contrast, dip into the desert next to face a huge dune, magical silence and plenty of camels, preferably on an overnight trip. Wrap up with a day in Al Ain and its Unesco-recognised heritage sites.

Essential Food & Drink

Restaurants serving Emirati food used to be rare but, thankfully, this is changing. If you do get a chance, try these typical dishes, and don't miss out on the succulent local dates!

- **Balaleet** Vermicelli blends with sugar syrup, saffron, rosewater and sauteed onions in this rich breakfast staple.
- **Fareed** Mutton-flavoured broth with bread; popular at Ramadan.
- **Hareis** Ground wheat and lamb slow cooked until creamy (a bit like porridge); sometimes called the 'national dish'.
- **Khuzi** Stuffed whole roasted lamb on a bed of spiced rice.
- **Madrooba** Salt-cured fish (*maleh*) or chicken mixed with raw bread dough until thick.
- **Makbous** A casserole of spice-laced rice and boiled meat (usually lamb) or fish garnished with nuts, raisins and fried onions.

At a Glance

- **Currency** UAE dirham (Dh)
- **Mobile phones** GSM network is widespread
- **Money** ATMs are common in urban areas
- **Visas** None required for 45 nationalities

Fast Facts

- **Capital** Abu Dhabi
- **Country Code** ☎ 971
- **Language** Arabic
- **Population** 9.5 million

Exchange Rates

Australia	A$1	Dh2.62
Bahrain	BD1	Dh9.74
Euro zone	€1	Dh3.95
Kuwait	KD1	Dh12.10
Oman	OR1	Dh9.53
Qatar	QR1	Dh1
Saudi Arabia	SR1	Dh0.97
UK	£1	Dh5.59
USA	US$1	Dh3.67

For current exchange rates see www.xe.com.

Resources

- **UAE Ministry of Information & Culture** (www.uaeinteract.com) Covers just about every aspect of life in the UAE.
- **Lonely Planet** (www.lonelyplanet.com/uae) Destination info, hotel booking and forum.
- **Zomato** (www.zomato.com) User-generated restaurant reviews around the UAE.

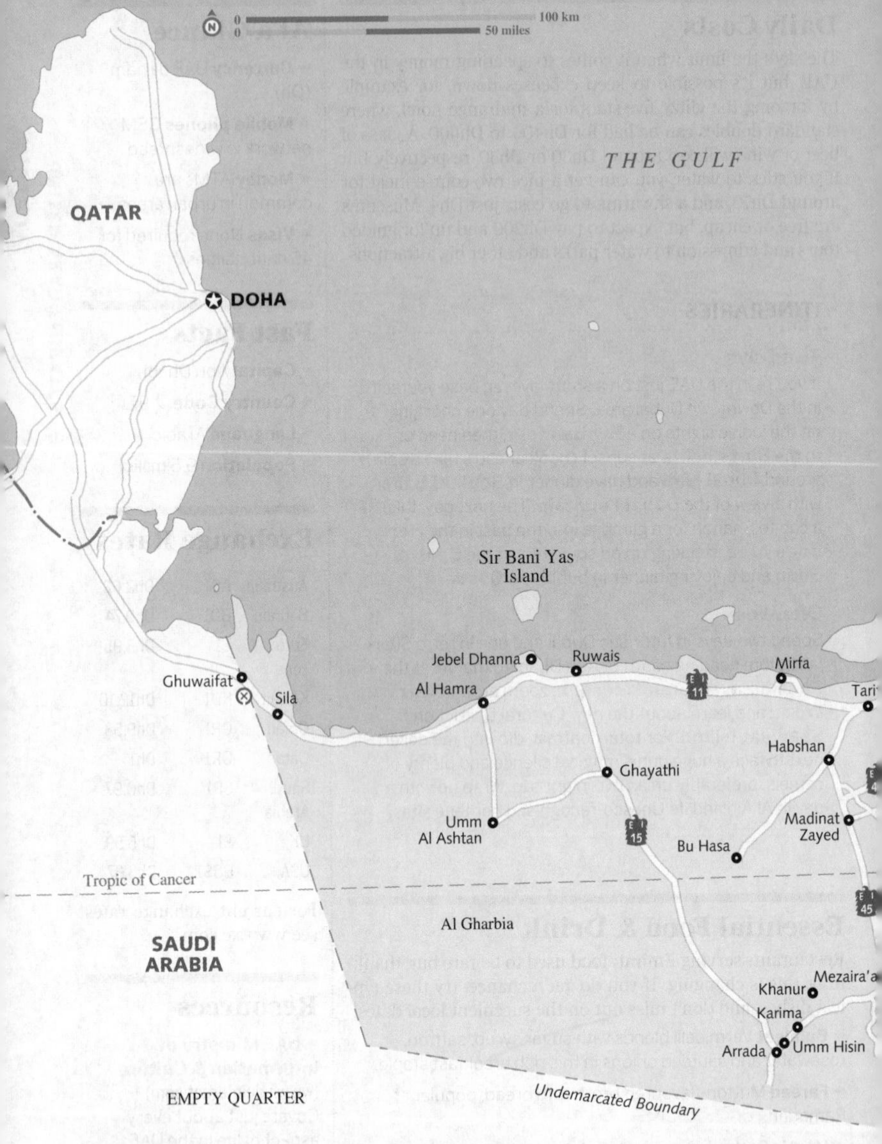

0 100 km
0 50 miles

THE GULF

QATAR

DOHA

Sir Bani Yas Island

Jebel Dhanna

Ruwais

Mirfa

Tari

Ghuwaifat

Sila

Al Hamra

E11

Habshan

Ghayathi

Madinat Zayed

Umm Al Ashtan

E15

Bu Hasa

Tropic of Cancer

E45

Al Gharbia

SAUDI ARABIA

Mezaira'a

Khanur

Karima

Umm Hisin

Arrada

EMPTY QUARTER

Undemarcated Boundary

United Arab Emirates Highlights

1. Shopping till you drop at **Dubai Mall** (p327), then soaring to the top of the **Burj Khalifa** (p311) and finishing up with cocktails at the iconic **Burj Al Arab** (p314) hotel.

2. Visiting Abu Dhabi's **Sheikh Zayed Grand Mosque** (p351) and getting some kicks at **Ferrari World Abu Dhabi** (p355).

3. Catching a glimpse of the pre-oil days in Sharjah's atmospheric **Heritage Museum** (p332).

4. Losing yourself in Al Ain's shady **date-palm oases** (p368) and visiting one of the

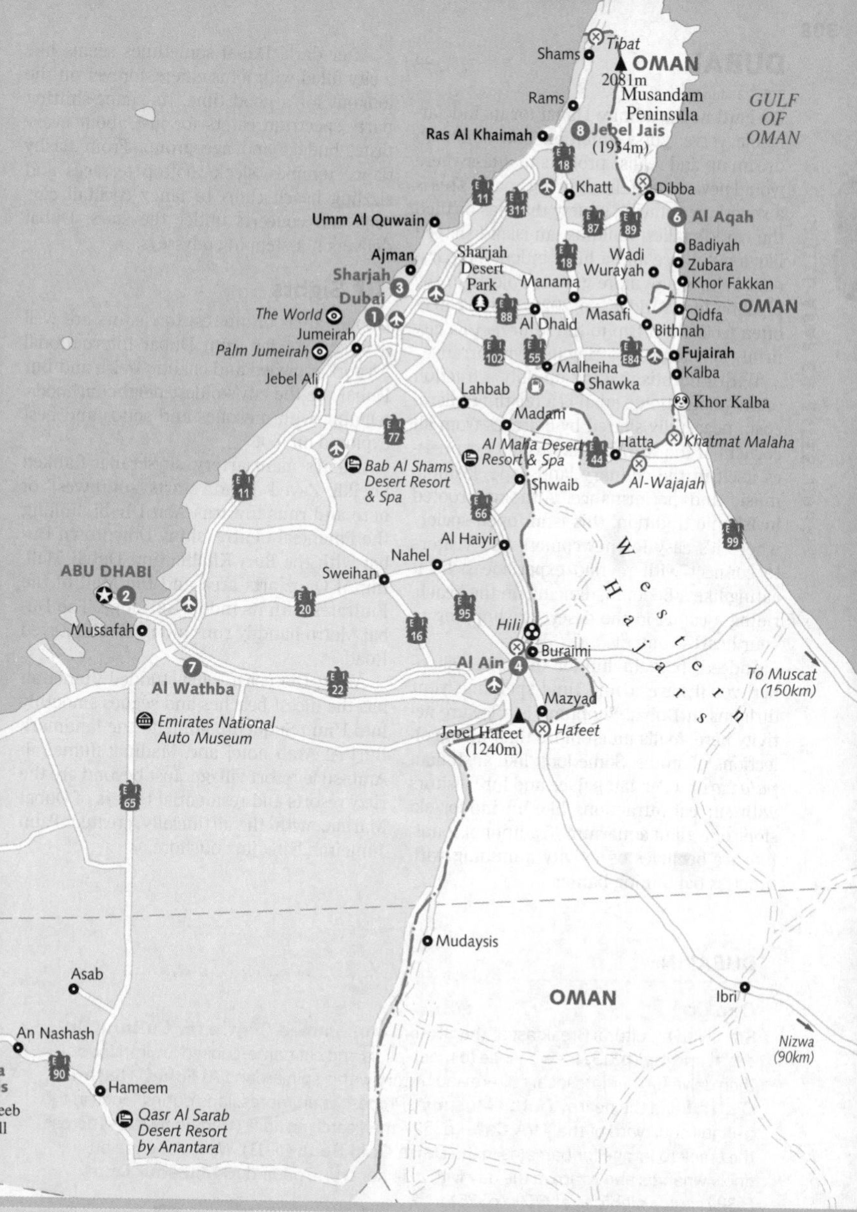

UAE's last **camel markets** (p366).

5 Wondering at the spectacle of shimmering sand dunes in the **Liwa Oasis** (p370).

6 Coming face to face with turtles and sharks in the fertile waters off **Al Aqah** (p378) on the east coast.

7 Seeing the 'ships of the desert' running like mad around a camel race track, for instance at **Al Wathba** (p383).

8 Taking the spectacular drive close to the top of **Jebel Jais** (p342), the UAE's highest mountain, in Ras Al Khaimah.

DUBAI دبي

POP 2.1 MILLION

It's hard not to admire Dubai for its indefatigable verve, gutsy ambition and ability to dream up and realise projects that elsewhere would never get off the drawing board. This is a superlative-craving society that has birthed the world's tallest building, an island shaped like a palm tree and a huge indoor ski paradise. With many more grand projects in the pipeline for World Expo 2020, visiting here often feels like a trip to the future – to a city firmly in charge of writing its own narrative.

With Emiratis making up only a fraction of the population, Dubai is a bustling microcosm peacefully shared by cultures from all corners of the world. This diversity expresses itself in the culinary landscape, fashion, music and performance. Although rooted in Islamic tradition, this is an open society where it's easy for newcomers and visitors to connect with myriad experiences, be it eating like a Bedouin, dancing on the beach, riding a camel in the desert or shopping to your heart's content.

Indeed, bargain hunter or power shopper, you'll have a fine time spending your dirhams in Dubai. Shopping is a leisure activity here, malls much more than mere collections of stores. Some look like an Italian *palazzo* or a Persian palace and lure visitors with surreal attractions like an indoor ski slope or a giant aquarium. Traditional souqs, too, are beehives of activity humming with timeless bargaining banter.

After dark, Dubai sometimes seems like a city filled with lotus eaters, forever on the lookout for a good time. Its shape-shifting party spectrum caters for just about every taste, budget and age group. From flashy dance temples, sleek rooftop terraces and sizzling beach clubs to fancy cocktail caverns and concerts under the stars, Dubai delivers hot-stepping odysseys.

Sights

Dubai's areas of interest to visitors are well defined. Not far from Dubai International Airport, crowded and chaotic Deira and Bur Dubai are the city's oldest neighbourhoods, teeming with mosques and souqs and best explored on foot.

Dubai's main artery, skyscraper-flanked Sheikh Zayed Road, starts southwest of here and runs towards Abu Dhabi, linking the Financial Centre, shiny Downtown Dubai with the Burj Khalifa and Dubai Mall, the Al Quoz arts area and the Mall of the Emirates with its indoor ski slope. The Dubai Metro handily runs along Sheikh Zayed Road.

Along the coast, villa-studded Jumeirah has the nicest beaches and segues smoothly into Umm Suqueim, home to the landmark Burj Al Arab hotel and Madinat Jumeirah Arab-style resort village. Just beyond are the ritzy resorts and residential towers of Dubai Marina, with the artificially created Palm Jumeirah lying just offshore.

DUBAI IN...

One Day

Start with a Cultural Breakfast at the **Sheikh Mohammed Centre for Cultural Understanding** (p313) for a chance to meet locals and eat home-cooked Emirati food, then delve further into local culture and history with a spin around **Al Fahidi Historic District** and the nearby **Dubai Museum**. Process your impressions during lunch in the tranquil courtyard of the **XVA Café** (p322), then catch an *abra* (traditional ferry) across the creek to forage for bargains in the **Deira Gold Souq** (p311). Walk along the busy dhow wharves and wrap up the day with a dinner cruise aboard **Al Mansour Dhow** (p322) and a nightcap at **QDs** (p325).

Two Days

Devote day two to modern Dubai, beginning with a guided visit of the **Jumeirah Mosque** (p314). Cab it down the coast to pick up souvenirs at the charming **Souk Madinat Jumeirah** (p328) before indulging in a canalside lunch while gazing at the iconic **Burj Al Arab** (p314). Next up, give your credit card a workout at the **Dubai Mall** (p327) and head up to the **Burj Khalifa** (p311) observation deck at sunset (book ahead). For dinner, pick any table with a view of the dancing **Dubai Fountain** (p313), then grab a nightcap at **Neos** (p325) with the glittering city below you. Magic!

LOCAL KNOWLEDGE

DUBAI'S COMING ATTRACTIONS

With the fiscal crisis firmly in the past, a number of temporarily shelved mega-projects in Dubai have picked up steam again and should open up in the coming years. Here's a glimpse at the top five under construction:

Dubai Frame Like a huge picture frame, this 150m-high rectangle looms above Za'abeel Park near the beginning of Sheikh Zayed Road and provides sweeping cityscape views from a glass-floor bridge reached by elevator. Opening in 2016.

Dubai Opera At the foot of the Burj Khalifa, this 2000-seat venue for opera, theatre, concerts, art exhibitions, film screenings and special events should be completed in 2016. It is part of a development known as the Dubai Opera District, which includes hotels, shops and apartment towers.

Dubai Safari Dubai will finally get a 21st-century zoo when this animal park opens, with critters making themselves at home in generous enclosures divided into four villages: Africa, Asia, Arabia and Safari. A butterfly park, petting zoo and botanical garden are also planned. Projected opening date is late 2016.

Dubai Parks & Resorts Three major theme parks are taking shape along Hwy E11 en route to Abu Dhabi: the world's first Bollywood Park (www.bollywoodparkdubai.com); Legoland Dubai (www.legoland.com/dubai), with 40 rides, shows and attractions in six themed areas; and Motiongate Dubai (www.motiongatedubai.com), a collaboration between Sony, DreamWorks and Lionsgate with 27 movie-themed attractions, many of them indoors for year-round appeal. Supposed to open in late 2016.

Bluewaters Island On land reclaimed opposite the Jumeirah Beach Residence, Bluewaters Island may be home to the world's tallest Ferris wheel, the 201m-high Dubai Eye, as early as 2016.

Deira & Bur Dubai

Straddling the creek, Deira and Bur Dubai offer an eye-opening peek into the city's past. Bur Dubai's neatly restored Al Fahidi and Shindagha historical quarters are wonderful for late-afternoon strolls, while a quick *abra* (traditional ferry boat) ride away, dazzlingly multicultural Deira is most famous for its cacophonous souqs and the colourful dhow wharfage. Loaded with everything from air-conditioners to chewing gum and car tyres, dhows are traditional trading vessels that have plied the waters between here and Iran, India and other far-flung locales for centuries.

In 2012 Dubai applied for the heritage quarters along Dubai Creek to be recognised as a Unesco World Heritage Site, but the bid was deferred in 2014.

★Dubai Museum MUSEUM

(Map p310; ☎04-353 1862; Al Fahidi St; adult/child Dh3/1; ⊙8.30am-8.30pm Sat-Thu, 2.30-8.30pm Fri; Ⓜ Al Fahidi) Dubai's best museum occupies the sturdy Al Fahidi Fort, built around 1800 and considered the city's oldest structure. The exhibit charts the emirate's turbo-evolution from fishing and pearling village to global centre of commerce, finance and tourism in engaging, multimedia fashion. A walk-through mock souq, exhibits on Bedouin life in the desert and a room highlighting the importance of the sea illustrate the days before the discovery of oil. The last room showcases archaeological findings from nearby excavation sites.

Al Fahidi Historic District AREA

(Map p310; Al Fahidi St; Ⓜ Al Fahidi) FREE Traffic fades to a quiet hum in the labyrinthine lanes of this nicely restored heritage area formerly known as the Bastakia Quarter. Its narrow walking lanes are flanked by sand-colored houses topped with wind towers, which provide natural air-conditioning. Today, there are about 50 buildings containing museums, craft shops, cultural exhibits, courtyard cafes, art galleries and two boutique hotels.

The quarter was built in the early 1900s by merchants from the Persian town of Bastak who settled in Dubai to take advantage of tax breaks granted by the sheikh. By the 1970s, though, the buildings had fallen into disrepair and residents began moving on to newer, more comfortable neighbourhoods. Dedicated locals, expats and even

Deira & Bur Dubai

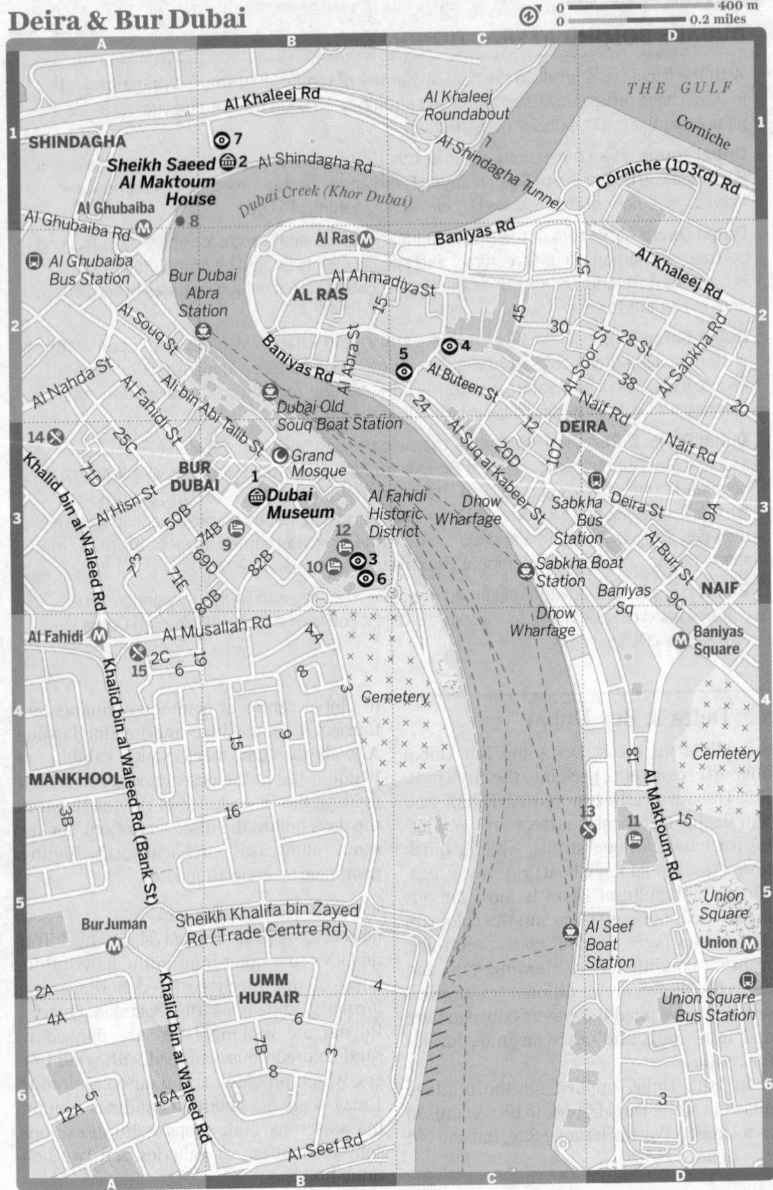

Prince Charles prevented the area's demolition in the 1980s. Hidden within the restored maze, which is easily explored on an aimless wander, is a short section of the old city wall from 1800. For a more in-depth experience, join a guided tour with the Sheikh Mohammed Centre for Cultural Understanding (p313).

Next to the district, a new waterfront tourist development called Marsa Al Seef is taking shape. Set to celebrate Emirati culture, it may be completed in 2017.

Deira & Bur Dubai

Shindagha Historic District AREA

(Map p310; Shindagha Waterfront; Ⓜ Al Ghubaiba) With a strategic location at the mouth of Dubai Creek, Shindagha was where the ruling sheikhs, their families and the city elite lived until the 1950s. Stately coral and gypsum homes wrapped around courtyards and cooled by wind towers have been reconstructed and recast as a heritage district flanked by a wide promenade paralleling the Creek. The nicest time to come here is at or after sunset, with the lights reflected in the water against the dhows heading out to sea.

★ Sheikh Saeed Al Maktoum House MUSEUM

(Map p310; ☎04-393 7139; Shindagha Historic District, Shindagha Waterfront; adult/child Dh3/1; ⏲8am-8.30pm Sat-Thu, 3-10pm Fri; Ⓜ Al Ghubaiba) This grand courtyard house served as the residence of Sheikh Saeed, the grandfather of current Dubai ruler Sheikh Mohammed bin Rashid, from 1912 until his death in 1958. The architectural marvel also houses an excellent collection of pre-oil boom photographs of Dubai taken in the souqs, on the Creek and at traditional celebrations. There are also some insightful private images of the ruling Al Maktoum clan. Other rooms feature coins, stamps and documents dating back as far as 1791.

Deira Gold Souq MARKET

(Map p310; Sikkat Al Khail St; ⏲10am-1pm & 3-10pm; Ⓜ Palm Deira) All that glitters is gold (and occasionally silver) at this colourful covered arcade where hundreds of stores overflow with every kind of jewellery imaginable, from tiny pearl earrings to giant golden wedding necklaces. Simply watching the goings-on is a treat. Settle down on a bench and take in the colourful street theatre of hard-working Afghanis dragging heavy carts of goods, African women in colourful kaftans and local women out on a shopping spree. Best in the evening.

Deira Spice Souq MARKET

(Map p310; btwn Baniyas Rd, Al Ras Rd & Al Abra St; ⏲roughly 9am-10pm Sat-Thu, 4-10pm Fri; Ⓜ Al Ras) Steps from the Deira Old Souq *abra* station, the sound of Arabic chatter bounces around the lanes of this small covered market as vendors work hard to unload cardamom, saffron and other aromatic herbs photogenically stored in burlap sacks alongside dried fruit, nuts, incense burners, henna kits and *sheesha* (water pipes). Away from the tourist-oriented main thoroughfare, the tiny shops also sell groceries, plastics and other household goods to locals and sailors from the dhows.

Downtown Dubai

Burj Khalifa is quite literally the pinnacle of this evolving urban hub that is also home to five-star hotels, restaurants and bars as well as the Dubai Mall (the world's biggest shopping temple) and the Burj Lake, with the mesmerising Dubai Fountain. Still under construction is the Opera District, anchored by a 2000-seat performing-arts centre. The bright red Dubai Trolley trundles along a section of Sheikh Mohammed Bin Rashid Blvd, the main thoroughfare encircling Downtown.

★ Burj Khalifa LANDMARK

(Map p312; ☎04-888 8888; www.atthetop.ae; 1 Sheikh Mohammed bin Rashid Blvd, entry lower ground fl, Dubai Mall; At the Top adult/child 4-12yr/fast track Dh125/95/300, At the Top Sky Dh300, audio-guide Dh25; ⏲At the Top 8.30am-midnight, At the Top Sky 11am-11pm Sun-Thu, 10am-11pm Fri & Sat, last entry 45min before closing; Ⓜ Burj Khalifa/Dubai Mall) The Burj Khalifa is a stunning feat of architecture and engineering, with two observation decks on the 124th and 148th floors and a restaurant-bar on the 122nd.

East Dubai

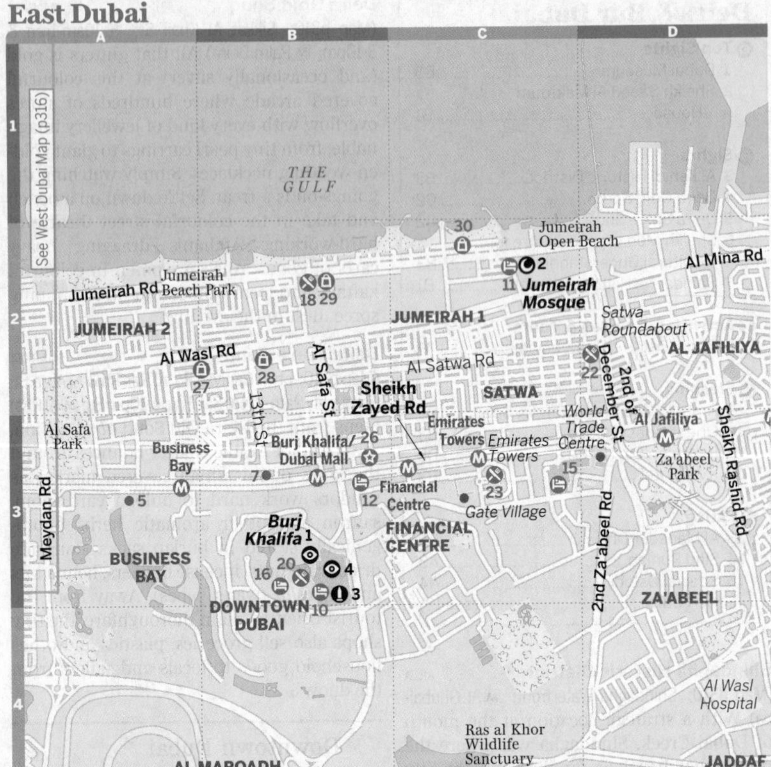

The world's tallest building pierces the sky at 828m and opened in January 2010, six years after excavations began. To avoid wait times or expensive fast-track admission, book tickets online as far as 30 days in advance. Note that high humidity often cloaks Dubai in a dense haze, making views less than breathtaking.

The most popular ticket is the one to the At the Top observation deck on the 124th floor (452m), where high-powered telescopes (extra fee) help bring even distant developments into focus (at least on clear days) and cleverly simulate the same view at night and 35 years back in time. Getting to the deck means passing various multimedia exhibits until a double-decker lift whisks you up at 10m per second.

To truly be on the world's highest observation platform, though, you need to spring for tickets to At the Top Sky on the 148th floor (555m). A visit here is set up like a hosted VIP experience, with refreshments, a guided tour and an interactive screen where you 'fly' to different city landmarks by hovering your hands over high-tech sensors. Afterwards, you're escorted to the 125th floor to be showered with interesting titbits about Dubai and the Burj and to take another virtual tour of major sights in an interactive attraction called A Falcon's Eye View.

Dubai Mall MALL

(Map p312; toll free 800 382 246 255; www.thedubaimall.com; Sheikh Mohammed bin Rashid Blvd; 10am-11am Sun-Wed, to midnight Thu-Sat; ; Burj Khalifa/Dubai Mall) The mother of all malls is much more than the sum of its 1200 stores: it's a veritable family entertainment centre with such crowd magnets as a huge aquarium, an amusement park with thrill rides and arcade games, an Olympic-sized ice rink and a genuine dinosaur skeleton. It also boasts a gorgeous souq, a designer-fashion avenue with catwalk and

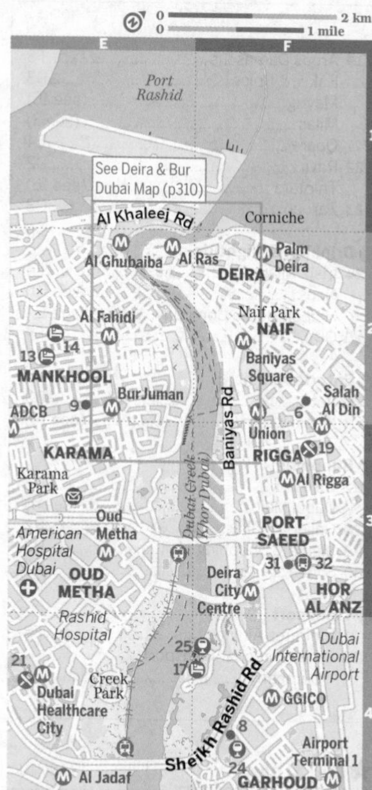

its own glossy monthly magazine. And as if that weren't enough, the mall was undergoing expansion when we visited.

Dubai Aquarium & Underwater Zoo AQUARIUM

(Map p312; ☎04-448 5200; www.thedubaiaquarium.com; ground fl, Dubai Mall, Sheikh Mohammed bin Rashid Blvd; packages Dh100-250; ⏲10am-11pm Sun-Wed, to midnight Thu-Sat; 👪; Ⓜ Burj Khalifa/Dubai Mall) Dubai Mall's most mesmerising sight is this gargantuan aquarium where thousands of beasties flit and dart amid artificial coral. Sharks and rays are top attractions, but other popular denizens include sumo-sized groupers and massive schools of pelagic fish. You can view quite a lot for free from outside or pay for access to the walk-through tunnel. Tickets also include access to the Underwater Zoo upstairs, whose undisputed star is a 5.1m-long Australian crocodile named King Croc.

Dubai Fountain FOUNTAIN

(Map p312; Burj Lake; ⏲shows 1pm & 1.30pm Sat-Thu, 1.30pm & 2pm Fri, every 30min 6-11pm daily; Ⓜ Burj Khalifa/Dubai Mall) FREE This dancing fountain is spectacularly set in the middle of a giant lake against the backdrop of the glittering Burj Khalifa. Water undulates as gracefully as a belly dancer, arcs like a dolphin and surges as high as 150m, all synced to stirring classical-, Arabic- and world-music soundtracks. There are plenty of great vantage points, including from some of the restaurants at Souk Al Bahar, the bridge linking Souk Al Bahar with Dubai Mall and the Dubai Mall waterfront terrace.

Dubai Dino PUBLIC ART

(Map p312; www.thedubaimall.com; Dubai Mall, Sheikh Mohammed bin Rashid Blvd; ⏲10am-11pm Sun-Wed, to midnight Thu-Sat; Ⓜ Burj Khalifa/Dubai Mall) FREE The Jurassic era meets the future in Dubai Mall's Souk Dome, the new home of *Amphicoelias brontodiplodocus*, an almost complete 155-million-year-old dinosaur skeleton unearthed in Wyoming in 2008. The long-necked lizard stands nearly 8m tall and measures 24m long – including its whip-like tail – thus filling up the better part of the exotic arched and dramatically lit atrium.

THE SHEIKH MOHAMMED CENTRE FOR CULTURAL UNDERSTANDING

'Open doors, open minds' is the motto of the **Sheikh Mohammed Centre for Cultural Understanding** (Map p310; ☎04-353 6666; www.cultures.ae; House 26, Al Musallah Rd; tours Dh65, breakfast & lunch Dh90, dinner & brunch Dh100; ⏲9am-5pm Sun-Thu, to 1pm Sat; Ⓜ Al Fahidi), founded by Dubai's current ruler, Sheikh Mohammed, in 1998 to build bridges between cultures and help visitors and expats understand UAE traditions and customs. The centre runs guided tours of the Al Fahidi Historic District and Jumeirah Mosque, and also hosts hugely popular communal meals where you can meet, ask questions of and exchange ideas with nationals while enjoying delicious Emirati food. All tours and meals must be booked in advance.

East Dubai

Top Sights
1 Burj Khalifa ... B3
2 Jumeirah Mosque ... C2

Sights
Dubai Aquarium & Underwater Zoo ... (see 4)
3 Dubai Dino ... B3
Dubai Fountain ... (see 1)
4 Dubai Mall ... B3

Activities, Courses & Tours
5 Arabian Adventures ... A3
Dubai Ice Rink ... (see 4)
6 Hormuz Tourism ... F2
7 Knight Tours ... B3
8 Orient Tours ... F4
9 Wonder Bus Tours ... E2

Sleeping
10 Address Downtown Dubai ... B3
11 Beach Hotel Apartment ... C2
12 Dusit Thani Dubai ... B3
13 Golden Sands Hotel Apartments ... E2
14 Majestic Hotel Tower ... E2
15 Novotel World Trade Centre ... C3
16 Palace Downtown Dubai ... B3
17 Park Hyatt Dubai ... F4

Eating
18 Al Fanar ... B2
19 Aroos Damascus ... F3
20 Baker & Spice ... B3
Mayrig ... (see 16)
Milas ... (see 3)
21 Qbara ... E4
22 Ravi ... D2
Thiptara ... (see 16)
23 Zaroob ... C3

Drinking & Nightlife
24 Irish Village ... F4
Neos ... (see 10)
Nippon Bottle Company ... (see 12)
25 QDs ... F4

Entertainment
26 Act ... B3
Music Room ... (see 14)

Shopping
27 BoxPark ... B2
Dubai Mall ... (see 4)
28 Galleria Mall ... B2
29 Mercato Shopping Mall ... B2
30 S*uce ... C2

Transport
31 Emirates Airlines ... F3
32 Oman National Transport Company ... F3

Jumeirah & Around

Bookended by Jumeirah Mosque and Burj Al Arab and hugging Dubai's best public beaches, villa-studded Jumeirah also offers excellent boutique shopping, copious spas and health clubs, and a growing number of excellent restaurants.

★ Jumeirah Mosque MOSQUE
(Map p312; ☎04-353 6666; www.cultures.ae; Jumeirah Rd; tours Dh10; ⏲tours 10-11.15am Sat-Thu; Ⓜ Emirates Towers, World Trade Centre) Snowy white and intricately detailed, Jumeirah is Dubai's most beautiful mosque and one of only a handful in the UAE that is open to non-Muslims, during one-hour guided tours operated by the Sheikh Mohammed Centre for Cultural Understanding (p313). Tours conclude with a Q&A session where you are free to ask any questions about Islamic religion and culture. There's no need to book. Modest dress is preferred, but traditional clothing may be borrowed for free before entering the mosque. Cameras are allowed.

★ Burj Al Arab LANDMARK
(Map p316; ☎04-301 7777; www.burj-al-arab.com; Jumeirah 3; Ⓜ Mall of the Emirates) The Burj's graceful silhouette – meant to evoke the sail of a dhow (traditional wooden cargo vessel) – is to Dubai what the Eiffel Tower is to Paris. Completed in 1999, this iconic landmark sits on an artificial island off Jumeirah Rd and comes with its own helipad and a fleet of chauffeur-driven Rolls Royce limousines. Beyond the striking lobby, with its gold-leaf opulence and attention-grabbing fountain, lie 202 suites with more trimmings than a Christmas turkey.

It's worth visiting if only to gawk at an interior that's every bit as garish as the exterior is gorgeous. The mood is set in the 180m-high lobby, which is decorated in a red, blue and green colour scheme and accented with pillars draped in gold leaf. The lobby atrium is tall enough to fit the Statue of Liberty within it.

If you're not staying, you need a restaurant reservation to get past lobby security. Don't expect any bargains: there's a minimum Dh350 spend for cocktails in the

Skyview Bar, while afternoon tea will set you back Dh620. Check the website for details and to make a (compulsory) reservation.

Madinat Jumeirah AREA

(Map p316; ☎04-366 8888; www.jumeirah.com; Al Sufouh Rd, Umm Suqeim; Ⓜ Mall of the Emirates) One of Dubai's most attractive developments, Madinat Jumeirah is a contemporary interpretation of a traditional Arab village, complete with a souq, palm-fringed waterways and desert-coloured hotels and villas festooned with wind towers. It's especially enchanting at night, when the gardens are romantically lit and the Burj Al Arab gleams in the background. There are exquisite details throughout, so if you see some stairs, take them – they might lead you to a hidden terrace with a mesmerising vista of the sprawling complex.

Dubai Water Canal

One of Dubai's latest mega-projects is the construction of the Dubai Canal, a 3km extension of the Dubai Creek all the way to the Gulf. The broad waterway originally ran 15km from its mouth in Deira/Bur Dubai down to the Ras Al Khor Wildlife Sanctuary, but it was extended by 2.2km to the new Business Bay district in 2007.

In December 2013, construction kicked off on the Dubai Canal, which will meander from Business Bay below Sheikh Zayed Road, through Al Safa Park and spill into the sea at Jumeirah Beach. As envisioned, it will add 6km of waterfront lined by a shopping mall, hotels, restaurants, cafes, residences, marinas, a public beach, a jogging track and other public spaces. Several bridges will link the banks. The projected completion date is 2017. Until then, there will be numerous traffic diversions, plus the closing of Jumeirah Beach Park and sections of Al Safa Park to contend with.

Dubai Marina & Palm Jumeirah

The Dubai Marina centres on a 3km-long canal flanked by a thicket of futuristic high-rises and lined by the Marina Walk promenade. A stroll along here is especially delightful after dusk, when you can gaze out at the glittering towers and bobbing yachts and find your favourite dinner, drink or *sheesha* spot. Just as pedestrian friendly is the nearby Walk at JBR, a nearly 3km-long strip of shops and family-oriented eateries paralleling a lovely sandy beach. Jutting into the Gulf is the Palm Jumeirah, a palm-shaped artificial island punctuated by the giant Atlantis The Palm resort with its crowd-pleasing water park and aquarium.

Walk at JBR WATERFRONT

(Map p316; Jumeirah Beach Residence; Ⓜ Jumeirah Lakes Towers, Damac, 🚋 Jumeirah Beach Residence 1, Jumeirah Beach Residence 2) In a city of air-conditioned malls, this attractive outdoor shopping and dining promenade was an immediate hit when it opened in 2008. Join locals and expats in strolling the 1.7km stretch, watching the world on parade from a pavement cafe, browsing the fashionable boutiques or ogling the shiny Ferraris and other fancy cars cruising by on weekends.

DUBAI'S GALLERY QUARTER

Hub of burgeoning arts precinct Al Quoz, the **Alserkal Avenue** (Map p316; www.alserkalavenue.ae; 8th St; Ⓜ First Gulf Bank) is the brainchild of local developer and arts patron Abdelmonem bin Eisa Alserkal. Roughly 20 galleries have turned high-ceilinged warehouses into pristine art spaces. Standouts include Gallery Isabelle van den Eynde, which has lifted some of the Middle East's and North Africa's most promising talent from obscurity into the spotlight, and Carbon 12, which presents the gamut of work by international contemporary artists, many with roots in the Middle East.

Since late 2015, an extension in a converted marble factory has added more galleries, including the prestigious New York–based Leila Heller Gallery, the Jean-Paul Najar Foundation from Paris and regional pioneer Third Line.

Complementing the art spaces are artist and design studios, a cultural radio project, two community theatres and urban-style cafes. Free gallery tours are offered on Saturday afternoon; check the website for details. Note that galleries are closed on Friday and that many don't open until the afternoon on Saturday (despite their advertised times).

Al Quoz is a dusty and chaotic industrial area south of Sheikh Zayed Road between Downtown Dubai and the Mall of the Emirates.

West Dubai

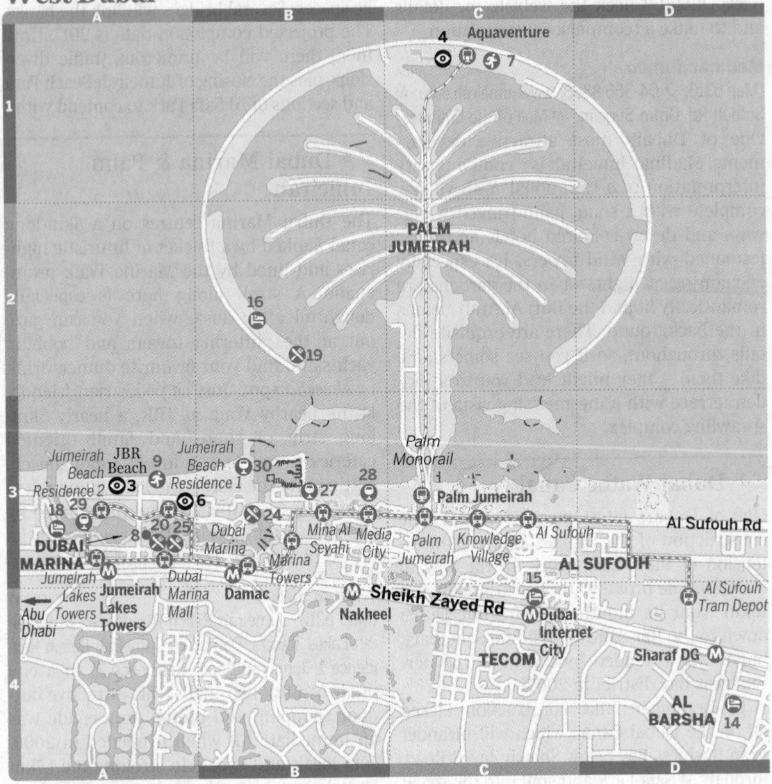

LOCAL KNOWLEDGE

GETTING AROUND THE DUBAI MARINA

The Dubai Marina is one of the most pedestrian-friendly areas in town and also has some convenient public transport. One way to get from A to B is aboard the air-conditioned **Dubai Tram** (www.rta.ae; Dubai Marina; tickets Dh3-5; ⏲6.30am-1am) that trundles between Dubai Internet City and Jumeirah Beach Residence, connecting with the Damac and Jumeirah Lakes Towers metro stations. The **Palm Monorail** (p330) travels along the entire trunk length of the Palm Jumeirah. For a bargain cruise, explore the Dubai Marina aboard a **water bus** (www.rta.ae; Dubai Marina; tickets Dh3-11, one-day pass Dh25; ⏲10am-11pm Sat-Thu, noon-midnight Fri), preferably after dark.

Beach at JBR WATERFRONT

(Map p316; www.thebeach.ae; Jumeirah Beach Residence; Ⓜ Jumeirah Lakes Towers, Damac, 🚊 Jumeirah Beach Residence 1, Jumeirah Beach Residence 2) Paralleling the beachfront for about 1km, the Beach is an open-plan cluster of low-lying, urban-style buildings wrapped around breezy plazas. Hugely popular with families on weekends, it mixes cafes and upmarket shops with a lively waterfront fun zone complete with a water park, a splash park, an outdoor gym, an outdoor cinema and plenty of other diversions. A beach club rents sunloungers, but you're free to spread your towel just about anywhere for free.

Lost Chambers Aquarium AQUARIUM

(Map p316; ☎04-426 1040; www.atlantisthepalm.com; Atlantis The Palm, Palm Jumeirah; adult/child 3-11yr Dh100/70; ⏲10am-10pm; 🚊 Aquaventure) Rare albino alligators Ali and Blue are the

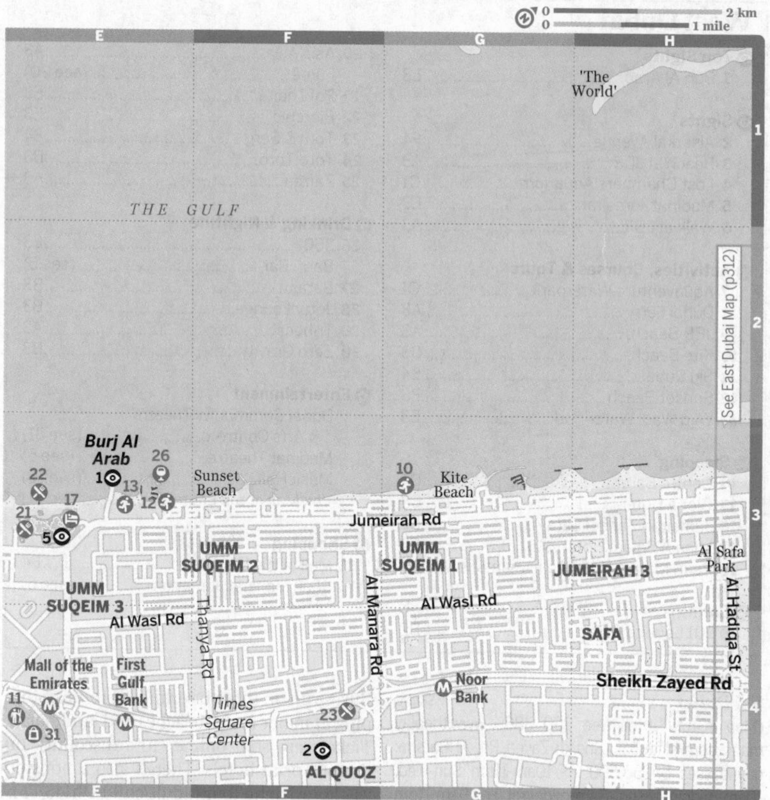

latest stars in this fantastic labyrinth of underwater halls, enclosures and fish tanks that recreates the legend of the lost city of Atlantis. Some 65,000 exotic marine creatures inhabit 20 aquariums, where rays flutter, jellyfish dance and giant groupers lurk. The centrepiece is the Ambassador Lagoon. For an extra fee you can snorkel or dive with the fishes in this 11.5-million-litre tank.

Activities

Wild Wadi Water Park WATER PARK

(Map p316; 04-348 4444; www.wildwadi.com; Jumeirah Rd, Jumeirah 3; over/under 110cm Dh285/240; 10am-6pm Nov-Feb, to 7pm Mar-Oct; ; Mall of the Emirates) It's liquid thrills galore at Wild Wadi, where you can ride a water roller coaster, plunge down death-defying slides and bodysurf huge waves. While these rides have a 110cm minimum height requirement, smaller kids can still have fun scooting down a lazy river or letting off steam in a vast water playground with smaller slides, water guns and a dumping bucket.

Aquaventure Waterpark WATER PARK

(Map p316; 04-426 0000; www.atlantisthepalm.com; Atlantis The Palm, Palm Jumeirah; over/under 120cm Dh250/205; 10am-sunset; ; Aquaventure) Adrenalin rushes are guaranteed at this water park at Atlantis The Palm resort. A 1.6km-long 'river' with rapids, wave surges and waterfalls meanders through vast grounds that are anchored by two towers. A highlight is the ziggurat-shaped Tower of Neptune, with three slides, including the aptly named Leap of Faith, a near-vertical plunge into a shark-infested lagoon.

Those under 120cm can keep cool with tamer rides, a wave pool and an enormous water playground. Tickets also include same-day access to a private beach.

West Dubai

Top Sights
1 Burj Al Arab ... E3

Sights
2 Alserkal Avenue ... F4
3 Beach at JBR ... A3
4 Lost Chambers Aquarium ... C1
5 Madinat Jumeirah ... E3
6 Walk at JBR ... A3

Activities, Courses & Tours
7 Aquaventure Waterpark ... C1
8 Dubai Ferry ... A3
9 JBR Beach ... A3
10 Kite Beach ... G3
11 Ski Dubai ... E4
12 Sunset Beach ... E3
13 Wild Wadi Water Park ... E3

Sleeping
14 Centro Barsha ... D4
15 Gloria Hotel ... C4
16 Jumeirah Zabeel Saray ... B2
17 Mina A'Salam Hotel ... E3
18 Pearl Marina Hotel Apartments ... A3

Eating
19 101 Lounge & Bar ... B2
20 Asia Asia ... A3
Fümé ... (see 20)
21 Pai Thai ... E3
22 Pierchic ... E3
23 Tom & Serg ... F4
24 Toro Toro ... B3
25 Zafran ... A3

Drinking & Nightlife
26 360° ... E3
Bahri Bar ... (see 5)
27 Barasti ... B3
28 Jetty Lounge ... B3
29 Tribeca ... A3
30 Zero Gravity ... B3

Entertainment
Dubai Community Theatre & Arts Centre ... (see 31)
Madinat Theatre ... (see 5)
MusicHall ... (see 16)
Vox Mall of the Emirates ... (see 31)

Shopping
31 Mall of the Emirates ... E4
Souk Madinat Jumeirah ... (see 5)

Ski Dubai SKIING

(Map p316; toll free 800 386; www.theplaymania.com/skidubai; Sheikh Zayed Rd, Al Barsha; day passes Dh250-500; 10am-11pm Sun-Wed, 10am-midnight Thu, 9am-midnight Fri, 9am-11pm Sat; ; Mall of the Emirates) Skiing in the desert? Where else but in Dubai. The city's most incongruous attraction is a faux winter wonderland built right into the gargantuan Mall of the Emirates. It comes complete with ice sculptures and live penguins, a tiny toboggan run, five ski runs (the longest being 400m) and a Freestyle Zone with jumps and rails.

Novices and kids will enjoy the snow park for its colour-lit igloo and tobogganing hill. The chemical-free snow is generated by snow guns at night. Passes include clothing and gear, except for hats and gloves. Bring your own or buy some on site.

Tours

Big Bus Dubai BUS TOUR

(04-340 7709; www.bigbustours.com; 24hr ticket adult/child Dh240/100, 48hr Dh295/130) These hop-on, hop-off city tours aboard open-topped double-decker buses are a good way for Dubai first-timers to get their bearings. Buses run on three interlinking routes, stopping at major malls, beaches and landmarks. Tickets are sold online (10% discount), on the bus or at hotels. There's also a nonstop 2¾-hour Night Tour (adult/child Dh145/75).

The tours include taped commentary in 12 languages and such extras as a souq walking tour or a dhow mini-cruise.

A similar Big Bus Tour (p356) is available in Abu Dhabi.

Wonder Bus Tours BOAT TOUR

(Map p312; 04-359 5656; http://wonderbusdubai.net; Khalid bin Al Waleed Rd; adult/child 3-11yr Dh160/115; several times daily; Bur Juman) These unusual sightseeing tours have you boarding the bright yellow amphibious Wonder Bus at the BurJuman Centre, driving down to the Creek, plunging into the water, cruising past historic Bur Dubai and Deira and returning to the shopping mall, all within the space of an hour.

Dubai Ferry BOAT TOUR

(04-284 4444; www.rta.ae; tickets from Dh50) Dubai Ferry runs 90-minute mini-cruises between its **Al Ghubaiba station** (Map p310; 800 9090; www.rta.ae; Al Ghubaiba Water Station, Shindagha Waterfront; gold/silver tickets Dh75/50, children 2-10 half-price; Ⓜ Al Ghubaiba) in Bur Dubai and the **Dubai Marina** (Map p316; ☎800 9090; www.rta.ae; gold/silver ticket Dh75/50; Ⓜ Damac), passing by Madinat Jumeirah, the Burj Al Arab and Port Rashid. Trips depart at 11am, 1pm and 6.30pm. Other options from either station include an afternoon-tea trip at 3pm and a sunset cruise at 5pm. Children get a 50% discount.

Frying Pan Adventures WALKING TOUR
(www.fryingpanadventures.com; tours Dh335-450) The narrow lanes of Bur Dubai and Deira are a feast for foodies, a beehive of shoebox-size restaurants where global expats cook up comfort food from home. Arva and Farida Ahmed open the doors to the most exciting eateries to introduce you to delicious fare from Morocco to Nepal to India on their small-group walking tours.

Festivals & Events

Dubai Shopping Festival SHOPPING
(www.mydsf.ae; ⊙Jan) Held throughout January, this shopping festival lures bargain-hunters from around the world. There are huge discounts in the souqs and malls, and the city is abuzz with activities, ranging from live concerts to fashion shows and fireworks.

Art Dubai ART
(www.artdubai.ae; ⊙Mar) Keep tabs on the rapidly evolving art scene in the Middle East and South Asia at this prestigious showcase of nearly 100 galleries from the UAE and around the world, exhibiting works at Madinat Jumeirah.

Dubai World Cup SPORTS
(www.dubaiworldcup.com; Meydan Racecourse, Nad Al Sheba; ⊙Mar) Horse racing has a long and vaunted tradition in the Emirates. Racing season kicks off in November and culminates in March with the Dubai World Cup, the world's richest horse race.

Dubai International Film Festival FILM
(DIFF; www.dubaifilmfest.com; ⊙Dec) This excellent non-competitive film festival is a handy chance to catch international indie flicks as well as new releases from around the Arab world and the Indian subcontinent.

Sleeping

When picking a place to stay in Dubai, identify what type of experience you're most keen to have, then base yourself in the area that best reflects your expectations in order to minimise time spent on the road. In other words, if you want to centre your explorations on Dubai Creek, the souqs and heritage areas, stay in Deira or Bur Dubai. For an immersion in Dubai's cutting-edge urbanity, find a place near Downtown Dubai. And if the beach beckons, head to Jumeirah or Dubai Marina.

Deira & Bur Dubai

Dubai Youth Hostel HOSTEL $
(☎04-298 8151; www.uaeyha.com; 39 Al Nahda Rd, Al Qusais; dm/s/d/tr HI members Dh110/220/260/330, non-members Dh120/230/270/360; ⊙reception 24hr; @ 🛜 ≋; Ⓜ Stadium) Dubai's only hostel is north of the airport, far from most Dubai attractions but only a short walk from a metro station and a mall. The range of facilities (pool, tennis court, coffee shop and laundry) is impressive. Private rooms in the newer wing (Hostel A) come with TV, fridge and bathroom.

Amenities in the four-bed dorms in the older wings (Hostels B and C) are minimal.

DUBAI FOR CHILDREN

Many hotels have kids clubs and activities, but there are also plenty of diversions around town. Both tots and teens can keep cool on the rides and slides at Wild Wadi Water Park (p317) or Aquaventure (p317), on the slopes at Ski Dubai or the **Dubai Ice Rink** (Map p312; ☎04-437 1111; www.dubaiicerink.com; ground fl, Dubai Mall; per session incl skates Dh60-80; ⊙10am-midnight; Ⓜ Burj Khalifa/Dubai Mall) at Dubai Mall. For fish encounters, head to Lost Chambers (p316) at Atlantis The Palm hotel or the Dubai Aquarium & Underwater Zoo (p313) in Dubai Mall. Just about every mall also has an indoor amusement park, such as Magic Planet at Mall of the Emirates and Sega Republic at Dubai Mall. Little kids may enjoy playing grown-ups at KidZania, also at Dubai Mall. A good online resource is www.uae4kidz.biz.

Formula and nappies (diapers) are widely available at supermarkets and pharmacies. Children under five travel for free on public transport.

It's located between Lulu Hypermarket and Al Bustan Mall. No smoking, alcohol or visitors allowed.

★XVA Hotel HERITAGE HOTEL $$
(Map p310; ☎04-353 5383; www.xvahotel.com; r from Dh300; 📶; Ⓜ Al Fahidi) This art-infused hotel occupies a century-old wind-tower house smack dab in the Al Fahidi Historic District, off Al Fahidi St. Its 13 compact rooms open onto a courtyard (making them rather dark) and sport classy decor inspired by local themes, such as the Henna Room and the Dishdash Room. All feature arabesque flourishes and rich colours. The charming cafe serves breakfast.

Orient Guest House HERITAGE HOTEL $$
(Map p310; ☎04-351 9111; www.orientguesthouse.com; r from Dh500; 📶; Ⓜ Al Fahidi) This romantic B&B in a former private home in the Al Fahidi Historic District beautifully captures the feeling of old Dubai. The 11 smallish rooms are entered via heavy wooden doors and surround a central courtyard where breakfast is served. Furnishings exude traditional Arabic flair and feature richly carved wooden armoires, four-poster beds with frilly drapes, and tiled floors.

Arabian Courtyard Hotel & Spa HOTEL $$
(Map p310; ☎04-351 9111; www.arabiancourtyard.com; Al Fahidi St, Meena Bazaar; r from Dh600; @📶🏊; Ⓜ Al Fahidi, Al Ghubaiba) Opposite the Dubai Museum, this hotel is an excellent launch pad for city explorers. The Arabian theme extends from the turbaned lobby staff to the design flourishes in the decent-sized rooms, some of which catch glimpses of the Creek across the souq. Facilities include a pub, several restaurants, swimming pool, spa and gym. One child under 11 stays free.

Majestic Hotel Tower HOTEL $$
(Map p312; ☎04-359 8888; www.dubaimajestic.com; Al Mankhool Rd; r from Dh600; P@📶🏊; Ⓜ Al Fahidi) Despite its ho-hum location on a busy street, this hotel scores high for comfort, design and a 'with it' vibe thanks to a happening Greek restaurant and the best live-music club in town. All rooms come with plush beds and heavy drapes in neutral colours; the 'classic' ones are tiny, so book 'deluxe' if you need more elbow room.

★Park Hyatt Dubai HOTEL $$$
(Map p312; ☎04-602 1234; www.dubai.park.hyatt.com; Dubai Creek Golf & Yacht Club, Dubai Creek Club St; d from Dh2200; P@📶🏊; Ⓜ Deira City Centre) The mile-long driveway through a lush date-palm grove is the first hint that the Park Hyatt is no ordinary hotel – an impression quickly confirmed the moment you step into the domed and pillared lobby. Tiptoeing between hip and haute, it has oversized pastel rooms with arabesque flourishes and balconies for counting the dhows plying the Creek.

The spa and restaurants are all top notch and the golf-course setting further lends it an air of exclusivity.

Radisson Blu Hotel HOTEL $$$
(Map p310; ☎04-222 7171; www.radissonblu.com/hotel-dubaideiracreek; Baniyas Rd; r from Dh1000; P@📶🏊; Ⓜ Union, Baniyas Sq) This Creekside stalwart was Dubai's first five-star hotel when it opened in 1975 and it fits as comfortably as your favourite jeans. Standard rooms won't hold a ton of luggage but boast a good range of amenities, an upbeat, contempory colour scheme and small, furnished balconies with water views.

Downtown Dubai

Dusit Thani Dubai HOTEL $$
(Map p312; ☎04-343 3333; www.dusit.com; 133 Sheikh Zayed Rd; r from Dh975; P@📶🏊; Ⓜ Financial Centre) Shaped like an upside-down tuning fork, one of Dubai's most architecturally dramatic towers hides traditional Thai decor behind its futuristic facade. Although it's geared towards the business brigade, urban nomads will also appreciate the lovely interplay of warm woods, earth tones and rich fabrics in the oversized rooms and the stellar views from the rooftop pool.

Novotel World Trade Centre HOTEL $$
(Map p312; ☎04-332 0000; www.novotel.com; Al Saada St; r excl breakfast from Dh700; P📶🏊; Ⓜ World Trade Centre) The no-nonsense Novotel adjoins the convention centre and comes with smallish but well-thought-out rooms with lots of desk space and a sofa. The rectangular swimming pool is sufficient for laps, and there's a pretty good gym with circuit-training equipment. The Blue Bar is one of the best places for jazz in town.

★Palace Downtown Dubai HOTEL $$$
(Map p312; ☎04-428 7888; www.theaddress.com; Sheikh Mohammed bin Rashid Blvd, Old Town Island; d from Dh1900; P@📶🏊; Ⓜ Burj Khalifa/Dubai Mall) City explorers with a romantic streak will be utterly enchanted by this low-lying, luxe lakefront contender with its winning

alchemy of old-world class and Arabic aesthetics. Rooms are chic and understated, styled in natural tones, and boast balconies overlooking Dubai Fountain. With the Burj Khalifa and Dubai Mall steps away, it's also a perfect launch pad for shopaholics.

Address Downtown Dubai HOTEL **$$$**
(Map p312; ☎04-436 8888; www.theaddress.com; Sheikh Mohammed bin Rashid Blvd; d from Dh2250; P@🛜≋; M Burj Khalifa/Dubai Mall) This hotel embodies everything Dubai has to offer: beauty, style, glamour and ambition. Since its opening, it has drawn the cognoscenti in droves, not only to its rooms but also to its edgy restaurants and bars. If you do stay, you'll find XL-size rooms dressed in rich woods and tactile fabrics, endowed with killer views and the latest communication devices.

If that's not enough, the 24-hour gym and five-tiered infinity pool beckon.

Jumeirah & Around

This section also includes a couple of lower-priced properties inland, near the Mall of the Emirates.

Centro Barsha HOTEL **$$**
(Map p316; ☎04-704 0000; www.rotana.com/centrobarsha; Rd 329, Al Barsha 1; d from Dh570; P@🛜≋; M Sharaf DG) An easy 10-minute walk from the Mall of the Emirates, this is the Rotana brand's entry into the budget design-hotel category. Rooms are compact but stylish and outfitted with all the key lifestyle and tech touches, including satellite TV and IP phones. Kick back in the comfy cocktail bar or the 24-hour gym, or by the pleasant outdoor pool.

Wi-fi is charged at Dh70 per 24 hours. It's behind the Mall of the Emirates.

Beach Hotel Apartment APARTMENT **$$**
(Map p312; ☎04-345 2444; http://beachhotelapartment.ae; Al Hudhaiba Rd & 10B St; apt from Dh950; P🛜≋; M World Trade Centre) Terrific service-minded staff, nice architecture, a sunny rooftop pool and a fantastic location give this place a considerable edge. You'll be steps from the beach, Jumeirah Mosque and trendy cafes and boutiques, as well as a Spinneys supermarket in case you want to make use of your kitchen.

Mina A'Salam Hotel RESORT **$$$**
(Map p316; ☎04-366 8888; www.jumeirah.com; Madinat Jumeirah, Al Sufouh Rd, Umm Suqeim 3; r excl breakfast from Dh1800; P@🛜≋; M Mall of the Emirates) The striking lobby is an overture to the full symphony of relaxed luxury awaiting in huge, amenity-laden rooms. Each has a balcony overlooking the romantic arabesque jumble that is Madinat Jumeirah or the striking Burj Al Arab. Guests have the run of the place and adjacent sister property Al Qasr, including the pools, the 2km-long private beach and the kids club.

Rates include free admission to Wild Wadi Water Park.

WORTH A TRIP

RAS AL KHOR WILDLIFE SANCTUARY

Pink flamingos steal the show at **Ras Al Khor Wildlife Sanctuary** (☎04-606 6822; www.facebook.com/wildlife.ae; cnr Oud Metha Rd & Ras Al Khor St; ⊙9am-4pm; M Dubai Healthcare City) in winter, but avid birdwatchers can spot more than 170 species in this pastiche of salt flats, mudflats, mangroves and lagoons spread over an area of around 6.2 sq km. Bordering Dubai Creek, the sanctuary is an important stopover on the east African–west Asian flyway. There are two accessible hides (platforms) with fantastically sharp binoculars. It's a 6km taxi ride from the nearest metro. No advance registration required for groups of fewer than five people.

The Flamingo Hide is on the sanctuary's western edge near the flamingo roost off the junction of Al Wasl and Oud Metha Rds, and the Mangrove Hide overlooks the mangrove forest off Ras Al Khor Rd on the southern edge.

Dubai Marina & Palm Jumeirah

Pearl Marina Hotel Apartments APARTMENT **$$**
(Map p316; ☎04-447 1717; www.pearlmarinahotel.com; Marina Waterfront; apt from Dh555; P🛜≋; M Jumeirah Lakes Towers) Tucked into the far end of the Dubai Marina, the Pearl may not be as flashy as its high-rise neighbours, but who cares? The price tag is only a fraction of that of the big boys, giving you more dirham to spend on fun, food and fashion. The fabulous beach and The Walk at JBR are only steps away.

Jumeirah Zabeel Saray HOTEL $$$

(Map p316; ☎04-453 0000; www.jumeirah.com; West Crescent Rd, Palm Jumeirah; r from Dh1680; P@🛜🏊; M Nakheel) With its domed ceiling, golden pillars and jewel-like lamps, Zabeel Saray's lobby is as lavish and majestic as an Ottoman palace. The rich decor transfers in subtler ways to the rooms, where everything is calibrated to take the edge off travel, including balconies to let in the ocean breeze and admire the sparkling Dubai skyline.

The Talise Spa, too, is a supreme relaxation station, complete with a Turkish hammam and a salt-water lap pool. A great selection of restaurants makes for contented tummies. The hotel is about 15-minute taxi ride from the nearest metro station (Dh40).

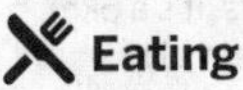

Eating

Deira & Bur Dubai

There's some fine dining here as well, but the real draw in these neighbourhoods are the tiny, unassuming cafes serving superb street food from Kerala to Kathmandu. Snag a pavement table beneath flickering neon, soak up the local colour and fill up for under Dh20.

Aroos Damascus SYRIAN $

(Map p312; ☎04-221 9825; cnr Al Muraqqabat Rd & Al Jazeira St; sandwiches Dh4-20, mains Dh15-60; ⌚24hr; M Salah Al Din) A Dubai restaurant serving Syrian food to adoring crowds since 1980 must be doing something right. One of our favourite dishes is *arayees* – a pita pocket stuffed with spice-laced ground lamb and grilled to crunchy perfection. Great tabbouleh, huge outdoor patio, cool flickering neon. Busy until the wee hours.

Special Ostadi IRANIAN $

(Map p310; ☎04-397 1469; Al Musallah Rd; mains Dh20-40; ⌚noon-4pm & 6.30pm-1am Sat-Thu, 6.30pm-1am Fri; M Al Fahidi) Sheikhs to shoe shiners clutter this funky, been-here-forever (since 1978, to be precise) kebab joint. Amid walls plastered in photographs of happy guests, a fleet of swift servers brings heaping plates of rice and yogurt-marinated chicken into a dining room humming with chatter and laughter.

Sind Punjab INDIAN $

(Map p310; ☎04-352 5058; Bukaz Bldg, Al Esbij St; mains Dh11-35; ⌚8am-2am; M Al Fahidi, Al Ghubaiba) Like a fine wine, some restaurants only get better over time and such is the case with Sind Punjab, the first family eatery to open in Meena Bazaar in 1977. Since then, the low-frills place has garnered a feverishly loyal following for its finger-lickin' butter chicken and *dal makhni* (a rich lentil and kidney-bean stew).

XVA Café CAFE $$

(Map p310; ☎04-353 5383; www.xvahotel.com/cafe; dishes Dh25-55; ⌚7am-9pm Nov-Apr; 🌿; M Al Fahidi) Escape Dubai's bustle at this artsy courtyard cafe in the Al Fahidi District where the menu eschews meat in favour of such offerings as eggplant burgers, burgul salad and *mojardara* (rice topped with sautéed veggies and yogurt). The mint lemonade is perfect on a hot day. Breakfast is served any time. It's off off Al Fahidi St.

★ **Qbara** MIDDLE EASTERN $$$

(Map p312; ☎04-709 2500; www.qbara.ae; Wafi Fort Complex, Oud Metha Rd; mains Dh95-325; ⌚6pm-1am; M Dubai Healthcare City) This Wafi hot spot is known for innovative, contemporary Arabic cuisine served in a sublime setting. Think dark, mysterious and sensuous, with a 10m-long bar, a huge glass-bubble chandelier, rich fabrics and projections on hand-carved timber panels. The upstairs lounge is lined with intimate nooks coveted by small groups. It's near the corner of 13th and 28th Sts.

Al Mansour Dhow INTERNATIONAL $$$

(Map p310; ☎04-222 7171; www.radissonblu.com/hotel-dubaideiracreek; Baniyas Rd; 2hr dinner cruise Dh185; ⌚8pm; 🛜; M Union, Baniyas Sq) For a traditional (albeit touristy) experience, book a table on this old wooden dhow cheerfully decorated with bands of twinkling lights and operated by the Radisson Blu Hotel. A house band plays as you enjoy the lavish buffet spread that's heavy on Middle Eastern and Indian choices before reclining with a *sheesha* in the upper-deck lounge. Board outside the hotel.

Downtown Dubai

Expect to pay top dirham for first-rate culinary indulgences at five-star hotel restaurants, or head to the Dubai Mall food court for a quick budget bite.

Zaroob LEBANESE $

(Map p312; ☎04-327 6060; www.zaroob.com; ground fl, Jumeirah Tower Building, Sheikh Zayed Rd; dishes Dh9-28; ⌚24hr; 🛜; M Emirates Towers) With its open kitchens, fruit-filled baskets,

LOCAL KNOWLEDGE

DUBAI'S TOP THREE PUBLIC BEACHES

If you're not staying at a beachfront five-star hotel but want to swim in the Gulf without shelling out mega dirham for beach-club admission, there are plenty of free public beaches. Most are almost deserted during the week but packed on weekends (Friday and Saturday).

Facilities range from non-existent to full beach infrastructure and have improved considerably over the years, especially with the opening of the 14km-long Jumeirah Corniche in late 2014. Stretching from Dubai Marine Beach Resort to the Burj Al Arab (with short sections interrupted by construction), it features a boardwalk, a spongy jogging track, changing facilities, kiosks, benches and, of course, pristine sand for tanning and frolicking. Here are our nominees for top three Dubai beaches (listed east to west):

Kite Beach (Sheikh Hamdan Beach; Map p316; Umm Suqeim 1; M Noor Bank) FREE Jam-packed with sporty types keen on kite surfing, soap football, beach tennis, beach volleyball, kayaking and other sports to show off those toned abs. There are showers, toilets, kiosks and changing facilities, plus great views of the Burj Al Arab. Turn off Jumeirah Rd opposite Saga World mall.

Sunset Beach (Map p316; Umm Suqeim 3; M First Gulf Bank, Mall of the Emirates) FREE Next to the Jumeirah Beach Hotel and with dreamy views of the Burj Al Arab, Sunset is popular with families, selfie-addicts and surfers, even though facilities are limited to a few changing cubicles and a playground.

JBR Beach (Map p316; Jumeirah Beach Residence; M Jumeirah Lakes Towers, Jumeirah Lakes Towers) FREE Though not the widest, this busy beach has state-of-the-art infrastructure and a number of pay-for-play attractions, including a water park, a kiddie splash zone, sunloungers and an outdoor gym. Food options abound at the adjacent The Beach at JBR outdoor mall and The Walk at JBR promenade.

colourful lanterns and graffiti-festooned steel shutters, Zaroob radiates the urban integrity of a Beirut street-food alley. Feast on such delicious no-fuss food as felafel (deep-fried chickpea balls), shwarma (spit-roasted meat in pita bread), flat or wrapped *manoush* (Lebanese pizza), *alayet* (tomato stew) or tabbouleh (parsley, tomato and bulgar-wheat salad), all typical of the Levant.

Mayrig ARMENIAN $$
(Map p312; 056-364 9794; www.mayrigdubai.com; Sheikh Mohammed bin Rashid Blvd; mains Dh55-74; noon-12.30am; ; M Burj Khalifa/Dubai Mall) Mayrig's Armenian food borrows from Lebanese cuisine while setting its own distinctive flavour accents. Menu stars include *sou beureg* (a flaky cheese-filled pastry), the mouthwatering *fishnah* kebab topped with wild sour-cherry sauce, and the lemon-zest chocolate cake. No alcohol but *sheesha* on the terrace.

Milas EMIRATI $$
(Map p312; 04-388 2313; http://milas.cc; ground fl, The Village, Dubai Mall, Sheikh Mohammed bin Rashid Blvd; mains Dh55-95; 9.30am-11.30pm Sun-Wed, to 12.30am Thu-Sat; M Burj Khalifa/Dubai Mall) Milas is how Emiratis pronounce *majlis* – the traditional guest reception room. This particular *majlis* has a sleek contemporary look (wood, glass, neon) that goes well with updated riffs on such traditional local dishes as *harees* (sugar-sprinkled cooked wheat) and *makbous* (beef stew). Thoughtful perks: wet handcloths, the complimentary *danqaw* (chickpea) appetiser and a post-meal perfume tray.

Baker & Spice INTERNATIONAL $$
(Map p312; 04-425 2240; www.bakerandspiceme.com; Souk Al Bahar; mains Dh68-152; 8am-11pm; ; M Burj Khalifa/Dubai Mall) Offering a seasonal bounty of intriguingly paired organic ingredients, the colourful salad bar is the undisputed star at this charming, country-style cafe imported from London. Mains like chicken pie and beef lasagna are more conventional but just as tasty. Also a good breakfast spot.

Thiptara THAI $$$
(Map p312; 04-888 3444; www.theaddress.com; Sheikh Mohammed bin Rashid Blvd; mains Dh120-290; 6-11.30pm; ; M Burj Khalifa/Dubai Mall) Thiptara means 'magic at the water' – very appropriate given its romantic setting in a lakeside pagoda with unimpeded views of

HALAL TRAVEL

What's a beach holiday without bikinis and booze? Well, still a grand old time if the fast-growing market in halal tourism is any indication. More and more hotels and resorts cater to the needs of Muslim travellers by providing services and facilities in accordance with Islamic beliefs and practices. They serve only halal foods and non-alcoholic drinks; their pool, spa and leisure facilities are segregated by gender; there are women-only beach areas, and mixed beach areas adhere to the Islamic dress code. On-site prayer facilities are as *de rigueur* as family-friendly entertainment.

The **Gloria Hotel** (Map p316; 04-399 6666; www.gloria-hotels.com; Sheikh Zayed Rd; r excl breakfast from Dh700; P @ ; Dubai Internet City) and the **Golden Sands Hotel Apartments** (Map p312; 04-355 5553; www.goldensandsdubai.com; Al Mankhool Rd; studio apt from Dh500; @ ; BurJuman), both in Dubai, and the **Oceanic Khorfakkan Resort & Spa** (p377) on the East Coast are among Sharia'a- (Islamic law-) compliant properties in the UAE.

the Dubai Fountain at the Palace Downtown Dubai hotel. The food is just as impressive, with elegant interpretations of classic Thai dishes perked up by herbs grown by the chef himself.

Jumeirah & Around

Jumeirah restaurants draw wealthy locals and tourists. Those at Madinat Jumeirah generally have good-quality food and are the most scenic, if pricey. For local flavour and superb ethnic eats, head inland to Satwa.

Ravi PAKISTANI $

(Map p312; 04-331 5353; Al Satwa Rd, Satwa; mains Dh8-25; 5am-2.30am; World Trade Centre) Everyone from cabbies to five-star chefs flocks to this legendary Pakistani eatery (dating from 1978) where you eat like a prince and pay like a pauper. The butter chicken is superb, but it's also worth loosening that belt for heaping helpings of mutton *tikka* and the chicken *masala biryani*. It's near the Satwa roundabout.

Tom & Serg INTERNATIONAL $$

(Map p316; 056-474 6812; www.tomandserg.com; Al Joud Center, 15A St, Al Quoz; mains Dh37-79; 8am-4pm Sun-Thu, to 5pm Fri & Sat; ; Noor Bank, First Gulf Bank) This loft-style urban cafe with concrete floors, exposed pipes and an open kitchen would fit right into London or Melbourne and is a great stop on an Al Quoz gallery hop. The menu teems with global feel-good food like tuna tacos, Moroccan chicken and eggs Benedict. Great coffee, too. It's near Ace Hardware.

Al Fanar EMIRATI $$

(Map p312; 04-344 2141; www.alfanarrestaurant.com; Jumeirah Rd, Jumeirah 1; mains Dh42-120; 8.30am-11.30pm; Burj Khalifa/Dubai Mall) Al Fanar lays on the old-timey Emirati theme pretty thick with a Land Rover parked outside, a reed ceiling and waiters dressed in traditional garb. Make your selection with the help of a picture menu depicting such classic local dishes as *biryani laham* (rice with lamb), *maleh nashef* (salted fish in tomato sauce) and *thereed deyay* (chicken stew).

★ **Pai Thai** THAI $$$

(Map p316; 04-432 3232; www.jumeirah.com; Madinat Jumeirah, Al Sufouh Rd, Umm Suqeim 3; mains Dh65-195; 6.30-11.30pm; Mall of the Emirates) An *abra* ride, a canalside table and candlelight are the hallmarks of a romantic night out and this enchanting spot sparks on all cylinders. If your date doesn't make you swoon, then such expertly seasoned Thai dishes as wok-fried seafood and steamed sea bass should still ensure an unforgettable evening. Early reservations advised.

★ **Pierchic** SEAFOOD $$$

(Map p316; 04-366 5866; www.jumeirah.com; Madinat Jumeirah, Al Sufouh Rd, Umm Suqeim 3; mains Dh100-240; 12.30-3pm & 6.30-11.30pm; Mall of the Emirates) Looking for a place to drop an engagement ring into a glass of champagne? Make reservations (far in advance) at this impossibly romantic seafood house capping a historic wooden pier with front-row views of the Burj Al Arab and Madinat Jumeirah. The menu is a foodie's daydream, from the champagne ceviche to the poached lobster.

Dubai Marina & Palm Jumeirah

There's plenty of high-end eating in the hotels plus reasonably priced fare with sidewalk seating along The Walk at JBR and The Beach at JBR.

Fümé INTERNATIONAL **$$**
(Map p316; ☎04-421 5669; www.fume-eatery.com; Pier 7, Dubai Marina; mains Dh50-95; ⏰noon-1am Sat-Wed, to 2am Thu & Fri; Ⓜ Damac, 🚊 Dubai Marina Mall) With its funky design, relaxed crew and global comfort food, Fümé brings more than a touch of urban cool to the marina. The menu features plenty of creative dishes to keep foodies happy. Bestseller: the super-juicy beef chuck ribs smoked for six hours in a closed charcoal oven. No reservations.

Zafran INDIAN **$$**
(Map p316; ☎04-399 7357; ground fl, Dubai Marina Mall; mains Dh30-130; ⏰noon-midnight Sat-Wed, to 1am Thu & Fri; 📶; Ⓜ Damac, 🚊 Dubai Marina Mall) Devoid of mall-setting sterility, this contemporary Indian restaurant packs a lot of sizzle into its kebabs, curries and biryanis, which are best enjoyed on the terrace. Menu stars include *dahee kebab* (dumplings), char-grilled lamb kebabs and tandoori king prawns.

Asia Asia FUSION **$$$**
(Map p316; ☎04-276 5900; www.asia-asia.com; 6th fl, Pier 7, Dubai Marina; mains Dh70-200; ⏰4pm-midnight or later; 📶; Ⓜ Damac, 🚊 Dubai Marina Mall) Prepare for a culinary journey along the Spice Route as you enter this lavish restaurant via a candlelit corridor that spills into an exotic booth-lined lounge with dangling birdcage lamps. The menu blends Asian and Middle Eastern flavours, usually with finesse and success. Signature dishes include the sambal chicken tagine and the Persian black cod. Full bar.

Toro Toro LATIN AMERICAN **$$$**
(Map p316; ☎04-399 8888; www.torotoro-dubai.com; Al Sufouh Rd; small plates Dh60-130; ⏰7.30pm-2am Sat-Wed, to 3am Thu & Fri; 📶; Ⓜ Damac, 🚊 Jumeirah Beach Residence 1) The decor has as much pizzazz as the food at this pan-Latin outpost conceived by star chef Richard Sandoval. Feast on such small-plate top picks as lamb shank in adobo sauce, seafood ceviche or grilled octopus, or opt for the *rodizio* menu (a series of grilled meats carved at your table; four-person minimum). Huge selection of spirits and cocktails.

101 Lounge & Bar MEDITERRANEAN **$$$**
(Map p316; ☎04-440 1030; thepalm.oneandonlyresorts.com; West Crescent Rd, Palm Jumeirah; mains Dh85-220, tapas selection of 3/6/9 Dh90/160/220; ⏰11.30am-2am) With to-die-for views of the Dubai Marina skyline, it may be hard to concentrate on the food at this marina-adjacent al fresco pavilion at the ultraswish One&Only The Palm resort. Come for nibbles and cocktails in the bar or go for the full dinner experience (paella, grills, pastas). Ask about the free boat shuttle when making reservations.

Drinking & Nightlife

Deira

★QDs BAR
(Map p312; ☎04-295 6000; www.dubaigolf.com; Dubai Creek Golf & Yacht Club, Garhoud; ⏰5pm-2am Sun-Wed, to 3am Thu & Sat, 1pm-3am Fri; Ⓜ Deira City Centre) Watch the ballet of lighted dhows floating by while sipping cocktails at this always-fun outdoor Creekside lounge deck where carpets and cushions set an inviting mood. In summer, keep cool in an air-conditioned tent. Great for *sheesha,* but skip the food (except for the pizza and Friday-afternoon barbecue).

Irish Village BEER GARDEN
(Map p312; ☎04-282 4750; www.theirishvillage.com; 31st St, Garhoud; ⏰11am-2am Sat-Wed, to 3am Thu & Fri; 📶; Ⓜ GGICO) This always buzzy pub, with its Irish-main-street facade made with materials imported straight from the Emerald Isle, has been a Dubai institution since 1996. There's Guinness and Kilkenny on tap, gardens around a petite lake, the occasional live concert and plenty of pub grub to keep your tummy happy (and brain balanced). It's located next to Dubai Tennis Stadium.

Downtown Dubai

Neos BAR
(Map p312; ☎04-888 3444; www.theaddress.com; Sheikh Mohammed bin Rashid Blvd; ⏰6pm-2.30am; 📶; Ⓜ Burj Khalifa/Dubai Mall) At this glamour vixen at The Address Downtown Dubai hotel, you can swirl your cosmo with the posh set 63 floors above Dubai Fountain. It takes two lifts to get to this urban den of shiny metal, carpeted floors, killer views and resident DJ.

LOCAL KNOWLEDGE

SHEESHA & MOCKTAILS

Most Emiratis don't drink alcohol, preferring to socialise over coffee, juice and mocktails. If you're not up for drinking, follow the locals to a mellow *sheesha* cafe and play a game of backgammon. Even if you don't smoke, it's tempting to recline languorously and sample a puff of the sweet flavours. *Sheesha* cafes are open until after midnight, later during the winter months. The going rate is Dh35 to Dh85 per pipe for a session. Remember though – popular and atmospheric as the pastime is, smoking *sheesha* isn't any better for your health than smoking cigarettes.

Nippon Bottle Company BAR

(Map p312; www.dusit.com/dusitthani/dubai; Sheikh Zayed Rd; ⌚noon-12.30am; Ⓜ Financial Centre) Finding this neon-lit Japanese bar, hidden speakeasy-style behind a bookcase off the lobby of the Dusit Thani Hotel, requires a clear head, which you may no longer have after sampling its potent cocktails and Japanese whiskeys.

Jumeirah & Around

★360° LOUNGE

(Map p316; ☎reservations 04-432 3232; www.jumeirah.com; Jumeirah Rd, Umm Suqeim 3; ⌚5pm-2am Sat-Thu, 4pm-3am Fri; 📶; Ⓜ Mall of the Emirates) Capping a long, curved pier, this fashionable al fresco lounge still hasn't lost its grip on the crowd after many years of music, mingling and magical views of the Burj Al Arab. On weekends top-notch DJs spin house for shiny, happy hotties; other nights are mellower. Must be 21 (ID required).

Bahri Bar BAR, LOUNGE

(Map p316; ☎04-366 5866; Madinat Jumeirah, Al Sufouh Rd; ⌚4pm-2am Sat-Mon, to 3am Tue-Fri; 📶; Ⓜ Mall of the Emirates) This chic bar drips with sultry Arabian decor and has a verandah laid with Persian rugs and comfy sofas perfect for taking in magical views of the Madinat waterways and the Burj Al Arab. Daily drink deals and bands or DJs playing jazz and soul make the place a perennial fave among locals and visitors.

Dubai Marina & Palm Jumeirah

★Barasti BAR

(Map p316; ☎04-318 1313; www.barastibeach.com; Al Sufouh Rd; ⌚11am-1.30am Sat-Wed, to 2.30am Thu & Fri; Ⓜ Nakheel) Seaside at Le Meridien Mina Seyahi Beach Resort, Barasti is the top spot for lazy days on the beach and is often jam-packed with shiny happy party people knocking back the brewskis. There's soccer and rugby on the big screen, a deck with pool tables, occasional bands and drink specials on Monday night.

★Jetty Lounge BAR, LOUNGE

(Map p316; ☎04-399 9999; www.royalmirage.oneandonlyresorts.com; Al Sufouh Rd; ⌚2pm-2am; 📶; Ⓜ Nakheel) From the moment you start following the meandering path through the One&Only's luxuriant gardens, you'll sense that you're heading for a pretty special place. Classy without the pretence, Jetty Lounge is all about unwinding (preferably at sunset) on plush white sofas scattered right in the sand. There's a full bar menu and snacks for nibbling.

Zero Gravity BAR, CLUB

(Map p316; ☎04-399 0009; www.0-gravity.ae; Al Seyahi St; day pass weekday/weekend Dh150/250, incl food & beverage Dh50/100; ⌚10am-2am Sun-Thu, to 3am Fri & Sat; Ⓜ Damac) Keep an eye on the Dubai Marina skyline and the daredevils jumping out of planes at this sleek beach club-bar next to Skydive Dubai, then cap a day of chilling and swimming in the sea and a new infinity pool with a night of drinks, snacks and international DJs. Nice touch: the Friday-afternoon 'brunch'.

Tribeca BAR

(Map p316; ☎050-345 6067; www.tribeca.ae; The Walk at JBR; ⌚5pm-1am Sat-Wed, 5pm-2am Thu, 2pm-2am Fri; 📶; Ⓜ Jumeirah Lakes Towers, 🚊 Jumeirah Lakes Towers) The concrete, steel and street-art decor may exude a New York–loft vibe, but the spirit of this happening if chilled lounge bar is distinctly local. A platform for home-grown DJs, musicians and artists, it serves cocktails, organic wines and healthy food, all best enjoyed on the terrace with Palm Jumeirah views.

☆ Entertainment

Music Room LIVE MUSIC

(Map p312; ☎04-359 8888; www.themusicroomdubai.com; Al Mankhool Rd; ⌚6pm-3am; Ⓜ Al

Fahidi) Arab hip-hop queen Malikah and English metal band Salem are among the many artists who've played gigs at Dubai's best place for indie and alt sounds. Great for dipping into the local music scene, it's the kind of spot that appeals to keeping-it-real music aficionados.

MusicHall LIVE MUSIC

(Map p316; ☎056-270 8670; www.jumeirah.com; West Crescent Rd, Palm Jumeirah; mains Dh170-290, minimum spend Dh450; ⏲9pm-3am Thu & Fri; Aquaventure) It's not a theatre, not a club, not a bar and not a restaurant – the lavishly designed MusicHall is all those things. The concept hails from Beirut, where it's had audiences clapping since 2003 with an eclectic line-up of live music – from Indian to country, and rock to Russian ballads. The food (fusion cuisine and international finger food) is an afterthought.

Act CABARET

(Map p312; ☎04-355 1116; www.theactdubai.com; Sheikh Zayed Rd; ⏲8.30pm-3am Sun & Thu, to 1am Mon-Wed; Ⓜ Financial Centre) No strippers and raunchy performances in the Dubai edition of this burlesque dinner theatre in a lush Victorian-styled venue with crimson walls, velvet curtains and baroque mirrors. Still, a mighty good time awaits, with shows featuring artistic and often sexy variety acts to go with your plate of ceviche and other Peruvian fare. Dancing after dinner. No phones, no cameras.

Dubai Community Theatre & Arts Centre THEATRE

(DUCTAC; Map p316; ☎04-341 4777; www.ductac.org; Mall of the Emirates, Sheikh Zayed Rd, Al Barsha; Ⓜ Mall of the Emirates) This thriving cultural venue puts on all sorts of diversions, from Shakespeare and classical concerts to Bollywood retrospectives, Arabic folklore and art exhibits. Much support is given to Emirati talent, making this a good place to keep tabs on the local scene. Drivers should take the Ski Dubai car-park entrance and park between rows S and T.

Madinat Theatre THEATRE

(Map p316; ☎04-366 6546; www.madinattheatre.com; Al Sufouh Rd, Umm Suqeim 3; Ⓜ Mall of the Emirates) The program at this handsome 442-seat theatre at Souk Madinat is largely calibrated to the cultural cravings of British expats. Expect plenty of crowd-pleasing entertainment ranging from popular West End imports to stand-up comedy, toe-tapping musicals and Russian ballet.

Vox Mall of the Emirates CINEMA

(Map p316; ☎600 599 905; www.voxcinemas.com; Mall of the Emirates, Sheikh Zayed Rd, Al Barsha; tickets Dh47-160; Ⓜ Mall of the Emirates) Forever upping this ante, this multiplex emerged from a makeover with 24 screens, including a 4-D cinema with motion chairs, and wind, light and water effects; the region's first IMAX laser cinema; and the superluxe Theatre by Rhodes, where you can enjoy a meal conceived by Michelin-starred chef Gary Rhodes. Skip the queue by buying tickets online.

Meydan Racecourse HORSE RACING

(☎04-327 0077, tickets 04-327 2110; www.dubairacingclub.com; Al Meydan Rd, Nad Al Sheba; general admission free, premium seating Dh50; ⏲races Nov-Mar) Dubai racing's home is the spectacular Meydan Racecourse, about 5km southwest of Downtown Dubai. Spanning 1.5km, its grandstand is bigger than most airport terminals and lidded by a crescent-shaped solar-panelled roof. It can accommodate up to 60,000 spectators and integrates a five-star hotel, restaurants, an IMAX theatre and a racing museum.

Shopping

Dubai has just about perfected the art of the mall, which is the de-facto, air-conditioned 'town common', the place to go with family and friends to chat, eat, shop and take in some entertainment. For local colour, head to the souqs in Deira and Bur Dubai, which can be a font for souvenirs, as is tourist-geared Souq Madinat Jumeirah. Jumeirah Beach Rd (near the Jumeirah Mosque) has some local indie boutiques, while Al Wasl Rd has become the domain of smaller designer malls.

★Dubai Mall MALL

(Map p312; ☎800-382 246 255; www.thedubaimall.com; Sheikh Mohammed bin Rashid Blvd; ⏲10am-11pm Sun-Wed, to midnight Thu-Sat; 📶; Ⓜ Burj Khalifa/Dubai Mall) With around 1200 stores, this isn't merely the world's largest shopping mall, it's a small city, with a giant ice rink and aquarium, a dinosaur skeleton, indoor theme parks and 150 food outlets. There's a strong European-label presence, along with branches of the French Galeries Lafayette department store, the British Hamley's toy store and the first Bloomingdale's outside the US.

★Mall of the Emirates MALL
(Map p316; ☎04-409 9000; www.mallofthe emirates.com; Sheikh Zayed Rd, Al Barsha; ⏲10am-10pm Sat-Wed, to midnight Thu & Fri; 📶; Ⓜ Mall of the Emirates) With 600 stores, MoE is (another) one of Dubai's mega malls, with retail options ranging from high street to haute couture. The indoor ski hall Ski Dubai is the main non-shopping attraction.

Mercato Shopping Mall MALL
(Map p312; ☎04-344 4161; www.mercatoshopping mall.com; Jumeirah Rd, Jumeirah 1; ⏲10am-10pm; Ⓜ Financial Centre, Burj Khalifa/Dubai Mall) With 140 stores, Mercato may be small by Dubai standards, but it's distinguished by attractive architecture that looks like a fantasy blend of a classic train station and an Italian Renaissance town. Think vaulted glass roof, brick arches, a giant clock and a cafe-lined piazza. Retail-wise, you'll find upscale international brands and a Spinneys supermarket.

Souk Madinat Jumeirah MALL
(Map p316; ☎04-366 8888; www.jumeirah.com; Madinat Jumeirah, Al Sufouh Rd, Umm Suqeim 3; ⏲10am-11pm; Ⓜ Mall of the Emirates) More tourist-geared boutique mall than traditional Arabian market, this handsomely designed souq is part of the Arab village-style Madinat Jumeirah resort and great for picking up souvenirs. Options include camel toys at Camel Company, Bedouin daggers at Lata's and quality pashmina shawls at Yasmine. The nicest of the numerous charming cafes, bars and restaurants overlook one of the resort's canals.

Galleria Mall MALL
(Map p312; Al Wasl Rd; ⏲10am-midnight; Ⓜ Burj Khalifa/Dubai Mall) The modern-Arabia design of this locally adored boutique mall is as much a draw as the shops, which include such rare gems as the first UAE branch of Saudi homeware store Cities and hip fashions from Valleydez. Wrap up a visit with a healthy lunch at South African cafe Tashas or gooey cakes from Emirati-owned Home Bakery. It's near 13th St.

BoxPark MALL
(Map p312; ☎800 637 227; boxpark.ae; Al Wasl Rd; ⏲10am-midnight; 📶; Ⓜ Business Bay) This 1.3km-long lifestyle mall is a mosaic of 220 colourful shipping containers, just like the London original. It's become an instant hot spot for promenading, picking up eclectic designer wares in trendy boutiques and relaxing over ice cream or eccentric eats from Azerbaijan to Argentina. Parking is at a premium.

S*uce FASHION
(Map p312; ☎04-344 7270; http://shopatsauce.com; Village Mall, Jumeirah Rd; ⏲10am-10pm Sat-Thu, 4-10pm Fri; Ⓜ Emirates Towers) The clothes and accessories at S*uce (pronounced 'sauce'), a pioneer in Dubai's growing lifestyle-fashion scene, are certainly not plain or simple. Join fashionistas picking through international designers you probably won't find on your high street back home (eg India's Anouk Grewal or Lebanon's Vanina).

ℹ Information

EMERGENCY

Ambulance (☎999)

Fire Department (☎997)

Police (☎999)

MEDICAL SERVICES

Pharmacies Hotline (☎04-223 2323) Pharmacies are generally open from 9am to 10pm, but some are open 24/7. Call the hotline for details.

American Hospital Dubai (Map p312; ☎appointments 04-377 5000, emergency 04-377 6645; www.ahdubai.com; Oud Metha Rd, Bur Dubai; ⏲primary-care walk-in clinic 8am-6pm Sat-Thu; Ⓜ Dubai Healthcare City, Oud Metha) One of the top hospitals in town. No appointments are needed for the walk-in clinic. The emergency room is open 24 hours.

Dubai Hospital (☎04-219 5000; http://web.dohms.gov.ae/dh; Al Khaleej Rd, Deira; Ⓜ Abu Baker Al Siddique) One of the region's best government hospitals, with 24/7 ER.

POST OFFICE

Central Post Office (Map p312; ☎04-337 1500; Zabeel Rd; ⏲7.30am-9pm Sat-Thu; Ⓜ BurJuman) In Bur Dubai's Karama district, between Zabeel and Umm Hurair Rds.

TOURIST INFORMATION

Dubai Tourism (www.visitdubai.com) Dubai's official tourism site.

ℹ Getting There & Away

AIR

Dubai International Airport (☎04-224 5555, flight enquiries 04-224 5777; www.dubaiairports.ae; Ⓜ Airport Terminal 1, Airport Terminal 3) Located on the border with the Sharjah emirate, Dubai International Airport has three terminals. Terminal 1 is the main terminal used by major international airlines, small and charter airlines are based at Terminal 2, and Terminal 3 is the sole domain of Emirates Airlines. There are duty-free shops in the arrival and departure halls.

INTERCITY BUS

The **Roads & Transport Authority** (p391) operates local buses within Dubai as well as buses on some inter-emirate routes. Buses are air-conditioned and dirt cheap but can get crowded.

Union Square Bus Station (Map p310; Union Sq; Ⓜ Union) E700 buses depart for Fujairah (Dh25, two hours, every 45 minutes), E400 buses for Ajman (Dh10, one to 1½ hours, every 30 minutes) and E303 buses for Sharjah (Dh10, 40 to 60 minutes, every 15 minutes) from this station handily located next to Union metro station.

Al Ghubaiba Bus Station (Map p310; Al Ghubaiba Rd; Ⓜ Al Ghubaiba) Al Ghubaiba station in Bur Dubai, next to Carrefour supermarket, has the E100 service to Abu Dhabi (Dh25, two hours, several hourly) and the E306 service to Sharjah (Dh10, 50 minutes, every 20 minutes).

Sabkha Bus Station (Map p310; cnr Al Sabkha Rd & Deira St; Ⓜ Baniyas) Hourly E16 buses to Hatta (Dh10, 2¼ hours) leave from this station in the Deira souqs.

CAR

Dubai has scores of car-rental agencies, from major global companies to no-name local businesses. All international agencies are based at the airport and have multiple branches around town. See p453 for websites.

TAXI

Taxis to Sharjah and the other northern emirates incur a Dh20 surcharge. Sample fares from Downtown Dubai to cities in other emirates are for a carload of passengers: Dh140 for Sharjah, Dh160 for Ajman, Dh225 for Umm Al Quwain, Dh380 for Ras Al Khaimah and Dh500 for Abu Dhabi or Al Ain. It is, however, possible to negotiate a better rate with your cabbie directly. To order a taxi call the **Dubai Taxi Corporation** (p330).

ℹ Getting Around

Negotiating most of Dubai by foot, even combined with public transport, is highly challenging, not only because of the heat but also due to the lack of pavements, traffic lights and pedestrian crossings.

Most visitors get around town by taxi. The Dubai metro is also an excellent mode of transport, with two lines and sparkling-clean trains. Although bus lines offer good coverage, they are slow and rarely run on time.

TO/FROM THE AIRPORT

Dubai Metro

The Red Line stops at Terminals 1 and 3. Luggage is limited to two pieces, one not exceeding 81cm by 58cm by 30cm and the other not exceeding 55cm by 38cm by 20cm. Getting caught with alcohol aboard (even if purchased at the airport duty-free shop) entails a Dh200 fine.

Taxi

Airport taxis have a starting meter of Dh25 and a per-kilometre charge of Dh1.75 (Dh25 plus Dh1.86 per kilometre for vans and 'ladies' taxis'). Sample fares:

DESTINATION	COST (DH)	TIME (MIN)
Deira Gold Souq	50	20
Bur Dubai	60	15
Downtown Dubai	65	15
Madinat Jumeirah	110	25
Dubai Marina	130	30

PUBLIC TRANSPORT

Dubai's local public transport is operated by the **RTA** (p391) and consists of the Dubai metro, buses, water buses and *abras* (traditional boats).

Abra

Abras are motorised traditional wooden boats linking Bur Dubai and Deira across the Creek on two routes:

Rte 1 Bur Dubai Abra Station to Deira Old Souq Abra Station; daily between 5am and midnight.

Rte 2 Dubai Old Souq Abra Station to Sabkha Abra Station around the clock.

Abras leave when full (around 20 passengers), which rarely takes more than a few minutes. The fare is Dh1 and you pay the driver en route. Chartering your own *abra* costs Dh120 per hour.

Dubai Metro

Dubai's metro (dubaimetro.eu) opened in 2010 and has proved a popular service.

Red Line Runs for 52.1km from near Dubai International Airport to Jebel Ali past Dubai Marina, mostly paralleling Sheikh Zayed Road.

Green Line Runs for 22.5km, linking the Dubai Airport Free Zone (Etisalat station) with Dubai Healthcare City (Creek station).

Intersection of Red and Green Lines At Union station in Deira and at BurJuman station in Bur Dubai.

Onward journeys At each station, cabs and feeder buses stand by to take you to your final destination.

BUS & METRO FARES & TICKETS

- The RTA network is divided into five zones, with fares depending on the number of zones traversed.
- Before you hop aboard a bus, train or water bus, you must purchase a rechargeable Nol card from vending machines or ticket offices in all stations.
- Short-term visitors should get the Red Card, which costs Dh2 and may be recharged for up to 10 journeys. Fares range from Dh2 to Dh6.50 per trip.
- If you intend to make more than 10 trips, get a Silver Card for Dh25 (including Dh19 of credit). Trips cost between Dh1.80 and Dh5.80 up to a daily maximum of Dh14.
- The Gold Card costs double and gives you access to the gold-class carriage.
- The correct fare is automatically deducted from your card when you swipe it upon entering and exiting a metro train or a bus.
- Children under age five and shorter than 90cm travel free.

Frequency Trains run roughly every 10 minutes from 6am to 11pm Saturday to Thursday, and 2pm to midnight on Friday.

Cars Each train consists of four standard cars and one car that's divided into a women-only section and a 'Gold Class' section where a double fare buys carpets and leather seats. Women may of course travel in any of the other cars as well.

Tickets Nol (fare) cards can be purchased at the station and must be swiped upon entry and exit.

Fares Vary from Dh1.80 for stops within a single zone to Dh6.50 for stops within five zones.

Routes All metro stations stock leaflets, in English, clearly mapping the zones.

Penalties If you exit a station with insufficient credit you will have to pay the equivalent of a day pass (Dh14).

Local Buses

Dubai has a clean, comfortable and air-conditioned bus network. The front of each bus is reserved for women and families. For information and trip planning, check www.rta.ae.

From Saturday to Thursday, most routes operate at 15- to 20-minute intervals between 6am and 11.30pm. Friday service is less frequent and may start later and finish earlier. Night buses operate at 30-minute intervals in the interim.

Palm Monorail

The **Palm Monorail** (Map p316; www.palm-monorail.com; one way/return Dh15/25; ⏰10am-10pm) is a 5.45km-long driverless train that runs along the trunk of the Palm Jumeirah between the Gateway station and the Atlantis Hotel in 10 minutes. It links to Dubai Tram's Palm Jumeirah station. It's not a bad ride, but taxis are no more expensive, even if you're travelling alone.

Water Buses

Air-conditioned water buses travel on two routes along the Creek and at Dubai Marina at 15-minute intervals. Tickets are Dh2 per trip. Nol cards are valid.

Rte B1 Bur Dubai Station to Al Seef via Dubai Old Souq, Sabkha and Baniyas stations (7am to 10pm Saturday to Thursday, 10am to midnight Friday).

Rte BM1 The Walk at JBR to Dubai Marina Mall (10am to midnight Thursday, noon to midnight Friday, noon to 10pm Saturday, 10am to 10pm Sunday to Wednesday).

TAXI

Taxis (☎04-208 0808; www.dubaitaxi.ae) are metered, quite inexpensive and the fastest and most comfortable way to get around, except during rush-hour traffic. Flag one down in the street or order it by phone.

- Daytime flagfall is Dh5 (Dh8 with advance booking, Dh12 during peak times) plus Dh1.71 per kilometre (Dh3.50 from 10pm to 6am or Dh7 when booked), including all tolls. The minimum fare is Dh12.
- Trips to Sharjah and the other northern emirates incur a Dh20 surcharge.
- Tip about 10%. Always carry small bills since most cabbies can't or won't give change.
- There's rarely a problem with women riding alone, even at night, although you can also request a woman driver (ask for a 'ladies' taxi') when booking. Eight-seaters (family vans) and special-needs taxis are also available.
- Many hotels operate a limo service, which may cost as much as double. Confirm the fare in advance and if you don't like it, ask the concierge to call you a regular cab.
- Most taxi drivers speak at least some English, but destinations are generally not given via a street address. Instead, mention the nearest landmark (eg a hotel, mall, roundabout, major building).
- If you're going to a private residence, phone your host and ask them to give the driver directions.

AROUND DUBAI

If you're tired of big-city mayhem and crave a little peace and quiet, these luxe desert resorts will show you a calmer, unhurried side of the emirate.

Al Maha Desert Resort & Spa

Al Maha Desert Resort & Spa RESORT **$$$**
(☎04-832 9900; www.al-maha.com; Dubai Desert Conservation Reserve, Al Ain Rd; full board from Dh2900;) It may only be 65km southeast of Dubai (on the Dubai to Al Ain Rd), but Al Maha feels like an entirely different universe. Gone are the skyscrapers, traffic and go-go attitude. At this remote desert eco-resort it's all about getting back to some elemental discoveries about yourself and where you fit into nature's grand design.

Part of the Dubai Desert Conservation Reserve (DDCR), Al Maha is one of the most exclusive hotels in the Emirates and named for the endangered Arabian oryx, which is bred as part of the DDCR's conservation program. The resort's 42 luxurious suites are all stand-alone, canvas-roofed bungalows with private plunge pools. Each one has its own patio with stunning vistas of the beautiful desert landscape and peach-coloured dunes, punctuated by mountains and grazing white oryx and gazelles.

Rates include two daily activities such as a desert-wildlife drive, an archery session or a camel trek. Private vehicles, visitors and children under 10 are not allowed.

Bab Al Shams Desert Resort & Spa

Bab Al Shams Desert Resort & Spa RESORT **$$$**
(☎04-809 6498, 04-381 3231; www.meydanhotels.com/babalshams; Al Qudra Rd; r from Dh1150;) Resembling a fort and blending into the desertscape, Bab Al Shams is a tonic for escapists seeking to indulge their *Arabian Nights* fantasies. Its labyrinthine layout reflects both Arabic and Moorish influences; the 115 rooms are gorgeous, spacious and evocatively earthy, with pillars, lanterns, paintings of desert landscapes and prettily patterned Bedouin-style pillows.

While this is the perfect place to curl up with a book or meditate in the dunes, those who enjoy a more active holiday will also find plenty to do. A wonderful infinity pool beckons, as do the luscious Satori Spa and eight restaurants. Children between five and 12 years old can make new friends in Aladdin's Kids Club. Off-site activities pay homage to Emirati heritage with desert tours, falconry, archery, and horse and camel rides. Bab Al Shams is about 45 minutes south of Dubai off Hwy E611, near Endurance Village.

Hatta حتا

Cradled by the craggy Hajar Mountains, Hatta, an enclave of Dubai emirate, is a popular weekend getaway. Its main attractions are its cool, humidity-free climate and magnificent mountain scenery. While it makes a good base for off-road trips, Hatta itself is a wonderful place to relax.

Sights

Hatta Heritage Village MUSEUM
(☎04-852 1374; www.dubaiculture.gov.ae; Hatta; ⏱7.30am-8.30pm Sat-Thu, 2.30-8.30pm Fri) FREE This sprawling village recreates the Hatta of yore. It is housed in the ruler's restored historic fort with a *majlis* (meeting room), a traditional courtyard house and various *barasti* (palm-leaf) buildings. Displays on weaponry, local music, palm-tree products, handicrafts, weaving, traditional dress and old village society illustrate the past. There are nice views from a restored defensive tower from 1880 whose doors are about 2.5m above the ground – guards had to use ropes to climb up there.

To get to the village, turn south at the main roundabout in Hatta, continue for about 3km and then turn left at the sign. If you're travelling by bus, it's about a 1.5km walk from the Hatta terminal.

LOCAL KNOWLEDGE

MASAFI MARKET

Despite the name, the **Friday Market** (Masafi; ⏱8am-10pm daily), a strip of nearly identical stalls on Hwy E88 from Dubai towards the eastern coast is actually a daily affair. Rugs, pottery, household goods and knick-knacks are for sale, but it's best for stocking up on local produce and also makes a nice photo-op. Masafi is famous for its mineral springs whose water is sold throughout the country.

Sleeping & Eating

Hatta Fort Hotel HOTEL $$$

(☎04-814 5400; www.jaresortshotels.com; Main Hatta Roundabout; d from Dh1100; P🛜🏊) The only lodging option in town, Hatta Fort Hotel is popular with expats at weekends and exudes a 1960s country-club feel thanks to its manicured lawns and expansive grounds. The 48 spacious and classy chalets brim with Arabic design flourishes amid stone walls and wood-beamed ceilings. All have a private patio or balcony with dreamy mountain views.

Overlooking one of the resort's two pools, Café Gazebo (mains Dh25 to Dh60) does breakfast, lunch and snacks until 8pm, while fine-dining restaurant Jeema (mains Dh60 to Dh130) opens for dinner and sometimes has live entertainment.

Getting There & Away

Hatta is about 125km east of Dubai. Bus E16 shuttles hourly between Dubai's Al Sabkha station and Hatta's bus terminal, about 2.5km south of the main roundabout (Dh10, 2¼ hours). The first bus from Hatta leaves at 5.35am, the last at 9.30pm. Buses from Dubai run between 6am and 10pm.

The 125km drive from Dubai via Hwy E44 is punctuated by roaming camels, rippling sand dunes and the occasional oasis, all set against a backdrop of the mighty mountains. Stretches of road pass through Oman and, although there are no immigration or customs formalities, you may be asked for your passport at soldier-staffed road blocks. This is largely an effort to stop illegal immigration. If you're driving a rental car, make sure you're allowed to take it into Omani territory and that you have insurance cover in Oman. You can avoid all this by taking the northerly route via Hwy E102.

NORTHERN EMIRATES

Sharjah الشارقة

☎06 / POP 946,000

Sharjah doesn't dazzle with glitz but with sensitivity towards its history and culture, which explains why Unesco declared it Cultural Capital of the Arab World in 1998, recognition reaffirmed in 2014, when it became Capital of Islamic Culture. Once you have penetrated the traffic-clogged outskirts of town, the historic old town is easy to navigate on foot. Plan on setting aside several hours to explore the Heritage and Arts Areas, as well as the souqs and excellent museums.

Aside from the main city of Sharjah, the enclaves of Dibba Al Hisn, Khor Fakkan and Kalba on the eastern coast also belong to the emirate.

One caveat: Sharjah takes its decency laws very seriously, so do dress modestly. That means no exposed knees, backs or bellies – and that goes for both men and women. It's also the only emirate that is 'dry' (ie no alcohol is available anywhere).

Sights

Many of Sharjah's top sights are scattered around the partly walled-in **Heritage Area** and the adjacent **Arts Area**, just off the corniche. Both are part of a historical preservation and restoration project called Heart of Sharjah that is expected to be completed in 2025. See www.heartofsharjah.ae for details.

★**Sharjah Heritage Museum** MUSEUM

(☎06-568 0006; www.sharjahmuseums.ae; Heritage Area; adult/child Dh5/free; ⏰8am-8pm Sat-Thu, 4-8pm Fri) This creatively curated museum goes a long way towards demystifying Emirati culture and traditions for visitors. Each of the five galleries zeroes in on different aspects of local life, from living in the desert, religious values, and birth and burial rituals to holiday celebrations, marriage and wedding ceremonies, and folk medicine. An abundance of quality original objects and excellent English panelling make a visit here a satisfying and educational experience.

Bait Al Naboodah HISTORIC SITE

(☎06-568 1738; www.sharjahmuseums.ae; Heritage Area; ⏰closed for restoration) This 1845 house, a former pearl trader's home with a grand entranceway, elaborately carved decorations and an ample courtyard, is a fine example of early Emirati architecture and daily living. It is expected to reopen in 2016 after extensive restoration.

Souq Al Arsah SOUQ

(Courtyard Souq; Heritage Area; ⏰9am-9pm Sat-Thu, 4-9pm Fri) One of the oldest souqs in the UAE (which in this case means about 50 years), Souq Al Arsah once crawled with traders from Persia and India and local Bedu stocking up on supplies, their camels fastened to posts outside. Despite a thorough facelift, it's still an atmospheric place, though vendors now vie for tourist dirham with pashminas, *dhallahs* (coffee pots), herbs and spices, old *khanjars* (daggers) and traditional jewellery in air-conditioned comfort.

Sharjah Art Foundation New Art Spaces GALLERY

(www.sharjahart.org; Heritage Area; ⏲information centre 9am-9pm Thu-Sat, 4-9pm Fri) Urban meets tradition in this cluster of white-cube galleries set within restored Emirati homes in the Heritage Area, behind Al Zahra Mosque. Inaugurated during the 2015 Sharjah Biennial, they present cutting-edge exhibits as well as art-related movies in an outdoor cinema. Drop by the information centre for a map.

Sharjah Fort Museum MUSEUM

(☎06-568 5500; www.sharjahmuseums.ae; Al Hisn Sq; adult/child Dh5/free; ⏲8am-8pm Sat-Thu, 4-8pm Fri) A row of cannons welcomes visitors to Sharjah's beautifully renovated 1823 Al Hisn fort, which reopened as a museum in 2015. Past its mighty teak gate well-presented exhibits help you study up on the history of Sharjah, the ruling Qasimi family and the history of the building itself. A highlight is the round prison tower. For a more in-depth experience, borrow a free audio-guide.

Sharjah Art Museum MUSEUM

(☎06-568 8222; www.sharjahmuseums.ae; Arts Area; ⏲8am-8pm Sat-Thu, 4-8pm Fri) FREE The Arts Area is anchored by one of the region's largest and most dynamic art museums and the organiser of the Sharjah Biennial. Upstairs, a permanent exhibit presents a comprehensive survey of art created in the Arab world over the past 50 years. Other galleries house visiting exhibits of international calibre, and there's a nice cafe to boot.

★Sharjah Museum of Islamic Civilisation MUSEUM

(☎06-565 5455; www.sharjahmuseums.ae; cnr Corniche & Arabian Gulf St; adult/child Dh5/free; ⏲8am-8pm Sat-Thu, 4-8pm Fri) Just about everything you always wanted to know about Islam is addressed in this well-curated museum in a stunningly converted souq right on the waterfront. Ground-floor galleries zero in on different aspects of the Islamic faith, including the ritual and importance of the hajj, and on Arab scientific accomplishments, especially in mathematics and astronomy. The upper floors navigate through 1400 years of Islamic art and artefacts, including ceramics, woodwork, textiles and jewellery. Don't miss the zodiac mosaic below the central dome.

AL NOOR MOSQUE VISITS

Among the most beautiful of Sharjah's 600 mosques, **Al Noor Mosque** (www.shjculture.com; Corniche, east Khalid Lagoon; ⏲tours 10am Mon) has a dream setting overlooking the Khalid Lagoon. It is the emirate's only mosque open to non-Muslims, on guided one-hour tours operated by the nonprofit Sharjah Centre for Cultural Communication. Tours conclude with a question-and-answer session. Dress modestly, of course, and do bring a camera and curiosity. No registration required.

Al Qasba AREA

(☎06-556 0777; www.alqasba.ae; Al Qasba Canal) FREE This car-free canalside development presents a family-friendly mix of cafes, carousels, boat rides, shops, a small musical fountain and a 60m-high Ferris wheel, the Eye of the Emirates. Come in the evening, but avoid Friday and Saturday nights if you don't like crowds. Art fans should check out the latest show at the Maraya Art Centre.

Al Majaz Waterfront PARK

(☎06-552 1552; www.almajaz.ae; Al Buheirah Corniche Rd) FREE The main attraction of this family fun zone at the bottom of the Khalid Lagoon is the Sharjah Fountain, which, after dark, combines music, lights, lasers and spurting water columns into impressive five-minute shows. Aside from a clutch of cafes and fast-food outlets, diversions include minigolf, a splash park, a playground, a camera obscura and boat rides.

Sharjah Aquarium AQUARIUM

(☎06-528 5288; www.sharjahaquarium.ae; Al Meena St; adult/child Dh25/15; ⏲8am-8pm Mon-Thu & Sat, 4-10pm Fri) Enter an 'abandoned dhow' for close-ups of maritime creatures from the UAE's west and east coast without getting your feet wet. Moray eels lurk, blacktip reef sharks prowl, eagle rays flop and jellyfish dance around tanks that recreate Dibba Rock, mangroves, Shark Island's coral reefs and other local watery habitats. We like the touchscreens, but a few more labels wouldn't hurt.

Sharjah Maritime Museum MUSEUM

(☎06-522 2002; sharjahmuseums.ae; Al Meena St; adult/child Dh10/5; ⏲8am-8pm Sat-Thu, 4-8pm Fri) For a salty introduction to the UAE, visit

Sharjah

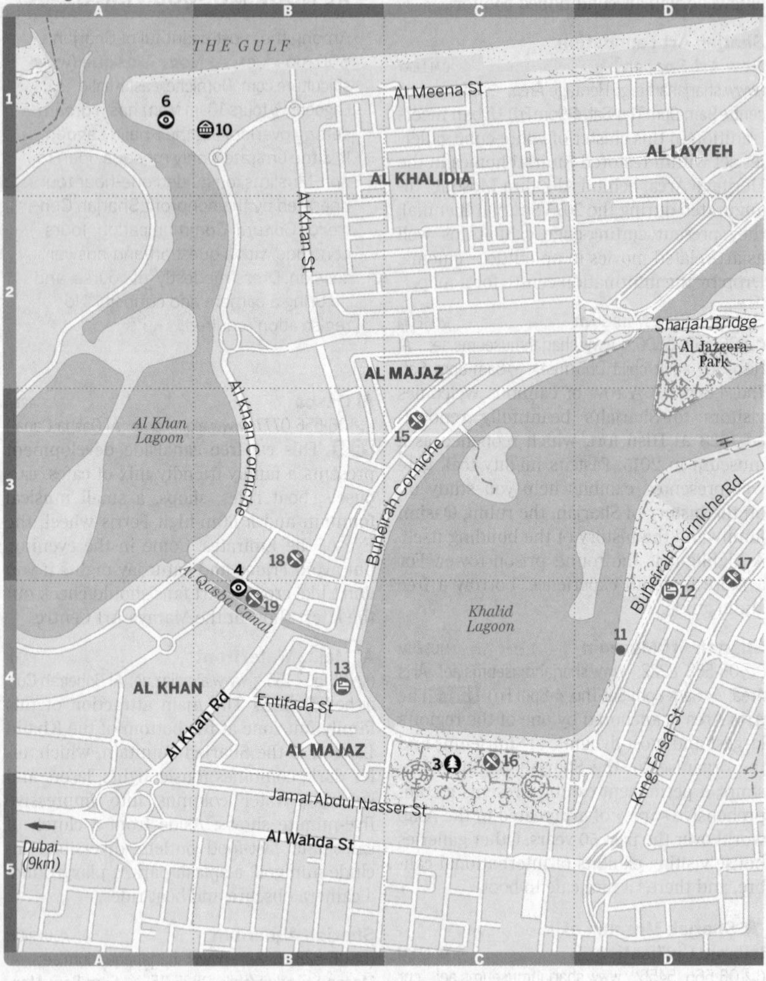

this charming museum that displays enough traditional dhows, exhibits on pearling and fishing equipment to keep your imagination afloat for a half hour or so.

Festivals & Events

Sharjah Biennial ART
(www.sharjahbiennial.org; ⏲ Mar-May) Held every two years (next in 2017), this is one of the most important art events in the Arab world.

Sharjah International Book Fair BOOKS
(www.sharjahbookfair.com; ⏲ Nov) Held since 1982, this major regional book fair, held over 11 days, brings together publishers, authors, translators and the public in presenting the latest tomes in Arabic, English and other languages.

Sleeping

Sharjah Heritage Hostel HOSTEL $
(☎ 06-298 8151; www.uaeyha.com; Heritage Area; dm per person without bathroom Dh75; ⏲ reception 9am-11pm; P) In a quiet location on the edge of the Heritage Area, this hostel occupies a nicely restored historic courtyard building. Carved wooden doors lead to eight clean, well-kept dorms with five or six single beds, air-con

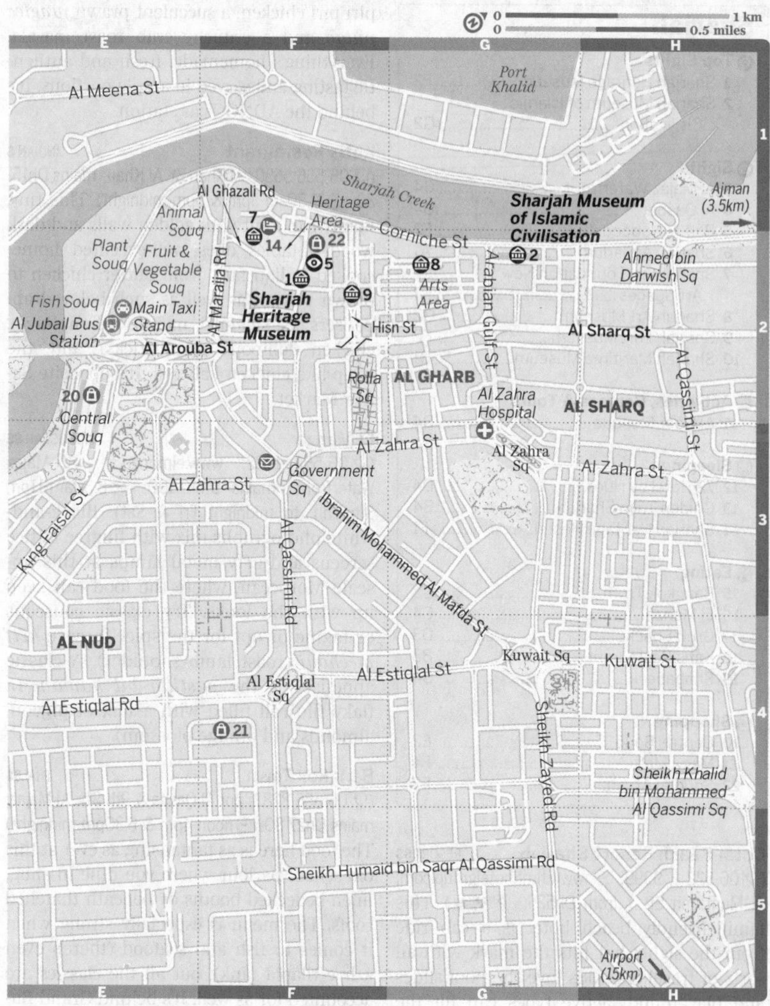

and a small fridge. There's a communal kitchen as well. It's behind the Al Zahra Mosque.

Golden Tulip Sharjah HOTEL $
(06-519 7777; www.goldentulipsharjah.com; Buheirah Corniche; r excl breakfast from Dh300; P) With a killer location mere steps from Al Qasba and Al Majaz Waterfront, the Golden Tulip has mostly good-size rooms with traditional furnishings and an earth-toned colour scheme; some have lagoon views. It's within the glass-fronted Al Fardan Shopping Centre and has a gym with separate workout facilities for men and women.

★ **72 Hotel by Hues** BOUTIQUE HOTEL $$
(06-507 9797; www.hueshotels.com/seventy-two-hotel; Corniche 110 St; r excl breakfast from Dh720; P @) This 72-unit hotel is as hip as it gets in Sharjah. Clearly a lot of thought has gone into the urban design, whose angularity is softened by warm colours, rich fabrics and atmospheric lighting. It's within walking distance of major sights and comes with indoor pool, gym, sauna and steam room. Spend a little extra for a room with lagoon view.

Sharjah

Top Sights

1 Sharjah Heritage Museum ... F2
2 Sharjah Museum of Islamic Civilisation ... G2

Sights

3 Al Majaz Waterfront ... C4
4 Al Qasba ... B4
5 Bait Al Naboodah ... F2
6 Sharjah Aquarium ... A1
7 Sharjah Art Foundation New Art Spaces ... F2
8 Sharjah Art Museum ... G2
9 Sharjah Fort Museum ... F2
10 Sharjah Maritime Museum ... B1

Activities, Courses & Tours

11 Al Noor Mosque ... D4

Sleeping

12 72 Hotel by Hues ... D4
13 Golden Tulip Sharjah ... B4
14 Sharjah Heritage Hostel ... F1

Eating

15 Bangkok Town ... C3
16 El Manza ... C4
17 Grub Shack ... D3
18 Katis Restaurant ... B3
19 Shababeek ... B4

Shopping

20 Central Souq ... E2
21 Mega Mall ... F4
22 Souq Al Arsah ... F2

Coral Beach Resort Sharjah RESORT $$

(06-522 9999; www.hmhhotelgroup.com; Al Muntazah St; r from Dh525; P) This family-friendly beach hotel is a cab ride from the sights but hits the mark with all sorts of travellers. Kids love the pool slides and playground; active types can hit the gym or the infinity pool; and couples can enjoy a massage or a romantic seaside dinner. Breezy rooms have ocean views, but the beach is quite small.

Eating

Grub Shack INDIAN $

(06-544 576; www.facebook.com/grubshackuae; King Faisal St, Al Majaz; mains Dh18-32; 11am-4pm (from 1pm Fri) & 6-11pm Mon-Sat) With its fire engine–red folding chairs and cute vintage decor, this little foodie fave serves great Goan food, including a meanly spiced piri piri chicken, a succulent prawn *junglee pulao* and a crunchy crab roast masala. Everything's homemade, fresh and authentic tasting and served in ample portions. It's behind the ADNOC gas station.

Katis Restaurant INDIAN $

(06-556 5650; Al Khan St, Al Khan; mains Dh15-33; 11.30am-3pm & 5pm-midnight) This tiny, family-run joint with golden walls and dark wooden tables does well-executed home-cooked Indian fare, from butter chicken to prawn biryani as well as such beloved appetisers as steamed momos (dumplings), chicken lollipops (drumsticks) and the wrap-like chicken kati roll. It's opposite Safeer Market.

El Manza MOROCCAN $$

(06-552 1882; www.elmanza.ae; Al Majaz Waterfront; mains Dh40-100; 8.30am-11pm Sun-Thu, to midnight Fri & Sat) Black-and-white photographs mix with filigree lattice screens and arty metal lamps at this upscale Moroccan, where the food can keep up with the looks. Try classic couscous or tagine or opt for the spice-intense *ketf mechoui* (roast lamb shoulder). A classic appetiser is the *pastilla bil hamam* (a flaky filo roll filled with a mix of pigeon, almonds and orange blossom).

Bangkok Town THAI $$

(06-556 8282; cnr Al Qasba & 9th Sts, Al Majaz; mains Dh27-80; noon-4pm & 6.30pm-midnight) The food here is as tantalising as ever at this old-school parlour where you dine in snug, linen-bedecked booths or beneath thatched roofs. The menu is especially strong when it comes to fish and seafood (there's even a live tilapia tank), but all the classics are accounted for as well. It's behind Grand Buhaira Cinema.

Shababeek LEBANESE $$

(06-554 0444; www.shababeek.ae; block B, Qanat Al Qasba; mezze Dh18-30, mains Dh32-70; noon-11.30am) With its deep-purple walls, black furniture and Arabic design flourishes, this chic and contemporary space is swish by Sharjah standards. Portions are not huge, but flavours are delicately paired and the creative selection goes way beyond the usual mezze and grills. Finish up with the tangy rosewater sherbet.

Shopping

Central Souq MARKET

(Blue Souq; Khalid Lagoon; ⌚9am-1pm & 4-11pm Sat-Thu, 4-11pm Fri) Near Al Ittihad Sq, the tile-festooned Central Souq occupies two long parallel buildings connected by indoor bridges. Shops on the ground floor hawk modern jewellery, watches and local and international clothing; upstairs is more regional flair, with rugs, pashminas and curios from around the Arab world. Try to visit in the evening, when the place fills with locals.

Mega Mall MALL

(☎06-574 2574; www.megamall.ae; Istiqlal St, Abu Shagara; ⌚10am-11pm Sun-Wed, 10am-midnight Thu & Sat, 2pm-midnight Fri) With 150 shops, this mall is diminutive compared with Dubai standards, but it comes with a multiplex cinema and an indoor theme park with roller coaster and haunted house. The supermarket is open 24 hours.

Information

Al Zahra Hospital (☎06-561 9999; www.alzahra.com; Al Zahra Sq, Al Ghuair) This clinic with 24/7 ER is near the Sharjah Clock Tower.

Sharjah Commerce & Tourism Development Authority (☎800 80000; www.sharjahmydestination.ae)

Getting There & Away

AIR

Sharjah International Airport (p390) is 15km east of the city centre and has increased its capacity since becoming the hub of budget airline **Air Arabia** (p390).

BUS

Sharjah's central **Al Jubail bus station** is next to the fish and vegetable souq.

DESTINATION	FARE (DH)	TIME (HOURS)	FREQUENCY
Abu Dhabi	30	3	every 30min
Ajman	5	½	every 20min
Al Ain	30	2	every 45min
Dubai (Bur Dubai)	5	1	every 15min
Fujairah	25	2½	every 60min
Ras Al Khaimah	20	2	every 60min
Umm Al Quwain	15	1	every 60min

HOP-ON, HOP-OFF TOURS

City Sightseeing Sharjah (☎06-525 5200; www.citysightseeing.ae; 24hr adult/child Dh85/45, 48hr Dh295/130; ⌚10am-6pm daily, plus 7-10pm Thu & Fri) Red double-decker buses deliver visitors to 20 of Sharjah's sightseeing hot spots, such as the Central Souq and the Heritage Area, on a hop-on, hop-off basis with taped commentary in seven languages, including English and German. The 48-hour ticket is also valid for the Dubai sightseeing tour operated by the same company. Buy tickets online, at hotels or on buses.

CAR

From Dubai, take Sheikh Rashid Rd across Garhoud Bridge and continue into Sharjah on Al Ittihad Rd. The drive should take between 30 and 60 minutes, depending on traffic and where in Dubai you started from.

TAXI

The **main taxi stand** is next to the bus station, but taxis can actually be flagged down anywhere in town. Trips to Dubai come with a Dh20 surcharge. Expect to pay about Dh50 to Dubai International Airport, Dh90 to Dubai Mall, Dh200 to Fujairah or Al Ain and Dh300 to Abu Dhabi.

If possible, avoid travelling between Dubai and Sharjah during peak rush hour (weekdays 7am to 10am, 1pm to 2pm and 5pm to 9pm), as roads can get frustratingly clogged.

Getting Around

TO/FROM THE AIRPORT

Buses 14, 15 and 99 link Sharjah airport with the city centre (Dh6). A taxi ride costs about Dh50, including a Dh20 airport surcharge.

BUS

Buses are operated by **Mowasalat** (☎600 522 282; www.mowasalat.ae) and travel on nine routes between 5.30am and 11.30pm at intervals ranging from 10 to 30 minutes. Regular tickets cost Dh4, express routes are Dh5.

TAXI

Taxis (☎600 525 252) can be flagged or booked. Flagfall is Dh3.50 (Dh4 from 11pm to 6am), plus Dh1 per 620m, with a Dh11.50 minimum fare. The average ride within town costs between Dh10 and Dh30. There's a Dh20 extra charge for rides originating at the airport and for trips to Dubai.

Sharjah Desert Park

This desert park packs four venues into a 1-sq-km package, including a natural-history museum, a botanical museum and a Children's Farm where kids get to meet, pet and feed goats, camels and ducks, and ride ponies and camels.

The main attraction, though, is the **Arabia's Wildlife Centre** (06-531 1999; www.breedingcentresharjah.com; Al Dhaid Rd; 9am-5.30pm Sun, Mon, Wed & Thu, 2-5.30pm Fri, 11am-5.30pm Sat), a zoo showcasing the diversity of local critters. Vipers, flamingos, wildcats, mongooses, hyenas, wolves and the splendid Arabian leopard all make appearances. Visitors get to observe the animals in air-conditioned comfort through glass panels, making the centre a year-round destination.

The park grounds also include a cafe and picnic facilities. It's on Al Dhaid Rd (Hwy E88), about 26km east of Sharjah.

Ajman عجمان

06 / POP 262,000

North of Sharjah, Ajman is the smallest of the seven emirates. Its pretty, palm-lined sandy beach, low-key vibe and value-for-money hotels make it an attractive getaway. Strolling along the Corniche, where locals like to barbecue and picnic in cooler weather, is a popular pastime, while a museum provides a heritage fix.

Ajman is also home to one of the few remaining dhow-building yards in the region. It's on the north side of Ajman Creek, where an entire new luxury township called Al Zorah is taking shape.

Sights

Ajman Museum MUSEUM
(06-742 3824; Central Sq; adult/child Dh5/1; 8am-8pm Sat-Thu) This late-18th-century fort served as the ruler's residence until 1970 and also saw a stint as the police station. Now a museum, it illustrates aspects of Ajman's past with an assortment of photographs, weapons, tools and archaeological artefacts.

Sleeping

Ramada Beach Hotel Ajman HOTEL $
(06-742 9999; www.ramadaajman.com; Sheikh Humaid bin Rashid Al Nuaimi St (Corniche Rd); r from Dh420; P) If you want to wake up to Gulf views without paying top dirham, book into this beachfront tower that may be a bit older but is still in respectable shape. Rooms are smartly decked out in desert colours, but the standard ones have city views and not much elbow room. Get a suite if you want a sea-facing balcony.

★ **Ajman Saray** HOTEL $$$
(06-714 2222; www.ajmansaray.com; Sheikh Humaid bin Rashid Al Nuaimi St (Corniche Rd); r from Dh1100; P) This swish newcomer makes for a lovely getaway thanks to its tranquil vibe, beachfront location and dreamy gardens. Rooms drip with elegant Arabic design touches and come with the gamut of mod-cons and a balcony. The huge and luxurious spa is a destination in itself.

Eating

★ **Themar Al Bahar** SEAFOOD $$
(06-747 0550; Sheikh Humaid bin Rashid Al Nuaimi St (Corniche Rd); fish per kilogram Dh50-160; noon-3am) It may not score high in the looks or service departments, but for well-priced fresh fish and seafood this beachside place is *the* go-to spot in Ajman. Head to a separate room to make your selection from the catch of the day, which is then weighed, cooked according to your preference and served with Arabic salads and sides.

It's next to the Al Owais Tower.

Attibrah MIDDLE EASTERN $$
(06-744 8383; www.facebook.com/attibrahrestaurant; Sheikh Humaid bin Rashid Al Nuaimi St (Corniche Rd); mains Dh30-70; 8am-1am Sat-Thu, 2pm-1am Fri) If your tummy is grumbling after a stroll along the Corniche, skip the abundant fast-food outlets and get a taste of traditional Arabic food instead, including such Emirati dishes as *gisheeda* (spicy fish) and *harris biliyan* (eggplant). After your meal, you can relax with a *sheesha*.

Bukhara INDIAN $$$
(06-714 5555; Sheikh Humaid bin Rashid Al Nuaimi St (Corniche Rd); mains Dh50-140; 12.30-3pm & 6.30-11.15pm;) This regally rustic restaurant at the Kempinski Hotel serves beautifully calibrated Indian fare prepared in an open kitchen. The *dal bukhara* (spicy lentils) is the meat-free signature dish, while the succulent *murgh malai kebab* gets top marks among the tandoori meals. You're encouraged to ditch the cutlery and eat with the help of your hands and heaps of fresh naan.

Ajman

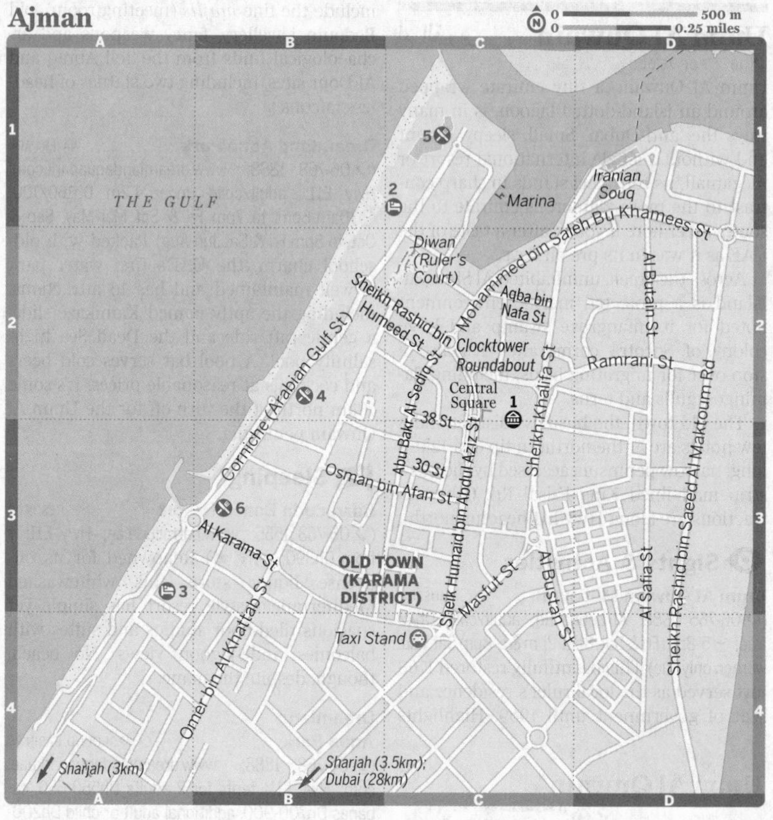

Ajman

Sights
1 Ajman Museum C2

Sleeping
2 Ajman Saray C1
3 Ramada Beach Hotel Ajman A3

Eating
4 Attibrah B2
5 Bukhara C1
6 Themar Al Bahar B3

Information

Ajman Tourism (☎06-711 6666; www.ajmantourism.ae)

Getting There & Around

BUS

Ajman Public Transport Corporation runs buses to Ras Al Khaimah (Dh20), Al Ain (Dh20), Sharjah (Dh3) and Dubai (Dh15). Buses leave from Liwara Station at the northern end of Sheikh Rashid bin Humaid St. There is no local bus service.

Dubai-based RTA E400 buses travel from Union Square bus station in Deira (Dubai) to Ajman (Dh7, 50 minutes) via Al Jubail station in Sharjah. Sharjah-based bus 112 also makes the trip from Al Jubail (Dh5, 30 minutes) several times hourly. Buses don't pick up passengers on the way back, so you'll need to take a taxi.

TAXI

Taxis in Ajman are plentiful and the only way to get around without your own transport. Flagfall is Dh3 (Dh4 between 10pm and 6am), plus Dh1 per 650m, with a Dh10 minimum fare. From hotels flagfall is Dh10 for trips within Ajman and Dh20 for trips outside Ajman. There's a central **taxi stand** (Sheikh Humaid bin Abdul Aziz St).

Umm Al Quwain أم القيوين

06 / POP 75,000

Umm Al Quwain, a tiny emirate wrapped around an island-dotted lagoon, is in many ways the 'anti-Dubai'. Small, sleepy, quaint and without a single international resort or megamall, its retro feel stands in sharp contrast to the more glamorous emirate to the south. Steer here if you're after a taste of the UAE as it was in its pre-oil days.

Across the creek, uninhabited Al Sinniyah Island is a protected marine environment noted for its mangrove swamp and large colony of Socotra cormorants. It's also a stop-over for migrating birds, including flamingos, gulls and terns.

The old town, the business district and a few hotels are at the northern tip of a 12km-long, narrow peninsula accessed by the busy, strip mall–lined King Faisal Rd. Other attractions are along Hwy E11 heading north.

Sights & Activities

Umm Al Quwain Museum MUSEUM
(06-765 0888; Al Lubna Rd; adult/child Dh4/free; 5-8pm Fri & Sat, 8am-2pm & 5-8pm Sat-Thu, women only Tue) This beautifully restored 1768 fort served as the local ruler's residence and seat of government until 1969. Highlights include the fine *majlis* (meeting room), old Bedouin jewellery, fancy weapons and archaeological finds from the Tell Abraq and Al Dour sites, including two statues of headless falcons.

Dreamland Aqua Park WATER PARK
(06-768 1888; www.dreamlandaquapark.com; Hwy E11; adult/child under 1.2m Dh160/100; 10am-6pm, to 7pm Fri & Sat Mar-May, Sep & Oct, to 8pm Fri & Sat Jun-Aug) Packed with old-school charm, the UAE's first water park is well maintained and has 16 attractions, including the aptly named Kamikaze slide, a gentle raft ride and the Dead Sea high-salinity pool. A pool bar serves cold beers and cocktails at reasonable prices. It's some 10km north of the turn-off for the Umm Al Quwain peninsula.

Sleeping

Barracuda Beach Resort RESORT $
(06-768 1555; www.barracuda.ae; Hwy E11; r from Dh390; P) Renowned for its off-license liquor store, this whitewashed Mediterranean-style resort has simple yet spacious tiled-floor studios and suites with balconies and lagoon views. No beach, though, despite the name.

Dreamland Aqua Park CAMPGROUND, CABIN $$
(06-768 1888; www.dreamlandaquaparkuae.com; Hwy E11; tents for 2 adults Dh550-650, cabanas Dh700-900, additional adult or child Dh200-250; P) Attached to the water park, this is the only organised campground on the beach in the UAE. Be the first one on the slides in the morning after spending the night in simple wooden cabins or in a tent. Rates include unlimited park access and three meals (BBQ dinner, breakfast and lunch).

Umm Al Quwain Beach Hotel RESORT $$
(06-766 6647; www.uaqbeachotel.com; Beach Rd; 1-bedroom villas from Dh900; P) Stresses melt pronto beneath a *barasti* (palm-leaf) umbrella on the beach, but this resort's biggest attraction is quite possibly the on-site liquor store. Lodging is in nicely furnished one- to three-bedroom villas set in lush gardens and overlooking the water. It's on the peninsula; turn west off King Faisal Rd just north of the Clocktower roundabout (near KFC).

Umm Al Quwain

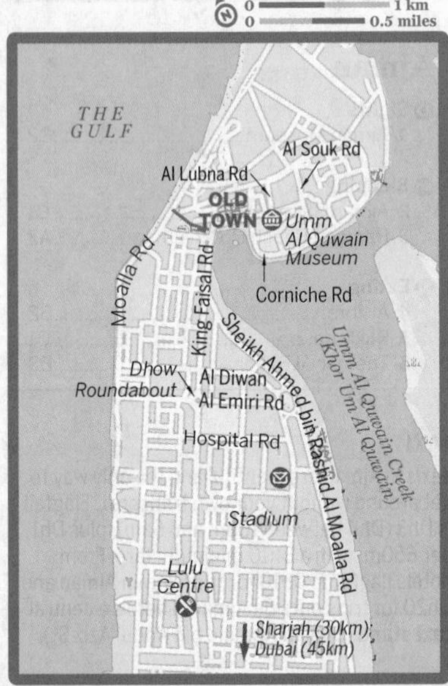

Eating

The best source for self-caterers is the giant **Lulu Centre** (06-766 6331; King Faisal Rd; 8am-11.30pm), near Al Kuwait roundabout.

Al Ayaam LEBANESE $

(06-766 6969; King Faisal Rd; mains Dh15-55; 8am-1am) It won't win design awards, but this family restaurant has some of the best Lebanese food in town. Start with some *baba ghanooj* and a watercress salad before tucking into big portions of mouthwatering grilled fish and meat, including camel and quail, all at very reasonable prices. It's across from KFC.

Aquarius INTERNATIONAL $$

(06-768 1555; www.barracuda.ae; Barracuda Beach Resort; mains Dh35-120; 8am-midnight) Match your mood to the food at this casual waterfront eatery, whose offerings run the gamut from burgers and kebabs to prawns and lobster.

Getting There & Away

BUS

Coming from Sharjah, catch bus 115 (Dh15, hourly) at Al Jubail bus station. From Dubai, bus E601 leaves from Itihad bus station in Deira (Dh10, every 45 minutes). Buses stop at UAQ's Union roundabout, where they are met by taxis. Both lines continue on to Ras Al Khaimah via Hwy E11 but don't pick up on the way back to Sharjah.

CAR

Umm Al Quwain is about 40km north of Dubai via Hwy E11. For the old town, turn off onto King Faisal Rd, just past the junction with the E55.

TAXI

Cab rides to Dubai or Ras Al Khaimah start at Dh120; for Sharjah budget Dh70 and for Ajman Dh50.

Getting Around

The only way to get around Umm Al Quwain is by taxi. They're cheap and plentiful; just flag one down. Most rides cost between Dh5 and Dh10.

Ras Al Khaimah راس الخيمة

07 / POP 300,000

Surrounded by the fierce Hajar Mountains, Ras Al Khaimah (or simply 'RAK') is the UAE's northernmost emirate. Outdoor enthusiasts love it here, thanks to diverse scenery ranging from sandy beaches to sprawling oases, hot springs to sun-baked desert, all backed by the rugged mountains.

Growth has been exponential in RAK in recent years, resulting in a free-trade zone, an artificial island with luxury resorts, new leisure facilities and a mountain road offering glorious views. Most of the development is based in an area called Al Hamra, some 15km south of RAK City.

In RAK City itself, the pearly-white and multidomed Sheikh Zayed Mosque overlooks the Al Qawasim Corniche, a paved promenade with kiosks, benches and restaurants fronting the creek.

RAK is also the gateway to the magnificent Musandam Peninsula, an enclave of Oman.

Sights

National Museum of Ras Al Khaimah MUSEUM

(07-233 3411; www.rakheritage.rak.ae; adult/child Dh5/free; 10am-5pm Wed-Mon Sep-May, 8am-noon & 4-7pm Wed-Mon Jun-Aug) This local-history museum occupies a 19th-century fort that was the residence of the Qawassim rulers until 1964. Behind ornate wooden doors awaits the usual ethnological assortment as well as artefacts from archaelogical digs in the area, including at Julfar, an important port between the 14th and 17th centuries. Gems include intricately patterned Iron Age softstone vessels and terracotta urns. Located off Al Hisn Rd.

Dhayah Fort FORTRESS

(24hr) FREE It's well worth climbing the zigzagging staircase to this twin-towered hilltop fortress to enjoy the sweeping 360-degree vistas of the RAK area, a vast date-palm oasis and the Hajar Mountains. Built in the early 19th century, the fort was the site of the last battle between British troops and local tribes in 1819. It's about 18km north of RAK City, off Al Rams Rd. Turn off at the sign for Dhayah Resthouse.

Jazirat Al Hamra Fishing Village VILLAGE

(24hr) FREE With roots in the 16th century, this deliciously spooky ghost town is one of the oldest and best preserved coastal villages in the UAE. Its people subsisted mostly on fishing and pearling until they suddenly picked up and left in 1968. To get there, turn off Hwy E11 opposite Majan Printing and drive towards Al Hamra Village. Turn right at the roundabout and right again, then take

Ras Al Khaimah

the dirt road immediately on your left and drive for about 1km.

Although the village is officially closed, you're free to peek through the fence at the remains of coral stone houses, wind towers, mosques, schools and shops.

Activities

★Jebel Jais Mountain Road DRIVING TOUR

FREE At 1934m, Jebel Jais is the highest peak in the UAE and is even occasionally dusted with snow. Since 2015 a mountain road has corkscrewed almost to the top, delivering great visual drama of artistically eroded cliffs, deep canyons and warped escarpments around every bend. There are plenty of pullouts with toilets but no other facilities (yet), so bring liquids and a snack.

The total drive is about 50km from the roundabout connecting Khuzam and Al Rams Rd in RAK City.

Iceland Water Park WATER PARK

(☎07-206 7888, toll free 800-969 725; www.icelandwaterpark.com; Hwy E11, Jazirat Al Hamra; adult Dh175, child under 120/80cm Dh100/free; ⊙10am-6pm Sun-Thu, to 7pm Fri & Sat, women only 8pm-midnight Fri) Penguins rule this 'Arctic' water park, challenging you to five rides down Polar Mountain, including a death-defying, near-vertical plunge down 40m-high Mt Attack. Most rides have a 1.2m height minimum. Food and drinks, including alcohol, are available. It's packed at weekends.

Bedouin Oasis Desert Camp CULTURAL TOUR

(☎055-228 4984, 04-266 6020; www.arabianincentive.com; Banyan Tree Al Wadi resort, Al Mazraa, Wadi Khadija; per person Dh380; ⊙7-10pm) Dinner in a recreated Bedouin desert camp, lit by candles and lanterns, certainly has the ring of romance to it. Rates include soft drinks, henna, camel rides, belly dancing and *sheesha*. It's also possible to spend the night 'glamping' in a comfortable tent.

Sleeping

Hotel Ras Al Khaimah HOTEL $$
(☎07-236 2999; www.rasalkhaimahhotel.com; Khuzam St; d from Dh565; P📶🏊) For an in-city location, this reliable hilltop stand-by won't break the bank. Furnishings and decor may not be of the latest vintage, but facilities include an outdoor pool and a 24-hour restaurant with good Lebanese fare. Rooms overlook the creek. No alcohol. Free wi-fi in public areas only.

★**Hilton Al Hamra Beach & Golf Resort** RESORT $$$
(☎07-244 6666; www.hilton.com; Vienna St, Jazirat Al Hamra; d from Dh1000; P📶🏊) With two pools, a 400m-long sandy beach, a Technogym, tennis courts and water sports, this sprawling resort feeds adrenaline and slothdom cravings. Rooms are either in the main tower or in traditional villas among palms and bougainvillea. All come with terrace or balcony and pack effortless sophistication and Arabesque flourishes into their generous frame. Great breakfast buffet and Friday brunch.

Banyan Tree Al Wadi RESORT $$$
(☎07-206 7777; www.banyantree.com; Al Mazraa, Wadi Khadija; villas from Dh2600; P📶🏊) This desert resort offers the ultimate in luxury with its Arabesque-style villas with private plunge pool. It's surrounded by a nature preserve where you may encounter gazelles, camels and oryxes on guided walks or safaris. Daily falconry shows (Dh275) provide a chance to learn more about these majestic birds. It's about 14km south of New RAK (7km south of Hwy E311).

Guests also have access to the private beach of sister property Banyan Tree Ras Al Khaimah Beach (whose contact details are as above), an equally romantic and exclusive peninsula retreat in Al Hamra.

Cove Rotana Resort RESORT $$$
(☎07-206 6000; www.rotana.com; Al Hamra Rd; r from Dh1450; P📶🏊) About 8km south of central RAK, off Hwy E11, this rambling full-service resort resembles a higgledy-piggledy Arab village wrapped around a lagoon and borders 600m of magnificent white sandy beach. Get a 'premium room' if you want a water view.

> **WORTH A TRIP**
>
> **KHATT HOT SPRINGS**
>
> Hot springs in the desert? Who needs 'em? Well, if your bones ache or your muscles are sore, the 40°C mineralised water gushing forth from the natural hot springs at the **Harmony Ayurveda Centre** (☎07-244 8141; Khatt Springs Rd, Khatt; admission Dh50; ⏱7am-9pm) apparently does wonders in limbering you up. Relax in gender-segregated pebble-floored pools or choose from the huge spa menu (honey-and-sesame body polish, anyone?). Admission is free if you're staying at the **Golden Tulip Khatt Springs** (☎07-244 8777; www.goldentulip-khattsprings.com; Khatt Springs Rd, Khatt; d from Dh360; P📶🏊) hotel above the springs. Rooms at this castle-shaped behemoth are a good size, come with balconies and comfy beds, and will treat you to date palm–dotted valley views.
>
> Khatt is about 25km southeast of RAK City. Follow Hwy E18 past the airport, then look for signs.

Eating & Drinking

Pure Veg Restaurant INDIAN $
(☎07-227 3266; Al Muntasir Rd; dishes Dh8-17; ⏱7.30am-3pm & 5pm-midnight; 🌿) Meat is a no-no at this clean and convivial eatery whose extensive menu hopscotches around India, featuring crispy dosas, tasty tandooris and creamy curries. It's opposite Al Manama Hypermarket.

Cafe La Luna ITALIAN $$
(☎07-243 4600; www.laluna.ae; Al Hamra Yacht Club & Marina, Minsk St, Al Hamra; mains Dh40-70; ⏱9am-11pm Sat-Wed, to midnight Thu & Fri) Snag an outside table and enjoy your pizza and pasta with a view of the bobbing yachts of Al Hamra Marina. This upbeat nosh spot also serves excellent coffees and a small breakfast selection (croissants, omelettes). The access road is off Hwy E11, opposite Majan Printing.

Madfoon Al Sada YEMENI $$
(Sheikh Mohammed bin Salem Rd; mains Dh20-60; ⏱11am-midnight) Don't be put off by the humble looks of this hospitable haunt: its *mandi*

CROSSING INTO THE MUSANDAM PENINSULA

RAK is the jumping-off point for the magnificent Musandam Peninsula, an Omani enclave, via the Shams/Tibat border post about 35km north of RAK City. Beyond the border await a dramatic coastal drive and the town of Khasab, where you can catch dhow cruises and go snorkelling with dolphins.

If you are from one of the currently 45 countries whose citizens are not required to have a UAE visa, you won't need to obtain a separate visa for Oman. Everyone else must pay a Dh35 exit fee at the UAE border post in Shams and OR6 upon entering Tibat.

If you have a rental car, make sure you are permitted to take it across the border and that you have insurance valid in Oman.

(a traditional dish originally from Yemen that pairs spiced rice with lamb, chicken or fish) is among the best in the country.

Trader Vic's Mai Tai Lounge INTERNATIONAL **$$**
(07-244 6666; www.hilton.com; Hilton Al Hamra Beach & Golf Resort, Vienna St, Jazirat Al Hamra; mains Dh40-125; noon-1am Sat-Wed, to 2am Thu & Fri;) Work your way through a menu of delectable *pupus* (Polynesian-style appetisers) like crispy prawns or baked crab and artichoke dip while kicking back with kick-ass tropical drinks in this chilled lounge where a band strikes up sultry Cuban sounds at night. A food star is the 'beef and reef' – a happy marriage of beef tenderloin and prawns.

Passage to Asia ASIAN **$$$**
(07-228 8844; www.3hilton.com; Al Maareedh St; sushi Dh85-147, mains Dh58-82; 6.30-11.30pm) The menu at this elegant restaurant at the Hilton Ras Al Khaimah Resort & Spa showcases two of Asia's most popular cuisines: Japanese and Thai. Kudos for the lovely setting amid tropical flowers and the wonderfully attentive service.

Drinking & Nightlife

Sho Fee Rooftop Bar BAR
(07-203 0000; Marjan Island Blvd; 9am-2am) This 9th-floor terrace at the Double Tree by Hilton on reclaimed Al Marjan Island is the perfect spot to cocoon with cocktails and watch the sun plop into the sea. After dark, a DJ spins into action and there's *sheesha* and mezze (Arabic snacks) as well.

Breakers on the Beach BAR
(07-206 6000; www.rotana.com; Hwy E11; 10am-10pm Sat-Wed, to midnight Thu & Fri) Chill with a coffee, cocktail or mocktail at this quintessential beach bar, where you can wriggle your toes in the sand or count the number of crashing waves. It's at the Cove Rotana Resort on the main highway about halfway between Jazirat Al Hamra and RAK City.

Club Acacia CLUB
(07-243 4421; http://acacia.binmajid.com; Acacia Hotel, Jazirat Al Hamra; 10pm-4am) Cut some rug on the dance floor of this stylish disco at the Acacia Hotel or come for karaoke, darts and snooker.

Getting There & Away

AIR

The grandly named but tiny **Ras Al Khaimah International airport** (p390) is about 18km south of RAK City via Hwy E18 (Airport Rd). It has regional flights with Air Arabia and charter flights from Russia and Germany.

BUS

Buses leave from the main taxi stand on Hwy E11 opposite the Cove Rotana Resort. Arriving buses are met by taxis for onward travel. Fares are Dh10 to Umm Al Quwain, Dh15 to Ajman and Dh20 to Sharjah and Dubai.

CAR

RAK is linked to the other emirates via coastal Hwy E11, called Sheikh Mohammad bin Salem St within city limits, and the much faster Hwy E311. Hwy E18 (Al Rams Rd) goes north to the Musandam Peninsula and south to the airport and the hot springs at Khatt.

TAXI

The main taxi stand is on Hwy E11 opposite Cove Rotana Resort. Approximate fares are Dh200 to Dubai, Dh150 to Sharjah and Dh130 to Ajman or Dibba on the eastern coast.

Getting Around

There is no public transport. **Taxis** (800 1700) can be flagged down or booked by phone. Flagfall is Dh3 plus Dh1 for every 650m, with a Dh10 minimum.

ABU DHABI أبو ظبي

☎02 / POP 1.5 MILLION

The world's largest hand-loomed carpet, the fastest roller coaster, the highest high tea, the tower with the greatest lean, the largest cluster of cultural buildings of the 21st century – UAE capital Abu Dhabi isn't afraid to challenge world records. Welcome to an exciting city where nothing stands still… except perhaps the herons in its mangroves.

For those looking to engage with Gulf culture, Abu Dhabi offers opportunities to understand the UAE's history through museums, exhibitions and tours. But thankfully Emirati heritage isn't boxed and mothballed; it's also experienced through strolls around the dhow harbour, haggling in markets and absorbing the atmosphere at *sheesha* cafes.

Sights

Al Markaziyah & Around

Although Abu Dhabi teems with vibrant districts, if you had to put your finger on the one that represents its centre, then the area around the city's oldest building, Qasr Al Hosn, is surely it. At the beating heart of this central district is the World Trade Center, built on the site of the city's original souq. The district is busy day and night with city traders, office workers, shoppers and visitors.

★Qasr Al Hosn FORT
(White Fort; Map p348; ☎02-697 6472; Sheikh Zayed the First St; ⏲9am-8pm) FREE Featured on the back of the Dh1000 note, this iconic fort started life in 1760 as a watchtower that safeguarded a precious freshwater well. After an expansion, it became the ancestral home of the ruling Al Nahyan family in 1793 and remained a royal residence until 1966. In a free exhibit, photographs, archaeological finds, models and other objects chart the history of Abu Dhabi and its people.

After a brief spell as an administrative centre, the palace was closed in 1990 and has been undergoing long-term restoration ever since.

Burj Mohammed bin Rashid BUILDING
(Map p348; Khalifa bin Zayed the First St) This 92-floor, 382m giant among tower blocks forms part of the World Trade Center and is an important landmark in this mixed-use development marking the middle of downtown. Not only is this Abu Dhabi's tallest building (at least for now) but it may just be unique in having an indoor terraced garden on the 90th floor! The tower is the tallest of two matching towers with distinctive sloping, elliptical roofs that look remarkable when lit at night.

Etisalat Head Office BUILDING
(Map p348; cnr Sheikh Zayed the First & Sheikh Rashid bin Saeed Al Maktoum Sts) This iconic 27-floor building, with a 'golf ball' as its crowning glory, makes an excellent landmark for navigating the city's grid system. Built in 2001, it houses the headquarters of the local telephone-service provider.

ABU DHABI IN...

One Day

Kick off the day with a tour of the stunning **Sheikh Zayed Grand Mosque** (p351), then head into town for lunch, perhaps at **Zyara Café** (p359), followed by a postprandial stroll along the **Abu Dhabi Corniche** (Map p348). Pop into the **World Trade Center Souk** (p363), then cab it over to the **Abu Dhabi Heritage Village** (p346) for a sense of society in the pre-oil days. Admire the out-of-this-world opulence of **Emirates Palace** (p346) next and treat yourself to a gold-dusted cappuccino.

Two Days

In the morning, find out what it takes to turn a desert island into a futuristic Cultural District at the **Manarat Al Saadiyat** (p349), then hop two islands further to have your eyeballs pressed into their sockets aboard the world's fastest roller coaster at **Ferrari World Abu Dhabi** (p355). Several hours later, stagger over to the **Yas Viceroy Abu Dhabi hotel** (p358) to marvel at the eccentric design and the fact that a Formula One racetrack runs right through it. Wrap up the day with a spin around the **Souk Qaryat Al Beri** (p364) and dinner at one of its fine restaurants.

Greater Abu Dhabi

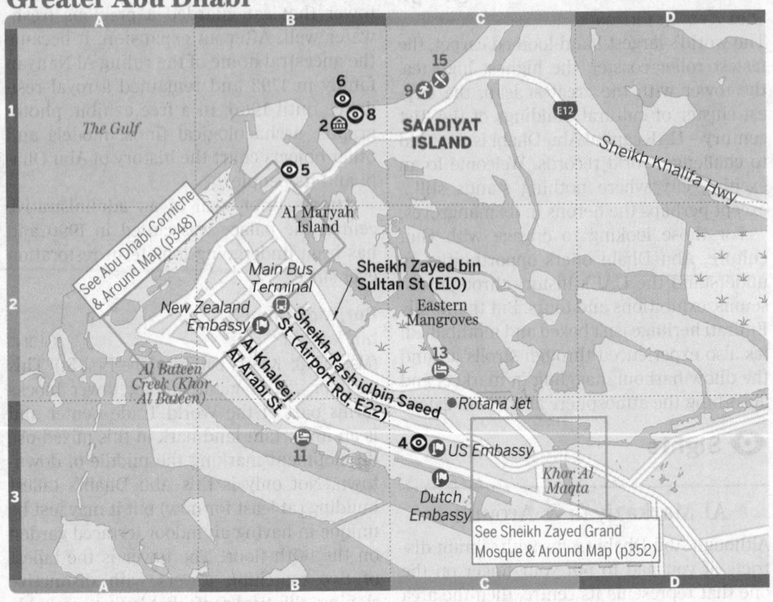

Breakwater & Around

The main attraction in this part of town is the Emirates Palace, one of the most opulent hotels in the Middle East. Lately it's been joined by other landmarks, including the clustered Etihad Towers and the lofty St Regis. Back down to earth, the landscaped Western Corniche is helping transform Abu Dhabi into an urban beach destination, while the Heritage Village is a reminder of the city's Bedouin roots.

★Emirates Palace — BUILDING

(Map p348; ☎02-690 9000; www.emiratespalace.com; Corniche Rd (West)) FREE What the Burj Khalifa in Dubai is to the vertical, the Emirates Palace is to the horizontal, with audacious domed gatehouses and flying ramps to the foyer, 114 domes and a 1.3km private beach. Built at a cost of Dh11 billion, this is the *big* hotel in the Gulf, with 1002 crystal chandeliers and 400 luxury rooms and suites. You don't have to check in to check out the Emirates Palace, as it doubles as a cultural hub of the city.

Hosting opera and renowned orchestras during the Abu Dhabi Classics concert season, and showing screenings during the Abu Dhabi Film Festival, the Emirates Palace has played its part in the cultural expansion of the capital. Other reasons to visit include the Barakat Gallery, which offers exquisite fine art from ancient China, Egypt, Africa, Greece and Rome; ever-popular afternoon high tea in the foyer (Dh160); and an ATM that dispenses gold bars.

Abu Dhabi Heritage Village — MUSEUM

(Map p348; ☎02-681 4455; Abu Dhabi Theater Rd; ⌚9am-5pm Sat-Thu, 3.30-9pm Fri) FREE This reconstructed village gives an insight into the pre-oil era in the UAE – a life that is still in evidence in many parts of the Arabian Peninsula to this day. The walled complex includes all the main elements of traditional Gulf life: a fort to repel invaders from the sea, a souq to trade goats for dates with friendly neighbours, and a mosque as a reminder of the central part that Islam plays in daily Arabic life.

Zayed Centre for Studies & Research — MUSEUM

(Baba Zayed's House; Map p348; ☎02-665 9555; Bainunah St, Al Bateen; ⌚8am-3pm Sun-Thu) FREE This eclectic collection of artefacts and personal memorabilia documents the life of Sheikh Zayed, the founding father of the Emirates. The collection is housed in a rare assembly of old villas sporting traditional

Greater Abu Dhabi

Sights

1	Abu Dhabi Grand Prix	E2
2	Abu Dhabi Louvre	B1
3	Aldar HQ	E2
4	Capital Gate	C3
5	Fruit & Vegetable Market	B1
6	Manarat Al Saadiyat	B1
7	Masdar City	E3
8	UAE Pavilion	B1

Activities, Courses & Tours

	Abu Dhabi Pearl Journey	(see 13)
	Ferrari World Abu Dhabi	(see 18)
9	Saadiyat Public Beach	C1
10	Yas Beach	E2
	Yas Marina Circuit	(see 1)
	Yas Waterworld	(see 18)

Sleeping

11	Aloft Abu Dhabi	B3
12	Centro Yas Island	E2
13	Eastern Mangroves Hotel & Spa	C2
	Yas Viceroy Abu Dhabi	(see 1)

Eating

	Aquarium	(see 1)
	Cipriani	(see 1)
14	Nolu's Café	E2
	Rogo's Rollercoaster Restaurant	(see 18)
15	Turquoiz	C1

Drinking & Nightlife

16	McGettigan's	E2
17	O1NE	E2
	Relax@12	(see 11)
	Stills Bar & Brasserie	(see 12)

Entertainment

	Burlesque Restaurant & Lounge	(see 1)

Shopping

18	Yas Mall	E2

wind towers, on the coast near the new Al Bateen developments. The museum complex, complete with 'Baba' (Father) Zayed's favourite blue Mercedes and beat-up Land Rover, is looking unloved, perhaps in anticipation of the new Zayed National Museum (p354) on Saadiyat Island.

The main hall has an interesting set of black-and-white photographs that capture pre–Arab Spring leaders Hosni Mubarak and Colonel Gaddafi. Also on display are various gifts from visiting dignitaries, including a stuffed leopard and anaconda skins. More poignant exhibits include Sheikh Zayed's used cologne bottle, a rifle that guests can handle, and his personal falcon clock.

Corniche – Al Khalidiyah WATERFRONT

(Map p348; Corniche Rd (West); 24hr) FREE It's hard to believe, while languishing on a sunlounger, swimming in the sea or strolling under a canopy of trees, that the Corniche was a dhow-loading bay for cargo and passengers until the 1970s. In 2004 land was reclaimed to form the 8km corniche and a decade later a major landscaping project transformed the seafront into a much-beloved public amenity. The western end of the Corniche, at Al Kahlidiyah, offers the most facilities.

Parks, fountains, cycle tracks, walking paths and beaches snake along the waterside. Lots of benches, shady spots and exercise stations make this a popular destination for strollers and joggers and there's a growing number of cafes.

UAE Flagpole LANDMARK

(Map p348; Abu Dhabi Theater Rd) At 122m, this giant flagpole was the tallest free-standing flagpole in the world when it was constructed in 2001. It lost its title to the Raghadan Flagpole in Jordan in 2004 and is now a long way short of the world's tallest. That said, the Emirati flag makes a fine landmark and the

Abu Dhabi Corniche & Around

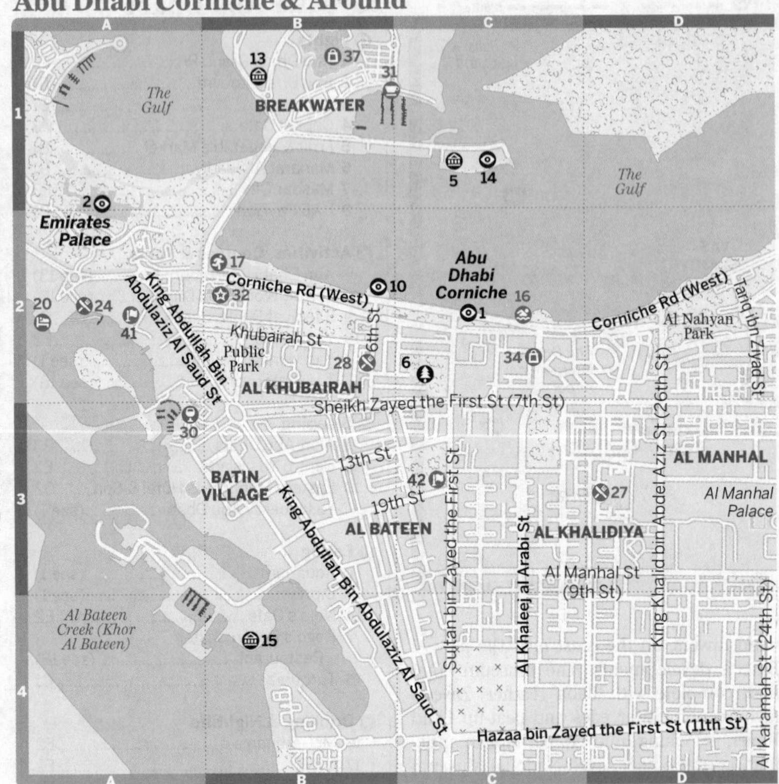

small promenade beneath the pole offers one of the best photo opportunities in the city for an uninterrupted view of the skyline.

Al Zahiyah & Al Maryah Island

The sights of Al Zahiyah, a district formerly known as 'Tourist Club Area' and still referred to by many as such today, now spill across to Al Maryah Island. It's a double neighbourhood where shopping remains one of the principal activities, whether you've come looking for camel kebabs for dinner, a pot to cook them in or designer plates to serve them on.

Abu Dhabi Global Market Square BUILDING

(formerly Sowwah Sq; Map p348; www.almaryahisland.ae; Al Falah St) Home to over 40 international companies, this cluster of glass-and-steel office monoliths on Al Maryah Island is the heart of Abu Dhabi's new financial centre. Also cradling the posh Galleria Mall and a couple of five-star hotels, it sits just off the Al Zahiyah district and offers striking views of the city skyline from the waterfront promenade. Various other feats of engineering also vie for attention, including the Cleveland Clinic with its catwalk podium, and a suspension bridge.

Al Maryah Island Promenade WATERFRONT

(Map p348; Al Maryah Island; 24hr) FREE This 5.4km-long promenade bends gently round the western shore of Al Maryah Island and offers fantastic views of Abu Dhabi and the busy channel of water in between. Used as a venue for a lavish Christmas market and New Year's fireworks, and linking an assortment of cafes and bistros, the promenade is already a meeting place for Abu Dhabi's elite. Notable buildings include the upmarket Galleria Mall and the Cleveland Clinic that almost manages to make healthcare look inviting.

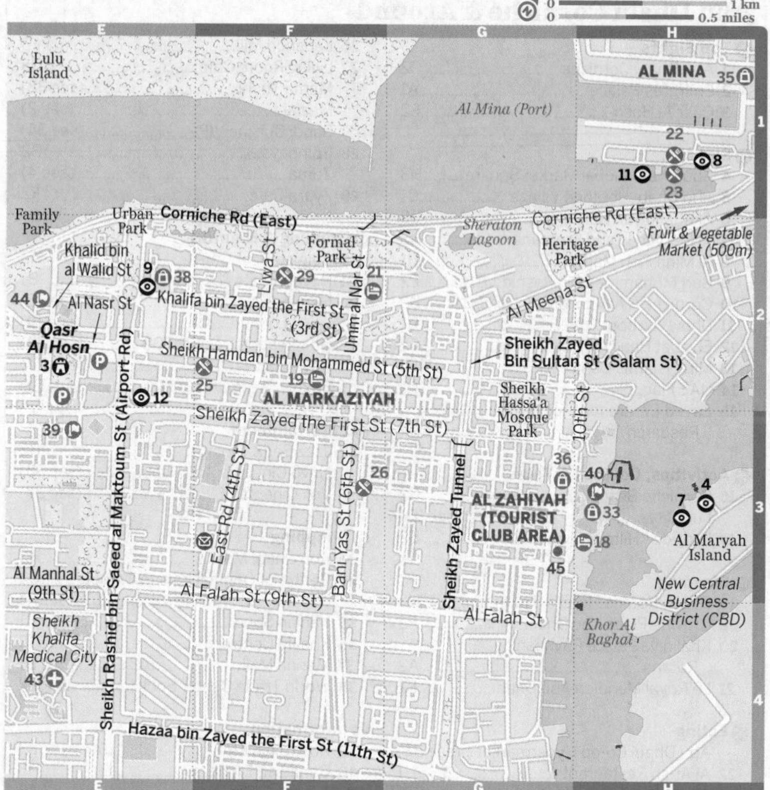

Al Mina & Saadiyat Island

These two neighbouring districts open up a window on Abu Dhabi's cultural inheritance, past and present. The port is home to the old dhow harbour and vibrant souqs, while Saadiyat Island's sandy beaches and protected coastal environment invite slowing down and plunging into a world removed from city life.

The development of Saadiyat Island is divided into various districts, the most attention grabbing of which is the **Cultural District** at its western point. This cluster of famous museums includes the Louvre Abu Dhabi and the Guggenheim Abu Dhabi, which are taking shape on off-shore islands. The opening dates of these prestigious projects have been postponed numerous times. The first one to be ready will be the Louvre, possibly in late 2016.

To the northeast of the museums, **Saadiyat Leisure** brims with five-star resorts, villas, a beach club and a golf course, while to the southeast is **Saadiyat Education**, which will be home to a branch of New York University and Cranleigh Abu Dhabi, a British-style prep school. An exhibit in the Manarat Al Saadiyat pavilion provides an overview of the development.

The Yas Express (p355) links Saadiyat with Yas Island via the Sheikh Khalifa Hwy (E12).

Manarat Al Saadiyat VISITOR CENTRE
(Map p346; ☎02-657 5800; www.saadiyatcultural district.ae; Cultural District, Saadiyat Island; ⌚9am-8pm) **FREE** Housed in a postmodern building with an eye-catching honeycomb mantle, Manarat Al Saadiyat ('place of enlightenment') is a multimedia exhibit called 'Saadiyat Experience'. It explains the vision behind the development of Saadiyat Island, which will include residential communi-

Abu Dhabi Corniche & Around

Top Sights
1 Abu Dhabi Corniche C2
2 Emirates Palace A1
3 Qasr Al Hosn E2

Sights
4 Abu Dhabi Global Market Square H3
5 Abu Dhabi Heritage Village C1
6 Al Khalidiyah Garden C2
7 Al Maryah Island Promenade H3
8 Al Mina Fish Market H1
9 Burj Mohammed bin Rashid E2
10 Corniche – Al Khalidiyah B2
11 Dhow Harbour H1
12 Etisalat Head Office E2
13 Miraj Islamic Centre B1
14 UAE Flagpole C1
15 Zayed Centre for Studies & Research B4

Activities, Courses & Tours
16 Corniche Beach C2
Fun City ..... (see 37)
17 Funride - Hiltonia Beach Club B2

Sleeping
18 Beach Rotana Hotel & Towers H3
19 Crowne Plaza Abu Dhabi F2
20 Khalidiya Palace Rayhaan by Rotana A2
21 Le Royal Méridien Abu Dhabi F2

Eating
Abu Dhabi Co-op Hypermarket ..... (see 33)
22 Al Arish Restaurant H1
23 Al Dhafra H1
Biryani Pot ..... (see 4)
24 Brasserie Angélique A2
Carrefour ..... (see 37)
Cho Gao ..... (see 19)
Finz ..... (see 18)
Kababs & Kurries ..... (see 38)
25 La Brioche Café F2
26 Lebanon Mill F3
27 Living Room Café D3
Mama Thani ..... (see 38)
Mezlai ..... (see 2)
Saudi Cuisine VIP ..... (see 34)
28 Spinneys B2
Zuma ..... (see 4)
29 Zyara Café F2

Drinking & Nightlife
30 Belgian Beer Café A3
31 Havana Café & Restaurant B1
Hemingway's ..... (see 32)
Level Lounge ..... (see 19)
Observation Deck at 300 ..... (see 24)
Ray's Bar ..... (see 24)
Sax ..... (see 21)

Entertainment
32 Jazz Bar & Dining B2
Novo Cinemas Abu Dhabi ..... (see 33)
Vox Cinemas ..... (see 37)

Shopping
33 Abu Dhabi Mall H3
34 Centre of Original Iranian Carpets C2
Galleria ..... (see 4)
35 Iranian Souq H1
36 Khalifa Centre G3
37 Marina Mall B1
38 World Trade Center Souk E2

Information
39 Australian Embassy E3
40 Canadian Embassy H3
41 French Embassy A2
German Embassy ..... (see 40)
42 Irish Embassy C3
43 Sheikh Khalifa Medical City E4
44 UK Embassy E2

Transport
45 City Terminal Check-In G3

ties, hotels, beaches, schools and, of course, a Cultural District with such headline-making museums as the Abu Dhabi Louvre, the Guggenheim Abu Dhabi and the Sheikh Zayed Museum.

A large model showing how the island's cultural, residential and leisure developments will fit together goes a long way towards understanding this ambitious project, as does an animation providing a virtual walkthrough and flyover. Another highlight is a detailed model of the Zayed National Museum, whose design takes inspiration from the wingtips of falcons, while Frank Gehry's Guggenheim picks up on traditional Emirati wind-tower architecture.

UAE Pavilion BUILDING
(Map p346; ☎02-406 1501; www.saadiyatculturaldistrict.ae; Cultural District, Saadiyat Island) FREE Shaped like two parallel sand dunes, smooth and curvaceous on the windward side, steep and rippled on the eroded side, this award-winning building by Sir Norman Foster and partners was designed for the 2010 Shanghai Expo. Now used as an exhibition space for touring cultural shows, this striking building is worth a visit for itself alone. It particularly comes into its own

in November, when it hosts the Abu Dhabi contemporary-art fair. It's next to Manarat Al Saadiyat.

Abu Dhabi Louvre MUSEUM
(Map p346; http://louvreabudhabi.ae; Cultural District, Saadiyat Island) The Abu Dhabi Louvre, designed by Jean Nouvel, is expected to open in late 2016. Already the theme of palm-tree shading is detectable in the elaborate filigree dome, whose geometric openings are intended to represent interlaced palm leaves used in traditional roofing. The gaps will create a shifting 'rain of light' in the galleries, which will present a world-class collection of paintings, sculpture and objects from antiquity to the present.

Works will be selected from the Louvre's vast repositories, and there will be loans from other leading French museums. Among the pieces expected to be displayed when doors first open is a 3000-year-old Egyptian statue of King Ramesses II, a Bronze Age breast plate from France, a medieval reliquary chest, Leonardo da Vinci's *Woman Portrait*, Van Gogh's *Self-Portrait* and Andy Warhol's *Big Electric Chair*.

Dhow Harbour HARBOUR
(Map p348; Al Mina) There's something fascinating about sitting by the harbourside watching the beautiful dhows (traditional wooden cargo boats) slip off to sea. At any time of day there's work going on as fishers mend their nets, pile up lobster pots, hang out colourful sarongs to dry, unload fish and congregate for communal chats. As you survey the resting dhows strung together five abreast, you can almost forget Abu Dhabi's modern backdrop as its ancient past as a fishing village is revealed.

Fruit & Vegetable Market MARKET
(Map p346; Al Mina; 7am-midnight) This vast wholesale market, part of which is open air, is the exchange point for melons from Jordan, potatoes from Turkey and onions from just about everywhere. A highlight is cruising along 'date alley', where shops sell around 45 varieties (from Dh25 per kilogram). Giant *medjool* dates from Saudi Arabia cost Dh65 per kilogram, while medicinal *ajwa* dates fetch Dh110 per kilogram. Try the plump, yellow *sucri* dates, which are prized for their sweetness.

The friendly vendors (from India mostly) are happy to let you sample, but it's polite to leave with a small purchase. If you buy fresh dates, choose half-ripe ones for the bittersweet contrast, and eat within a couple of days. Dried dates last a lifetime (well, almost)!

Sheikh Zayed Grand Mosque & Around

Three bridges straddle the approach from the mainland to Abu Dhabi Island, and from each there is one sight that dominates the view: Sheikh Zayed Grand Mosque. This exquisite building is not just an exceptional piece of architecture, it also represents the living soul of this heritage-minded emirate by providing a place of worship for residents and a memorial to the nation's founding father. While for visitors the mosque is clearly the key attraction of the district, other sights vie for attention in and around the south-eastern end of the island, including the new developments of Bain al Jessrain. The Big Bus tour links the exhibition centre with the mosque and the Eastern Corniche but doesn't stray across to the mainland, so taxi or car is the most efficient means of visiting this area.

★**Sheikh Zayed Grand Mosque** MOSQUE
(Map p352; 02-419 1919; www.szgmc.ae; 9am-10pm Sat-Thu, 4.30-10pm Fri, tours 10am, 11am & 5pm Sun-Thu, additional tours 2pm & 7pm Sat, 5pm & 7pm Fri) FREE Rising majestically from beautifully manicured gardens and

ABU DHABI FOR CHILDREN

Keep tempers cool by taking the kids to **Yas Waterworld** (p355), a state-of-the-art water park. A huge indoor amusement park with a jungle theme, **Fun City** (Map p348; 02-681 5527; funcity.ae; Marina Mall, Breakwater; admission from Dh55; 10am-10pm) will keep tots entertained with bumper cars, a roller coaster, carousels and arcade games. If you prefer the outdoors, take them to the beaches along the Corniche or to **Al Khalidiyah Garden** (Map p348; Sheikh Zayed the First (7th) St; 8am-1am Mon-Sat, to midnight Sun) FREE, which has large grassy areas perfect for picnics, as well as inflatable slides, trampolines and pony rides. Older kids might also enjoy a visit to the **Falcon Hospital** (p357) or a desert safari, while teenage speed freaks will love you for treating them to **Ferrari World** (p355).

Sheikh Zayed Grand Mosque & Around

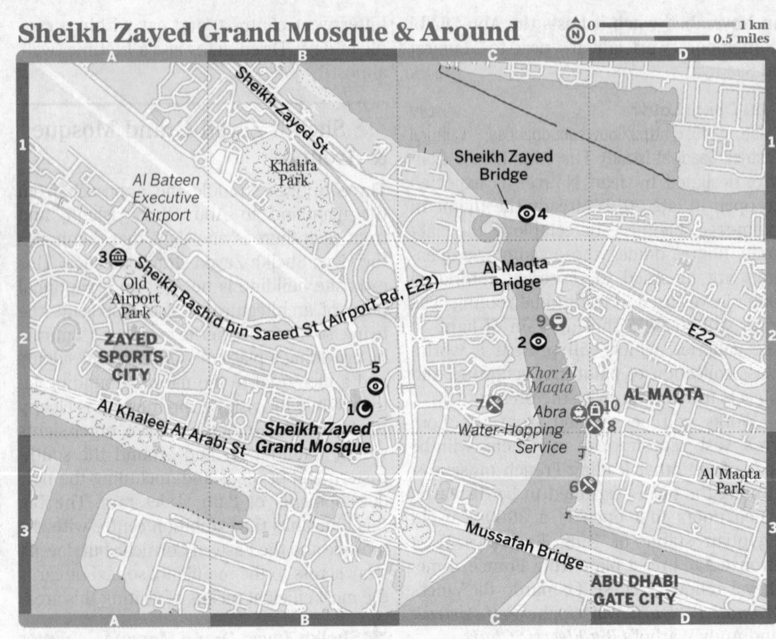

Sheikh Zayed Grand Mosque & Around

Top Sights
1 Sheikh Zayed Grand Mosque........ B2

Sights
2 Khor Al Maqta........ C2
3 Miraj – The Museum........ A2
4 Sheikh Zayed Bridge........ C1
5 Sheikh Zayed Grand Mosque Centre Library........ B2

Sleeping
Traders Hotel, Qaryat al Beri........ (see 10)

Eating
6 Bord Eau........ C3
7 Mijana........ C2
Milas........ (see 10)
8 Ushna........ D2

Drinking & Nightlife
9 Chameleon........ C2

Shopping
10 Souk Qaryat Al Beri........ D2

visible from each of the bridges joining Abu Dhabi Island to the mainland, the Sheikh Zayed Grand Mosque represents an impressive welcome to the city. Conceived by the first president of the UAE, Sheikh Zayed, and marking his final resting place, the mosque accommodates 41,000 worshippers and is one of the few in the region open to non-Muslims.

With more than 80 marble domes on a roofline held aloft by over 1000 pillars and punctuated by four 107m-high minarets, Sheikh Zayed Grand Mosque is a masterpiece of modern Islamic architecture and design. Over 100,000 tons of pure white Greek and Macedonian marble were used in its construction. Delicate floral designs inlaid with semi-precious stones, such as lapis lazuli, red agate, amethyst, abalone, jasper and mother-of-pearl, decorate a variety of marbles and contrast with the more traditional geometric ceramic details.

While it includes references to Mamluk, Ottoman and Fatimid styles, the overwhelming impression of the breathtaking interior is contemporary and innovative, with three steel, gold, brass and crystal chandeliers filling the main prayer hall with shafts of primary-coloured light. The chandeliers, the largest of which weighs approximately 12 tons, sparkle with Swarovski crystals and shine with 40kg of 24-carat galvanised gold.

One of the prayer hall's most impressive features is the world's largest loomed carpet. The medallion design with elaborate arabesque motifs took 1200 craftsmen two years to complete, half of which was spent on hand knotting the 5700 sq metres of woollen thread on a cotton base. That translates as two billion, 268 million knots!

Visitors are welcome to enter the mosque except during prayer times. A worthwhile free 45- to 60-minute guided tour (in English and Arabic) helps explain some fundamentals of the Islamic religion while pointing out some of the stylistic highlights of the interior. Check the website for prayer times, which change daily. Mosque etiquette requires all visitors to wear long, loose-fitting, ankle-length trousers or skirts, long sleeves and a headscarf for women. Those not dressed appropriately are asked to go to the basement, where hooded *abeyyas* and kanduras can be borrowed for free.

Sheikh Zayed's mausoleum is on the approach to the mosque entrance. Prayers are continually recited by attendants here. While photographs of the mausoleum are not permitted, visitors are free to photograph all other parts of the mosque, but sensitivity should be shown towards those in prayer.

The mosque is located off Sheikh Rashid bin Saeed St.

Sheikh Zayed Grand Mosque Centre Library LIBRARY
(Map p352; ☎02-419 1919; www.szgmc.ae; ⏲10am-5pm Sat, 9am-9pm Sun-Wed, 9am-4pm Thu) FREE With rare collections of Arabic calligraphy and copies of the Quran dating back to the 16th century, this priceless collection of manuscripts is intended primarily as a research centre but is also open to public view. Part of the magic of the collection is its location in the mosque's minaret, giving an aerial view of the mosque's magnificent domes and the city and outlying islands beyond.

The library is located off Sheikh Rashid bin Saeed St.

Miraj – The Museum MUSEUM
(Map p352; ☎02-449 1041; www.mirajabudhabi.com; Sheikh Rashid bin Saeed St; ⏲9am-7pm) FREE Showcasing beautiful objects from around the Islamic world, including Persian carpets, calligraphy, ceramics and textiles, this private, museum-quality collection is open for view, with some pieces also for sale. It's next to the Hilton Abu Dhabi Capital Grand Hotel. A **second venue** (Map p348; ☎050-250 3950; www.mirajabudhabi.com; Villa 14, Marina Office Park; ⏲9am-7pm) FREE in the south-facing villas on the Breakwater, near Marina Mall, has a lovely rooftop cafe with views of Emirates Palace.

Khor Al Maqta WATERFRONT
(Map p352; Bain al Jessrain) This historic waterway separates Abu Dhabi from the mainland, guarded by the now somewhat hidden Al Maqta Fort and a small watchtower, on a rocky promontory in the middle of the *khor*. Luxury hotels and the charming Souk Qaryat Al Beri line the banks. Walking paths and *abras* (small traditional ferries) help visitors move between hotels and sights, while the snowy-white Sheikh Zayed Grand Mosque looms in the background.

Sheikh Zayed Bridge BRIDGE
(Map p352) Said to symbolise the flow of energy into the capital, this 842m-long modern bridge designed by Zaha Hadid is one of three gateways to Abu Dhabi. Its curvilinear form is reminiscent of sand dunes and at

LOCAL KNOWLEDGE

DINNER CRUISES

The Abu Dhabi Corniche and skyline form a magical backdrop for a leisurely dinner aboard a traditional dhow. Based next to the fish market at the port, Al Dhafra (p360) runs two-hour dinner cruises with a fixed three-course Arabic meal, including nonalcoholic beverages. Sit in air-conditioned comfort downstairs or alfresco on the *majlis*-style upper deck.

ABRA WATER-HOPPING SERVICE

Abra Water-Hopping Service
(☎050-636 5227; http://captaintonys.ae; ⏲Red Rte usually 4-10.30pm) Traditional wooden boats, called *abras*, ferry passengers around the Khor Al Maqta, stopping at the Shangri-La Hotel, the Ritz-Carlton Hotel, the Fairmont Hotel and the Souk Qaryat Al Beri (Red Rte; Dh20), on a hop-on, hop-off basis. With pre-booking, boats also travel from the Eastern Mangroves Marina to Souk Qaryat Al Beri (Yellow Rte; Dh50, five-person minimum) and to Yas Island (Blue Rte; Dh100, five-person minimum).

ABU DHABI'S NEW MUSEUMS & GALLERIES

Art lovers, take note: one of the world's most ambitious cultural construction projects is taking shape on Saadiyat Island off the coast of Abu Dhabi. When all is said and built, the new Cultural District (www.saadiyatculturaldistrict.ae) will consist of three museums and a performing-arts centre, making it (what else?) the largest artistic oasis in the world.

Construction has been fraught with delays but finally picked up again in early 2013.

Abu Dhabi Louvre (p351) This will be the first building to open, perhaps in late 2016. Designed by Jean Nouvel, its most distinctive feature is a perforated white dome that appears to hover above the water.

Zayed National Museum (www.zayednationalmuseum.ae) Set to be another visual jewel, this museum will tell the story of UAE founding father Sheikh Zayed bin Sultan Al Nayhan within the context of the history of the region and its cultural connections with other parts of the world. Architect Norman Foster translated Sheikh Zayed's love of falconry into an avant-garde structure with jutting steel-and-glass galleries inspired by flight and feathers. Each 'feather' will contain a gallery highlighting different historical and cultural aspects of the country.

Guggenheim Abu Dhabi (www.guggenheim.org/abu-dhabi) Designed by Frank Gehry, this promises to be a similarly exciting building: a cacophonous composition of geometrical shapes, from cuboids to cones, cylinders to prisms. It will showcase international art from the 1960s to today.

Performing Arts Centre Envisioned for the second phase of the district's development is this spaceship-like design by Iraqi-British architect Zaha Hadid.

Maritime Museum Also part of the second phase of development, this building by Japanese architect Tadao Ando will explore the Emirati relationship with the sea.

For a sense of the ambition of the project, visit the Manarat Al Saadiyat exhibition centre (p349) on Saadiyat Island.

night the lighting scheme gives a sense that the dunes are on the move.

Capital Gate LANDMARK

(Map p346; ☎02-596 1234; http://abudhabi.capitalgate.hyatt.com; Al Khaleej Al Arabi St) Look out of the window from many points in Abu Dhabi at night and you could be forgiven for thinking you've had one too many at the bar: reaching skyward in the city's southeast is this 35-floor, dramatically listing skyscraper that holds the Guinness world record as the world's most leaning building (at 18 degrees westwards, it's over four times more wayward than the Leaning Tower of Pisa).

It's the focal point of the Abu Dhabi National Exhibition Centre (Adnec) and also houses a Hyatt hotel.

Eastern Corniche WATERFRONT

(New Corniche; Sheikh Zayed bin Sultan St; E10) The seaward side of Sheikh Zayed bin Sultan St has been developed into a promenade to rival Abu Dhabi's original downtown Corniche, with a series of landscaped gardens, parking bays, picnic areas and paths. Offering excellent views of the mangroves, this is a good place to watch birds or dangle a line in the water. It gets busy on winter nights.

Yas Island & Around

Helping to define Abu Dhabi as a dynamic destination, Yas Island has blossomed into the capital's activities hub. While the Grand Prix brings in a global audience every November, there's much more to Yas Island than Formula 1. Enjoy engineering wizardry in Ferrari World rides and simulations, in the wave makers of Waterworld (p355) and in a restaurant (p361) where the burgers arrive by roller coaster. As a rewarding contrast, explore the beautiful natural environment of the mangroves dotted along the edge of the Gulf in a number of eco-friendly adventures. Retail therapy beckons in the form of the light-flooded Yas Mall (p364), while salty types can admire the yachts moored at **Yas Marina**.

Yas Island is connected to the mainland via the Yas Tunnel to Al Raha Beach and the Sheikh Khalifa Hwy (E12).

Aldar HQ BUILDING

(Map p346; Shahama Rd, Al Raha) Visible from afar, this futuristic landmark building has been dubbed 'The Coin' thanks to its distinctive penny-shaped architecture. The world's first circular skyscraper, this slender monument to modern design houses Aldar, one of the largest property developers in the Emirates.

Activities

Yas Island is revving up to reel in the testosterone crowd. Since 2009, the world's racing elite has descended in November for the Formula 1 race on the 5.5km Yas Marina Circuit, which features 21 wicked turns and straightaways leading to top speeds above 300km/h. Uniquely, it runs straight through the futuristic Yas Viceroy Abu Dhabi hotel.

★Ferrari World Abu Dhabi AMUSEMENT PARK

(Map p346; ☎02-496 8000; www.ferrariworldabudhabi.com; Yas Leisure Dr; adult/child under 1.3m Dh250/205; ⏰11am-8pm Sun-Wed, to 10pm Thu-Sat) If you want bragging rights to having 'done' Formula Rossa, the world's fastest roller coaster, visit this temple of torque and celebration of all things Ferrari in a spectacular building on Yas Island. Accelerating from 0km/h to 240km/h in 4.9 seconds, this is as close to an F1 experience as most of us are likely to get.

Tamer diversions include a flume ride through a V12 engine, a motion simulator that lets you ride shotgun with a race-car champion, and an imaginative 4D adventure. There's also a somewhat saner roller coaster that has you 'race' a Ferrari F430 Spider around the track. Between thrills, check out the car exhibitions or live shows.

Funride - Hiltonia Beach Club CYCLING

(Map p348; ☎02-441 3264; www.funridesports.com; Corniche Rd (West); per hour adult/child Dh30/20; ⏰4pm-midnight) A great way to appreciate the modern skyline of Abu Dhabi's western shore is to cycle the dedicated bike path along the Corniche. Bicycles (men's, women's and children's) are available for rent at four stations along the road, with this one near the Hiltonia Beach Club being the most reliably staffed.

It's 8km from here to the Dhow Harbour and there's a Dh10 surcharge for collecting the bike at one station and dropping it off at another.

Yas Marina Circuit ADVENTURE SPORTS

(Map p346; ☎02-659 9800; www.yasmarinacircuit.ae; venue tours Dh120, driving & passenger experiences Dh250-1600; ⏰2hr tours 10am & 2pm Tue-Sat) Even if you're not in town in November for the Formula 1 Grand Prix, it's possible to experience the track year round. Fancy yourself Lewis Hamilton as you drive the concourse at the wheel of – or as a passenger in – an Aston Martin GT4. Take a ride in a drift taxi or go from 0km/h to 100km/h in two seconds in a dragster.

Tamer types can take a leisurely behind-the-scenes tour with stops in the grandstand, the race control centre and the media centre. The circuit is off Yas Leisure Dr.

Yas Waterworld WATER PARK

(Map p346; ☎02-414 2000; www.yaswaterworld.com; Yas Leisure Dr; adult/child Dh240/195, fast pass Dh460/415; ⏰10am-6pm Nov-Feb, to 7pm Mar-May, Sep & Oct, to 8pm Jun-Aug) The UAE's most elaborate water park offers opportunities to get soaked on 45 rides, slides and other liquid attractions as you follow Emirati cartoon character Dana on her quest for a magical pearl. A wave pool, two lazy rivers and sunbeds offer relaxing alternatives to the rides if you're just looking to beat the Gulf heat.

With four thrill levels, there are rides for the fearful as well as the fearless. Top draws include the Bandit Bomber roller coaster with water and laser effects; a hair-raising slide called Liwa Loop; and Dawwama, a

YAS EXPRESS

A great way to get around Yas Island is aboard the free **Yas Express** (☎02-496 8110; www.yasisland.ae; ⏰9am-9pm) FREE, a shuttle bus that links major attractions at least once hourly on three routes. See the website for route maps and the schedule.

Blue Rte Operates from 9am to 9pm and connects Yas Waterworld with the hotels at Yas Plaza, the Yas Viceroy Abu Dhabi hotel, Yas Marina Circuit and Ferrari World Abu Dhabi.

Red Rte Runs from 9am until 2am between Yas Plaza, the Viceroy, Yas Beach, Yas Marina and the Yas Links golf course.

Saadiyat Rte Links Yas and Saadiyat Islands between 10am and 7pm.

wild tornado ride through a 20m-high funnel that takes a gravity-defying 1½ minutes. Body sliding is also on offer. The attractive date-palm landscaping, pearl-diving show, *barasti* (palm) shelters and souq create a pleasant heritage theme.

Tours

Big Bus Abu Dhabi BUS TOUR

(☎02-449 0026; www.bigbustours.com; 24hr adult/child Dh230/100, 48hr adult/child Dh260/130; ⏱9am-8pm) This hop-on, hop-off bus tour with recorded commentary is an easy way to get the lay of the land. The route passes all the major sights, including Sheikh Zayed Grand Mosque, the Corniche, the Heritage Village, Emirates Palace Hotel and Yas Island. Tickets include headphones and are sold online (at a discount) as well as at hotels and on the bus.

A separate shuttle, leaving every 90 minutes, covers Yas Island and Masdar City between 9am and 5.30pm daily. There is also a night bus (adult/child Dh115/75) that leaves from the Marina Mall (at the Breakwater) at 7.15pm every evening and takes two hours. You can board the bus at any stop, but the nominal starting point is the Marina Mall.

Abu Dhabi Pearl Journey BOAT TOUR

(Map p346; ☎02-656 1000; www.adpearljourney.com; Sheikh Zayed bin Sultan St; adult/under 12yr Dh500/400; ⏱cruises 9am-8pm) Based at the Eastern Mangroves Hotel & Spa, these walk-in tours ply the mangrove channels on a traditional dhow and leave when the boat reaches its maximum capacity of 18 passengers. Cruises include informative descriptions of Abu Dhabi's past as a pearling village, demonstrate traditional seafaring songs and offer coffee and dates. Tours end with oyster opening until you find one with a pearl!

Noukhada Adventure Company KAYAKING

(☎02-558 1889; http://noukhada.ae; various launching points; kayaking tours adult/child from Dh155/120; ⏱office hours 8.30am-5.30pm) Specialising in local exploration by paddle, this tour company runs popular kayaking trips through the local mangrove swamps. A 90-minute tour (Dh155) is a great way to experience this unusual habitat. The two-hour Eco Tour (Dh220) gives an even deeper understanding of this unique environment and there's even a monthly full-moon tour (adults only, Dh200).

Festivals & Events

Abu Dhabi Grand Prix SPORTS

(Map p346; ☎02-659 9800; www.yasmarinacircuit.com; Yas Marina Circuit; ⏱Nov) The Formula 1 Abu Dhabi Grand Prix is a major event, attracting visitors from across the region as well as international racing fans. Offering one of the most impressive circuits on the race calendar, including a marina setting

TOP THREE ABU DHABI PUBLIC BEACHES

Corniche Beach (Map p348; www.bakeuae.com; Corniche Rd (West); adult/under 12yr Dh10/5; ⏱8am-8pm) There are several gates to this spotlessly maintained, blue-flagged public beach. The turquoise sea, view of Lulu Island, palm trees and gardens make it an unexpected pleasure in the heart of a capital city. A lifeguard is on duty until sunset.

The beach is divided into three sections: Al Sahil is for singles and groups, Gate 2 is for families and a quiet zone and Gate 3 is for families and children. The latter two beaches are shielded from view by a fence. Showers, changing rooms and cabanas are available; towels can be rented for Dh10, sunloungers and umbrellas for Dh25.

Saadiyat Public Beach (Map p346; www.bakeuae.com; Saadiyat Island; adult/child Dh25/15; ⏱8am-8pm) A boardwalk leads through a protected zone of coastal vegetation to this beautiful powdery white beach, home to nesting turtles, on the north-west coast of Saadiyat Island (near Park Hyatt Abu Dhabi). There's a lifeguard until sunset and a cafe but no alcohol. Towels rent for Dh10, sunloungers for Dh25.

Yas Beach (Map p346; ☎056-242 0435; www.yasbeach.ae; Yas Island; adult/8-16yr/under 8yr Dh100/50/free, Sun-Thu half-price; ⏱10am-7pm Sun-Wed, to 10pm Fri & Sat) A surprisingly low-key corner of this high-tech island, Yas Beach is a lovely place to relax and enjoy the sea views, dabble in some water sports or generally chill with a cool beer. The kitchen rustles up grilled local fish and other tasty light bites. A DJ plays soothing sounds on Friday. Day admission includes towel, sunbed, parasol and showers. Alcohol available.

WORTH A TRIP

ABU DHABI FALCON HOSPITAL

Standing outside **Abu Dhabi Falcon Hospital** (☎02-575 5155; www.falconhospital.com; Sweihan Rd; 2hr tour adult/child Dh170/60; ⏱tours 2pm Sat, 10am & 2pm Sun-Thu), watching anxious owners from across the region delivering their hooded 'patients' in person, you will quickly realise that this is a much-needed and much-loved facility. Falcons are an integral part of traditional Gulf culture and no expense is spared in restoring these magnificent birds to full health. Tours include a visit to the falcon museum, the examination room and the free-flight aviary. Tour reservations (bookable online) are mandatory. If you're willing to brave an arm, the well-behaved raptors will even perch for a photograph.

The hospital is about 6km southeast of Abu Dhabi airport. Coming from central Abu Dhabi, follow Airport Rd (E20) to Sweihan Rd in the direction of Falah City; about 3km past the junction with Hwy E11, turn right after the water tank (before exit 30A) and follow the signs to the hospital.

and a section of track that passes through the Yas Viceroy Abu Dhabi hotel, this day-night race is held annually.

Sleeping

Abu Dhabi doesn't have a youth hostel, and budget accommodation is practically nonexistent, although most hotels listed here offer steep discounts when business is slow (including summer, Ramadan and non-European holiday times). Since the city is so spread out, it makes sense to find a hotel location that matches your needs. Stay in the city centre to be close to historic sights and urban life; head east to Khor Maqta for upscale stays with great dining and superb Grand Mosque views; or settle in on Yas Island to be close to Ferrari World and other activities.

City Centre

★**Crowne Plaza Abu Dhabi** HOTEL $$
(Map p348; ☎02-616 6166; www.crowneplaza.com; Sheikh Hamdan bin Mohammed St; r from Dh570; P@🛜🏊) This thoroughly amenable hotel, with its generous rooms and grand views of the city, knows exactly how to please its guests. The emphasis is on providing excellent service and a sociable experience, which is accomplished through its highly popular pan-Asian restaurant and lounge, Cho Gao (p358), Heroes bar and a rooftop cocktail bar.

Khalidiya Palace Rayhaan by Rotana HOTEL $$
(Map p348; ☎02-657 0000; www.rotana.com; Corniche Rd (West); r from Dh975; P@🛜🏊) With its giant pool, landscaped gardens, facilities aimed at children (such as 'mini-me' climbing frames, swings and a crèche) and a relaxed atmosphere, this alcohol-free beachfront hotel has established a following among local families seeking a weekend getaway. There's an authentic Arabic restaurant, Kamoon, equally popular with locals.

Le Royal Méridien Abu Dhabi HOTEL $$
(Map p348; ☎02-674 2020; www.leroyalmeridienabudhabi.com; Khalifa bin Zayed the First St; r from Dh850; P@🛜🏊) Not to be confused with family-friendly Le Méridien, this hotel is where the well connected come to sign on the dotted line. The diplomatically termed 'leisure guest' could well feel intimated by the purposeful comings and goings of the designer-suited, the bathing-suited and for that matter the ill-suited. For those who enjoy being seen, however, Le Royal is where it's at.

Beach Rotana Hotel & Towers HOTEL $$$
(Map p348; ☎02-697 9000; www.rotana.com; 10th St; r from Dh1100; P@🛜🏊) Joined at the hip to Abu Dhabi Mall, this hotel is as much a favourite with leisure travellers as with conference-goers. Staff manage to keep several hundred guests happy when they have just spent a harrowing day with the credit card at the mall next door.

Sheikh Zayed Grand Mosque & Around

★**Aloft Abu Dhabi** HOTEL $$
(Map p346; ☎02-654 5000; www.aloftabudhabi.com; Al Khaleej Al Arabi St; d from Dh615; P🛜🏊) The loft-like rooms, landscaped pool and high-tech gadgetry in this hotel scream urban chic. Free wi-fi in all rooms, large TVs and iPod docking stations make this a

ABU DHABI'S CLEAN-TECH CITY

Near Abu Dhabi airport, **Masdar City** (Map p346; ☎toll free 800 627 327; www.masdar.ae; btwn Hwys E10 & E20; ⏰8.30am-4.30pm Sun-Thu) is the world's first carbon-neutral, zero-waste city powered entirely by renewable energy. However, this is not your regular residential neighbourhood but rather a science community with a graduate-research university and companies focused on sustainability, clean tech and renewable energy. It's a great place to visit for the architecture and the sci-fi vibe.

Part of the fun is hopping on a podlike driverless Personal Rapid Transit (PRT) vehicle at the car park for the short ride to the main campus. Pick up a map at the information desk upstairs from the PRT terminal (or download it from the website) for a self-guided tour. Several cafes and restaurants provide sustenance.

convenient choice for getting some work done while attending a function at the adjoining ADNEC Exhibition Centre. The popular rooftop bar Relax@12 has killer views and cocktails.

Traders Hotel, Qaryat al Beri HOTEL $$
(☎02-510 8880; www.shangri-la.com/traders; Khor Al Maqta; r from Dh750; P@🛜🏊) With a Pop Art vibe and bright colours in the lobby, this offers a funky alternative to the standard marble and crystal of neighbouring hotels. After frolicking by the two pools or on the beach, guests can retreat to rooms that are subdued but spacious. Use of the facilities of the related and nearby Shangri-La Qaryat Al Beri is free, and top restaurants a mere stroll away.

★Eastern Mangroves Hotel & Spa HOTEL $$$
(Map p346; ☎02-656 1000; www.abu-dhabi.anantara.com; Sheikh Zayed bin Sultan St; d from Dh1000; P@🛜🏊) Stepping into the lobby, with its *mashrabiya* patterns and *oud* player, it's clear that Arab hospitality is taken seriously at this luxe lair. Rooms overlook the eponymous mangroves (kayak tours available) and are soothingly furnished in matching nature tones. Work up an appetite in the infinity pool before grazing on international small plates in the rooftop Impressions restaurant-lounge.

Yas Island & Around

Centro Yas Island HOTEL $$
(Map p346; ☎02-656 4444; www.rotana.com; Yas Plaza, Yas Island; r from Dh700; P@🛜🏊) A good-value option in the hotel cluster on Yas Island, this upbeat place with compact rooms is a decent choice for the budget conscious and attracts a younger crowd. Rates include shuttle service to Yas Beach and access to the luxurious leisure facilities at the adjacent Yas Island Rotana.

Yas Viceroy Abu Dhabi HOTEL $$$
(Map p346; ☎02-656 0000; www.viceroyhotelsandresorts.com; Yas Marina Circuit; r from Dh1000; P@🛜🏊) This extravagantly shaped hotel sits in pole position on Yas Island, literally straddling the Yas Marina Circuit. The avant-garde, steel-and-glass structure with its corrugated mantel flung over the race track is dramatically studded with lights at night, and the blue-white interior, reminiscent of an ice hotel, is a haven of cool in the Gulf heat.

Eating

Al Markaziya & Around

Mama Thani EMIRATI $
(Map p348; Khalifa bin Zayed the First St; sandwiches Dh22-35; ⏰10am-10pm; 🛜) What baguette is to the French, khameer is to Emiratis. This little cafe on the ground floor of the World Trade Center Souk serves the traditional bread sandwich-style, stuffed with all sorts of savoury and sweet ingredients, from the Rose (rose cream, pistachios and figs) to the Italiano (rucola, bresaola, egg and feta). Also try a yummy camel-milk shake.

★Cho Gao ASIAN $$
(Map p348; ☎02-616 6149; www.facebook.com/ChoGaoAsianExperience; Sheikh Hamdan bin Mohammed St; mains Dh50-150; ⏰noon-1am; 🛜) This upbeat joint at the Crowne Plaza Abu Dhabi is a favourite as much for the tasty fare as for its highly sociable ambience. The menu hopscotches from Japan to Singapore, China to Thailand and other Asian countries without missing a step. Whether it's curry, stir-fry or Peking duck, it all tastes fresh and flavourful.

Zyara Café LEBANESE $$

(Map p348; 02-627 5007; dishes Dh20-60; 24hr;) Red is the overwhelming impression of this fun little eatery: scarlet cushions, ruby drapes, carmine tablecloths and Eastern-patterned fabrics make the interior a riot of colour. Breakfast is served all day, and the mezze and home-baked cakes are delicious. Near the corner of Khalifa bin Zayed the First and 4th Sts, it has lovely Corniche views. Avoid the lunchtime crush.

La Brioche Café FRENCH $$

(Map p348; 02-677 0905; www.labriocheuae.com; Sheikh Hamdan bin Mohammed St; breakfast Dh23-52, mains Dh20-90; 7am-midnight;) A slice of Paris in the UAE, this mini-chain charmer is famous for its breakfasts but also makes healthy salads, bulging sandwiches and some of the best bread, croissants and pastries (baked fresh and local) in town. Service is swift and smiling, making this ideal for a takeaway to eat at Capital Gardens, which are within walking distance.

Kababs & Kurries INDIAN $$

(Map p348; 02-628 2522; Khalifa bin Zayed the First St; mains Dh28-73; noon-11.30pm) This appealing place on the ground floor of the Norman Foster–designed World Trade Center Souk serves up an extensive menu of tasty and refined Indian food inside and on the terrace.

Breakwater & Around

★Living Room Café CAFE $$

(TLRC; Map p348; 02-639 6654; www.thelivingroomcafeabudhabi.com; Khalidiya Village, Khalifa bin Shakhbout St (28th St); snacks Dh10-20, mains Dh35-80; 7.30am-11.30pm Sun-Thu, 8.30am-11.30pm Fri & Sat;) This award-winning, family-run venue began as a coffee-and-cake experience and has grown by word of mouth into a beloved restaurant. The emphasis is on family-friendly fare (there's a VIP children's menu and kids' corner), and the home-baked cakes, all-day breakfasts, toasted sandwiches and healthy salads will please those with a craving for something from mum's kitchen. It's inside the Sarouh Compound.

Saudi Cuisine VIP ARABIAN $$

(Map p348; 02-665 5355; 3rd St; mains Dh40-100; noon-midnight) A snug little den behind Corniche Towers that's decked out with sheepskins and partitioned tables, this restaurant is the perfect place to try lamb dishes from the heart of the Peninsula. Roasted slowly for many hours and served with rice and chilli sauce, the lamb falls easily off the bone. Hands are the best utensils in this local favourite.

★Mezlai EMIRATI $$$

(Map p348; 02-690 7999; www.kempinski.com; Corniche Rd (West); mains Dh110-210; 1-10.30pm;) Meaning 'old door lock', Mezlai at the sumptuous Emirates Palace delivers a rare chance to enjoy local flavours. The Emirati food is prepared from organic and locally sourced ingredients. Favourites include *lamb medfoun* (shoulder of lamb, slow cooked in a banana leaf) and *chicken makbus* with spiced rice. The potato mashed with camel's milk makes an interesting side dish.

Brasserie Angélique FRENCH $$$

(Map p348; 02-811 5666; www.jumeirah.com; Corniche (West); mains Dh75-225; noon-3.30pm & 7-11.30pm) This award-winning fine-dining restaurant at Jumeirah at Etihad Towers has taken the city by storm. Even if the opulent chandeliers scream 'Gulf', the food is thoroughly Gallic, with seared squab breast, stuffed saddle of lamb and Armagnac-smoked veal cutlet making appearances alongside foie gras, *escargot* and quiche.

Al Zahiyah & Al Maryah Island

Lebanon Mill LEBANESE $

(Map p348; 02-677 7714; 9th St; sandwiches Dh5-15, mains Dh18-37; noon-1am) Empty tables are as rare as hen's teeth in this simple but clean cafeteria that spoils palates with five types of shwarma, grilled kebabs and spit-roast chicken. Pair your meat with a plate of hummus, Arabic salad and a fruit juice, and you're in for one fine dining experience. It's on 9th St, near Fatima bint Mubarak St.

Biryani Pot INDIAN $$

(Map p348; 02-676 6555; www.biryanipot.ae; Galleria Mall, Al Falah St, Al Maryah Island; mains Dh22-44; 10am-11pm Sat-Wed, to midnight Thu & Fri;) Billed as gourmet Indian fast food, the 'pot' does indeed do yummy biryanis, including a gluten-free organic version with quinoa, alongside curries, tandoor grills and salads. The food-court setting isn't conducive to lingering unless you camp out on the terrace, which has water views.

LOCAL KNOWLEDGE

DIY FISH SUPPER

Never mind the prospect of lots of tasty seafood, **Al Mina Fish Market** (Map p348; Dhow Harbour, Al Mina; 5am-11pm) is a visual feast of colour, texture and design. Rhythmical arrangements of prawns, orange-spotted trevally, blue-shelled crabs, red snappers, pink Sultan Ibrahims and a host of unlikely edibles from the sea grace the ice bars here.

For a memorable lunch or supper for under Dh20, buy your fish at the market from the folk in blue, and take it to the folk in red in the gutting and filleting station. Take the fillets next door (alongside the dry fish section) and jostle with seafarers for your favourite spices. At the back of the spice area, give your purchases to the cooks, who will make it into a firey-hot Kerala fish curry or simply grill it rubbed in salt and dried chillies. Take the finished dish onto the dhow harbour outside, and sit on a lobster pot to eat it!

★Zuma JAPANESE $$$
(Map p348; 02-401 5900; www.zumarestaurant.com; Galleria Mall, Al Maryah Island; mains Dh80-180; noon-3pm & 7pm-midnight;) Zuma is quite possibly the summit of Japanese cuisine in Abu Dhabi. Book ahead to enjoy the superb sushi and sashimi selections, or indulge in the signature miso-marinated black cod or a hunk of meat cooked to perfection on the robata grill. A four-course business lunch, served Sunday to Thursday, costs Dh140. Alcohol served. Buzzy bar to boot.

Finz SEAFOOD $$$
(Map p348; 02-697 9011; www.rotana.com; 10th St; small plates Dh40-90, mains Dh130-350; 5pm-1am Sun-Wed, 12.30pm-3am Thu & Fri, 12.30pm-1am Sat;) Amble down the jetty to this A-frame with terraces above the sea, order a cocktail and prepare for some of the finest seafood in town. Whether grilled, wok-cooked, baked or prepared in the tandoor oven, the results are invariably delicious. Also good for midday nibbles. Alcohol available. It's at the Beach Rotana Hotel & Towers, next to Abu Dhabi Mall.

Al Mina & Saadiyat Island

Al Arish Restaurant MIDDLE EASTERN $$
(Map p348; 02-673 2266; Al Mina Port, near Fish Market; lunch & dinner buffet Dh175; noon-4pm & 7pm-midnight) This aged, flamboyant gem, with its fading Arabian decor, *barasti* (palm-leaf) ceiling and hand-carved furniture, sports a sumptuous *majlis* (lounge) that has entertained princes and sheikhs over the decades. The lunch buffet offers one of the best opportunities in Abu Dhabi to sample local dishes, including *ouzi* (baked lamb) and *majboos* (chicken baked in rice). It's near the fish market.

Turquoiz SEAFOOD $$$
(Map p346; 02-498 8001; www.turquoizabudhabi.com; Saadiyat Island; mains Dh80-170; noon-3pm & 6.30-11pm Sun-Thu, noon-4pm & 6.30-11pm Fri & Sat;) It would be hard to find a more romantic venue for a sunset drink, a bowl of mussels and an ambient waft of *sheesha*. Housed in a set of wooden pavilions with decked terraces overlooking the sea, this lovely restaurant at the St Regis Saadiyat Island Resort feels a world away from the city beyond.

Al Dhafra ARABIAN $$$
(Map p348; 02-673 2266; Dhow Harbour, Al Mina; dinner cruise per person Dh180; cruise 8-10pm) This floating restaurant is on board a traditional dhow. The popular Al Arish Restaurant supplies the buffet for the nightly dinner cruise from Al Mina to the Breakwater and back. Al Dhafra offers a fun setting for sampling Arabic dishes while sitting cross-legged on sedans and cushions and enjoying stunning views of Abu Dhabi's night-time skyline.

Sheikh Zayed Grand Mosque & Around

Milas EMIRATI $$
(02-558 0425; www.milas.cc; Khor Al Maqta; mains Dh30-95; 9am-11.30pm;) Dark wood, black glass and neon announce that this is an Emirati restaurant for the 21st century. Traditional dishes such as chicken *makbous* (stew) and *deyay shiwa* (chicken marinated in saffron-yoghurt) have been given a contemporary makeover. Thought-

ful perks: wet handcloths, a complimentary *danqaw* (chickpea) appetiser and a post-meal perfume tray. It's on the 1st floor of Souk Qaryat Al Beri.

Ushna INDIAN $$

(☎02-558 1769; Khor Al Maqta; mains Dh50-110; ⌚12.30-11.30pm) Romantic and elegant, this place at Souk Qaryat Al Beri hums with appreciation for the complex cuisine of India, brought to the UAE by a large expat community. There are many curry houses across town, but this restaurant offers some of the most luscious variations, alongside beautiful views across the canal to the Sheikh Zayed Grand Mosque.

★Bord Eau FRENCH $$$

(☎02-509 8511; www.shangri-la.com; Khor Al Maqta; mains Dh180-320, 5-course blind tasting menu Dh500; ⌚6.30-11.30pm; 📶) Bord Eau at the Shangri-La Hotel is *le* restaurant for French fine dining in Abu Dhabi. The classic French fare (onion soup, foie gras, chateaubriand) is flawlessly executed with a modern twist and the flavours are calibrated to perfection. With simple elegance (including reproduction Degas ballerinas gracing the walls), the ambience matches the refined quality of the food.

★Mijana LEBANESE $$$

(☎02-818 8282; www.ritzcarlton.com; Khor Al Maqta; mains Dh80-160; ⌚4pm-1am) At the Ritz-Carlton, this swish venue offers contemporary Lebanese cuisine with interesting twists on favourite themes, such as beetroot *moutabel* (smoked-aubergine dip), six varieties of hummus and *habra niyah* (raw mince lamb 'cooked' in fresh mint and garlic). Leave space for a camel-milk smoothie or a *sheesha* on the terrace with live Arabic music.

Yas Island & Around

Aquarium SEAFOOD $$

(Map p346; ☎02-565 0007; www.yasmarina.ae/aquarium; Yas Marina; mains Dh65-130; ⌚noon-1am; 📶) With stunning floor-to-ceiling aquariums gracing the interior of this casual-dining restaurant, there's no doubting its speciality. Tables on the terrace are the most coveted at night, when views of the marina and the eccentric Yas Viceroy Abu Dhabi hotel team up with Arabian-caught, Asian-prepared seafood for a memorable experience. *Sheesha* available.

Nolu's Café CAFE $$

(Map p346; ☎02-557 9500; Al Raha Beach, Al Bandar; mains Dh50-125; ⌚8am-10pm Sat-Wed, to 11pm Thu & Fri) With its starburst abstract panels, lime-green decor and a wholesome menu, this charmer feels more California than Abu Dhabi, but the secret recipes of the owner's Afghani mother add a delightfully regional spin. Try such little-known specialities as *aushak* (dumplings) and *bolani* (stuffed flatbread). Also popular for breakfast. Next to Spinneys.

Rogo's Rollercoaster Restaurant BURGERS $$

(Map p346; ☎02-565 0888; www.rollercoasterrestaurant.com; Town Sq, Yas Mall, Yas Island West; meals around Dh55; ⌚noon-10pm Sat-Wed, to midnight Thu & Fri) If you haven't got the stomach for Ferrari World, you may muster more of an appetite for this novel roller-coaster restaurant. Two conveyor belts deliver your meal from the kitchen via a pair of 12m-high tornado (spiral) double-loops, lifts and other engineering wizardry. Food of indifferent flavour is delivered in metal pots on plastic trays, and ordered via tablet.

Cipriani ITALIAN $$$

(Map p346; ☎02-657 5400; www.cipriani.com; Yas Marina; mains Dh100-260; ⌚6pm-midnight) The cuisine at this renowned restaurant may be Italian (including a lot of signature dishes from world-famous Harry's Bar in Venice), but the view is distinctly Emirates. The terrace looks out over the grandstands of the Yas Marina Circuit, designer yachts moored alongside, and the Yas Viceroy Abu Dhabi hotel, with its mantle of amethyst and diamond lights.

Self-Catering

Big, central supermarkets with convenient opening hours include **Carrefour** (Map p348; ☎02-681 4266; www.carrefouruae.com; Marina Mall; ⌚9am-midnight Sat-Wed, to 1am Thu), which has lots of products from Europe. North American expats tend to prefer **Spinneys** (Map p348; ☎02-681 2897; www.spinneys-dubai.com; cnr 5th & 6th Sts, Khalidiya; ⌚24hr). A popular local chain is **Abu Dhabi Co-op** (Map p348; ☎02-645 9777; www.abudhabicoop.com/english; ground fl, Abu Dhabi Mall, 10th St; ⌚8am-midnight). All have additional branches around town (see the websites for locations).

Drinking & Nightlife

Al Markaziyah & Around

Level Lounge BAR

(Map p348; 02-616 6101; www.crowneplaza.com; Sheikh Hamdan bin Mohammed St; 5pm-2am;) This relaxing poolside rooftop lounge at the Crowne Plaza Abu Dhabi is open to the stars and offers a piece of tower-top calm in the middle of the hectic city. It makes a good local haunt for *sheesha* and a chat with chill-out music.

Sax CLUB

(Map p348; 02-674 2020; www.leroyalmeridienabudhabi.com; Khalifa bin Zayed the First St; 5pm-2am Sun-Wed, to 3am Thu-Sat;) In the early evening Sax lures chatty jet-setters huddled in intense tête-à-têtes, then cranks up the superb sound system to pack the dance floor with a glamtastic international crowd. Different promotions – Ladies' Night, Cabin Crew Night, Lebanese Weekend – keep things dynamic at this venue inside Le Royal Méridien Abu Dhabi.

Breakwater & Around

★**Observation Deck at 300** CAFE

(Map p348; 02-811 5666; www.jumeirah.com; Corniche Rd (West); entry Dh75, high tea Dh175; 10am-6pm) This chic coffee shop on the 74th floor of Tower 2 of the iconic Jumeirah at Etihad Towers hotel serves the highest high tea in Abu Dhabi with a sublime panorama of city, sea and surrounds. The '300' refers to the metres above ground. The admission price includes Dh50 towards food and drink.

★**Belgian Beer Café** BAR

(Map p348; 02-666 6888; www.belgianbeercafe.com; InterContinental Hotel, Bainunah St; 5pm-1am;) Not convinced there's more to beer than a canned lager? Head to the Belgian Beer Café, overlooking the marina at the InterContinental, and the specialist draughts and bottles behind the bar may just convince you otherwise. Follow the expat lead and order *frites* (fries) with a very Belgian pot of mussels – reputedly the best in town.

Hemingway's BAR

(Map p348; 02-681 1900; www.abudhabi.hilton.com; Hilton Abu Dhabi, Corniche Rd (West); noon-1am) A Tex-Mex cantina popular with long-term expats, Hemingway's is the place to lounge in front of the big screen with beer, chips (albeit nacho chips) and football. There's a live band from Monday to Saturday, happy hour from 4pm to 8pm and quiz night on Sunday.

Ray's Bar BAR

(Map p348; 02-811-5666; www.jumeirah.com; Corniche Rd (West); 5pm-3am;) For a prime perspective on Abu Dhabi's audacious architectural vision, let the lift whisk you up to this 62nd-floor bar at Jumeirah at Etihad Towers. If you arrive at sunset, you'll be dazzled by the light bouncing off these grand edifices. If the views and cocktails make you dizzy, the Asian tapas menu will restore balance to the brain.

Havana Café & Restaurant CAFE

(Map p348; 02-681 0044; Corniche Rd (West); sheesha from Dh35; 9am-12.30am) With one of the very best views of night-time Abu Dhabi, the outside terrace at this highly popular *sheesha* cafe is always teeming with appreciative puffers, smokers and gurglers. The service is attentive despite the crowds.

Sheikh Zayed Mosque & Around

Relax@12 BAR

(Map p346; 02-654 5183; Al Khaleej Al Arabi St; 5pm-2am Sun-Wed, to 3am Thu-Sat) This stylish rooftop bar at the Aloft Abu Dhabi hotel indeed puts you in the mood for relaxing, with mellow sounds, comfy seating and an extensive drinks menu that won't eviscerate your wallet. Sushi, mezze and tapas are available to help you stay stable, and there are different promotions almost every night.

Chameleon BAR

(02-654 3238; www.fairmont.com; Khor Al Maqta; 6pm-1am) Cool cucumber mojitos, flaming rosemary gimlets, and Smitten Watermelon Ritas are just some of the signature cocktails shaken but not stirred by the entertaining mixologists in this sophisticated lounge bar on the ground floor of the Fairmont Bab Al Bahr. A resident DJ adds to the fun from 10pm onwards (11pm on Thursday and Friday).

Yas Island & Around

★**O1NE** CLUB

(Map p346; 052-788 8111; www.o1neyasisland.com; Yas Leisure Dr; 11pm-late Thu & Fri) This Beirut transplant has taken up in residence in a purpose-built venue near the entrance to Yas Tunnel. It became an instant landmark thanks to 19 international graffiti artists, who aerosolled their visions onto the facade of the Coliseum-inspired building. Inside, top technology and dizzying 3D projections fuel the high-octane vibe.

Stills Bar & Brasserie BAR

(Map p346; ☎02-656 3053; Yas Island Golf Plaza; ⏲noon-1am Fri-Wed, to 3am Thu, happy hour 5-8pm) Boasting the longest bar in Abu Dhabi and with live entertainment, this is a happening spot for beer, cocktails and a satisfying selection of upscale pub grub, from burgers to fresh mussels. Based at the Crowne Plaza on Yas Island.

McGettigan's IRISH PUB

(Map p346; ☎02-652 4333; www.mcgettigans.com; Channel St; ⏲noon-3am; 📶) Irish pubs tend to be a prescription for a good time and this Dublin-to-desert import is no exception. If a pint of Guinness doesn't keep you entertained, then the quiz night, happy hour, Premier-League soccer on 18 screens or solid pub-grub menu should do the trick. It's off Hwy E10, next to Al Raha Beach Hotel.

☆ Entertainment

Jazz Bar & Dining LIVE MUSIC

(Map p348; ☎02-681 1900; www.abudhabi.hilton.com; Corniche Rd (West); mains Dh85-165; ⏲7pm-12.30am, to 1.30am Tue & Fri; 📶) Cool cats flock to this sophisticated supper club at the Hilton Abu Dhabi that serves international cuisine in a modern art deco–inspired setting. But the venue is less about the food and more about the music – a seven-piece jazz band plays on a stage to an audience of sagely nodding aficionados. It's ladies' night on Monday and Wednesday.

Burlesque Restaurant & Lounge CABARET

(Map p346; ☎056-498 7580; www.burlesqueuae.com; Marina Wing, Yas Viceroy Abu Dhabi; mains Dh65-225; ⏲7pm-2am Sat-Mon & Wed, to 4am Tue, Thu & Fri) This red-velvet venue with scarlet, high-backed sofas and opulent drapes channels slightly naughty 1920s glamour. Two hours of cabaret-style live singing and dancing are followed by differently themed dance parties after 11.30pm.

Abu Dhabi Classics CLASSICAL MUSIC

(☎toll free 800-555; www.abudhabiclassics.com; tickets Dh80-350; ⏲Nov-May) This concert series brings top classical performances – including renowned international soloists and famous orchestras – to such venues as the Emirates Palace and Manarat Al Saadiyat in Abu Dhabi and the historic Al Jahili Fort in Al Ain.

Vox Cinemas CINEMA

(Map p348; ☎02-681 8464; uae.voxcinemas.com; Marina Mall; tickets from Dh35) Ultracomfortable cinema with Hollywood and Bollywood blockbusters in 2D, 3D and 4D. Tickets can be booked online.

Novo Cinemas Abu Dhabi CINEMA

(Map p348; ☎02-645 8988; www.novocinemas.com; 3rd fl, Abu Dhabi Mall, 10th St; tickets Dh35) This multiplex shows the latest Hollywood films, some in 3D.

Shopping

World Trade Center Souk MALL

(Map p348; ☎02-810 7814; www.wtcad.ae; Khalifa bin Zayed the First St; ⏲10am-10pm Sat-Thu, to 11pm Thu & Fri; 📶) Norman Foster's reinterpretation of the traditional souq is a stylish composition of warm lattice woodwork, stained glass, walkways and balconies. On the site of the old central market, it connects with the modern World Trade Center mall via a footbridge. Enticing stores include the Persian Carpet House & Antiques, Kashmir Cottage and the Rocky Mountain Chocolate Factory.

Marina Mall MALL

(Map p348; ☎02-681 2310; www.marinamall.ae; Breakwater; ⏲10am-10pm Sat-Wed, to midnight Thu & Fri; 📶) Aside from more than 400 stores, this popular mall has plenty of entertainment options, including a multiplex cinema, a Fun City indoor playground, the Emirates Bowling Village and the new Marina Eye Ferris wheel.

Centre of Original Iranian Carpets CARPETS

(Map p348; ☎02-681 1156; www.coicco.com; Al Khaleej Al Arabi St; ⏲9.30am-1.30pm & 5-9.30pm Sat-Thu) Spread over three floors, this carpet gallery has over 4000 carpets to choose from, making it one of the largest collections of carpets in the Middle East. The shop's detailed website has a useful buyer's guide and glossary.

Abu Dhabi Mall MALL

(Map p348; ☎02-645 4858; www.abudhabi-mall.com; 10th St; ⏲10am-10pm Sat-Wed, to 11pm Thu & Fri) This elegant mall has the expected 200 stores, cinemas and children's amusements, but it also has shops with a local twist. On level 3, buy sweets and nuts from Arabesq and Al Rifai, while on level 1 Bateel's dates make good gifts.

The discerning Emirati browser will buy *ouds* (perfumes) from Cambodia and India in the celebrated store called Yas – The Royal Name of Perfumes (level 1). Also on level 1, *abeyyas* (women's outer garments) cost around Dh1700 from Khunji, while men's delicate *bishts* (outer garments worn on ceremonial occasions) cost anything from Dh300 to Dh2000.

Iranian Souq HOMEWARES
(Map p348; Al Mina; ⏲7am-midnight) If you've never been to a regional wholesale hardware market before, then this cramped collection of stalls huddled around the harbour edge is a fun destination. Giant aluminium cauldrons, floral melamine trays, Chinese plastic decorations, wickerware, thermoses and copper coffeepots are just some of the assorted imports in this lively souq.

Look out for a few local crafts like rice mats (around Dh40).

Khalifa Centre SOUVENIRS, HANDICRAFTS
(Map p348; 10th St, Al Zahiyah; ⏲10am-1pm & 4-10pm Sat-Thu, 4-10pm Fri) For a wide range of souvenirs (*sheesha* pipes, camel-bone boxes, stuffed leather camels, carpets and cushion covers), head to the Khalifa Centre, across the road from the Abu Dhabi Mall, where you'll find a dozen independent stores, mostly run by the expat Indian community, selling handicrafts and carpets.

Most of the goods on sale are from India, Turkey and Syria and many are made in China, but it's a fun place to root around and try your bargaining skills.

Galleria MALL
(Map p348; ☎02-616 6999; www.thegalleria.ae; Al Falah St, Al Maryah Island; ⏲10am-10pm Sat-Wed, 10am-midnight Thu, noon-midnight Fri) This flashy contender in the new business district on Al Maryah Island has dramatic looks (cathedral-high ceilings, sculptural roof) and a line-up of brands that should appeal to deep-pocketed couture lovers. Think Jimmy Choo, Prada and Dior. Nice touch: two food courts with terraces overlooking a pond.

Souk Qaryat Al Beri MARKET
(☎02-558 1670; www.soukqaryatalberi.com; Khor Al Maqta; ⏲10am-10pm Sat-Wed, to 11pm Thu, 3-11pm Fri) This 21st-century take on the classic souq gets a thumbs-up for its appealing Arabian architecture and waterfront location. The shops, which are popular with tourists and locals, stock many items with roots in Arabia, including oil-based perfumes, cookies made with camel milk, chocolate-covered dates and hand-crafted jewellery. Some small stalls sell souvenirs and craft items. Next to Shangri-La Hotel.

Yas Mall MALL
(Map p346; ☎toll free 800 927 6255; www.yasmall.ae; Yas West; ⏲10am-10pm Sat-Wed, to midnight Thu & Fri; 📶) Bright and spacious and with trees and a growing plant wall, Yas Mall is the latest addition to the Abu Dhabi mega-shopping scene. Look out for two 12m-high tree-themed sculptures by acclaimed South African artist Marco Cianfanelli, with leaves inspired by Arabic calligraphy. There's access to Ferrari World, cinemas, Xtreme Zone entertainment and a Géant hypermarket.

ℹ Orientation

The city of Abu Dhabi occupies an island connected to the mainland by three bridges: Sheikh Zayed Bridge, linking Hwy E10 (Abu Dhabi–Dubai Rd) with Sheikh Zayed bin Sultan St, which culminates in an eponymous 4.2km-long tunnel in the city centre; Al Maqta Bridge, which connects Hwy E22 (Abu Dhabi–Al Ain Rd) and Hwy E20 (Airport Rd) with Rashid bin Saeed (2nd) St; and Mussafah Bridge, which links Hwys E20 and E22 with Al Khaleej Al Arabi (30th) St. All main roads run through the Abu Dhabi city centre and culminate at the Corniche.

The airport is about 30km east of the Corniche, close to Yas Island, which is accessed by Hwy E12 (Sheikh Khalifa Hwy) and continues to Saadiyat Island to eventually link up with the Corniche via Sheikh Khalifa Bridge.

ℹ Information

Abu Dhabi Tourism Authority (ADTA; ☎toll free 800 555; www.visitabudhabi.ae) Maintains information desks in the airport arrivals hall (7am to 1am), in Yas Mall (near the entrance to Ferrari World, ☎11am to 8pm Tuesday to Sunday) and at the World Trade Center Souk (☎10am to 8pm).

Abu Dhabi Central Post Office (Map p348; ☎600 599 599; http://epg.gov.ae; cnr Al Sharqi & 4th Sts; ⏲7.30am-9pm Sat-Thu, 5-9pm Fri) Main post office.

Sheikh Khalifa Medical City (Map p348; ☎02-819 0000; www.seha.ae; cnr Al Karama St) One of many well-equipped hospitals in Abu Dhabi with 24-hour emergency service.

Getting There & Away

AIR

Abu Dhabi International Airport (p390) is about 30km east of the city centre and served by over 50 airlines flying to 85 cities. It has three terminals, including Etihad's exclusive base, Terminal 3. A vast expansion, the Midfield Terminal, is expected to be completed in 2017. Free wi-fi throughout.

BUS

The central **bus terminal** (Map p346; Sheikh Rashid bin Saeed St), at the corner of 4th and 11th Sts, is about 4km south of the Corniche. RTA bus E100 leaves for Dubai's **Al Ghubaiba bus station** (p329) in Bur Dubai every 30 minutes from 5.30am to 10.30pm (Dh25, two hours).

The Abu Dhabi Department of Transportation operates numerous services within the emirate. Destinations include:

DESTINATION	FARE (DH)	TIME (HOURS)	FREQUENCY
Al Ain (X90)	25	2¼	half-hourly
Jebel Dhanna (X87)	35	3½	up to 4 daily
Madinat Zayed (X60)	25	2½	every 2hr
Mezaira'a (X60)	30	3¼	every 2hr

CAR

Abu Dhabi is 150km south of Dubai via Hwy E11. All the international car-rental agencies have branches at the airport and within the city.

TAXI

A **taxi** (☎600-535 353; www.transad.ae) ride to Dubai or Al Ain costs between Dh250 and Dh300 and can be booked in advance.

Getting Around

TO/FROM THE AIRPORT

Air-conditioned bus A1 picks up from outside the arrivals area of all terminals every 40 minutes around the clock (one hour, Dh4) and travels via the central bus station all the way into town as far as Al Zahiyah.

Etihad passengers can use free shuttle buses to and from Dubai and Al Ain (show your boarding pass).

Taxis cost Dh70 to Dh80 for the half-hour trip to the city centre, including flagfall of Dh20.

If you're leaving on Etihad, Gulf, Cathay Pacific, Air Berlin and a few other airlines, you may be able to check your luggage and pick up a boarding pass between four and 24 hours before departure at four remote check-in locations: the **City Terminal** (Map p348; ☎02-644 8434; www.abudhabiairport.ae; 10th St; fare Dh4; ⏲24hr, buses every 40min) near Abu Dhabi Mall, Adnec, Park Rotana and the Crowne Plaza on Yas Island.

BUS

Abu Dhabi City Bus (☎800 55 555; dot.abudhabi.ae; within Abu Dhabi Dh2) operates on 14 routes around the clock. Useful services include bus 5, which links the Marina Mall with Al Maryah Island via Al Zahiya, and bus 54, which travels from Al Zahiya to the Sheikh Zayed Grand Mosque. For more routes and other details, call or check the website.

The fare is Dh2 per ride. In 2015, a new rechargeable smart card called Hafilat was introduced. Of several card types available, the Temporary Card (Dh5, valid for 14 days) is the most useful to visitors. It is available from vending machines at bus stops, shopping malls and customer-care centres. Hold up your Hafilat card to the validator upon boarding and exiting the bus.

TAXI

Taxis (☎600 535 353) are metered and charge Dh3.50 at flagfall plus Dh1.60 per kilometre. Between 10pm and 6am rates climb to Dh4 and Dh1.69, respectively, and a Dh10 minimum fare comes into effect. Cabs can be flagged down or ordered through the call centre (Dh8 fee).

Uber (www.uber.com) operates a chauffeur service with a minimum fare of Dh35 plus Dh2.50 per kilometre or Dh1.50 if travelling under 18km/h. You need to download the free Uber app to use this service.

Careem (www.careem.com) matches customers to private drivers closest to them. Cars can be booked online or via the free app. Fares are the same as Uber's and are charged to a credit card.

Al Ain العين

☎03 / POP 650,000

About two hours east of Abu Dhabi, Al Ain is fed by natural springs and set among oases and plantations, garnering it the nickname 'Garden City'. The birthplace of UAE founding father Sheikh Zayed was once a vital stop on the caravan route between Oman and the Gulf. Visitors flock to its forts, museums, zoo, Unesco sites and central date-palm oasis. A highlight is the drive up the mountain road serpentining to the top of Jebel Hafeet, treating you to sweeping views of the arid splendour that is the Empty Quarter along the way.

Al Ain rubs up against the town of Buraimi across the Omani border. Those who are not citizens of the Gulf Cooperation Council (GCC) must use the Hili border crossing in northern Al Ain. However, don't expect to make a quick dip across the border. You first need to pay a fee of Dh35 to leave the UAE and drive (or take a cab) east 40km to the Omani border post at Wadi Al Jizi to obtain your Omani visa for OR5. There is no fee to re-enter the UAE. GCC citizens can use the more central Al Mudeef crossing.

Sights

Al Ain is quite tough to navigate thanks to its many roundabouts. Brown signs directing visitors to the major tourist attractions are helpful, but a few more wouldn't hurt.

★ Al Jahili Fort HISTORIC SITE

(☎03-784 3996; Mohammed bin Khalifa St; 9am-5pm Tue-Sun) FREE Surrounded by a lush park, this fairytale fort was constructed in the 1890s as the summer residence of Sheikh Zayed I (1836–1909) and expanded by the British in the 1950s. The original parts are the square fort in the far-left corner of the courtyard and the wedding-cake-tiered tower opposite. Today the compound houses a tourist centre and a superb exhibit of photographs taken by British explorer Sir Wilfred Thesiger during his multiple crossings of the Empty Desert in the 1940s.

Al Ain Palace Museum MUSEUM

(☎03-751 7755; Al Ain St; ⏲8.30am-7.30pm Sat, Sun & Tue-Thu, 3-7.30pm Fri) FREE This nicely restored, rambling palace was Sheikh Zayed's residence from 1937 until 1966. The simple yet elegant cinnamon-coloured compound is divided into private, guest and official quarters by courtyards and landscaped with cacti, magnolia trees and palms. You can step inside the *majlis* (meeting room) where Zayed received visitors, roam around the huge kitchen, see the canopied matrimonial bed and snap a photo of the Land Rover he used to visit the desert Bedu.

Al Ain National Museum MUSEUM

(☎03-764 1595; Zayed bin Sultan St; adult/child Dh3/1; ⏲8.30am-7.30pm Sat, Sun & Tue-Thu, 3-7.30pm Fri) This charmingly old-fashioned museum is perfect for boning up on the ancient past of the Al Ain region. Highlights of the archaeological section include weapons, jewellery, pottery and coins excavated from 4000-year-old tombs at nearby Al Hili and Umm Al Nar. The ethnography galleries zero in on various aspects of the daily life of the Bedu and settled people, including education, marriage and farming.

There is some beautiful silver jewellery, traditional costumes and a harrowing display of simple surgical instruments with lots of sharp points and hooks – ouch!

★ Al Ain Zoo ZOO

(☎03-799 2000; www.alainzoo.ae; adult/child Dh30/10; ⏲9am-8pm Sat-Wed, to 9pm Thu & Fri Oct-Apr, 4-10pm May-Sep) The region's largest and most acclaimed zoo has modern, spacious enclosures inhabited by indigenous and exotic species. Observe grazing Arabian oryx, big-horned Barbary sheep, lazy crocodiles, tigers and lions and dozens of other species, some of them born at the zoo, which has a well-respected conservation and breeding program. Special treats for tots include the petting zoo, bird shows and giraffe feedings. The zoo is off Zayed Al Awwal and Nahyan Al Awwal Sts.

Al Ain Camel Market MARKET

(Zayed bin Sultan St; ⏲7am-sunset) FREE It's dusty, noisy, pungent and chaotic, but never mind: Al Ain's famous camel market is a wonderful immersion in traditional Arabic culture. All sorts of camels are holed up in pens, from wobbly legged babies that might grow up to be racers to imposing studs kept for breeding. The intense haggling is fun to watch. Trading takes place in the morning, but it's usually possible to see the corralled animals all day long.

Some traders may offer to give you a tour (for money), but you're totally free to walk around on your own. Taking photographs will also elicit requests for payment. Haggling should bring the often exorbitant asking price down to Dh10 or Dh20. Women should dress conservatively.

The market is about 8km south of central Al Ain, behind Bawadi Mall.

Activities

Wadi Adventure WATER PARK

(☎03-781 8422; www.wadiadventure.ae; Jebel Al Hafeet St; adult/child Dh50/25, attractions Dh25-150; ⏲11am-8pm Sun-Thu, 10am-8pm Fri & Sat) Unleash your inner daredevil at this water park. Admission buys access to pools, restaurants and low-ropes course only. Make reservations to brave white water aboard a raft (Dh100 per 1½ hours), ride the 200m-long zip line (Dh50 per hour) or ride

Al Ain & Buraimi

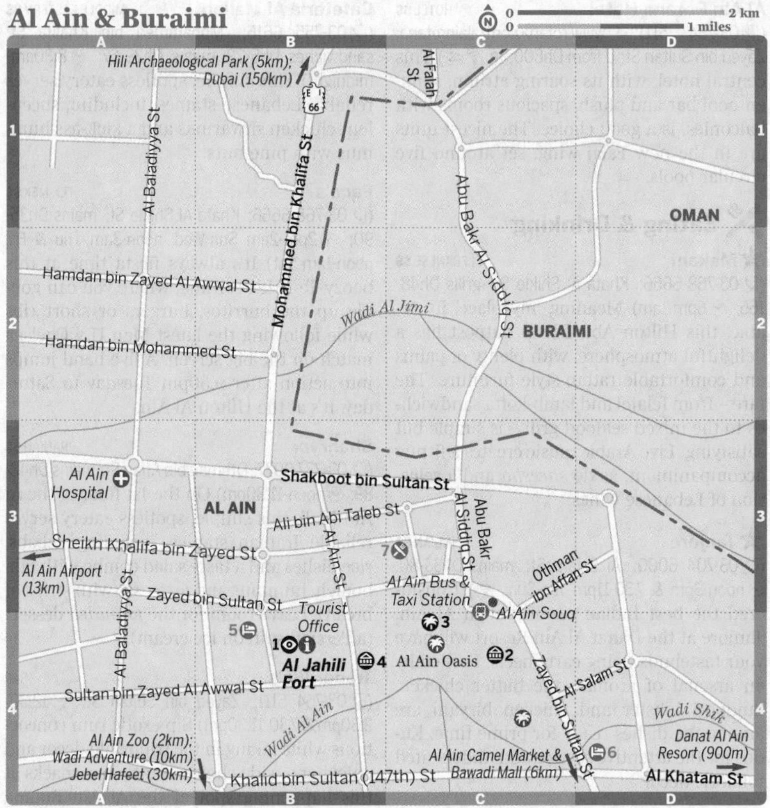

the giant swing with its stomach-turning 14m drop (Dh25).

Sleeping

★Hilton Al Ain HOTEL $$

(☎03-768 6666; www.placeshilton.com/al-ain; Khata Al Shikle St; d from Dh700; @☎≋) Al Ain's sentimental favourite has the usual comforts and amenities plus loads of character and smiley staff. Kick back in spacious rooms with balconies or work up an appetite in the big gym, the tennis court or the lap pool. Families like the kids' activities and separate pool with slides. It's near the junction of Khalid bin Sultan and Zayed bin Sultan Sts.

Danat Al Ain Resort RESORT $$

(☎03-704 6000; http://alain.danathotels.com; Al Salam St; r from Dh850; P☎≋) Set within flowery gardens, this family-friendly resort has an attractive pool with slides and a separate one for swimming laps. Newly slicked-up rooms sparkle in sophisticated shades of cream and chocolate and come with balcony, goosedown bedding and a coffee- and tea-making station.

Al Ain & Buraimi

Top Sights
1 Al Jahili Fort B4

Sights
2 Al Ain National Museum C4
3 Al Ain Oasis C4
4 Al Ain Palace Museum B4

Sleeping
5 Al Ain Rotana Hotel B4
6 Hilton Al Ain D4

Eating
7 Cafeteria Al Mallah C3
Paco's .... (see 6)

Al Ain Rotana Hotel HOTEL $$
(03-754 5111; www.rotana.com/alainrotana; Zayed bin Sultan St; d from Dh800; P) This central hotel, with its soaring atrium, sunken pool bar and plush, spacious rooms with balconies, is a good choice. The nicest units are in the new Falaj wing, set around five circular pools.

Eating & Drinking

★Makani LEBANESE $$
(03-768-6666; Khata Al Shikle St; grills Dh48-165; 6pm-1am) Meaning 'my place' in Arabic, this Hilton Abu Dhabi outpost has a delightful atmosphere, with plenty of palms and comfortable rattan-style furniture. The fare – from felafel and lamb-kofta sandwiches to the mixed seafood grill – is simple but satisfying. Live Arabic music creates a fitting accompaniment, as do *sheesha* and a selection of Lebanese wines.

★Tanjore INDIAN $$
(03-704 6000; Al Salam St; mains Dh33-80; noon-3pm & 7.30-11pm Tue-Sun;) Considered the best Indian restaurant in Al Ain, Tanjore at the Danat Al Ain Resort will have your tastebuds doing cartwheels. Fuelled by an arsenal of aromas, the butter chicken, tandoori lobster and chicken biryani are among the dishes ready for prime time. Kudos for the attentive service and understated folkloric decor.

Cafeteria Al Mallah MIDDLE EASTERN $$
(03-755 6616; Mohammed bin Khalifa St; sandwiches Dh5-22, mains Dh29-67; 8.30am-midnight) This simple, spotless eatery serves reliable Lebanese staples, including succulent chicken shwarmas and a kick-ass hummus with pine nuts.

Paco's TEX-MEX $$
(03-768 6666; Khata Al Shikle St; mains Dh35-90; 2pm-2am Sun-Wed, noon-3am Thu & Fri, noon-1am Sat) It's always fiesta time at this boozy Tex-Mex cantina, where you can gobble up the burritos, burgers or short ribs while following the latest Man U v Chelsea match on the big screen. A live band jumps into action after 9.30pm Tuesday to Saturday. It's at the Hilton Al Ain.

Shahryar IRANIAN $$
(03-737 0077; Othman bin Affan St; mains Dh48-89; noon-11.30pm) On the 1st floor of the Al Ain Mall, this simple, spotless eatery serves reliable Iranian staples, including kebabs, rice dishes and a tasty salad combo with tabbouleh, hummus and *fattoosh* (with strips of bread). Leave room for the *faloudeh* dessert (a Persian spin on ice cream).

Trader Vic's BAR
(03-754 5111; Zayed bin Sultan St; 12.30-3.30pm & 7.30-11.30pm) Sip exotic rum concoctions while taking in the trippy tiki decor and enjoying a wide choice of tasty bar snacks at this happening spot at the Al Ain Rotana Hotel. Still hungry? Then consider booking

AL AIN'S WORLD HERITAGE SITES

In June 2011, four sites in Al Ain became the first in the UAE to be inscribed on Unesco's World Heritage list thanks to their archaeological, cultural and historical significance. Aside from the locations described below, the honour includes the ancient dome-shaped tombs at the foot of Jebel Hafeet and the tombs at Bida Bint Saud, which are not yet open to visitors.

Al Ain Oasis (03-712 8429) FREE Eight gates lead into the great date plantations of this famous oasis, with some 150,000 trees of around 100 varieties. Simply wander around this tranquil, jungly maze, away from the hubbub of the city, and keep an eye out for the 3000-year-old falaj natural irrigation system lacing the grounds. It's easy to get lost – if you do, ask a security guard for a lift on a buggy (offer a tip). The oasis is off Zayed bin Sultan St.

Hili Archaeological Park (Mohammed Bin Khalifa St, Hili; 4.30am-9.30pm Sat-Thu, 10am-10pm Fri) FREE In the village of Al Hili, vestiges of a settlement and tombs dating back some 5000 years to the Umm Al Nar period open a window on early life in the region. Some 12km north of Al Ain, en route to Dubai, they've been integrated into a peaceful park. A highlight is the Great Hili Tomb, whose two entrances are decorated with carvings of humans and antelopes. Many of the items found here, including pottery and vessels, are now displayed at the Al Ain National Museum.

WORTH A TRIP

JEBEL HAFEET جبل حفيت

This jagged 1240m-high limestone mountain rears out of the plain south of Al Ain. Its arid crags are home to red foxes, feral cats and the rock hyrax, which resembles a large rabbit but is, improbably, related to the elephant. A 12km-long paved road, which is completely lit after dark, corkscrews to the **Mercure Grand Jebel Hafeet** (☎03-783 8888; www.mercure.com; nr top of Jebel Hafeet; r Dh850; P 🛜 ≋) and a couple of coffee shops at the summit. There are several pull-outs to admire the views along the way.

The green slopes at the bottom of the mountain are fed by natural hot mountain springs. A small resort with a lake and a giant fountain has grown up around the springs, with segregated bathing, camping and picnicking opportunities.

The mountain top is about 30km from central Al Ain, including the 12km stretch of mountain road. From the town centre, head west on Khalifa bin Zayed St towards the airport, then follow the brown signs.

a table for dinner, when a live Cuban band will get your toes tapping between courses.

ℹ Information

Tourist Office (☎03-784 3996; www.visitabudhabi.ae; Al Jahili Fort; ⊙9am-5pm Tue-Thu, Sat & Sun, 3-5pm Fri) Al Ain's tourist office is located inside the Al Jahili Fort and has lots of printed material about the town and the entire emirate of Abu Dhabi.

ℹ Getting There & Away

BUS

Al Ain's central **bus station** (off Zayed bin Sultan St) is off the Al Murabba roundabout opposite the Lulu Centre. Express bus X90 shuttles back and forth to Abu Dhabi every 30 minutes between 4.30am and 2.20am (Dh15, 1½ hours). Al Gazal runs minibuses between Al Ain and Dubai's Al Ghubaiba bus station in Bur Dubai hourly from 6.30am to 11.30pm (Dh20). From Sharjah's Al Jubail bus station, bus 117 departs every 45 minutes between 7am and 10.45pm (Dh30).

CAR

From Dubai, it's 150km south to Al Ain via Hwy E66. Coming from Abu Dhabi, head east on Hwy E22 for about 160km. Europcar, Avis and Hertz are among the car-rental agencies with branches in Al Ain.

TAXI

Taxis to Dubai or Abu Dhabi are about Dh200.

ℹ Getting Around

Al Ain has an extensive network of public buses that run roughly every 30 minutes from 5am to midnight at Dh2 per trip. Check dot.abudhabi.ae (click through to Eastern Region Bus Services) for routes and schedules.

Taxis are metered; most in-town rides cost between Dh10 and Dh20.

Al Gharbia الغربية

The desert is a land of contradictions: vast yet intimate, barren yet beautiful, searing yet restorative. In short, it's a special, spiritual, almost mystical place that's often so whisper-quiet it feels as though someone has pushed the mute button. So if you really want to get away from it all, steer your pony south and west of Abu Dhabi into the Al Gharbia region, which is all desert, all the time. There are two main areas: the Liwa Oasis and Sir Bani Yas Island on the far western coast.

Madinat Zayed مدينة زايد

En route to the Liwa Oasis, you'll likely pass through Madinat Zayed, the largest town in the Al Gharbia region. Along the main commercial strip, you'll find ATMs, internet cafes, a hospital, a petrol station, Al Dhafra Co-op supermarket and the City Mall.

Madinat Zayed is famous for its **Al Dhafra Festival** (www.aldhafrafestival.com; Madinat Zayed; ⊙late Dec), which runs for 11 days and brings up to 25,000 long-legged dromedaries into town. Aside from camel races and a camel beauty contest, there are other competitions involving falcons, classic cars, Arabian horses and Arabian salukis (dogs), along with heritage activities, auctions, a traditional souq and merriment of all sorts.

Madinat Zayed also has its own **camel race track** just south of town, with races usually taking place on Fridays between October and March. Overlooking the dunes is the **Tilal Liwa Hotel** (☎02-894 6111; tilalliwa.danathotels.com; Million St, Madinat Zayed; r from Dh550; P 🛜 ≋), a modern and comfortable fort-style retreat where you can count the colours of the desert through a giant arch spanning the infinity pool.

About 6km south, en route to Liwa, you'll drive past the **Shams 1 solar plant**, one of the largest in the world, which went live in 2013 and provides power for thousands of homes.

Madinat Zayed is about 180km southwest of Abu Dhabi via Hwy E11 west and E45 south. From here, it's another 45km to Mezaira'a, the main town in the Liwa Oasis. Bus X60 from Abu Dhabi stops in Madinat Zayed en route to Mezaira'a (Dh25, every two hours).

Liwa Oasis ليوا

Approximately 250km south of Abu Dhabi, the Liwa Oasis is a 150km arc of villages and farms hugging the edge of Saudi Arabia's Empty Quarter (Rub' al-Khali), which truly lives up to its name: the odd roaming camel or small verdant oasis magnifies just how magnificent this endless landscape of undulating sand dunes, shimmering in shades of gold, apricot and cinnamon, really is.

This is the Arabia described by explorer Sir Wilfred Thesiger, but it's also the birthplace of the Al Maktoum and Al Nahyan families, now the rulers of Dubai and Abu Dhabi respectively. Once you visit, you'll understand why the Liwa Oasis has a special place in the hearts of nationals, who come here to get back to their roots, relax and just take in the arid splendour of this glorious landscape.

The commercial heart of the oasis is Mezaira'a, with activity centered on the junction of Hwy E43 from Madinat Zayed and Hwy E90, the main road through the oasis. Here you'll find a gas station, an ATM, a supermarket and a hospital.

Sights & Activities

The Liwa Oasis is best visited in your own vehicle, as the joy of travelling here is to be able to drive through the villages and stop spontaneously to photograph a lone camel, a proud fort or a beautiful 'desert rose' (flower-like crystallised gypsum).

Along the main road (Hwy E90), the most spectacular stretch is between Hameem and Mezaira'a. The dunes here are like shifting mountain ranges of sand, with green farms creating an occasional and unexpected patchwork effect. The landscape west of Mezaira'a, towards Karima, is flatter and more open.

Moreeb Dune LANDMARK

Soaring almost 300m high, Moreeb (whose name translates as 'scary mountain') is one of the world's tallest dunes. To get there, turn left at the second roundabout, about 5km west of central Mezaira'a, and keep right when you reach the Liwa Resthouse. Continue along this well-signposted, paved road for about 20 minutes; signs will say 'Moreeb Dune' or 'Tal Mireb'. The dune is where the road ends – you can't miss it!

Fish Farm FARM

At this fish farm near Khanur, you can buy fresh tilapia, carp and other fish and grill it up at your campsite later on. The turn-off for Khanur is about 20km west of Mezaira'a. Ask locally for directions to the farm.

Festivals & Events

Liwa International Festival SPORTS

(www.agsc.ae; usually Jan) The large, flat area at the base of the Moreeb Dune is the staging ground of the Liwa International Festival, featuring car and bike races alongside shooting competitions, falcon and camel racing and a classic car show.

Liwa Date Festival FOOD

(Liwa Oasis; Jul) The quest for the best date is on at this weeklong festival, which also features cooking competitions, a souq and a kids' tent. These are accompanied by various competitions, including one for the most beautiful date (the fruit, that is).

Sleeping & Eating

Camping is hugely popular in the Liwa Oasis, although there are no designated campgrounds. If you do decide to camp, make sure to take out all your trash. Discarded rubbish, especially anything made of plastic, is highly dangerous when ingested by camels and other local wildlife. If you don't have camping gear, you can get fully kitted out at **Liwa Oasis Picnic** (050-812 0288; Mezaira'a), with three branches in the oasis: one in central Mezaira'a, another in the Jefn industrial area en route to Moreeb Hill and one at the dune itself.

The best place to stock up on food and water is **Al Dhafra Hypermarket** (02-884 6065; www.adcs.ae; Mezaira'a; 8am-9pm), at the end of a commercial strip on the road to Madinat Zayed, next to the 24-hour petrol station. The market also has an ATM.

OFF THE BEATEN TRACK

EMIRATES NATIONAL AUTO MUSEUM

Like a kooky mirage, a pyramid-shaped structure rises from the desert sands some 45km south of Abu Dhabi on the lonely highway that leads to the Liwa Oasis. **Emirates National Auto Museum** (☎055-749 2155; www.enam.ae; Hwy E65; adult/child Dh50/free; ⏲10am-6pm) holds the private car collection of Sheikh Hamad bin Hamdan Al Nahyan, aka the 'Rainbow Sheikh': some 200 vehicles – from prototypes to concept cars to American classics – the oldest being a steam-powered Mercedes from 1885. The newest addition is a wall of glass-encased SUVs outside the facility.

In 1983 Sheikh Hamad bought seven Mercedes 500 SELs, painted in the colours of the rainbow for each day of the week. The car park is the resting place of several iconic vehicles, including the sheikh's monster truck, an eight-bedroom motor home complete with balcony, and the Globe Trailer dubbed the 'earth on wheels'.

Liwa Resthouse GUESTHOUSE $
(☎02-882 2075; fax 02-882 9311; Mezaira'a; d from Dh200; P) This government-run resthouse is frill-free and functional but run by friendly folk. Faded furnishings, including an ancient TV and a fridge, characterise the big rooms. A cafeteria serves three meals a day. To get here, head west of Mezaira'a and pass through the unmarked gate at the second roundabout, just past the local police office. Cash only.

★**Qasr Al Sarab Desert Resort by Anantara** RESORT $$$
(☎02-886 2088; http://qasralsarab.anantara.com; 1 Qasr Al Sarab Rd; r from Dh1740; P 📶 🏊) This discreet retreat near Hameem perfectly captures the desert vibe and blends seamlessly into its surroundings. Earth-toned rooms are decorated with original Bedouin artefacts – as is the resort throughout – and have balconies looking out over the dunes. There are three restaurants, two bars, a relaxing spa, a library, a huge free-form swimming pool with canopied day beds and various outdoor activities.

There's nothing at all around here, but with so many amenities, you're at no risk of getting bored.

Liwa Hotel HOTEL $$$
(☎02-882 2000; www.almarfapearlhotels.com/liwa; Mezaira'a; r from Dh1750; P 📶 🏊) This hilltop contender set amid gardens offers dust-free respite after a day in the desert. Enjoy sunset drinks on your balcony facing a palace of the late Sheikh Zayed's (itself on a green sand dune!). Even the standard rooms are huge and have subdued colours and retro-chic charm. A 24-hour coffee shop serves light meals and international favourites. Alcohol available.

ℹ Getting There & Around

BUS

Bus X60 travels every two hours to Mezaira'a from Abu Dhabi's central bus station via Madinat Zayed (Dh30, 3¼ hours). From Mezaira'a, local bus 640 travels west along Hwy 90 as far as Arrada Farms, while bus 650 goes east to Hammeem Farms. There is no public transport to Moreeb Hill.

CAR

All the main roads are fit for 2WD vehicles, but you'll need a 4WD to go off-road.

Coming from Abu Dhabi, head west on Hwy E11 and turn south on Hwy E65 to Hameem or E45 to go via Madinat Zayed. The total trip is 250km either way. There are petrol stations on Hwy E65 at the Emirates National Auto Museum, in Tarif on Hwy E11 and in Madinat Zayed. In the Liwa Oasis you'll find gas in Hameem, in Mezaira'a, near the Khanur turnoff, and in Umm Hisin.

From Jebel Dhanna/Ruwais, the long and lonely Hwy E15 also goes to the oasis; gas is available in Ghayathi.

Abu Dhabi to Sila

Linking Abu Dhabi with Sila on the border with Saudi Arabia is Hwy E11, a mind-numbing, 350km-long, dual-carriage highway. The road is flanked by palm trees and fences, beyond which lie the emirate's rich oil and gas fields. The main reason to travel along here is to get to Sir Bani Yas Island.

A good spot to break the journey after a couple of hours is **Mirfa**, a low-key, sleepy fishing village with a nice sandy beach. The town comes to life in April during the 10-day **Al Gharbia Watersports Festival** (www.algharbiafestivals.com; Mirfa; ⏲Apr/May), which sees kite-surfing, sailing and

SUBLIME SAND DUNES

Avoid dull drives on drab roads by taking the following routes through stunning desert scenery.

Liwa: Abu Dhabi to Hameem (mostly Hwy E65) Take pleasure in the peach-and-cinnamon dunes dotted with date-palm oases. Take the road to Hameem instead of the main route via Madinat Zayed; the turn-off is about 20km out of Abu Dhabi on the Mussafah to Tarif road.

Liwa: Liwa Resthouse to Moreeb Hill (Tal Mireb) Marvel at these enormous apricot-coloured dunes on the edge of the Empty Quarter – the largest you'll see in the UAE.

Mahafiz: Sharjah to Kalba Rd (Hwy E102) Count the camels, if you can! See how they blend into the sands along the S116 as it winds east past camel farms to Kalba on the Gulf of Oman.

Al Ain: Dubai to Al Ain Rd (Hwy E66) Be amazed by the big tangerine dunes on the approach to Al Ain around Shabat. To truly appreciate them you'll have to pull over to get a look through the roadside greenery.

Shwaib: Al Ain to Hatta Rd (Hwy E55) Graceful gazelles leap through desert shrubs on the big, red dunes in the grounds of a sheikh's palace at Shwaib. From Al Ain, head north on E66 towards Dubai for about 50km, then cut right to Shwaib; drive down into the town to see rugged mountains on your right and gazelles on your left.

swimming competitions along with dhow and dragon-boat racing. If you want to stay, steer towards the falcon-shaped **Mirfa Hotel** (☎02-895 3000; www.almarfapearlhotels.com/mirfa; Hwy E11, Mirfa; r from Dh870; P 📶 🏊), which has big rooms with sea views and a nice pool with a swim-up bar.

If you had any doubt as to the oil wealth of the UAE, it'll evaporate when you see **Ruwais**, an industrial town about an hour past Mirfa that exists only to service the massive refineries set up along there. Needless to say, there's little reason to stop.

Not far from Ruwais is **Jebel Dhanna**, the jumping-off point for Sir Bani Yas Island. It has absolutely gorgeous white sandy beaches and shallow azure water perfect for the kids to splash around. An unexpected high-end treat is the five-star **Danat Jebel Dhanna Resort** (☎02-801 2222; jebeldhanna.danathotels.com; Jebel Dhanna; r from Dh1900; P 📶 🏊), where you can lounge in hammocks, relax by the pool, hit the tennis courts or rent a kayak. There's a cafe, a buffet restaurant, fine Italian fare at **Zaitoun** (☎02-801 2222; jebeldhanna.danathotels.com/en/zaitoun; pizza & pasta Dh60-100, mains Dh90-200), a bar and a club that's popular with expat workers from Ruwais.

Workers are also the main clientele of the adjacent **Dhafra Beach Hotel** (☎02-801 2000; dhafrabeach.danathotels.com; Jebel Dhanna; r from Dh720; P 📶), which does little to hide the fact that it's three decades old. Staying here gives you full access to the Danat Jebel Dhanna Resort's facilities, though.

As remote as it is, there are buses going out here from Abu Dhabi's central bus station. Bus X87 makes the trip all the way to the ferry terminal in Jebel Dhanna in 3½ hours (Dh35, up to four daily). Bus X80 goes to Mirfa (Dh25, every two hours).

If you're driving, note that, even though the region is surrounded by oil fields, there's a dearth of petrol stations, so take every opportunity to refuel – Hwy E11 is not a good place to run out of gas.

Sir Bani Yas Island جزيرة صير بني ياس

A great way to shake off the stresses nibbling at your psyche is by taking a trip to Sir Bani Yas Island and contemplating life surrounded by a luxurious resort, free-roaming animals and the calm azure waters of the Gulf.

In the remote far west of the country, this 87-sq-km desert island was originally Sheikh Zayed's private retreat. It was his love of animals that inspired him to turn it into a nature reserve and to bring many native species back from the brink of extinction. Today, 60% of the island is home to 13,000 free-roaming indigenous and introduced animals, including sand gazelles, Barbary sheep, ostriches and even giraffes and cheetahs. Rarities include the Indian blackbuck, an antelope that can reach speeds of up to 90km/h, and several species of oryx, including the Arabian oryx, one of the world's most endangered animals.

Abu Dhabi's royal family still maintains two palaces in the island's south, but if they forgot to send your invitation, you can still visit by staying at one of the island's three full-service resorts. Activities on the island range from archery and snorkelling to horse riding and nature walks and drives.

A limited number of day trips can be arranged, although usually on weekdays only. Check details with the property directly. Note that you cannot visit the island without a reservation at a resort or at least for a tour or activity.

Activities

Nature & Wildlife Drive DRIVING TOUR

(02-801 5266; Sir Bani Yas Island; adult/2-12yr Dh250/100; tours 7am, 9am, 11am, 2pm & 4pm) If you only do one thing while on the island, make it this two-hour safari around the savannah-like interior. Guides are very knowledgeable about the fauna and flora and will often go out of their way to find critters for you to look at. Try to get an early-morning or late-afternoon tour, when the animals are at their most active.

Sir Bani Yas Stables HORSE RIDING

(Sir Bani Yas Island; rides Dh250-500; rides 7am, 9am & 4pm) For an intimate nature encounter, book a horseback ride at the state-of-the-art Sir Bani Yas Stables. Guides will match the horse to your level of experience and kit you out with shoes, chaps and a helmet before taking you on a ride along the beach or through the bush.

Anantara Spa SPA

(02-801 5400; desertislands.anantara.com/spas; Desert Islands Resort & Spa by Anantara, Sir Bani Yas Island; massages from Dh450; 10am-10pm) A great relaxation station is the lush Anantara Spa, where you can choose from an extensive massage and treatment menu to work out the kinks and turn you into a glowing centre of tranquility. Options include a jet-lag massage, a mother-to-be massage and an emerald-gemstone massage.

Sleeping

Desert Islands Resort & Spa by Anantara RESORT $$$

(02-801 5400; desertislands.anantara.com; Sir Bani Yas Island; r from Dh2650;) At this ultra-deluxe resort you'll sleep sweetly in elegantly exotic, oversized rooms hued in calming brown, beige and dark red. There's tasteful regional art throughout and private balconies overlooking the flower-filled garden, free-form infinity pool and the shimmering sea. Deep-pocket types in need of extra privacy can rent their own pool villa.

Al Yamm Villa Resort RESORT $$$

(02-801 4200; al-yamm.anantara.com; Sir Bani Yas Island; r from Dh2350;) This villa cluster on the eastern shore of Sir Bani Yas Island sports breezy Mediterranean flair. Wriggle your toes in the soft, white sand from your private porch and count the flamingos flapping over the open sea. Bonus points for the stylish freestanding oval tubs. The on-site restaurant serves fine Italian fare.

Al Sahel Villa Resort RESORT $$$

(02-801 4300; al-sahel.anantara.com; Sir Bani Yas Island; r from Dh2100;) On the island's western side, in the middle of the savannah, this luxe complex pretty much guarantees you animal sightings from your African-themed chalet. Each of the 30 villas has a thatched roof with open-beam cathedral ceiling, a four-poster bed and a colour scheme that perfectly matches the surroundings. The on-site restaurant specialises in grilled meats and fish.

Eating

Al Shams INTERNATIONAL $$

(02-801 5400; desertislands.anantara.com/al-shams; Desert Islands Resort & Spa by Anantara, Sir Bani Yas Island; mains Dh40-90; noon-10.30pm;) This casual all-day eatery and lounge-bar at the Desert Islands Resort & Spa overlooks the pool and serves fresh salads, pasta, a great burger, fish and chips and other snacks and light meals. After 5pm you can also relax with a *sheesha*.

Olio ITALIAN $$$

(02-801 4200; al-sahel.anantara.com/olio; Al Sahel Villa Resort, Sir Bani Yas Island; mains Dh95-195; 7am-10.30pm;) Expect a festival of flavours at this cosily elegant charmer with seaside views where stars on the Italian menu range from roast black cod to traditional tiramisu.

Getting There & Away

AIR

Rotana Jet (www.rotanajet.com) flies to Sir Bani Yas in about an hour from Terminal 2 at Abu Dhabi International Airport from Tuesday to Saturday and from Dubai's new Al Maktoum International Airport in Jebel Ali every Monday, Thursday and Saturday. The round trip starts at Dh400.

You can also charter a private seaplane with **Seawings** (www.seawings.ae) for a cool Dh11,500.

BOAT

From the Jebel Dhanna ferry jetty, boats make the 20-minute trip to the island at 7pm and then every two hours between 10am and 8pm. From Thursday to Saturday, there's also a boat at 10.30pm. A minivan will take you to the Desert Islands Resort & Spa in another 20 minutes.

BUS

Bus X87 makes it out to the ferry jetty from Abu Dhabi's central bus station four times daily (Dh35, 3½ hours).

CAR

The Jebel Dhanna ferry jetty is about a 250km drive west of Abu Dhabi and 370km southwest of Dubai via Hwy E11. Past Ruwais, follow the signs to the jetty.

If you want someone else to do the driving, ask the resort to arrange a limo service, which starts at Dh650 from Abu Dhabi and Dh1000 from Dubai.

EAST COAST

Time seems to move at a much slower pace on the UAE's eastern coast, whose beaches are a popular getaway for nationals and expats keen to escape the razzmatazz in their daily lives. Although there are a few five-star resorts, the vibe is decidedly old school and low key. International tourism has suffered, as visitors prefer the glitzy resorts of Dubai or the new properties of up-and-coming neighbouring emirate of Ras Al Khaimah.

Facing the Indian Ocean (more specifically, the Gulf of Oman), the east coast belongs almost entirely to the emirate of Fujairah, interrupted only by the three small Sharjah enclaves of Dibba Al Hisn, Khor Fakkan and Kalba. While the businesslike capital, Fujairah, has a couple of heritage sites, tourism is concentrated further north, especially around Al Aqah, where the rugged Hajar Mountains dip down to long, sandy beaches with excellent swimming, snorkelling and diving.

South of Khor Fakkan, industry replaces idyll thanks to massive container ports and a new oil-export terminal just outside Fujairah. Nearly two million barrels of oil from fields in the UAE's western desert arrive here daily via a 370km-long pipeline.

Several archaological sites, some dating back 4000 years, provide evidence of the coast's long and turbulent history. The legacy of the Portuguese, who swarmed the area in the 16th century to control the spice trade, survives in a handful of forts.

Fujairah City الفجيرة

09 / POP 192,000

Fujairah City is the emirate's business and commercial hub. Office buildings line its main strip, Hamad bin Abdullah Rd, while its northern waterfront is hemmed in by vast fields of circular oil-storage containers. Still, the town is worth a stop, if only to get a sense of Fujairah's past at the restored fort and the adjacent museum. Locals are also proud of several developments: the massive, gleaming white Sheikh Zayed Mosque, the emirate's first big shopping mall (Fujairah City Centre mall) and the Sheikh Khalifa Hwy to Dubai.

Sights

★Fujairah Fort HISTORIC SITE

(cnr Al Nakheel & Al Salam Rds; usually 9am-1pm) FREE Draped over a rocky mound above vestiges of Fujairah's old village and a date-palm oasis, this restored fort looks splendid, especially when floodlit at night. Built from mud, gravel, wood and gypsum in the 16th century, it's a compact composition of circular and square towers that aided in its defence. There's usually a caretaker around in the morning to open the heavy teak door, so you can climb up the towers and ramparts for great views.

Fujairah Museum MUSEUM

(09-222 9085; cnr Al Nakheel & Al Salam Rds; adult/child Dh5/1; 8am-6.30pm Sat-Thu, 2.30-6.30pm Fri) This old-school local-history museum does little to meaningfully display and label its significant collection of archae-

DIVING THE EAST COAST

The East Coast offers the best diving in the UAE, mainly reefs and a few wrecks, with many fun sites close to shore. If you're lucky you'll encounter green sea turtles and black-tip reef sharks among large schools of fish. The best time to go is in the morning, as the tide may cloud the water around midday, and afternoon winds may make it choppy. Also watch out for jellyfish.

Most resorts along here have a PADI-accredited dive centre that rents snorkelling gear, does diving certification and organises diving and snorkelling trips, including to the Musandam Peninsula. Rates vary slightly, but expect to pay from Dh350 for a two-dive trip including full equipment. Snorkelling gear rents for around Dh100 per day. More experienced divers should check out locally owned **Scuba 2000** (☎09-238 8477; www.scuba-2000.com; Al Badiyah Beach, Hwy 99; ⏰9am-7pm), about 1km north of Badiyah's mosque, which also provides simple lodging for Dh200 (nondivers Dh250).

ological finds from such tombs as those at Badiyah, Dibba and Qidfa (including vessels, arrowheads and carnelian beads), thus leaving visitors scratching their heads as to what they're actually looking at. Other halls, including the last two, with ornate baroque-style ceilings, are crammed with ethnographic items like weapons, costumes and Bedouin jewellery.

Sheikh Zayed Mosque MOSQUE
(cnr Al Ittihad & Al Salam Sts) After the one in Abu Dhabi, Fujairah's grand new mosque is the second largest in the UAE. Festooned with six 100m-high minarets, the white granite and marble edifice can accommodate up to 28,000 worshippers. It's not open to non-Muslims, but the impressive exterior alone warrants a look.

Al Hayl Fort HISTORIC SITE
(Al Hayl) FREE Built around 1830, this well-preserved fort is tucked deep into the jagged Hajar Mountains near the village of Al Hayl, about 13km southwest of Fujairah. There's usually a caretaker to show you around (tip appreciated). To get there (usually possible without 4WD), turn south off Sheikh Khalifa bin Zayed Hwy near the new Fujairah City Centre mall and follow signs. Best when the sun is low.

Sleeping

Novotel Fujairah HOTEL $
(☎09-203 4851; Hamad bin Abdullah Rd; r from Dh250; P 📶 🏊) Central and well run, this newish hotel offers copious comforts typically reserved for posher players, including a large and modern gym, a swimming pool and a kids' club. Rooms are comfortable and come with blue and purple colour accents and modern art.

★**Hilton Fujairah Resort** RESORT $$
(☎09-222 2411; www.hilton.com; Al Faseel Rd; r from Dh650; P 📶 🏊) Easygoing and impeccably maintained, this characterful property packs all the amenities of a full resort into a compact frame, including a gym, tennis courts and a children's playground. It's also your only in-town beachfront choice. Other assets include a killer breakfast buffet, a fall-over-backwards staff and the Breezes lounge-restaurant above a sandy strip. Space cravers and families should book a chalet.

Eating & Drinking

Nalukettu SOUTH INDIAN $
(☎09-222 3070; Hamad bin Abdullah Rd; mains Dh13-36; ⏰noon-3pm & 6.30pm-midnight; 📶) The decor is a bit worn, but the pungently flavoured dishes from the South Indian province of Kerala are fresh and authentic in this licensed restaurant at the City Plaza Hotel. Menu stars include the prawns masala and the deep-fried chicken. During busy times, the staff can be a bit overwhelmed.

★**Breezes** INTERNATIONAL $$
(☎09-222 2411; www.hilton.com; Al Faseel Rd; dishes Dh50-160; ⏰noon-11pm; 📶) On a balmy night, there's no better place for cocktails or a meal than Breezes at the Hilton Fujairah Resort. At the town's only beachfront restaurant, the menu revolves around pasta, burgers and salads, although top honours go to the big seafood platter. At night, the sparkling string of container ships waiting to enter Fujairah port make the setting strangely romantic. *Sheesha* is available.

Fujairah

Fujairah

Top Sights
1 Fujairah Fort C1

Sights
2 Fujairah Museum C2
3 Sheikh Zayed Mosque B2

Sleeping
4 Hilton Fujairah Resort D1
5 Novotel Fujairah B3

Eating
6 Al Meshwar B3
7 Breezes D1
8 Nalukettu B3
9 Sadaf D2

Shopping
10 Central Souq D3

★ **Sardinia** ITALIAN $$
(☎09-228 3601; The Club, Sakamkam area; mains Dh40-70; ⏰noon-3.30pm & 7pm-midnight; 📶) Never mind the ho-hum looks and location: this is Italian food at its most authentic, thanks to chef Angelo Usai. His homemade pasta, wood-fired pizza and creamy risotti are superb and can even be enjoyed with a glass of Chianti. Great tiramisu. It's about 4km north of the city centre via the coastal road (E99), next to the gate of Free Zone N2.

Sadaf IRANIAN $$
(☎09-223 3400; www.sadaffood.com; Corniche Rd; mains Dh35-60; ⏰noon-3pm & 7pm-midnight) A branch of the popular Sadaf franchise, this always-busy eatery serves up traditional Iranian fare, including grilled kebabs and delicately spiced *zereshk polo* (rice with barberries) with meat or chicken, amid hilariously retro-kitsch decor. It's near the Coffeepot Roundabout.

Al Meshwar LEBANESE $$
(☎09-222 1113; Hamad bin Abdullah Rd; mezze Dh15-33, mains Dh33-95; ⏰9am-1am; 📶) With its Fred Flintstone exterior, this perennially popular local restaurant is easily spotted. Just as well, for the Lebanese fare is finger licking, from the tangy hummus and copious other mezze to grilled meats and fluffy *sambousek* (meat pies). *Sheesha* lounge downstairs, family dining upstairs.

McGettigan's FJR IRISH PUB
(☎09-224 4880; www.mcgettigans.com; Tennis & Country Club; mains Dh50-85; ⏰noon-1am; 📶) The opening of McGettingan's has injected some much-needed pizzazz into Fujairah's nightlife. Events like happy hour, quiz night

and open-mic night bring in the punters, as does the soulful pub fare, from burgers to fish and chips. It's near Fujairah City Center mall, behind Ajman University.

Shopping

Central Souq MARKET
(8am-9pm) At the bottom of the main strip, Hamad bin Abdullah Rd, locals shop for meat, fish, produce, dates and spices at the traditional Central Souq, set up in a no-nonsense market hall.

Fujairah City Centre MALL
(www.citycentrefujairah.com; Sheikh Khalifa bin Zayed Hwy; 10am-11pm Sun-Wed, to midnight Thu & Fri;) The first big, modern mall in Fujairah sits on the outskirts of town and is much beloved for its multiplex 3D cinema and Magic Planet indoor amusement park.

Getting There & Away

BUS

Hourly bus E700 runs between Dubai's **Union Square station** (p329) in Deira to central Fujairah in about two hours (Dh25). From Sharjah's Al Jubail station, bus 116 departs for Fujairah (Dh25) via Dhaid (Dh15) and Masafi (Dh20) every 60 minutes.

CAR

Locals rejoiced when the opening of the scenic Sheikh Khalifa Hwy (Hwy E84) through the Hajar Mountains in December 2011 cut the trip between Fujairah and Dubai to about an hour. It meets the old Hwy E89 (via Masafi) near Al Hayl on the western outskirts of Fujairah.

TAXI

Taxis (09-223 3533) between Fujairah and Dubai or Sharjah cost about Dh180 to Dh250. Budget about Dh80 to Dh100 to Al Aqah or Badiyah and about Dh120 to Dibba. Most rides within Fujairah cost no more than Dh15.

Khor Fakkan خورفكان

About 25km north of Fujairah, Khor Fakkan is dominated by its super-busy container port. At times, an entire armada of ships can be seen on the horizon, queuing to dock, unload or refuel. Still, Khor Fakkan is not without charm, especially along the family-friendly **Corniche**, which is flanked by beach, palm trees, gardens, kiosks and playgrounds. Several kilometres long, it links the port and the fish market with the Oceanic Hotel.

Note that, since Khor Fakkan is an enclave of the Sharjah emirate, it's 'dry' as a bone.

Sleeping & Eating

Oceanic Khorfakkan Resort & Spa HOTEL $$
(09-238 5111; oceanichotel.com; Al Mufidi St; r from Dh550;) After a major facelift, this Khor Fakkan landmark with its distinctive rooftop rotunda once again sparkles, with handsome carpeted rooms decked out in dark-wood furniture and a natural colour scheme. A spa, yoga on the private, sickle-shaped beach and an outdoor pool provide diversions, while five restaurants, including the excellent Bab Al Bahr for seafood, give your tummy a workout.

LOCAL KNOWLEDGE

BULL BUTTING

Every Friday an unusual spectacle takes place throughout the day in a muddy patch off the Fujairah Corniche, just south of the 'Hand Roundabout' (look for the huge fleet of parked SUVs): the ancient sport of bull butting. Dozens of sumo-sized animals tethered to posts await their turn in the ring, snorting derisively and kicking up dirt. In the arena, two humpbacked specimens lock horns and pit their strength against each other as hundreds of locals cheer them on. The first animal to back away loses, which usually takes a couple of minutes. If neither does, handlers will separate the beasts with ropes. Little harm comes to the bull beyond a sore head and dented pride. There is no prize money, but a win increases the value of the bull and brings honour to its owner.

The origin of the sport, which is even more popular in Oman, is disputed, with one theory saying that it was introduced by the Portuguese, although it's possible that the tradition goes back a lot further. Today it is upheld by two local clubs, who take turns to host the fights.

Irani Pars Restaurant IRANIAN $$
(☎09-238 7787; Corniche Roundabout; mains Dh20-75; ⏰9.30-12.30am) Locals give this simple restaurant the thumbs up for its generous portions of grills served with fluffy rice. Also try the classic stews like the herb-based *ghorm sabzi.*

Badiyah بادية

Al Badiyah Mosque MOSQUE
(Dibba Rd (Hwy E99); ⏰9am-5pm) FREE Badiyah (also spelt Bidyah and Bidiya), 8km north of Khor Fakkan, is famous for its teensy mosque. The modest stone and mud structure, adorned with four pointed domes and resting on a single internal pillar, dates to 1446 and is considered the oldest mosque in the UAE.

Non-Muslims are free to take a peek but must be modestly dressed and take off their shoes; women must also cover their hair. Free *abeyyas* (black robes for women) may be borrowed from the attendant.

The prayer hall has a lovely contemplative feel, enlivened by a red carpet with white dots and leatherbound books stacked into wall niches. There is a small mihrab (niche pointing in the direction of Mecca) and simple minbar (stepped pulpit).

The mosque is built into a low hillside along the coastal road just north of Badiyah village and guarded by two ruined watchtowers. It's well worth walking up here for sweeping views of the Hajar Mountains and the Gulf.

Al Aqah العقة

Al Aqah has the East Coast's best beaches, flanked by mostly high-end hotels with an unhurried vibe. Waters are generally calm and temperatures pleasant even in winter. This is prime snorkelling and diving territory, and beginners can have a satisfying experience thanks to Snoopy Island, named by some clever soul who thought the shape of this rocky outcrop about 100m offshore resembled the *Peanuts* cartoon character sleeping atop his doghouse.

Sleeping & Eating

Le Méridien Al Aqah Beach Resort RESORT $$
(☎09-244 9000; www.lemeridien-alaqah.com; Dibba Rd (Hwy E99); d Dh800; P 📶 🏊) With a beautiful location embracing a private beach, this resort is practically a destination in its own right. Spend days diving, waterskiing, playing volleyball or simply lazing by the pool or in the sand, then pick your favourite from among the five on-site restaurants at dinnertime.

Sandy Beach Hotel & Resort RESORT $$
(☎09-244 5555; sandybeachhotel.ae; Dibba Rd (Hwy E99); r from Dh725; P 📶 🏊) On a wide sandy beach opposite diving destination Snoopy Island, this low-key, family-oriented place was one of the first beach resorts in the UAE and oozes delightful retro charm, especially in the little bungalows dotted around the flowery gardens. The on-site PADI dive centre rents equipment and organises boat trips.

OFF THE BEATEN TRACK

BIRDING IN KALBA

About 15km south of Fujairah City on the Omani border, the Sharjah enclave of Kalba is famous for its creek (Khor Kalba), a pastiche of mangroves, tidal creeks and sandy beaches that is a birders' paradise. A key breeding ground of rare bird species, including the white-collared kingfisher and the Sykes's warbler, the area is also a wintering spot of the Indian pond heron.

In 2012, the Sharjah government closed access to Khor Kalba, whose fragile habitat had become threatened by a growing influx of off-road drivers and dune bikers. With strong binocularss, you might still be able to spot the birds from the bridge overlooking the creek and mangroves. Check www.uaebirding.com for updates.

Meanwhile, Sharjah's plans to develop Kalba into an ecotourism destination with a visitor centre, a sea-turtle rehabilitation centre, a campground and sustainable outdoor adventures have not yet come to fruition.

WADI WURAYAH وادي الوريعة

Tucked into the Hajar Mountains between Dibba, Khor Fakkan and Masafi, Wadi Wurayah (Wurayah Canyon) is a true natural treasure that was designated the UAE's first Mountain Protected Area by the World Wildlife Fund (WWF) in 2009. One of the few places in the country with a freshwater source, the 127-sq-km area boasts extraordinary biodiversity that includes such endemic mammals as the mountain gazelle, the caracal and the Blanford's fox. The canyon also hides archaeological vestiges dating as far back as 300 BC.

Alas, since this fragile habitat was under constant threat from human interference (littering, hunting, fires, etc), the park was closed indefinitely in December 2014. The WWF, together with the Emirates Wildlife Society, is developing a conservation plan that will restore and sustainably manage this ecosystem. Find out more at uae.panda.org.

Gonu Bar & Grill INTERNATIONAL $$$
(09-244 9000; www.lemeridien.com; Le Meridien Al Aqah Resort; mains Dh60-250; noon-midnight) Watch the waves crash onto the narrow private beach of this swish hotel as you tuck into your perfectly grilled steak or go into battle against an Omani lobster at this charming venue. Also a lovely spot for sunset cocktails.

Dibba دبا

Dibba was put on the map in 633 as the site of one of the battles of the Ridda wars, a series of campaigns launched by the caliph Abu Bakr shortly after Mohammed's death in order to quash anti-Muslim rebellions and enforce religious unity across Arabia. By some estimates, as many as 10,000 members of the local Azd tribe lost their lives in the uprising. Bones found in a cemetery just outside Dibba are believed to belong to some of the rebels.

Today the town is unique in that its territory is shared by two emirates and the Sultanate of Oman. The most commercial part is the southernmost, Dibba Al Fujairah, whose main thoroughfare is lined by small shops and cafes.

Dibba Al Hisn, in the middle, belongs to Sharjah, and its face has changed almost beyond recognition thanks to major government investment in recent years. New developments include a row of government buildings along Al Fareed St, and there are plans to develop a fun zone of restaurants, a canal, parks and playgrounds on Al Hisn Island.

Dibba Al Baya, across the border in Oman, is a launch pad for exploring the ruggedly beautiful Musandam Peninsula. Local operator **Sheesa Beach Dive Centre** (in Oman +968 26 836551; www.sheesabeach.com; Dibba Baya, Oman; 8am-5pm), on the waterfront about 3km north of the Corniche border crossing, organises dhow cruises and dive trips, while **Absolute Adventure** (04-345 9900; www.adventure.ae; day trips from Dh350; Oct-Apr) specialises in trekking, mountain biking and kayaking tours.

At press time, visitors eligible for a free UAE tourist visa did not require an Omani visa to cross into Musandam (bring your passport, though); however, it's best to get the latest information before heading out, for instance by calling a hotel or tour operator.

Sleeping

There's camping along Dibba Al Baya beach as well as in the dunes north of the Golden Tulip Hotel on the Omani side.

Royal Beach Hotel HOTEL $$
(09-244 9444; www.royalbeach.ae; Dibba Rd (Hwy E99), Dibba Al Fujairah; d from Dh820;) This friendly, old-school resort sits on a stretch of sand facing Dibba Rock, a popular diving and snorkelling site thanks to its shallow coral gardens. On-site Freestyle Divers rents gear, and does dive trips and PADI courses. All rooms have a private terrace facing a manicured lawn and the private beach strewn with *barasti* (palm-leaf) umbrellas. It's 8km south of Dibba.

Radisson Blu Resort, Fujairah RESORT $$
(09-244 9700; www.radissonblu.com/resort-fujairah; Dibba Rd (Hwy E99), Dibba Al Fujairah; d from Dh840;) With its modest entrance and generic lobby, the Radisson may not wow instantly, but it's actually an immaculately kept, full-service resort with five swimming pools, a super-long private beach and several good restaurants. Even standard rooms are large, and all have sea-facing balconies. It's 7km south of Dibba.

UNDERSTAND THE UNITED ARAB EMIRATES

History

Early History

The earliest significant settlements in the UAE date back to the Bronze Age. In the 3rd millennium BC, a culture known as Umm Al Nar arose near modern Abu Dhabi. Its influence extended well into the interior and down the coast to today's Oman. There were also settlements at Badiyah (near Fujairah) and at Rams (near Ras Al Khaimah) during the same period.

The Persians and, to a lesser extent, the Greeks were the next major cultural influences in the area. The Persian Sassanid empire held sway until the arrival of Islam in AD 636, and Christianity made a brief appearance in the form of the Nestorian Church, which had a monastery on Sir Bani Yas Island, west of Abu Dhabi, in the 5th century.

During the Middle Ages, the Kingdom of Ormus controlled much of the area, including the entrance to the Gulf, as well as most of the regional trade. The Portuguese arrived in 1498 and by 1515 they occupied Julfar (near Ras Al Khaimah). They built a customs house and taxed the Gulf's flourishing trade with India and the Far East, but they ended up staying only until 1633.

British Rule

The rise of British naval power in the Gulf in the mid-18th century coincided with the consolidation of two tribal factions along the coast of the lower Gulf: the Qawassim and the Bani Yas, the ancestors of the rulers of four of the seven emirates that today make up the UAE.

The Qawassim, whose descendants now rule Sharjah and Ras Al Khaimah, were a seafaring clan based in Ras Al Khaimah whose influence extended at times to the Persian side of the Gulf. This brought them into conflict with the British, who had forged an alliance with the Al Busaid tribe, the ancestors of today's rulers of Oman, to prevent the French from taking over their all-important sea routes to India.

The Qawassim felt that Al Busaid had betrayed the region and they launched attacks on British ships to show that they weren't going to be as compliant. As a result, the British dubbed the area the 'Pirate Coast' and launched raids against the Qawassim in 1805, 1809 and 1811. In 1820 a British fleet destroyed or captured every Qawassim ship it could find, imposed a peace treaty on nine Arab sheikhdoms in the area and installed a garrison.

This was the forerunner of another treaty, the 1835 Maritime Truce, which greatly increased British influence in the region. In 1853 the treaty was modified yet again and renamed the Treaty of Peace in Perpetuity. It was at this time that the region became known as the Trucial States. In subsequent decades, the sheikhs of each tribal confederation signed agreements with the British under which they accepted formal British protection.

Throughout this period, the main power among the Bedouin tribes of the interior was the Bani Yas tribal confederation, made up of the ancestors of the ruling families of modern Abu Dhabi and Dubai. The Bani Yas were originally based in Liwa, an oasis deep in the desert, but moved their base to Abu Dhabi in 1793. In the early 19th century, the Bani Yas divided into two main branches when around 800 of its members moved north and took charge of a tiny fishing settlement along the Dubai Creek. This laid the foundation for the Al Maktoum dynasty that rules Dubai to this day.

Black Gold

Until the discovery of oil in the first half of the 20th century the region remained a backwater, with the sheikhdoms nothing more than tiny enclaves of fishers and pearl divers. Rivalries between the various rulers occasionally erupted into conflict, which the British tried to thwart. During this time the British also protected the federation from being annexed by Saudi Arabia.

After the collapse of the world pearl market after the Japanese discovery in 1930 of a method of artificial pearl cultivation, the Gulf coast sank into poverty. While Abu Dhabi threw in its lot with the exploration for oil, Dubai embraced the concept of re-export. This exporting involved the importing of goods (particularly gold), which entered and exited Dubai legally but which were sold on to other ports abroad tax free.

The wealth generated from trade in yellow gold in Dubai was quickly trumped by the riches earned from black gold in Abu Dhabi. The first commercial oil field was discovered at Babi in Abu Dhabi in 1960 and, six years later, Dubai struck it lucky, too. The discovery of oil greatly accelerated the modernisation of the region and was a major factor in the formation of the UAE.

The Road to Unification

In 1951 the British set up the Trucial States Council, for the first time bringing together the rulers of the sheikhdoms of what would eventually become a federation. When Britain announced its departure from the region in 1968, Sheikh Zayed bin Sultan al Nahyan took the lead in forming alliances among the seven emirates that made up the Trucial States.

On 2 December 1971, thanks to Sheikh Zayed's persistence, the United Arab Emirates was created. It consisted of the emirates of Dubai, Abu Dhabi, Ajman, Fujairah, Sharjah and Umm Al Quwain; Ras Al Khaimah joined in 1972. Impressively, given the volatility in the region, the UAE remains to this day the only federation of Arab states in the Middle East. In fact, if anything, the financial bailouts by oil-rich Abu Dhabi of Dubai during the 2009 economic crisis tightened the bond and demonstrated the emirates' commitment to – and interdependence on – each other.

Government & Politics

The UAE is a federation of seven autonomous states – Abu Dhabi, Dubai, Sharjah, Ras Al Khaimah, Ajman, Umm Al Quwain and Fujairah – each governed by a hereditary absolute monarch called a sheikh. The seven rulers form the Supreme Council, the highest body in the land. The council ratifies federal laws and sets general policy. There is also a Council of Ministers, or cabinet, headed by the prime minister (the ruler of Dubai), who appoints ministers from across the emirates. Naturally, the more populous and wealthier emirates like Abu Dhabi and Dubai have greater representation.

The cabinet and Supreme Council are advised, but can't be overruled, by a parliamentary body called the Federal National Council (FNC). Since 2006, half of its 40 members are elected; the other 20 are directly appointed by each emirate. The number of eligible voters catapulted from 6595 in 2006 to 224,000 in the 2015 elections. However, at 35.29%, turnout was low. There are plans to grant the FNC some legislative powers and eventually to give the vote to all UAE citizens.

Economy

The UAE has the world's seventh-largest oil reserves (after Venezuela, Saudi Arabia, Canada, Iran, Iraq and Kuwait), with the vast majority of it concentrated in the emirate of Abu Dhabi. It is thought that, at current levels of extraction, reserves will last for another century, but – as the dramatic drop in oil prices in 2015 has shown – the country cannot afford to be complacent about preserving its wealth.

In common with Gulf neighbours, therefore, the UAE is looking at alternative sources of energy and ways of diversifying the economy. Dubai has been especially successful in this, largely thanks to the vision and ambition of its ruler, Sheikh Mohammed bin Rashid al Maktoum. Dubai's reserves of oil and gas were never that large, but the resources were used wisely to finance a modern and efficient infrastructure for trade, manufacturing and tourism. Today, revenues for oil and gas account for less than 2% of Dubai's GDP.

Until September 2008 it looked as though Dubai had the Midas touch. But then the world financial crisis struck and the emirate's economy collapsed like the proverbial house of cards. After real-estate prices plummeted by as much as 50%, the emirate was unable to meet its debt commitments, but markets stabilised after Abu Dhabi rode to the rescue with a US$10-billion loan.

FUN FACTS ABOUT CAMELS

Camels...

- can reach a top speed of 40km/h
- are pregnant for 13 to 15 months
- can go up to 15 days without drinking
- soak up water like a sponge when thirsty, guzzling up to 100L in 10 minutes
- don't store water in their humps
- have a life expectancy of 50 to 60 years
- have a three-part stomach
- in Arabia are one-humped dromedaries
- can travel 160km without drinking
- move both legs on one side of the body at the same time

Dubai climbed quickly out of recession, proving its perennial critics wrong. Despite appearances, however, Dubai is playing the long game, investing in enduring strategies that will help it weather future storms. Abu Dhabi has realised the power of this strategy and is catching up on non-oil enterprises, particularly in the tourism sector.

The free-trade zones have also been significant factors in the rebound. Companies are enticed here by the promise of full foreign ownership, full repatriation of capital and profits, no corporate tax for 15 years, no currency restrictions, and no personal income tax. One of the largest free-trade zones is Jebel Ali in Dubai, which is home to 5500 companies from 120 countries.

People & Society

The UAE population is one of the most diverse, multicultural and male (three quarters of the population) in the world. It is, overall, a tolerant and easygoing society. Most religions are tolerated (Judaism being an exception), and places of worship exist for Christians, Hindus and Sikhs. Notwithstanding, traditional culture and social life are firmly rooted in Islam, and day-to-day activities, relationships, diet and dress are very much dictated by religion.

Islamic Values

Islam is not just the official religion in the UAE, it is the cultural lifeblood. Religion is more than something performed on a Friday and put aside during the week; it is part of everyday life. It guides the choices an individual makes and frames the general context in which family life, work, leisure, care of the elderly and responsibility towards others take place. As such, Islam has played a socially cohesive role in the rapidly evolving UAE, providing support where old structures (both physical and social) have been dismantled to make way for a new urban experience.

For the visitor, understanding this link between religion and daily life can help make better sense of often misunderstood practices. Take dress, for example. Islam prescribes modest dress in public places for both men and women. The origin of the custom of covering the body is unclear – it certainly pre-dates Islam and to a large degree makes excellent sense under the ravaging tropical sun. Similarly, Muslims are forbidden to consume anything containing pork or alcohol. These strictures traditionally made good sense in a region where tapeworm was a common problem with pork meat and where the effects of alcohol are exaggerated by the extreme climate.

Role of Women

Modern life has provided new opportunities for women beyond care of the family, largely thanks to the equitable nature of education in the country. Emirati women constitute 77% of total university students, which is the highest percentage in the world. Many go on to work in a variety of roles, including as doctors, engineers, government ministers, innovators and corporate executives. In fact, 66% of the public-sector workforce (compared with 48% globally) and 30% of senior decision-makers are women. In 2012 the UAE became only the second country in the world to introduce the mandatory appointment of women to UAE boards. Since September 2014, it also has the region's first military college for women.

Five women serve in the UAE cabinet, including Minister for Foreign Trade Sheikha Lubna Al Qasimi, who was ranked among the world's 100 most powerful women by *Forbes* magazine. In 2015, she received the Clinton Global Citizen Award. Alas, Emiratis still seem reluctant to elect female politicians (cabinet members are appointed): during the 2015 Federal National Council elections only one of the 20 seats went to a woman.

Marriage

A Muslim man is permitted by Islam to have up to four wives (but a woman may have only one husband). As with many practices within Islam, this one originally came about due to practical considerations: the ability of a man to take more than one wife enabled men to marry women who had been widowed (and thus left without a provider) due to war, illness or natural disaster. Most Emiratis have only one wife, however, not least because Islam dictates that each spouse must be loved and treated equally. Besides, housing and child rearing are expensive – perhaps that's why the average number of children in a modern Emirati family has declined from five to two.

CAMEL RACING

Camel racing is deeply rooted in the Emirati soul and attending a race is hugely popular with locals and visitors alike. It's quite an exhilarating sight when hundreds of one-humped dromedaries fly out of their pens and onto the dirt track, jostling for position in a lumbering gallop with legs splayed out in all directions, scrambling towards the finish line at top speeds of 40km/h.

Pure-bred camels begin daily training sessions when they're about two years old. The local Mahaliyat breed, Omaniyat camels from Oman, Sudaniyat from Sudan and inter-bred Muhajanat are the most common breeds used in competition.

Over 100 animals participate in a typical race. Each camel is outfitted with 'robot jockeys', which have remote-controlled whips operated by the owners while driving their white SUVs on a separate track alongside the animals. The camels used to be piloted by child jockeys, but this practice was outlawed in the UAE in 2005.

Racing season runs between October and early April. There's no fixed schedule, although two- or three-hour meets usually take place from around 7am on Friday, sometimes with a second race around 2.30pm. Training sessions can sometimes be observed at other times. For exact times, check the local newspapers or call the numbers below. Admission is free.

Here's a rundown of the main tracks where you can see these great desert athletes go nose to nose:

Al Wathba (02-583 9200; Al Wathba; 7.30am & 2.30pm Thu-Sat Oct-Apr) FREE Abu Dhabi – about 45km east of town via the E22 towards Al Ain; take exit 47, turn right to Al Wathba Palace and right again to the track.

Al Marmoum (04-832 6526; www.dcrc.ae; off Hwy E66; Oct-Apr) Dubai – about 40km south of town en route to Al Ain, near Al Lisaili; go past the Dubai Outlet Mall and the Sevens rugby stadium and turn right at exit 37.

Al Sawan (Hwy E18, Ras Al Khaimah; usually 6.30am-9.30am Fri & Sat Nov-Mar) Ras Al Khaimah – about 15km southeast of RAK City via E18. Drive towards RAK airport as far as Digdagga, turn off opposite the big World Discount Store (just before the free-standing minaret) and drive for about 5km.

Urban life puts a particular strain on city marriages, with the high divorce rate (three per day in Dubai alone) revealing a fault line between traditional and modern values. Growing infidelity between partners, unrealistic expectations about living the urban dream, the difficulties of cross-cultural unions and long commutes are some of the many reasons cited for marriage break-ups.

The Workplace

Most Emiratis work in the public sector, as the short hours, good pay, benefits and early pensions make for an attractive lifestyle. The UAE government is actively pursuing a policy of 'Emiratisation', which involves encouraging Emiratis to work in the private sector. Until more locals take up the baton of small and medium enterprise, it will be hard for the government to decrease its dependence on an imported labour force, which accounts for about 80% of the population. Indeed, the visitor experience is largely defined by interaction with the myriad nationalities that have been attracted to the Gulf in search of a better (or at least more lucrative) life.

Different nationalities have tended to dominate specific sectors of the workforce: those from the Philippines are often employed in health care; construction workers hail from Pakistan and financial advisers from India; people from western Europe and the US have traditionally supplied technical know-how. One enduring topic is concern about the welfare of workers, particularly those employed in construction and as maids and nannies.

Arts

Owing to its Bedouin heritage, the most popular art forms in the UAE are traditional dance, music and poetry, although of late other forms of artistic expression have seen a surge in popularity. Sizeable art communities have sprouted in Dubai and Sharjah alongside world-class galleries and such international art festivals as Art Dubai, Abu Dhabi Art and the Sharjah Biennial. Abu Dhabi is especially ambitious when it comes to positioning itself as an art-world leader, building outposts of the Louvre and the Guggenheim on Saadiyat Island.

The UAE also hosts the Dubai International Film Festival (p319).

Poetry

In Bedouin culture a facility with poetry and language is greatly prized. Traditionally, a poet who could eloquently praise his own people while pointing out the failures of other tribes was considered a great asset. One of the most important poets in the region was Mubarak Al Oqaili (1880–1954). There's an entire museum dedicated to him in a traditional building in the Deira Spice Souq in Dubai. Modern UAE poets of note include Sultan al-Owais (1925–2000) and Dr Ahmed Al Madani (1931–95).

Nabati (vernacular poetry) is especially popular and has traditionally been in spoken form. Sheikh Mohammed bin Rashid al-Maktoum, Dubai's ruler, is a well-respected poet in this tradition, as is the award-winning contemporary female poet Ousha Bint Khalifa. The Women's Museum (Bait Al Banat) in Dubai's Deira district devotes an entire room to her work.

There are scores of well-known male poets in the UAE who still use the forms of classical Arab poetry, though they often experiment by combining it with other styles. Well-known female poets writing in the modern *tafila* (prose) styles include Rua Salem and her sister Sarah Hareb as well as Sheikha Maisoon Al Qasimi.

Music & Dance

Emiratis have always acknowledged the importance of music in daily life. Songs were traditionally composed to accompany different tasks, from hauling water to diving for pearls. The Arabic music you're most likely to hear on the radio, though, is *khaleeji*, the traditional Gulf style of pop music. Alongside this, an underground rock and metal music scene is increasingly taking shape, especially in Dubai.

The UAE's contact with East and North African cultures through trade, both seafaring and by camel caravan, has brought many musical and dance influences to the country. One of the most popular dances is the *ayyalah*, a typical Bedouin dance performed throughout the Gulf. The UAE has its own variation, performed to a simple drumbeat, with anywhere between 25 and 200 men standing with their arms linked in two rows facing each other. They wave walking sticks or swords in front of themselves and sway back and forth, the two rows taking it in turn to sing. It's a war dance and the words expound the virtues of courage and bravery in battle.

A traditional dance performed by women is the *al naashat*, where the dancers roll their heads from side to side to show off their long, jet-black hair to songs that pay tribute to the love, honour or bravery of the men of the tribe.

Environment

Environmental awareness is increasing at the macro level in the UAE, due in no small part to the efforts of the late Sheikh Zayed, who was posthumously named a 'Champion of the Earth' by the UN Environment Programme (UNEP) in 2005. With his efforts in wildlife preservation, such as Sir Bani Yas Island, which operates a breeding program for endangered Arabian wildlife species, as well as the ban on hunting with guns decades ago, Sheikh Zayed foresaw the acute threats to the endangered native species of the region.

In Dubai, the Dubai Desert Conservation Reserve (DDCR) comprises 225 sq km (5% of the area of the Dubai emirate) and integrates both a national park and the super-luxe Al Maha Desert Resort & Spa. One of the DDCR's most notable achievements is the successful breeding of the endangered scimitar-horned oryx. Migrating birds and flamingos are the darlings of the Ras Al Khor Wildlife Sanctuary, at the head of Dubai Creek within view of the Burj Khalifa and the high-rises on Sheikh Zayed Road. Sharjah has a successful breeding centre at Sharjah Desert Park, as does Al Ain Zoo.

In terms of going green at the micro level, much work needs to be done in the UAE. Water and energy wastage (nearly all water comes from desalination plants) and littering are major issues. Resources are consumed at a much faster rate than they can be replaced, which is why the ecological footprint of the Gulf cities is so high. It is no easy feat to reverse the trend and achieve environmental sustainability when the UAE relies so heavily on imported goods and urban dwelling has become the norm.

There are a few projects aimed at reducing the impact, such as the Shams 1 solar plant south of Madinat Zayed, and Masdar City, Abu Dhabi's flagship environmental project, which strives to become the world's first carbon-neutral, zero-waste community powered entirely by renewable energy.

For more information, check the website of the UAE's leading environmental organisation, the nonprofit, nongovernmental **Emirates Environmental Group** (☎04-344 8622; www.eeg-uae.org).

SURVIVAL GUIDE

Directory A–Z

ACCOMMODATION

The UAE has the gamut of places to unpack your suitcase, from ultra-posh beach resorts, romantic boutique hotels, buttoned-up business properties and furnished hotel apartments with kitchens to basic hostels and inns where bathrooms may be shared. Midrange options are usually the best value for money.

Camping

Although the UAE has no official public campgrounds, pitching a tent on a beach or in the desert is very popular with locals and expats and is a free and safe way to spend the night. Be prepared to take everything in (and out), don't litter and bring a shovel to bury your 'business'. For camping destinations consult the locally published specialist guides widely available in bookstores. There is also 'glamping' in supplied tents and cabins at the Dreamland Aqua Park (p340) in Umm Al Quwain.

Hostels

There are four hostels affiliated with Hostelling International in the UAE: one each in Dubai and Fujairah and two in Sharjah. All are open to men and women, although solo women are a rare sight. Facilities are basic and shared, and smoking and alcohol are prohibited. Accommodation is in dorms or family rooms, which may be available to small groups and couples depending on availability and the manager's mood.

Hotel Apartments

Although designed for long-term stays, hotel apartments are a great way for wallet-watching travellers to economise in comfort. Available in various configurations from studios to two-bedroom apartments, they come with cooking facilities and room cleaning. Facilities like a gym or pool are fairly standard, but on-site restaurants or bars are not. Rates start at Dh300 per night.

Rates

Room rates fluctuate enormously, spiking during festivals, holidays and big events and dropping in the summer months (May to September). The best beds often sell out fast, so make reservations as early as possible if you've got your eye on a particular place. Most properties now have an internet booking function with a best-price guarantee.

Rates are subject to a municipality fee and a service charge, which vary by emirate but are usually around 10% each. Dubai and Ras Al Khaimah also tack on a 'tourism tax' ranging from Dh7 to Dh20 per room per night, depending on the property's star rating.

CHILDREN

It's easy to travel through the UAE with children. Many top-end hotels and some midrange ones have kids' clubs, pools and playgrounds. There are plenty of beaches, parks, playgrounds and activity centres (many in shopping malls) to keep kids amused; many restaurants have children's menus and high chairs.

Formula is readily available in pharmacies, and disposable nappies at grocery stores and supermarkets. High chairs are available in restaurants and babysitting facilities are available in some midrange and all top-end hotels, as well as at some shopping malls.

CUSTOMS REGULATIONS

UAE airports have duty-free shops in the arrivals and departure areas. Allowances are subject to change but at the time of writing visitors over 18 arriving at Dubai International Airport were allowed to bring in the following duty-free:

- 4L of wine or spirits or two cartons of beer at 24 cans each (non-Muslims only).
- 400 cigarettes plus 50 cigars plus 500g of loose tobacco.
- Gifts up to the value of Dh3000.

Allowances may be slightly different at other UAE airports.

SLEEPING PRICE RANGES

The following price ranges refer to an air-conditioned standard double room with private bathroom in peak season (November to March). Unless otherwise stated, breakfast and taxes are included in the price.

$ less than Dh500

$$ Dh500–Dh1000

$$$ more than Dh1000

EATING PRICE RANGES

The following price ranges refer to an average main course. Prices may or may not include VAT and a service charge, as this varies by emirate. Details are almost always spelled out (in fine print) in restaurant menus.

$ less than Dh30

$$ Dh30–Dh90

$$$ more than Dh90

You are generally not allowed to bring in:

- Alcohol if you cross into the UAE by land.
- Materials (eg books) that insult Islam.
- Firearms, pork, pornography and Israeli products.

EMBASSIES & CONSULATES

All embassies listed below are in Abu Dhabi, but most countries also maintain a consular office in Dubai. Call or check the relevant website for details.

Australian Embassy (Map p348; ☎02-401 7500; www.uae.embassy.gov.au; Zayed the First St) On the 8th floor of the Al Muhairy Centre.

Canadian Embassy (Map p348; ☎02-694 0300; www.canadainternational.gc.ca; Abu Dhabi Trade Towers (Abu Dhabi Mall), 10th St) On the 9th and 10th floors of the West Tower.

Dutch Embassy (Map p346; ☎02-695 8000; http://uae.nlembassy.org; Al Khaleej Al Arabi St) On the 14th floor of Building 11 of the Centro Capital Centre Office Tower.

French Embassy (Map p348; ☎02-813 1000; www.ambafrance-eau.org; Corniche Rd (West)) On the 22nd floor of Etihad Tower 3.

German Embassy (Map p348; ☎02-596 7700; www.abu-dhabi.diplo.de; Towers at the Trade Center (Abu Dhabi Mall), 10th St) On the 14th floor of the West Tower.

Irish Embassy (Map p348; ☎02-495 8200; www.embassyofireland.ae; Al Yasat St) Off 6th St in the Al Bateen area.

New Zealand Embassy (Map p346; ☎02-441 1222; www.nzembassy.com/united-arab-emirates; Villa 235, Al Karamah St) On 14th St between 11th and 13th Sts in the Al Karamah area.

UK Embassy (Map p348; ☎02-610 1100; http://ukinuae.fco.gov.uk/en/; Khalid bin Al Waleed St) Near Adnec.

US Embassy (Map p346; ☎emergencies only 02-414 2200; abudhabi.usembassy.gov; Plot 38, Sector W59-02, 4th St) Off Airport Rd in the Embassies District.

FOOD

Filling your tummy in the UAE is an extraordinarily multicultural experience with a virtual UN of ethnic cuisines to choose from. Lebanese and Indian fare are the most prevalent, but basically you can feast on anything from Afghan kebabs to British fish and chips, German sauerkraut to South African *boerewors* (sausage). And thanks to the vast number of Asian and subcontinental restaurants, vegetarians have no problem sourcing delicious meals.

In cosmopolitan Dubai – and to a lesser degree also in Abu Dhabi – taking global fare local has been a recent trend. Following the farm-to-table credo, many chefs now grow their own herbs or vegetables, pick up fresh produce from the farmers' market and source their eggs from farms in Al Ain and their fish from Ras Al Khamaih. The last couple of years have also brought a profileration of food trucks, restaurants serving Emirati cuisine, health-conscious cafes and products made from camel milk.

Pork is available for non-Muslims in a special room at some larger supermarkets such as Spinneys. In many hotel restaurants, pork is a menu item and is clearly labelled as such.

GAY & LESBIAN TRAVELLERS

A useful read is *Gay Travels in the Muslim World* by Michael Luongo.

- Homosexual acts are illegal under UAE law and can incur a jail term. You will see men walking hand in hand, but that's a sign of friendship and not an indication of sexual orientation.
- You can't access gay- and lesbian-interest websites from inside the UAE. Public displays of affection between partners are taboo regardless of sexual orientation.
- Sex outside marriage is against the law.
- Sharing a room is likely to be construed as companionable or cost cutting, but being discreet about your true relationship is advisable.

INTERNET ACCESS

- Places in the UAE are well wired and you should not have a problem getting online.
- Nearly every hotel has in-room internet access, either broadband or wi-fi, usually for free. Most restaurants and cafes offer their own wi-fi, usually free with purchase.
- Most shopping malls also offer free wi-fi, but you may need a UAE mobile-phone number to access this service.
- Pornography, gay-interest sites, websites considered critical of Islam or the UAE's leaders, dating and gambling sites, drug-related material and the entire Israeli domain are banned in the UAE, as is software such as Skype.

LEGAL MATTERS

Locals are tolerant of cultural differences – to a point. Go beyond that point and you could find you are subject to some of the harshest penalties in the region. This section lists the various infringements commonly committed by visitors and the penalties that can be expected.

➡ Attempting to use drugs in Dubai and Abu Dhabi is simply a bad, bad idea. The minimum penalty for possession of even trace amounts is four years in prison, and the death penalty is still on the books for importing or dealing in drugs (although in fact the sentence usually ends up being a very long jail term). Just being in a room where drugs are used, even if you are not partaking, could land you in trouble. The secret police are pervasive, and they include officers of many nationalities.

➡ There are import restrictions for prescription medications that are legal in most countries, such as diazepam (Valium), dextromethorphan (Robitussin), fluoxetine (Prozac) and anything containing codeine. Check with the UAE embassy in your home country for the full list. If you need to take such medications, carry the original prescription and a letter from your doctor.

➡ Penalties for breaching the code of conduct or breaking the law include warnings or fines (for littering, for example), or jail and deportation (for example, for drug possession and criticism of Islam). Ignorance is no defence.

➡ If arrested, you have the right to a phone call, which you should make as soon as possible (ie before you are detained in a police cell or prison pending investigation, where making contact with anyone could be difficult). Call your embassy or consulate first so they can get in touch with your family and possibly recommend a lawyer.

➡ The UAE police have established a **Department of Tourist Security** (☎ toll free 04-800 243; www.dubaipolice.gov.ae) to help visitors with any legal complications they may face on their trip – this may also be helpful if you get into difficulties.

MONEY

ATMs

Credit and debit cards can be used for withdrawing money from ATMs that display the relevant symbols, such as Visa and MasterCard. A charge (around 1.5% to 2%) on ATM cash withdrawals abroad is levied by some banks.

Changing Money

If you need to change money, exchange offices tend to offer better rates than banks. Reliable exchanges include **Al Rostamani** (www.alrostamaniexchange.com) and **UAE Exchange** (☎ 04-229 7373; www.uaeexchange.com), with multiple branches in Dubai and Abu Dhabi.

The currencies of regional countries are all recognised and easily changed, with the exception of Yemeni riyal.

Credit Cards

Visa, MasterCard and American Express are widely accepted at shops, hotels and restaurants throughout Dubai and Abu Dhabi, and debit cards are accepted at bigger retail outlets.

Tipping

By law, only food and beverage outlets in hotels (ie not independent restaurants) are entitled to tack a service charge (usually 10%) onto bills. The service charge rarely ends up in the pockets of the person who served you, so a few dirhams are appreciated for a job well done.

PRACTICALITIES

Currency The UAE dirham (Dh) is fully convertible and pegged to the US dollar. One dirham is divided into 100 fils. Notes come in denominations of five, 10, 20, 50, 100, 200, 500 and 1000 dirham. Coins are Dh1, 50 fils, 25 fils, 10 fils and five fils.

News and magazines Widely read English-language dailies are *The National*, *Gulf News*, *Gulf Today* and *Khaleej Times*. Content is government controlled. *Time Out* produces the most popular weekly listings magazine, with separate editions for Dubai and Abu Dhabi. *What's On* is an insightful monthly alternative. International magazines and newspapers are readily available.

Radio Popular stations include BBC Worldwide (87.9) and Dubai Eye (103.8) for news and talk, and Dubai FM (92), Channel 4 FM (104.8) and Emirates Radio 1 (104.1) and 2 (99.3) for music.

Smoking Dubai and Abu Dhabi have a comprehensive smoking ban in all public places, with the exception of nightclubs and enclosed bars. The fine for lighting up in a non-smoking area can range from Dh1000 to Dh8000. There are fines for throwing cigarette butts onto the street. There's a ban on smoking in public-access parks, beaches and recreation areas. Smoking is not permitted in cars where children are present.

ALCOHOL

Buying When arriving by air, you may, as a non-Muslim visitor over 18, buy 4L of spirits, wine or beer in the airport duty-free shop. With the exception of the 'dry' emirate of Sharjah, where alcohol and even *sheesha* smoking are banned, you can also purchase alcohol in licensed bars and clubs that are generally attached to four- and five-star hotels; alcohol purchased here is for on-site consumption.

Non-Muslim expats may obtain an alcohol licence, which entitles them to a fixed monthly limit of alcohol sold in such places as the African & Eastern liquor stores and some branches of Spinneys. Visitors are not permitted to legally purchase alcohol in these places and staff members are supposed to ask to see the licence. The only stores where visitors can legally buy alcohol are at the Barracuda Beach Resort and the Umm Al Quwain Beach Hotel, both in Umm Al Quwain. Note that you are not officially allowed to transport alcohol through Sharjah, although most people just seem to take the risk anyway.

Driving There is zero tolerance in the UAE when it comes to drinking and driving. And we mean zero: under no circumstances should you get behind the wheel of a car if you've had even one sip of alcohol. Getting caught could get you a one-month stint in jail, a fine and deportation. Even being drunk in public is illegal and may also result in jail time and a fine of several thousand dirham. Also note that, even if you are the victim of a crime (eg sexual assault or robbery), police protection may be limited if you are found to be under the influence.

OPENING HOURS

The UAE weekend is on Friday and Saturday. Hours are more limited during Ramadam and in summer.

Banks 8am to 1pm (some until 3pm) Sunday to Thursday, 8am to noon Saturday.

Government offices 7.30am to 2pm (or 3pm) Sunday to Thursday.

Restaurants noon to 3pm and 7.30pm to midnight.

Shopping malls 10am to 10pm Sunday to Wednesday, 10am to midnight Thursday and Friday.

Souqs 9am to 1.30pm and 4pm to 9pm (often later in Dubai and Abu Dhabi), closed Friday morning.

Supermarkets 9am to midnight daily, some open 24 hours.

PHOTOGRAPHY

Memory cards, batteries and other accessories for digital cameras are available in major supermarkets, at shopping malls and in electronics stores. Taking video or photographs of airports, government offices, or military and industrial installations may result in arrest and/or prosecution. Also ask permission before photographing people, especially Muslim women.

POST

Your hotel should be able to send mail for you, but otherwise stamps are available at local post offices operated by **Emirates Post** (☎600 599 999; www.emiratespost.com) and found in every city and town.

PUBLIC HOLIDAYS

As well as the major Islamic holidays (see p446), the UAE observes the following public holidays:

New Year's Day 1 January

Martyrs' Day 30 November

National Day 2 December

A mourning period of up to one week usually follows the death of a royal-family member, a government minister or a head of a neighbouring state. Government offices, some businesses and state-run tourist attractions (such as museums) may be closed on these days. Events may be cancelled.

SAFE TRAVEL

Crime The UAE has a low incidence of crime and even pickpocketing and bag snatching are rare. One very real danger is bad driving. Courtesy on the road rarely exists. People will cut in front of you, turn without indicating and race each other on highways.

Driving Out of the cities, the left lane is for passing only – block people at your own risk as speeds of up to 200km/h are not unusual. Some drivers also have a tendency to zoom into roundabouts at frightening speeds and try to exit them from inside lanes. Pedestrian crossings are no guarantee that drivers will stop or even slow down.

Traffic accident If you have an accident, even a small one, you must call the police (☎999) and wait at the scene. If it's a minor accident, move your car to the side of the road. You cannot file an insurance claim without a police report.

Swimming If you are swimming at an unpatrolled (ie public) beach, be very careful. Despite the small surf, there may be dangerous rip tides and drownings are not uncommon.

Knockoffs Do not buy counterfeit and pirated goods, even if they are widely available. Not only are these goods illegal in many countries, purchasing them is a violation of local law.

TELEPHONE

The UAE has an efficient communications network. Both mobile networks – Etisalat and Du – are government owned. Local calls within the same area code are free.

Mobile Phones

- The UAE's mobile-phone network uses the GSM 900 MHz and 1800 MHz standard, the same as Europe, Asia and Australia. Mobile numbers begin with either 050 (Etisalat) or 055 (Du).
- If you don't have a worldwide roaming service but do have an unlocked phone, consider buying a prepaid SIM card with a local number at a telecommunications or licensed mobile-phone shop. Good-value visitor packages may be available. You'll need a credit card and a passport to obtain a SIM card.
- Recharge cards in various denominations are sold at grocery stores, supermarkets and petrol stations.

Phone Codes

- When calling the UAE from another country, dial the country code ☎971, followed by the area code (minus the zero) and the subscriber number.
- To call abroad from the UAE, dial ☎00 followed by the country code.
- For directory enquiries call ☎181; for international directory assistance call ☎151.
- When making calls within the UAE, dial the seven-digit local number if already in the city and using a landline. If dialling a number in another city – or using a mobile phone – dial the two-digit area code provided throughout this book first.

Phonecards

Coin phones have been almost completely superseded by card phones. Phonecards are available in various denominations from grocery stores, supermarkets and petrol stations.

TOILETS

- Public toilets in shopping centres, museums, restaurants and hotels are Western-style sit-down affairs and are generally clean and well maintained.
- Those in souqs and bus stations are usually only for men. Outside the cities you might have to contend with hole-in-the-ground loos at the back of restaurants or petrol stations, although these are increasingly rare.
- You'll always find a hose and nozzle next to the toilet, which is used for rinsing (left hand only if you want to go native); toilet paper is used for drying only.

VISAS

- Entry requirements to the UAE are in constant flux, so all information here can only serve as a guideline. Always obtain the latest requirements from the UAE embassy in your home country.
- At the time of writing, citizens of 45 nations, including the UK, the US, Canada, Australia and most European countries do not require a tourist visa to enter the UAE.
- Everyone else must have a visitor visa arranged through a sponsor – such as your UAE hotel or tour operator – prior to arrival in the UAE. The nonrenewable visas cost Dh100 and are valid for 30 days.
- Visas can be extended for a further 30 days at a cost of Dh500 at an immigration office in the emirate in which you arrived.
- If you're transiting via the UAE and are a citizen of one of the 45 countries exempt from tourist visas, you do not need to pre-arrange a transit visa. Other nationalities need to get the airline or a local hotel to organise a 96-hour visa. The official fee is Dh100.
- Gulf Cooperation Council (GCC) citizens only need a valid passport to enter the UAE and stay indefinitely.
- Note that passports must be valid for at least six months from the date of arrival.

WOMEN TRAVELLERS

Dispelling the Myths

Many women imagine that travel to the Gulf cities and within the UAE is much more difficult than it is. Some key facts:

- You don't have to wear a burka, headscarf or veil.
- You won't be constantly harassed.
- It's safe to take taxis, stay alone in hotels (although you may want to avoid the fleabag hotels in Deira and Bur Dubai) and walk around on your own in most areas.
- However, you are likely to receive unwanted male attention and long, lewd stares on public beaches.

Attitudes Towards Women

Some of the biggest misunderstandings between Middle Easterners and people from other parts of the world occur over the issue of women. Half-truths and stereotypes exist on both sides: foreigners sometimes assume that all Middle Eastern women are veiled, repressed victims, while some locals see Western women as sex-obsessed and immoral.

Traditionally, the role of a woman in this region is to be a mother and matron of the household, while the man is the financial provider. However, as with any society, the reality is far more nuanced. There are thousands of middle- and upper-middle-class professional women in the UAE, who, like their counterparts elsewhere in the world, juggle work and family responsibilities.

The issue of sex is where the differences between the cultures are particularly apparent. Premarital sex (or indeed any sex outside marriage) is taboo, although, as with anything forbidden, it still happens. Emirati women are expected to be virgins when they marry, and a family's reputation can rest upon this point. The presence of foreign women provides, in the eyes of some Arab men, a chance to get around these norms with ease and without consequences – hence the occasional hassle foreign women experience.

What to Wear

Even though you'll see plenty of female tourists wearing skimpy shorts and tank tops in shopping malls and other public places (especially in Dubai), you should not assume that it's acceptable to do so. While as hosts they're too polite to say anything, most Emiratis find this disrespectful. Despite the UAE's relative liberalism, you are in a country that holds its traditions dear and it's prudent not to parade a different set of values. A bit of common sense (such as covering up to and from a beach party or when taking a taxi to a nightclub) helps keep the peace.

Generally speaking, dressing 'modestly' has the following advantages: it attracts less attention to you; you will get a warmer welcome from locals (who greatly appreciate your willingness to respect their customs); and it'll prove more comfortable in the heat. Dressing modestly means covering your shoulders, knees and neckline. Baggy T-shirts and loose cotton trousers or below-the-knee skirts will not only keep you cool but will also protect your skin from the sun. If you travel outside Dubai and Abu Dhabi, keep in mind that everywhere else in the UAE is far more conservative.

ℹ Getting There & Away

Flights, cars and tours can be booked online at lonelyplanet.com/bookings.

ENTERING THE UAE

If you're a citizen of the currently 45 countries exempt from obtaining a tourist visa, simply proceed straight to the immigration desk or border post and get your passport stamped. If you are entering on a sponsored visa, you'll need to go to the clearly marked visa-collection counter at the airport when you arrive.

Passports

All passports must be valid for at least six months from the date of arrival. It is generally not possible to enter with an Israeli passport, but anyone entering the UAE with an Israeli stamp in a non-Israeli passport should have no problem.

AIR

Airports & Airlines

Dubai International (p328) and **Abu Dhabi International** (Map p346; ☎02-505 5555; www.abudhabiairport.ae) are the UAE's main airports. A small number of flights, especially charters, also land at **Sharjah International Airport** (☎06-558 1111; www.shj-airport.gov.ae) and **Ras Al Khaimah International Airport** (☎07-207 5200; www.rakairport.com; Hwy 118 (Airport Rd)). Passenger flights have also started using Dubai's new megasized Al Maktoum International. Departure tax is included in the ticket price.

Emirates Airlines (Map p312; www.emirates.com) Dubai-based; has extensive route network, excellent service and good safety record.

Etihad Airways (www.etihad.com) Based in Abu Dhabi; has extensive route network, excellent service and good safety record.

Air Arabia (www.airarabia.com) Sharjah-based low-cost carrier flying to North African, Middle Eastern, Asian and select European destinations, including Amsterdam, London and Barcelona.

FlyDubai (www.flydubai.com) Discount carrier with around 50 destinations, mostly within the Middle East, India and Central Asia. Has some flights to and from Dubai's new Al Maktoum International.

LAND

Border Crossings

- The UAE shares borders with Oman and Saudi Arabia, but only Gulf Cooperation Council (GCC) citizens are permitted to cross into Saudi Arabia at the Ghuwaifat/Sila border post in the far west of the UAE.
- The handiest border crossings for non-GCC citizens headed for mainland Oman are the Hili checkpoint in Al Ain, the Hatta checkpoint east of Dubai and the tiny coastal Khatmat Malaha crossing south of Fujairah.
- If you're headed for Khasab on the Musandam Peninsula, use the Shams/Tibat checkpoint north of Ras Al Khaimah. There's another border crossing to the Musandam in Dibba on the east coast, but military checkpoints make it impossible to drive to Khasab from there.
- There's a Dh35 fee when leaving the UAE and a OR6 visa fee at the Omani entry point.
- Thanks to a common visa facility between Oman and the emirate of Dubai, tourists from around 60 countries (there's a list at www.rop.

gov.om/english/dg_pr_visas_dubai.asp) who entered the UAE through Dubai don't have to pay the exit fee or the Omani visa fee – but *only* when using the Hatta checkpoint. However, there have been reports that not all Hatta border personnel honour this agreement.

Bus

Oman National Transport Company (ONTC; Map p312; ☎ in Dubai 04-252 5909; www.ontocoman.com; each way Dh55) ONTC runs comfortable buses with televisions and toilets on board between Muscat (Oman) and Dubai. Buses leave Ruwi station in Muscat at 6am, 3pm and 11pm and take about six hours for the trip to the bus stop near the Deira City Centre. Buses for Muscat leave at 7am, 3pm and 11pm.

Car & Motorcycle

If you intend to drive into the UAE, bring your passport, visa (if any), driving licence, car registration and proof of adequate insurance cover. Make sure you have enough gas since petrol stations are few and far between.

Getting Around

AIR

Rotana Jet (Map p346; ☎ 02-444 3366; www.rotanajet.com; Al Bateen Executive Airport) This Abu Dhabi–based airline offers executive travel from Al Bateen airport some 10km east of Abu Dhabi's city centre. There are three weekly flights to Dubai and four weekly trips to Sir Bani Yas Island.

INTERCITY BUS

The following companies provide travel between the emirates. See individual sections for details.

Abu Dhabi Department of Transportation (☎ toll free 800 55555; www.dot.abudhabi.ae) Service within the emirate, eg to Al Ain, Mezaira'a (for the Liwa Oasis) and Jebel Dhanna (for Sir Bani Yas Island).

Roads & Transport Authority (RTA; ☎ 24hr hotline 800 9090; www.rta.ae) Based in Dubai; service to Sharjah, Al Ain, Abu Dhabi and Ras Al Khaimah from several bus stations in Bur Dubai and Deira.

Sharjah Roads & Transport Authority (☎ 06-562 4444; www.st.gov.ae) Destinations include Dubai, Ajman, Ras Al Khaimah, Abu Dhabi, Al Ain, Masafi, Fujairah, Khor Fakkan and Dibba.

CAR

Having your own wheels is a great way to see the UAE, allowing you to get off the major highways and to stop as you please. Well-maintained multi-lane highways link the cities, often lit along their entire length. For off-road driving, you need a 4WD. If you have a breakdown call the **Arabian Automobile Association** (☎ 04-266 9989; www.aaauae.com).

Hire

- To hire a car, you'll need a passport, a credit card and a valid driving licence. International driving licences are not usually compulsory, but it's better to have one.
- Daily rates start at about Dh200 for a small manual car such as a Toyota Yaris, including comprehensive insurance and unlimited miles.
- Expect surcharges for airport rentals, additional drivers, one-way hire and drivers under 25. Most companies have child and infant safety seats for a fee, but these must be reserved well in advance.
- GPS devices are also available for hire for about Dh35 per day. Although somewhat useful, their data (especially outside of Dubai) is not usually current and should not be relied upon entirely.
- Local agencies may be cheaper, but the major international ones have the advantage of larger fleets and better emergency backup.
- For longer rentals, prebooked and prepaid packages, arranged in your home country, may work out cheaper than on-the-spot rentals. Check for deals with online travel agencies, travel agents or brokers such as Auto Europe (www.autoeurope.com) or Holiday Autos (www.holidayautos.com).
- If you plan on taking the car to Oman, bring written permission from the car-rental company in case you're asked for it at the border. You'll also need car insurance that's valid in Oman. Omani insurance is available at most border crossings.

PUBLIC TRANSPORT

Dubai, Abu Dhabi and Sharjah are the only emirates with public bus services. Dubai also has the high-tech Dubai Metro, which links some of the major attractions and malls and is an inexpensive, efficient way to get across town. New in Dubai is the Dubai Tram, which trundles around the Dubai Marina.

TAXIS

Taxis are cheap, metered and ubiquitous and – given the dearth of public transportation in some emirates – often the only way of getting around.

Most drivers can also be hired by the hour. In that case, rates should be negotiated unless fixed fees are set in place. In Dubai, for instance, the fee for six hours is Dh300, for 12 hours Dh500.

Most cabs can also be engaged for long-distance travel to other emirates, in which case you should negotiate the fee at the beginning of the trip.

Few drivers are fluent English speakers and many are more familiar with landmarks than street names. It helps if you mention parks, shopping malls or hotel names when giving directions for your desired destination. Tip about 10% for good service.

TOURS

The following companies are all well established and are licensed by the Department of Tourism & Commerce Marketing (DTCM). They offer a wide choice of tours, ranging from city excursions of Dubai, Al Ain and Abu Dhabi to more active trips, such as trekking in the Hajar Mountains or overnight desert safaris. Check the websites for details and prices. Note that some tours only depart with a minimum number of passengers. If you have a choice, Arabian Adventures has a particularly good reputation and repeatedly receives positive feedback from tourists.

Alpha Tours (☎04-294-9888; www.alphatoursdubai.com) Covers dune trips, safaris, ballooning, cruises, deep-sea fishing and helicopter tours.

Arabian Adventures (Map p312; ☎04-303 4888; www.arabian-adventures.com) Wider range of tours, including sundowner tours, which include 4WD drives, barbecues and Arab-style entertainment. Also does day trips to the East Coast and into the mountains.

Desert Rangers (☎04-456 9944; www.desertrangers.com) This is one of the oldest adventure-sports-and-activities outfits in Dubai. It offers a wide variety of tours, including overnight desert safaris, dhow dinner cruises, mountain safaris, canoe expeditions and desert-driving courses.

Hormuz Tourism (Map p312; ☎04-229 2138; www.hormuztourism.com) Specialises in desert safaris, including desert dinners, dune bashing, sand skiing and camel riding, alongside urban and water adventures.

Knight Tours (Map p312; ☎04-343 7725; www.knighttours.co.ae) Offers tours led by local guides/drivers who know the desert like the back of their hand. Activities include a day at the camel races, a camel caravan, Hajar Mountain treks and a falcon show.

Orient Tours (Map p312; ☎04-282 8238; www.orient-tours-uae.com) Sharjah-based outfit runs desert, city and mountain tours as well as comprehensive five-night tours of all seven emirates.

Understand Oman, UAE & Arabian Peninsula

Oman, UAE & Arabian Peninsula Today

With the exception of Yemen, the Arabian Peninsula is enjoying what is termed in Oman as a 'renaissance' – a rebirth of former confidence and strength, marked by investment in culture, education, health care and infrastructure, and a gentle relaxation of the strictly autocratic regimes of the mid-20th century. Guided by the Islamic faith, each country on the Peninsula is feeling its way towards a modern society, sharing many of the aims of the wider world while endeavouring to maintain an Arab identity.

Rapid Change

It is hard to think of another region where the pace of change has been so phenomenal. Grandparents across Arabia remember travelling by donkey, studying under a tree and sleeping in hot and inadequate housing. Infant mortality rates were high, and life expectancy low.

Within the space of 50 years, the Peninsula has changed beyond recognition. Icons of the region's success are visible from the superhighways of Saudi Arabia to the soaring towers of Gulf cities. This rapid growth is largely due to the discovery of oil, but it is also due to a willingness to embrace modernity and complex technologies it involves. Computer competence, e-governance and a mobile-phone culture are the norm across the region.

Political Disenchantment

Rapid growth inevitably has social and political repercussions and in 2011 the Arabian Peninsula witnessed its own Arab Spring. Mostly propelled by students who felt sympathy with the democratic aspirations of their Arab neighbours, there were minor protests in Oman and Kuwait and more pronounced problems in Bahrain.

Despite the unrest, many Peninsula Arabs glanced at the chaos in Yemen (the Peninsula's only democracy) and questioned the desirability of democratic governance. They looked to their own regimes and saw other ways of effecting positive change: as Hilary Clinton identified, strong leadership and a mandate to govern is behind the phenomenal growth and modernisation of Gulf countries. The promise of higher education and jobs further helped quell the unrest, while a groundswell of interest in canvassing for local elections to *majlis ashura* (equivalent to a Western parliament) has laid the groundwork for greater participation in government by elected representatives across the region.

Today political disenchantment, where it exists, is less about ideology and more about domestic concerns such as religious sectarianism and high youth unemployment.

Best on Film

Lawrence of Arabia (1962) David Lean's classic desert epic.

A Dangerous Man: Lawrence after Arabia (1991) An unofficial sequel to *Lawrence of Arabia*.

Lessons of Darkness (1992) Werner Herzog's exploration of apocalypse in Kuwait's oil fields after the Gulf War.

The Kingdom (2007) Action film examining Saudi Arabia's relationship with USA.

Best in Print

Seven Pillars of Wisdom (TE Lawrence; 1935) Evocative desert descriptions during the Arab Campaign of 1915 to 1918.

Arabian Sands (Wilfred Thesiger; 1959) Captures the Bedouin way of life before it is lost forever.

Orientalism (Edward Said; 1978) The book that redefined the Western love affair with the Middle East.

The Travels of Ibn Battutah (ed Tim Mackintosh-Smith; 2002) Includes illuminating commentary on the great Arab traveller's lifework.

Nine Parts of Desire: The Hidden World of Islamic Women (Geraldine Brooks; 1994) Probing account by an Australian journalist of what it means to be a woman living in an Islamic country.

In 2015 the Arab region continued to have the highest youth unemployment rate in the world, an issue that has contributed to the placement of Qatar at 32 and Oman at only 52 on the UN's Human Development Index (global standard-of-living benchmark).

Diversification & Cooperation

Providing more employment opportunities is difficult when all countries across the region have been hit by falling oil prices prompted by new methods of extraction and a resulting oversupply. This has placed greater emphasis on economic diversification through trade, commerce and tourism. Dubai is the obvious success story in this regard, with only 5% of the emirate's GDP based on oil revenue.

Hindering local employment is the continued reliance on a largely expatriate workforce. It takes time for the benefits of a modern education system to produce home-grown expertise and there is resistance from some immigrant communities to train local replacements. Without progress in the human-resource development of the region, however, there is concern that a two-tier society will inevitably lead to further resentment and instability.

A strengthening of ties between the countries of the Gulf Cooperation Council (GCC) has helped find regional solutions to employment issues, permitting migration of indigenous workers across the region. Although a shared currency has been put on hold, a new railway spanning the region from Kuwait to Oman is underway, symbolising the underlying sense of unity between GCC member states.

Problematic Neighbour

Perhaps the biggest challenge facing the region today is Yemen. The complex conflict in Yemen is fuelled by a sectarian dimension in the form of a Shiite insurgency, carried out by Houthi rebels. To date they have succeeded in ousting the former president and have taken over much of the country. This in turn has provoked Saudi Arabia and allies to launch air strikes aimed at restoring the internationally recognised regime. Some fear that Saudi's Arab coalition, involving the UAE, may spill across the wider region as competing ideologies battle for a foothold in the only impoverished corner of the Peninsula.

Balancing the Future

Peninsula Arabs have braved the shock of the new, but now each country needs to find a way in which to honour its heritage and give a greater sense of inclusion to its citizens. The establishment of *majlis ashura* (public representation) in public policy is a good start and the inclusion of women as they join the ranks of government ministers is also viewed favourably.

In 2015 Saudi Arabia made history by electing 14 women as local councillors. Propelled ahead of male colleagues by a proven propensity for education and with less commitment to *wasta* (nepotism), Arabia's women are seen as the change agents of the future.

POPULATION: **78 MILLION**

LITERACY: **86.5%**

UNEMPLOYMENT: **AVERAGE 9%**

AREA: **3,097,988 SQ KM**

LAND MASS: **WORLD'S LARGEST PENINSULA**

if the Arabian Peninsula were 100 people

70 would identify as indigenous Arab
17 would identify as Sub-continental
8 would identify as other Arab
3 would identify as Eastern expatriate
2 would identify as Western expatriate

belief systems
(% of population)

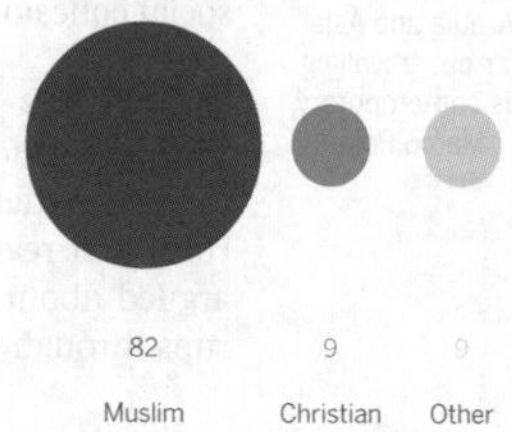

population per sq km

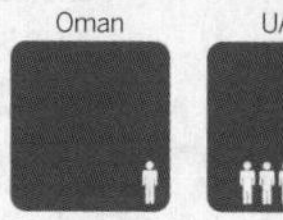

≈ 10 person

History

In the 1950s the countries of the Arabian Peninsula were a collection of impoverished, disparate states, more easily defined by tribe than by nation. Any sense of the former glory days of incense routes and East African empires was lost in the sands of time. So how did the region suddenly reinvent itself as a major economic powerhouse with a strong sense of identity? The answer lies in Arabia's inheritance of trading excellence and social coherence, two subjects worth further investigation within the context of the region's history.

Tropical Roots (66,000,000–10,000 BC)

Stand in the middle of Wadi Fanja on the outskirts of Muscat and you may just uncover more than the toads and grasshoppers of today's arid vista. This was where archaeologists discovered a herbivorous dinosaur, not unlike Zalmoxes or Rhabdodon dinosaurs from France and Romania. What is interesting about this discovery is that it shows the climate of eastern Arabia some 66 million years ago was far more verdant than it is today, with savannah-like grasslands and abundant rainfall. Crocodiles also inhabited places such as Wadi Fanja, suggesting that permanent rivers helped to cut the deeply incised mountain ranges of today's Peninsula.

Staying in religious schools to avoid expensive hostelries, 14th-century Muslim pilgrim Ibn Battuta set the standard for budget travel. Intending to perform hajj at the age of 20, his 'gap year' lasted 24 years. He clocked up an impressive 120,000km in Arabia and Asia, far out-travelling his contemporary, Marco Polo.

Homo erectus was attracted to the rich hunting and gathering grounds of southern Arabia more than a million years ago. Homo sapiens arrived on the scene around 100,000 BC and began more organised settlement. Visitors to museums across the region, particularly the national museums in Bahrain and Muscat, will see charcoal burners, flint axes and spearheads, dating from 10,000 BC, as evidence of the earliest forms of social cohesion.

Born to Trade (10,000 BC–AD 500)

Visit any souq across the Peninsula, or attend a meeting between doctor and patient, teacher and pupil, and you will realise instantly that rules and regulations are fluid, negotiable entities to be haggled over, argued about and artfully manipulated. Perhaps this is because trade runs through the blood of Peninsula people, shaping modern daily inter-

TIMELINE

c 66,000,000 BC

Unlike the deserts of modern Arabia, the Peninsula is covered in savannah-like grasslands, rainfall is abundant and permanent rivers are home to crocodiles and herbivorous dinosaurs.

c 100,000 BC

Homo sapiens live a hunter-gatherer life across the Peninsula, burning fires and rearing their own livestock. They form the first organised communities in the region.

6000–3200 BC

Loose groups of Stone Age and Bronze Age individuals occupy the Peninsula, setting up intricate trade routes between Arabia and Mesopotamia (Iraq) and the Indus Valley.

The Incense Route

actions as it has shaped each country's ancient heritage. Not surprisingly then, trade informed the very earliest aspects of the region's history.

Copper was where it all began. It was mined in Majan (the ancient name of Oman) and traded through the mighty Dilmun Empire. It's easy to simplify the lives of the ancients, but the early seafaring traders of Dilmun were no barbarians. They spent their mineral wealth on fine glass, ate too many dates and suffered bad teeth, took the time to thread beads of carnelian to hang round their beloveds' necks, enjoyed complex legends and expressed their interest in life through their administrations of death – much like their contemporaries in Egypt.

The Peninsula's early wealth wasn't founded on ore alone, however. It was due in large part to a tree, and a particularly ugly one at that. Frankincense, the aromatic resin of the *Boswellia sacra* tree, was the chief export and economic mainstay of the region. Grown in southern Arabia and carried by caravan across the desert interior, it helped fund powerful civilisations for 500 years. Indeed, the Nabataeans, famed for

Books: Early History

Arabia & the Arabs: From the Bronze Age to the Coming of Islam (Robert Hoyland)

Frankincense & Myrrh (Nigel Groom)

c 3000 BC

Dilmun, the first great civilisation on the Peninsula, is founded off the coast of Bahrain; it extends from Failaka Island (near present-day Kuwait) towards the mountains of Oman.

3000–2000 BC

In Oman, tombs at Bat and Gaylah are erected along mountain ridges by the Hafit and the Umm an Nar cultures – people belonging to the low-lying territories of the Gulf.

323 BC

Alexander the Great, attracted to Arabia's wealth, dies, leaving his plan to mount an expedition to the region unfulfilled. His admiral, Nearchus, establishes an important trading colony on Failaka Island.

c 200 BC–AD 100

The Nabataean Empire controls northwestern Arabia, growing rich by taxing frankincense caravans travelling between southern Arabia and Damascus. The Gulf comes under the influence of Persian dynasties.

carving spectacular tombs into the desert cliffs at Madain Saleh (Saudi Arabia), similar to those of their capital Petra (Jordan), controlled much of northwestern Arabia from 200 to 100 BC, sustained by the precious sap. Along ancient trade routes, frankincense found its way into the inner sanctum of temples in Egypt, Jerusalem and Rome and was recorded in the Bible and the Quran. It is used to this day in many of the world's most sacred ceremonies. According to Pliny, writing in the 1st century AD, it was thanks to the frankincense trade that the people of southern Arabia became the richest on Earth.

The Queen of Sheba is fabled to have laid frankincense at the feet of King Solomon and the three wise men took it to Jerusalem. According to Pliny, only 3000 families had the right of harvesting frankincense – but with exclusions as men were forbidden to cut trees after contact with women.

Tradition dictated that the frankincense tree was a gift from Allah and was thus not to be propagated, bought or sold, and only harvested if it happened to be within your plot of land. Needless to say, that didn't stop people from trying. In an attempt to protect their precious resources, the Jibbali, the caretakers of Omani frankincense groves, honed the art of misinformation. Flying red serpents and toxic mists were just some of the mythical tribulations rumoured to protect trees from evil eye and thieving hand. Gathering the aromatic gum was fraught with danger due to deadly indigenous infections and the harsh environment beyond the monsoon catchment. Little wonder the collectors were often slaves, or those banished to the area as punishment.

The frankincense trade was centred on Sumhuram, which the Greeks called Moscha and which is now known as Khor Rouri. Today the ruins of this once-great port are a short drive from Salalah, the capital of Dhofar and the second-largest city in Oman. Looking out to sea on a wet and windy July day, when the grazing camels and flamingos shelter in the upper reaches of the lagoon and leave the violent shore to the ghost crabs, it's little wonder that easier ports would eventually be found for readier cargo, and Khor Rouri left to slip back to nature.

Travel to museums in Pakistan and around the Mediterranean and you'll be sure to find the small round seals that were the hallmark of Dilmun traders. These seals represented their personal signatures and their wide distribution is evidence of the extent of their trading influence, far beyond the Arabian Peninsula.

The Birth & Growth of Islam (570–1498)

Given that today one out of every four people in the world are Muslim, there can be no greater moment of historical importance on the Arabian Peninsula than the birth of the Prophet Mohammed in AD 570.

As one of the world's most influential spiritual leaders, it is easy to focus on Mohammed's teachings and forget his historical context, but in many ways the limited descriptions of his childhood give a good indication of life in the desert at that time. As his father died before he was born, Mohammed became the poor ward of his grandfather. Although his family were settled Arabs, he was given to a Bedouin foster mother, as was the custom at the time, to be raised in the desert. Perhaps it was this experience that gave him a sense of moderation and the preciousness of resources. In the desert, too, there were no intermediaries, no priests and no prescribed places of worship – nothing separating the people from the things they believed in.

c 300

Central and western Arabia develop into a patchwork of independent city states, sustained by the frankincense trade or by farming, while the Gulf is subsumed into the Sassanian Empire from Persia.

570

The Ma'rib dam, upon which the livelihoods of 50,000 people depend, bursts its banks, scattering the people of Adz in the Peninsula's most significant migration. Prophet Mohammed is born.

610

Mohammed receives his first revelation. Considered by Muslims as the word of God, the Quran subsequently lays the foundations of a new, monotheistic religion that condemns the worship of idols.

622–632

Mohammed and his followers flee Mecca for Medina in 622, marking the beginning of the first Islamic state. The new religion spreads across the Peninsula, despite Mohammed's death in 632.

Mohammed went on caravans and became a trusted trader before returning to Mecca, which at that time was a large and prosperous city that profited from being the centre of pilgrimage. Mecca was the home of the Kaaba, a sanctuary founded by Abraham but occupied by the images and idols of many other tribes and nations.

The worship of the one true god and the condemnation of idols was at the heart of Mohammed's teaching and inevitably the Meccans took fright, forcing Mohammed to flee to Medina in 622. Mohammed's mighty legacy, however, transcended his personal history and the new religion of Islam quickly spread across the Peninsula and to the world beyond. Ironically, as Islam expanded, the fortunes of Arabia waned, but to this day the Peninsula holds a special place in history as the birthplace of one of the world's great monotheistic religions.

THE FRANKINCENSE TREE

Drive along the road from Salalah to the Yemeni border and you may be forgiven for missing one of the most important aspects of the Arabian Peninsula's history. Sprouting from the limestone rock as if mindless of the lack of nutrition, leafless and (for much of the year) pretty much lifeless, *Boswellia sacra* must be one of the least spectacular 'monuments' on a traveller's itinerary. Indeed, with its peeling bark and stumped branches, the frankincense tree looks more like something out of *The Day of the Triffids* than a tree that established the early fortunes of the region.

What makes the tree so special, of course, is its aromatic sap, known as 'lubban' in Arabic or 'frankincense' in English. The sap oozes in white- or amber-coloured beads from incisions made in the bark and is left to harden in the sun. Frankincense has a natural oil content, allowing it to burn well, and the vapour is released by dropping a bead of the sap onto hot embers.

To this day the pungent aroma is used locally with great enthusiasm, wafted at the entrance of a house to ward away evil spirits, guard against the evil eye or perfume garments. It has other traditional uses, too. The sap has medicinal qualities and was used in just about every prescription dispensed by the Greeks and the Romans. It is still used in parts of the Peninsula to treat a wide range of illnesses, including coughs and psychotic disorders, believed to be the result of witchcraft. Internationally, frankincense remains a part of many (particularly Christian) religious rites and is included as an ingredient in exotic perfumes.

Although the frankincense tree grows in Wadi Hadramawt in Yemen, as well as in northern Somalia, the specimens of Dhofar in southern Oman have been famed since ancient times for producing the finest-quality sap. The tree favours the unique weather system of this corner of southern Arabia, just beyond the moisture-laden winds of the *khareef* (summer season), but near enough to enjoy their cooling influence. As such it is notoriously difficult to root elsewhere.

632–850

The Muslim capital moves to Damascus, heading an empire that extends from Spain to India. Mecca and Medina lose their earlier political importance, but grow as the spiritual homes of Islam.

850–1300

Arabia's old trade routes collapse and the Peninsula declines in wealth and importance. Petty sheikhdoms bicker over resources, under the control of Tartar moguls, Persians and Ottoman Turks.

1498

In a generous but ominous gesture, a celebrated sailor from Oman, Ahmed bin Majid, helps Vasco da Gama navigate the Cape of Good Hope, leading a decade later to occupation.

1507

Portugal annexes the Yemeni island of Suqutra. It uses this vantage point to complete an occupation of Oman and goes on to colonise the island of Bahrain.

Europeans Arrive (1498–1650)

Nicknamed 'Ruffian Dick' by his contemporaries, famed 19th-century traveller Richard Burton learned Arabic and entered Mecca disguised as a *hajji* (pilgrim), an adventure he recorded in a vast tome entitled *Personal Narrative of a Pilgrimage to Al Madinah and Meccah*.

There is something satisfying about standing under the Tomb of Bibi Miriam in Qalhat, Oman, knowing that two of the world's great medieval travellers, Marco Polo and Ibn Battuta, also stood there. Their travels prefigured a revival in Western trading interests in Arabia and it wasn't long before the pilgrim caravans of Mecca were once again transporting spices and drugs from the Orient to Europe via the ports of Istanbul and Venice.

Meanwhile, a great Omani seafarer, Ahmed bin Majid, helped Vasco da Gama navigate the Cape of Good Hope in 1498 and, in good faith, told him of his own wondrous country on the Straits of Hormuz. The Portuguese quickly understood the strategic significance of their 'discovery' and by 1507 Portugal had annexed the Yemeni island of Suqutra, occupied Oman and colonised Bahrain. Travel along the coast of the Gulf today and Portuguese forts appear with regularity – cut inland and there's no trace of them. The Portuguese were only interested in protecting their trade routes and made no impact on the interior of these countries at all – a suitable metaphor for the negligible cultural exchange that took place. When they were eventually ousted by the mid-17th century, they left little more than a legacy of military architecture – and the Maria Theresa dollar.

British 'Protection' (1650–1914)

'One great distinguishing feature of Muscat ... is the respect and civility shown by all classes of its inhabitants to Europeans,' wrote the English diplomat James Silk Buckingham in his 1816 book, *Travels*. It is an interesting comment because it appears to show that the intimate British involvement with Oman and the 'Trucial States' (the countries along the southern rim of the Gulf) over the next two centuries was founded on mutual benefit rather than solely on colonisation and exploitation. On the one hand, the various treaties and 'exclusive agreements' that Britain signed with the sultan and emirs of the region kept the French at bay and thereby safeguarded British trading routes with India. On the other hand, the British helped maintain the claims to sovereignty of the emerging Gulf emirates against marauding Turkish and Persian interests and from the powerful ambitions of the eventual founder of Saudi Arabia, Ibn Saud.

The pearling season began each year in late May. Fishermen remained at sea, through the blistering summer, without interruption until mid-October. Supplies were ferried out by dhow.

During WWI British interests in the Gulf were threatened by the Ottomans. The sultan, siding with the Germans, declared jihad (holy war), calling on Muslims everywhere to rise up against the Allied powers of Britain, France and Russia. In response, the British persuaded Hussein

1902

Abdul Aziz bin Abdul Rahman al Saud, known as Ibn Saud, begins a series of conquests that eventually lead to the formation of the state of Saudi Arabia.

1912

The Saudis pose a serious threat to the Gulf sheikhdoms. British protection saves Kuwait, Qatar and the UAE from being subsumed into Saudi Arabia.

1916

Hussein bin Ali al Hashimi leads an Arab revolt against the Ottomans in anticipation of being crowned 'King of the Arabs'. The British sign the Balfour Declaration instead, favouring the establishment of Israel.

1932

Ibn Saud combines the two crowns of Hejaz and Najd, renaming his country the 'Kingdom of Saudi Arabia'. In the same year, oil is struck in commercial quantities in Bahrain.

bin Ali, the Grand Sherif of Mecca, to lead an Arab revolt against the Ottomans in exchange for a promise to make him 'King of the Arabs' once the conflict was over. To the famous disgust of British army officer TE Lawrence, the British negotiated with the French on the carving up of the Ottoman Empire and assisted the Zionist movement instead.

Despite this monumental sell-out, visit any corner of the Arabian Peninsula today and you are bound to meet a pink-faced Brit, basking in the desert sun. Equally, talk to leaders across the region and chances are they were educated in part in the UK. The special relationship between the British and the Arabs of the Peninsula has endured the trials and tribulations of history, and is one of the positive legacies of 19th-century colonialism.

LAWRENCE OF ARABIA

If there is one name in Arab history that most Western people will recognise, it's surely that of TE Lawrence, better known as Lawrence of Arabia – the same Lawrence, in fact, who wrote to his sceptical biographer that 'history isn't made up of the truth anyhow, so why worry'. This is an interesting question when it comes to the history of the Arabian Peninsula as there appears to be no definitive version of events. The story assumes a different shape, particularly since the beginning of the 20th century, according to whose account you read.

Lawrence's own account of Arabian history, so eloquently described in *The Seven Pillars of Wisdom,* is a case in point. You might imagine, from what he writes, that Lawrence and General Allenby, the senior British Officer responsible for the Arab Campaign, single-handedly brought the modern Arabian Peninsula into being during the Arab Revolt from 1915 to 1918. 'On my plan, by my effort,' he states triumphantly on the taking of Aqaba.

But where are the Arabs in Lawrence's account? What did they make of the pale-skinned, blue-eyed eccentric? Read Suleiman Mousa's account of the campaign in *TE Lawrence: An Arab View* and you barely recognise the same moment in history. While Lawrence is busy taking credit for little skirmishes, larger battles led by the Arabs are only briefly mentioned, and Lawrence arrives triumphant in cities where Arab leaders Feisal and Auda have been waiting for days. Far from the great white hunter, he is remembered in many Arab accounts as a sickly individual with boils who, like a spoof in a Western, mistakenly shot his own camel. But then such is history from an Arab perspective.

We'll never know whether Lawrence was centre stage or sideshow. What the example illustrates, however, is the caution with which you need to approach the history of the Peninsula. In the early 21st century this must surely sound familiar to anyone following current events in the region in local and Western media. It's tempting to agree with Lawrence that history can at times be more about fiction than fact.

1948

The Gulf rupee replaces the Indian rupee as the common currency of all Gulf States, reflecting a shift away from the jurisdiction of the British Raj after India's independence.

1960

The Middle East produces 25% of the non-Communist world's oil. The 1960s bring the winds of change and hand-in-hand with independence comes a sense of national and regional identity.

1961–71

In 1961 Kuwait gains independence from Britain. In late 1971 Bahrain and Qatar follow suit, followed by the sheikhdoms of the lower Gulf, which combine to form the United Arab Emirates.

1973

The Gulf States' embargo of oil to the West – the 'oil weapon' – is first used to powerful effect during the Arab-Israeli War to protest against the West's support for Israel.

The Pearling Industry (1914–1930)

One of the mixed pleasures of visiting a Gulf jewellery shop is to hold a natural pearl in the palm of one's hand and see reflected in its gorgeous lustre the not-so-illustrious history of the region.

Although pearls have come to be associated with Bahrain, they were harvested throughout the Gulf and each region gave rise to a specific type of pearl. Pteria shells, or winged oysters, were extensively collected for their bluish mother-of-pearl off the coast of Ras al Khaimah. The large shells known in the trade as 'Bombay Shells' were found in Omani waters and chiefly exported to London for pearl inlay and decorative cutlery. With an annual export of 2000 tonnes, worth UK£750,000, the most common pearl oyster of the Gulf was *Pinctada radiata,* collected off the coasts of Kuwait, Bahrain and the UAE.

Books: Modern Regional History

- *Inside Al Qaeda: Global Network of Terror* (Rohan Gunaratna)
- *A History of the Middle East* (Peter Mansfield)

Given the volume of the trade, it is not surprising that it supported the local economies of much of the Gulf. Trading in pearls has existed since the 3rd millennium BC, but it was only in the 19th century, with the collapse of other trade routes in the region, that pearls assumed their economic value. In the 1920s, with what seemed like an insatiable international appetite for pearls, the trade reached its apex.

Pearling was brutally hard work. Workers were divided into divers (who descended for the shells with a weight between their feet) and pullers (who would hoist the divers to the surface by rope). Neither were paid wages. Instead they would receive a share of the total profits for the season. A puller's share was half to two-thirds of a diver's. Boat owners would usually advance money to their workers at the beginning of the season. But the divers were often unable to pay back these loans and got further into debt each year. As a result they were often bound to a particular boat owner for life. If a diver died, his sons were obliged to work off his debts. It was not unusual to see quite elderly men still working as divers.

The American journalist Lydell Hart made TE Lawrence into a media superhero. The *Sunday Times* of June 1968 hailed Lawrence as a 'Prince of Mecca, riding across Arabia'. Hollywood did the rest.

Suddenly, around 1930, the unthinkable happened. The Japanese invented a method of culturing pearls. This, combined with the Great Depression, caused the bottom to drop out of the international pearl market. The Peninsula's great pearling industry petered out almost overnight. Although the collapse brought great hardship to the Gulf in the decades before the discovery of oil, few had the heart to regret it.

Impact of Oil and Modernisation (1930–Today)

Early in the 20th century a rare resource was discovered on the Peninsula that was to change the face of the region forever. It is upon this resource that the super-modern cities of the Gulf have been crafted out

1981

In May Saudi Arabia, Kuwait, Bahrain, Qatar, UAE and Oman form the Gulf Cooperation Council (GCC) to increase economic cooperation and in response to the perceived threat from Iran.

1990

Iraq invades Kuwait in August and annexes the state. King Fahd of Saudi Arabia appeals to the US for help and the US and Allied forces launch Operation Desert Storm.

1991

The Gulf States eye up developments in Yemen as it makes regional history by becoming the first multiparty democracy on the Arabian Peninsula.

2006

The Asian Games are hosted in Doha – a coup for Qatar and the region as a whole. Oman pulls out of the proposed single currency, a setback for greater GCC integration.

of the sea on reclaimed land, and upon which the nations of Arabia have been pulled by the sandal straps into the 21st century.

Within a few years almost every ruler in the Gulf had given some kind of oil concession in an attempt to bolster their finances. The region's nascent industry was suspended temporarily during WWII but resumed soon after, increasing output to rival that of Iran, the world's biggest producer by 1960.

In the 1960s and '70s the new wealth, and the threat of cutting off oil supplies to Europe and the US, gave Middle Eastern countries an international influence they hadn't enjoyed for centuries. After each embargo, a surge in oil prices increased both their wealth and their power, triggering the first wave of an enormous building boom in the Gulf that has continued almost unabated for half a century. Western expatriates flocked to the region, providing engineering and financial expertise while hundreds of thousands of Asian expatriates were brought in as manual labour. This change in demographics has left a legacy that continues to have profound effects on the indigenous populations. On the one hand it has resulted in tolerant, multicultural societies and greatly enhanced infrastructure; on the other hand it has led to an outnumbering in some countries of the indigenous Arab population and a difficulty in all countries of ensuring work opportunities for locals.

Each time the bottom falls out of the oil market (through global recession or the threat of new technologies such as fracking), Gulf countries have trouble maintaining their building programs and the generous welfare support their people have come to expect. Each crisis has had hidden benefits, however, forcing the countries of the Gulf Cooperation Council (GCC) to diversify their economies.

But the days of black gold are not over yet. Exploration continues across the region, together with investment in research into ever-more-sophisticated ways of extraction. Despite the hunt for renewable energies such as solar, wind, wave and waste-to-energy power, it's unlikely that any of these green technologies will replace oil in the collective memory of the region. Oil, after all, has given Arabia its place in the modern world.

Gulf pearls have been traded for centuries as the gems of celebrities. A magnificent multi-stranded pearl necklace, gifted by Sheik Zaid, founder of the UAE, to the famous Arab singer Umm Khalthum, sold for US$1.4 million in 2008.

2007

The building boom across the Peninsula reaches its peak as multibillion-dollar projects, almost unthinkable elsewhere in the world, reach fruition in all Peninsula countries except Yemen.

2008

The global recession starts to bite on the Arabian Peninsula with catastrophic effect in Dubai by 2009. Qatar and Oman remain relatively unscathed.

2011

The Arab Spring erupts across the region, leaving Bahrain in particular in turmoil. Peninsula governments crack down on corruption and review their policies to quell local restiveness.

2015

Conflict between elected government forces and Houthi rebels plunges Yemen into virtual civil war, attracting air strikes from neighbouring Saudi Arabia and threatening to destabilise an otherwise peaceful Peninsula.

People & Society

Although Peninsula countries cover a large area, and vary considerably in terms of geography, history and recent fortunes, they nonetheless share a strong continuity of culture quite distinct from neighbouring Arab regions. Whether this arises out of a shared desert experience, from being at the crossroads of East–West trade, or from proximity to the birthplace of Islam, it makes for a coherent experience for visitors, who are likely to sense Bedouin roots as equally in a mall as a souq.

People

Those who live on the Arabian Peninsula are not so much distinguished between one country and the next (although national and tribal allegiances are fiercely maintained) as between those who live there for work and those who are native to the region. That may sound obvious, but given that expats outnumber the indigenous population in many quarters, this takes on a particular significance in the region, fuelling the social debates in the coffeehouses and affecting policy in and between Gulf states. Distinctions are also drawn between city dwellers who have made their fortunes in the era of oil, and those who have either chosen or been obliged to continue living the harsh desert life of their forebears. All indigenous Arabs share, and are proud of, the Peninsula's Bedouin roots, but only a very few would welcome to live a life of such hardships today.

The Arabs: Myth and Reality by Gerald Butt, the ex-BBC Middle East correspondent, traces the geopolitical history of the region and examines its complex relationship with the West, including the stereotypical images of the Peninsula Arab.

Lifestyle

Drive through the suburbs of Peninsula cities and you'll see domed villas with spangled concrete that glistens in the sun. Walk through the gold souqs and you'll see women with Gucci handbags, buying diamonds and pearls. Park outside the Ritz-Carlton in Manama, or the Burj al Arab in Dubai, and you'll be embarrassed to be driving a Toyota Echo. Undoubtedly, huge private fortunes have been made in the oil rush and building expansion.

But that isn't the whole picture. Universal education and the mass media have increased expectations, and people who were content with little now want more. Cement and steel prices have doubled in a decade and the burgeoning Arab middle class frets over securing loans to finish the house or pay college fees. If shopping before payday is anything to go by, most families are left with little at the end of the month.

The rest of the picture is completed by stepping out of the city altogether. Lives in mountain villages, in desert oases, on the dunes, or in coastal fishing villages may seem to have been little impacted by city incomes, but then you spot the satellite dish attached to the *barasti* (palm frond) walls; the electricity poles marching up the wadis; the communally owned truck that has allowed settlement to replace nomadic existence. Water, electricity, roads, education and healthcare: this is the real wealth of the region today and it is remarkably evenly spread given the challenges of geography and topography.

Minority Population Statistics

- *Pastoral nomads: less than 5% of Arabia's Bedouin population*
- *Emiratis in UAE: 18% of population*
- *Qataris in Qatar: 12% of population*

Health & Life Expectancy

A more modern lifestyle, be it in the city or the interior, together with immunisation and improved healthcare systems, have brought radical benefits to the health of many Peninsula people. Life expectancy has risen, child mortality reduced and diseases such as malaria eradicated. On the terraces of southern Arabia 20 years ago, women were bent double

A COSMOPOLITAN POPULATION

Although officially treated equally, expatriates who work on the Peninsula are often discriminated against, either positively or negatively, depending on their ethnicity. Middle-income workers from other Middle Eastern countries, for example, are given a friendly reception as brother Arabs and fellow Muslims, but are viewed somewhat condescendingly as poor relations and it is partially true that these expats often stay only long enough to build a house back home and send their children to college. Indeed, in some countries, such as Egypt, Jordan and Yemen, remittances from nationals working abroad constitute the backbone of the home economy.

The number of Europeans and Americans in the region has declined over the past few decades, now that the military and much of the oil and gas industry has been transferred into local hands. Often viewed as a necessary, but not altogether welcome, route to rapid modernisation, employment of these expats focused on those with advanced educational qualifications, specific skills, or teaching and training abilities. This group, with its larger disposable income, is now somewhat making way for the rise of professionals from India and China, who often command smaller salaries for similar experience and accomplishment.

Expats from India (and to a lesser extent, Pakistan and Bangladesh) have traditionally formed the middle management of the region, particularly in trade, commerce and industry, and the new generations of indigenous graduates look to them for inspiration as entrepreneurs and small business owners. The majority of expats from these countries, however, tend to be employed as manual labourers, for whom life is unremittingly hard. Long hours, poor conditions, unsafe working practices, daily exposure to 45°C heat, visa restrictions and lengthy periods without permission to return home all contribute to often-miserable lives. Most of these migrant workers are on bachelor-status visas and their plight has been the subject of much media coverage, especially in the wake of the decision to host the FIFA World Cup in Qatar in 2022. Despite their treatment being condemned by some human rights organisations, many of these expats find that the benefits outweigh the hardships of a life without work back home and they continue to be recruited in ever-larger numbers. Many return home to a hero's welcome, their meagre remittances capable of transforming the lives of their families.

Women expats, largely from the Philippines, play an important role in the healthcare industry, working as nurses and healthcare teachers. Many of the region's domestic workers are from Muslim countries such as Malaysia and Indonesia. Often required to work long hours for wages much lower than those paid to other expats, and with the risk of sexually related abuse, many nonetheless manage to support an entire extended family from their wages.

It is fair to say that, despite the negative media coverage, not all low-income expats are unhappy with their lot, with many remaining on the Peninsula for 20 years or more, bonding with the families they help to bring up, or attaining satisfaction in the infrastructure they helped build. Equally, their employers are not uniformly callous in their regard for workers' rights, and progress is being made to safeguard the rights of migrant workers across the region. Gulf Cooperation Council labour ministers met in 2014 and agreed a standardised employment contract for domestic workers that, for example, discards the controversial sponsorship system. In future, employees will not have to surrender their passports, will have the freedom to change employment and their hours will be regulated by law. It is yet to be seen how this will affect their lot, and indeed their future job prospects, but it has been welcomed by the expat community as a step in the right direction.

in the fields, baked by the sun, arthritic in the mud, or weighed down with herbage, trudging back to their homes, pausing to stack stones in the crumbling terrace walls. For many Peninsula inhabitants, it's pointless being nostalgic about the demise of hard manual labour, even if a modern lifestyle comes at the price of 'modern' diseases such as diabetes, hypertension and stroke.

Less exercise, more stress and a fast-food diet high in fats, sugar and salt have led to an increase of diabetes in Arabia. Alarmingly, five of the 10 countries with the world's highest rates of diabetes are on the Peninsula, namely the United Arab Emirates, Qatar, Bahrain, Kuwait and Saudi Arabia.

Population & Ethnic Diversity

In the Gulf, names are all important. Names tell a lot about who is from where, and each country is acutely mindful of such distinctions: 'with a name like that, he must be a Baluchi (not real Emirati)'; 'he speaks Swahili so he must be Zanzibari (not real Omani)'; 'he's from the coast (not real Saudi)'. And so it goes on until you wonder if there's any such thing as a 'real anybody'. Such snipes at ethnicity make you realise that Arab allegiances are linked to tribe before nation. Centuries of trading and pilgrimage have resulted in an extraordinarily mixed population and only a few pockets of people, such as the Jibbalis of southern Oman, can claim ethnic 'purity'.

For the visitor, Arabs are often less in evidence anyway. The indigenous population of the entire Peninsula numbers less than 50 million out of a total population of 78 million. In Saudi and Oman, non-nationals account for 33% and 44% respectively of the population, but this figure rises to 52% in Bahrain, 69% in Kuwait, 82% in the UAE and 88% in Qatar.

The large presence of other nationals on the Peninsula came about after the discovery of oil. Hundreds of thousands of expatriate workers were brought in to help develop the region's industries and provide skills and knowledge in creating a modern infrastructure. Although none of these nationals were originally permitted citizenship, many have stayed a lifetime, raising families and setting up businesses under local sponsorship, changing the demographics of the entire Peninsula.

The issue now is how to reduce the dependence on expatriate labour and train the local population to fill their place. Inevitably, few expats willingly train locals to take over their jobs. Equally, in some of the wealthier Gulf countries, there is a reluctance from locals to take on manual labour and a traditional distaste for jobs in the service industry.

In a region where petrol is cheaper than water, Peninsula Arabs love their cars and are great travellers – to family members at weekends, to foreign countries for honeymoons and, of course, to Mecca for hajj or *umrah* (literally 'little pilgrimage'). The concept of commuting solely for work is something of an alien concept, reflected in the lack of a coherent transport system.

Bedouin Roots

It's easy to underestimate the Bedouin heritage of Arab society if your visit is concentrated on the big cities of the Gulf. Yet even here there are weekend escapes to the desert (in Oman), an enormous falcon souq (in Doha) and tents set up outside the house (in Kuwait). These are all indicative of a strong attachment to an ancient culture that runs through all the countries of the Peninsula.

The attitude towards the camel is an interesting case in point. The donkey played just as important a role in transport in the mountains of the Peninsula, but no one breeds donkeys for fun. Camels, on the other hand, are as prevalent as ever and in some corners of Arabia (such as Dhofar in Oman) are proliferating at such a speed, due to their leisurely modern lifestyle, they are threatening the fragile ecology of their habitat. Of course, racing has something to do with the obsession with camel ownership, but the animal is more deeply involved in the Arab psyche than mere racing. Camels evoke ancient nomadic lifestyles, the symbol of community through hardship and endurance – the inheritance, in short, of Bedouin roots.

The term 'Bedu' (Bedouin in singular and adjectival form) refers not so much to an ethnic group as to a lifestyle. City Arabs today, stressed by familiar modern anxieties regarding wealth and how to keep it, are wistful about a bygone era to which they claim lineage, even if they are more likely to be the descendants of townspeople and seafarers.

Society

Marriage & the Role of Women

Although polygamy is legal, and the marrying of two wives is reasonably common, few Peninsula Arabs exercise their Islamic right to four wives, unable or unwilling to afford the emotional, physical and financial cost of multiple households. This is particularly burdensome given that, according to the Quran, each wife must be treated equally, in as much as this is possible.

Divorce is easily enacted and is becoming less of a taboo, especially in Oman and the Gulf countries. Modern Peninsula women are educated, usually far harder working at university than men and therefore often more successful in the workplace. They are entitled to earn and keep their own income (unlike the man, who surrenders his salary to the household) and as such have an independence unthinkable to their grandmothers.

On the one hand, discussion in Saudi Arabia focuses on fundamental women's rights – to vote (they earned this opportunity for the first time in 2015), drive, travel unescorted by male relatives, represent and be represented in a public forum. On the other hand, in the UAE and Oman, where equality of education has led to an equality of expectation, it focuses on issues such as breaking through the glass ceiling and how to train in traditionally male-oriented disciplines such as engineering, but still be able to pick and choose over shift hours or working on site.

With more women than men graduating from some of the top universities across the region, inevitably questions are being asked about primary carers in the family and the psychological fallout on men, whose once-unquestioned authority is being undermined by poor performance relative to their female counterparts.

Nine Parts of Desire by the journalist Geraldine Brooks was a ground-breaking investigation into the lives of women under Islam in the 1990s, covering various countries of the Middle East and exposing some of the many myths regarding the treatment of women in the Arab world.

Family Size & Welfare

The family, guided by Muslim principles, is still at the centre of the Arab way of life. The family is an extended unit often comprising whole villages, united around a common tribal name. Avoiding actions that may bring shame to the family is of paramount importance. Saving face is therefore more than a reluctance to admit a mistake; it's an expression of unwillingness to make a family vulnerable to criticism. Equally, promotion or success is not calculated in individual terms, but in the benefits

Encounter the Bedu in...

Sharqiya Sands, Oman

Khor Al Adaid, Qatar

Interior, Kuwait

Rub al Khali, Saudi Arabia, Oman & UAE

THE MODERN BEDOUIN

Most Bedouin have modernised their existence with 4WD trucks (it's not unusual to find the camel travelling by truck these days), fodder from town (limiting the need to keep moving) and purified water from bowsers. Most have mobile phones and satellite TV and everyone listens to the radio. Many no longer move at all. Bedouin customs, dating from the earliest days of Islam, remain pretty much unchanged, however, especially their legendary hospitality towards strangers.

Living arrangements tend to stay the same too, with tents generally divided into a *haram* (forbidden area) for women and an area reserved for the men. The men's section also serves as the public part of the house, where guests are treated to coffee and dates, or meals. It's here that all the news and gossip – a crucial part of successful survival in a hostile environment – is passed along the grapevine.

The Bedouin family is a close-knit unit. The women do most of the domestic work, including fetching water (sometimes requiring walks of many kilometres), baking bread and weaving. They are also often the first to help pull, dig and drive a tourist's stuck 4WD out of the soft sand. The men are traditionally the providers in times of peace, and fierce warriors in times of war.

it bestows on the family. Of course, everyone knows someone who can help in the collective good, and accruing *wasta* (influence) is a Peninsula pastime.

The 18th-century traveller Lady Montague noted that Arab women were more at liberty to follow their own will than their European counterparts and that the *abeyya* (which she described as the 'black disguise') made it easier for women to take a lover.

The efforts of one generation are reflected in the provision of education and opportunity for the next. This comes at a cost and few Arabs these days can afford the large families of up to 12 children of a decade ago; indeed the average in the Gulf States is now around 2.5 children.

The governments of each country have made generous provision for families across the region in terms of free education and healthcare, but the resources won't last forever and the younger generation are beginning to see that they have to work hard to secure the same opportunities for their children.

Dress & Fashion

Men take huge pride in their costume, which, in its simplicity and uniformity, is intended to transcend wealth and origin. A loose headscarf, known as *gutra,* is worn by many Peninsula males. In the Gulf States it is of white cloth, while in western Kuwait and Saudi Arabia it is checked. The black head rope used to secure the *gutra* is called *agal.* It's said to originate in the rope the Bedu used to tie up their camels at night. The Omanis usually wear a turban, wrapped deftly about a cap. In Oman these are pastel-hued and decorated with intricate and brightly coloured embroidery.

Most Peninsula men also wear the floor-length shirt-dress, which in Saudi Arabia, Bahrain and Qatar is known as a *thobe,* and in Kuwait, the UAE and Oman as a *dishdasha.* Most are white and some have collars and cuffs, while others are edged with tassels and white-thread embroidery at the neck. On ceremonial occasions the dress is completed with a finely wrought belt and ceremonial dagger and a silk outer garment.

Why the Low Crime Rate?

Strict codes of moral conduct expounded by Islam

A legal system rigorously enforced

Traditional Arab values

Ancient concepts of honour

Women's dress is more varied. It often comprises a colourful long dress or an embroidered tunic with trousers and heavily decorated ankle cuffs. In the cities, modern clothing is common. Over the top, women usually wear a black gown known as an *abeyya.* This can either be worn loose and cover the head (as in Saudi Arabia) or it can be worn as a fashion item, tailored to the body and spangled with diamantes (as in Oman).

Almost all women on the Arabian Peninsula cover their hair, but they don't all wear the burka (veil) – in Oman and the UAE, they mostly do not cover the face. Veils can be of a thin gauze completely covering the face; a cloth that covers the face but not the eyes; or a mask concealing the nose, cheeks and part of the mouth. Women often choose such coverings

THE BEDU – SURVIVAL OF THE MOST GENEROUS

Meaning 'nomadic', the name Bedu is today a bit of a misnomer. Though thought to number several hundred thousand, very few Bedu are still truly nomadic, though a few hang on to the old ways. After pitching their distinct black, goat-hair tents – the *beit ash-sha'ar* (literally 'house of hair') – they graze their goats, sheep or camels in an area for several months. When the sparse desert fodder runs out, it's time to move on again, allowing the land to regenerate naturally.

The hospitality of the Bedu is legendary, even in a region known for its generosity. Part of the ancient and sacrosanct Bedouin creed is that no traveller in need of rest or food should be turned away. Likewise, a traveller assumes the assured protection of his hosts for a period of three days and is guaranteed a safe passage through tribal territory.

The philosophy is simple: you scratch my back, I'll scratch yours – only in the desert, it's a matter of survival. Such a code of conduct ensures the survival of all in a difficult environment with scant resources. It allows the maintenance of a nomadic lifestyle and the continuation of trade. It's a kind of survival, in other words, of the most generous.

TEA & TALK

A *diwaniya* (gathering), usually conducted at someone's home – in a tent or on cushions just outside it, to be precise – is an important aspect of Gulf life, and any visitor who has the chance to partake in one will find it the best opportunity to observe Arab social life first-hand. The object of the gathering, which has its origin in Bedouin traditions of hospitality, is to drink endless cups of hot, sweet tea – oh, and to chew the political cud, of course. It is usually a 'man thing'. As one Kuwaiti woman explained, the women of the house are usually too busy living life to waste time discussing it.

in order to pass more comfortably through male company, or to protect prized pale skin and glossy hair from the harsh penalties of sun and sand. This is a custom that predates Islam.

Guests are usually seen to the door, or even to the end of the corridor or garden. Traditionally this represents the safe passage of guests across your tribal territory. If you have Arab visitors, make sure you do the same!

Religious Zeal

Only a tiny minority of people on the Peninsula are involved in religious fundamentalism, and most of those channel their zeal into peaceful attempts to reconcile the liberties of modern life with the traditional values of Islam. Those who resort to violence to accomplish largely political aims are mistrusted by their own communities and considered misguided by most religious leaders in the region. It is unfortunate that this small minority gain maximum media coverage and are the people upon whom the entire culture of the mostly peaceful, amiable, adaptable and tolerant Arabian Peninsula is judged.

Arts, Sports & Leisure

If you chose one feature that distinguishes art on the Arabian Peninsula (and Arab art generally) from other traditions, it is the close integration of function with form. In other words, most Arab art has evolved with a purpose. That purpose could be as practical as embellishing the prow of a boat with a cowrie shell to ward off 'evil eye', or as nebulous as creating intricate and beautiful patterns to intimate the presence of God and invite spiritual contemplation.

Arts

Poetry

The Son of a Duck is a Floater by Arnander and Skipworth is a fun collection of Arab sayings with English equivalents. It's worth buying just to see how wisdom is universal – not to mention the thoroughly enjoyable illustrations.

Poetry is part and parcel of the great oral tradition of storytelling that informs the literature of all Peninsula countries, the roots of which lie with the Bedu. Stories told by nomadic elders to the wide-eyed wonder of the young serve not just as after-dinner entertainment, but as a way of binding generations together in a collective oral history. As such, storytelling disseminates the principles of Islam and of tribal and national identity. It extols the virtues of allegiance, valour, endurance and hospitality, virtues that make life in a harsh environment tolerable.

All the best-known figures of classical Arabic and Persian literature are poets, including the famed Omar Khayyam, the 11th-century composer of *rub'ai* (quatrains), and the 8th-century Baghdadi poet, Abu Nuwas. The great Arab poets were regarded as possessing knowledge forbidden to ordinary people and, as such, they served the purpose of bridging the human and spirit worlds. To this day, poetry recitals play an important part in all national celebrations, and even the TV-watching young are captivated by a skilfully intoned piece of verse.

Music

The Thousand and One Nights, translated by Richard Burton, is a collection of tales (including Ali Baba and Aladdin) that originate from Arabia, India and Persia. They are told, night by night, by the beautiful, beguiling narrator, Sheherazade, to save herself from beheading by a vengeful king.

Arabian song and dance have evolved for a purpose. Generally, music was employed to distract from hardship – like the songs of the seafarers marooned on stagnant Gulf waters, or the chanting of fishermen hauling in their nets. There are also harvest songs and love ballads, all of which are either sung unaccompanied or to syncopated clapping or drum beats. East African rhythms, introduced into Arab music from Arab colonies, lend much Peninsula music a highly hypnotic quality, and songs can last for over an hour.

While the austere Wahhabi and Ibadi sects discourage singing and dancing, no wedding or national celebration on the Peninsula would be the same without them. Men dance in circles, flexing their swords or ceremonial daggers while jumping or swaying. If they get really carried away, volleys of gunfire are exchanged above the heads of the crowd. Women have a tradition of dancing for the bride at weddings. Unobserved by men, they gyrate suggestively in their revealing dresses as if encouraging the bride towards the marital bed.

While traditional music plays a big part in contemporary Arab life, it is not the only form of music. Arab pop, especially of the Amr Diab type, is ubiquitous, while radio stations and nightclubs featuring DJs show-

ORAL TRADITION

For the nomadic Bedu, life is lived on the move. Permanence is virtually unknown – even the footsteps that mark their passing shift with the sands. The artistic expression of their culture has evolved to be similarly portable – weaving that can be rolled up and stowed on a camel, beadwork that can be tucked in a pocket, stories unfurled around the campfire.

Bedu tales, with their endless digressions, allegories and parables, are used to clarify a situation, to offer tactful advice to a friend, or to alert someone diplomatically to trouble or wrongdoing. More often, they lampoon corrupt leaders and offer a satirical commentary on current affairs, particularly those of the mistrusted 'townspeople'. They can be very funny, highly bawdy and verging on the libellous, depending on the persuasions of the teller.

There is said to be a tale for every situation. Travellers may be surprised at how often the Bedu resort to proverbs, maxims or stories during the course of normal conversation. It is said that the first proverb of all is: 'While a man may tell fibs, he may never tell false proverbs'!

Sadly, the modern world has encroached on storytelling. The advent of TV and other forms of entertainment has led some to fear that this valuable oral patrimony is in danger of disappearing forever, but look at any national-day gathering and it's clear that it still has the power to touch Arab hearts.

casing the latest international trends are also popular, particularly in the UAE, Qatar and Bahrain. A classical orchestra in Oman and military drum and pipe (bagpipes) bands have won international acclaim.

Crafts

Function and form are most noticeably linked in the rich craft heritage of the Peninsula, encompassing jewellery, silversmithing, weaving, embroidery and basket making. Take jewellery, for example – the heavy silver jewellery, so distinctively worn by Bedouin women, was designed not just as a personal adornment, but as a form of portable wealth. Silver amulets, containing rolled pieces of parchment or paper, bear protective inscriptions from the Quran, to guarantee the safety of the wearer. Jewellery is traditionally melted down rather than handed on – the ultimate pragmatic gesture.

In the souqs of eastern Arabia, silver jewellery was often sold according to weight, measured in *tolahs* (11.75g). *Tolahs* are sometimes called *thallers* after the Maria Theresa dollar, an 18th-century Austrian coin used in much of Arabia's currency in the 19th and early 20th centuries.

The sad fact of practical craft is that once the need for it has passed, there is little incentive to maintain the skills. What is the point of potters in Al Hofuf and Bahla making clay ewers when everyone drinks water from branded plastic bottles? Many regional governments encourage local craft associations in the hope of keeping the craft heritage alive, resulting in successful ventures such as the Bedouin weaving project at Sadu House in Kuwait City and the women's centres in Manama and Abu Dhabi. The Omani Heritage Documentation Project is another worthwhile enterprise. Launched in 1996 to document Oman's great craft heritage, it resulted after eight years of study in a two-volume definitive guide, *The Craft Heritage of Oman*.

Architecture

In common with other arts, Peninsula architecture is also steered by purpose. The local climate plays an important role: the wind towers of the Gulf, for example, not only look attractive, they function as channels of cooler air; gaily painted adobe walls and window frames help waterproof homes in the Asir. Positioning forts around rocky outcrops gives them solid foundations. And then there's the question of space: in the mountains whole villages appear to be suspended in air, storeys piled high to save from building on precious arable land.

The love of the tower block in modern architecture stems perhaps from this common heritage, but the use of materials such as glass and concrete, inappropriate to the desert heat, have corrupted the balance between function and form. It will take more than traditional Arab motifs, such as a pointed window or a wooden screen, to bring back a harmony between architecture and its environment, but this is a challenge taken up across the region, resulting in energy-efficient urban projects such as Masdar City in Abu Dhabi.

Books on Arab Arts

Arab Contemporary: Architecture & Identity (Kallehauge, Tøjner & Holm, 2014)

Islamic Art (Luca Mozatti, 2010)

Craft Heritage of Oman (Richardson & Dorr, 2004)

Islamic Art

There is no greater example of the marriage of function and form than Islamic art. For a Muslim, Islamic art remains first and foremost an expression of faith, and many Peninsula Arabs are cautious of art for art's sake, or art as an expression of the self without reference to community.

The prime example of instructive, inspirational art is calligraphy. Arabic is not just a language for Arabs – for Muslims throughout the world it is the language of the Quran and, as such, plays a cohesive, unifying role. Islamic calligraphy, the copying of God's own words, is seen by many as a pious act and remains to this day the highest aesthetic practiced in the Arab world. In all the museums of Arabia there are magnificent examples of this highly refined art with its repetition of forms and symmetry of design.

The most visible expression of Islamic art, however, is surely the mosque. It too is built on mostly functional principles. In fact, the first mosques were modelled on the Prophet Mohammed's house. To this day the basic plan (with courtyard, domed prayer hall and vaulted niche indicating the direction of Mecca) provides a safe, cool and peaceful haven for worship and has changed little, although the first minarets appeared long after Mohammed's death. Prior to that time, the muezzin (prayer caller) often stood on a rooftop or some other elevation so that he could be heard by as many townsfolk as possible. Traditionally mosques had an ablution fountain at the centre of the courtyard, often fashioned from marble. Today most modern mosques have a more practical row of taps and drains alongside.

The mosque in Arabian countries serves the community in many ways. Young children run on a hand-loomed carpet, their siblings receive Quranic lessons beneath tiled domes, their parents sit in quiet contemplation of carved panels, and the elders enjoy a peaceful nap in the cool of flowering gardens. Art, in other words, remains at the service of people.

Contemporary Art

Not all artistic expression on the Peninsula shares the same Islamic roots and increasingly there is a trend across the region to explore international lines of aesthetic enquiry through challenging contemporary exhibitions and the opening of museums that showcase a broader tradition. The most obvious example of this is the cluster of contemporary buildings taking shape on Saadiyat Island in the UAE, which include Jean Nouvel's Abu Dhabi Louvre. Due to open towards the end of 2016 this magnificent gallery, with a canopy issuing a rain of light inspired by palm fronds, will exhibit work from the Paris Louvre and other museums in France.

The Bedu are known for their mischievous sense of humour, which they list – alongside courage, alertness and religious faith – as one of the four secrets of life, encouraging tolerance and humility.

Cinema

Recently, Arab cinema has attracted world attention, largely thanks to the growing popularity of international film festivals held in Dubai, Abu Dhabi and Doha. Around 75% of all Arab films are made in Egypt, the unchallenged Hollywood of Arab film, but with the encouragement of well-funded initiatives such as the Doha Film Institute, Gulf film-makers are starting to make a name for themselves.

Sports & Leisure

The people of the Arabian Peninsula love sport, and Qatar and the UAE in particular have become major hosts and patrons of international events. An interest in sport is no new phenomenon. For centuries Arab men have been demonstrating their prowess in agility, speed and courage. Most of these traditional games, which involve barefoot running, ball games, wrestling and even rifle throwing, are hard for a visitor to fathom, but since 2007 the Gulf Cooperation Council (GCC) countries have been trying to encourage greater participation in these kinds of sports and they may well receive more popular promotion in future.

During the flying season, October to February, 10,000 birds are tended at Doha's Falcon Hospital, a measure of how popular the sport remains. Top falcons can cost up to US$1 million.

Camel Racing

Camel racing is a grumbling affair of camels (who'd really rather not run) and owners (who make sure they do). The rider, traditionally, is almost immaterial. Racing usually involves a long, straight track (camels are not very good at cornering) with very wide turns. Camel fanciers race alongside in their 4WDs to give their favourite camel encouragement.

Camel racing can be seen throughout the region from October to May. Authorities, sensitive about the bad press associated with the traditional recruitment of young jockeys, have mostly insisted on replacing child riders with lightweight adults, or even with something more imaginative (see boxed text below). Visitors can see races in Al Shahaniya in Qatar and Al Marmoum Camel Racecourse en route to Al Ain from Dubai.

Horse Riding

The breeding of horses, shipped from ports such as Sur in Oman, has been a source of income in Arabia for centuries. Now, partly thanks to the efforts of Lady Anne Blunt, a 19th-century British horse breeder, the fleet-footed, agile Arab horse is raced all over the world.

Horse racing is a major spectator event for Peninsula people and the event is at its most expensive and glamorous at the Dubai Cup. Heads of states, royalty, celebrities and top international jockeys gather for the occasion. Like Ascot in the UK it's *the* place to be seen. The Meydan Racecourse in Dubai holds regular events.

Betting is against Islamic principles, but at camel races, vast sums of money change hands in terms of prize money, sponsorship and ownership. A prize-racing camel can fetch more than US$100,000.

Falconry

The ancient art of falconry is still practiced across the Peninsula. It dates back at least to the 7th century BC, when tradition has it that a Persian ruler caught a falcon to learn from its speed, tactics and focus. Modern owners continue to admire their birds and lavish love and respect upon them.

CAMEL ON COMMAND

Traditionally, camels were raced by child jockeys, who were often 'bought' from impoverished families in Pakistan and Bangladesh, trained in miserable conditions, kept deliberately underweight and then exposed to the dangers of regular racing. The plight of these young boys attracted international condemnation, with the result that the practice has now all but died out.

A novel solution to the problem of finding something similarly lightweight to replace child jockeys can be described as the 'robo-rider'. These robotic jockeys are remote controlled, look vaguely humanoid and can crack an electronic whip. The camels appear to respond just as well (or just as badly) to their new mounts, and future versions of this gadget will sport robotic eyes, through which the owner can take virtual strides at 60km/h around the racetrack.

LEISURE & THE CORNICHE

Until very recently there was no time in the lives of the indigenous population, beyond the demands of work and family, to devote to other pursuits. With the wealth that oil brought to the region, however, the concept of leisure has become a reality.

Alas, it's fair to say that the infrastructure to support the new-found leisure time has been slow to catch up. Take the seaside as an example. Two decades ago the coast was considered a place of work for fishermen; now it is teeming with walkers and joggers, swimmers and footballers, but still few facilities exist to allow these activities.

This is beginning to change, however, and most capital cities now sport a corniche – a road with a wide footpath running along the coast, giving access to sandy beaches, cafes, water sports and toilets. For the visitor, one of the best ways to watch each nation at play is to walk or cycle along these attractive thoroughfares. Sit nearby long enough and you're bound to be seconded to the local volleyball team.

Many raptors are bred for falconry on the Asir escarpment in Saudi, but the easiest place to see a peregrine up close is in the Falcon Souq in Doha. The magical spectacle of birds being flown can be seen in Dubai and at most festivals, such as the Jenadriyah National Festival in Riyadh.

Bull-Butting

A curiosity of the east coast of Arabia, bull-butting is the pitching of one Brahman bull against another in a contest of strength. Much effort is taken to ensure the animals are not harmed, but occasional injuries occur to ears or necks. Bull-butting takes place in a dusty arena where the animals are nudged into a head-down position, and push and shove from one side of the arena to the other.

The bulls are precious to their owners and much beloved so the minute the going gets tough, thankfully the tough get going. As such, it isn't exactly the most spectacular sport to watch, though it always draws a huge crowd of locals. The best places to see bull-butting are near Muscat in Oman and at Fujairah in the UAE.

Football International

Reading (goalkeeper Omani Ali al Habsi from Oman)

Manchester City (owned by Abu Dhabi and Etihad in football's biggest-ever sponsorship deal)

FC Barcelona (sponsored by Qatar Airways)

Modern Sports

A range of modern sports are popular in the region, including rally driving, quad biking, volleyball and even ice skating. At Ski Dubai there are even five ski runs with real snow. You can't possibly talk about sports in the area, however, and not mention football. At 4pm on a Friday, the men of just about every village in Arabia trickle onto the local waste ground to play, all hopeful of joining international European clubs one day like some of their compatriots. Football is usually a shoeless business, on a desert pitch, played in *wizza* (cotton underskirt) and nylon strip, but it is taken just as seriously as if it were played in a multi-million-dollar stadium…which of course at least one Gulf country owns in another part of the world!

Islam in Arabia

On the Arabian Peninsula, as distinct from other countries with mainly Muslim populations, such as Turkey, there's little distinction between politics, culture and religion: each flows seamlessly through the other. Recognising the religious integrity of Peninsula people makes sense of certain customs and manners. In turn it guides the traveller in appropriate conduct and minimises the chance of giving offence.

The Islamic Legacy

Social Cohesion

You don't have to stay on the Arabian Peninsula for long to notice the presence of a 'third party' in all human interaction. Every official occasion begins with a reading from the Holy Quran. A task at work begins with an entreaty for God's help. The words *al-hamdulillah* (thanks be to God) frequently lace sentences in which good things are related. Equally, the words *insha'allah* (God willing) mark all sentences that anticipate the future. The concept of *mash'allah,* said when giving a compliment or celebrating good news, is a reminder that all good things extend from the will of God.

These common expressions are not merely linguistic decoration. They evidence a deep connection between society and faith, a shared lexicon of social experience that extends beyond the common language. In other words, for most Muslims on the Peninsula, Islam is not just a religion, it's a way of life. It suggests what an Arab should wear and eat, how income should be spent, who should inherit and how much. It guides behaviour and social intercourse, and punishment for transgression.

Shades of Difference: Sunnis & Shiites

The Peninsula's social cohesion, built on the Islamic faith, stems not just from the religion itself but from the particular sect of Islam followed by most Peninsula Arabs. Most Arab people across the region are Sunnis, with only Bahrain encompassing a majority Shiite population.

Islam split into the two main sects shortly after its foundation in the early 7th century. The division was based not so much on theological interpretation, but on historical event. When Prophet Mohammed died in 632, he left no instructions as to who should be his successor, or the manner in which future Islamic leaders (known as caliphs) should be chosen. The community initially

ISLAM'S PENINSULA ORIGINS

AD 570

Prophet Mohammed, founder of Islam, is born in Mecca in modern-day Saudi Arabia.

610

Mohammed receives his first revelation. Considered by Muslims as the word of God, the revelations gathered in the Quran lay the foundations of a new, monotheistic religion.

622

Mohammed and his followers flee Mecca for Medina, marking the beginning of the first Islamic state. The new religion spreads across the Peninsula.

632

Mohammed dies. The Muslim capital moves to Damascus. Mecca and Medina grow as the spiritual homes of Islam.

656

Ali bin Abi Taleb, Mohammed's cousin and son-in-law, becomes caliph as the fourth of Mohammed's successors. His followers are known as Shiites ('partisans' of Ali).

661

Ali is assassinated by troops loyal to a distant relative of Mohammed. From this point on, the Muslim community separates into two competing factions, Sunnis and Shiites.

680

Ali's son Hussein is murdered at Karbala (in today's southern Iraq), an event that further widens the gap between the two sects. Today, only Bahrain has a Shiite majority among Peninsula nations.

chose Abu Bakr, the Prophet's closest companion and father-in-law, as the new leader of the Muslim faith, but not everyone agreed with this approach, preferring the claim of Ali bin Abi Taleb, Mohammed's cousin and son-in-law. Ali's supporters became known as Shiites ('partisans' of Ali). Ali eventually became the fourth of Mohammed's successors, but was assassinated after five years as caliph.

Over the centuries Sunnism has developed into the 'orthodox' strain of Islam and today comprises about 90% of the world's more than 1100 million Muslims. There are large Shiite minorities, however, spread across the Middle East. Bahrain is notable for its Shiite majority.

From that point the Muslim community separated into two competing factions, the Sunnis and the Shiites, who believed that only a descendant of Mohammed should lead the Muslims. As with any religion approaching one billion adherents, Islam has produced many sects within the traditional Sunni–Shiite division. The two most important Sunni sects in the Gulf States are the Wahhabis, whose austere doctrines are the official form of Islam in Saudi Arabia, and the Ibadis, who also espouse a strict interpretation of Islam and are the dominant sect in Oman.

The Five Pillars of Islam in Arabia

With its emphasis on direct relationship with God, Islam historically appealed to the scattered people of the Peninsula, who were given access to a rich spiritual life without having to submit to incomprehensible rituals administered by hierarchical intermediaries. Believers needed only to observe the transportable Five Pillars of Islam in order to fulfil their religious duty.

Shahada

In a region where almost the entire population espouses a single religion, there is a tangible sense of *shahada,* or the profession of faith. In many secular countries the declaration 'There is no God but Allah and Mohammed is his Prophet' represents a private or even internalised act, but in Arabia it is a lived daily experience that is knitted into the fabric of society.

Salat

No one can miss *salat,* or the five-times-daily call to prayer. It is an audible part of the Arabian soundscape, hovering above the noise of daily lives, even in the Gulf cities where one eye is kept on Mammon. Whole communities across the Peninsula stop work, stop study and stop by the side of the road with an unfurled prayer mat facing Mecca in Saudi and let their prayers stream across the desert wind.

Zakat

On the Peninsula the duty of alms giving, where Muslims must give a portion of their salaries to those in greater need, is carried out through formal schemes. One-fortieth of each person's annual income is deducted for this.

Ramadan

Perhaps it is because of the proximity to the Prophet Mohammed's birthplace, perhaps it is because of the shared experience of hardship in the

DISTRIBUTION OF SUNNIS & SHIITES

This table shows the approximate distribution of Sunni and Shiite Muslims across the Arabian Peninsula. For updates of this information, consult www.populstat.info.

COUNTRY	SUNNI MUSLIMS	SHIITE MUSLIMS	OTHER RELIGIONS
Bahrain	25%	57%	18%
Kuwait	45%	30%	25%
Oman	74% (Ibadi)	14%	12%
Qatar	92%	0%	8%
Saudi Arabia	93%	4%	3%
UAE	80%	16%	4%

AND YOUR RELIGION IS...?

After exchanging pleasantries with acquaintances on the Peninsula, the conversation inevitably tends towards three subjects from which many people around the world shy away: sex, politics and religion. The level of frankness involved in some of these discussions can come as a surprise. Forewarned is forearmed, however, and there's no better way of getting under the skin of a nation than talking about the things that matter most in life.

While all three subjects may seem like potential minefields (don't talk about sex with the opposite gender, especially if you're male; if you're talking politics, avoid saying 'you' when you mean 'your government'), religion is the one topic that takes a bit of practice.

For most Muslims, tolerating Christians, Jews (both 'People of the Book'), Buddhists or Hindus is easy – knowing what to do with a heretic is the problem. Stating you don't believe in God is as good as saying you doubt the very foundation of a Muslim's life. So how do you say you're an atheist in Arabia without causing offence? Try saying 'I'm not religious'. This will likely lead to understanding nods and then, on subsequent meetings, a very earnest attempt at conversion. Phrases such as 'You'll find God soon, God willing' should be seen as a measure of someone's like for you and not as a rejection of your 'position'. A reasonable response would be *'shukran'* ('thank you').

heat of a desert climate, but Ramadan has a particular resonance across the Peninsula. This holy month, with its dawn-to-dusk fasting, marking the time when Mohammed received his first revelation in AD 610, isn't a lifestyle choice: for most people across the region it is a fervent act of communal worship, as evidenced by joyous *iftar* (fast-breaking) suppers in tents across the region.

Hajj

Although many Peninsula people have a greater opportunity to visit Mecca at other times of the year (in a journey known as *'umrah',* the 'lesser pilgrimage' or 'visitation'), the undertaking of a 'true' hajj (p34), performed during a few specific days of the Muslim year, is considered a crowning achievement. During the *eid* (holiday) that follows hajj, towns across the Arabian Peninsula come alive with convoys of pilgrims, their car horns hooting, cheered on by those welcoming the *hajjis'* return. Of course, hajj is richly rewarded: all past sins are forgiven and the prefix of Al Haj evokes much respect across Peninsula communities.

Islam's Peninsula Context

The Quran

For many Muslims the Quran, believed to be the literal word of God, is not just the principal source of doctrine in Islam, but also a source of spiritual rapture in its own right. It is recited often with emotional elation, as a blessing to the reciter and the listener. For Arabs on the Peninsula, there is the added connection that the 'sacred' language of the holy book is their mother tongue.

Arabic, with its unique rhythms, gives the recitation a sacramental quality that eludes translation, and many Muslims around the world still learn large portions of the Quran in its original form (*fus-ha,* or formal Arabic) to feel closer to God's words. Those who can recite the Quran well are highly respected across the region and many formal occasions, including conferences, government meetings and graduations, commence with a reading from the Holy Quran.

Books on Islam

Muhammed: A Biography of the Prophet (Karen Armstrong)

The Concise Encyclopedia of Islam (Cyril Glasse)

Sharia'a

The Arabian Peninsula has a reputation, not wholly deserved, for extreme forms of punishment meted out to transgressors in the strict interpretation of Sharia'a law: amputation of limbs for repeat-offending thieves, flogging of those caught committing adultery, public beheading for murderers. In fact, these punishments are associated mostly with the austere Hanbali school of jurisprudence practiced in Saudi Arabia and are intended as a deterrent first and foremost. As such, they are only occasionally enforced.

Across all Peninsula countries, Sharia'a is quite specific in areas of inheritance law and the punishments for certain offences, but in many other cases it provides only guidelines.

A scholar or judge learned in Sharia'a law has to determine the proper 'Islamic' position or approach to a problem using his own discretion. This partly explains the wide divergence in Muslim opinion on some issues – such as with regard to jihad today.

Jihad

In Arabia most Arabs are inclined to associate the word 'jihad' with its literal meaning of 'striving' or 'struggle'. Far from 'holy war', it more often means 'striving in the way of the faith' – struggling against one's own bad intentions, or rooting out evil, indecency or oppression in society. Islam dictates that this struggle should occur through peaceful, just means so that wisdom prevails, not through anger and aggression.

If the local papers are anything to go by, the rise of militancy in neighbouring countries is viewed mostly with fear and consternation. Much has been gained in terms of peace and prosperity over the past 50 years and the common sentiment expressed on social media within the region shows a fear of losing these gains through sectarian violence fuelled by religious intolerance.

Keeping the Faith Today

Modern life requires daily compromises with religion, but then it always has. As such, there's not much that separates a Peninsula life from any other life, except perhaps in the degrees of temptation and opportunity. But even that is changing as access to foreign cultures becomes more prevalent in the region.

Except in Saudi and Kuwait, alcohol is widely available and has become a source of curiosity and experimentation for many youngsters and a way of life for some Arabs who have studied and worked abroad. Drugs, largely smuggled in from across the Gulf, have led to addiction (together with the familiar misery, shame in the community and family disruption) in a small but growing number of Arabian youths who seek to emulate the kind of rock-star lifestyles they see celebrated on satellite TV.

All of these temptations and opportunities are causing a new generation, educated to think and research the truth for themselves, to question the knowledge handed down from their elders. The uprisings of the Arab Spring of 2011 were partly symptomatic of the pull in two directions between a traditional life, governed by Islamic principles and concern for society, and the realities of a modern life, where the individual and his or her own personal needs and satisfactions take priority.

Websites on Islam

Al-Bab (www.al-bab.com) Comprehensive site providing links to information on and discussions of Islam.

Islamicity (www.islamicity.com) Good reference for non-Muslims interested in Islam.

Other Religions on the Peninsula

All the indigenous people of the Peninsula today are Muslim. One or two Muslim converts to Christianity wander in a state of miserable purgatory on the periphery of society, barred from all social interaction with family and friends by a decision that most Muslims would consider not just heretical but also a rejection of common sense, history and culture.

This is not the case with expatriate Christians, whose religion is respected and provision for worship catered for in church services across the region. There are also Hindu and Buddhist temples tucked away in small suburbs of the region's big cities and travelling missions visit expat camps in rural areas to bring comfort to those separated from the familiar props of their home communities. Small enclaves of Jewish people have lived on the Peninsula for centuries.

Saudi, as keeper of Islam's holiest shrines, is the exception: no religious observance is formally permitted other than Islam.

Flavours of Arabia

Bedouin feasts of lavish meats stuffed with rice and sultanas, served with chilled sherbets defying the desert heat, may be largely the product of a hunger-ravished imagination but eating is nonetheless a central part of Peninsula life. Few social interactions take place without sharing 'bread and salt', or at least Arabic coffee (*qahwa*) and dates. The staple dishes may not immediately appeal to Western palates, but with knowledge of the customs informing their preparation, they assume a whole new flavour.

Staples & Specialities

Arabian

Breakfast

For most Arab people on the Peninsula, breakfast means eggs in some shape or form and locally produced salty white cheese with a glass of buttermilk or labneh (thick yogurt) and tahini sweetened with date syrup. It might come with *fuul madamas,* a bean dish lubricated with olive oil, garnished on high days and holidays with pickles and eased along with olives. There may be lentils, heavily laced with garlic, to the chagrin of co-workers, and, of course, bread.

Known generically as *khobz,* bread (in up to 40 different varieties) is eaten in copious quantities with every meal. Most often it's unleavened and comes in flat discs about the size of a dinner plate (not unlike an Indian chapatti). It's traditionally torn into pieces, in lieu of knives and forks, and used to pinch up a morsel of meat, a scoop of dip and a nip of garnish.

Lunch

Lunch means one word only: rice. It is often flavoured with a few whole cardamom pods (one of which always lurks beguilingly in the last mouthful) and at feasts with saffron and sultanas. Buried in or sitting on top of the rice will be some kind of delicious spiced stew with okra or grilled and seasoned chicken, lamb, goat or even camel – but of course never pork, which is haram (forbidden) for Muslims. Popular seasoning includes some or even all of the following: cardamom, coriander, cumin, cinnamon, nutmeg, chilli, ginger, pepper and the all-important, health-giving and almost-flavourless

SEASONAL TREATS

January–February

Start atop Oman's Green Mountain for citrus delights such as oranges, sweet lemons and limes. Descend to the Dhofar coast for the sea's annual harvest of abalone and conches.

March–April

Head for the coastal plains to sample corn, tomatoes, capsicums and chillies.

May–June

Visit Al Hasa plantations to sink your teeth into Saudi's *bukayyirah,* or early dates; there are around 300 varieties to choose from. Select a Ramadan tent for *iftar* specialities at a Gulf hotel.

July–August

Spend *eid* in the interior desert towns, where killing the fatted calf is more than a metaphor. Papayas and green mangoes, salted and pickled, are eaten with celebratory lamb.

September–October

Watch offloaded watermelons burst like fireworks on roads that follow ancient caravan routes. Taste honey-dipped sweetmeats with returning pilgrims on the same routes.

November–December

Return to the Omani mountains for pomegranates, almonds and walnuts. Enjoy international delicacies, including turkey and chestnuts, imported in time for Christmas.

turmeric. Chillies are not often used, although they sometimes put a punch in a minimal broth or bean dish when least expected.

Unsurprisingly for a Peninsula with such a rich coastline, fish (fresh or dried) is an equally important lunchtime staple. Hamour (a species of grouper), beya (mullet), kingfish, Sultan Ibrahim and tuna are grilled, fried or barbecued and served with rice and chopped raw cabbage with the essential half lime or lemon. Sardines, piles of which spangle the shore in season and are raked into malodorous heaps between houses, are seldom eaten: they're usually dried for animal fodder.

Pork is haram (forbidden) to Muslims, but it's sometimes available in Gulf supermarkets. Pork sections are easy to spot: customers slink out with wrapped sausages as if they're top-shelf items.

Dinner

The evening meal is a ragged affair of competing interests – children clamouring for hot dogs or burgers, maids slipping them 'keep-quiet food', mothers going for a sandwich in Starbucks and grandmothers making sweetmeats and aubergine dips, nibbling on dates and trying to persuade fathers to enjoy the company of the family instead of going out for a kebab.

City people on the Peninsula enjoy going out and a diversity of international dishes, from Mongolian lamb chops and crab rangoon to spaghetti bolognese, is readily available. Lebanese food, with its copious selections of hot and cold appetisers known as mezze, is a particular regional favourite, lending itself to lengthy chats over selective grazing. The peeled carrots, buffed radishes, whole lettuces and bunches of peppery spinach leaves, provided complimentary, are a meal in themselves.

Arab families invariably entertain guests at home and go out to eat something different. For travellers to the region, it can therefore be difficult finding indigenous food. Ask locally where to sample 'real' Peninsula food and you may find you're taken home for supper.

The world's oldest cultivated fruit has been the staple of Arabs for centuries. Of the world's 90 million date palms, 64 million are in Arab countries.

Snacks & Sweets

Fast food has caught on among Peninsula people, with the consumption of burgers and fries verging on epidemic proportions. The concept has translated easily from traditional practices of visiting small eateries that sell kebabs, felafel and other types of sandwiches. *Shwarma* (meat sliced off a spit and stuffed in a pocket of pita-type bread with chopped tomatoes and garnish), usually served with some form of salad, is the snack of choice across the whole region. Outings to the coffeeshops that sell these traditional fast foods are more about sharing time with friends than eating and men in particular may spend all night on the same plastic chair, puffing on *sheesha* tobacco and sipping tea.

Peninsula people are not big on 'puddings', preferring fruit after (or often before) the meal, and thick fruit juices. On high days and holidays,

There are more than 600 species of date. The best come from Al Hasa in Saudi Arabia, where a variety called *khlas* is pre-sold to regular customers before it's even harvested.

RECORD-BREAKING SWEET

People in all countries in the region have a legendary sweet tooth and various sticky, sweet confections are prepared for high days and holidays. In 2015, in honour of Oman's 45th National Day, marking the point at which His Majesty Sultan Qaboos came to the throne in the country, an enterprising novice confectioner made a 675kg halwa in the shape of the Sultanate of Oman.

The glutinous sweet was made of a whopping 67.5kg of starch, 405kg of white sugar, 270kg of black sugar, almonds, cashews, walnuts, saffron, rosewater, cardamom and butter and 135 eggs. Guinness World Records is reviewing the project for possible inclusion as a bone fide world record.

Halwa crops up in various forms across the Peninsula and is served with *qawa* (Arabic coffee) on ceremonial occasions.

COFFEE CUSTOMS

Throughout the Peninsula there is an old and elaborate ritual surrounding the serving of coffee. In homes, offices and even at some hotels, you may well be offered a cup. To refuse is to reject an important gesture of welcome and hospitality and you risk offending your host. 'Arabic' or 'Bedouin' coffee, as it's known, is usually poured from an ornate, long-spouted pot known as a *dalla* into tiny cups without handles. You should accept the cup with your right hand.

It's considered polite to drink at least three cups (the third is traditionally considered to bestow a blessing). More may be impolite; the best advice is to follow your host's lead. To show you've had sufficient, swivel the cup slightly between fingers and thumb.

however, baklava (made from filo and honey) or puddings, including *mahallabiye* (milk based) and *umm ali* (bread based), might put in an appearance after lunch or supper.

Every town has a baklava or pastry shop selling syrupy sweets made from pastry, nuts, honey and sometimes rosewater. Sweets are ordered by a minimum weight of 250g.

Drinks

Nonalcoholic Drinks

If you want to try camel's milk without the stomach ache, you can often find it in supermarkets – next to the labneh, a refreshing drink of yogurt, water, salt and sometimes crushed mint.

One of the best culinary experiences in the region is sampling the fresh juices of pomegranate, hibiscus, avocado, sugar cane, mango, melon or carrot – or a combination of all sorts – served at juice stalls known as *aseer*. Mint and lemon or fresh lime is a refreshing alternative to soda.

Tea, known as *shai* or *chi libton,* could be tea *min na'ana* (with mint, especially in Saudi Arabia), tea with condensed milk (in the Gulf) or plain black tea (in Oman), but whatever the flavour of the day it will contain enough sugar to make a dentist's fortune. The teabag is left dangling in the cup and water is poured from maximum height as proof of a host's tea-making skills.

Coffee, known locally as *qahwa,* is consumed in copious quantities on the Peninsula and is usually strong. Arabia has a distinguished connection with coffee. Though no longer involved in the coffee trade, Al Makha in Yemen gave its name to the blend of chocolate and coffee popularly known as 'mocha' that spread across the region. The traditional Arabic or Bedouin coffee is heavily laced with cardamom and drunk in small cups. Turkish coffee, which floats on top of thick sediment, is popular in the Gulf region.

Nonalcoholic beer is widely available. Incidentally, travellers shouldn't think that cans of fizzy drink will suffice for hydration in the desert: they often induce more thirst than they satisfy.

If as a traveller you try to opt out of the fifth spoonful of sugar in your tea or coffee, you will inevitably be assumed to have diabetes.

Coffeehouses & Coffeeshops

Across the Arabian Peninsula, there are bastions of old-world Arab hospitality that go by the name of 'coffeehouses'. These relics of an era when people had more time to sit and chat are places of male camaraderie and tend often to be no more than a mere hole-in-the-wall, a bench up against a souq alleyway, or even a favourite perch under a tree. These coffeehouses dispense coffee from copper pots, or tea in disposable paper cups, while *sheibas* (old men) with beards dish out dates, advice and opinions in equal measure to anyone who'll listen. For a male visitor, they offer a unique engagement with Arab society. Women are politely tolerated, but it is more sensitive to leave the men to their bonding.

'Coffeeshops', on the other hand, welcome all comers. These ubiquitous cafes, with their plastic chairs and compulsory string of fairy lights, are dotted across Arabia. They are usually run by expatriates from the subcontinent and they form the social hub of many small villages, selling kebabs, roasted chickens or omelettes rolled up in flat Arabic bread. Most are simple shopfronts with seating on the pavement, but the more upmarket coffeeshops stretch to a plate and a napkin and are scented with the regional passion for *sheesha* (waterpipe).

Saudi 'champagne' is less exciting than it sounds: it's a mixture of apple juice and Perrier water, but that doesn't stop it being used to anoint sporting winners.

Alcoholic Drinks

Despite its reputation as a dry region, alcohol is available in all Peninsula countries, except Saudi Arabia, Kuwait and some of the Emirates (where both possession and consumption for locals and foreigners is strictly forbidden).

In the more liberal countries, such as Bahrain and some parts of the UAE, bars, cocktail bars and even pubs can be found. In others, such as Qatar and Oman, usually only certain mid- or upper-range hotels are permitted to serve alcohol. Wine is served in most licensed restaurants in Bahrain, Oman, Qatar and the UAE.

Officially, no Peninsula country produces its own alcoholic drinks, though rumours abound where grapes and dates ferment. The high prices of imported alcohol are intended to keep consumption low – not very successfully (alcoholism is a small but growing social problem). The legal age to be served alcohol is usually 18 years old. You can't buy alcohol to take off the premises unless you are a resident and are eligible for a monthly quota.

Asian

All across Arabia large populations of expatriates have brought their own cuisine to the Peninsula, with the result that it dominates the menus of the region. For many Asian expats – often men on 'bachelor' contracts – breakfast, lunch and dinner consists of the same thing: rice and dhal, or rice and vegetable, or so-called 'non-veg' curry, separated into three round metal lunchboxes, stacked one on top of the other, and including a bag of rolled-up chapatti.

Providing a cheap and cheerful alternative to the 'lunchbox', and serving samosas, biryani or spicy mutton curry, a string of Indian and Pakistani restaurants have sprung up across the region, catering for hungry workers who would normally be looked after by wives and daughters. Those who do have their families with them enjoy as varied a cuisine as their nationality and local supermarket allow. British teachers can find roast-beef brunches at local hotels, Filipino restaurants make chicken *adobo,* Sri Lankan maids win over their adoptive families to furious fish curries. In many of the big cities, travellers can sample all these delights too, often in world-class restaurants.

For an exquisite tang on the palate, dates should be eaten half ripe, biting the fruit lengthwise and savouring the bitter zest with the mellow ripe part. Don't forget to discard the pip discreetly in a napkin – Sinbad spat his out and blinded a genie's son, who claimed mischievous revenge.

Bedouin

When round him mid the burning sands he saw
Fruits of the North in icy freshness thaw
And cooled his thirsty lip beneath the glow
Of Mecca's sun, with urns of Persian snow.

Thomas Moore, Lalla Rookh

Thomas Moore's 19th-century description of Bedouin delicacies, elaborated with sherbets and dainties, sounds enticing, but the reality is far more prosaic. TE Lawrence memorably describes a feast with the Arab Sheikh Sherif Nasir of Medina, in which he dips his fingers into a mess of boiling-hot lamb fat while ripping the meat from the carcass. This was

THE SHEESHA EXPERIENCE

In any city across the Peninsula, two sensations mark the hot and humid air of an Arabian summer's evening: the wreaths of scented, peach-flavoured smoke that spiral above the corner coffeehouse and the low gurgle of water, like a grumbling camel, in the base of the water pipe. Periodically banned by governments concerned for public morality (the pipes are not narcotic, only time-wasting), and inevitably returned to the street corners by the will of the people, these *sheesha* establishments are an indispensable part of Arabian social life.

In the region's traditional coffeehouses, *sheesha* is an entirely male affair. Men sprawl on cushions in Jeddah, or lounge on benches in the souqs of Doha. They indolently watch the football on TV, occasionally breaking off from the sucking and puffing to pass a word of lazy complaint to their neighbour, snack on pieces of kebab, or hail the waiter for hot coals to awaken the drowsy embers of the *sheesha* bottle.

In Dubai, Manama and Muscat, *sheesha* has long since spread to the more family-oriented coffeeshop. It has even become a fashionable occupation in international-style cafes. Here, women in black *abeyyas* (full-length black robes) and sparkling diamante cuffs drag demurely on velvet-clad mouthpieces, their smoking punctuating a far more animated dialogue as they actively define the new shape of society.

probably *kebsa,* a whole lamb stuffed with rice and pine nuts. The most prized pieces of this dish are the sheep's eyeballs, which irreverent hosts delight to this day in waving towards horrified non-native guests.

Bedouin food mostly consists of whatever is available at a particular time, and hunger and thirst are far more attendant on a day's travelling in the desert than sumptuous feasting. Camel's milk and goat's cheese are staple parts of the diet, as are dried dates and, of course, water. Water takes on a particularly precious quality when it is rationed and the Bedouin are renowned for consuming very little, particularly during the day when only small sips are taken, mostly to rinse the mouth.

As an extravagant gesture in a Bedouin emir's tent, a camel is stuffed with a sheep, which is stuffed with a goat, which is stuffed with a chicken.

The legendary hospitality of the Bedu means that travellers in the Empty Quarter (in Saudi) or the Sharqiya Sands (Oman) who bump into a Bedouin camp are bound to be invited to share 'bread and salt'. At the least this will involve Arabic coffee, camel's milk and a thatch of dried meat, usually with a host of flies dancing in the bowl. The flies don't harm the Bedu and it's unlikely they'll bother the traveller much either, but the milk can upset a sensitive stomach.

Habits & Customs

The main meal for most Peninsula people is usually a home-cooked family affair involving rice at lunchtime – but there the region's similarities end. There is huge diversity in the kinds of food prepared and the habits practiced across the Peninsula. Learning about regional customs associated with shopping for food, as well as cooking and preparing it, helps give insight into the important place that dining has within the Arab community as a whole.

Books: Arabian Recipes

The Arab Table: Recipes & Culinary Traditions (May Bsisu)

Medieval Arab Cookery (Maxime Rodinson)

Shopping

Catering for food is largely a man's job and brothers are often dispatched to Thursday wholesale markets to find fresh produce. Giant shopping malls such as Carrefour have met with instant success among city locals, perhaps because they resemble an air-conditioned version of the wholesale market. For many, however, buying meat from the livestock market is a matter of male pride and the animal will be taken home live, ready for dispatch under specific Islamic guidelines.

Cooking

Dining is essentially a communal affair and it's traditional at weekends for many families who work in the city to travel long distances back to their villages to enjoy 'mum's cooking'. Women almost exclusively prepare food: grinding spices, peeling vegetables and plucking chickens is seen as an opportunity to chat with female relatives and catch up on the news.

When it comes to customs and manners, there's one thing most Peninsula people agree upon: after you eat, you go. Talking is conducted over mezze. During the main course, focus is on the food. After eating, once coffee has been served, all anyone wants to think about is sleeping.

Eating

In more traditional towns and villages, men and women will eat separately, with the eldest son helping to serve the men first while the women await their turn in another room. It's considered good manners for men to reserve the best parts of the meal for the women. Arab people assert that eating is enjoyed best, even by city dwellers with Western-style furniture, on the floor from shared dishes using bread and the right hand as utensils. This makes eating very easily transferable to an outdoor setting and indeed picnics are the number-one regional pastime.

Relaxing

A dish of rosewater, the petals harvested from Arabian mountains, marks the traditional end of a meal; diners rinse their hands in the scented water. Sleep is generally enjoyed by all after the midday meal.

EATING ETIQUETTE

Sharing a meal with Arab friends is a great way of cementing a newly formed friendship. But Peninsula eating etiquette is refined and complex. Note that food is traditionally shared by all from the same serving dishes, spread on a cloth on the floor, without the use of cutlery.

Pre-Meal

➡ If you're eating in someone's house, bring a small gift of flowers, chocolates or pastries, fruit or honey.

➡ Carry out your ablutions – it's polite to be seen to wash your hands before a meal.

➡ Don't sit with your legs stretched out – it's considered rude during a meal.

During the Meal

➡ Use only your right hand for eating or accepting food; the left is reserved for ablutions.

➡ Don't take the best part of the meal, such as the meat, until offered; it is usually saved until last.

➡ Mind your manners – your host will often lay the tastiest morsels in front of you; it's polite to accept them.

➡ Don't put unwanted food back on the plate. Discard it in a napkin.

Post-Meal

➡ It's traditional to lavish food upon a guest – if you're full, pat your stomach contentedly.

➡ Leave a little food on your plate. Traditionally, a clean plate was thought to invite famine.

➡ Feel free to pick your teeth after a meal – it is quite acceptable and toothpicks are often provided.

➡ Stay for coffee – it's polite to accept a cup of coffee after a meal and impolite to leave before it's served.

➡ Know when to go. The chatting is usually done before the meal, so once the meal is over it's time to leave – but don't go before the chief guest.

Ramadan

The holy month is a time of great conviviality and perhaps somewhat surprisingly, given that the month is about fasting and abstinence, many Arab people put on weight at this time. The reason for this is the long Ramadan nights, which are generally marked by bonhomie and socialising and the sharing of seasonal delicacies and sweetmeats. The fast (between dawn and dusk) is broken each day with a communal 'break-fast' comprising something light (such as dates and *laban* – an unsweetened yogurt drink) before prayers. Then comes *iftar,* at which enough food is usually consumed to compensate for the previous hours of abstinence with socialising that continues well into the early hours. The venue for this communal meal is often the wali's office (equivalent to a town hall), the mosque precinct or a specially erected Ramadan tent. People then rise again before dawn to prepare a meal to support them through the day.

In Lebanese restaurants the number of mezze can run to 50 or more dishes and include delicacies such as chopped liver, devilled kidney, sheep brain and other offal.

Where to Eat & Drink

One of the undoubted pleasures of the Peninsula's modern cities is the variety and quality of the restaurants. In the Gulf in particular, world-class dining in magnificent surroundings is a highlight.

On the whole, restaurants are open (mostly for expats) during lunch. They're closed in the afternoon and open from about 6pm to the early hours of the morning to cater for the late-night eating habits of most people across the region. In Saudi Arabia restaurants must comply with certain strict regulations (regarding segregation of men and women and the observation of prayer hours, for example).

In most Peninsula countries, mixed dining is common in more expensive or modern city restaurants. In smaller establishments, men eat on the ground floor, while women and families eat upstairs in a section reserved for them.

Expatriate & Local Cuisine

Lebanese and Indian restaurants are the most prevalent throughout the region, followed by Chinese and Thai in bigger towns. Food from all over the world is available in the Gulf cities.

The hardest food to find in a restaurant is local, traditional fare, but chains such as Bin Ateeq in Muscat, and restaurants in Souq Waqif in Doha or the Heritage Village in Abu Dhabi, try to redress that imbalance. In very local restaurants, seating is sometimes on the floor on mats and food is served from a communal plate placed on a tray. Shoes should be left outside the perimeters of the mats.

Friday Brunch

One of the best ways to experience local dishes and regional delicacies on the Peninsula is to skip breakfast on a Friday and visit the nearest five-star hotel for brunch – a regional speciality much beloved by locals and expats alike. A spectacular array of local, Middle Eastern and international dishes will be on display, decorated with ice carvings and garnished extravagantly, for a relatively modest price.

Surrounded by the Red Sea, the Gulf and the Arabian Sea, it's little surprise that fish is such a staple of the Peninsula diet. Kingfish, pomfret and hamour are local favourites. Lobsters and prawns, now widely eaten, used to be discarded as bottom feeders, not fit for human consumption!

Seafood Nights

Seafood is a highlight of the region and many hotels arrange weekly seafood nights, often with belly dancing or local entertainment. This is often a more economic way of sampling the Peninsula's famous oysters, lobsters and prawns than reserving a table at an exclusive seafood restaurant. The latter, however, usually offer the opportunity to select your own fish from the specimens swimming in the restaurant's tanks, a way of guaranteeing its freshness in the often-intense heat.

A visit to the local fish market (in every seaboard town) is a good way of becoming acquainted with the bewilderingly large variety of seafood available. Don't shy away from the dried-fish counters: the dried crustaceans and sardines make a tasty, if pungent, equivalent of biltong or jerky.

FOOD & DRINK GLOSSARY

Note that because of the imprecise nature of transliterating Arabic into English, spellings will vary. For example, what we give as *kibbeh* may appear variously as *kibba, kibby* or even *gibeh*.

Middle Eastern Mezze

baba ghanooj	smokey-flavoured dip of baked, mashed aubergine (eggplant), typically mixed with tomato and onion and sometimes pomegranate
batata hara	hot, diced potatoes fried with coriander, garlic and capsicum
börek	pastry pockets stuffed with salty white cheese or spicy minced meat with pine nuts; also known as *sambousek*
fatayer	small pastry triangles filled with spinach
fattoosha	fresh salad of onions, tomatoes, cucumbers, lettuce and shards of crispy, thin, deep-fried bread
fuul	paste made from beans, tomatoes, onions, and chilli; also spelled foul, fool
hummus	chickpeas ground into a paste and mixed with tahini, garlic and lemon
kibbeh	minced lamb, bulgur wheat and pine nuts mixed into a lemon-shaped patty and deep fried
kibbeh nayye	minced lamb and cracked wheat served raw
kibda	liver, often chicken liver (*kibda firekh* or *kibda farouj*), usually sautéed in lemon or garlic
labneh	yogurt paste, heavily flavoured with garlic or mint
lahma bi-ajeen	small lamb pies
loubieh	French bean salad with tomatoes, onions and garlic
mashi	baked vegetables such as courgettes (zucchini), vine leaves, capsicums or aubergines stuffed with minced meat, rice, onions, parsley and herbs
mujadarreh	traditional 'poor person's' dish of lentils and rice garnished with caramelised onions
muttabal	similar to baba ghanooj, but the blended aubergine is mixed with tahini, yogurt and olive oil to achieve a creamier consistency
shanklish	salad of small pieces of crumbled, tangy, eye-wateringly strong cheese mixed with chopped onion and tomato
soojuk	fried, spicy lamb sausage
tabouleh	bulgur wheat, parsley and tomato–based salad, with a sprinkling of sesame seeds, lemon and garlic
tahini	thin sesame-seed paste
waraq aynab	vine leaves stuffed with rice and meat

Middle Eastern & Arabian Main Courses

bamiya	okra-based stew
fasoolyeh	green-bean stew

felafel	deep-fried balls of mashed chickpeas, often rolled in Arabic bread with salad and hummus
hareis	slow-cooked wheat and lamb
kabbza	lamb or chicken cooked with onion, tomato, cucumber, grated carrot and fruit
kebab	skewered, flame-grilled chunks of meat, usually lamb, but also chicken, goat, camel, fish or squid; also known as *sheesh* or shish kebab
kebab mashwi	meat paste moulded onto flat skewers and grilled
kebsa	whole stuffed lamb served on a bed of spiced rice and pine nuts; also known as *khuzi*
kofta	ground meat peppered with spices, shaped into small sausages, skewered and grilled
makbus	casserole of meat or fish with rice
mashboos	grilled meat (usually chicken or lamb) and spiced rice
mashkul	rice served with onions
mihammar	lamb cooked in yogurt sauce and stuffed with nuts, raisins and other dried fruit
muaddas	rice served with lentils
mushkak game	seasoned camel meat grilled on a skewer – usually tough as old boots!
samak mashwi	fish barbecued over hot coals after basting in a date puree
shish tawooq	kebab with pieces of marinated, spiced chicken
shuwa	lamb cooked slowly in an underground oven
shwarma	Middle Eastern equivalent of Greek *gyros* or Turkish *döner kebap;* strips are sliced from a vertical spit of compressed lamb or chicken, sizzled on a hot plate with chopped tomatoes and garnish and then stuffed or rolled in Arabic bread
ta'amiyya	see *felafel*

Middle Eastern Pastries & Desserts

asabeeh	rolled filo pastry filled with pistachio, pine and cashew nuts and honey; otherwise known as 'ladies' fingers'
baklava	a generic term for any kind of layered flaky pastry with nuts, drenched in honey
barazak	flat, circular cookies sprinkled with sesame seeds
isfinjiyya	coconut slice
kunafa	shredded wheat over a creamy, sweet cheese base baked in syrup
labneh makbus	sweet yogurt cheese balls, sometimes made into a frittata-like creation or rolled in paprika; sometimes eaten for breakfast
mahallabiye	milk-based pudding
mushabbak	lacework-shaped pastry drenched in syrup
umm ali	bread-based pudding made with sultanas and nuts, flavoured with nutmeg
zalabiyya	pastries dipped in rosewater

Quick Bites

Traditional snacks (such as *shwarma* and kebabs) are quick, cheap and usually safe to eat, as the food is prepared and cooked in front of you. There's also a good range of well-stocked supermarkets (selling many international foods) in the large cities and extensive food halls are found in all the malls.

Vegetarians beware! Some Peninsula chefs may regard vegetarianism as an incomprehensible Western indulgence, or a kind of culinary apostasy. To avoid uncomfortable conversations about soup ingredients, stick to Indian restaurants.

Ramadan Tents

During Ramadan most hotels set up elaborate buffets of Ramadan specialities that non-Muslims are free to join. These buffets are generally in air-conditioned tents, which helps evoke the sense of community in breaking the fast under one roof. Alcohol is not available in Ramadan except as room service at hotels.

Vegetarians & Vegans

While Arab people are traditionally thought of as full-blooded, red-meat eaters, the reality is that for many of modest income across the region, meat is a treat for high days and holidays. This fact, coupled with the influence of southern Indian cuisine introduced by large expat communities of vegetarian Hindus, means that vegetable dishes appear more often than might be expected on a restaurant menu.

Vegetarian staples include many bean and pulse dishes such as soup, *fuul* (fava bean paste) and dhal, or lentil stews. Chickpeas, either fried into felafel or ground into a paste with oil and garlic (hummus), are a common supplement. Aubergines and okra are used in many delicious stews, and salad vegetables are usually locally grown and organic.

Eating with Kids

The venue of preference for 'that special meal' for many Peninsula families is a well-lit grassy verge on a highway with kebabs brought in by the kilo.

Eating out as a family is a popular pastime on the Peninsula for Arabs and expats. Whole minibuses of relatives arrive at the outdoor, seaboard city venues, particularly in the winter months when huddling round a mobile stove is part of the fun. Equally, many parents join their children for a halal 'MacArabia' chicken roll-up, or a beef pepperoni pizza in the spreading rash of fast-food outlets.

Children are welcome in restaurants across the Peninsula, except in the more exclusive, chic establishments of the Gulf, and many midrange restaurants provide children's menus. High chairs are not commonly available.

Fresh or powdered milk is widely available, except in remote areas. Labneh and yogurt are generally considered safe for children.

The Natural Environment

Spend time in Arabia after rain and it becomes immediately apparent that the Peninsula is far from a barren wasteland of undulating sands. On the contrary, the diverse desert landscapes support uniquely adapted plants and animals, particularly in the region's wadis (valleys) and oases. This extraordinary environment forms the backdrop for dramas of survival and endurance by the hardiest of inhabitants and is a revelation and a joy to visitors.

The Land

Geology

The Arabian Peninsula is a treasure trove for geologists. Though not particularly rich in minerals or gems (except the copper that is found in northern Oman), the Peninsula reveals the Earth's earliest history, supporting theories of plate tectonics and continental drift. Indeed, geologists believe the Peninsula originally formed part of the larger landmass of Africa. A split in the continent created Africa's Great Rift Valley (which extends from Mozambique up through Djibouti, into western Yemen, Saudi Arabia and Jordan) and the Red Sea.

As Arabia slipped away from Africa, the Peninsula began to tilt, with the western side rising and the eastern edge dropping, a process that led to the formation of the Gulf.

Extensive flooding millions of years ago led to the remains of marine life being deposited in layers of sediment across the tilted landmass – as the rich fossil remains found across Arabia indicate. When sufficient dead organic matter is laid down and trapped under the surface, where a lack of oxygen prevents it from decaying to water and carbon dioxide, the raw material of hydrocarbons is produced – the origin, in other words, of oil and gas. The conversion from dead organic matter to hydrocarbons is subject to many other conditions such as depth and temperature. Arabia's geology is uniquely supportive of these conditions, and 'nodding donkeys' (drilling apparatus, capable of boring holes up to 5km deep) can be seen throughout the interior.

Governments across the region speculate endlessly on the quantity of reserves remaining. Given that the economies of all the Peninsula countries rely to a lesser or greater extent on oil and gas, this is one issue that can't be left to *insha'allah* (God's will). As such, Peninsula countries are busy diversifying their economic interests in case their reserves run out sooner rather than later.

The Al Hasa Oasis, near the town of Al Hofuf in eastern Saudi Arabia, is the largest oasis in the world. Covering 2500 sq km, it's home to over three million palm trees.

Geologists speak of the Peninsula in terms of the Arabian shield and Arabian shelf. The shield, which consists of volcanic sedimentary rock, comprises the western third of the landmass. The shelf comprises the lower-lying areas that slope away from the shield, from central Arabia to the waters of the Gulf.

Geography

Stand on top of Kuwait Towers and the eye roams unhindered along flat country. The low-lying coastal plains and salt flats stretch along the limp waters of the northern Gulf until the Mussandam Peninsula brings the plain to an abrupt close. This is the environment of mudhoppers, wading birds and long stretches of dazzling-white sands.

Much of the interior is flat too, but some major mountain ranges, such as the Hajar Mountains of Oman and the Asir Mountains of Saudi Arabia, bring an entirely different climate and way of life to the high ground.

There are no permanent river systems on the Peninsula. Water-laden clouds from the sea break across the mountains, causing rainfall to slide along wadis with dramatic speed. Smaller tributaries of water collect in the wadis from natural springs and create oases in the desert. On much of the Peninsula, the water table is close enough to the surface to hand dig a well, a fact not wasted on the Bedu who, until very recently, survived on a system of wells and springs discovered or made by their ancestors. Irrigation, in the form of elaborate ducts and pipes (called *aflaj* in Oman), helps channel water through plantations, allowing more extensive farming in the region than might be supposed.

The stoic early 20th-century traveller Charles Doughty described the Harra as 'iron desolation...uncouth blackness... lifeless cumber of volcanic matter!' in the book *Arabia Deserta*. Even camels have trouble crossing the Harra as the small rocks heat in the sun and catch in their feet.

Ecosystems

Desert

The harsh lands of Arabia have for centuries attracted travellers, from the 14th-century Moroccan Ibn Battutah, to a host of Europeans from the 18th-century onwards. According to Sir Richard Burton in *Personal Narrative of a Pilgrimage to El Medinah and Meccah*, they were curious to see 'a haggard land infested with wild beasts, and wilder men... What can be more exciting? what more sublime?' Indeed, there is such awe in the words 'Arabian desert', it has been described by so many famous writers and travellers, and it is bound up so inseparably in fantasies of escape, that it is hard to begin a description of it. The very words 'Empty Quarter' (a sea of dunes that lies at the heart of the Peninsula, straddling Saudi, Oman and the UAE) invite imaginative speculation, exploration and discovery.

To this day, people come to the desert expecting 'sand, sand, sand, still sand, and only sand, and sand and sand again'. The traveller who wrote those words (Alexander William Kinglake, in *Eothen*) curiously had only passed through gravel plains at that point (in 1834), but so strong is the connection between the words 'desert' and 'sand', he felt obliged to comment on what he thought he should see, rather than on what was there.

In fact, the sand dunes of the Empty Quarter, or Rub al Khali as it is known locally, may be the most famous geographical feature, but they are not the only desert of interest. Much of the Peninsula is made up of flat, gravel plains dotted with outcrops of weather-eroded sandstone in the shape of pillars, mushrooms and ledges. Fine examples of these desert forms can be seen in Saudi Arabia, near Al Ula, Bir Zekreet in Qatar and Duqm and the Huqf Escarpment in Oman.

There are many other kinds of desert too, including flat coastal plains and the infamous volcanic black Harra of northern Arabia.

Nowadays, camels (few of which are wild) and feral donkeys dominate the landscape of thorny acacia (low, funnel-shaped bushes) and life-supporting *ghaf* trees. Sheltering under these trees, sustained by dew from the leaflets in the morning, are gazelle, protected colonies of oryx and a host of smaller mammals – hares, foxes and hedgehogs – that provide a food source for the land's many raptors. Easier to spot are the lizards, snakes and insects that provide the building blocks of the desert ecosystem.

Books on the Desert

In the Deserts of the Earth, Uwe George (1977)

Desert: Nature and Culture, Roslynn Haynes (2013)

Desert Adaptations

One of the remarkable aspects of life in the desert is the very existence of life here. Some species go to enormous lengths to cope with the searing heat of the summer sun and the minimal presence of water. Officially, a desert refers to land that receives less than 250mm of rain per year. In these conditions, animals have had to evolve remarkable adaptations

DESERT, YES – DESERTED, NO

Visiting any wilderness area carries a responsibility and no more so than a desert, where the slightest interference with the environment can wreak havoc with fragile ecosystems. The rocky plains of the interior may seem like an expanse of nothing, but that is not the case. Red markers along a road, improbable as they may seem on a cloudless summer day, indicate the height of water possible during a flash flood. A month or so later, a flush of tapering grasses marks the spot, temporary home to wasp oil beetles, elevated stalkers and myriad other life forms.

Car tracks scar a rock desert forever, crushing plants and insects not immediately apparent from the driver's seat. Rubbish doesn't biodegrade as it would in a tropical or temperate climate. The flower unwittingly picked in its moment of glory may miss its first and only opportunity for propagation in seven years of drought.

With a bit of common sense, however, and by taking care to stick to existing tracks, it's possible to enjoy the desert without damaging the unseen communities it harbours. It also pays to turn off the engine and just sit. At dusk, dramas unfold: a fennec fox chases a hedgehog, a wild dog trots out of the wadi without seeing the snake slithering in the other direction, tightly closed leaves relax in the brief respite of evening and a dung beetle rolls its reward homewards.

to drought conditions to survive. These include nocturnal living (foxes and hedgehogs), hairy paws and big ears that give protection against hot surfaces (jerboas), the ability to survive on dew (gazelle) and remaining dormant in the ground for years in a state of semi-hibernation (toads).

The sand cat, sand fox and desert hare have large ears, giving a large surface area from which to release heat, and tufts of hair on their paws that enable them to walk on blistering desert floors.

Mountains

They may not be the mightiest mountains in the world, but the ranges of the Peninsula are nonetheless spectacular. This is partly because they rise without preamble from flat coastal plains.

The Peninsula has two main mountain ranges. The Hejaz range runs the length of Saudi Arabia's west coast, generally increasing in height as it tends southwards. The term 'mountain' may seem a misnomer for much of the range. Saudi's landmass looks like a series of half-toppled books, with flat plains ending in dramatic escarpments that give way to the next plain. The last escarpment drops spectacularly to the sea. If you follow the baboons over the escarpment rim, from the cool, misty, green reaches of Abha to Jizan on the humid, baking plains of the Tihama, the effect of this range is immediately felt. The settlers of the fertile mountains in their stone dwellings live such a different life to the goat herders in their mud houses on the plains, they may as well belong to different countries – and indeed the Tihama shares much in common with Eritrea and Ethiopia's Tigré region on the opposite side of the Red Sea.

Arabia's other principal mountain range is found in the east of the Peninsula. Here, Oman's Hajar Mountains protect the communities around the Gulf of Oman from the encroachment of deserts from the interior. Terracing similar to that of southern Saudi Arabia can be seen on Jebel Akhdar and on pocket-handkerchief scraps of land in the Musandam. The hills of Dhofar, in the south of Oman, catch the edge of the monsoon from India, bringing light rains that cause the arid hills to burst into life during the summer when most of the rest of the Peninsula is desiccated by heat.

Ostriches once roamed the savannah-like plains of Arabia and crocodiles inhabited the rivers, but changing climate and human encroachment resulted in a change of resident wildlife.

Dhofar is home to the elusive leopard, one of Arabia's most magnificent animals. It is the largest but not the only predatory mammal of the Peninsula. Caracals, wolves, striped hyenas and sand cats are all resident (though in small and diminishing numbers) in the mountains and wadis of Oman in particular, where they prey on snakes and the plentiful rodents.

The mountains are the best (though far from the only) place to see wildflowers. After rains they bloom in abundance. In the wadis, pink-flowering oleander and tall stands of Sodom's apples flower year-round. On the mountainsides, juniper trees, wild olives, lavenders and many plants with medicinal properties flourish.

Books on Seashells

Collectable Eastern Arabian Seashells (Donald Bosch)

Seashells of Eastern Arabia (Donald Bosch et al)

Seas

The Peninsula is bordered by three distinct seas, each of which has its own character.

The Red Sea, with its world-renowned underwater landscape and great diversity of tropical fish, is mostly calm and its shores are flat and sandy. Groupers, wrasse, parrotfish and snapper inhabit the colourful gardens of coral, sea cucumbers and sponge, while sharks and barracuda swim beyond the shallows, only venturing into the reefs to feed or breed.

The Arabian Sea, home to dolphins and whales and five species of turtle, many of which nest along the eastern Arabian shore, has a split personality. Calm for much of the year, it becomes violently rough in the *khareef* (summer monsoon), casting up shells on some of the most magnificent, pristine, uninterrupted beaches in the world. Rimmed by cliffs for much of its length, this sea is punctuated with fishing villages that continue a way of life little changed in centuries, supported by seas rich in sardine and tuna.

The Gulf has a completely different character to the other two seas. Flat, calm, so smooth that at times it looks solid like a piece of shiny coal, it tends to be shallow for up to 1km from the shore. With lagoons edged with valuable mangroves, this is an important habitat for birds. It is also conducive to human development and much of the rim of the Gulf has been paved over or 'reclaimed' for the improbable new cities at its edge.

National Parks & Protected Areas

The idea of setting aside areas for wildlife runs contrary to the nature of traditional life on the Peninsula, which was, and to some extent still is, all about maintaining a balance with nature, rather than walling it off. The Bedu flew their hunting falcons only at certain times of the year and moved their camels on to allow pasture to regrow. Fishermen selected only what they wanted from a seasonal catch and threw the rest back. Goat and sheep herders of the mountains moved up and down the hillside at certain times of the year to allow for regrowth. Farmers let lands lie fallow so as not to exhaust the soil.

Modern practices, including settlement of nomadic tribes, sport hunting, trawler fishing and the use of pesticides in modern farming, have had such an impact on the natural environment over the past 50 years, however, that all governments in the region have recognised the need to actively protect the fragile ecosystems of their countries. This has resulted in the creation of protected areas (10% of the regional landmass) but, with tourism on the increase, there is a strong incentive to do more.

Books on Arabian Plants

Handbook of Arabian Medicinal Plants (SA Ghazanfar)

Vegetation of the Arabian Peninsula (SA Ghazanfar)

Most countries have established conservation schemes, with the UAE leading the way. Five per cent of the emirate of Dubai is a protected area, thanks to the example set by the late Sheikh Zayed, posthumously named 'Champion of the Earth' by the UN Environment Programme (UNEP) in 2005. Sir Bani Yas Island has an important and growing collection of Arabian wildlife and Al Ain Zoo has been transformed into a sustainable wildlife centre. Saudi Arabia's Asir National Park is the largest on the Peninsula, comprising 450,000 hectares of Red Sea coast, escarpment and desert. In addition, Saudi authorities have designated 13 wildlife reserves (amounting to more than 500,000 hectares) as part of a plan for more than 100 protected areas. The Hawar Islands, home to epic colonies of cormorants and other migrant birds, are protected by the Bahrain government.

Although it has no national parks as such, Oman has an enviable record with regard to protection of the environment, a subject in which the sultan has a passionate interest. His efforts have repeatedly been acknowledged by the International Union for the Conservation of Nature. Sanctuaries for oryx, the internationally important turtle nesting grounds of Ras al Jinz, tahr (a mountain-dwelling, goat-like mammal) and leopard sanctuaries provide protection for these endangered species.

The Breeding Centre for Endangered Arabian Wildlife is dedicated to programs preserving the endangered species of the Peninsula. Some of the animals can be seen in Arabia's Wildlife Centre in Sharjah's Desert Park, the largest of its kind.

Environmental Issues

Water

The major concern for all Peninsula countries, particularly those of the Gulf, is water – or rather, the lack of it. Sustained periods of drought and dramatically increased water consumption over the past two decades have led to a depleted water table. Saudi Arabia will run out of groundwater long before it runs out of oil.

Bahrain's freshwater underground springs have already dried up, leaving the country reliant on expensive desalinated water. Higher demand for residential use is another factor forcing countries to rethink ways of managing water. Desalination and modernisation of irrigation systems appears to be the way forward, though public awareness also has a role to play. At present, it would be unthinkable to impose a hose-pipe ban on municipal and private gardens, as flowering borders are considered the ultimate symbol of a modern, civilised lifestyle.

That said, mostly gone are the days when you could cross parts of Saudi and see great green circular fields dotted across the desert. There was much to regret in the attempt to make the desert bloom. While Saudi became an exporter of grain, it used up precious mineral deposits and lowered the water table, and to no great useful purpose – the country can easily afford to import grain at the moment. There may be times to come when it cannot, and many experts are of the opinion it's better to retain precious resources, if not for the proverbial rainy day, then at least for the expected prolonged drought.

Pollution & Rubbish

In a region where oil is the major industry, there is always a concern about spillage and leakage, and the illegal dumping of oil from offshore tankers is a constant irritation to the countries of the Gulf. The oil spillage, following the deliberate release of oil by Iraq during the Gulf War, resulted in an environmental catastrophe that, though not quite as bad as initially predicted, caused significant damage that is still being addressed today.

The oil industry isn't the only sector responsible for environmental degradation. As one of the Peninsula's fastest-growing industries, tourism is becoming a major environmental issue – as seen at the turtle beaches of Ras al Jinz, where many tourists show a dismal lack of respect for both the turtles and their environment. The irresponsible use of 4WD vehicles in dune bashing is another lamentable problem.

Arabian Wildlife (www.arabianwildlife.com) is the online version of the Arabian Wildlife Magazine and covers 'all facets of wildlife and conservation in Arabia'.

By far the biggest concern created by larger numbers of visitors to the desert is the discarding of rubbish. Indeed, for several decades the Arabian Peninsula has been afflicted by the scourge of plastic bags and tin cans. These are unceremoniously dumped out of car windows or discarded at picnic sites and can be seen drifting across the desert, tangled in trees or floating in the sea. Expatriates and many Peninsula Arabs don't feel it is their responsibility to 'bag it and bin it' – that would be

GO LIGHT ON LITTER

There's a wonderful tale in *The Thousand and One Nights* that describes the inadvertent chain of devastation caused by a merchant spitting out his date pip and unknowingly blinding the son of a genie.

It may not be immediately apparent to a visitor watching pink and blue plastic bags sailing in the breeze that Peninsula authorities are making concerted efforts to clean up the countryside. And they have a stiff task: according to some estimates, the average person uses 300 plastic bags a year, prompting Friends of the Earth Middle East to run a 'Say No to Plastic Bags' campaign. It's immensely difficult to avoid adding to the rubbish, especially when local attitude still maintains that every soft-drink can thrown on the ground represents one more job for the needy.

Attitudes are beginning to change, however, thanks in part to educational schemes that target children and the adoption of environment days in Oman, the UAE and Bahrain. 'Bag it' and 'out it' is a pretty good maxim as, hardy as it seems, the desert has a surprisingly fragile ecosystem that, once damaged, is as difficult to mend as the eye of a genie's son.

stealing the job, so the argument goes, of the road cleaner. You can see these individuals on a scooter, or even walking in the middle of summer, with a dustpan and brush and a black bin liner, 100km from the nearest village. The idea that Arabs have inherited the throwaway culture from the Bedu and can't distinguish between organic and non-biodegradable is often cited, but lacks credibility. The Bedu know very well that an orange peel, let alone a Coke can, does not decompose in a hurry in the dry heat of the Peninsula.

The Arab response to litter, like the Arab response to conservation in general, probably has more to do with a lack of interest in the great outdoors for its own sake. But times are changing, and school trips to wild places may just be the answer. In the UAE, recycling was made mandatory in 2010 and Masdar City in Abu Dhabi is taking the lead on carbon-neutral living.

Survival Guide

Safe Travel

PRE-TRIP ADVICE

The following government websites offer travel advisories and information on current hot spots.

British Foreign & Commonwealth Office (www.fco.gov.uk)

Canadian Department of Foreign Affairs & International Trade (www.dfait-maeci.gc.ca)

Smart Traveller (www.smarttraveller.gov.au)

US State Department (www.travel.state.gov)

Rightly or wrongly, the Arabian Peninsula has historically earned a reputation as a high-risk destination, marked by hard-line political regimes, Islamic fundamentalism and home-grown terrorism. Added to that, the uprisings of 2011 left a legacy of unrest that increased the negative impression of security in the region.

This is a reputation, however, that is not wholly deserved and today the threats to safety are largely confined to one or two trouble spots in Bahrain and some sensitive areas in Kuwait and Saudi Arabia. With a war raging across the border with Saudi Arabia, and entrenched internal conflicts, Yemen is currently the only country on the Peninsula that poses a high risk, and for this reason it should be entirely off-limits for visitors.

Politics aside, the Peninsula overall represents a very safe destination, boasting one of the lowest average crime rates in the world. That doesn't mean you should take unnecessary risks, but it does mean you can largely travel without worrying about theft, mugging and scams.

COUNTRY BY COUNTRY SAFETY STATUS

Safety is a subjective topic. As far as security on the Peninsula is concerned, most peoples' perceptions are shaped by media stories of Islamic fundamentalism. It's a picture that bears little relation to reality. Interestingly, Arabs travelling abroad share similar safety fears, bearing in mind *Al Jazeera* reports of violent gun crime, carjacking and theft that appear to plague many cities around the world. Needless to say, day-to-day life on the Peninsula revolves around violence about as much as it does in Kentucky, Kent or Kerala.

Fortunately, the people of the Middle East are ready and willing to distinguish between foreign travellers and the policies of their governments. You might receive the occasional question about politics, but you'll never be held personally accountable. Keep abreast of current events, and visit your embassy for travel advice if you're feeling cautious, but otherwise (with the current exception of Yemen) just go.

Bahrain & Kuwait

At the time of writing (late 2015), political tensions following the Arab Spring uprisings in Bahrain of 2011 and 2012 were still simmering under the surface. A ban on public demonstrations is in place and there are no-go areas in and around the capital cities. Sporadic violent outbursts, fuelled by frustration from opposition groups at what is regarded as a lack of government reform, remain commonplace.

That said, this has little impact on the visitor and the areas of tourist interest in Bahrain and Kuwait remain safe to visit. As a precaution, however, it is worth keeping an eye on international news for any further unrest and checking with your consulate before booking a visit.

While visiting either country, remain vigilant, keep abreast of local news and avoid large gatherings.

Oman, Qatar & the UAE

These are some of the safest countries in the entire Middle East to visit and though there were minor skirmishes during the Arab Spring of 2011, the unrest was localised.

The main danger is from the weather: flash floods, particularly in the mountains of Oman and the UAE, often catch visitors unaware. Wadis should be avoided during and immediately after rain. Visitors also sometimes underestimate the strength of the current in the Gulf and the Arabian Sea, so local guidelines should be observed.

In the desert, getting a vehicle stuck in soft sand in remote areas can be life-threatening, but if you have plenty of water with you, remain with the vehicle and keep calm as there is a strong likelihood of being noticed within a few days. In popular tourist spots, it is more an inconvenience than a hazard.

Saudi Arabia

Despite the pivotal role Saudi Arabia has played in engendering Al-Qaeda, the government in Riyadh has made a concerted effort to stamp our terrorism in the kingdom. This has not eradicated it entirely, however, and sectarian violence sometimes flares up, most recently targeting mosques.

Tourism (almost exclusively in groups, as independent travel remains virtually impossible) has increased in recent years and the security of these visitors is taken very seriously as the authorities seek to grow this nascent industry.

DANGERS & ANNOYANCES

Road Accidents

Traffic accidents are the largest threat to safety on the Peninsula, with a high incidence of fatalities on the road. Some cities across the region suffer from congestion, with rush-hour traffic rivalling that of major cities abroad. With the increase in traffic, accidents have become a major issue (particularly in Kuwait, Saudi Arabia and the UAE, which have some of the highest accident rates per capita in the world) and are a cause for concern for visitors and residents alike.

The standard of driving on the Peninsula is poor, largely because driving tests are less exacting or are illegally dodged. Poor driving habits include tailgating, queue jumping, pushing in, lack of indication, not using mirrors, jumping red lights and turning right across the traffic when sitting in the left lane. Car horns, used at the slightest provocation in some cities, take the place of caution and courtesy and almost no one likes to give way, slow down or wait.

AVOIDING TROUBLE

Do...

➡ Be vigilant in the cities, keeping clear of large public gatherings.

➡ Cooperate politely with security checks in hotel foyers and at road checkpoints.

➡ Keep abreast of the news in English-language newspapers published locally.

➡ Check the latest travel warnings online through your country's state department or ministry.

➡ Consult your embassy/consulate in the region for specific concerns.

➡ Register with your embassy/consulate on arrival if there have been recent issues around public order.

➡ Trust the police, military and security services. They are overwhelmingly friendly, honest and hospitable, in common with their compatriots.

Don't...

➡ Be paranoid – the chances of running into trouble are no greater than at home.

➡ Get involved if you witness political protests or civil unrest.

➡ Strike up conversations of a stridently political nature with casual acquaintances.

➡ Forget to carry some form of identification with you at all times, including some or all of the following: passport, labour card, residence card, driving licence and travel permit (Saudi). It's helpful to carry something with the contact details of your next of kin and your blood type.

➡ Touch any unidentified objects in the wilds – ordnance from earlier conflicts is still an occasional issue in Dhofar (in Oman) and Kuwait.

IF BITTEN BY A SNAKE...

Snakes are some of the most remarkable creatures of the desert and deserve considerable respect for their survival skills. Most are non-venomous, or only mildly toxic, but a few are a bit more challenging. The only time you're likely to encounter them is camping in the sands or walking up wadis, where they will make every attempt to avoid a confrontation – and you should do the same. If you are unlucky enough to get bitten, follow this advice:

➡ Don't panic: half the people bitten by venomous snakes are not actually injected with poison (envenomed).

➡ Immobilise the bitten limb with a splint (eg a stick).

➡ Apply a bandage over the site, with firm pressure, similar to bandaging a sprain.

➡ Do not apply a tourniquet, or cut or suck the bite.

➡ Seek medical help as soon as possible so that antivenin can be given if necessary.

➡ If you have the presence of mind, take a photo of the snake for identification to aid doctors in giving the appropriate antivenin.

During Ramadan, drivers are often tired, thirsty, hungry and irritable (due to the day's fasting) and everyone is in that much more of a hurry – generally to get home for a nap.

The one good news story of the region is Oman, where (on the whole) drivers stick to the speed limits, let people into their lane and thank others for the same courtesy. Use of the horn is forbidden, except in an emergency, and you can be fined for having a dirty car.

Hazards to look out for while driving in the region include:

➡ animals on the road (particularly camels)

➡ dust storms that loom out of nowhere and obscure the road ahead

➡ cars travelling without lights on

➡ heavy rain washing out sections of road

➡ sudden flash floods that sweep away vehicles

➡ corrugated surfaces (like a rumble strip) on graded roads that damage tyres

➡ batteries that run out of juice without warning as they are quickly exhausted in high temperatures

IF YOU HAVE AN ACCIDENT...

➡ Don't move the car until the police arrive.

➡ Don't sign anything you don't understand in the accident report (as you may be accepting responsibility for an accident that wasn't your fault).

➡ Call your insurance or car-hire company immediately.

➡ Try at all costs to remain calm. Aggression may be held against you and will only worsen the situation.

➡ The traffic police are generally helpful and friendly, and it's customary for men to shake hands with policemen before commencing discussions.

Extreme Temperatures

Visitors should be aware that most of the Arabian Peninsula comprises desert and this extreme environment can bring its own hazards, especially in temperatures that exceed 50°C in summer. With common sense and a few precautions, however, encountering this unique environment is one of the highlights of a Peninsula visit.

The major hazard of the region is undoubtedly the heat. At any time of year, the high midday temperatures, combined with high humidity, can quickly lead to heat exhaustion, sunstroke and serious sunburn. If you are travelling in summer, breaking down on an empty road without water can literally be life-threatening. You should bear this in mind when planning a trip outside urban areas and think twice about travelling alone unless you are highly resourceful.

Avoiding problems is largely a matter of common sense: always carry more water than you think you'll need; cover your head and neck; wear sunglasses; cover up, especially between 11am and 3pm; and avoid too much activity in the summer months – in other words, do as the locals do!

Hazards at Sea

The waters of the Red Sea and the northern part of the Arabian Sea are usually calm and safe for swimming, but there are a few hazards to avoid.

Strong Currents During summer (July to September) in eastern and southern Oman, huge swells occur, making swimming very dangerous. Every year there are casualties associated with the strong tides and powerful undercurrents. On some stretches of the normally quieter Gulf and Red Sea coasts, lifeguards using internationally recognised flags patrol the beach at weekends. Make sure you obey the red-flag directives: in Dubai there are frequent casualties, with tourists being swept out to sea in unexpected currents.

Pollution Litter affects many public beaches, despite the best efforts of local authorities, and tar, released from irresponsible tankers, can be a nuisance on a few wild beaches. The practice is illegal, but hard to police. Occasionally, raw sewage is illegally dumped in the sea to avoid queues and fees at sanitation depots.

Dangerous Marine Life Most problems can be avoided by wearing shoes and a t-shirt when swimming (also useful against sunburn).

Common hazards of the sea include the following:

Stonefish Have a highly venomous sting.

Jellyfish Deliver a fairly innocuous but persistent sting.

Urchins Most are not toxic, but spines break off easily if brushed against and can embed in the skin for months.

Sea snakes Highly toxic but thankfully shy.

Cones Some species of these beautiful molluscs deliver a paralysing sting if handled.

Coral Can inflict cuts that can easily lead to infection in this climate.

Sharks While sharks are common, only very rare incidents of aggressive behaviour have been reported and generally in predictable circumstances (such as in waters where fishermen are gutting fish).

Red tide This bloom of blood-coloured algae can affect the waters of the Gulf and Arabian Sea for months at a time, making swimming unappealing. It is not fully understood if these tides are harmful.

KEEPING WOULD-BE SUITORS AT BAY

Engaging with locals is always a highlight of travel in the Middle East and it's easy for women to strike up a conversation if travelling alone. The key when interacting with local men is to realise that initiating conversation can be misinterpreted. Report serious harassment to the local police, who are likely to take the matter very seriously. Here are some tips to deter would-be suitors:

➡ Master the art of detachment by remaining aloof in a conversation rather than animated; local women are good role models in this.

➡ Keep eye contact to a minimum – unless delivering the killer cold stare if someone oversteps the mark.

➡ Approach a woman for help first (for directions and so forth) rather than a man.

➡ Ask to be seated in the 'family' section if dining alone.

➡ Avoid sitting in the front seat of taxis and the back seat of buses.

➡ Invent or borrow a husband if the situation feels alarming, but beware that this may lead to uncomfortable questions about abandoning the home and kids.

➡ Retain your self-confidence and keep a sense of humour in compromising situations. This is far more effective than losing your temper or showing vulnerability.

➡ Insist on being told the family name of pestering individuals and their place of work – the threat of shame is often enough to dampen their ardour.

Hazards on Land

Most of the hazards of the desert are related to overexposure to the sun and the danger of getting caught in a flash flood. This is when a wall of water rolls quickly across land too hard-baked to absorb it, sweeping away everything that gets in its path. The key strategy to staying safe is to avoid camping in wadis, not to approach the mountains during rains, don't travel alone and never cross roads where water is flowing over the red marker signs, however shallow that appears to be.

There are a few other land hazards to watch out for, such as poisonous plants (eg pink oleander in the wadis, the Sodom's apples that strew the desert floor), camel spiders, scorpions that deliver a nasty but non-fatal bite, large ants with painful bites, and annoying clusters of mosquitoes and wasps at certain times of the year. Snakes are also common in the region. Most problems can be avoided by wearing shoes and resisting the temptation to prod holes and overturn rocks.

WOMEN TRAVELLERS

Many women imagine that travel on the Peninsula will be a lot more difficult and stressful than it actually is.

Unaccompanied women will certainly attract curious stares and glances, and occasionally comments too, but they will receive hospitable treatment almost universally. Be aware that some religiously devout men prefer not to shake hands with a woman, so be ready to put your hand on your heart instead.

Gender Segregation

It is important to be aware that there are 'men areas' and 'women areas' and that this is something that is enforced mainly by women, not by men. As such, it can be quite uncomfortable for both sexes if a woman sits in a male area. In some instances, it could compromise a woman's safety.

Traditional coffeehouses, cheaper restaurants, budget hotels, the front seat of taxis and the back seats of buses all tend to be men-only areas and it's culturally sensitive to avoid them. At some budget Gulf hotels, unaccompanied women may be refused a room and insisting otherwise will likely attract the wrong kind of attention in the middle of the night. Women areas include family rooms in better restaurants, public beaches on certain days of the week and the front rows of buses.

Rather than seeing segregation as being excluded from male company, it is regarded locally as providing a safe haven for women to relax and enjoy their own company with or without the kids and without worrying about harassment or unwanted attention. For the female visitor, it presents a great opportunity to see into the lives of Arab women, an opportunity rarely, if ever, afforded to a male visitor.

Harassment

Sometimes women may be followed (particularly on beaches) or find unwanted visitors in a hotel, but this is far less prevalent than in other parts of the Middle East where there is more exposure to tourists. Sexual harassment in some Peninsula countries is considered a serious crime, but verbal harassment and sexual innuendo can be more common.

Modesty

Modesty is one of those culturally defined concepts that is hard to define, but it is highly prized by men and women in all Peninsula societies. A lack of this so-called virtue is likely to bring trouble to women travellers, especially those travelling alone.

Inappropriate, tight clothing that reveals shoulders, knees and cleavage is the quickest way to earn the opprobrium of local women. It will also send conflicting messages to men who, especially in rural areas, often confuse attractive dress with sexual invitation.

Modesty includes, but isn't restricted to, clothing. Drinking and smoking copiously in public, talking in a loud voice in mixed company, partying and dancing suggestively with male friends, engaging in conversations of innuendo, flirtatiousness of any kind – all these modes of conduct may well be harmlessly intended, but they often give offence and may result in disdain from men and women and/or unwanted male advances.

Modesty should not be confused with attempting to dress and behave like local women. Wearing an *abbeya* is only expected in Saudi Arabia and it is not necessary to cover hair in any of the Peninsula countries. Similarly, foreign women are welcome to mingle publicly in mixed company, providing they remain sensitive to the cultural environment. Within reason, women may dress and behave as they please inside Gulf resorts and top-end hotels.

Directory A–Z

Accommodation

During local holiday periods (particularly over *eid*, the Islamic feast) and popular festivals (such as the shopping festivals in Dubai and Kuwait), as well as Western holidays (Christmas and New Year) and major fixtures (such as the Dubai Rugby Sevens), travellers should book well in advance. Discounts in summer (except in Salalah in Oman) are common.

Outside the big cities, accommodation is scarce and choice limited. Rooms in all categories generally have air-conditioning, hot water, telephone, fridge, some form of internet connection and TV (usually with satellite channels, including BBC and CNN).

BOOK YOUR STAY ONLINE

For more accommodation reviews by Lonely Planet authors, check out http://lonelyplanet.com/hotels. You'll find independent reviews, as well as recommendations on the best places to stay. Best of all, you can book online.

Camping

➡ Key areas for desert camping include Khor Al Adaid in Qatar and Sharqiya Sands and Jebel Shams in Oman.

➡ With a 4WD and your own equipment, wild camping (without any facilities) is a highlight of the region.

➡ Avoid camping in wadis, Bedouin areas and turtle beaches (ones with large pits at the top of the tide line) and remove all rubbish.

Budget Hotels

➡ The cheapest rooms are not suitable for women; in the Gulf, very cheap hotels may double as brothels.

➡ There's no established network of backpacker hotels in the region and prices are much higher than international norms.

➡ Dormitory-style hostels (men-only) are only available in the UAE and Qatar.

Midrange Hotels

➡ Generally offer good value for money and are often family-run.

Top-end Hotels

➡ Ranked as some of the best in the world with spas, personal fitness and shopping services, infinity pools, fine dining, world-class architecture and palatial interior designs.

➡ Often the only venues in town with a licence to serve alcohol in countries where alcohol is permitted, so they tend to double as entertainment venues for non-residents.

Resorts

➡ Growing concept across the region, offering retreats from the city but often in isolated locations with few surrounding amenities.

➡ Most are sumptuous and palatial with activity centres.

Activities

The Peninsula offers many opportunities for engaging with the sea and with the desert interior, though many of these activities require resourcefulness (such as survival and map-reading skills) or the help of a specialist agency (especially for rock climbing, caving and desert safaris). **Outward Bound Oman** (☎+968 2469 6525; www.outwardbound.net) offers life-changing leadership opportunities for youngsters in the deserts of Oman. The Arabian and Red Seas offer some of the best diving and snorkelling in the world.

Customs Regulations

Customs regulations vary from country to country, but in most cases they don't differ significantly. All luggage is X-rayed and sometimes also opened. That said, with greater numbers of tourists arriving, and in the drive to appear more tourist friendly, many of the old customs nightmares (such as long queues while officials check the contents of your soap box) are things of the past.

Alcohol It is strictly forbidden to take alcohol into dry or semi-dry regions (Kuwait, Qatar, Sharjah, Abu Dhabi and Saudi Arabia). Alcohol can only be taken into Oman by air. If you're caught attempting to smuggle in even small quantities of alcohol, punishments range from deportation and fines to imprisonment. In most other countries, foreigners (but not Muslims) are permitted a small duty-free allowance.

Drugs Syringes, needles and some medicinal drugs (such as tranquillisers and even some antidepressants and sleeping pills) are banned, unless you have a doctor's prescription to prove you need them.

Israel & 'Incendiary' Material Books critical of Islam, Peninsula governments or their countries, or pro-Israeli books may be confiscated (though the days of removing labels from M&S underwear are thankfully now gone).

Money There are no restrictions on the import and export of money (in any currency) in and out of Peninsula countries.

Pork products Some countries make allowances for foreigners, but it's better not to get stopped with a pork chop in your pocket.

Pornography Officials may construe images in style magazines, or women in swimwear, as pornographic and remove the offending page from the magazine.

Video Material & DVDs Censors may well want to examine these and then allow you to collect them after a few days.

Electricity

All countries in the region have an electrical supply of 220 to 240V, except Saudi Arabia, which also has 110V.

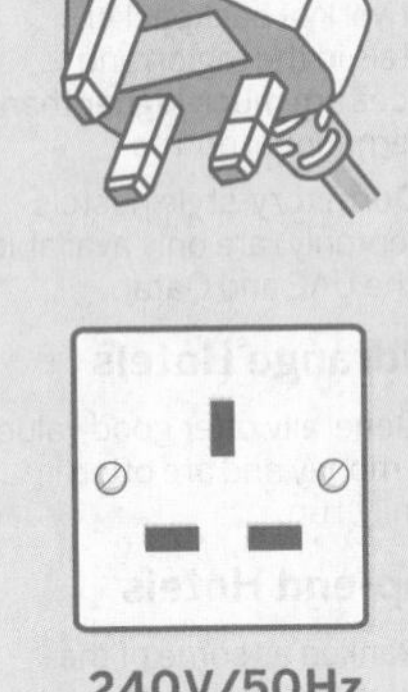

Embassies & Consulates

Embassies are a fairly good, if somewhat cautious and at times alarmist, source of information on current hotspots and dangers. Many embassies advise travellers to register with them upon arrival, especially if you're staying in the country for an extended period: if you should disappear, have a serious accident, or suddenly need to be evacuated from the country, you will at least be in a better position to receive help. If you break the law, you're on your own!

See the Directory sections of each individual destination chapter for lists of embassies and consulates.

Gay & Lesbian Travellers

Homosexual practices are illegal in all of the Peninsula countries. Under Sharia'a (Islamic) law, homosexuality incurs the death penalty in some countries, though punishment usually ranges from flogging to imprisonment or deportation. In other countries infractions are punished by fines and/or imprisonment.

Visitors are unlikely to encounter outright prejudice or harassment so long as they remain discreet. However, this may well change if you become involved with a local. Room sharing is generally not a problem (it will be assumed you're economising). Condoms are fairly widely available, though may be limited in selection.

Useful Resources

Global Gayz (www.globalgayz.com/middle-east) Country-by-country guide to gay and lesbian activity.

Barra (www.barramag.com) A news-and-views forum for the LBGT community based in the Middle East.

Insurance

Travel insurance covering accidents and medical problems is strongly advised, particularly as traffic accidents are a major hazard of the region and problems can easily occur if visiting the desert (particularly on off-road excursions). Although

GET ACTIVE

WHAT	WHERE	HOW	NOTES
Camel Treks	Sharqiya Sands, Khor Al Adaid	Arrange through local desert camps	Choose a mounted rather than a walking guide for a more authentic experience.
Diving & Snorkelling	Jeddah, Muscat, Musandam	Contact Extra Divers (www.extradivers.com)	The Red Sea is one of the world's top diving destinations; the Arabian Sea offers easier access but has less coral. Both are wows in the water, but low-key experiences on land.
Dhow Rides & Dolphin Spotting	Manama, Doha, Musandam, Abu Dhabi, Dubai, Muscat	Most tour companies offer half- or whole-day trips, or turn up at the local marina and see what's heading out to sea!	Go early in the morning for the best chance to see pods of dolphins in action.
Fishing	Manama, Doha, Abu Dhabi, Dubai, Muscat	Negotiate an hourly rate with local fishermen, or book through the local marina	Common catches include yellow-fin tuna (weighing between 25kg and 60kg), sail fish, barracuda and shark. Fishing licences are not needed on the Peninsula.
Golf	Manama, Doha, Abu Dhabi, Dubai, Muscat	Consider a Peninsula cruise (www.perrygolf.com/golfcruising), taking in the best courses	Designer golf courses with grass are becoming a signature feature of modern Gulf cities.
Hiking	Oman, Saudi Arabia	Book through local tour agencies	Oman has an established network of walking paths, but signposts are limited. Most hiking on the Peninsula is ad hoc, passing through small villages. Allow 1L of water per person per hour, wear light-coloured clothing and stay out of wadis during and after rain.
Off-Road Driving	UAE, Oman	Pick up a locally published off-road guidebook for routes and their challenges	Beware flash floods, soft sand and salt flats. Stay on tracks to protect the fragile desert ecology.
Turkish Baths	UAE, Saudi Arabia	Ask at your hotel for a local recommendation	A great antidote for aching muscles, the hammam is otherwise known as a Turkish bath. Women should call ahead for a female assistant.
Water Sports	All seaboard cities	Organise through any of the seaboard five-star hotels and resorts	Water sports on offer include jet skiing, kite surfing, windsurfing, sailing and kayaking. Avoid southern Arabia during the summer, when currents are ferocious.

some regional hospitals do not charge for emergency treatment, you cannot rely on this. The cost of complicated surgery (for a fracture, for example) is comparable with international rates.

A policy that pays doctors or hospitals directly rather than you having to pay on the spot and claim later is a better option for the region. If you have to claim later, make sure you keep all documentation.

Note that some policies specifically exclude 'dangerous activities', which can include activities you may want to engage in on the Peninsula, such as scuba diving, rock climbing, motorcycling and even trekking.

Car insurance does not usually include automatic off-road coverage. Specify that you need this if hiring a 4WD for off-road adventure.

Internet Access

Staying connected on the Peninsula is easy. All countries have International Direct Dialling (IDD) facilities

BARGAINING & BARTERING

Arabs are committed shoppers and they make an art form out of it, promenading the main street and popping into shops to vex the owners without any intention of buying. Buying, meanwhile, is a whole separate entertainment, focused on the business of bartering and bargaining.

Bartering implies that items do not have a value per se – their value is governed by what you are willing to pay balanced against the sum for which the vendor is happy to sell. This subtle exchange, often viewed with suspicion by those from a fixed-price culture, is dependent on many factors, such as how many other sales the vendor has made that day, whether the buyer looks like a person who can afford an extra rial or two, and even whether the vendor is in a good mood or not.

As with all social interaction, there's an unwritten code of conduct that keeps negotiations sweet:

- Bartering is your chance to decide what you are willing to pay for an item, so use your interpersonal skills to see if you can persuade the vendor to match it.
- Haggling is a sociable activity, often conducted over refreshments, so avoid causing offence by refusing hospitality.
- Don't pay the first price quoted. This is often considered arrogant.
- Start below the price you wish to buy at so you have room to compromise – but don't quote too low or the vendor may be insulted.
- If negotiations aren't going to plan, simply smile and say goodbye – you'll be surprised how often the word *ma'a salaama* (goodbye) brings the price down.
- Resist comparing prices with other travellers. If they were happy with what they paid, they certainly won't be if you tell them you bought the same thing for less. Besides, you can't put a price on the thrill of the deal.

via satellite links. Mobile phones are easy to buy and local SIM cards are widely available in all cities and most airports across the region. Roaming charges apply for non-local SIM cards and it is worth checking the rates before travelling. Internet access is generally offered free in most midrange hotels and free wi-fi is becoming the norm in many coffeeshops and hotels. Unless you are off road in the desert or camping in the mountains, use of all connectivity devices (smartphones, tablets and so forth) is virtually guaranteed.

Legal Matters

Although the law varies in specifics from country to country, it does share certain similarities. The legal system in all Peninsula countries is based wholly or partly on Sharia'a law, derived mainly from the Quran.

Sharia'a law is often perceived as notoriously harsh and inflexible, but in reality it shares many commonly held legal values, such as the presumption of innocence until proven guilty. The severest punishment for a crime is in practice rarely exacted (even in Saudi Arabia).

Visitors should remember that they are subject to the laws of the country they find themselves in, and that ignorance of the law does not constitute a defence. In Saudi Arabia, in particular, it is vital that travellers (particularly women) acquaint themselves with the local laws.

If you are arrested and detained, call your embassy or consulate and wait until a representative arrives before you sign anything. In a car accident you should not move the car, even if you're causing a traffic jam, until the police arrive.

Those caught in possession of drugs (including ecstasy, amphetamines, cannabis and cocaine) can face the death penalty, which in Saudi Arabia, with its policy of zero tolerance, means what it says.

Money

The best way to carry money on the Peninsula is to take a supply of US dollars, pounds sterling or euros and rely on ATMs to withdraw additional funds.

The Peninsula used to be famous as a low-tax area. Nowadays, however, a mixture of taxes, often reaching 17%, is added to hotel and restaurant prices.

ATMs

Virtually all banks in the region, from big cities to small villages, have ATMs from which you can withdraw funds from an overseas bank or gain a cash advance with a credit card. ATMs are also widespread in shopping malls and petrol stations.

Cash

Cash in US dollars, pounds sterling or euros is easily exchanged anywhere in the region.

In small businesses, including cheap restaurants, bus stations and budget hotels, and in rural areas, you will need cash for most transactions.

Change money before leaving one Peninsula country for another as neighbouring currency is not often accepted across borders (with the possible exception of Emirati dirhams in northern Oman).

Credit Cards

Credit cards are widely accepted on the Peninsula and almost everything can be paid for by plastic, including your morning cup of coffee.

Visa and MasterCard are the most popular credit cards; Amex is less widely accepted. It's possible to get cash advances on credit cards.

Moneychangers

Moneychangers are easy to find in all Peninsula cities, but the rates do not differ much from banks.

Tipping

Tips are not generally expected in the Gulf and the concept of *baksheesh*, common throughout the rest of the Middle East, is little known on the Peninsula. That said, those who have contact with tourists (such as guides and hotel porters) have grown to expect tips.

Note that the service charge added to most hotel and restaurant bills is not an automatic gratuity that goes to the waiters. It usually goes into the till and is often the restaurant's way of making the prices on the menu look 10% to 15% cheaper than they really are. Waiters in the Gulf tend to be paid derisory wages, so a small tip discreetly left on the table, while not required, is greatly appreciated if the service is good. The practice of automatic, lavish tip giving, however, can backfire as many establishments simply reduce the wages of their employees if they know that tips are expected.

Travellers Cheques

These are virtually a thing of the past on the Peninsula. With low levels of theft in the region, it is hard to find a good reason to recommend them.

SECURITY

On the whole, theft is rare in the region. Scams involving ATMs sometimes occur, so beware of any unusual-looking keypads or signs of tampering.

Opening Hours

Regional & Seasonal Variations

Opening hours vary from country to country. They also vary from institution to institution and from season to season (especially during Ramadan). Above all, Arabs are not known for blind obedience to rules, and opening hours are often taken with a pinch of salt.

Weekends In Bahrain, Kuwait, Oman, Qatar and the UAE, the weekend is Friday and Saturday; in Saudi Arabia it is Thursday and Friday. Shops stay open for six days a week in all countries and many open for a limited period on Friday evening, too. Major tourist sights usually open during the weekend.

Banks Opening hours vary throughout the region, but usually banks operate from 8am or 9am to noon or 1pm, either five or six days a week. Some reopen for a couple of hours in the afternoon. Foreign-exchange facilities usually keep longer hours.

Ramadan Government offices work shorter hours during Ramadan and businesses tend to open much later and close earlier, or else not open at all during the day but remain open for much of the night. Note that most restaurants close during the day throughout Ramadan, or even remain closed for the month.

Tourist Attractions You can't rely on tourist sites opening as prescribed. If you're determined to see a particular museum or other attraction and haven't time to waste, it's worth calling ahead to make sure it's open as stated. That, alas, is still no guarantee!

OPEN SESAME

Nothing causes quite so much disappointment as finding a sight closed when the guidebook states it should be open. Unfortunately on the Peninsula, even at major city sites, such as forts and mosques, the tour timings or opening hours can change on a whim. Despite information taken from notices posted at the sites, or definitive timings being given by ministries of tourism, the reality on the ground is that sites open pretty much when the gate-guard feels like it. On a good day he'll be there an hour early, on a bad day he won't turn up at all. Who can blame him when little-touristed sites, like some of those in Saudi or Oman, may not see a visitor for days? All opening hours must be prefaced, therefore, with a hopeful *insha'allah* (God willing). The good news is that often sites that are scheduled to be closed can suddenly spring open with the magic words 'please' and the kind heart of the gate-guard.

Photography

Restricted Areas Do not photograph anything vaguely military in nature (including the police), or anything construed as strategic (including airports, bridges and ports). In general terms, Bahrain and the UAE are the most relaxed countries on the Peninsula when it comes to photography, while Kuwait and Oman seem to have the broadest definitions of what constitutes a strategic site. In Saudi Arabia it often seems that the authorities just don't like cameras.

Photographing People Do not photograph anyone without their permission, especially women. In the more conservative countries, such as Saudi Arabia and Kuwait, you can cause real offence in this way and may risk having stones thrown at you.

Photographing Poverty People on the Peninsula are often offended when you take photographs of run-down houses or anything that resembles poverty, as the tendency is to emphasise what their country has achieved in the last few decades.

Religious Sites Photography is usually allowed inside religious and archaeological sites (when entry is permitted), unless there are signs indicating otherwise. Avoid taking photos of religious observance.

PRACTICALITIES

Discount Cards Student, youth and senior-citizens cards are of little use anywhere on the Peninsula.

Smoking In Peninsula countries smoking is banned in indoor public spaces (including taxis in the UAE). With the exception of Qatar, these bans are mostly well enforced, especially in cities.

Time Saudi Arabia, Kuwait, Bahrain and Qatar are three hours ahead of GMT/UTC. The UAE and Oman are four hours ahead of GMT/UTC. Daylight-saving time is not observed in any of the Gulf countries (in other words, the time remains constant throughout the year).

Public Holidays

All Peninsula countries observe the main Islamic holidays. Some of the Peninsula countries also observe the Gregorian New Year (1 January). Every country has its own national days and other public holidays.

Islamic New Year Also known as Ras as-Sana, it literally means 'the head of the year'.

Ashura The anniversary of the martyrdom of Hussein, the third imam (religious teacher) of the Shiites.

Prophet's Birthday Known as Moulid an-Nabi, it's 'the feast of the Prophet'.

Ramadan The ninth month of the Muslim calendar, this is when Muslims fast during daylight hours. How strictly the fast is observed depends on the country, but most Muslims conform to some extent. Foreigners are not expected to follow suit, but visitors should not smoke, drink or eat (including gum chewing) in public during Ramadan. Hotels make provision for non-Muslim guests by erecting screens for discreet dining. Opening hours tend to become more erratic and usually shorter and many restaurants close for the whole period. Alcohol is not available in Ramadan, except as room service. Once the sun has set each day, the fast is broken with something light (such as dates and *laban*) before prayers. Then comes *iftar* (breakfast), at which enough food is usually consumed to compensate for the previous hours of abstinence. People then rise again before dawn to prepare a meal to support them through the day.

Eid al Fitr The festivities mark the end of Ramadan fasting; the celebrations last for three days and are a time of family feasting and visiting.

Eid al Adha This feast marks the time that Muslims make the pilgrimage to Mecca.

Islamic Calendar

Although most secular activities and day-to-day life are planned on the Peninsula according to the Gregorian calendar (the most commonly used system internationally), all Islamic holidays are calculated according to the Muslim calendar. For visitors this can cause confusion, such as when trying to decipher official documents, including the date of expiry of travel permits and visas. Calendars showing parallel systems are available.

The Muslim year is based on the lunar cycle and is divided into 12 lunar months, each with 29 or 30 days. Consequently, the Muslim year is 10 or 11 days shorter than the Christian solar year, and Muslim festivals gradually move around the common year, completing the cycle in roughly 33 years.

Year zero in the Muslim calendar was when Muhammed and his followers fled from Mecca to Medina (AD 622 in the Christian calendar). This Hejira, or migration, is taken to mark the start of the new Muslim era, much as Christ's birth marks year zero in the Christian calendar. Just as BC denotes 'Before Christ', so AH denotes 'After Hejira'.

Solo Travellers

Travel for Arabic people and Asian expats entails large convoys of family groups and great gatherings at the airport. As such, solo male travellers are often regarded either with sympathy or with suspicion, as it is inconceivable to most Arabian Peninsula people that someone might choose to travel alone.

A woman travelling on her own is an even hotter topic of discussion. Women will want to adopt you, men will either ignore you (out of respect) or treat you as a token man. Either way, you will inevitably be showered with well-meaning solicitations for your safe keeping, extra help on public transport and even offers of accommodation.

Without Arabic, travelling on the Arabian Peninsula can be quite lonely at times – the roads are long and the deserts wide. Without an established network of tourism facilities, you may spend days without seeing another traveller.

Single rooms are available in most hotels, though they're often just a few dollars cheaper than double rooms. Walking around alone seldom presents a safety problem.

One word of caution: if you drive away from urban areas by car alone, you need to be quite resourceful. Many roads see very little traffic and you could wait hours before help arrives. It is not recommended that you go off-road alone.

Telephone

All the Peninsula countries have good networks and International Direct Dialling (IDD) facilities via satellite links.

Most cities and large towns have public telephone offices (either part of the post office, or privately run) from where you can make international calls and send faxes if you lose your phone.

International calls cost up to US$1 for two minutes for most destinations. Rates don't usually vary during the day or night, but in some countries there are reductions at weekends. Public phones accept coins, phonecards and, in the main cities, credit cards.

Mobile Phones

The use of mobile phones is widespread throughout the Peninsula and every country has its own (state-owned) national network. Some of these run on the GSM system (as in Europe), so if your phone works on GSM and your account allows you to roam, you'll be able to use your mobile on the Peninsula. In other places you'll have to buy prepaid SIM cards.

Toilets

Outside the midrange and top-end hotels and restaurants of the Peninsula, where Western-style toilets are found, visitors will encounter the Arab-style squat toilet (which interestingly, according to physiologists, encourages a far more natural position than the toilet-seat invention!).

It's a good idea to carry a roll of toilet paper with you on your travels if you normally use this. Most toilets only provide water and the use of paper is considered barbaric except for drying hands.

Beyond the towns you're unlikely to find public toilets, except poorly maintained ones at petrol stations.

Tourist Information

Despite the fact that tourism is a growing industry on the Peninsula, there are surprisingly few tourist offices. Staff training and office facilities are equally minimal. Sometimes the most you'll find is a free map (often very outdated) or an aged brochure.

There are two good, unofficial sources of information on the Peninsula: your hotel and local travel agents, many of whom generously offer information without necessarily expecting you to engage their services in return.

Travellers with Disabilities

Generally speaking, scant regard is paid to the needs of disabled travellers on the Peninsula. Steps, high kerbs and other assorted obstacles are everywhere. Roads are made virtually uncrossable

ISLAMIC HOLIDAYS 2015–2020

Dates of Islamic holidays are dependent on moon sightings and consequently may occur a day later, but not generally earlier, than listed. Not all countries spot the moon on the same day (cloud cover doesn't count), so regional differences between countries occur each year. In fact, speculation regarding whether tomorrow will bring *eid* is the subject of great public debate and private expat exasperation. The following is therefore to be treated as a guide only!

YEAR HEJIRA	NEW YEAR	ASHURA	PROPHET'S BIRTHDAY	RAMADAN BEGINS	EID AL FITR	EID AL ADHA
1437	15 Oct 2015	24 Oct 2015	24 Dec 2015	6 Jun 2016	7 Jul 2016	12 Sep 2016
1438	3 Oct 2016	12 Oct 2016	12 Dec 2016	26 May 2017	26 Jun 2017	1 Sep 2017
1439	22 Sep 2017	1 Oct 2017	1 Dec 2017	15 May 2018	16 Jun 2018	21 Aug 2018
1440	12 Sep 2018	21 Sep 2018	21 Nov 2018	6 May 2019	5 Jun 2019	12 Aug 2019
1441	1 Sep 2019	10 Sep 2019	10 Nov 2019	24 Apr 2020	24 May 2020	31 Jul 2020

THE ISRAELI STAMP STIGMA

The game of wits played between travellers and diplomatic consulars across the Middle East is ratcheted up by what's known as the 'Israeli Stamp Stigma'. On the Arabian Peninsula, all countries refuse to admit anyone whose passport has evidence of a visit to the Jewish state – even though, from time to time, rumours abound of a relaxation of this rule in some Gulf countries. Israeli immigration officials do not stamp your passport, but if you are crossing into Jordan or Egypt overland, the entry/exit stamps into those countries (marked, for example 'Taba' or 'Aqaba') will be no less incriminating than an Israeli stamp.

The safest option is to arrange your itinerary so that any visit to Israel is the final stop on your tour of the Middle East.

by heavy traffic, while some doorways are narrow and many buildings have steep staircases and no lifts.

In top-end hotels facilities are usually better (with lifts, ramps and more-accommodating bathrooms), but still leave much to be desired. Trips have to be planned carefully and may be restricted to luxury-level hotels and private, hired transport.

Elderly people with physical difficulties will find that every effort will be made to welcome them. Arab people are highly respectful of the elderly.

Useful Resources

Before setting off for the Middle East, disabled travellers can get in touch with their national support organisation (preferably with the travel officer, if there is one). In the UK try www.disabledtravelers.com or contact **RADAR** (☎020-7250 3222; www.radar.org.uk; 250 City Rd, London EC1V 8AS) or **Holiday Care Service** (☎0845 1249971; www.tourismforall.org.uk).

Visas

All countries except Saudi Arabia issue tourist visas on arrival for most nationalities. Some countries, such as the UAE and Oman, facilitate e-visas obtainable in advance. The rules change frequently, however, and it is imperative to check with the relevant embassy or consulate for the latest information.

Currently those with a UAE tourist visa may visit Oman overland (and visa versa) without paying for an Omani visa, but this often changes.

The flow of foreigners in, out and around the Peninsula is carefully monitored and strictly controlled. As a result the visa-application process ranges from fairly simple and straightforward (Oman) to nightmarishly complicated (Saudi Arabia). It also means that if you plan to travel from one country to another, passing through Saudi as you go, you need to plan ahead.

An Israeli passport, or an Israeli stamp in your passport, can be a problem. If you have either of these, it is unwise to leave it to chance as to whether an official will notice it or not.

Passports need to be valid for at least six months beyond your expected departure date from the region. Note also that most Peninsula countries require you to carry your passport with you at all times. Spot checks occasionally occur.

Collecting Visas

If you've arranged your visa in advance of arrival, make sure you have some proof of it with you before setting off (a fax or email with the visa number), or you may not be allowed to board your plane, let alone enter the country of your destination.

Transit Visas

Saudi Arabia issues transit visas for people travelling overland between Jordan and Bahrain, Kuwait, Oman, Qatar and the UAE. These transit visas can be sought from Saudi Arabian embassies in any of these countries with proof of onward connections beyond Saudi borders. They are not easy to obtain, however, as you often have to show you can't reach your destination by other means.

Visa Sponsorship

If you cannot obtain a visa to the Peninsula on arrival, or through an embassy, you can try to obtain one through a sponsor. This can be the hotel where you're planning to stay, or a tour company.

In theory, a sponsor is a national of the country you are visiting, who is willing to vouch for your good behaviour and take responsibility for your departure when you're due to leave. You'll need to send details of your passport and itinerary a couple of weeks in advance to your sponsor. Make sure you obtain confirmation *in writing* (a fax is suitable) that your visa will be awaiting your arrival at the relevant airport before you leave.

The sponsorship process varies greatly from country to country (and is also liable to change – check current regulations with the local embassy). The documentation required also varies with each country and processing can take anything from a few days to a few weeks.

Transport in the Arabian Peninsula

GETTING THERE & AWAY

Flights and tours can be booked online at www.lonelyplanet.com/bookings.

Entering the Region

Visas are available on arrival for many nationalities, except in Saudi Arabia. Check with embassies ahead of time as this information changes frequently in the region. Note that getting a visa for Saudi is highly challenging for independent travellers, including the elusive transit visa. Those with an Israeli passport, or an Israeli stamp in their passport, may be refused entry. Passports must be valid for six months from the date of entry. See p448 for more details.

Air

The cities of the Gulf have developed into major international air hubs.

Airports & Airlines

The Peninsula, and the Gulf in particular, has some of the world's best airlines and most modern and impressive airports.

All major European, Asian and Middle Eastern airlines (with the obvious exception of El Al, the Israeli airline) serve the principal cities of the Arabian Peninsula, and routes to the Americas and Australasia are increasing.

The national carriers of each Peninsula country link one country to another, with regular flights at reasonable prices.

Tickets

Dubai, Abu Dhabi, Bahrain and Doha are the major transport hubs in the region. Dubai, the main link between Europe, Southeast Asia and Australasia, is the destination that offers the best hope of picking up cheaper fares.

Dubai grew as a city by attracting and entertaining stopover travellers between Europe and Asia and it has made an art of the stopover market. Airlines support this continuing trend by offering stopover packages that include hotel accommodation, airport transfers and a short tour, all for a very reasonable price.

Land

Border Crossings

Travelling overland from Jordan or Egypt and travelling between the countries of the Arabian Peninsula is hampered by the fact that it is very difficult to get a transit visa through Saudi Arabia. In addition, many border crossings are closed to non-nationals.

The only really feasible overland route is between Oman and the UAE. There several borders between these countries, but crossings may take anything from 30 minutes to more than two hours. Showing patience, politeness and good humour is likely to speed up the process and it also helps to have pre-paid insurance if you're driving, or to have a pen if you're travelling by bus!

Bus

The only bus routes entering the region are from Jordan through the Al Umari border crossing, south of Azraq; Ad Durra, south of Aqaba; and Al Mudawwara, east of Aqaba. Services link Riyadh, Jeddah and Dammam with Aqaba and Amman.

Jordan Express Tourist Transport (JETT; ☎00962 6585 4679; www.jett.com.jo) The Jordanian national bus company has a reliable website and operates air-conditioned, modern coaches.

Car & Motorcycle

The following documents are required if you are hoping to enter the region with your own transport.

Green Card Issued by insurers. Insurance for some countries is only obtainable at the border.

International Driving Permit (IDP) Compulsory for foreign drivers and motorcyclists in Bahrain and Saudi Arabia. Most foreign licences are acceptable

TRAVELLING BY LAND ON THE ARABIAN PENINSULA

Travelling between the countries of the Arabian Peninsula is challenging, but not impossible.

BETWEEN		BORDER CROSSING NOTES	VISA AT BORDER?
Oman	Saudi Arabia	There was no border crossing open between Oman and Saudi at the time of writing	n/a
Oman (mainland)	UAE	The Wajaja border crossing is the most commonly used	yes
Oman (Musandam)	UAE	The Al Darah/Tibat border crossing was the only one open at the time of writing	yes
Saudi Arabia	Bahrain	The border crossing is on King Fahd Causeway	to Saudi, no; to Bahrain, yes
Saudi Arabia	Kuwait	The border crossing is at Al Khafji and is usually only used by those on public transport	to Saudi, no; to Kuwait, yes
Saudi Arabia	Qatar	The border crossing is at Salwah and is usually only used by those on public transport	to Saudi, no; to Qatar, yes
Saudi Arabia	UAE	The border crossing is at Sila	to Saudi, no; to UAE, yes
Bahrain, Qatar, Kuwait, UAE	Bahrain, Qatar, Kuwait, UAE	A Saudi transit visa must be obtained before travelling overland between any of these countries. Application forms can be obtained from a Saudi embassy. Travellers must have a ticket with confirmed reservations and a visa for the country of final destination. Transit times cannot exceed 72 hours. Women can only apply for a transit visa if accompanied by a male relative – proof of kinship (marriage certificate etc) is required. Children need a copy of birth certificate. If travelling by your own vehicle you are required to register your carnet at the embassy.	to Saudi, no; to others, no (you need to show your visa for your final destination at the Saudi border to transit through the country)

in the other Peninsula countries, but even in these places an IDP is recommended.

Vehicle Registration Documents Check with your insurer whether you're covered for the countries you intend to visit and whether third-party cover is included.

AAA (www.aaauae.com) The Arabian Automobile Association can provide advice on documentation.

Sea

Cargo boats call erratically at Aden, Muscat and Jeddah on their way to Europe and Asia. Getting aboard is mostly a question of luck and being in the right place at the right time. Your passage may well be dependent on the whim of the captain. Ask at the port of departure to see what boats are headed where. Some offer comfortable passenger cabins (intended for crew's family); for others you may need to come equipped with food, drink and bedding.

Some cruise ships call at Salalah, Muscat, Dubai and Doha and these ports offer passengers the opportunity to go ashore.

Several ferry services operate between the Peninsula and Egypt and Iran, but they are not geared up for tourists. If you're in for an adventure then bear the following in mind:

- In summer, conditions may be impossibly hot for many people, especially in deck class.
- Many passengers prefer to take their own food rather than rely on that served on board.
- Vehicles can be shipped on ferry services, but advance arrangements should be made.
- Ferry destinations and their timetables change frequently, but most ferry companies have good websites where you can check current fares, routes and contact details.
- Be aware of migrant routes and avoid paying a third party for your fare in case you find yourself dealing with people traffickers.

Egypt

The Alexandria-based **Misr Edco Shipping Company** (☎00203 4843901; www.acs.org.eg/members/misr-edco-shipping-co-s-a-e) and four Saudi companies sail between Jeddah and Suez. The journey takes about 36 hours direct, and about 72 hours via Aqaba. Misr Edco also sails about twice weekly between Port Safaga (Egypt) and Jeddah.

Iran

If you're travelling to/from the east and want to avoid Iraq and Saudi Arabia, you can cross the Gulf Sea from Iran into Kuwait, Dubai or Sharjah.

Ferries only have 1st-class (cabin) accommodation, but are much cheaper than the equivalent airfare, and most are overnight journeys. They are operated by **Valfajr Shipping Company** (www.valfajr.ir) in Tehran, which has a good online booking service.

Tours

Tours to the Peninsula are gaining in popularity, and some offer two-country trips between the UAE and Oman.

On the Peninsula itself there are a host of reputable tour agencies offering good trips at competitive prices. Additionally, most regional airlines usually offer short tours of Peninsula cities for a reasonable supplement to an airfare.

For many would-be visitors, unless they are undertaking hajj, tours are often the only way of visiting Saudi Arabia.

Adventure World (☎1300 363 055; www.adventureworld.com.au) Has branches in Adelaide, Brisbane, Melbourne and Perth and is the agent for the UK's Explore Worldwide.

Kuoni (www.kuoni.co.uk) Offers comprehensive tours of the UAE and Oman; UK-based.

Original World (www.originalworld.com) Offers multi-destination tours of the UAE and Oman.

Passport Travel (☎03-9500 0444; www.travelcentre.com.au) Australia-based Middle East specialist, assisting in tailor-made itineraries for individuals and groups.

Reiseservice Graw (www.firstclasstravel.de) Germany-based, offering comprehensive tours to the Peninsula. Its website is in English and the service is available across Europe.

GETTING AROUND

As fuel is cheap throughout the region and vehicles are relatively inexpensive to buy, road transport is the most popular means of travel within the Peninsula. Car hire (with or without driver) is inexpensive and travel by taxis and bus is cheap. A train service operates in Dubai. There is also an intercity service in Saudi Arabia connecting Dammam with Riyadh via Hofuf. Work has also begun on an interstate railway between Kuwait and Oman.

The need to obtain a transit visa for Saudi Arabia hampers transport from one Gulf country to another. With the exception of driving between UAE and Oman, it's often easier to move around by air and there's a good flight network linking all major Peninsula cities.

If you do decide to try your luck overland, bear in mind that rules change frequently and you are strongly advised to check the latest information with relevant embassies before travelling.

Air

Reputable travel agencies in all major Peninsula cities can advise you about the best intercity deals and it's better to use their services than go directly to the airlines. Note that prices fluctuate considerably according to the season, or if there's a public holiday (such as *eid*).

Airlines on the Arabian Peninsula

The Peninsula boasts some world-class airlines with good safety records, modern aircraft and well-trained crew. Dubai offers a famously slick international airport with superb facilities, including hotels, business centres and extensive duty-free sections. Abu Dhabi and Doha have excellent modern airports, too. Some other key information:

- For detailed information on safety records, visit www.airsafe.com.
- Award-winning Gulf Air, Emirates, Qatar Airways, Etihad and Oman Air increase their direct-flight networks regularly.
- Saudi Arabia, Oman and the UAE have reasonably priced domestic flight networks.
- Smaller regional airports are adequate and many are in the process of being modernised and expanded.
- Arrival procedures are straightforward, quick and efficient. Note, however, the prohibition on various items at customs (p441), particularly in Saudi Arabia.

Budget Airlines

The arrival of budget airlines in the region revolutionised intercity transport on the Peninsula. As elsewhere, the airlines tend to use less-frequented cities as their hubs to avoid the high taxes of major airports. This minor inconvenience is worth considering for the cheap travel they offer.

Air Arabia (www.airarabia.com)

Al Jazeera Airways (www.jazeeraairways.com)

Bahrain Air (☎17 463 330; http://en.bahrainair.net)

Bicycle

The Peninsula offers good cycling opportunities, cyclists are made welcome (the

CLIMATE CHANGE & TRAVEL

Every form of transport that relies on carbon-based fuel generates CO_2, the main cause of human-induced climate change. Modern travel is dependent on aeroplanes, which might use less fuel per kilometre per person than most cars but travel much greater distances. The altitude at which aircraft emit gases (including CO_2) and particles also contributes to their climate change impact. Many websites offer 'carbon calculators' that allow people to estimate the carbon emissions generated by their journey and, for those who wish to do so, to offset the impact of the greenhouse gases emitted with contributions to portfolios of climate-friendly initiatives throughout the world. Lonely Planet offsets the carbon footprint of all staff and author travel.

annual Tour of Oman attracts international cyclists, including celebrities such as Tour de France winner Bradley Wiggins) and police are helpful and friendly to all road users. Repair shops are easy to come by, and local expats are able bush mechanics. Post any queries on the Thorn Tree on lonelyplanet.com, under the Activities branch. Some difficulties to consider:

- In most cities, especially in the Gulf, it is very hazardous to cycle as car drivers are not used to anticipating cyclists.
- Most bicycles on the Peninsula are simple machines, so spare parts for mountain or touring bikes are only available in major cities.
- The heat is a major challenge and cycling is not recommended from June to August, or during the middle of the day at other times of the year.

Cyclists Touring Club (CTC; www.ctc.org.uk) is a UK-based organisation offering good tips and a helpful website. It has useful information sheets on cycling in different parts of the world.

Bus

Car ownership levels are so high across the Peninsula that little demand for public bus services exists. Where services do exist, they are often primarily intended for expat workers getting to and from their place of work. It's not too difficult to get between the main towns in Saudi Arabia and Oman by bus, but Qatar, Bahrain, Kuwait and the UAE have fewer (if any) domestic services that meet the needs of tourists. Modern bus services have been developed in several capital cities, including Doha and Abu Dhabi.

Of the major regional routes, there are four principal ones currently open to foreigners: Saudi Arabia to Bahrain; Saudi Arabia and Bahrain to Kuwait; Saudi Arabia and Bahrain to the UAE via Qatar; and the UAE to Oman.

Bus travel is usually comfortable, cheap and on schedule, roads are good, and air-conditioned buses are the norm. Loud music or videos, as well as heavy smoking, can be unpleasant for many on some services. Check which services are the norm and take a warm layer as the air-conditioning systems are generally brutal.

Women accompanied by men can usually sit anywhere, but women travelling alone are expected to sit in the front seats.

Reservations

It's always advisable to book bus seats in advance at bus stations, and it's a must over the Muslim weekend (especially Friday), as well as during public holidays such as *eid*.

Car & Motorcycle

Car ownership is virtually a must for expats in most Peninsula countries, where cities cover large distances and there's little public transport. Motorcycles are also popular for getting around town. Spare parts are easier to find for Japanese models. The summer months are not conducive to motorcycling.

Bringing Your Own Vehicle

Unless you're coming to live on the Peninsula for an extended duration, bringing your own vehicle may prove more trouble than it's worth. Obtaining a *carnet de passage* is expensive and progressing through the Peninsula (due to visa regulations and paperwork) can be challenging. For most short-term visitors, it makes more sense to hire a car locally. For long-term residents it is cheaper and more straightforward to buy a car in the country and sell it before leaving.

Driver's Licence

Travellers from the West can use their own national driver's licences for a limited period in some Peninsula countries (including Oman and Saudi Arabia).

For longer stays an International Driving Permit (IDP), obtainable from your own country, is recommended (and required) by some countries.

To obtain a local licence you'll need to have a residency visa, plus the following documents:

- a valid foreigner's licence (and sometimes an IDP)
- a no-objection certificate (NOC) from your employer
- your accommodation rental contract
- photocopies of your passport
- passport-sized photos
- sometimes a certificate confirming your blood group
- some countries (such as Saudi Arabia) insist on Arabic translations of foreign documents
- for some expats a driving test may be required

Car Hire

Availability & Cost Car hire is possible in all Peninsula countries, with international as well as local companies represented at international airports and five-star hotels. Costs are comparable to international rates. Reservations are necessary in some countries during peak tourism times, particularly during hajj, or major national or religious holidays.

Vehicle Type For off-road driving in the desert, a 4WD is essential; these are available from all hire companies. Don't cut costs by hiring a 2WD for off-road driving – for one thing, your insurance will be null and void as soon as you leave the sealed road and secondly, you won't know whether the previous person who hired your car similarly abused the vehicle. If you break down, the hire company won't help you. Motorcycle hire is near unheard of, but bicycle hire is becoming popular in some cities, including Abu Dhabi and Muscat.

Documentation To hire a vehicle you'll need your driver's licence and, for some Peninsula countries, an IDP and copies of both your passport and visa. The minimum age varies between 21 to 25. Invariably, credit cards are now a prerequisite.

Insurance

Insurance is compulsory. Given the large number of traffic accidents, fully comprehensive insurance (as opposed to third-party) is strongly advised. This covers the ancient law of paying blood money in the event of the injury or death of a person (and sometimes livestock). Car-hire companies automatically supply insurance, but check carefully the cover and conditions.

Make certain you're covered for off-road travel, as well as travel between Peninsula countries if you're planning cross-border excursions. If you are taking the car outside Gulf Cooperation Council (GCC) borders, you'll need separate insurance.

In the event of an accident, don't move the vehicle until the police arrive and make sure you submit the accident report as soon as possible to the insurance or car-hire company.

Road Conditions & Driving Amenities

Road Quality The Peninsula's road system is one of the best in the world, with high-quality two- or four-lane highways. Few roads are unsealed (except in Oman) and 4WDs are, on the whole, only necessary for driving off-road in the desert.

Off-road Routes The term 'off-road' refers to unsealed roads that have been graded, or levelled, with a roller, or tracks that have simply been made by cars driving along old camel or donkey tracks. To drive on any of these roads you need a 4WD. Responsible drivers stick to prior tracks and never cut new routes.

Fuel Petrol stations are widespread along major roads and in cities. On desert roads they can be few and far between. Away from the main towns it's advisable to fill up whenever you get the chance, as remote stations sometimes run out of fuel. Fuel remains extremely cheap throughout the region. Most cars run on unleaded petrol.

CARNETS

A *carnet de passage* is a booklet that is stamped on arrival and at departure to ensure that the vehicle leaves the country and has not been misappropriated. It's usually issued by a motoring organisation in the country where the vehicle is registered. Contact your local automobile association for details about required documentation at least three months in advance and bear the following in mind.

- You have to lodge a deposit to secure a carnet.
- If you default (ie you don't have an import and export stamp that match) then the country in question can claim your deposit, which can be up to 300% of the new value of the vehicle.
- Bank guarantees or carnet insurance are available.
- If your vehicle is irretrievably damaged or stolen, you may be suspected by customs officials of having sold the vehicle, so insist on police reports.
- The carnet may need to specify any expensive spare parts, such as a gearbox, you bring with you. This is designed to prevent spare-part importation rackets.

DESERT DRIVING

The following tips may help if going off-road, but there's no substitute for experience.

Pre-departure Planning

- Travel with another vehicle if you're heading for sandy areas so that you can pull each other out if you get stuck.
- Don't travel alone unless you can change a tyre (very heavy on 4WD vehicles).
- Use the services of a local guide if planning an extended dune trip – navigation is not as easy as it seems.
- Take a map and compass. A GPS and fully charged GSM phone are also helpful, but remember that GPS is only useful for knowing exactly where you're lost (and not how to find the way out) and phones don't work in some mountainous or remote areas.
- Bring the equivalent of at least 5L of water per passenger per day and sufficient food to last several days. Dried dates are a good source of energy and keep well in high temperatures.
- Bring a tool kit with a tow rope, shovel, sand ladders, spanner, jack, wooden platform (on which to stand the jack), tyre inflator (and preferably a gauge) and jump leads. Also pack a first-aid kit.
- Tell someone (and in some countries the local authorities, too) where you're going.

Driving Tips

- In all desert areas follow prior tracks.
- Keep the acceleration up through areas of soft sand and under no circumstances stop!
- Never camp at the bottom of a wadi, even on a clear day. Be wary of wadis when rain threatens. Flash flooding rips through the narrow channels of a wadi with huge force. Each year many people lose their lives this way.
- Engage low gear on extended mountain descents, even if it slows your progress to walking speed: many people run into trouble by burning out their brakes.

Getting Stuck in Sand

- In sand the minute you feel the wheels are digging in, stop driving. The more you accelerate, the deeper you'll sink.
- If your wheels are deeply entrenched, don't dig; the car will just sink deeper.
- Partially deflate the tyres (for greater traction), clearing the sand away from the wheel in the direction you want to go (ie behind if you're going to try to reverse out).
- Collect brushwood (you'll wish you brought the sand ladders!) and anything else available, and pack under the tyres, creating as firm a launch pad as possible.
- Plan your escape route or you'll flip out of the sand only to land in the next dune. In most dune areas, there are compacted platforms of sand. Try to find one of these on foot so that you have somewhere safe to aim.
- Engage low ratio and remember that going backwards can be as effective as going forwards, especially if you stalled going uphill – gravity is a great help.
- Keep your eye on the petrol gauge: low ratio consumes a lot. Reinflate your tyres before rejoining a sealed road.

What to Do if You're Lost

- Stay with your vehicle, where there's shade and water. The Bedu or local villagers will find you before you find them. It's easier for a search party to spot a vehicle than people wandering in the desert.
- Use mirrors, horns or fires to attract attention, and construct a large sign on the ground that can easily be seen from the air.

Garages Found even in the smallest towns and villages in most countries. Spare parts (and servicing) are available for the most popular car models (Toyota and Land Rover, especially).

Signposting Good throughout the region and uses international symbols. English spelling of place names, however, is erratic and seldom matches the maps. Most countries indicate places of interest to a visitor on dedicated brown or green road signs.

Parking A challenge in the cities. Traffic inspectors and parking meters are now more prevalent.

Hazards See the Safe Travel chapter (p436).

Road Rules

Non-compliance to the following common road rules can lead to a hefty fine – although that may be of surprise considering the generally poor standard of driving.

➡ Driving is on the right side of the road in all Peninsula countries.

➡ Speed limits range between 100km/h and 120km/h on highways and 40km/h and 60km/h in towns and built-up areas. Speed cameras are in operation in most city areas and on highways.

➡ Wearing a seat belt is a legal requirement.

➡ The use of hand-held mobile phones while driving is an offence.

➡ The use of the horn is discouraged except in an emergency.

➡ Running a red light often carries a two-day jail sentence.

➡ You should keep your licence with you at all times.

➡ Carrying a first-aid kit, fire extinguisher and warning triangle is required in some Peninsula countries.

➡ Driving under the influence of either alcohol (of any quantity) or drugs is not only considered a grave offence with serious consequences, but also automatically invalidates your insurance and makes you liable for any costs in the event of an accident, regardless of fault.

➡ Women are not permitted to drive in Saudi Arabia.

Hitching

Hitching is never entirely safe in any country and can't be recommended. Travellers who still decide to hitch should understand that they are taking a small but potentially serious risk. This is particularly the case on the Peninsula, where distances are great between towns and you can be marooned in isolated places with literally life-threatening consequences (for example, if you run out of water in summer). You may also find you end up spending days at someone's remote desert settlement because your driver wanted you to meet the family. Beware: the novelty of communal living quickly wears off! Women travelling alone should not hitch.

Despite the above, hitching is legal and in many places it is common practice among locals. It's considered not so much an alternative to the public transport system as an extension of it. Throughout the Peninsula a raised thumb is a vaguely obscene gesture – instead, the right hand is extended, palm down and wagged up and down briskly.

While it's normal for locals and Asian expats to hitch, it isn't something visitors are expected to do. It can lead to suspicion from local police and can cause some resentment in local communities, where there's an expectation that tourism will bring income – watching tourists hitch along with the locals isn't returning anticipated dividends.

Hitching isn't free. The going rate is usually the equivalent of the bus or shared taxi fare, but may be more if a driver takes you to an address or place off their route – even if you didn't ask to go there! Negotiate a fare *before* you get into the vehicle and be clear about your destination and that you're not on a sightseeing trip.

As a driver you'll often be flagged down for a ride. You might need to think what this might entail before offering one – an excursion to the extended family for coffee and dates is usually the norm. Women drivers should never give a lift to a man.

Local Transport

As cars are relatively cheap to buy and run, public transport (particularly buses and minibuses in towns) tends to be used by less-affluent members of the population.

Minibus & Bus

In most cities and towns, a minibus or bus service operates. Fares are cheap, regular and run on fixed routes. However, unless you're familiar with the town, they can be difficult to use (not all display their destination) and they're often crowded.

Doha, Abu Dhabi and Dubai have modern, air-conditioned bus networks that run on time and extend across the city; some networks even boast air-conditioned bus stops. Such networks are presently the exception rather than the rule. More usually, minibus or local bus services tend to connect residential or commercial areas. An alternative to public bus routes are the Big Bus routes that operate in some cities, offering a hop-on, hop-off service linking the main sites of interest, accompanied by an audio tour.

Few countries have public minibuses to/from the airport, but top-end hotels and travel agents (if you're taking a tour) can usually provide a complimentary minibus with advance notice. Some hotels also provide

TAXI TIPS

On the whole, taxi drivers on the Peninsula are helpful and honest, with a good sense of humour, but that said, new arrivals are tempting bait for a bit of overcharging. Here are a few tips to avoid being scammed:

- Be aware that not all taxi drivers speak English.
- Negotiate a fare, or insist that the meter is used if it works, before jumping in.
- Don't rely on street names (there are often several versions) – landmarks are more useful.
- In many places it's safest to ask the taxi driver to wait to avoid being stranded.
- Avoid using unlicenced cab drivers at airports.

bus services to city centres, and limousines organised by the airline (in some classes of travel) are a popular feature of the region.

Taxi

In many countries taxis are an avoidable luxury, but on the Peninsula they are often the best way for travellers to get about town. Many cities have no other form of urban public transport, while there are also many rural routes that are only feasible in a taxi or private vehicle.

The way in which taxis operate varies widely from country to country, and often even from place to place within a country. So does the price. As a general rule, it's best to establish the price in advance.

REGULAR TAXI

The regular taxi (also known as 'contract', 'agency', 'telephone', 'private', 'engaged' or 'special taxi') is found in all the main Peninsula towns or cities, coexisting alongside less-expensive means of transport (such as shared taxis or minibuses).

Its main purpose is for transport within a town, or on a short rural trip. It is also often the only way of reaching airports or seaports and is generally considered safe for women travellers, who should always sit in the back.

SHARED TAXI

Known also as 'collect', 'collective' or 'service taxi' in English, and *servees* in Arabic, most shared taxis can take up to four or five passengers, but some seat up to 12 and are indistinguishable from minibuses.

Shared taxis are far cheaper than private taxis and, once you get the hang of them, can be just as convenient. They're usually a little dearer than buses, but run more frequently and are usually faster (they don't stop as often or for as long). They also tend to operate for longer hours than buses. Shared taxis function as urban, intercity and rural transport.

Fixed-route taxis wait at the point of departure until full or nearly full. Usually they pick up or drop off passengers anywhere en route, but in some places they have fixed stops or stations. Generally a flat fare applies for each route, but sometimes it's possible to pay a partial fare.

On 'routeless' taxis, fares depend largely on time and distance and the number of passengers on board.

Beware of boarding an empty shared taxi. The driver may assume you want to hire the vehicle as a 'regular taxi' and charge accordingly. You may also have to wait a long time (sometimes several hours) for it to leave, particularly if it's destined for a remote place.

Passengers are expected to know where they are getting off. '*Shukran*' means 'thank you' in Arabic and is the usual cue for the driver to stop. Make it clear to the driver or other passengers if you want to be told when you reach your destination.

Train

The only train services in the region at present are in Saudi Arabia, connecting the capital with the east of the kingdom (running from Riyadh to Dammam, via Hofuf and Dhahran, among other places), and a metro service in Dubai. Decisions have been taken to build a railway from Kuwait to Salalah in Oman.

Health

While prevention is better than cure, medical facilities in Peninsula countries are of a high standard (ambulance services are available in capital cities, but emergency and specialised treatment is less readily or extensively so).

Problems particular to the Peninsula include respiratory complaints (due to the arid climate and high levels of dust), sunburn and sunstroke, heat exhaustion and prickly heat, eye problems and injuries resulting from the exceptionally high incidence of traffic accidents – it pays to be extra vigilant on the roads, especially as a pedestrian.

> **CALL ME A CAB!**
>
> If you find you suddenly require urgent medical treatment outside major Peninsula cities, don't call an ambulance, call a cab. The ambulance services – where they exist – are usually reserved for road accidents when the victim is unconscious or immobile. It's common (and much quicker) to take a taxi.

BEFORE YOU GO

Pre-Trip Registration

- Register with the **International Association for Medical Advice to Travellers.** (IAMAT; www.iamat.org)
- Check IAMAT's website to find a doctor, or to find recommended advice by country or by health issue.
- First-aid courses offered by the Red Cross and St John Ambulance are helpful if planning lengthy off-road trips on the Peninsula.
- The Royal Geographical Society gives links to training providers in a number of first-aid and remote-area physical and psychological health training.

Insurance

You are strongly advised to have insurance (p442) before travelling to the region. Check it covers the following:

- direct payments to health providers (or reimbursement later)
- emergency dental treatment
- evacuation or repatriation, or access to better medical facilities elsewhere

Recommended Vaccinations

The World Health Organization (WHO) recommends that all travellers, regardless of the region in which they are travelling, should be covered for diphtheria, tetanus, measles, mumps, rubella, polio and hepatitis B.

Many vaccines take four to eight weeks to provide immunity. Ask your doctor for an International Certificate of Vaccination, listing all the vaccinations you've received.

Peninsula countries require proof of yellow-fever vaccination upon entry for travellers who have recently visited a country where yellow fever is found.

Travelling with Medication

Bring medications in their original, clearly labelled containers with a signed and dated letter from your physician describing your medical condition and the medications (including generic names).

If carrying syringes or needles, carry a physician's letter documenting their medical necessity.

Websites

Lonely Planet (www.lonelyplanet.com) A good place to start.

Centers for Disease Control & Prevention (www.cdc.gov)

Useful guide to health issues related to specific regions.

MD Travel Health (www.mdtravelhealth.com) Complete travel-health recommendations for every Peninsula country. It's updated daily and is free.

World Health Organization (www.who.int/ith) Publishes a free, online book, *International Travel and Health*, revised annually.

It's a good idea to consult your government's travel-health website before departure.

Australia (http://smartraveller.gov.au/tips/health.html)

UK (www.doh.gov.uk)

US (www.cdc.gov/travel)

Further Reading

- *Travel with Children* (Lonely Planet)
- *Traveller's Health* (Dr Richard Dawood)
- *International Travel Health Guide* (Stuart R Rose)
- *The Travellers' Good Health Guide* (Ted Lankester)

MEDICAL CHECKLIST

Consider packing the following items:

- ☐ acetaminophen/paracetamol or aspirin
- ☐ antibacterial ointment for cuts and abrasions
- ☐ antibiotics (if travelling off the beaten track)
- ☐ anti-diarrhoeal drugs
- ☐ antihistamines (for allergic reactions)
- ☐ anti-inflammatory drugs
- ☐ bandages, gauze and gauze rolls
- ☐ DEET-containing insect repellent for the skin
- ☐ iodine tablets (for water purification if hiking or staying in remote areas)
- ☐ oral rehydration salts
- ☐ permethrin-containing insect spray for clothing, tents and bed nets
- ☐ steroid cream or cortisone (for allergic rashes)
- ☐ sunscreen

ON THE ARABIAN PENINSULA

Availability & Cost of Healthcare

Though some Peninsula countries allow travellers access to free state medical treatment in emergencies, you should not rely on this and are strongly advised to have insurance cover. The availability of healthcare in Arabia can be summarised as follows:

- High ratio of doctors to patients.
- Modern, well-equipped hospitals with well-qualified, English-speaking staff in all cities and most of the larger towns throughout the Peninsula.
- Emergency units in most hospitals.
- Limited and less-well-equipped clinics in rural areas.
- Pharmacies (signposted with green crosses) able to dispense advice by well-trained, English-speaking staff who may assist in place of doctors in very remote areas.
- High standards of dental care in the larger towns and cities.

Infectious Diseases

Dengue Fever

- Known as break-bone fever.
- Spread through mosquito bites.
- Causes a feverish illness, with a headache and muscle pains, that's like a bad, prolonged attack of influenza. There may also be a rash.
- Take precautions to avoid being bitten by mosquitoes.

Diphtheria

- Spread through close respiratory contact.
- Causes a high temperature and a severe sore throat. Sometimes a membrane forms across the throat, requiring a tracheotomy to prevent suffocation.
- Vaccination is recommended for those likely to be in close contact with the local population in infected areas. The vaccine is given as an injection by itself, or with tetanus, and lasts 10 years.

Hepatitis A

- Spread through contaminated food (particularly shellfish) and water.
- Causes jaundice; rarely fatal but can cause prolonged lethargy and delayed recovery. Symptoms include dark urine, a yellow colour to the whites of the eyes, fever and abdominal pain.
- Hepatitis A vaccine (Avaxim, VAQTA, Havrix) is given as an injection. A single

dose will give protection for up to a year, while a booster 12 months later will provide protection for a subsequent period of 10 years. Hepatitis A and typhoid vaccines can also be given as a single-dose vaccine in the form of Hepatyrix or Viatim.

Hepatitis B

- Transmitted by infected blood, contaminated needles and sexual intercourse.
- Causes jaundice and affects the liver, occasionally causing liver failure.
- All travellers should make this a routine vaccination – many countries now give hepatitis B vaccination as part of routine childhood vaccination. The vaccine is given by itself, or at the same time as the hepatitis A vaccine. A course protects for at least five years and can be given over four weeks or six months.

HIV

- Spread via infected blood and blood products, sexual intercourse with an infected partner, and from an infected mother to her newborn child. It can also be spread through blood-to-blood contacts such as contaminated instruments used during medical, dental, acupuncture and other body-piercing procedures, as well as from sharing intravenous needles.
- All Peninsula countries except Bahrain require a negative HIV test as a requirement for some categories of visas (particularly employment visas).

Malaria

- Spread by bite from infected mosquito.
- Causes shivering, fever and sweating. Muscle pains, headache and vomiting are also common. Symptoms may occur any time from a few days up to three weeks or more after being bitten. Symptoms can occur even if taking preventative tablets.
- The prevalence of malaria varies throughout the Peninsula. The risk is considered minimal in most cities, but may be more substantial in rural areas. Check with your doctor or local travel-health clinic for the latest information.
- Antimalarial tablets are essential if the risk is significant.

Meningitis

- Spread through close respiratory contact.
- A meningococcal vaccination certificate covering the A and W135 strains is required as a condition of entry if embarking on a hajj pilgrimage to Mecca and Medina in Saudi Arabia, and for all travellers arriving from the meningitis belt of sub-Saharan Africa.
- Visas for pilgrimages are not issued unless proof of vaccination is submitted with the visa application.

Rabies

- Spread through bites or licks (on broken skin) from any warm-blooded, furry animal.
- Rabies can be fatal. Seek immediate medical assistance if bitten by an animal suspected of being infected with rabies. Clean skin immediately and thoroughly. A course of five injections starting within 24 hours, or as soon as possible after the injury, is needed. Vaccination does not provide immunity; it buys more time to seek appropriate medical help.
- Animal handlers and those travelling to remote areas where a reliable source of postbite vaccine is not available within 24 hours should be vaccinated. Three injections are needed over a month.

Tuberculosis (TB)

- Spread through close respiratory contact and occasionally through infected milk or milk products.
- Can be asymptomatic or can include a cough, weight loss or fever, months or even years after exposure. An X-ray establishes the presence of TB.
- BCG vaccine is recommended for those likely to be mixing closely with the local population. BCG gives a moderate degree of protection against TB. It's usually only given in specialised chest clinics and is not available in all countries. As it's a live vaccine, it should not be given to pregnant women or immunocompromised individuals.

Typhoid

- Spread through food or water contaminated by infected human faeces.

AIDS ON THE PENINSULA

Though it's strictly illegal for AIDS or HIV sufferers to visit or to live on the Peninsula (and detection of the disease usually results in instant deportation), the region is not the AIDS-free place you might imagine. In recent years prostitutes have flowed into the area under the guise of tourists. Locals have also returned infected after sexual adventures abroad. Additionally, there is something of a cultural taboo about condom use among many Arab men. Travellers who form new relationships should also note that fornication, adultery and homosexuality are considered grave crimes in some Peninsula states.

TAP WATER

Tap water is safe to drink in Gulf cities and main towns in Oman. Avoid tap water in Saudi and in rural areas where water is delivered by tanker. Bottled water is available everywhere, or boil water for 10 minutes, use water-purification tablets or a filter. Never drink from wadis (valleys or riverbeds) or streams as animals are invariably watered in them.

- Causes fever or a pink rash on the abdomen. Septicaemia (blood poisoning) may also occur.
- Typhoid vaccine (Typhim Vi, Typherix) gives protection for three years. In some countries, the oral vaccine Vivotif is also available.

Yellow Fever

- Does not occur on the Peninsula, but any traveller coming from a country where yellow fever is found will need to show a vaccination certificate at immigration.
- Vaccination must be given at an approved clinic, and is valid for 10 years. It is a live vaccine and must not be given to immunocompromised or pregnant travellers.

Environmental Hazards

Diarrhoea

Prevention

- Avoid tap water.
- Eat fresh fruit or vegetables you have peeled yourself, or eat cooked produce.
- Avoid dairy products that might contain unpasteurised milk, or have been refrozen after defrosting.

Treatment

- Drink plenty of fluids.
- Take an oral rehydration solution containing salt and sugar.
- If you start having more than four or five loose stools a day, take an antibiotic (usually containing quinolone) and an antidiarrhoeal agent (such as loperamide).
- Seek medical attention if the diarrhoea is bloody, persists for more than 72 hours, or is accompanied by fever, shaking, chills or severe abdominal pain.

Heat Illness

Heat exhaustion Occurs following heavy sweating and excessive fluid loss. In summer, temperatures can reach 50°C, making even a round of golf dangerous without drinking. Symptoms include headache, dizziness and tiredness. Drink sufficient water to produce pale, diluted urine. To treat heat exhaustion, drink lots of water, cool down in an air-conditioned room and add a little more salt to foods than usual.

Heatstroke A serious condition that occurs when the body's heat-regulating mechanism breaks down. An excessive rise in body temperature leads to the cessation of sweating, irrational and hyperactive behaviour and, eventually, loss of consciousness and death. Rapid cooling of the body by spraying with water or fanning is an effective treatment. Emergency fluid and electrolyte replacement (by intravenous drip) is also usually required.

Insect Bites & Stings

- Using DEET-based insect repellents helps prevent mosquito bites.
- Bed bugs and sometimes scabies are occasionally found in hostels and cheap hotels. Cause very itchy lumpy bites. Spray the mattress or find new lodgings!
- Scorpions and snakes are common in the desert. Although their bite can be painful, it's rarely life threatening. Avoid walking on sand dunes in bare feet, don't prod holes in wadis and check shoes for unwanted wildlife.

Travelling With Children

- Poses no specific health problems between the months of November and March.
- In summer (April to October) extreme temperatures, often combined with high humidity, pose high threats of dehydration and heat exhaustion.
- Avoid prolonged exposure to the sun at all times of the year.

Women's Health

Some health considerations for women travelling in the region:

- Condoms should be checked before use as they crack in the hot climate.
- The **International Planned Parent Federation** (www.ippf.org) can advise about the availability of contraception in each Peninsula country.
- Tampons are not always available outside the major cities; sanitary towels are more widespread.
- High standards of obstetric and antenatal facilities are offered throughout the Peninsula, particularly in Gulf cities.

Language

Arabic is the official language on the Arabian Peninsula, but English is widely understood. Note that there are significant differences between the MSA (Modern Standard Arabic) – the official lingua franca of the Arab world, used in schools, administration and the media – and the colloquial language, ie the everyday spoken version. The Arabic variety spoken throughout the Arabian Peninsula (and provided in this chapter) is known as Gulf Arabic.

Read our coloured pronunciation guides as if they were English and you'll be understood. Note that a is pronounced as in 'act', aa as the 'a' in 'father', ai as in 'aisle', aw as in 'law', ay as in 'say', ee as in 'see', i as in 'hit', oo as in 'zoo', u as in 'put', gh is a throaty sound (like the Parisian French 'r'), r is rolled, dh is pronounced as the 'th' in 'that', th as in 'thin', ch as in 'cheat' and kh as the 'ch' in the Scottish *loch*. The apostrophe (') indicates the glottal stop (like the pause in the middle of 'uh-oh'). The stressed syllables are indicated with italics and (m) and (f) refer to the masculine and feminine word forms respectively.

BASICS

Hello.	اهلا و سهلا.	*ah*·lan was *ah*·lan
Goodbye.	مع السلامة.	ma' sa·*laa*·ma
Yes.	نعم.	*na*·'am
No.	لا.	la
Please.	من فضلك.	min *fad*·lak (m)
	من فضلِك.	min *fad*·lik (f)
Thank you.	شكران.	*shuk*·ran
Excuse me.	اسمح.	is·*mah* (m)
	اسمحي لي.	is·mah·*ee* lee (f)

WANT MORE?

For in-depth language information and handy phrases, check out Lonely Planet's *Middle East Phrasebook*. You'll find it at **shop.lonelyplanet.com**.

Sorry.
مع الاسف. ma' al·*as*·af

How are you?
كيف حالك/حالك؟ kayf *haa*·lak/*haa*·lik (m/f)

Fine, thanks. And you?
بخير الحمد الله. bi·*khayr* il·*ham*·du·li·laa
و انت/و انتِ؟ *win*·ta/*win*·ti (m/f)

What's your name?
اش اسمَك/اسمِك؟ aash *is*·mak/*is*·mik (m/f)

My name is ...
اسمي ... *is*·mee ...

Do you speak English?
تتكلم انجليزية؟ tit·*kal*·am in·glee·*zee*·ya (m)
تتكلمي انجليزية؟ tit·*ka*·la·mee in·glee·*zee*·ya (f)

I don't understand.
مو فاهم. moo *faa*·him

Can I take a photo?
ممكن اتصور؟ *mum*·kin at·*saw*·ar

ACCOMMODATION

Where's a ...?	وين ... ؟	wayn ...
campsite	مخيم	moo·*khay*·am
hotel	فندق	*fun*·dug
Do you have a ... room?	عندك/عندك غرفة ... ؟	*'and*·ak/*'and*·ik *ghur*·fa ... (m/f)
single	لشخص واحد	li·*shakhs waa*·hid
double	لشخصين	li·shakh·*sayn*
twin	مع سريرين	ma' sa·ree·*rayn*
How much is it per ...?	بكم كل ... ؟	bi·*kam* kul ...
night	ليلة	*lay*·la
person	شخص	shakhs

Can I get another (blanket)?
احتاج الى (برنوس) الثاني من فضلك؟ ah·*taaj* i·la (bar·*noos*) i·*thaa*·nee min *fad*·lak

SIGNS

Entrance	مدخل
Exit	خروج
Open	مفتوح
Closed	مقفول
Toilets	المرحاض
Men	رجال
Women	نساء

The (air conditioning) doesn't work.
(الكنديشان) (il·kan·*day*·shan)
ما يشتغل. ma yish·*ta*·ghil

DIRECTIONS

Where's the ...?	من وين ...؟	min wayn ...
bank	البنك	il·*bank*
market	السوق	i·*soog*
post office	مكتب البريد	*mak*·tab il·ba·*reed*

Can you show me (on the map)?
لو سمحت وريني law sa·*maht* wa·ree·nee
(علخريطة)؟ ('al·kha·*ree*·ta)

What's the address?
ما العنوان؟ ma il·'un·*waan*

Could you please write it down?
لو سمحت اكتبه لي؟ law sa·*maht* ik·ti·*boo* lee (m)
لو سمحت اكتبيه لي؟ law sa·*maht* ik·ti·*bee* lee (f)

How far is it?
كم بعيد؟ kam ba·'*eed*

How do I get there?
كيف ممكن اوصل kayf *mum*·kin *aw*·sil
هناكا؟ *hoo*·naak

EATING & DRINKING

Can you recommend a ...?	ممكن تنصح/ تنصحي ...؟	*mum*·kin *tan*·sah/ *tan*·sa·hee ... (m/f)
cafe	قهوة	*gah*·wa
restaurant	مطعم	*ma*·ta'm

I'd like a/the ..., please.	اريد... من فضلك.	a·*reed* ... min *fad*·lak
nonsmoking section	المكان ممنوع تدخين	il·ma·*kaan* mam·*noo*·a' tad·*kheen*
table for (four)	طاولة (اربعة) اشخاص	*taa*·wi·lat (*ar*·ba') ash·*khaas*

What would you recommend?
اش تنصح؟ aash *tan*·sah (m)
اش تنصحي؟ aash *tan*·sa·hee (f)

What's the local speciality?
اش الطبق المحلي؟ aash i·*ta*·bak il·*ma*·ha·lee

Do you have vegetarian food?
عندك طعم نباتي؟ '*an*·dak *ta*·'am na·*baa*·tee

I'd like (the) ..., please.	عطني/ عطيني الـ ... من فضلك.	'*a*·ti·nee/ '*a*·*tee*·nee il ... min *fad*·lak (m/f)
bill	قائمة	*kaa*·'i·ma
drink list	قائمة المشروبات	*kaa*·'i·mat il·mash·roo·*baat*
menu	قائمة الطعام	*kaa*·'i·mat i·ta·'*aam*
that dish	الطبق هاذاك	i·*tab*·ak *haa*·dhaa·ka

Could you prepare a meal without ...?	ممكن تطبخها/ تطبخيها بدون ...؟	*mum*·kin *tat*·bakh·ha/ *tat*·bakh·ee·ha bi·*doon* ... (m/f)
butter	زبدة	*zib*·da
eggs	بيض	bayd
meat stock	مرق لهم	ma·*rak la*·ham

I'm allergic to ...	عندي حساسية لـ ...	'*an*·dee ha·saa·see·ya li ...
dairy produce	الألبان	il·al·*baan*
gluten	قمح	*ka*·mah
nuts	كرزات	ka·ra·*zaat*
seafood	السمك و المحارات	i·*sa*·mak wa al·ma·haa·*raat*

Drinks

coffee ...	نقهوة ...	*kah*·wa ...
tea ...	شاي ...	shay ...
with milk	بالحليب	bil·ha·*leeb*
without sugar	بدون شكر	bi·*doon shi*·ker

bottle of beer	بوتل بيرة	*boo*·til *bee*·ra
glass of beer	قلاس بيرة	glaas *bee*·ra
(orange) juice	عصير (برتقال)	'*a*·*seer* (bor·too·*gaal*)
(mineral) water	ماي (معدني)	may (*ma'a*·da·nee)

... wine	... خمر	... *kha*·mar
red	احمر	*ah*·mer
sparkling	فوار	fa·*waar*
white	ابيض	*ab*·yad

EMERGENCIES

Help! مساعد! moo·*saa*·'id (m)
مساعدة! moo·*saa*·'id·a (f)

Go away! ابعد! *ib*·'ad (m)
ابعدي! *ib*·'ad·ee (f)

I'm lost. انا ضعت. *a*·na duht

Call ...! تصل على ...! ti·*sil* 'a·la ... (m)
تصلي على ...! *ti*·*si*·lee 'a·la ... (f)

a doctor طبيب ta·*beeb*

the police الشرطة i·*shur*·ta

Where are the toilets?
وين المرحاض؟ wayn il·mir·*haad*

I'm sick.
انا مريض. *a*·na ma·*reed* (m)
انا مريضة. *a*·na ma·*ree*·da (f)

SHOPPING & SERVICES

Where's a ...? من وين ...؟ min wayn ...

department store محل ضخم ma·*hal dukh*·um

grocery store محل ابقالية ma·*hal* ib·gaa·*lee*·ya

newsagency محل يبيع جرائد ma·*hal* yi·*bee*·a' ja·*raa*·id

souvenir shop محل سياحي ma·*hal* say·*aa*·hee

supermarket سوبرمركت *soo*·ber·mar·ket

I'm looking for ...
مدور على ... moo·*daw*·ir 'a·la ... (m)
مدورة على ... moo·*daw*·i·ra 'a·la ... (f)

Can I look at it?
ممكن اشوف؟ *mum*·kin a·*shoof*

Do you have any others?
عندَك اخرين؟ '*and*·ak ukh·*reen* (m)
عندِك اخرين؟ '*and*·ik ukh·*reen* (f)

It's faulty.
فيه خلل. fee *kha*·lal

How much is it?
بكم؟ bi·*kam*

Can you write down the price?
ممكن تكتبلي/ تكتبيلي السعر؟ *mum*·kin tik·*tib*·lee/ tik·*tib*·ee·lee i·*si'r* (m/f)

That's too expensive.
غالي جدا. *ghaa*·lee *jid*·an

What's your lowest price?
اش السعر الاخر؟ aash i·*si'r* il·*aa*·khir

There's a mistake in the bill.
فيه غلط في الفطورة. fee *gha*·lat fil fa·*too*·ra

QUESTION WORDS

When?	متى؟	*ma*·ta
Where?	وين؟	wayn
Who?	من؟	man
Why?	لاش؟	laysh

Where's ...? من وين ...؟ min wayn ...

a foreign exchange office صراف si·*raaf*

an ATM مكينة صرف ma·*kee*·nat sarf

What's the exchange rate?
ما هو السعر؟ maa *hoo*·wa i·*sa'r*

Where's the local internet cafe?
من وين انترنيت كفي؟ min wayn *in*·ter·net ka·*fay*

How much is it per hour?
بكم كل ساعة؟ bi·*kam* kul *saa*·a'

I'd like to buy a phonecard.
اريد اشري كرت لتلفون. a·*reed ish*·ree kart li·til·*foon*

NUMBERS

1	١	واحد	*waa*·hid
2	٢	اثنين	ith·*nayn*
3	٣	ثلاثة	tha·*laa*·tha
4	٤	اربع	ar·*ba'*
5	٥	خمسة	*kham*·sa
6	٦	ستة	*si*·ta
7	٧	سبعة	*sa*·ba'
8	٨	ثمانية	tha·*maan*·ya
9	٩	تسعة	*tis*·a'
10	١٠	عشرة	*'ash*·ar·a
20	٢٠	عشرين	'ash·*reen*
30	٣٠	ثلاثين	tha·la·*theen*
40	٤٠	اربعين	ar·ba'·*een*
50	٥٠	خمسين	kham·*seen*
60	٦٠	ستين	sit·*een*
70	٧٠	سبعين	sa·ba'·*een*
80	٨٠	ثمانين	tha·ma·*neen*
90	٩٠	تسعين	ti·sa'·*een*
100	١٠٠	مية	*mee*·ya
1000	١٠٠٠	الف	alf

Note that Arabic numerals (in the second column), unlike letters, are read from left to right.

TIME & DATES

What time is it?
الساعة كم؟ i·*saa*·a' kam

It's (two) o'clock.
الساعة (ثنتين). i·*saa*·a' (thin·*tayn*)

Half past (two).
الساعة (ثنتين) و نس. i·*saa*·a' (thin·*tayn*) wa nus

At what time ...?
الساعة كم ...؟ i·*saa*·a' kam ...

At ...
الساعة ... i·*saa*·a'...

yesterday ...	البارح ...	il·*baa*·rih ...
tomorrow ...	باكر ...	*baa*·chir ...
morning	صباح	sa·*baah*
afternoon	بعد الظهر	ba'd a·*thuhr*
evening	مساء	*mi*·saa

Monday	يوم الاثنين	yawm al·ith·*nayn*
Tuesday	يوم الثلاثة	yawm a·tha·*laa*·tha
Wednesday	يوم الاربعة	yawm al·*ar*·ba'
Thursday	يوم الخميس	yawm al·kha·*mees*
Friday	يوم الجمعة	yawm al·*jum*·a'
Saturday	يوم السبت	yawm a·*sibt*
Sunday	يوم الاحد	yawm al·*aa*·had

TRANSPORT

Is this the ... (to Riyadh)?	هاذا ال ... يروح (لرياض)؟	*haa*·dha al ... yi·*roh* (li·ree·*yaad*)
boat	سفينة	sa·*fee*·na
bus	باص	baas
plane	طيارة	tay·*aa*·ra
train	قطار	gi·*taar*
What time's the ... bus?	الساعة كم الباص ...؟	a·*saa*·a' kam il·*baas* ...
first	الاول	il·*aw*·al
last	الاخر	il·*aa*·khir
next	القادم	il·*gaa*·dim

One ... ticket (to Doha), please.	تذكرة ... (الدوحة) من فضلك.	*tadh*·ka·ra ... (a·*do*·ha) min *fad*·lak
one-way	ذهاب بص	dhee·*haab* bas
return	ذهاب و اياب	dhee·*haab* wa ai·*yaab*

How long does the trip take?
كم الرحلة تستغرق؟ kam i·*rah*·la tis·*tagh*·rik

Is it a direct route?
الرحلة متواصلة؟ i·*rah*·la moo·ta·*waa*·si·la

What station/stop is this?
ما هي المحطة هاذي؟ maa *hee*·ya il·ma·*ha*·ta *haa*·dhee

Please tell me when we get to (Al-Ain).
لو سمحت خبرني/خبريني وقت ما نوصل الي (العين). law sa·*maht* kha·*bir*·nee/kha·*bir*·ee·nee wokt ma *noo*·sil i·*la* (al·*'ain*) (m/f)

How much is it to (Sharjah)?
بكم الى (شارقة)؟ bi·*kam* i·la (*shaa*·ri·ka)

Please take me to (this address).
من فضلك خذني (علعنوان هاذا). min *fad*·lak *khudh*·nee ('al·'un·*waan* *haa*·dha)

Turn left/right.
لف يسار/يمين. lif yee·*saar*/yee·*meen* (m)
لفي يسار/يمين. li·fee yee·*saar*/yee·*meen* (f)

Please stop here.
لو سمحت وقف هنا. law sa·*maht* wa·gif *hi*·na

Please wait here.
لو سمحت استنا هنا law sa·*maht* is·ta·na *hi*·na

Driving

I'd like to hire a ...	اريد استأجر ...	a·*reed* ist·*'aj*·ir...
4WD	سيارة فيها دبل	say·*aa*·ra *fee*·ha *da*·bal
car	سيارة	say·*aa*·ra

with ...	مع ...	ma'...
a driver	دريول	*dray*·wil
air conditioning	كنديشان	kan·*day*·shan

How much for ... hire?	كم الإيجار ...؟	kam il·ee·*jaar* ...
daily	كل يوم	kul yawm
weekly	كل اسبوع	kul us·*boo*·a'

Is this the road to (Abu Dhabi)?
هاذا الطريق الى (ابو ظبي)؟ *haa*·dha i·ta·*reeg* i·*la* (a·*boo* *da*·bee)

I need a mechanic.
احتاج ميكانيك. ah·*taaj* mee·kaa·*neek*

I've run out of petrol.
ينضب البنزين. *yan*·dab al·ban·*zeen*

GLOSSARY

Following is a list of some unfamiliar words you might meet in the text. For a list of common foods you may encounter, see p426.

abeyya – woman's full-length black robe; also *abaya*
abra – water taxi
agal – black head-rope used to hold a *gutra* in place; also *igal*
ardha – traditional Bedouin dance
attar – rosewater

badghir – wind tower
barasti – palm-frond material used in building the traditional coastal houses of the Gulf region, especially along the coast of Oman
barjeel – wind tower
Bedouin – (pl Bedu) a nomadic desert dweller
beit ash-sha'ar – Bedouin goat-hair tent
bijou – service taxi
bukhnoq – girl's head covering
burda – traditional Qatari cloak
burj – tower
burka – *see* hijab

compound – residential area of expats, usually with high security (Gulf States)
corniche – seaside road

dalla – traditional copper coffeepot
dhow – traditional Arab boat rigged with a *lateen* (triangular) sail; also *sambuq* or *sambuk*
dishdasha – man's floor-length shirt-dress, usually of white cotton cloth, worn in Oman
diwan – Muslim meeting room or reception room
diwaniya – gatherings, usually at someone's home

eid – Islamic feast
Eid al-Adha – Feast of Sacrifice marking the pilgrimage to Mecca
Eid al-Fitr – Festival of Breaking the Fast, celebrated at the end of Ramadan
emir – literally 'prince'; Islamic ruler, military commander or governor

falaj – traditional irrigation channel

GCC – Gulf Cooperation Council; members are Saudi Arabia, Kuwait, Bahrain, Qatar, Oman and the UAE
gutra – white head-cloth worn by men in Saudi Arabia and the Gulf States; also *shemaag*

hajj – annual Muslim pilgrimage to Mecca; one of the Five Pillars of Islam
halal – literally 'permitted'; describes food permitted to Muslims including animals slaughtered according to the prescribed Islamic customs; also *halaal*
hammam – bathhouse
haram – literally 'forbidden'; anything forbidden by Islamic law; also prayer hall
hijab – woman's head scarf or veil, worn for modesty
Hejira – Islamic calendar; Mohammed's flight from Mecca to Medina in AD 622

iftar – the breaking of the day's fast during Ramadan
imam – preacher or prayer leader; Muslim cleric
insha'allah – 'If Allah wills it'; 'God willing'
iqama – residence permit and identity document (Saudi Arabia)

jambiya – tribesman's ceremonial dagger (Yemen and southern Saudi Arabia)
jamrah – pillars
jebel – hill, mountain; also *jabal*, *gebel*
jihad – literally 'striving in the way of the faith'; holy war
jizari – people of the Gulf

Kaaba – the rectangular structure at the centre of the Grand Mosque in Mecca (containing the Black Stone) around which hajj pilgrims circumambulate; also *Kabaa* and *Qaaba*
khanjar – tribal curved dagger; also *khanja* (Oman and southern Saudi Arabia)
khareef – southeast monsoon, from mid-June to mid-August in Oman
khor – rocky inlet or creek
kilim – flat, woven mat
kohl – eyeliner
Kufic – type of highly stylised old Arabic script
kuma – Omani cap

madrassa – Muslim theological seminary; also modern Arabic word for school
mafraj – (pl mafarej) 'room with a view'; top room of a tower house (Yemen)
majlis – formal meeting room; also parliament
mandoos – Omani wooden chest
manzar – attic; room on top of a tower house (Yemen)
mashrabiyya – ornate carved wooden panel or screen; feature of Islamic architecture
masjid – mosque
medina – city, town, especially the old quarter
midan – city or town square
mihrab – niche in a mosque indicating the direction of Mecca
mina – port
minaret – mosque tower
minbar – pulpit used for sermons in a mosque
misbah – prayer beads
muezzin – cantor who sings the call to prayer
mutawwa – religious police charged with upholding Islamic orthodoxy (Saudi Arabia)

Nabataeans – ancient trading civilisation based around Petra in Jordan

qat – mildly narcotic plant, the leaves of which are chewed

Ramadan – Muslim month of fasting; one of the Five Pillars of Islam

ras – cape or headland; also head

sabkha – soft sand with a salty crust

sadu – Bedouin-style weaving

salat – prayer; one of the Five Pillars of Islam

sambuq – see *dhow*; also *sambuk*

shahada – the profession of faith that Muslims publicly declare in every mosque, five times a day; one of the Five Pillars of Islam

shai – tea

sharia – street

Sharia'a – Islamic law

sheesha – water pipe used to smoke tobacco; also *nargileh* or hubble-bubble

sheikh – head of a tribe; religious leader; also *shaikh*

Shiite – one of the two main branches of Islam

souq – market

stele – (pl stelae) stone or wooden commemorative slab or column decorated with inscriptions or figures

sultan – absolute ruler of a Muslim state

Sunni – one of the two main branches of Islam

suras – chapters of the Quran

tawaf – circling required during the pilgrimage to Mecca

thobe – men's floor-length shirt-dress similar to a *dishdasha*, but more fitting, worn in the Gulf; also *thawb*

umrah – Islamic ritual performed outside of hajj; literally 'little pilgrimage'

wadi – valley or river bed, often dry except after heavy rainfall

Wahhabi – conservative and literalist 18th-century Sunni orthodoxy prevailing throughout Saudi Arabia and Qatar

wali – regional head in Oman, similar to mayor

wusta – influence gained by way of connections in high places

yashmak – veil

zakat – the giving of alms; one of the Five Pillars of Islam

Behind the Scenes

SEND US YOUR FEEDBACK

We love to hear from travellers – your comments keep us on our toes and help make our books better. Our well-travelled team reads every word on what you loved or loathed about this book. Although we cannot reply individually to your submissions, we always guarantee that your feedback goes straight to the appropriate authors, in time for the next edition. Each person who sends us information is thanked in the next edition – the most useful submissions are rewarded with a selection of digital PDF chapters.

Visit **lonelyplanet.com/contact** to submit your updates and suggestions or to ask for help. Our award-winning website also features inspirational travel stories, news and discussions.

Note: We may edit, reproduce and incorporate your comments in Lonely Planet products such as guidebooks, websites and digital products, so let us know if you don't want your comments reproduced or your name acknowledged. For a copy of our privacy policy visit lonelyplanet.com/privacy.

OUR READERS

Many thanks to the travellers who used the last edition and wrote to us with helpful hints, useful advice and interesting anecdotes:

Hao Yan, Jens Riiis, Johann Schelesnak, Jonas Wernli, Margret van Irsel, Nicole Smoot, Peter Schentler, Richard Bradbury, Richard Moss, Tessa Tennant

AUTHOR THANKS

Jenny Walker

I'm always touched by the humour and goodwill of Omani friends and colleagues. Thanks to Maj Gen Fattorini and Alex Celini for triangulating information in remote corners of Oman. Biggest thanks to beloved Sam (Owen), husband, co-researcher and fellow traveller in the odyssey of a volume dear to our hearts.

Anthony Ham

Thanks to Helen Elfer for such wise oversight of this difficult region and to Jenny Walker, a much-valued, long-term virtual companion of Middle Eastern trails. Numerous Qataris, Kuwaitis and Bahrainis were generous with their time and unfailingly patient with my questions. To Jan – much strength to you in the days (and hopefully journeys) that lie ahead. Special, heartfelt thanks to Marina, Carlota and Valentina for enduring my absences again and again and welcoming me home with such love. And to Ron: I missed having you here upon my return.

Andrea Schulte-Peevers

Big heartfelt thanks to the many wonderful people who have plied me with tips, insights, information, ideas and encouragement, with special thanks to Abhi Sen, Rashi Sen, Jojo Jose, Suzette Tabora, Matthias Narr and Ali Mohammed Al Mansouri.

ACKNOWLEDGMENTS

Climate map data adapted from Peel MC, Finlayson BL & McMahon TA (2007) 'Updated World Map of the Köppen-Geiger Climate Classification', Hydrology and Earth System Sciences, 11, 163344

Cover photograph: A camel caravan near Dubai, UAE; Kami/amanaimages ©.

THIS BOOK

This fifth edition of Lonely Planet's *Oman, UAE & Arabian Peninsula* guidebook was researched and written by Jenny Walker, Anthony Ham and Andrea Schulte-Peevers. Rob Wagner and Mariam Nihal contributed to the Saudi Arabia chapter and Rob also wrote the Hajj chapter. The previous edition was written by Jenny, Anthony, Andrea, and Stuart Butler, while the third edition was written by Jenny, Andrea, Stuart, and Iain Shearer. This book was produced by the following:

Destination Editor Helen Elfer

Product Editors Kate Chapman, Kate Kiely

Book Designer Mazzy Prinsep

Senior Cartographer David Kemp

Assisting Editors Sarah Bailey, Andrew Bain, Paul Harding, Victoria Harrison, Rosie Nicholson, Vicky Smith, Jeanette Wall

Assisting Cartographer Gabe Lindquist

Assisting Layout Designer Jessica Rose

Cover Researcher Naomi Parker

Thanks to Carolyn Boicos, Chris Love, Ilana Myers, Ryan Evans, Karyn Noble, Luna Soo, Angela Tinson, Tony Wheeler

Index

ABBREVIATIONS

B	Bahrain
K	Kuwait
O	Oman
Q	Qatar
SA	Saudi Arabia
UAE	United Arab Emirates

Map Pages **000**
Photo Pages **000**

Map Pages **000**
Photo Pages **000**

Map Pages **000**
Photo Pages **000**

Map Pages **000**
Photo Pages **000**

S

Mechanics' Institute Library
3 1750 03425 2869

Map Legend

Sights

- Beach
- Bird Sanctuary
- Buddhist
- Castle/Palace
- Christian
- Confucian
- Hindu
- Islamic
- Jain
- Jewish
- Monument
- Museum/Gallery/Historic Building
- Ruin
- Shinto
- Sikh
- Taoist
- Winery/Vineyard
- Zoo/Wildlife Sanctuary
- Other Sight

Activities, Courses & Tours

- Bodysurfing
- Diving
- Canoeing/Kayaking
- Course/Tour
- Sento Hot Baths/Onsen
- Skiing
- Snorkelling
- Surfing
- Swimming/Pool
- Walking
- Windsurfing
- Other Activity

Sleeping

- Sleeping
- Camping

Eating

- Eating

Drinking & Nightlife

- Drinking & Nightlife
- Cafe

Entertainment

- Entertainment

Shopping

- Shopping

Information

- Bank
- Embassy/Consulate
- Hospital/Medical
- Internet
- Police
- Post Office
- Telephone
- Toilet
- Tourist Information
- Other Information

Geographic

- Beach
- Hut/Shelter
- Lighthouse
- Lookout
- Mountain/Volcano
- Oasis
- Park
- Pass
- Picnic Area
- Waterfall

Population

- Capital (National)
- Capital (State/Province)
- City/Large Town
- Town/Village

Transport

- Airport
- Border crossing
- Bus
- Cable car/Funicular
- Cycling
- Ferry
- Metro station
- Monorail
- Parking
- Petrol station
- S-Bahn/S-train/Subway station
- Taxi
- T-bane/Tunnelbana station
- Train station/Railway
- Tram
- Tube station
- U-Bahn/Underground station
- Other Transport

Note: Not all symbols displayed above appear on the maps in this book

Routes

- Tollway
- Freeway
- Primary
- Secondary
- Tertiary
- Lane
- Unsealed road
- Road under construction
- Plaza/Mall
- Steps
- Tunnel
- Pedestrian overpass
- Walking Tour
- Walking Tour detour
- Path/Walking Trail

Boundaries

- International
- State/Province
- Disputed
- Regional/Suburb
- Marine Park
- Cliff
- Wall

Hydrography

- River, Creek
- Intermittent River
- Canal
- Water
- Dry/Salt/Intermittent Lake
- Reef

Areas

- Airport/Runway
- Beach/Desert
- Cemetery (Christian)
- Cemetery (Other)
- Glacier
- Mudflat
- Park/Forest
- Sight (Building)
- Sportsground
- Swamp/Mangrove

OUR STORY

A beat-up old car, a few dollars in the pocket and a sense of adventure. In 1972 that's all Tony and Maureen Wheeler needed for the trip of a lifetime – across Europe and Asia overland to Australia. It took several months, and at the end – broke but inspired – they sat at their kitchen table writing and stapling together their first travel guide, *Across Asia on the Cheap*. Within a week they'd sold 1500 copies. Lonely Planet was born.

Today, Lonely Planet has offices in Franklin, London, Melbourne, Oakland, Beijing and Delhi, with more than 600 staff and writers. We share Tony's belief that 'a great guidebook should do three things: inform, educate and amuse'.

OUR WRITERS

Jenny Walker

Oman Jenny Walker has written extensively on the Middle East in Lonely Planet publications, is a member of the British Guild of Travel Writers and a Fellow of the Royal Geographic Society. She has a long academic engagement with the region (undergraduate dissertation, postgraduate thesis from Oxford University and current PhD studies at NTU on perception of Arabic Orient). Associate Dean and an executive at Oman's leading engineering college since 2008, Jenny has travelled in 120 countries from Mexico to Mongolia. Jenny also wrote the Plan, Understand and Survival Guide chapters (with the exception of the Hajj).

Anthony Ham

Kuwait, Saudi Arabia, Qatar, Bahrain Anthony has written more than 100 guidebooks for Lonely Planet, including *Saudi Arabia*, the *Middle East*, *Jordan* and *Iran*, and writes for magazines and newspapers around the world. He has a Masters degree in Middle Eastern politics, has travelled to 16 of the 22 countries of the Arab League and never ceases to be surprised by the kindness of anything-but-ordinary people wherever he goes.

Read more about Anthony at:
lonelyplanet.com/members/anthony_ham

Andrea Schulte-Peevers

UAE Born and raised in Germany and educated in London and at UCLA, Andrea has travelled the distance to the moon and back in her visits to dozens of countries, including several in North Africa and the Middle East. She's authored or contributed to some 90 Lonely Planet titles, including the last edition of this guide, the *Dubai & Abu Dhabi* city guide and the *Pocket Dubai* guide. After years of living in LA, Andrea now happily makes her home in Berlin.

Contributing Writers

Mariam Nihal contributed to the Saudi Arabia chapter.

Robert Wagner contributed to the Saudi Arabia chapter and wrote the Hajj chapter.

Published by Lonely Planet Global Limited
CRN 554153
5th edition – Sept 2016
ISBN 978 1 78657 104 5

10 9 8 7 6 5 4 3 2 1
Printed in China